AF769506

Drug Formulation Design and Drug Delivery

Drug Formulation Design and Drug Delivery

Editor: Ned Burnett

FOSTER ACADEMICS
www.fosteracademics.com

www.fosteracademics.com

FOSTER ACADEMICS

Cataloging-in-Publication Data

Drug formulation design and drug delivery / edited by Ned Burnett.
p. cm.
Includes bibliographical references and index.
ISBN 978-1-63242-572-0
1. Drugs--Design. 2. Drug delivery systems. 3. Pharmaceutical chemistry. I. Burnett, Ned.
RS420 .D78 2018
615.19--dc23

© Foster Academics, 2018

Foster Academics,
118-35 Queens Blvd., Suite 400,
Forest Hills, NY 11375, USA

ISBN 978-1-63242-572-0 (Hardback)

This book contains information obtained from authentic and highly regarded sources. Copyright for all individual chapters remain with the respective authors as indicated. All chapters are published with permission under the Creative Commons Attribution License or equivalent. A wide variety of references are listed. Permission and sources are indicated; for detailed attributions, please refer to the permissions page and list of contributors. Reasonable efforts have been made to publish reliable data and information, but the authors, editors and publisher cannot assume any responsibility for the validity of all materials or the consequences of their use.

Trademark Notice: Registered trademark of products or corporate names are used only for explanation and identification without intent to infringe.

Printed and bound in China.

Contents

Preface

It is often said that books are a boon to mankind. They document every progress and pass on the knowledge from one generation to the other. They play a crucial role in our lives. Thus I was both excited and nervous while editing this book. I was pleased by the thought of being able to make a mark but I was also nervous to do it right because the future of students depends upon it. Hence, I took a few months to research further into the discipline, revise my knowledge and also explore some more aspects. Post this process, I begun with the editing of this book.

Drug delivery is an important part of medicinal studies as it deals with the study, formulation, and transformation of drugs into reaching their optimum therapeutic effect. The subject includes study of dosage form and administrative route. This book includes some of the vital pieces of work being conducted across the world, on various topics related to drug delivery and drug formulation. It consists of contributions made by international experts. It strives to provide a fair idea about this discipline and to help develop a better understanding of the latest advances within this field. This book is appropriate for students seeking detailed information in this area as well as for experts.

I thank my publisher with all my heart for considering me worthy of this unparalleled opportunity and for showing unwavering faith in my skills. I would also like to thank the editorial team who worked closely with me at every step and contributed immensely towards the successful completion of this book. Last but not the least, I wish to thank my friends and colleagues for their support.

Editor

1

Reassessing the Role of Intra-Arterial Drug Delivery for Glioblastoma Multiforme Treatment

Jason A. Ellis,[1] Matei Banu,[1] Shaolie S. Hossain,[2] Rajinder Singh-Moon,[3] Sean D. Lavine,[1] Jeffrey N. Bruce,[1] and Shailendra Joshi[4]

[1]*Department of Neurological Surgery, Columbia University Medical Center, New York, NY 10032, USA*
[2]*Department of Molecular Cardiology, Texas Heart Institute, Houston, TX 77030, USA*
[3]*School of Engineering and Applied Science, Columbia University, New York, NY 10032, USA*
[4]*Department of Anesthesiology, Columbia University Medical Center, New York, NY 10032, USA*

Correspondence should be addressed to Shailendra Joshi; sj121@cumc.columbia.edu

Academic Editor: S. P. Vyas

Effective treatment for glioblastoma (GBM) will likely require targeted delivery of several specific pharmacological agents simultaneously. Intra-arterial (IA) delivery is one technique for targeting the tumor site with multiple agents. Although IA chemotherapy for glioblastoma (GBM) has been attempted since the 1950s, the predicted benefits remain unproven in clinical practice. This review focuses on innovative approaches to IA drug delivery in treating GBM. Guided by novel *in vitro* and *in vivo* optical measurements, newer pharmacokinetic models promise to better define the complex relationship between background cerebral blood flow and drug injection parameters. Advanced optical technologies and tracers, unique nanoparticles designs, new cellular targets, and rational drug formulations are continuously modifying the therapeutic landscape for GBM. Personalized treatment approaches are emerging; however, such tailored approaches will largely depend on effective drug delivery techniques and on the ability to simultaneously deliver multidrug regimens. These new paradigms for tumor-selective drug delivery herald dramatic improvements in the effectiveness of IA chemotherapy for GBM. Therefore, within this context of so-called "precision medicine," the role of IA delivery for GBM is thoroughly reassessed.

1. Introduction

Although drugs directed against glioblastoma may be delivered by a number of routes, from a physiological standpoint, intra-arterial (IA) drug delivery is an appealing method (Table 1) [1]. Drugs are distributed through the capillary network within a narrow volume of distribution, physically restricted by local factors. Tissue drug perfusion is theoretically very efficient following a path of nutrient diffusion [2]. However, the pharmacokinetics of IA drug delivery is exceedingly complex [3–6]. For effective IA drug delivery, drugs have to be rapidly and, preferably, irreversibly taken up during their first pass through the tissue circulation, lasting between 1 and 10 seconds in the brain [7–9]. Therefore, IA pharmacokinetics requires an understanding of several important parameters including (1) physiologic and anatomic factors that influence regional blood flow, (2) hydrodynamic factors that affect drug delivery, (3) injection parameters and endothelium-drug interactions, (4) kinetics of uptake and transfer across the blood brain barrier (BBB), and (5) site- or tissue-specific pharmacokinetics [3, 6, 10–13].

The lack of robust experimental and theoretical models, leading to inadequate optimization of injection parameters as well as a lack of rationalization in drug selection, further hinders improvements in IA drug delivery [5, 14–16]. However, IA drugs have been widely used in recent years, either off-label or as part of clinical trials [14, 17–26]. Most of these attempts rely on the general belief that local injections, transiently generating high arterial blood concentrations, will lead to the desired pharmacodynamic effects. Poor rationalization and selection for IA interventions could lead to treatment failure as well as significant adverse

Table 1: Methods of targeting drugs to glioblastoma.

	Example agent	FDA approved	Advantages	Disadvantages
Oral	Temozolomide	Yes	Noninvasive administration	Systemic toxicity, myelosuppression
Intravenous	Bevacizumab	Yes	Minimally invasive administration	Systemic toxicity, CNS hemorrhage, and thromboembolic events
Local polymers	Carmustine implant (Gliadel)	Yes	Delivery directly to tumor resection bed	Craniotomy for implantation required, small volume of drug distribution, and relying on diffusion, seizure, and infection
Intra-arterial	Bevacizumab	No	Minimally invasive superselective delivery to tumor feeding arteries	High first-pass drug extraction necessary
Intraventricular	Methotrexate	No	Ideal for intraventricular and leptomeningeal disease	Neurotoxicity, aseptic meningitis, need for ventricular access device, and limited value for parenchymal tumor
Intrathecal	Methotrexate	No	Ideal for intraspinal and leptomeningeal disease	Neurotoxicity, aseptic meningitis, need for lumbar infusion, and limited value for parenchymal tumor
Microdialysis	Methotrexate	No	Limiting systemic and neurotoxicity, tissue delivery, and sampling possible	Small volume of drug distribution, relying on diffusion
Convection-enhanced	Topotecan	No	Limiting systemic and neurotoxicity, diffusion independent, and continuous infusion with implantable pumps possible	Surgical implantation required
Intranasal	Perillyl alcohol	No	Noninvasive administration	Unpredictable targeting and volume of distribution, mucosal irritation

events. This is even more disconcerting since IA interventions are generally performed in extremis, in recurrent or even end-stage cases, with a severely skewed risk-benefit ratio.

IA anesthetic drugs have been used to localize brain functions since 1948, providing a robust platform for the safe use of this delivery method [27]. Attempts to treat GBM with IA chemotherapy began soon after the Second World War, with no significant impact on outcomes [28]. On the other hand, IA chemotherapy is now routinely used for the treatment of retinoblastoma and advanced liver cancer, improving quality of life and extending overall survival [29–33]. Beyond these two well-established applications, IA chemotherapy has been also used, with variable success, in the treatment of other cancers such as breast cancer, head and neck cancer, colorectal cancer, penile cancer, and pancreatic cancer [34–39].

The failure of previous IA chemotherapies to effectively treat GBM is not unique, however. Numerous other treatment modalities have had little impact on the clinical course of this disease. Several recent clinical trials have or currently are assessing IA drugs for GBM treatment (Table 2). Given the failure to affect outcomes over the last several decades, the question arises whether one should persist in evaluating IA chemotherapy for brain tumor treatment. In light of recent technological and therapeutic advances in GBM treatment, what is the role of IA therapy?

The following review supports revisiting IA drug delivery for the treatment of GBM. Emerging optical technologies offer novel insight into the complex pharmacokinetics of IA drug delivery and may lead to improved clinical effectiveness [40–43]. Concurrent reduction of blood flow appears to enhance the regional effectiveness of IA drug delivery [41, 42, 44]. New tumor targeting strategies using computational analysis of phenotypic and genotypic characteristics as well as nanodelivery platforms may further improve GBM treatment [45]. Thus, we believe that the insights provided by these novel technologies will improve drug targeting while significantly minimizing complications that have plagued the field in the past.

2. Brief History

Warner Frossman's development of cardiac catheterization was driven, in part, by the hope of locally targeting drug treatments for heart failure. His concept of local pharmacological intervention using catheters appealed to many at the time [46–48]. The interest in IA drugs received a significant boost in 1948, after Wada demonstrated the effectiveness of local anesthetic drug delivery in generating cortical electrical quiescence [27, 49]. The Wada test for localization of neurological functions has been used virtually unchanged over the past sixty years [50]. Targeted IA chemotherapy was first used in the years following the Second World War [51]. Calvin Klopp at George Washington University used IA chemotherapy for head and neck tumors as well as glioblastoma, in

TABLE 2: Recent clinical trials employing IA chemotherapy for CNS tumors.

Trial	Drugs	Tumor type
NCT01811498	Bevacizumab	GBM
NCT01238237	Cetuximab	GBM, anaplastic astrocytoma
NCT01180816	Temozolomide	GBM, anaplastic astrocytoma
NCT01269853	Bevacizumab	GBM, anaplastic astrocytoma
NCT00075387	Carboplatin-based chemotherapy	High grade glioma
NCT01083966	Bevacizumab	Vestibular schwannoma
NCT00253721	Melphalan	Brain and CNS tumors, lymphoma, and metastatic cancer
NCT01386710	Bevacizumab, Carboplatin	GBM, anaplastic astrocytoma
NCT00983398	Melphalan, Carboplatin, Sodium Thiosulfate, Filgrastim, and Pegfilgrastim	CNS embryonal tumors and germ cell tumors
NCT02285959	Bevacizumab	GBM
NCT01884740	Erbitux, Bevacizumab	GBM and other tumors

1950 [28, 52]. In the 1960s, Charles Wilson systematically investigated IA chemotherapy for glioma treatment [53–55]. In 1972, Stanley Rapport demonstrated hyperosmotic disruption of the BBB [56, 57]. Significant advances were made at the NIH by Oldfield and others in the 1980s [15, 58–60]. Most IA therapies focused on nitrogen mustards; their high lipid solubility and rapid onset of action made these drugs particularly appealing for IA administration [61]. However, unexplained neurotoxicity, in particular white matter infarction, emerged as serious complications with IA nitrogen mustards, thereby limiting their usage [62–65]. By the 1990s, interest in IA chemotherapy for brain tumors started to wane. Edward Neuwelt was a fervent advocate of IA chemotherapy throughout the 1990s, incorporating it into his BBB disruption program [66, 67]. Unfortunately, the loss of drive to further advance IA therapeutics for GBM and other brain neoplasms could not have been more untimely. Modern endovascular technology was rapidly advanced in the 1990s and continues to make significant technological strides. Furthermore, the past decade has seen advances in optical imaging and nanoparticle engineering, both with the potential to impact IA drug delivery immensely.

In sharp contrast to the treatment of GBM, interest in IA chemotherapy as a treatment modality for certain other malignancies has been steadily increasing. Reese et al. first used IA chemotherapy for the treatment of retinoblastoma in 1954 [68]. Today, IA chemotherapy is widely used as a treatment for this tumor. Data demonstrates that IA chemotherapy extends organ survival, avoids disfiguring ablative surgery, and may promote functional recovery [32, 69–71]. Sullivan et al. introduced hepatic artery (HA) chemotherapy in 1964 [72]. HA chemotherapy via implanted infusion pumps is now routinely used for the treatment of unresectable hepatic metastases [73, 74]. In the 1980s, complete breast tumor remission was reported following internal mammary artery infusions of chemotherapy drugs over several days [75]. IA chemotherapy is currently being used in cases of locally advanced breast cancer [39, 76, 77].

Why has IA chemotherapy been so successful in other organs but not in the brain? The challenges for GBM treatment stem from the unique anatomical and physiological characteristics of the brain. Characteristics of the brain including its high resting blood flow, its susceptibility to embolic injury, and its relative environmental isolation provided by the BBB increase the risks and challenges associated with IA drug delivery. However, with safer drugs, advanced imaging methods, and modern endovascular techniques, these hurdles to IA treatment for GBM are not insurmountable.

3. Challenges to IA Drug Delivery for GBM

3.1. Biological Hurdles. Critical examination of GBM tissue reveals numerous impediments to its treatment with any single modality. GBM is heterogeneous, at both the molecular-genetic and the cellular-tissue levels [78, 79]. To date, there are no consistent tumor-specific phenotypic or genotypic targets. There is always extensive tissue infiltration preventing complete surgical resection. Following surgery, recurrence is universal and generally occurs at the surgical margins. Extensive areas of tumor infiltration, necrosis, hemorrhage, and thrombosis impede effective drug delivery. Certain regions of the tumor are hypoperfused due to ineffective tumor angiogenesis, while others are highly vascular [80]. Given this structural variability, it is likely that drug penetration is variable in different regions of the same tumor [81]. Furthermore, certain regions of the tumor might be inaccessible to IA drugs. Although transient radiographic evidence of IA chemotherapy treatment response in high grade glioma has been reported, no studies have shown durable patient benefit [44]. Furthermore, the question of whether clinical improvements can be made with removal of structural impediments to drug delivery by performing surgery remains unanswered.

3.2. Clinical Experience. It is estimated that over 2000 patients have been treated with IA chemotherapy for GBM, mostly in the setting of Phases I and II trials [82]. Thus far, there has been little evidence of significantly improved outcomes during these trials. Several series report prolonged survival by a few weeks, with ocular toxicity or neurotoxicity occurring in 7–50% of the patients [82]. These toxicities were more evident with carmustine. In many instances, IA

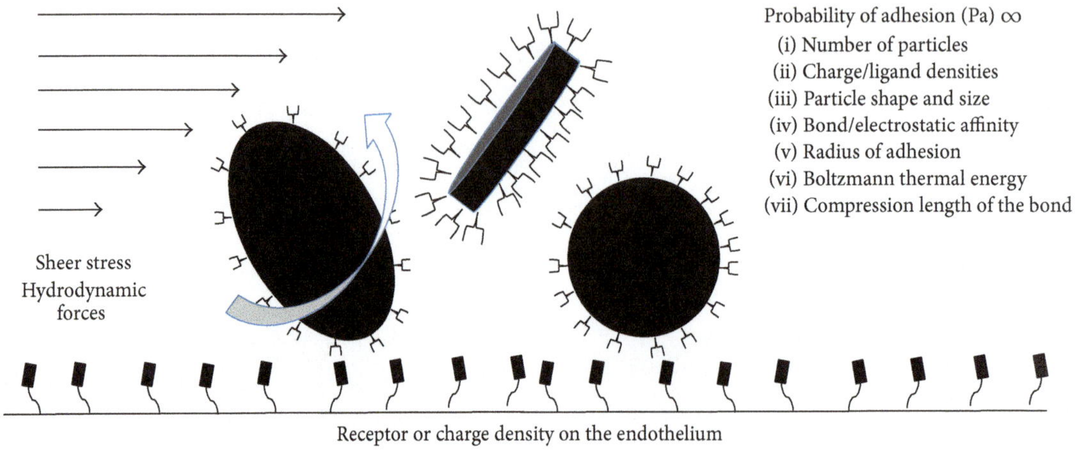

FIGURE 1: Hydrodynamic forces on drug particles. Shear stress, particle shape, and ligand-receptor interactions are the dominant forces that affect the delivery of particles to their target site.

chemotherapy was delivered proximally to the entire hemisphere via intracarotid injections. Subsequently, supraophthalmic injections were used to decrease toxicity.

The clearance of highly diffusible compounds from brain tissue is directly proportional to the regional blood flow [83]. With hemispheric drug infusion, diffusible compounds pose an elevated risk of injury to white matter tracts. Due to lower blood flow in the white matter as compared to gray matter, this may explain the occurrence of white matter lesions with the administration of IA nitrosoureas. Thus, unless drugs are specifically selected and formulated for tumor uptake, the benefits of IA drug delivery will not be fully reaped.

3.3. Treatment Goals. Studies on IA chemotherapy differ significantly in drug injection protocols with respect to the site, dose, timing, anesthetic management, and underlying rationale. Due to this lack of consistency, it is often difficult to compare outcomes from various studies. Lack of standardization is, in part, due to our incomplete understanding of the pharmacokinetics of IA drug injections [5, 82]. Although the primary goal of IA drug delivery is to selectively target the tumor tissue, this goal is often difficult to achieve due to a lack of drug-tumor selectivity and the complex angioarchitecture of GBM. Unlike conventional cerebrovascular lesions, such as an arteriovenous malformation, a GBM's vascular supply may arise from adjacent vascular territories or even from the contralateral hemisphere. Such diffuse vascular input impedes selective drug delivery. Therefore, with IA delivery, drugs are often delivered to both the tumor and the neighboring brain tissue. Complications resulting in neurological deterioration, blindness, cognitive impairment, and seizures are often due to iatrogenic brain injury from nontarget delivery. Without a comprehensive tumor targeting strategy, the goal of IA chemotherapy often becomes a quest for safe delivery of systemic drug doses. Gobin et al. used fractionated algorithms to decrease local toxicity [14]. With this approach, the dose of drug is proportional to the regional blood flow. Therefore, the benefits of the high transient arterial blood concentrations have to be combined with pharmacokinetic or pharmacodynamic selectivity to the tumor tissue. The goal of IA treatments should be tumor-selective drug delivery such that local and systemic complications can be mitigated.

3.4. Lack of Reliable Pharmacokinetic Models. One of the fundamental problems in translating IA treatment into the clinical setting is the lack of robust pharmacokinetic models. Models used to assess the benefits of IA delivery rely on simplistic concepts and have repeatedly failed to predict tissue drug concentrations [5, 84, 85]. The relevance of these models is further challenged by the evolution of nanotechnology, with larger particles subject to considerably greater hydrodynamic forces [10, 86]. Hydrodynamic forces, as determined by vascular geometry, shear stress, and rate constants of endothelium-drug interactions are critical in determining the probability of the drug to adhere to the endothelium (Figure 1). However, preclinical models thus far have failed to take such parameters into account. Most studies have used snapshot methods to determine tissue drug concentrations at a fixed time point. Technologies for real-time tracking of tissue drug distribution and concentrations, such as PET, were seldom used [87, 88]. Concurrent blood flow measurements are also required for adequate monitoring of drug uptake [89].

In recent years, optical methods have emerged with the capability of tracking tissue tracer concentrations of drugs in subsecond time domains (Table 3) [41, 43, 90–93]. These methods can be combined with complementary techniques to simultaneously assess cerebral blood flow [11, 41, 42, 94–96]. Experimental data tracking tissue concentrations and blood flow changes could generate more accurate pharmacokinetic models that include hydrodynamic factors largely ignored in the past.

3.5. Streaming. Cerebral blood flow plays an integral role in IA drug delivery. However, in most clinical studies, parameters such as the cerebral blood flow are not monitored or modified. Some investigators have recommended that blood flow should be increased to improve regional drug delivery. In a series of experiments performed *in vitro* and in primates,

TABLE 3: Optical methods employed to study IA drug pharmacokinetics.

Method	Depth	Advantage	Disadvantage
Diffuse reflectance spectroscopy	1-2 mm	(i) Insensitive to scattering changes (ii) Low cost (iii) High spectral resolution	(i) Recovery of relative absorption (ii) Low spatial resolution
Diffuse optical tomography	up to ~4 cm	3D reconstruction of absolute optical pharmacokinetics (OP)	(i) Expensive (ii) Bulky (iii) Low spectral resolution
Frequency domain photon migration	up to ~4 cm	Recovery of absolute OP	(i) Low spectral resolution (ii) Expensive (iii) Low spatial resolution (iv) Not suitable for small geometries
Diffuse optical spectroscopic imaging	up to ~4 cm	(i) 3D reconstruction of absolute OP (ii) High spectral resolution	(i) Expensive (ii) Not suitable for small geometries
Spatial frequency domain imaging	up to ~1 cm	(i) Noncontact (ii) High spatial resolution (iii) Depth sensitivity	(i) Long acquisition times (ii) Expensive (commercial)
Multispectral imaging	up to ~1 cm	(i) Low cost (ii) High spatiotemporal acquisition rate	(i) Relative absorption values (ii) Susceptible to scattering effects (iii) No depth resolution

Saris and Lutz showed the negative effects of streaming on drug distribution after low volume internal carotid artery (ICA) injections [4, 97, 98]. Streaming was less likely to affect distal injections in the cerebral circulation, for example, after supraophthalmic infusion. Streaming can be decreased by injecting volumes exceeding 20% of the background blood flow rate, by injecting during the diastole, or by injecting using catheters with side ports [4, 97, 99]. It is clear that subtle differences in injection protocols can have profound effects on both the therapeutic response and the occurrence of adverse events. Standardization of delivery protocols and defining concurrent blood flow conditions could have an important impact on the results of clinical studies.

3.6. Safety Concerns. IA drug delivery carries risks such as complications related to catheter placement and vascular access, local and systemic complications due to chemotherapeutic drug infusion, and complications due to blood brain barrier disruption. On the other hand, the safety of endovascular procedures has increased tremendously and short-term IA drug delivery is now considered to be generally safe [100, 101]. Local reactions to chemotherapeutic drug infusions, such as ocular erythema with cisplatin, can be minimized by superselective catheter placement upstream of the ophthalmic artery [102]. Although superselective IA chemotherapy can result in streaming, employing specific delivery techniques, as previously described, can mitigate this phenomenon [97]. Selective tumor targeting is perhaps the best way to prevent inadvertent neurological injury and minimize systemic complications.

4. Advantages of IA Drug Delivery for GBM

4.1. Local Drug Delivery. IA injections rely on drug delivery through capillary networks and eventually into the perfused tissue. The tissue concentrations achieved by IA delivery are considerably higher than those achieved after IV delivery [82, 88]. This high concentration can further increase the tissue diffusion gradient. For highly lipid soluble drugs, such as nitrogen mustards, rapid targeting of tumor tissue is possible [88]. The key to effective IA drug delivery lies in proper drug selection as well as in optimizing the delivery technique based on specific controllable parameters (Figure 2). As discussed later, this can be achieved by increasing the probability that drug molecules attach to the endothelium [10].

4.2. Unique Pharmacokinetics. Hydrodynamic factors related to background blood flow, injection characteristics, and vascular geometry play a major role in determining tissue concentrations after IA drug injections. In computational models and in preclinical experiments, reduction of cerebral blood flow improved regional drug delivery [11, 41, 42, 89, 95, 96]. When a bolus of drug is injected during transient cerebral hypoperfusion (TCH), tissue concentrations can be significantly increased (Figure 3). Cerebral hypoperfusion decreases hydrodynamic stress on the injected molecules. It increases drug transit time through the cerebral circulation. Furthermore, it delivers pure drug to the vascular endothelium and decreases opsonization by serum proteins and blood cells.

4.3. Dose Advantages. The net advantage of IA drug injection over IV injection depends on a number of factors such as the method of injection, the rate of injection, and the duration of infusions. Comparing IA to IV by using PET measurements in human subjects has revealed a 50-fold increase in tumor tissue concentrations after IA injections [88]. In rabbits, when BCNU concentrations were measured 5 minutes after drug injection, there was a 6-fold improvement in drug delivery [96]. With cationic liposomes, we have observed a similar 50-fold improvement in liposome delivery with IA versus

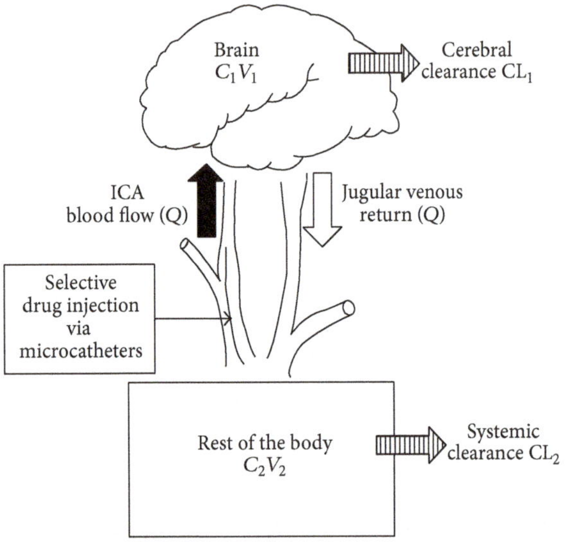

FIGURE 2: Dedrick model of intracarotid delivery. This pictorial representation of the mathematical model demonstrates that IA drug delivery is most efficient when regional flow (Q) is low, regional extraction is high, and systemic clearance is rapid. C: concentration, V: volume, CL: clearance, and Q: regional blood flow.

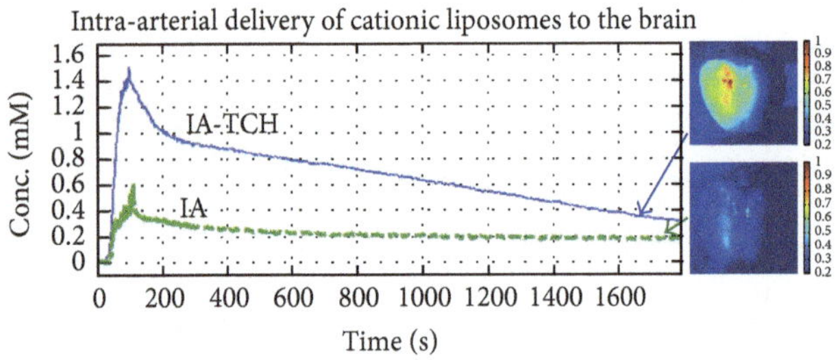

FIGURE 3: Hypoperfusion-assisted intra-arterial drug delivery. Transient cerebral hypoperfusion (TCH) significantly facilitates the delivery of cationic liposomes to the brain. Multispectral images (MSI) show that cationic liposomal uptake is significantly improved by utilizing intra-arterial delivery with TCH (right panel). Corresponding concentration-time curves obtained by diffuse reflectance spectroscopy quantitatively corroborate these optical phenomena (left panel).

IV injection [42, 95]. We noticed an additional 3- to 10-fold improvement in tissue concentrations by injecting drugs during TCH compared to IA injections without flow arrest.

4.4. Systemic Rescue. One of the potential advantages of IA drug delivery is the ability to neutralize the recirculating drug with an antidote or to physically remove drugs by hemoperfusion [15, 58–60]. Such an approach can decrease the chances of systemic side effects. Ototoxicity and nephrotoxicity are known complications of IA cisplatin therapy which can be reduced with concurrent thiosulfate infusion [103, 104]. Trials are underway to evaluate the effectiveness of this combination.

5. Investigating the Kinetics of IA Drugs

Critical to the development of the field of IA therapeutics is the understanding of first-pass kinetics during drug delivery. Most conventional methods (see below) do not provide the subsecond time resolution needed to investigate first-pass kinetics. These methods usually do not assess cerebral blood flow and lack adequate spatial resolution. Furthermore, these methods require complicated chemical drug extraction techniques, pose radiation and magnetic hazards, and can be resource- and cost-intensive. However, dramatic advances have been made in optical drug and tracer concentration measurements. Many of these methods can measure tissue drug concentration and blood flow. Provided that the drug has a suitable spectral profile, one can track drug delivery in real-time, map distribution in gross postmortem samples and even track drug and metabolites at a cellular level.

5.1. Brain/Plasma Partition Ratio. In this method, the relative concentration of the drug in the brain tissue and plasma is simultaneously determined at a specified time point [105]. The drug remaining in the vascular dead space is not flushed and that amount is therefore included as part of the brain drug concentration. This approach provides a snapshot measurement and is resource-intensive. Additionally, several animals have to be sacrificed to obtain a concentration-time curve.

5.2. In Situ Perfusion. In this method, the internal carotid artery is isolated and drugs are infused over time (Figure 4). The carotid is flushed out and brain tissue drug concentration is determined. There are two pharmacokinetic parameters that describe brain drug uptake: K_{in} and PS. K_{in} is the net inwards flux of a drug. PS is permeability surface area product; it is the plasma volume that is cleared of a drug during its passage through the cerebral circulation. With the in situ method, $K_{in} = C_{br}/(C_{pf} \times T)$, where C_{br} is the concentration of compound in the brain (mg/g), C_{pf} is the concentration of compound in the perfusion fluid (mg/mL), and T is the time. Using this method, PS can be determined by the Renkin Crone equation: $PS = Q\ln(1 - K_{in}/Q)$, where Q is the cerebral blood flow [106].

5.3. Brain Uptake Index (BUI). The classical method to determine BUI as described by Oldendorf in the 1970s involves injection of the isotope labeled drug into the common carotid artery of a rat [6, 108, 109]. The typical volume is 200 μL and the injection is made over 0.5 s. Fifteen seconds after injection, the animal is sacrificed and the brain tissue is harvested. The drugs are labeled with ^3H and the uptake of the drug is normalized to the uptake of ^{14}C labeled butanol that is freely diffusible into the brain tissue. BUI is then calculated using the following equation: $BUI = (^3H\ brain/^{14}C\ brain)/(^3H\ injection/^{14}C\ injection)$. BUI is a fraction but can also be expressed as a percentage. BUI represents net uptake of a drug during the first pass through the cerebral circulation [85]. Hardebo and Nilsson have challenged this view, suggesting that recirculation of a drug can occur in 15 s, thereby recommending obtaining tissue samples 5 s after

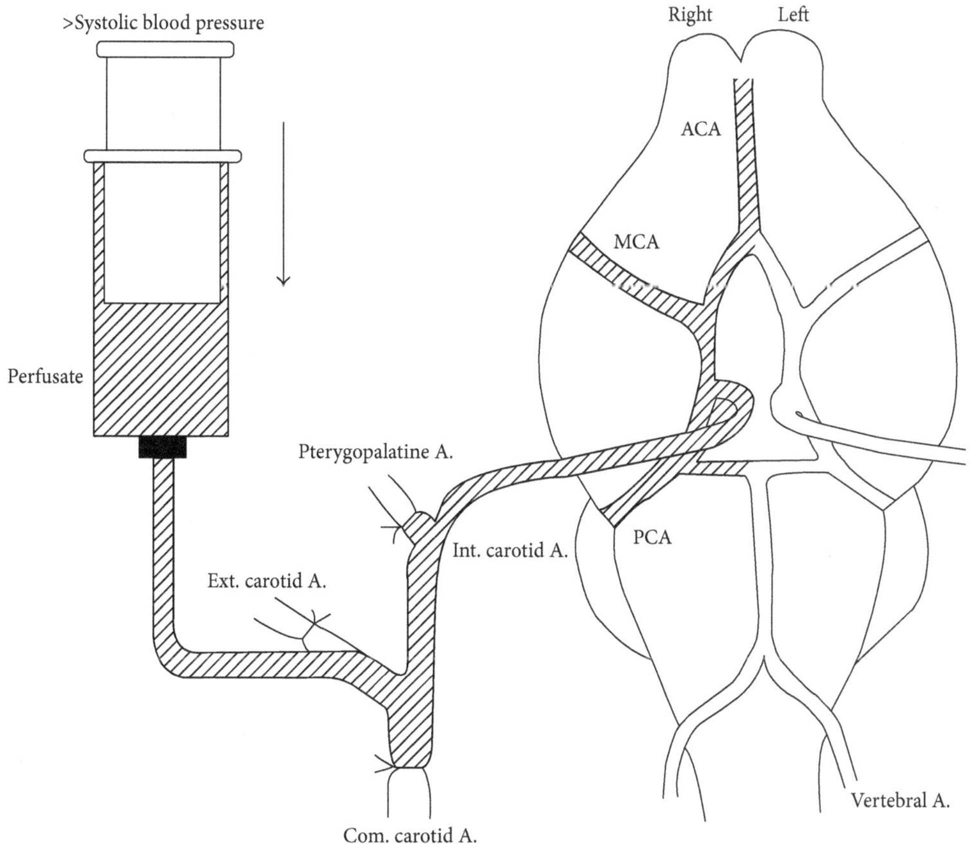

FIGURE 4: In situ perfusion in an animal model. Used with permission from Takasato et al. [107].

intracarotid injection [6]. BUI provides a good measure for compounds that rapidly diffuse into the brain and are well retained by the brain tissue.

5.4. Microdialysis. For intravenous drug delivery with steady state infusion, brain tissue concentrations can be determined by microdialysis. The technique can be used with steady state IA injections as well [110, 111]. However, with bolus IA injections, changes in tissue drug concentration might be too rapid to obtain a sample and injection of the drug could potentially destabilize the probe. Hence, microdialysis is rarely used to investigate the kinetics of IA drugs. The main advantage of microdialysis is its ability to obtain multiple measurements over extended time periods.

5.5. Autoradiography. Using radiolabeled drugs, it is possible to obtain a map of drug delivery following IA infusion. The method provides only a single data point per animal. It has been used in both large and small animal models [98, 99, 112].

5.6. Positron Emission Tomography (PET). PET imaging is a very useful tool to investigate the kinetics of IA drugs. This method can track drug delivery in a single animal. However, it is resource-intensive, requires a cyclotron, and has poor spatial resolution [88].

5.7. Novel Optical Approaches. The key to the understanding of IA drug kinetics is to be able to track tracer concentrations within a subsecond time frame and to concurrently assess cerebral blood flow either directly or by using an additional device. Newly available optical tools such as diffuse reflectance spectroscopy permit simultaneous measurements of blood flow as well as optical tracer and drug concentrations [113–116]. Optical measurements are possible in a subsecond time frame and are site-specific, and the method is tissue nondestructive. Table 3 summarizes some of the advantages and disadvantages of these novel optical methods. These methods are cost effective and relatively simple to execute once optimized, and they do not carry the hazards of radiation and magnetic fields. Such optical tools can generate pharmacokinetic insights and generate models that could guide future drug development.

6. Pharmacokinetics of IA Drugs

Many investigators use simple flow and volume calculations to determine the pharmacokinetic benefits of IA drugs. However, these simple models of IA drug delivery overlook the underlying hydrodynamic complexity. The complex conceptual framework of IA drug delivery requires an understanding of fluid dynamics of both cerebral blood flow and the drug injection. One must simultaneously take

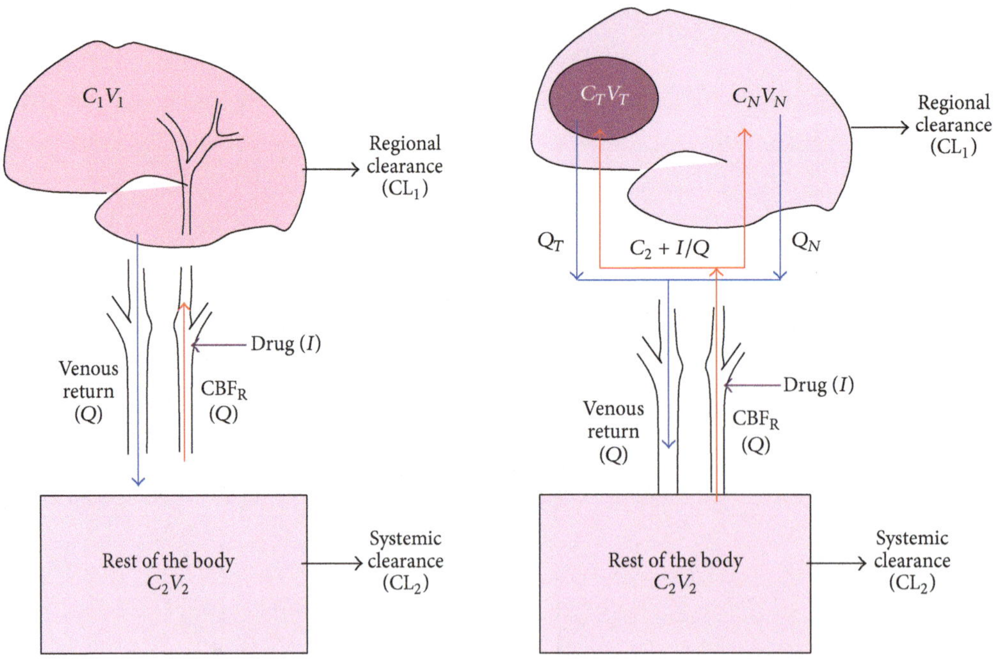

FIGURE 5: Models of intracarotid drug delivery with and without brain tumor.

into account the rapid first-pass uptake of the drug by the endothelium, transfer across the blood brain barrier, the local release of drug from potential carriers, the tissue pharmacokinetics including local metabolism, and finally the first-pass elimination and recirculation of the drug.

6.1. Basic Model of IA Drug Delivery. The significance of the Dedrick model lies in clearly defining when IA drug delivery truly works (Figure 5) [3]. If the advantage of IA regional drug delivery (Rd) is defined as the $(C_1/C_2)_{IA}/(C_1/C_2)_{IV}$, then Rd can be also represented as follows: $Rd = 1 + (CL_{TB}/Q \times (1 - E))$, where CL_{TB} is the total body clearance of the drug, Q is the regional blood flow, and E is the fraction of drug extracted in the first pass through the cerebral circulation. This basic model has several implications. First, it shows that Rd is increased under the following circumstances: reduced regional blood flow (Q), high first-pass regional extraction (E) or a high BUI, or a high systemic clearance CL_{TB}. Thus, it shows the disadvantage of applying IA therapies to treating brain disorders in which the blood flow is 50 mL/100 g/min, with the BBB generally preventing drug uptake. Second, the model shows that IA drug delivery will be useful for a drug that has high regional extraction (K_{in} or BUI), if the blood flow to the brain can be safely decreased or if the systemic clearance of the drug is low. However, this model has several inherent limitations due to assumptions made. First, the model assumes that there is uniform mixing of drug in the arterial blood, thereby ignoring regional variations in drug concentrations due to streaming. A second assumption is that there is no drug efflux and therefore highly diffusible molecules may have a rapid uptake and high first-pass extraction, but will rapidly wash out once the arterial concentrations decline. Moreover, the model also assumes homogeneous retention of drugs by the brain tissue, which is not always the case. Highly diffusible tracers and drugs are likely to be washed out directly proportional to regional blood flow. Despite these concerns, the model is very useful in understanding the applications of IA drugs. This model was also compartmentalized into tumor and normal tissue and by varying the relative blood flow in these two compartments the model could then be altered to investigate how blood flow and tumor drug delivery could be improved.

6.2. Computational Fluid Dynamic Models of Regional Drug Delivery. With the advent of nanotechnology, much greater emphasis is being placed on developing models of drug delivery that include fluid dynamic factors. The uptake of the nanoparticles is described as a function of the probability of adhesion. Hossain et al. provide an accurate description of regional drug delivery of nanoparticles in the coronary circulation [10]. This model uses human MR data to acquire vascular dimensions and then applies isogeometric corrections to the dimensions of the vascular lumen. It assumes Newtonian properties of blood. It describes the movement of nanoparticles on the parabolic wave front as they are presented to the vascular endothelium. The probability of adhesion of a nanoparticle in this model is determined by several key factors including the number of nanoparticles released, vascular geometry, input flow function, and the size and shape of the nanoparticles. The flow function, along with the properties of the nanoparticles such as the size and the shape, determines hydrodynamic and shear stress that tend to dislodge the particles from the vascular endothelium. Other intrinsic properties of the nanoparticle, such as ligand density of the nanoparticle and the density of receptors on the endothelium, determine the likelihood of particles binding to the endothelial

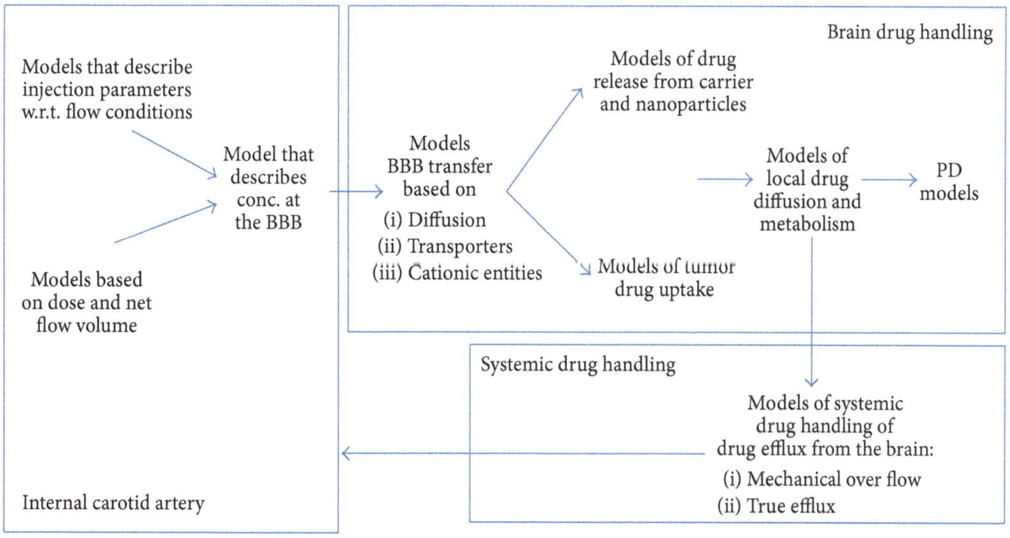

FIGURE 6: Integrated framework for characterizing intra-arterial delivery models.

surface. The net uptake of the nanoparticles is a balance of two opposing forces: the force with which the particle attaches to the endothelium and the hydrodynamic force that tends to dislodge it. The model was tested *in vitro* to determine the effects of shear forces and particle size. The experimental data was consistent with the model predictions. A similar model describing nanoparticle delivery reported by Liu et al. revealed how the shape of the particles, for a given particle volume, further affects the probability of adhesion [86].

The Hossain and Liu et al. models are limited to the description of particle delivery to the vascular endothelial surface. These models describe IV delivery. However, these models provide valuable insight into the hydrodynamic factors that will, probably even more profoundly, affect IA drug delivery. Older models of IA drug delivery completely overlooked the hydrodynamic factors. As of yet, there is no model taking into account all aspects of IA drug delivery. Many models applying limited components of IA drug delivery are currently available and are being applied in the clinical setting. Attempts are currently underway to integrate several of these models into a composite descriptor of IA drug delivery (Figure 6) [10, 86].

7. Recent Studies

The pharmacological rationale for IA chemotherapy has not changed significantly over the past five decades. The scope of IA therapies remains that of targeted drug delivery. There have been numerous improvements that could have bearing on modern IA chemotherapy trials. Several important advancements in technology and patient selection have significantly changed the landscape of IA drug delivery. Table 4 summarizes the most recent published clinical trials employing IA chemotherapy for GBM.

TABLE 4: Studies using intra-arterial chemotherapy for brain tumors.

Author, year	Drugs	Pathology
Fortin et al., 2014 [20]	Carboplatin and Melphalan	Recurrent GBM
Jeon et al., 2012 [23]	Bevacizumab	Recurrent GBM
Shin et al., 2012 [25]	Bevacizumab, Temozolomide, and Cetuximab	Recurrent GBM
Boockvar et al., 2011 [17]	Bevacizumab	Recurrent GBM
Imbesi et al., 2006 [22]	Nimustine (ACNU)	Newly diagnosed GBM
Hall et al., 2006 [21]	Carboplatin, Methotrexate	Recurrent pontine GBM
Fortin et al., 2005 [19]	Carboplatin, Methotrexate	GBM and other tumors
Qureshi et al., 2001 [24]	Carboplatin + Cereport	GBM and other tumors
Gobin et al., 2001 [14]	Carboplatin + Cereport	GBM and other tumors
Chow et al., 2000 [18]	Carboplatin + Cereport	Recurrent GBM

7.1. Patient Selection. With increased experience and availability of new biomarkers defining patient specific characteristics, tailored therapeutic strategies will certainly be the modus operandi in the not so distant future. Genetic markers, such as MGMT gene expression, could further aid in selecting those patients that would benefit most from IA temozolomide [117, 118]. Using appropriate adjuvant measures in conjunction with careful patient selection could enhance the safety and efficacy of IA treatments. Although IA GBM treatment has shown relatively little clinical benefit thus far, the good results seen with primary central nervous system lymphomas, low-grade astrocytomas, and oligodendrogliomas give hope.

7.2. Catheter Technology. In the early years, polyethylene catheters were surgically implanted to deliver drugs, such that infusions were performed over a period of several days. Hemorrhage, thrombosis, and vasospasm were reported with such placement. As expected, catheter technology has significantly improved over the years. Drugs can now be delivered superselectively, above the ophthalmic artery, thereby minimizing ocular complications. Thrombotic catheter complications can also be mitigated by newly developed anticoagulant/antiplatelet drugs [119, 120].

7.3. Imaging Technology. A major advancement that could impact IA chemotherapy is the capability to assess regional blood flow from angiographic transit time [121]. Ability to assess blood flow could prove extremely valuable in determining the injection profile of chemotherapeutic drugs in order to enhance safety and efficacy of the procedure.

7.4. Drug Selection. Due to its high lipid solubility, short biological half-life, and rapid onset of action, nitrogen mustard compounds (BCNU, ACNU, and HeCNU) have been investigated in past clinical trials. These compounds have had significant neurological complications. Recent studies have therefore focused on drugs with reduced local toxicity and are therefore safer for IA delivery, such as carboplatin and methotrexate.

8. New Paradigms in IA Chemotherapy

Several key points have led to a paradigm shift in IA chemotherapy for GBM in recent years. The emphasis has shifted from traditional chemotherapeutic compounds to relatively nontoxic biological interventions. The availability of biological agents, such as the VEGF antagonist bevacizumab, has led to a considerable increase in the safety profile of IA chemotherapy [17]. However, the impact of such drugs on survival is still debatable. On the other hand, new biological compounds and improved IA delivery methods could potentially have a tremendous impact on the efficacy and safety of IA treatments. For example, flow arrest during IA delivery of drugs has several important benefits including better targeting of the drugs to the tumor site, achieving higher cerebral arterial concentrations, achieving more consistent concentrations in the arterial distribution, and increased transit time with decreased shear stress and avoidance of binding of drugs to blood proteins or other cellular elements. The Dedrick model shows the importance of blood flow in influencing the kinetics of IA drugs. Reduction of blood flow has been used to augment the effects of drugs in the IA treatment employed for liver and breast cancer. The brain can safely tolerate up to three minutes of ischemia in healthy normothermic individuals. Therefore, we strongly advocate for flow arrest during IA chemotherapy for GBM, as an essential part of optimizing drug delivery to brain tumors.

Improvements in IA drug delivery can be further enhanced by developing better drug delivery protocols that account for anatomic and physiologic variables. In preclinical research, this can be done by optically monitoring and correcting for the variable degree of BBB disruption and, ultimately, monitoring the response of brain tissue during treatment. Clinically safe and reversible means of decreasing cerebral blood flow, such as hyperventilation, hypothermia, or deep anesthesia, could be used to improve drug delivery.

Another important component is the design of drugs specifically tailored for IA delivery.

The conventional design of drugs relies on pharmacokinetic properties of compounds that result in preferential uptake by the target site. However, if a drug is directly delivered to the target site by IA injections, the emphasis on such characteristics becomes redundant. Classical preclinical screening of drug isomers does not adequately select for IA use; drug isomers and formulations for effective IA delivery are likely fundamentally different from those administered systemically. For IA delivery, drug design has to ensure maximum tumor uptake and adequate retention of drugs, in order to achieve the desired therapeutic effects while avoiding regional toxicity. The uptake has to be rapid, virtually within the transit time through the capillary network. The problem of drug delivery is further compounded by the presence of the BBB that severely restricts the uptake of many therapeutic compounds.

Specific methods can be used to improve IA drug design in order to augment delivery. Small molecule chemotherapy (<400 Daltons) significantly facilitates uptake across the BBB [122]. Increasing lipid solubility, either by adding methyl groups, replacing polar groups, or adding halogenated alkane chains, such as tributyl chlorambucil, further increases diffusivity [123]. Alternatively, using liposomal carrier systems optimized for size and surface charge with rapid drug offloading characteristics may be effective [124]. Furthermore, another novel alternative is immunoliposomes, nonspecifically targeted to the vascular endothelium (CD 31, ACE, or Factor VIII/vWF-Ag), to the transport systems (OX-26 antibody to transferrin receptor), or to the pathology specific antigens (ICAMs) [125–128]. Immunoconjugated drugs, such as OX26-methotrexate and OX26-daunorubicin, chimeric drugs using high capacity transporter systems, or drugs with exceedingly brief duration of actions that are hydrolyzed during transit through cerebral/regional circulation by ubiquitous enzymes, such as esterases or alkaline phosphatases, are also intriguing options that should be considered for IA delivery [128].

Osmotic disruption of the BBB is often employed to augment IA drug delivery. Although the blood brain barrier is already compromised around the tumor bed, disruption of the BBB further improves drug permeability and tumor response. Alternatives to mannitol are being actively developed but are not yet available in the clinical setting. Bradykinin analogues have been a promising alternative but have given way to focused ultrasound in recent years [14, 129, 130]. Perhaps a better alternative to BBB disruption might be the use of cell-penetrating peptides [131]. There is some evidence that IA delivery of cell-penetrating peptides can penetrate the BBB and preliminary results suggest that they can lead to tumor specific drug uptake. Similarly, OX-26 antitransferrin receptor antibody also targets the vascular endothelium of the tumor cells after IA injections. Both anionic ligands and transferrin receptors are relatively overexpressed in the tumor tissue compared to normal brain and they provide convenient targets for tumor-specific drug delivery [132]. These preliminary results suggest that it might be possible to bypass the BBB and achieve tumor-selective drug delivery.

Temozolomide (TMZ) is currently the first-line drug for GBM treatment after surgery. It is a relatively small molecule capable of easily diffusing across the BBB [133]. To that end, increased permeability is an important advantage for systemic chemotherapy. TMZ also acts synergistically with radiation, with both being part of a combined treatment regimen. However, despite its theoretical advantages, TMZ also provides a good example of the shortcomings of systemic chemotherapy. Systemic administration can only achieve 10% of the observed *in vitro* tumoricidal concentrations. Furthermore, currently prescribed doses of TMZ have been demonstrated to cause immunosuppression. Gliomas are notorious for suppressing the local immune response. Therefore, systemic TMZ may aggravate this immunosuppressive effect, further affecting outcomes [25].

To overcome the problem of systemic drug delivery, a concerted effort is now underway to develop nanoparticles that could be injected either systemically, reaching the tumor site due to the intrinsic homing capabilities, or via novel routes such as IA or intranasally. Yet, complex theoretical and practical hurdles to delivery remain. Increased capillary permeability lowers the diffusion barrier while also creating a fluid flux away from the lesion. In addition, within the tumor mass, there are areas of necrosis and hemorrhage, with capillary networks compressed by malignant cells. The tumor stroma also poses a barrier to drug diffusion, particularly in the case of larger nanoparticles. Therefore, full tumor penetration of drugs is extremely difficult, irrespective of delivery method. The microscopic tumor characteristics will hinder complete eradication of tumor cells through purely chemotherapeutic means, with certain populations of malignant cells remaining beyond the reach of drugs.

9. Conclusion

Given the complexity of drug delivery to the brain, conventional pharmacokinetic approaches cannot be applied to the delivery of large and complex molecules, genes, and peptides. Hence, innovative approaches, such as intra-arterial delivery, have to be considered to ensure effective tumor targeting of such novel pharmaceuticals. GBM, in particular, requires a coherent treatment strategy simultaneously targeting multiple mechanisms of tumorigenesis and progression. IA delivery is a well-conceived strategy for delivering such agents that may prove to be an integral component of the protocol for combating this uniformly fatal disease.

Conflict of Interests

The authors declare that there is no conflict of interests regarding the publication of this paper.

References

[1] S. Joshi, P. M. Meyers, and E. Ornstein, "Intracarotid delivery of drugs: the potential and the pitfalls," *Anesthesiology*, vol. 109, no. 3, pp. 543–564, 2008.

[2] J. Siepmann, F. Siepmann, and A. T. Florence, "Local controlled drug delivery to the brain: mathematical modeling of the underlying mass transport mechanisms," *International Journal of Pharmaceutics*, vol. 314, no. 2, pp. 101–119, 2006.

[3] R. L. Dedrick, "Arterial drug infusion: pharmacokinetic problems and pitfalls," *Journal of the National Cancer Institute*, vol. 80, no. 2, pp. 84–89, 1988.

[4] R. J. Lutz, R. L. Dedrick, J. W. Boretos, E. H. Oldfield, J. B. Blacklock, and J. L. Doppman, "Mixing studies during intracarotid artery infusions in an in vitro model," *Journal of Neurosurgery*, vol. 64, no. 2, pp. 277–283, 1986.

[5] R. L. Dedrick, "Interspecies scaling of regional drug delivery," *Journal of Pharmaceutical Sciences*, vol. 75, no. 11, pp. 1047–1052, 1986.

[6] J. E. Hardebo and B. Nilsson, "Estimation of cerebral extraction of circulating compounds by the brain uptake index method: influence of circulation time, volume injection, and cerebral blood flow," *Acta Physiologica Scandinavica*, vol. 107, no. 2, pp. 153–159, 1979.

[7] A. Cenic, D. G. Nabavi, R. A. Craen, A. W. Gelb, and T.-Y. Lee, "Dynamic CT measurement of cerebral blood flow: a validation study," *American Journal of Neuroradiology*, vol. 20, no. 1, pp. 63–73, 1999.

[8] W. H. Oldendorf, "Measurement of the mean transit time of cerebral circulation by external detection of an intravenously injected radioisotope," *Journal of Nuclear Medicine*, vol. 25, no. 2, pp. 253–269, 1984.

[9] K. L. Zierler, "Occupancy principle: identity with that of mean transit time of tracers in biological systems," *Science*, vol. 163, no. 3866, pp. 491–492, 1969.

[10] S. S. Hossain, T. J. R. Hughes, and P. Decuzzi, "Vascular deposition patterns for nanoparticles in an inflamed patient-specific arterial tree," *Biomechanics and Modeling in Mechanobiology*, vol. 13, no. 3, pp. 585–597, 2014.

[11] S. Joshi, M. Wang, J. J. Etu, E. V. Nishanian, and J. Pile-Spellman, "Cerebral blood flow affects dose requirements of intracarotid propofol for electrocerebral silence," *Anesthesiology*, vol. 104, no. 2, pp. 290–298, 2006.

[12] W. M. Pardridge, "Drug transport across the blood-brain barrier," *Journal of Cerebral Blood Flow and Metabolism*, vol. 32, no. 11, pp. 1959–1972, 2012.

[13] W. M. Pardridge, "Drug targeting, drug discovery, and brain drug development," in *Brain Drug Targeting. The Future of Drug Development*, W. M. Pardridge, Ed., chapter 1, pp. 1–12, Cambridge University Press, Cambridge, UK, 2010.

[14] Y. P. Gobin, T. F. Cloughesy, K. L. Chow et al., "Intraarterial chemotherapy for brain tumors by using a spatial dose fractionation algorithm and pulsatile delivery," *Radiology*, vol. 218, no. 3, pp. 724–732, 2001.

[15] E. H. Oldfield, R. L. Dedrick, R. L. Yeager et al., "Reduced systemic drug exposure by combining intra-arterial chemotherapy

with hemoperfusion of regional venous drainage," *Journal of Neurosurgery*, vol. 63, no. 5, pp. 726–732, 1985.

[16] H. A. Riina, J.-K. Burkhardt, A. Santillan, L. Bassani, A. Patsalides, and J. A. Boockvar, "Short-term clinico-radiographic response to super-selective intra-arterial cerebral infusion of bevacizumab for the treatment of vestibular schwannomas in neurofibromatosis type 2," *Interventional Neuroradiology*, vol. 18, no. 2, pp. 127–132, 2012.

[17] J. A. Boockvar, A. J. Tsiouris, C. P. Hofstetter et al., "Safety and maximum tolerated dose of superselective intraarterial cerebral infusion of bevacizumab after osmotic blood-brain barrier disruption for recurrent malignant glioma. Clinical article," *Journal of Neurosurgery*, vol. 114, no. 3, pp. 624–632, 2011.

[18] K. L. Chow, Y. P. Gobin, T. Cloughesy, J. W. Sayre, J. P. Villablanca, and F. Viñuela, "Prognostic factors in recurrent glioblastoma multiforme and anaplastic astrocytoma treated with selective intra-arterial chemotherapy," *American Journal of Neuroradiology*, vol. 21, no. 3, pp. 471–478, 2000.

[19] D. Fortin, A. Desjardins, A. Benko, T. Niyonsega, and M. Boudrias, "Enhanced chemotherapy delivery by intraarterial infusion and blood-brain barrier disruption in malignant brain tumors: the Sherbrooke experience," *Cancer*, vol. 103, no. 12, pp. 2606–2615, 2005.

[20] D. Fortin, P.-A. Morin, F. Belzile, D. Mathieu, and F.-M. Paré, "Intra-arterial carboplatin as a salvage strategy in the treatment of recurrent glioblastoma multiforme," *Journal of Neuro-Oncology*, vol. 119, no. 2, pp. 397–403, 2014.

[21] W. A. Hall, N. D. Doolittle, M. Daman et al., "Osmotic blood-brain barrier disruption chemotherapy for diffuse pontine gliomas," *Journal of Neuro-Oncology*, vol. 77, no. 3, pp. 279–284, 2006.

[22] F. Imbesi, E. Marchioni, E. Benericetti et al., "A randomized phase III study: comparison between intravenous and intraarterial ACNU administration in newly diagnosed primary glioblastomas," *Anticancer Research*, vol. 26, no. 1, pp. 553–558, 2006.

[23] J. Y. Jeon, I. Kovanlikaya, J. A. Boockvar et al., "Metabolic response of glioblastoma to superselective intra-arterial cerebral infusion of bevacizumab: a proton MR spectroscopic imaging study," *American Journal of Neuroradiology*, vol. 33, no. 11, pp. 2095–2102, 2012.

[24] A. I. Qureshi, M. F. K. Suri, J. Khan et al., "Superselective intra-arterial carboplatin for treatment of intracranial neoplasms: experience in 100 procedures," *Journal of Neuro-Oncology*, vol. 51, no. 2, pp. 151–158, 2001.

[25] B. J. Shin, J.-K. Burkhardt, H. A. Riina, and J. A. Boockvar, "Superselective intra-arterial cerebral infusion of novel agents after blood-brain disruption for the treatment of recurrent glioblastoma multiforme: a technical case series," *Neurosurgery Clinics of North America*, vol. 23, no. 2, pp. 323–329, 2012.

[26] S. Joshi, J. A. Ellis, E. Ornstein, and J. N. Bruce, "Intraarterial drug delivery for glioblastoma mutiforme: will the phoenix rise again?" *Journal of Neuro-Oncology*, vol. 124, no. 3, pp. 333–343, 2015.

[27] J. Wada, "A new method for the determination of the side of cerebral dominance. A preliminary report of intracarotid injection of sodium amytal in man," *Igaku to Seibutsugaku*, vol. 14, pp. 221–222, 1949.

[28] C. T. Klopp, T. C. Alford, J. Bateman, G. N. Berry, and T. Winship, "Fractionated intra-arterial cancer; chemotherapy with methyl bis amine hydrochloride; a preliminary report," *Annals of Surgery*, vol. 132, no. 4, pp. 811–832, 1950.

[29] D. H. Abramson, I. J. Dunkel, S. E. Brodie, J. W. Kim, and Y. P. Gobin, "A phase I/II study of direct intraarterial (ophthalmic artery) chemotherapy with melphalan for intraocular retinoblastoma initial results," *Ophthalmology*, vol. 115, no. 8, pp. 1398–1404.el, 2008.

[30] D. H. Abramson, J. H. Francis, I. J. Dunkel, B. P. Marr, S. E. Brodie, and Y. P. Gobin, "Ophthalmic artery chemosurgery for retinoblastoma prevents new intraocular tumors," *Ophthalmology*, vol. 120, no. 3, pp. 560–565, 2013.

[31] V. Cristina, M. Pracht, Y. Lachenal et al., "Interventional radiology procedures for malignancies of the liver treatment: intraarterial procedures," *Revue Medicale Suisse*, vol. 10, no. 431, pp. 1130–1135, 2014.

[32] J. H. Francis, C. A. Barker, S. L. Wolden et al., "Salvage/adjuvant brachytherapy after ophthalmic artery chemosurgery for intraocular retinoblastoma," *International Journal of Radiation Oncology Biology Physics*, vol. 87, no. 3, pp. 517–523, 2013.

[33] Y. P. Gobin, I. J. Dunkel, B. P. Marr, J. H. Francis, S. E. Brodie, and D. H. Abramson, "Combined, sequential intravenous and intra-arterial chemotherapy (bridge chemotherapy) for young infants with retinoblastoma," *PLoS ONE*, vol. 7, no. 9, Article ID e44322, 2012.

[34] P.-H. Chiang, C.-H. Chen, and Y.-C. Shen, "Intraarterial chemotherapy as the first-line therapy in penile cancer," *British Journal of Cancer*, vol. 111, no. 6, pp. 1089–1094, 2014.

[35] H. Homma, T. Doi, S. Mezawa et al., "A novel arterial infusion chemotherapy for the treatment of patients with advanced pancreatic carcinoma after vascular supply distribution via superselective embolization," *Cancer*, vol. 89, no. 2, pp. 303–313, 2000.

[36] L. J. Jiang, Z. L. Zhang, P. Dong et al., "Efficacy of radical cystectomy plus adjuvant intraarterial chemotherapy with gemcitabine and cisplatin on locally advanced bladder cancer," *Chinese Medical Journal*, vol. 127, no. 7, pp. 1249–1254, 2014.

[37] T. Nakasato, K. Katoh, M. Sone et al., "Superselective continuous arterial infusion chemotherapy through the superficial temporal artery for oral cavity tumors," *American Journal of Neuroradiology*, vol. 21, no. 10, pp. 1917–1922, 2000.

[38] O. M. Rashid, S. Sloot, and J. S. Zager, "Regional therapy in metastatic melanoma: an update on minimally invasive intraarterial isolated limb infusion and percutaneous hepatic perfusion," *Expert Opinion on Drug Metabolism & Toxicology*, vol. 10, no. 10, pp. 1355–1364, 2014.

[39] X. Wang, C. Gan, H. Li et al., "Main complications and results of treatment with intra-arterial infusion chemotherapy through the subclavian and thoracic arteries for locally advanced breast cancer," *Molecular and Clinical Oncology*, vol. 1, no. 4, pp. 745–748, 2013.

[40] A. Ergin, M. Wang, J. Zhang, I. Bigio, and S. Joshi, "Noninvasive in vivo optical assessment of blood brain barrier permeability and brain tissue drug deposition in rabbits," *Journal of Biomedical Optics*, vol. 17, no. 5, Article ID 057008, 2012.

[41] R. P. Singh-Moon, D. M. Roblyer, I. J. Bigio, and S. Joshi, "Spatial mapping of drug delivery to brain tissue using hyperspectral spatial frequency-domain imaging," *Journal of Biomedical Optics*, vol. 19, no. 9, Article ID 096003, 2014.

[42] S. Joshi, R. P. Singh-Moon, J. A. Ellis et al., "Cerebral hypoperfusion-assisted intra-arterial deposition of liposomes in normal and glioma-bearing rats," *Neurosurgery*, vol. 76, no. 1, pp. 92–100, 2015.

[43] R. Reif, M. Wang, S. Joshi, O. A'Amar, and I. J. Bigio, "Optical method for real-time monitoring of drug concentrations facilitates the development of novel methods for drug delivery to brain tissue," *Journal of Biomedical Optics*, vol. 12, no. 3, Article ID 034036, 2007.

[44] H. A. Riina, J. Knopman, J. P. Greenfield et al., "Balloon-assisted superselective intra-arterial cerebral infusion of bevacizumab for malignant brainstem glioma. A technical note," *Interventional Neuroradiology*, vol. 16, no. 1, pp. 71–76, 2010.

[45] D.-Y. Cho and T. M. Przytycka, "Dissecting cancer heterogeneity with a probabilistic genotype-phenotype model," *Nucleic Acids Research*, vol. 41, no. 17, pp. 8011–8020, 2013.

[46] W. Hollmann, "Werner Forssmann, Eberswalde, the 1956 Nobel Prize for medicine," *European Journal of Medical Research*, vol. 11, no. 10, pp. 409–412, 2006.

[47] R. Forssmann-Falck, "Werner Forssmann: a pioneer of cardiology," *The American Journal of Cardiology*, vol. 79, no. 5, pp. 651–660, 1997.

[48] M. G. Bourassa, "The history of cardiac catheterization," *The Canadian Journal of Cardiology*, vol. 21, no. 12, pp. 1011–1014, 2005.

[49] J. Wada and T. Rassmussen, "Intracarotid injection of sodium amytal for the lateralization of cerebral speech dominance: experimental and clinical observations," *Journal of Neurosurgery*, vol. 17, no. 2, pp. 266–282, 1960.

[50] K. Wagner, C. Hader, B. Metternich, F. Buschmann, R. Schwarzwald, and A. Schulze-Bonhage, "Who needs a Wada test? Present clinical indications for amobarbital procedures," *Journal of Neurology, Neurosurgery and Psychiatry*, vol. 83, no. 5, pp. 503–509, 2012.

[51] C. D. Bonner, A. Thurman, and F. Homburger, "A critical study of regional intra-arterial nitrogen mustard therapy in cancer," *Annals of Surgery*, vol. 136, no. 6, pp. 912–918, 1952.

[52] J. D. French, P. M. West, F. K. Von Amerongen, and H. W. Magoun, "Effects of intracarotid administration of nitrogen mustard on normal brain and brain tumors," *Journal of Neurosurgery*, vol. 9, no. 4, pp. 378–389, 1952.

[53] C. B. Wilson, "Chemotherapy of brain tumors by continuous arterial infusion," *Surgery*, vol. 55, no. 5, pp. 640–653, 1964.

[54] C. B. Wilson, "Chemotherapy of brain tumors," *Advances in Neurology*, vol. 15, pp. 361–367, 1976.

[55] C. B. Wilson, P. Gutin, E. B. Boldrey, D. Drafts, V. A. Levin, and K. J. Enot, "Single-agent chemotherapy of brain tumors. A five-year review," *Archives of Neurology*, vol. 33, no. 11, pp. 739–744, 1976.

[56] S. I. Rapoport, M. Hori, and I. Klatzo, "Reversible osmotic opening of the blood-brain barrier," *Science*, vol. 173, no. 4001, pp. 1026–1028, 1971.

[57] S. I. Rapoport, M. Hori, and I. Klatzo, "Testing of a hypothesis for osmotic opening of the blood-brain barrier," *American Journal of Physiology*, vol. 223, no. 2, pp. 323–331, 1972.

[58] R. L. Dedrick, E. H. Oldfield, and J. M. Collins, "Arterial drug infusion with extracorporeal removal. I. Theoretic basis with particular reference to the brain," *Cancer Treatment Reports*, vol. 68, no. 2, pp. 373–380, 1984.

[59] E. H. Oldfield, W. C. Clark, R. L. Dedrick et al., "Reduced systemic drug exposure by combining intraarterial cis-diamminedichloroplatinum(II) with hemodialysis of regional venous drainage," *Cancer Research*, vol. 47, no. 7, pp. 1962–1967, 1987.

[60] E. H. Oldfield, R. L. Dedrick, D. C. Chatterji et al., "Arterial drug infusion with extracorporeal removal. II. Internal carotid carmustine in the rhesus monkey," *Cancer Treatment Reports*, vol. 69, no. 3, pp. 293–303, 1985.

[61] S. J. Hassenbusch, J. H. Anderson, and D. M. Whiting, "Intra-arterial chemotherapy for brain tumors," *Cleveland Clinic Journal of Medicine*, vol. 57, no. 6, pp. 513–520, 1990.

[62] G. Di Chiro, E. Oldfield, D. C. Wright et al., "Cerebral necrosis after radiotherapy and/or intraarterial chemotherapy for brain tumors: PET and neuropathologic studies," *American Journal of Roentgenology*, vol. 150, no. 1, pp. 189–197, 1988.

[63] L. Pickrell and V. Purvin, "Ischemic optic neuropathy secondary to intracarotid infusion of BCNU," *Journal of Clinical Neuro-Ophthalmology*, vol. 7, no. 2, pp. 87–92, 1987.

[64] K. Suda, S. Nakasu, and A. Saito, "Ocular complication of combined intracarotid chemotherapy and osmotic blood-brain barrier disruption," *Nihon Geka Hokan. Archiv fur Japanische Chirurgie*, vol. 54, pp. 359–363, 1985.

[65] J. C. Tonn, K. Roosen, and W. Schachenmayr, "Brain necroses after intraarterial chemotherapy and irradiation of malignant gliomas—a complication of both ACNU and BCNU?" *Journal of Neuro-Oncology*, vol. 11, no. 3, pp. 241–242, 1991.

[66] E. Neuwelt, N. J. Abbott, L. Abrey et al., "Strategies to advance translational research into brain barriers," *The Lancet Neurology*, vol. 7, no. 1, pp. 84–96, 2008.

[67] E. Neuwelt, *Implications of the Blood-Brain Barrier and Its Manipulation*, Plenum Press, New York, NY, USA, 1988.

[68] A. B. Reese, G. A. Hyman, G. R. Merriam Jr., A. W. Forrest, and M. M. Kligerman, "Treatment of retinoblastoma by radiation and triethylenemelamine," *AMA Archives of Ophthalmology*, vol. 53, no. 4, pp. 505–513, 1954.

[69] C. L. Shields, F. P. Manjandavida, S. E. Lally et al., "Intra-arterial chemotherapy for retinoblastoma in 70 eyes: outcomes based on the international classification of retinoblastoma," *Ophthalmology*, vol. 121, no. 7, pp. 1453–1460, 2014.

[70] J. H. Francis, Y. P. Gobin, S. E. Brodie, B. P. Marr, I. J. Dunkel, and D. H. Abramson, "Experience of intra-arterial chemosurgery with single agent carboplatin for retinoblastoma," *The British Journal of Ophthalmology*, vol. 96, no. 9, pp. 1270–1271, 2012.

[71] J. H. Francis, Y. P. Gobin, I. J. Dunkel et al., "Carboplatin +/− topotecan ophthalmic artery chemosurgery for intraocular retinoblastoma," *PLoS ONE*, vol. 8, no. 8, Article ID e72441, 2013.

[72] R. D. Sullivan, J. W. Norcross, and E. Watkins Jr., "Chemotherapy of metastatic liver cancer by prolonged hepatic-artery infusion," *The New England Journal of Medicine*, vol. 270, pp. 321–327, 1964.

[73] L. M. Boehm, T. T. Jayakrishnan, J. T. Miura et al., "Comparative effectiveness of hepatic artery based therapies for unresectable intrahepatic cholangiocarcinoma," *Journal of Surgical Oncology*, vol. 111, no. 2, pp. 213–220, 2015.

[74] T. De Baere and P. Mariani, "Surgical or percutaneous hepatic artery cannulation for chemotherapy," *Journal of Visceral Surgery*, vol. 151, supplement 1, pp. S17–S20, 2014.

[75] F. O. Stephens, P. Crea, G. J. Harker, B. A. Roberts, and C. K. Hambly, "Intra-arterial chemotherapy as basal treatment in advanced and fungating primary breast cancer," *The Lancet*, vol. 2, no. 8192, pp. 435–438, 1980.

[76] W. Zhang, R. Liu, Y. Wang et al., "Efficacy of intraarterial chemoinfusion therapy for locally advanced breast cancer patients: a retrospective analysis of 28 cases," *OncoTargets and Therapy*, vol. 6, pp. 761–765, 2013.

[77] Y. Koike, K. Takizawa, Y. Ogawa, and Y. Nakajima, "Bilateral approach of redistributed subclavian arterial infusion chemotherapy for locally advanced breast cancer spreading to the contralateral chest wall," *Acta Radiologica*, vol. 53, no. 7, pp. 750–753, 2012.

[78] C. L. Appin and D. J. Brat, "Molecular pathways in gliomagenesis and their relevance to neuropathologic diagnosis," *Advances in Anatomic Pathology*, vol. 22, no. 1, pp. 50–58, 2015.

[79] M. Ranjit, K. Motomura, F. Ohka, T. Wakabayashi, and A. Natsume, "Applicable advances in the molecular pathology of glioblastoma," *Brain Tumor Pathology*, vol. 32, no. 3, pp. 153–162, 2015.

[80] R. C. Rockne, A. D. Trister, J. Jacobs et al., "A patient-specific computational model of hypoxia-modulated radiation resistance in glioblastoma using ^{18}F-FMISO-PET," *Journal of the Royal Society Interface*, vol. 12, no. 103, 2015.

[81] F. Yuan, H. A. Salehi, Y. Boucher, U. S. Vasthare, R. F. Tuma, and R. K. Jain, "Vascular permeability and microcirculation of gliomas and mammary carcinomas transplanted in rat and mouse cranial windows," *Cancer Research*, vol. 54, no. 17, pp. 4564–4568, 1994.

[82] H. B. Newton, "Intra-arterial chemotherapy of primary brain tumors," *Current Treatment Options in Oncology*, vol. 6, no. 6, pp. 519–530, 2005.

[83] W. D. Obrist and W. E. Wilkinson, "Regional cerebral blood flow measurement in humans by xenon-133 clearance," *Cerebrovascular and Brain Metabolism Reviews*, vol. 2, no. 4, pp. 283–327, 1990.

[84] S. Joshi, W. L. Young, J. Pile-Spellman et al., "Intra-arterial nitrovasodilators do not increase cerebral blood flow in angiographically normal territories of arteriovenous malformation patients," *Stroke*, vol. 28, no. 6, pp. 1115–1122, 1997.

[85] D. R. Jones, S. D. Hall, E. K. Jackson, R. A. Branch, and G. R. Wilkinson, "Brain uptake of benzodiazepines: effects of lipophilicity and plasma protein binding," *Journal of Pharmacology and Experimental Therapeutics*, vol. 245, no. 3, pp. 816–822, 1988.

[86] Y. Liu, S. Shah, and J. Tan, "Computational modeling of nanoparticle targeted drug delivery," *Reviews in Nanoscience and Nanotechnology*, vol. 1, no. 1, pp. 66–83, 2012.

[87] S. Mitsuki, M. Diksic, T. Conway, Y. L. Yamamoto, J.-G. Villemure, and W. Feindel, "Pharmacokinetics of 11C-labelled BCNU and SarCNU in gliomas studied by PET," *Journal of Neuro-Oncology*, vol. 10, no. 1, pp. 47–55, 1991.

[88] J. L. Tyler, Y. L. Yamamoto, M. Diksic et al., "Pharmacokinetics of superselective intra-arterial and intravenous [^{11}C]BCNU evaluated by PET," *Journal of Nuclear Medicine*, vol. 27, no. 6, pp. 775–780, 1986.

[89] T. Satou, M. Shibata, T. Kawaguchi, and S. Takenoshita, "Intraarterial chemotherapy combined with the concept of pharmacoangiogram using noradrenalin," *Gan to Kagaku Ryoho. Cancer & Chemotherapy*, vol. 39, no. 12, pp. 1863–1866, 2012.

[90] D. A. Boas and R. D. Frostig, "Optics in neuroscience," *Journal of Biomedical Optics*, vol. 10, no. 1, Article ID 011001, 2 pages, 2005.

[91] A. Devor, S. Sakadžić, V. J. Srinivasan et al., "Frontiers in optical imaging of cerebral blood flow and metabolism," *Journal of Cerebral Blood Flow and Metabolism*, vol. 32, no. 7, pp. 1259–1276, 2012.

[92] E. M. C. Hillman, "Optical brain imaging in vivo: techniques and applications from animal to man," *Journal of Biomedical Optics*, vol. 12, no. 5, Article ID 051402, 2007.

[93] V. J. Srinivasan, D. N. Atochin, H. Radhakrishnan et al., "Optical coherence tomography for the quantitative study of cerebrovascular physiology," *Journal of Cerebral Blood Flow and Metabolism*, vol. 31, no. 6, pp. 1339–1345, 2011.

[94] S. Joshi, R. Singh-Moon, M. Wang et al., "Cationic surface charge enhances early regional deposition of liposomes after intracarotid injection," *Journal of Neuro-Oncology*, vol. 120, no. 3, pp. 489–497, 2014.

[95] S. Joshi, R. P. Singh-Moon, M. Wang et al., "Transient cerebral hypoperfusion assisted intraarterial cationic liposome delivery to brain tissue," *Journal of Neuro-Oncology*, vol. 118, no. 1, pp. 73–82, 2014.

[96] S. Joshi, M. Wang, J. J. Etu et al., "Transient cerebral hypoperfusion enhances intraarterial carmustine deposition into brain tissue," *Journal of Neuro-Oncology*, vol. 86, no. 2, pp. 123–132, 2008.

[97] S. C. Saris, R. G. Blasberg, R. E. Carson et al., "Intravascular streaming during carotid artery infusions. Demonstration in humans and reduction using diastole-phased pulsatile administration," *Journal of Neurosurgery*, vol. 74, no. 5, pp. 763–772, 1991.

[98] S. C. Saris, D. C. Wright, E. H. Oldfield, and R. G. Blasberg, "Intravascular streaming and variable delivery to brain following carotid artery infusions in the Sprague-Dawley rat," *Journal of Cerebral Blood Flow and Metabolism*, vol. 8, no. 1, pp. 116–120, 1988.

[99] S. C. Saris, D. R. Shook, R. G. Blasberg et al., "Carotid artery mixing with diastole-phased pulsed drug infusion," *Journal of Neurosurgery*, vol. 67, no. 5, pp. 721–725, 1987.

[100] A. Haag, S. Knake, H. M. Hamer et al., "The Wada test in Austrian, Dutch, German, and Swiss epilepsy centers from 2000 to 2005: a review of 1421 procedures," *Epilepsy & Behavior*, vol. 13, no. 1, pp. 83–89, 2008.

[101] J. T. Fifi, P. M. Meyers, S. D. Lavine et al., "Complications of modern diagnostic cerebral angiography in an academic medical center," *Journal of Vascular and Interventional Radiology*, vol. 20, no. 4, pp. 442–447, 2009.

[102] H. M. Wu, A. G. Lee, D. E. Lehane, T. L. Chi, and R. A. Lewis, "Ocular and orbital complications of intraarterial cisplatin. A case report," *Journal of Neuro-Ophthalmology*, vol. 17, no. 3, pp. 195–198, 1997.

[103] N. D. Doolittle, L. L. Muldoon, A. Y. Culp, and E. A. Neuwelt, "Delivery of chemotherapeutics across the blood-brain barrier: challenges and advances," *Advances in Pharmacology*, vol. 71, pp. 203–243, 2014.

[104] R. B. Vance, J. Pittisapu, and J. P. Kapp, "Experiences with sodium thiosulfate after intracarotid infusion of cisplatin and BCNU for malignant gliomas," *Journal of Neuro-Oncology*, vol. 4, no. 2, pp. 151–154, 1986.

[105] H. Nakagawa, T. Fujita, S. Izumoto, S. Kubo, Y. Nakajima, and K. Turuzono, "Distribution of cis-diamminedichloroplatinum in patients with metastatic brain tumors after intravenous or intracarotid administration," *Cancer & Chemotherapy*, vol. 18, pp. 103–109, 1991.

[106] I. van Rooy, S. Cakir-Tascioglu, W. E. Hennink, G. Storm, R. M. Schiffelers, and E. Mastrobattista, "In vivo methods to study uptake of nanoparticles into the brain," *Pharmaceutical Research*, vol. 28, no. 3, pp. 456–471, 2011.

[107] Y. Takasato, S. I. Rapoport, and Q. R. Smith, "An in situ brain perfusion technique to study cerebrovascular transport in the rat," *The American Journal of Physiology*, vol. 247, no. 3, pp. H484–H493, 1984.

[108] W. H. Oldendorf, "Measurement of brain uptake of radiolabeled substances using a tritiated water internal standard," *Brain Research*, vol. 24, no. 2, pp. 372–376, 1970.

[109] W. H. Oldendorf, "Lipid solubility and drug penetration of the blood brain barrier," *Proceedings of the Society for Experimental Biology & Medicine*, vol. 147, no. 3, pp. 813–815, 1974.

[110] M. Nakashima, S. Shibata, Y. Tokunaga et al., "In-vivo microdialysis study of the distribution of cisplatin into brain tumour tissue after intracarotid infusion in rats with 9L malignant glioma," *Journal of Pharmacy and Pharmacology*, vol. 49, no. 8, pp. 777–780, 1997.

[111] Y. Tokunaga, M. Nakashima, H. Sasaki et al., "Local distribution into brain tumor and pharmacokinetics of 4-pyridoxate diammine hydroxy platinum, a novel cisplatin derivative, after intracarotid administration in rats with 9L malignant glioma: simultaneous brain microdialysis study," *Biological and Pharmaceutical Bulletin*, vol. 23, no. 12, pp. 1491–1496, 2000.

[112] Y. Sawada, R. Kawai, M. McManaway et al., "Kinetic analysis of transport and opioid receptor binding of [3H](−)-cyclofoxy in rat brain in vivo: implications for human studies," *Journal of Cerebral Blood Flow and Metabolism*, vol. 11, no. 2, pp. 183–203, 1991.

[113] I. J. Bigio and S. G. Bown, "Spectroscopic sensing of cancer and cancer therapy: current status of translational research," *Cancer Biology and Therapy*, vol. 3, no. 3, pp. 259–267, 2004.

[114] I. J. Bigio, J. R. Mourant, and G. Los, "Noninvasive, in-situ measurement of drug concentrations in tissue using optical spectroscopy," *Journal of Gravitational Physiology*, vol. 6, no. 1, pp. 173–175, 1999.

[115] J. R. Mourant, T. M. Johnson, G. Los, and I. J. Bigio, "Non-invasive measurement of chemotherapy drug concentrations in tissue: preliminary demonstrations of in vivo measurements," *Physics in Medicine and Biology*, vol. 44, no. 5, pp. 1397–1417, 1999.

[116] E. Reichenthal, P. H. Hollis, G. J. Senior, M. L. Cohen, and R. S. Zappulla, "The feasibility of low dose barbiturate administration by intra-carotid infusion to achieve EEG burst suppression—a preliminary report," *Neurochirurgia*, vol. 31, no. 2, pp. 50–53, 1988.

[117] C. Iaccarino, E. Orlandi, F. Ruggeri et al., "Prognostic value of MGMT promoter status in non-resectable glioblastoma after adjuvant therapy," *Clinical Neurology and Neurosurgery*, vol. 132, pp. 1–8, 2015.

[118] Y. Wang, X. Chen, Z. Zhang et al., "Comparison of the clinical efficacy of temozolomide (TMZ) versus nimustine (ACNU)-based chemotherapy in newly diagnosed glioblastoma," *Neurosurgical Review*, vol. 37, no. 1, pp. 73–78, 2014.

[119] A. Charidimou, J.-C. Baron, and D. J. Werring, "Transient focal neurological episodes, cerebral amyloid angiopathy, and intracerebral hemorrhage risk: looking beyond TIAs," *International Journal of Stroke*, vol. 8, no. 2, pp. 105–108, 2013.

[120] A. K. Vellimana, Y. Kadkhodayan, K. M. Rich et al., "Symptomatic patients with intraluminal carotid artery thrombus: outcome with a strategy of initial anticoagulation," *Journal of Neurosurgery*, vol. 118, no. 1, pp. 34–41, 2013.

[121] C. N. Ionita, V. L. Garcia, D. R. Bednarek et al., "Effect of injection technique on temporal parametric imaging derived from digital subtraction angiography in patient specific phantoms," in *Medical Imaging: Biomedical Applications in Molecular, Structural, and Functional Imaging*, vol. 9038 of *Proceedings of SPIE*, International Society for Optical Engineering, San Diego, Calif, USA, March 2014.

[122] S. Hoelder, P. A. Clarke, and P. Workman, "Discovery of small molecule cancer drugs: successes, challenges and opportunities," *Molecular Oncology*, vol. 6, no. 2, pp. 155–176, 2012.

[123] N. H. Greig, E. M. Daly, D. J. Sweeney, and S. I. Rapoport, "Pharmacokinetics of chlorambucil-tertiary butyl ester, a lipophilic chlorambucil derivative that achieves and maintains high concentrations in brain," *Cancer Chemotherapy & Pharmacology*, vol. 25, no. 5, pp. 320–325, 1990.

[124] D. C. Drummond, O. Meyer, K. Hong, D. B. Kirpotin, and D. Papahadjopoulos, "Optimizing liposomes for delivery of chemotherapeutic agents to solid tumors," *Pharmacological Reviews*, vol. 51, no. 4, pp. 691–743, 1999.

[125] A. S. Y. Chan, S. Y. Leung, M. P. Wong et al., "Expression of vascular endothelial growth factor and its receptors in the anaplastic progression of astrocytoma, oligodendroglioma, and ependymoma," *The American Journal of Surgical Pathology*, vol. 22, no. 7, pp. 816–826, 1998.

[126] Y.-S. Chen and Z.-P. Chen, "Vasculogenic mimicry: a novel target for glioma therapy," *Chinese Journal of Cancer*, vol. 33, no. 2, pp. 74–79, 2014.

[127] P. M. Friden, T. S. Olson, R. Obar, L. R. Walus, and S. D. Putney, "Characterization, receptor mapping and blood-brain barrier transcytosis of antibodies to the human transferrin receptor," *Journal of Pharmacology and Experimental Therapeutics*, vol. 278, no. 3, pp. 1491–1498, 1996.

[128] P. M. Friden, L. R. Walus, G. F. Musso, M. A. Taylor, B. Malfroy, and R. M. Starzyk, "Anti-transferrin receptor antibody and antibody-drug conjugates cross the blood-brain barrier," *Proceedings of the National Academy of Sciences of the United States of America*, vol. 88, no. 11, pp. 4771–4775, 1991.

[129] M. Kinoshita, N. McDannold, F. A. Jolesz, and K. Hynynen, "Targeted delivery of antibodies through the blood-brain barrier by MRI-guided focused ultrasound," *Biochemical and Biophysical Research Communications*, vol. 340, no. 4, pp. 1085–1090, 2006.

[130] H.-L. Liu, H.-W. Yang, M.-Y. Hua, and K.-C. Wei, "Enhanced therapeutic agent delivery through magnetic resonance imaging-monitored focused ultrasound blood-brain barrier disruption for brain tumor treatment: an overview of the current preclinical status," *Neurosurgical Focus*, vol. 32, article E4, 2012.

[131] S. Joshi, M. Wang, and R. Singh-Moon, "Feasibility of intra-arterial drug delivery to brain tissue using cell penetrating peptides," *Journal of Neurosurgical Anesthesiology*, vol. 25, article 465, 2013.

[132] W. M. Pardridge, J. L. Buciak, and P. M. Friden, "Selective transport of an anti-transferrin receptor antibody through the blood-brain barrier in vivo," *Journal of Pharmacology and Experimental Therapeutics*, vol. 259, no. 1, pp. 66–70, 1991.

[133] S. S. Agarwala and J. M. Kirkwood, "Temozolomide, a novel alkylating agent with activity in the central nervous system, may improve the treatment of advanced metastatic melanoma," *The Oncologist*, vol. 5, no. 2, pp. 144–151, 2000.

2

Formulation of Bilayer Benzydamine HCl Patch Targeted For Gingivitis

Piyush Sanghai, Tanaji Nandgude, and Sushilkumar Poddar

Department of Pharmaceutics, Dr. D. Y. Patil Institute of Pharmaceutical Science and Research, Pimpri, Pune, Maharashtra 411018, India

Correspondence should be addressed to Tanaji Nandgude; tanajinandgude@gmail.com

Academic Editor: Philippe Maincent

In the present study bilayer patch of benzydamine HCl was developed using solvent casting method. Different substrates were attempted like Petri dish, glass-and-ring, and teflon-and-ring for selection of the proper option to formulate patch that should give easily peelable film with adequate mechanical properties. HPMC E15 LV was used in different concentrations for obtaining proper viscosity of solution for pouring on to surface and ring, that it should not leak from ring. The second layer was optimized by using different polymer like eudragit RSPO, eudragit RSPO + EC, and eudragit NE30 D for efficient layer bonding. The minimum release from backing membrane was established by diffusion study as compared to from drug loaded layer. The optimized batches were evaluated for folding endurance, weight variation, thickness, drug content, drug release, tensile strength, layer separation, mucoadhesion, moisture uptake, and layer bonding. The novel gingival patch of benzydamine HCl developed would be beneficial in optimizing the therapy.

1. Introduction

The concentration of drugs, when taken orally or by intramuscular route, in the blood increases and reaches its peak value in few minutes to hours. After reaching the peak blood level the drug then starts decreasing in concentration and hence must be readministered when the concentration is thought to be reduced, discussed by Kornman, Carranza [1, 2].

Pharmaceutical technologists today are able to provide drug delivery systems with very precise control over drug release for a prolonged period of time, eliminating the need for a frequent dosing and minimizing side effects, thereby increasing patient compliance and comfort. In conventional mode of administration, many drugs do not reach the target area in the body in sufficient concentration because many are prematurely inactivated and excreted. This problem can be overcome by administering the drugs directly into the intended site of action with lesser dose, discussed by Venkatesh, Jain [3, 4].

Localized drug delivery to tissues of the oral cavity has been investigated for the treatment of periodontal disease and bacterial and fungal infection, amongst the various routes in the novel drug delivery systems. Optimizing localized drug delivery mucoadhesion has potential, by retaining a dosage form at the site of action or systemic delivery. Bioadhesion is the ability of a material (synthetic or biological) to adhere to a biological tissue for a significant period of time. The biological surface can be epithelial tissue or it can be the mucus membrane over the tissue. Discussed by Raghavendra Rao, Poddar [5, 6], Nonsteroidal Anti-Inflammatory Drugs (NSAID) have been widely used for their application in dentistry which consists of analgesic and anti-inflammatory effects [6]. These drugs are used for relieving pain in periodontal disease and retarding the disease process. NSAID act by inhibiting inflammatory enzymes triggered by cytokines, which are important immune factors in periodontal disease.

A number of NSAID have been reported to reduce gingivitis and slow progression of periodontal disease, discussed by Slots and Rams [7].

Prostaglandin synthetase inhibitor benzydamine HCl is an anti-inflammatory, antimicrobial, and local anaesthetic. It is free of adverse systemic effects and is not ulcerogenic. Gingivitis involves inflammation of gums which leads to

Table 1: Composition of double layer patch by using 3^2 factorial design.

(a) First Layer

Batches	Benzydamine HCl (mg)	HPMC E15 LV (mg)	PEG 400 mL	IPA mL	Dist. water mL
DL1	32.14	600	—	12	8
DL2	32.14	650	0.5	12	8
DL3	32.14	700	1	12	8
DL4	32.14	600	—	12	8
DL5	32.14	650	0.5	12	8
DL6	32.14	700	1	12	8
DL7	32.14	600	—	12	8
DL8	32.14	650	0.5	12	8
DL9	32.14	700	1	12	8

(b) Second layer

Batches	Eudragit RSPO mg	Eudragit RSPO + EC mg	Eudragit NE30 D mL	Acetone mL	TEC %
DL1	1680	—	—	20	—
DL2	1680	—	—	20	2
DL3	1680	—	—	20	3
DL4	—	1428 + 272	—	20	—
DL5	—	1428 + 272	—	20	2
DL6	—	1428 + 272	—	20	3
DL7	—	—	2	—	—
DL8	—	—	2	—	—
DL9	—	—	2	—	—

destruction and breakdown of periodontal structures resulting in increased pocket depth, clinical attachment loss, and destruction of alveolar bone. Therefore the benzydamine HCl would be an ideal choice to treat the gingival infection. Benzydamine HCl is available as mouth wash in concentration of 0.15%. The objective of the present study was to design suitable periodontal double layer patch of benzydamine HCl by using teflon as a casting substrate and HPMC E15 LV as a drug releasing polymer (first layer) and eudragit NE 30D as a backing polymer (second layer) to avoid loss of drug through back side of the patch and to evaluate for the physicochemical characteristics, including in vitro drug release.

2. Material and Method

2.1. Material. Benzydamine HCl was provided as gift sample from Alkem Laboratories Pvt. Ltd., Mumbai, India. Eudragit NE 30D was obtained as gift sample from Evonik India Pvt. Ltd. HPMC E15 LV was purchased from Colorcon Asia, Goa, India, and PEG 400 was purchased from Research Labs Finechem Industries, Mumbai, India.

2.2. Method

2.2.1. Preparation of Double Layer (DL) Patches. Patches were prepared using the solvent casting method. The film forming polymer was dissolved by solvating overnight. Clear bubble-free solutions were poured on a film casting substrate arranged horizontally with the help of a spirit level. Pool of liquid with uniform thickness was evaporated. The dried film that resulted was peeled off.

2.2.2. Casting of First Layer (FL). The first layer was developed as a film by using teflon coated surface of an iron and stainless steel ring by the solvent casting method. For avoiding leakage the fitment of the ring and the viscosity of solution were optimized by taking different concentration of HPMC, namely, 600 mg, 650 mg, and 700 mg. The HPMC was dissolved in distilled water and IPA in ratio of 40 : 60. The PEG 400, 1 mL, was included as plasticizer. The quantity of drug was taken based on quantity in mouth wash. Mouth wash contains 22.5 mg of drug; therefore 2 mg of drug was taken to formulate patch. The resultant solution was poured on teflon coated iron surface confined by stainless steel ring. It was allowed to dry in air overnight.

2.2.3. Casting of Second Layer (SL). Second layer was cast on the surface of first layer which was obtained by confining with a ring. Eudragit NE 30D 2 mL was poured on the surface of first layer. It was allowed to dry overnight.

2.2.4. Design of Experiment. See Table 1.

2.2.5. Physicochemical Properties of Drug and Polymer. Characterisation of drug and polymer was performed by using FTIR (Shimadzu-8400S) discussed by Nandgude and Bhise

[8] and DSC (PerkinElmer-4000) discussed by Nandgude et al. [9].

2.2.6. Evaluation of Double Layer (DL) Patches. This was discussed by Agarwal, Singh, Prabhushankar, and Beetha Rohini [10–14].

(1) Physical Evaluation

(a) Thickness [11, 12]. The thickness of film was measured by digital vernier caliper Schr.Lab/DSR II (184)/1. The thickness was measured at five different sites and average was taken.

(b) Percent Flatness [10, 11]. The percent flatness was measured by cutting a film into strips from centre of the film. The strips were so cut that each should have had 4 cm length and 0.5 cm breadth. Each strip was put on a clean surface without applying any pressure and measured for length by digital vernier caliper Schr.Lab/DSR II (184)/1.

(c) Moisture Uptake [10, 11]. Desiccators were used for humidity creation, one for 58% RH and another for 79% RH. Saturated solution of sodium bromide and aluminium chloride at RT (approx. 35°C) was used, respectively.

The patches were dried for 24 hours in a desiccators containing calcium chloride. Then the patches were kept in desiccators of 58% RH and 79% RH, respectively. The patches were equilibrated at respective RH for 48 hours.

(d) Weight Uniformity [11, 12]. Five patches of $2 \times 2\,cm^2$ were taken from different areas of cast; each was weighed on an electronic balance and the mean weight was recorded. Uniformity in the weight of the patches was determined.

(e) Surface pH [11, 12]. Agar plates were prepared by dissolving 2% (w/v) agar in warmed water and pouring into a Petri dish to solidify at room temperature. The patches were left to swell for 1 hour on the surface of the agar plate. The surface pH was measured by means of pH paper placed on the surface of the soaked patch.

(2) Mechanical Properties

(a) Tensile Strength [12]. The tensile strength was determined by an apparatus. Three strips of patch were cut having 4 cm length and 0.5 cm breadth. The thickness and breadth of strips were noted at three sites and average value was taken for calculation. The strips were marked with ink 2 cm apart and 1 cm from each end. Each strip was kept in the clips such that the markings were visible. The rate of change of stress was kept constant with increment. The elongation was observed and the total weight taken was used for calculation. The tensile strength was calculated using the following formula:

$$(S) = \frac{m \times g}{b \times t}, \quad (1)$$

where S is tensile strength in dynes/cm^2, m is mass in grams, g is acceleration due to gravity (980 cm/sec^2), b is breadth of strip in cm, and t is thickness of strip in cm.

The strain undergoes change in size after a force is applied. Therefore, the strain can be given as

$$\text{Strain } (E) = \frac{L - L_0}{L_0}, \quad (2)$$

where L is length after force was applied and L_0 is original length.

(b) Elongation [13, 14]. The percent elongation at break was measured by the formula given below:

$$\%\ \text{elongation} = \frac{L - L_0}{L_0} \times 100, \quad (3)$$

where L is length after force was applied and L_0 is original length.

(c) Mucoadhesion Study. The mucoadhesion study was performed by using goat gingiva. The study was performed using a texture analyser method. The sample contact time was 10 sec and load was 10 g.

(d) Content Uniformity [11, 12, 15]. The patch of area 4.0 cm^2 was dissolved in 10 mL methanol and transferred to 100 mL volumetric flask, volume made up by freshly prepared phosphate buffer having pH 6.8 and kept at room temperature. After disintegration of patch, drug and polymer had got dissolved. An aliquot of 1 mL was withdrawn from the solution and diluted to 10 mL with phosphate buffer pH 6.8. The absorbance of the solution was taken at λ_{max} 214 nm against the solvent phosphate buffer pH 6.8 as blank.

(e) Microscopy. TS was prepared with a sharp blade. It was observed for the status of the two layers and their bonding under optical microscope at 100x.

(3) Drug Release Studies

(a) Dissolution Studies [10, 15]. The dissolution study was performed by using USP type 1 basket type six station dissolution apparatus where previously wet patch of each batch was kept inside the basket. The dissolution medium consisted of phosphate buffer of pH 6.8 at 37±1°C and 50 rpm rotation was maintained throughout the experiment. Samples were withdrawn at the intervals of 30 min. and replaced with equal volume of dissolution medium each time.

The release study was carried out for 5 hours. Withdrawn samples were filtered, diluted with phosphate buffer of pH 6.8, and then analysed spectrophotometrically at λ_{max} 214 nm. The patches were also noted critically for maintenance of layer bonding.

(b) Diffusion Studies [10]

Diffusion Cell. Diffusion studies are performed to obtain an idea of permeation of a drug through a barrier from a system. Usually, two types of diffusion cells are used, namely, horizontal and vertical. Franz and Keshary-Chien (K-C) type diffusion cells are of vertical type. In this work, Franz type of diffusion cell was used.

TABLE 2: Physical evaluation of double layer patches.

Batches	Appearance	Thickness (mm)	Flatness (%)	Surface pH	Moisture Loss (%)	Moisture uptake (%)	
						At 58% RH	At 79% RH
DL1	Thin, rigid, transparent	0.3 ± 0.015	90.3	6-7	1.36	2.4	5.4
DL2	Thin, rigid, transparent	0.29 ± 0.019	91.9	6-7	2.41	3.2	7.1
DL3	Thin, rigid, transparent	0.31 ± 0.019	92.1	6-7	3.54	3.8	7.5
DL4	Thin, flexible, transparent	0.28 ± 0.020	98.20	6-7	3.67	5.8	7.5
DL5	Thin, flexible, opaque	0.30 ± 0.018	96.9	6-7	3.20	6.2	7.8
DL6	Thin, flexible, transparent	0.32 ± 0.13	95	6-7	4.26	6.5	4.3
DL7	Thin, flexible, transparent	0.27 ± 0.16	98.45	6-7	4.35	3.4	7.1
DL8	Thin, flexible, transparent	0.30 ± 0.11	97.94	6-7	3.98	4.6	5.1
DL9	Thin, flexible, transparent	0.25 ± 0.21	98.93	6-7	3.55	5.4	6.4

Diffusion cells generally comprise two compartments, receiver and donor compartment containing the API to dissolve and diffuse. Acceptor compartment contains a medium to receive the diffused API. The compartments are separated by barrier which was dialysis membrane.

3. Result and Discussion

3.1. Physicochemical Characterisation

3.1.1. FTIR. IR spectra of drug and polymer indicated the purity of drug and polymer and absence of interaction between drug and polymer. Results are shown in Figure 1.

3.1.2. DSC. Figure 2(a) shows endotherm of pure benzydamine HCl was found as 161.29°C. This represented the melting point for the drug.

Figure 2(b) shows the DSC graph of physical mixture of the drug and the polymer. There was no change in the endotherm drug. The melting point of drug was 161.04°C. The graph showed the compatibility of the drug and polymer.

Figure 2(c) shows the DSC graph of a formulated patch. It did not show the drug peak. This meant drug might have got changed into another form like amorphous.

3.2. Results of Patches of Factorial Design

3.2.1. Physical and Mechanical Evaluation. The double layer patches were studied using different polymers, individually and in combinations. Eudragit RSPO gave rather brittle layer on the surface of first layer. Batches from DL4–DL6 were of combination of ethyl cellulose and eudragit RSPO with different concentration of TEC as plasticizer. The patches obtained of this combination were opaque in nature and nonuniformly spread over the first layer. Batches number DL7–DL9 contained the second layer of eudragit NE30 D. These were thin, flexible, and transparent and gave maximum percent elongation. The pH of patches from batches number DL1–DL9 was found to be in range of 6-7.

As the proportion of HPMC and PEG 400 increased in the first layer moisture uptake increased significantly. HPMC being hydrophilic in nature increased in the moisture uptake which might be due to the increase in the concentration of HPMC.

The percent moisture loss was also found to be proportional to the concentration of HPMC. In case of second layer acetone was used as solvent in batches DL1–DL6; therefore these did not show maximum percent moisture loss. This indicated that water holding was more in case of aqueous operation. Some moisture would be essential for the desirable mechanical properties. At the same time lesser moisture in the patch especially FL would make them water "thirsty." This quality would be helpful when the patch would be applied on the gingival mucosa, helping in mucoadhesion (Table 2).

Batches DL1–DL3 gave the minimum percent elongation. This could be due to the brittle nature of second layer. The batches from DL4 to DL9 had percent elongation more as the concentration of PEG 400 and TEC was higher in them.

Batches from DL1–DL3 gave the layer separation because of the brittle nature of second layer. Second layer of these batches consisted of eudragit RSPO. As the combination of eudragit and ethyl cellulose was used it gave the weak bonding in between first and second layer, though it needed the plasticizer. Batches from DL7 to DL9 consisted of eudragit NE30 D dispersion as second-layer forming agent. There was no need of plasticizer in them as there were good plasticity and bonding of the layer.

Tensile strength was found to be changing as the use of the polymer changed. In case of eudragit RSPO it was observed

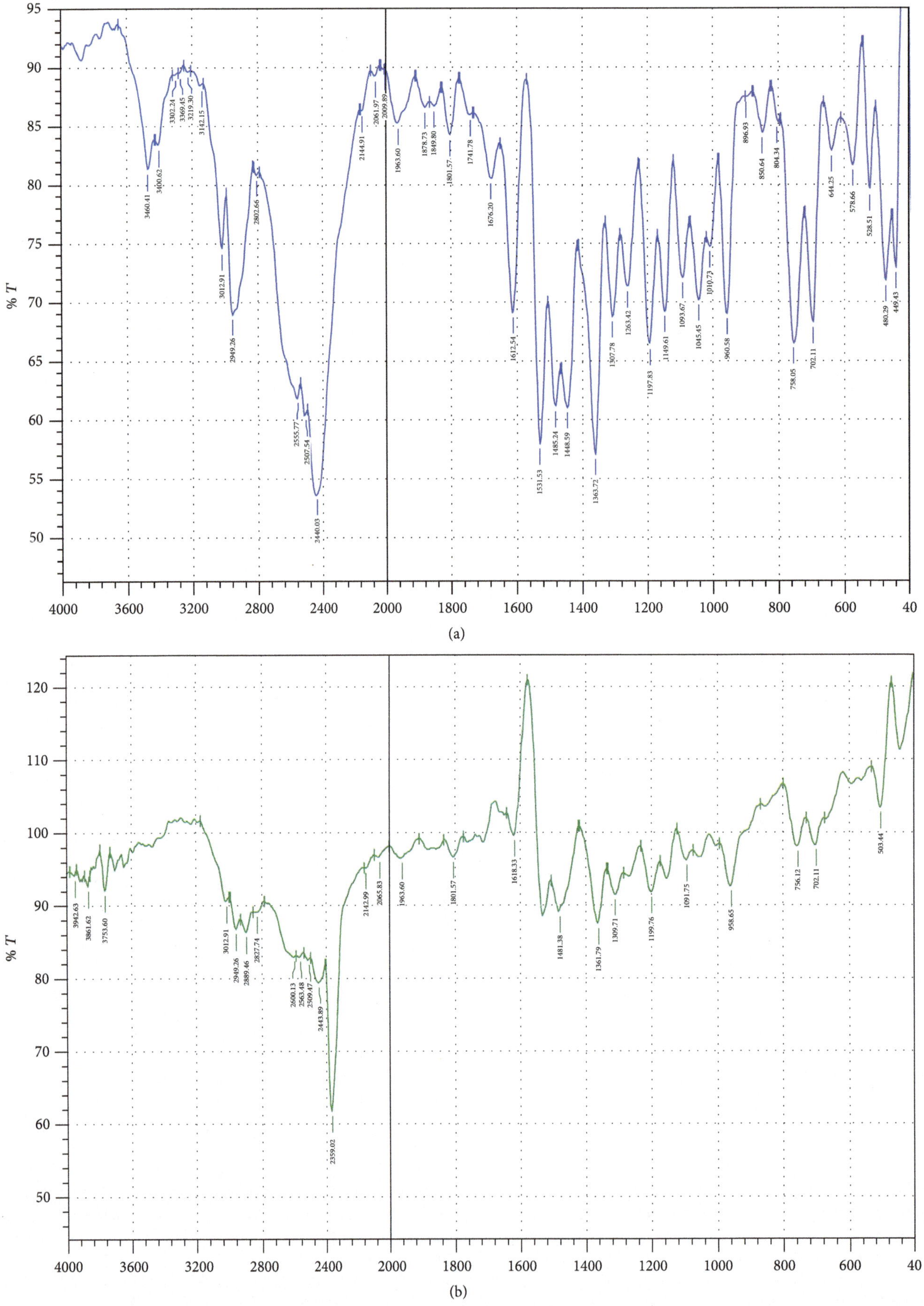

FIGURE 1: IR spectra of drug and polymer, (a) IR of benzydamine HCl, and (b) IR of physical mixture of benzydamine HCl and HPMC E15 LV.

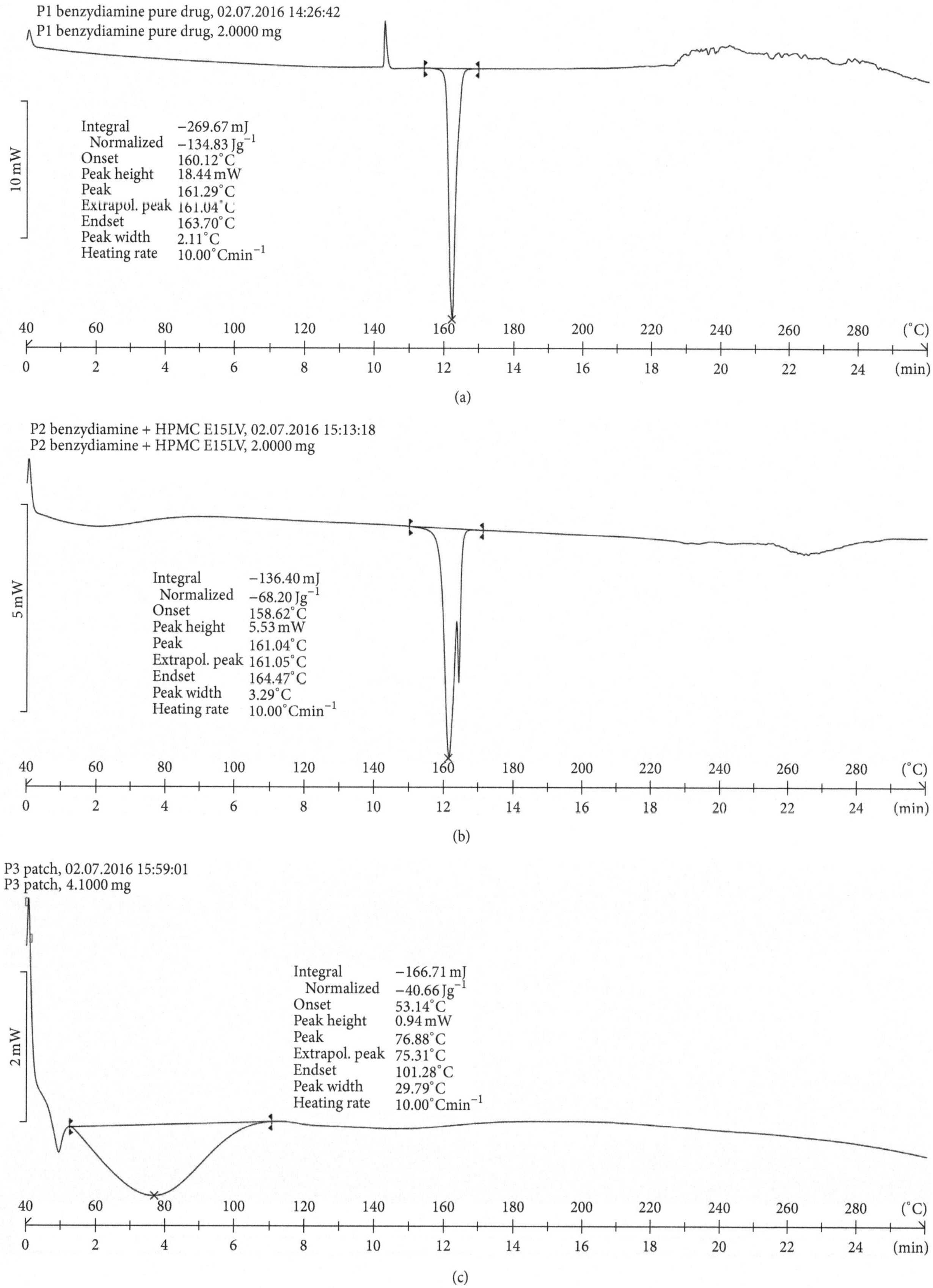

FIGURE 2: DSC patterns of (a) benzydamine HCl, (b) physical mixture of benzydamine HCl and HPMC E15 LV, and (c) patch (batch DL9).

TABLE 3: Mechanical evaluation of double layer patches.

Batches	Tensile strength (dynes/cm^2)	Elongation (%)	Weight (mg)	Folding endurance		Drug content (%)
				Layer separation	Yield number of folds	
DL1	$33.7 \times 10^6 \pm 21.7$	46 ± 0.8	105	Yes	>120	94.21
DL2	$36.9 \times 10^6 \pm 1.7$	44 ± 0.8	108	Yes	>125	94.70
DL3	$37.5 \times 10^6 \pm 1.7$	48 ± 0.8	110	Yes	>130	95.01
DL4	$39.8 \times 10^6 \pm 2.0$	52 ± 1.8	106	No	>125	95.32
DL5	$42.1 \times 10^6 \pm 2.0$	55 ± 1.8	109	No	>135	94.65
DL6	$43.14 \times 10^6 \pm 2.0$	58 ± 1.8	112	No	>145	96.2
DL7	$45.02 \times 10^6 \pm 1.5$	56 ± 1.8	111	No	>150	95.11
DL8	$44.1 \times 10^6 \pm 1.5$	59 ± 1.8	114	No	>150	96.98
DL9	$46.26 \times 10^6 \pm 1.5$	60 ± 1.8	115	No	>160	98.5

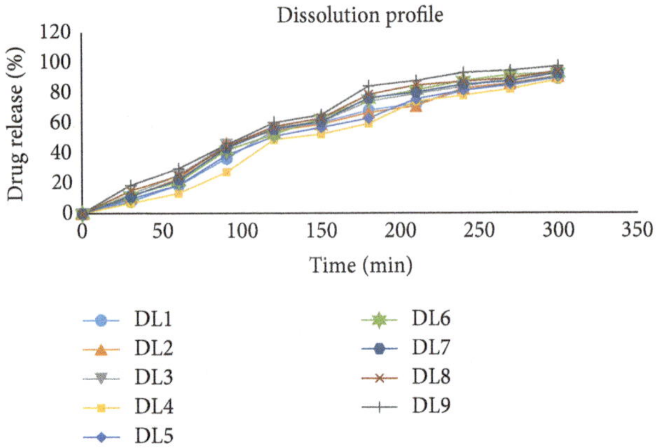

FIGURE 3: Drug release from double layer patches by dissolution study.

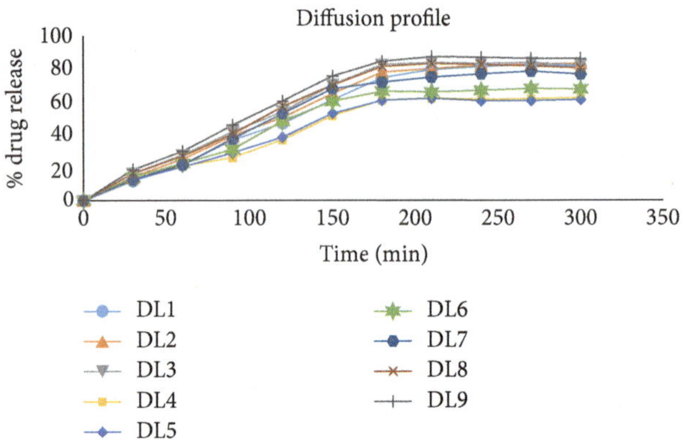

FIGURE 4: Drug diffusion from front side of double layer patches.

that required force was low as compared to eudragit NE30 D and the combination of EC and eudragit RSPO.

As the concentration of HPMC E15 LV increased the weight also increased. This might be because of moisture retention by the HPMC E15 LV. As the concentration of HPMC increased the moisture uptake increased, and that resulted in increase in weight (Table 3).

3.3. Dissolution Study. The dissolution study of the double layer patches is shown in Figure 3. The release of drug was in the range 88–96%. Batch DL9 gave a 96.4% drug release. During dissolution study layer separation study was executed. It was observed that there was no layer separation during and at the end of the dissolution period. This indicated significant layer bonding.

3.4. Diffusion Study

(a) Front Release. Drug release by diffusion study of front layer of double layer patch gave less diffusion as compared to the monolayer. It might be because of the presence of second layer. The release obtained was found to be in the range of 61–87% in 5 hours. The batches from DL1 to DL6 gave lesser release as compared to DL7–DL9. This indicated that as the concentration of HPMC increased release also increased. The remaining 10–15% of drug might have penetrated into the second layer.

In DL1–DL3 backward diffusion was higher due to improper layer bonding. The 10–15% of drug might have penetrated in the second layer because of dissolution of HPMC in solvent of the second layer. The nature of second layer in batches DL1–DL3 was brittle and layer separation was observed in them.

It was observed that there was no layer separation during and at the end of dissolution period in DL7–DL9. DL4–DL6 showed the separation of the layer, and it might be because of weak bonding in FL and SL (Figure 4).

(b) Back Release. It could be concluded that the 13–16% of drug diffused into and through the second layer. Batches from DL7 to DL9 gave minimum drug diffusion from second layer.

Eudragit RSPO gave back release up to 17%. The combination of eudragit RSPO and ethyl cellulose gave up to 15%. The eudragit NE30 D gave release up to 13%.

The eudragit NE30 D was found to have lowest permeability as compared to the eudragit RSPO and combination of eudragit RSPO and EC in case of benzydamine HCl. Therefore the batches from DL7 to DL9 were considered as the optimized batches giving the minimum release from

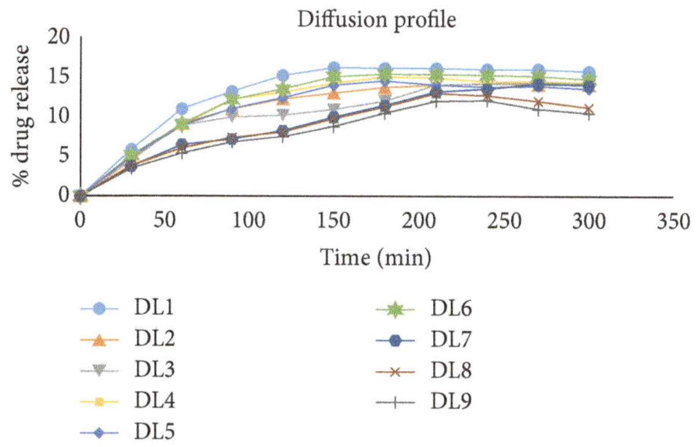

FIGURE 5: Drug diffusion from back side of double layer patches.

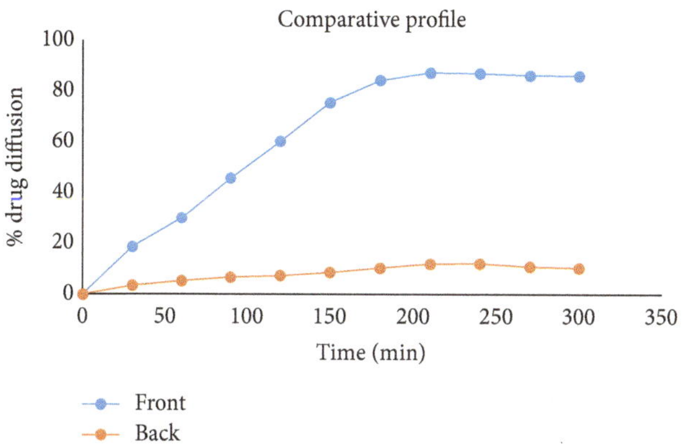

FIGURE 6: Comparative drug release from both sides of double layer patches by diffusion study.

backing layer and probably helping to have maximum release from front side (Figure 5).

(c) Comparative Study. The comparative release of drug from front and back surfaces of batch DL9 showed that up to 13% drug was released from backing layer and up to 87% of drug was released from front layer. From the above results it could be concluded that passage of drug could be minimum through the backing acrylate layer through fabrication of double layer patches (Figure 6).

3.5. Mucoadhesion Study. It is the ex vivo mucoadhesion with Brookfield Texture Analyser on goat gingival mucosa. Adhesion for formulation DL9 containing PEG 400 1 mL was found to be 1.9 g/cm^2. The adhesive force generated with formulation DL9 was found to be 7.6 g (Table 4).

3.6. Microscopy. Layer bonding status was reported through optical microscopy at 100x, the bonding between first layer and second layer. Fine channels indicated intermixing and interpenetration of layer. This might have happened due to the addition of the second-layer solution over the dry first layer as well as during the subsequent drying. Interpenetration of layer might be due to dissolving of HPMC in second-layer liquid. Interpenetration of layers leads to good layer bonding but might lead to back release. Though it might have led to good layer bonding, it also gave a bit higher drug release through the second layer (Figure 7).

TABLE 4: In vitro mucoadhesion strength measurement with Brookfield Texture Analyser.

Batch	Adhesive force	Adhesiveness
DL9	7.6 g	1.9 g/cm^2

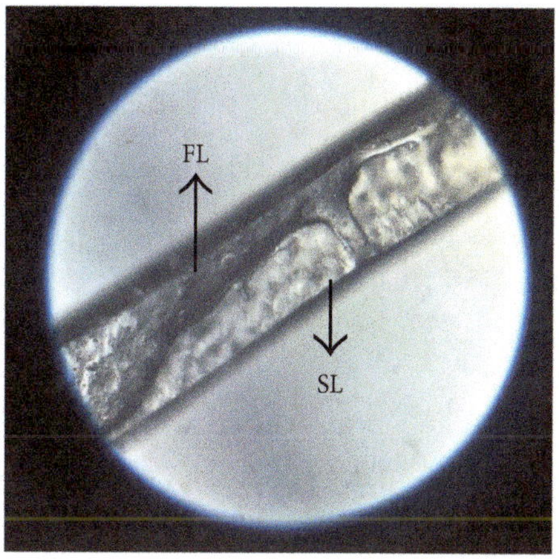

FIGURE 7: Layer bonding study by optical microscope, where FL is first layer and SL is second layer.

4. Conclusion

From the obtained results, it could be concluded that periodontal bilayered patches of benzydamine HCl were formulated by solvent casting technique using teflon coated iron and ring. The IR spectra revealed that there was no interaction between polymers and drug. All the polymers used were compatible with the drug. DSC showed purity of drug by thermogram. Evaluation parameters like thickness, tensile strength, folding endurance, and percentage moisture loss indicate that patches were mechanically stable. Percentage weight variation and content uniformity were found to be uniform in all the patches. In vitro drug release showed an abrupt release after 2 to 2.5 h. and there after the release profile was controlled and extended till the end of static release study. It also did not show layer separation of double layer patch. All the patches were found to be stable over the storage period and conditions tested. Drug release from backing membrane was minimum that would result in less loss of drug in GI track. The high % drug release of the patch indicated that these patches could be real alternative to traditional OTC product like tablets, mouth washes, gels, and capsules. This could be helpful for the treatment of gingivitis. Further investigation is required to establish in vivo and clinical efficiency of these patches.

Competing Interests

The authors declare that there is no conflict of interests regarding the publication of this paper.

References

[1] K. S. Kornman, "Controlled-release local delivery antimicrobials in periodontics: prospects for the future," *Journal of Periodontology*, vol. 64, no. 8, pp. 782–791, 1993.

[2] F. A. Carranza and G. Michel, *New Man. Clinical Periodontology*, Prism Books Pvt. Ltd, New Delhi, India, 1996.

[3] S. A. Venkatesh M and N. Udupa, "Controlled-drug delivery systems for periodontitis," *The Pharm Review*, pp. 61–82, 2004.

[4] N. K. Jain, "Advances in controlled and novel drug delivery," in *Controlled and Novel Drug Delivery*, pp. 130–147, CBS Publication, New Delhi, India, 1st edition, 1997.

[5] N. G. Raghavendra Rao, R. Neelagiri, and M. S. Reddy, "Muccoadhesive Patch as Drug Delivery System: an overview," *International Journal of Current Pharmaceutical Research*, vol. 5, no. 2, pp. 40–47, 2010.

[6] R. S. Patel and S. S. Poddar, "Development and characterization of mucoadhesive buccal patches of salbutamol sulphate," *Current Drug Delivery*, vol. 6, no. 1, pp. 140–144, 2009.

[7] J. Slots and T. E. Rams, "Antibiotics in periodontal therapy: advantages and disadvantages," *Journal of Clinical Periodontology*, vol. 17, no. 7, pp. 479–493, 1990.

[8] T. D. Nandgude and K. Bhise, "Characterization of drug and polymers for development of colon specific drug delivery system," *Asian Journal of Biomedical and Pharmaceutical Sciences*, vol. 1, no. 4, pp. 17–21, 2011.

[9] T. D. Nandgude, K. S. Bhise, and V. B. Gupta, "Characterization of hydrochloride and tannate salts of diphenhydramine," *Indian Journal of Pharmaceutical Sciences*, vol. 70, no. 4, pp. 482–486, 2008.

[10] R. K. Agarwal, D. H. Robinson, G. I. Maze, and R. A. Reinhardt, "Development and characterization of tetracycline-poly(lactide/glycolide) films for the treatment of periodontitis," *Journal of Controlled Release*, vol. 23, no. 2, pp. 137–146, 1993.

[11] N. Singh and R. Malviya, "Formulation and evaluation of different polymer based periodontal," *Film of Ofloxacin der Pharmacia Lettre*, vol. 2, no. 3, pp. 297–303, 2010.

[12] G. L. Prabhushankar, B. Gopalkrishna, K. M. Manjunatha, and C. H. Girisha, "Formulation and evaluation of levofloxacin dental films for periodontitis," *International Journal of Pharmacy and Pharmaceutical Sciences*, vol. 2, no. 1, pp. 162–168, 2010.

[13] U. S. Beetha Rohini, "Formulation and evaluation of dental films for periodontitis," *Journal of Chemical and Pharmaceutical Research*, vol. 4, no. 6, pp. 2964–29710, 1994.

[14] W. M. M. Jenkins and C. J. Allan, *Pathogenesis Guide to Periodontics*, 3rd edition, 1994.

[15] N. Choudhary and J. Avari, "Formulation and evaluation of taste mask pellets of granisetron hydrochloride as oro dispersible tablet," *Brazilian Journal of Pharmaceutical Sciences*, vol. 51, no. 3, pp. 569–578, 2015.

3

Formulation and *In Vitro* Evaluation of Bilayer Tablets of Nebivolol Hydrochloride and Nateglinide for the Treatment of Diabetes and Hypertension

Harika Ryakala,[1] S. Dineshmohan,[1] Alluri Ramesh,[1] and V. R. M. Gupta[2]

[1] *Vishnu Institute of Pharmaceutical Education and Research, Vishnupur, Narsapur, Medak, Telangana 502313, India*
[2] *Department of Pharmaceutics, Pulla Reddy Institute of Pharmacy, Annaram, Hyderabad 502313, India*

Correspondence should be addressed to S. Dineshmohan; akinesh@yahoo.co.in

Academic Editor: Sri Rama K. Yellela

Diabetes mellitus (DM) and hypertension are two common diseases that often coexist. The most common cause of death in the diabetic patient is heart disease. In the present investigation we combine Nebivolol and Nateglinide for better patient compliance. IR layer was formulated using various superdisintegrants like Crospovidone, Croscarmellose sodium, and sodium starch glycolate and SR layer was formulated using polymers and gums like HPMC E_{15}, ethyl cellulose, Gaur gum, and Xanthan gum. The disintegration and dissolution study of both layers showed that inclusion of surfactant (sodium lauryl sulphate) to the tablet formulation (IR) and dissolution medium (SR) enhanced the release of drugs from both layers. Kinetic studies of optimized IR layer (NBL8) and SR layer (N9) showed good linearity with regression coefficient of 0.9714 (Higuchi model) and 0.9931 (zero order kinetics), respectively. The above results reveal that the optimized IR layer of Nebivolol (NBL8) and SR layer of Nateglinide (N9) might be suitable for the treatment of diabetes and hypertension by sequential release of the two drugs in a bilayer tablet. IR-immediate release, SR-sustain release, NBL8-Nebivolol 8, N9-Nateglinide 9.

1. Introduction [1–11]

Type 2 diabetes mellitus and hypertension are among the most common chronic noncommunicable diseases and multifactorial disorders affecting both developed and developing countries. Lifestyle and genetic factors are responsible for diabetes mellitus and hypertension. In India, currently we have around 40 million cases of DM and it is projected to increase to 87 million by the year 2030. The prevalence of type 2 DM has raised from 1.2% to 11% over last three decades. A patient who suffers from type 2 DM has 2–4 times greater risk of death from cardiovascular causes than the patient without diabetes mellitus. The most common cause of death in the diabetic patient is heart disease. In addition, peripheral vascular disease, end-stage renal disease, blindness, and amputations are common comorbidities in diabetic patients. Therefore, combination therapy is important for the prevention of diabetes in patients with hypertension. Nebivolol hydrochloride is a BCS class-2 drug and β_1 receptor blocker with nitric oxide-potentiating vasodilator effect. It is used in treatment of hypertension and is highly cardioselective. It lowers blood pressure by reducing peripheral vascular resistance and significantly increases stroke volume with preservation of cardiac output. Nebivolol has reduced typical beta-blocker related side effects such as fatigue, clinical depression, bradycardia, and impotence. Nateglinide is a novel D-phenylalanine derivative that inhibits ATP-sensitive K+ channels in pancreatic beta-cells in the presence of glucose and thereby stimulates the prandial release of insulin. It is selective blocker of pancreatic beta-cells with a short half-life of 1.5–2.5 hrs. Therefore, in order to prolong its effect in the body and to decrease oscillations in concentration level in plasma, a modified drug delivery system is needed for Nateglinide.

The aim of present research work was undertaken to formulate bilayer tablets of Nebivolol and Nateglinide through its incorporation of an oral dosage form that is able to release Nebivolol immediately as well as sustained release of

TABLE 1: Scale of flowability (USP).

Flow character	Angle of repose (θ)	Compressibility index (%)	Hausner's ratio
Excellent	25–30	≤10	1.00–1.11
Good	31-35	11–15	1.12–1.18
Fair	36–40	16–20	1.19–1.25
Passable	41–45	21–25	1.26–1.34
Poor	46–55	26–31	1.35–1.45
Very poor	56–65	32–37	1.46–1.59
Very, very poor	>66	>38	>1.60

Nateglinide for 12 hrs to enhance the oral bioavailability of Nateglinide. The main objective of this work was formulation of bilayer tablets composed of two different classes of drugs by using a simple and easy-to-scale-up formulation strategy.

2. Materials and Methods

Nateglinide and Nebivolol were obtained as gift samples from Hetero Drugs Ltd. Hyderabad, India. Xanthan gum, Guar gum, and HPMC E15 were gifted by Ashland Labs, Hyderabad, India. Sodium starch glycolate, Crospovidone, and Croscarmellose sodium were procured from SD Fine Chemicals, Mumbai, India. Talc and magnesium stearate were purchased from Nice Chemie Pvt. Ltd., Mumbai, India. Ethyl cellulose N 50 was gifted by Aurobindo Pharma, Hyderabad, India.

2.1. Characterization of IR/SR Granules [12–14]. Solubility studies of the drugs were carried out in various aqueous solutions and buffers. Drug excipient compatibility studies were done using FTIR. The granules of both the layers of IR/SR were evaluated for various precompression parameters. The angle of repose was measured by fixed funnel method. Bulk and tapped densities were determined by tapped density apparatus from which compressibility index and Hausner's ratio values were calculated and from the values obtained flow property of granules was determined from Table 1.

2.1.1. Drug-Excipient Compatibility Studies by FT-IR. The compatibility of drugs with their respective excipients was studied by FT-IR spectroscopy (Model number 02437, Shimadzu, India). The scanning was performed 20 times at scanning speed 2 mm/sec with resolution of 4 cm^{-1} over the region 4000–400 cm^{-1}. The scans were evaluated for presence of principle peaks of drug, shifting and masking of drug peaks, and appearance of new peaks due to polymer interaction.

2.2. Analytical Method Development [15–18]

2.2.1. Construction of Calibration Curve of Nebivolol and Nateglinide. Standard dilutions were prepared in the range of 2–10 μg/mL using 0.1 N HCl for Nebivolol and absorbance was determined at λ_{max} (282 nm) in UV spectrophotometer (UV-1700, Shimadzu, India). Similarly standard dilutions were prepared in the range of 2–10 μg/mL using 0.01 N HCl with 0.5% w/v SLS for Nateglinide and absorbance was determined at λ_{max} (210 nm) in UV spectrophotometer. From the values obtained, standard graph can be plotted between concentration and absorbance values.

SLS: Sodium Lauryl Sulfate.

2.3. Preparation of Immediate Release Nebivolol Tablets [19]. Immediate release layer of Nebivolol (NBL1–NBL9) was prepared by direct compression method. Nebivolol and other excipients like microcrystalline cellulose, Crospovidone, Croscarmellose sodium, and sodium starch glycolate and sodium lauryl sulfate were accurately weighed and sifted through sieve #40 and mixed in a polybag and these formulations are given in Table 2. The sifted powders were thoroughly mixed for approximately 5 min and again passed through sieve #40 to get uniform particle size. Magnesium stearate was added into the powder mixture for lubrication after passing through sieve #40 and 0.125% w/w of iron oxide red previously sifted to sieve #100 was added to the above mixture and blended thoroughly to ensure uniform color.

2.4. Preparation of Sustained Release Nateglinide Tablets [19]. Sustained release layer of Nateglinide (N1–N13) was prepared by wet granulation technique by adding 5% concentration of PVP K 30 dissolved in isopropyl alcohol as a binding agent and these formulations are represented in the Table 3. Required quantities of Nateglinide and other excipients like HPMC E_{15}, Guar gum, Xanthan gum, ethyl cellulose, mannitol, and microcrystalline cellulose were weighed accurately and were sifted through sieve #40 and were mixed thoroughly and a sufficient volume of binding agent was added slowly to get cohesive mass. Then mass was passed through sieve #20 to obtain the granules. Next the granules were dried at 50°C in a hot air oven until dry the dried granules were lubricated uniformly with magnesium stearate; then talc was added and mixed properly. The above granules were compressed into tablets by 10-station tablet compression machine (Mini Press I, Karnavati, Gujarat, India) using 9 mm punch. In batches N1 to N3, HPMC E_{15} was used as the sustained release polymer and in batches N4 to N7 Guar gum was used, and in N8 Xanthan gum, in N9 combination of HPMC E_{15} and Guar gum, and in N10 to N12 combination of Guar gum and ethyl cellulose, and finally in N13 combination of Guar gum and Xanthan gum was used as sustained release polymer.

2.5. Preparation of Bilayer Tablets [19]. In order to prepare bilayer tablets, the dissolution test was conducted for both layers of IR/SR separately with the aim of selecting the best formulations. Based on dissolution behavior, formulations NBL-8 and N-9 were selected for bilayer tablet. First, sustained release Nateglinide layer was placed in the die cavity and punched with low compression force. Then the immediate release Nebivolol layer was placed in the die cavity and allowed for punching with optimum hardness of 6–8 kg/cm^2 to form bilayer tablets. Compression was made

TABLE 2: Composition of Nebivolol immediate release tablets (150 mg).

Batch code	Ingredients in mg/tablet							
	Drug	MCC	CP	CCS	SSG	Mg. stearate	SLS	Fe_2O_3
NBL-1	10	131	7.5	—	—	1.5	—	Qs
NBL-2	10	123.5	15	—	—	1.5	—	Qs
NBL-3	10	131	—	7.5	—	1.5	—	Qs
NBL-4	10	123.5	—	15	—	1.5	—	Qs
NBL-5	10	131	—	—	7.5	1.5	—	Qs
NBL-6	10	123.5	—	—	15	1.5	—	Qs
NBL-7	10	119.5	—	—	18.75	1.5	—	Qs
NBL-8	10	131	—	—	7.5	1.5	0.3	Qs
NBL-9	10	123.5	—	—	15	1.5	0.3	Qs

MCC: microcrystalline cellulose, CP: Crospovidone, CCS: Croscarmellose sodium, SSG: sodium starch glycolate, SLS: sodium lauryl sulfate.

TABLE 3: Composition of Nateglinide sustained release tablets.

Ingredients	N1	N2	N3	N4	N5	N6	N7	N8	N9	N10	N11	N12	N13
Drug	60	60	60	60	60	60	60	60	60	60	60	60	60
HPMC	30	45	60	—	—	—	—	—	45	—	—	—	—
Guar gum	—	—	—	30	45	60	75	—	—	60	60	60	60
X-gum	—	—	—	—	—	—	—	75	45	45	—	—	—
EC	—	—	—	—	—	—	—	—	—	—	15	30	15
Mannitol	—	—	—	—	—	—	—	—	—	—	—	—	72
MCC	180	165	150	180	165	150	135	135	120	129	135	120	72
PVP	15	15	15	15	15	15	15	15	15	15	15	15	15
Mg. st.	7.5	7.5	7.5	7.5	7.5	7.5	7.5	7.5	7.5	6	7.5	7.5	6
Talc	7.5	7.5	7.5	7.5	7.5	7.5	7.5	7.5	7.5	—	7.5	7.5	—
Total wt.	**300**	**300**	**300**	**300**	**300**	**300**	**300**	**300**	**300**	**300**	**300**	**300**	**300**

HPMC: hydroxy propyl methyl cellulose; X-gum: Xanthan gum; EC: ethyl cellulose; MCC: microcrystalline cellulose; PVP: polyvinyl pyrrolidone, Mg. st.: magnesium stearate.

by using 10 mm punches (Mini Press I, Karnavati, Gujarat, India). The total weight of each bilayer tablet was adjusted to 450 mg, containing 10 mg of Nebivolol in fast-release layer and 60 mg of Nateglinide in sustained release layer. Prepared bilayer tablets were evaluated for various postcompression parameters and *in vitro* dissolution studies.

2.6. Evaluation of IR/SR Tablets [19–22]. The prepared tablets were subjected to various evaluation tests like thickness, hardness, weight variation, friability, and drug content. Thickness of the tablets was determined by using vernier calipers. Randomly 10 tablets were selected and used for determination of thickness. Hardness is termed as the tablet crushing strength and it is the force required to break a tablet diametrically. Hardness of tablets was measured by selecting 6 tablets randomly and the hardness of each tablet was measured with Monsanto hardness tester. The hardness was noted. The hardness is usually measured in terms of kg/cm^2. For weight variation test individual weight of 20 tablets was taken; then their average weight and their mean and standard deviation were calculated and compared with the standards. The weight of the tablet being made is measured to ensure that it contains predetermined amount of drug. The tablet friability is a measure of loss due to abrasion. The preweighed tablets were exposed to repeated shocks in Roche friabilator in which they are initially weighed (W_0) and kept in a tumbling and rotating apparatus drum and were subjected to fall from 6 inches height. After completion of 100 rotations, the tablets were reweighed (W) and the percent loss in weight or friability (f) was calculated by the formula given below:

$$\%\text{Friability} = \frac{\text{Initial weight} - \text{Final weight}}{\text{Initial weight}} \times 100. \quad (1)$$

2.7. Drug Content [23]. Twenty tablets were selected randomly and average weight was calculated. The tablets were crushed in a mortar and accurately weighed amount of average tablet weight was taken from the crushed blend and transferred in to a 100 mL volumetric flask. To this little amount of methanol was added to dissolve the drug and volume was made up to the mark with concerned medium. The content was shaken periodically and kept for 1 hour to allow the drug to dissolve completely. Then it was filtered and appropriate dilutions were made. Finally dilutions were observed using spectrophotometer to determine % drug content. The drug content should be within the range between 90 and 110% of standard amount.

2.8. Disintegrating Time [24]. The disintegration test is carried out in an apparatus (Electro lab, Mumbai) containing a basket rack assembly with six glass tubes of 7.75 cm in length and 2.15 mm in diameter, the bottom of which consists of a #10 mesh sieve. The basket is raised and lowered 28–32 times per minute in a medium of 900 mL water which is maintained at 37 ± 2°C. Six tablets were placed in each of the tubes and the time required for complete passage of tablet fragments through the mesh (#10) was considered as the disintegration time of the tablet.

2.9. In Vitro Dissolution Studies [17, 18]. The release of drug from different batches of prepared tablets was studied using USP dissolution apparatus type II. The dissolution medium used was 500 mL of 0.1 N HCl for first 30 minutes for immediate release layer and then 900 mL of 0.01 N HCl with 0.5% w/v SLS was used up to 12 hours for sustained release layer. The temperature was maintained at 37 ± 0.5°C and the stirring rate was 50 rpm. The samples were withdrawn at regular intervals and this withdrawn volume was replaced with fresh medium. The collected samples were filtered using Whatman filter paper and observed using spectrophotometer at respective λ_{max} against a blank (respective medium).

2.10. Evaluation of Bilayer Tablet [17, 18, 25]. Evaluation parameters of bilayer tablet were performed according to I.P. specifications. Parameters such as weight variation were performed by taking average weight of 20 tablets and hardness test was performed by Monsanto hardness tester. Thickness of the tablet was measured using vernier caliper. Friability test was performed by taking 6 tablets in Roche friabilator and % friability was calculated. *In vitro* drug release studies of bilayer tablets were carried out uvusing USP dissolution apparatus type II in 500 mL of 0.1 N HCl for first 30 minutes and in 900 mL of 0.01 N HCl with 0.5% SLS up to 12 hours. Samples were collected at regular intervals of time and filtered. The medium in bowl was discarded after 30 minutes and replaced with another medium which was preferred for dissolution of sustain release layer. The collected samples were filtered and observed in UV spectrophotometer. The results were calculated using simultaneous equation method as given below:

$$Cx = \frac{A_2 ay_1 - A_1 ay_2}{ax_2 ay_1 - ax_1 ay_2},$$
$$Cy = \frac{A_1 ax_1 - A_2 ax_2}{ax_2 ay_1 - ax_1 ay_2} \qquad (2)$$

where

Cx and Cy are concentrations of Nebivolol and Nateglinide,

A_1 is absorbance value at wavelength λ_1,

A_2 is absorbance value at wavelength λ_2,

ax_1 is absorptive value of Nebivolol at λ_1,

ax_2 is absorptive value of Nebivolol at λ_2,

ay_1 is absorptive value of Nateglinide at λ_1,

ay_2 is absorptive value of Nateglinide at λ_2.

Table 4: Diffusion exponent and solute release mechanism (Korsemeyer equation/Peppas model).

Diffusion exponent (n)	Drug release mechanism
0.45	Fickian diffusion
$0.45 < n = 0.89$	Anomalous (non-Fickian) diffusion
0.89	Case-II transport
$n > 0.89$	Super case-II transport

2.11. Kinetic Data Analysis [15, 19]. The drug release kinetic studies were carried out for bilayer tablets of Nebivolol and Nateglinide and were evaluated using the linear regression method:

(1) zero order kinetic model—cumulative % of drug released versus T;

(2) first order kinetic model—log cumulative percent drug remaining versus T;

(3) Higuchi's model—cumulative percent drug released versus square root of T;

(4) Korsmeyer equation/Peppa's model—log cumulative percent drug released versus log T.

2.12. Stability Studies [19]. The purpose of stability testing is to provide evidence on how the quality of drug product varies with time under the influence of a variety of environmental factors such as temperature, humidity, and light. The optimized bilayer tablets were subjected to stability studies (as per ICH guidelines) at 40°C ± 2°C/75% ± 5% RH in a humidity chamber. The products were evaluated for their physical characteristics and *in vitro* drug release profiles over a period of 3 months.

3. Results and Discussion

3.1. Analytical Method Development. Calibration curves were plotted for both Nebivolol and Nateglinide based on the data obtained in UV spectrophotometer and these curves showed regression coefficient of 0.9999 and 0.9996 for the respective drugs.

3.1.1. Construction of Calibration Curve of Nebivolol and Nateglinide. See Tables 5 and 6 and Figures 1 and 2.

3.2. Characterization of IR/SR Granules

3.2.1. Solubility Studies. Solubility studies were carried out for both Nebivolol and Nateglinide in various solvents and buffers and results were found to be as in Table 7.

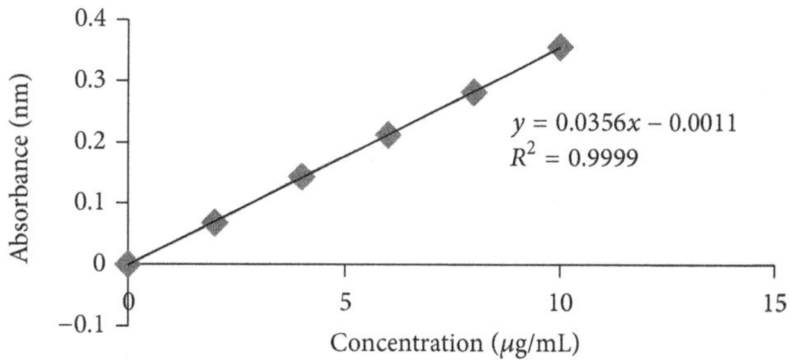

FIGURE 1: Calibration curve of Nebivolol in 0.1 N HCl.

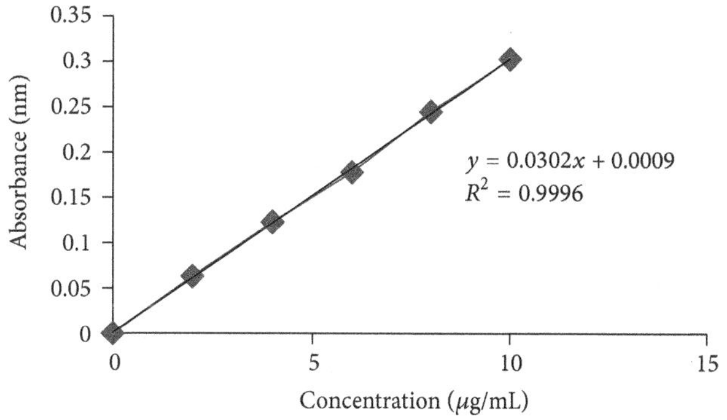

FIGURE 2: Calibration curve of Nateglinide in 0.01 N HCl with 0.5% w/v SLS.

TABLE 5: Data for calibration curve of Nebivolol in 0.1 N HCl.

Concentration (μg/mL)	Absorbance (nm)
0	0
2	0.068
4	0.143
6	0.212
8	0.282
10	0.356

TABLE 6: Data for calibration curve of Nateglinide in 0.01 N HCl with 0.5% w/v SLS.

Concentration (μg/mL)	Absorbance (nm)
0	0
2	0.063
4	0.123
6	0.178
8	0.245
10	0.303

3.2.2. Drug-Excipient Compatibility Studies by FT-IR. As part of compatibility studies, FT-IR studies were performed as shown in Figures 3, 4, 5, and 6 for both drugs along with the excipients to detect any major interference between drug and excipients.

TABLE 7: Solubility study data of Nebivolol and Nateglinide in various solvents and buffers.

Name of solvent/buffer	Nebivolol (mg/mL)	Nateglinide (mg/mL)
Water	0.0017	0.001
HCl buffer pH 1.2	1.2234	0.105
Phosphate buffer pH 6.8	0.0012	0.021
PEG	0.9102	—
DMSO	0.4567	0.574
Methanol	0.0814	0.342

As per the data tabulated in Tables 8 and 9, there was no significant shift in the positions of wave numbers when compared to that of the pure drugs. As there is no interaction observed between the drugs and excipients of the formulations, these excipients were chosen for the formulations.

3.2.3. Micromeritics Studies. Flow properties of Nebivolol and Nateglinide were carried out and results are shown in the Tables 10 and 11 which were found to be as per the limits given in the Table 1.

3.3. Evaluation of IR/SR Tablets. Immediate release tablets of Nebivolol were successfully prepared by direct compression method using various concentrations of superdisintegrants like Crospovidone, Croscarmellose sodium, sodium starch

Table 8: Characteristic peak of Nebivolol pure drug and optimized formula.

Functional groups	Reported value (cm^{-1})	Observed value (cm^{-1}) Pure drug	Observed value (cm^{-1}) Optimized formula
COOH	3300–2500	3195.59	3196.12
Nitro compounds	1550–1475	1493.30	1493.05
Alkyl halides	1300–1150	1214.62	1215.17
Aliphatic amines	1250–1020	1074.87	1074.47

Table 9: Characteristic peak of Nateglinide pure drug and optimized formula.

Functional groups	Reported value (cm^{-1})	Observed value (cm^{-1}) Pure drug	Observed value (cm^{-1}) Optimized formula
COOH	3300–2500	3123.24	3126.84
Carbonyls	1760–1665	1690.97	1691.56
Nitro compounds	1550–1475	1487.80	1488.00
Aliphatic amines	1550–1475	1150.20	1150.63

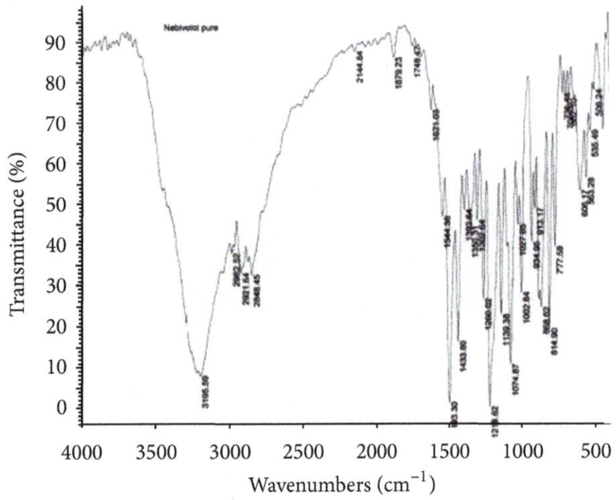

Figure 3: FT-IR (Nebivolol pure drug).

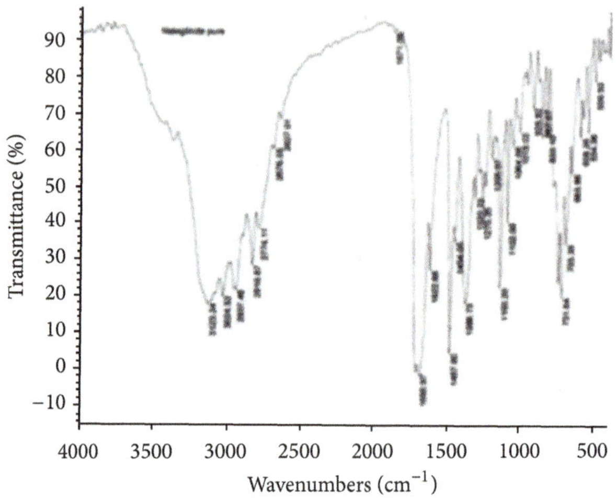

Figure 5: FT-IR (Nateglinide pure drug).

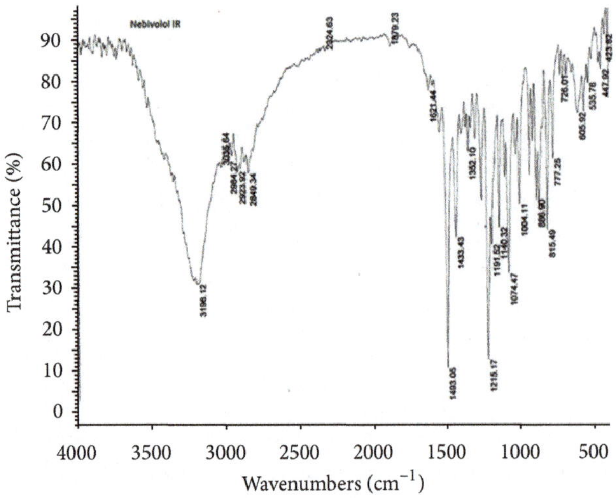

Figure 4: FT-IR (Nebivolol optimized formula).

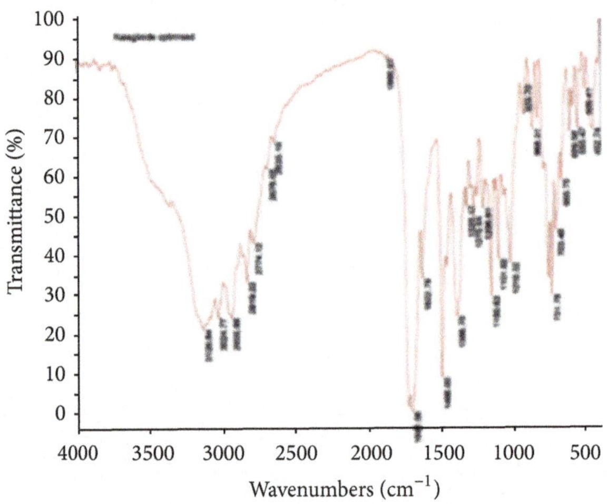

Figure 6: FT-IR (Nateglinide optimized formula).

TABLE 10: Flow properties of Nebivolol immediate release layer.

Batch code	Angle of repose	Bulk density (g/cm^3)	Tapped density (g/cm^3)	Carr's index (%)	Hausner's ratio
NBL-1	30.17	0.34	0.40	15.00	1.17
NBL-2	34.70	0.35	0.47	25.53	1.34
NBL-3	26.10	0.34	0.41	17.07	1.20
NBL-4	29.12	0.34	0.40	15.00	1.17
NBL-5	28.47	0.34	0.39	12.82	1.14
NBL-6	26.96	0.35	0.43	18.60	1.22
NBL-7	26.10	0.36	0.41	12.19	1.13
NBL-8	**27.92**	**0.35**	**0.42**	**16.66**	**1.20**
NBL-9	28.01	0.35	0.40	12.50	1.14

TABLE 11: Flow properties of Nateglinide sustained release layer.

Batch code	Angle of repose	Bulk density (gm/cm^3)	Tapped density (gm/cm^3)	Carr's index (%)	Hausner's ratio
N1	35.12	0.32	0.37	13.50	1.15
N2	32.15	0.31	0.40	22.50	1.29
N3	31.18	0.34	0.38	10.52	1.11
N4	32.20	0.38	0.44	13.63	1.15
N5	34.80	0.30	0.35	14.28	1.16
N6	33.15	0.36	0.42	14.28	1.16
N7	30.00	0.29	0.33	12.12	1.13
N8	28.55	0.30	0.35	14.28	1.16
N9	**27.50**	**0.31**	**0.35**	**11.42**	**1.13**
N10	31.85	0.39	0.46	15.21	1.18
N11	27.90	0.34	0.40	15.00	1.17
N12	34.55	0.39	0.45	13.33	1.15
N13	34.41	0.33	0.38	13.15	1.15

TABLE 12: Evaluation parameters of Nebivolol immediate release tablets.

Batch code	Weight variation (%)	Hardness (kg/cm^2)	Thickness (mm)	Friability (%)	Drug content (%)	Disintegration time (min)
NBL-1	0.53	4.3	2.83	0.13	95.56	3.40
NBL-2	1.19	4.5	3.29	0.15	97.20	2.55
NBL-3	2.51	4.0	3.18	0.14	96.45	4.10
NBL-4	1.19	5.0	3.30	0.13	90.84	3.28
NBL-5	1.25	3.5	2.85	0.16	103.01	3.56
NBL-6	3.18	4.3	2.91	0.12	97.62	2.45
NBL-7	0.53	4.2	3.10	0.15	100.94	1.50
NBL-8	**1.25**	**4.5**	**3.05**	**0.18**	**98.19**	**3.45**
NBL-9	0.53	4.5	3.20	0.16	99.42	2.40

TABLE 13: *In vitro* drug release data of Nebivolol immediate release tablets (NBL1–NBL9).

Time	NBL-1	NBL-2	NBL-3	NBL-4	NBL-5	NBL-6	NBL-7	NBL-8	NBL-9
0	0	0	0	0	0	0	0	**0**	0
5	11 ± 3.12	16 ± 3.26	14 ± 3.11	19 ± 3.80	16 ± 3.57	19 ± 3.85	19 ± 24	**25 ± 3.96**	27 ± 3.68
10	21 ± 3.45	28 ± 3.40	25 ± 4.25	28 ± 3.54	29 ± 4.20	32 ± 3.15	31 ± 3.20	**43 ± 3.56**	41 ± 3.24
15	35 ± 3.08	36 ± 4.05	34 ± 4.50	38 ± 3.69	42 ± 4.22	46 ± 4.12	48 ± 4.01	**50 ± 3.94**	58 ± 3.80
20	49 ± 4.15	50 ± 4.91	47 ± 3.75	52 ± 4.52	58 ± 3.75	59 ± 3.46	60 ± 4.23	**66 ± 4.25**	73 ± 4.31
25	55 ± 3.89	61 ± 3.89	53 ± 3.90	59 ± 3.96	64 ± 3.58	66 ± 4.29	70 ± 3.99	**80 ± 3.98**	88 ± 3.78
30	64 ± 4.52	69 ± 3.68	65 ± 4.82	68 ± 4.95	74 ± 4.52	80 ± 4.42	84 ± 4.58	**96 ± 3.80**	97 ± 3.94

Table 14: Evaluation parameters of Nateglinide sustained release tablets.

Batch code	Weight variation (%)	Hardness (kg/cm^2)	Thickness (mm)	Friability (%)	Drug content (%)
N1	0.22	7.0	3.97	0.59	96.12
N2	0.89	5.8	3.95	0.62	97.45
N3	0.55	7.2	3.99	0.60	98.10
N4	1.55	6.8	3.85	0.54	95.53
N5	1.20	6.2	3.57	0.70	98.63
N6	0.89	5.5	3.84	0.69	98.84
N7	0.22	6.5	3.73	0.72	97.14
N8	0.22	5.5	3.69	0.54	101.15
N9	**0.55**	**6.8**	**3.89**	**0.52**	**98.68**
N10	1.55	5.4	3.91	0.63	102.42
N11	0.89	6.5	4.11	0.71	97.85
N12	1.88	7.0	3.90	0.51	96.81
N13	1.20	6.0	3.66	0.56	100.65

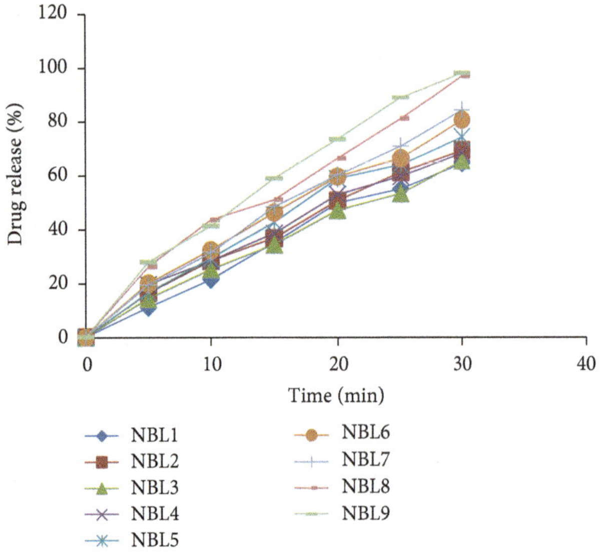

Figure 7: Comparison of % drug release of Nebivolol immediate release tablets (NBL1–NBL9).

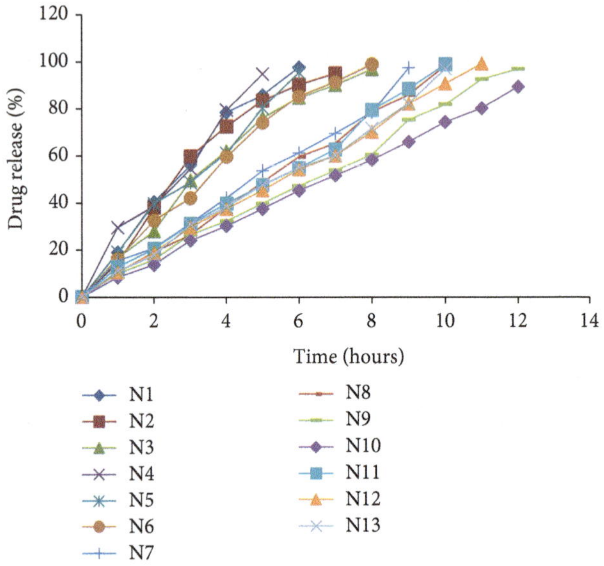

Figure 8: Comparison of % drug release of Nateglinide sustained release tablets (N1–N13).

glycolate, and other tableting excipients. The prepared formulations were evaluated for postcompression parameters. The results of all formulations were found to be within limits (weight variation ±7.5%, hardness range 4.5–7 kg/cm^2, friability <1%, drug content 90–110%, and disintegration time 5–30 minutes) and all the values were reported in Table 12. *In vitro* drug release studies of immediate release tablets were carried out using USP type II dissolution apparatus in 500 mL of 0.1 N HCl at 50 rpm up to 30 minutes. Except formulation code NBL7, all other formulations contain same concentrations of different superdisintegrants (5–10%). Formulation NBL7 has increased amount (12.5%) of sodium starch glycolate as a superdisintegrant. Formulation batches NBL1–NBL7 have shown an immediate release profile between 64 and 84% within 30 minutes. The formulations NBL1–NBL6 showed lesser drug release 64–80% and NBL7 showed 84% of drug release. Hence to further increase the drug release SLS was

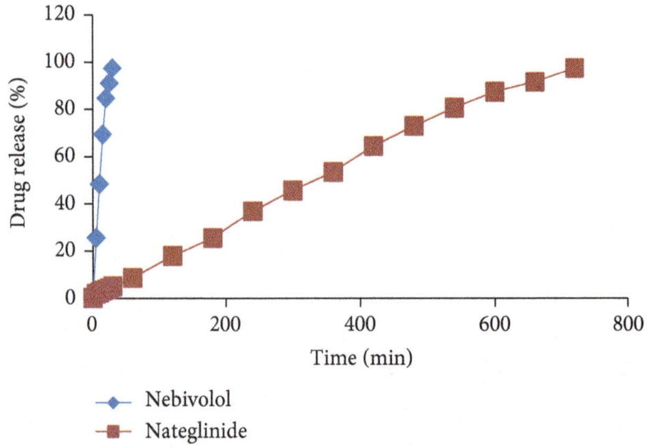

Figure 9: Cumulative % drug release of Nebivolol and Nateglinide bilayer tablet.

TABLE 15: *In vitro* drug release data of Nateglinide sustained release tablets (N1 to N13).

Time (hrs)	N1	N2	N3	N4	N5	N6	N7	N8	N9	N10	N11	N12	N13
0	0	0	0	0	0	0	0	0	**0**	0	0	0	0
1	18 ± 3.99	14 ± 3.45	16 ± 3.51	29 ± 3.68	19 ± 4.03	16 ± 4.02	15 ± 3.38	10 ± 3.37	**9 ± 3.90**	8 ± 3.25	12 ± 3.64	10 ± 3.31	10 ± 3.96
2	40 ± 3.46	38 ± 4.14	28 ± 4.07	38 ± 3.72	39 ± 3.72	32 ± 3.61	20 ± 3.64	18 ± 3.99	**15 ± 3.68**	13 ± 3.63	20 ± 3.36	18 ± 3.61	17 ± 3.64
3	56 ± 3.14	59 ± 3.78	49 ± 3.54	54 ± 3.58	48 ± 3.80	41 ± 3.94	31 ± 437	26 ± 3.42	**26 ± 3.42**	24 ± 4.01	31 ± 4.24	29 ± 3.64	30 ± 3.76
4	78 ± 4.44	72 ± 3.45	61 ± 3.92	79 ± 4.45	61 ± 4.19	59 ± 4.55	42 ± 4.11	37 ± 3.98	**32 ± 4.20**	30 ± 4.25	39 ± 3.31	37 ± 4.29	38 ± 3.22
5	85 ± 3.83	83 ± 4.42	75 ± 3.96	94 ± 3.83	80 ± 3.27	73 ± 3.93	53 ± 3.67	48 ± 3.71	**39 ± 3.63**	37 ± 3.45	47 ± 3.53	45 ± 4.23	47 ± 3.61
6	97 ± 4.56	90 ± 4.28	84 ± 3.52		95 ± 3.36	85 ± 4.19	61 ± 4.10	59 ± 4.45	**47 ± 3.06**	45 ± 3.23	54 ± 3.69	53 ± 3.98	54 ± 3.83
7		95 ± 4.01	90 ± 4.08			91 ± 3.40	69 ± 3.36	65 ± 3.23	**53 ± 3.67**	51 ± 3.64	62 ± 3.58	59 ± 3.87	60 ± 4.09
8			96 ± 3.81			98 ± 3.79	78 ± 3.44	78 ± 3.44	**60 ± 3.27**	58 ± 4.21	79 ± 4.34	70 ± 4.01	71 ± 3.56
9							97 ± 3.43	85 ± 3.87	**75 ± 4.14**	65 ± 3.82	88 ± 3.46	81 ± 3.97	82 ± 4.13
10								98 ± 3.30	**81 ± 3.74**	74 ± 4.30	98 ± 3.97	90 ± 3.64	96 ± 3.98
11									**92 ± 3.48**	80 ± 4.16		99 ± 4.15	
12									**96 ± 3.92**	89 ± 4.43			

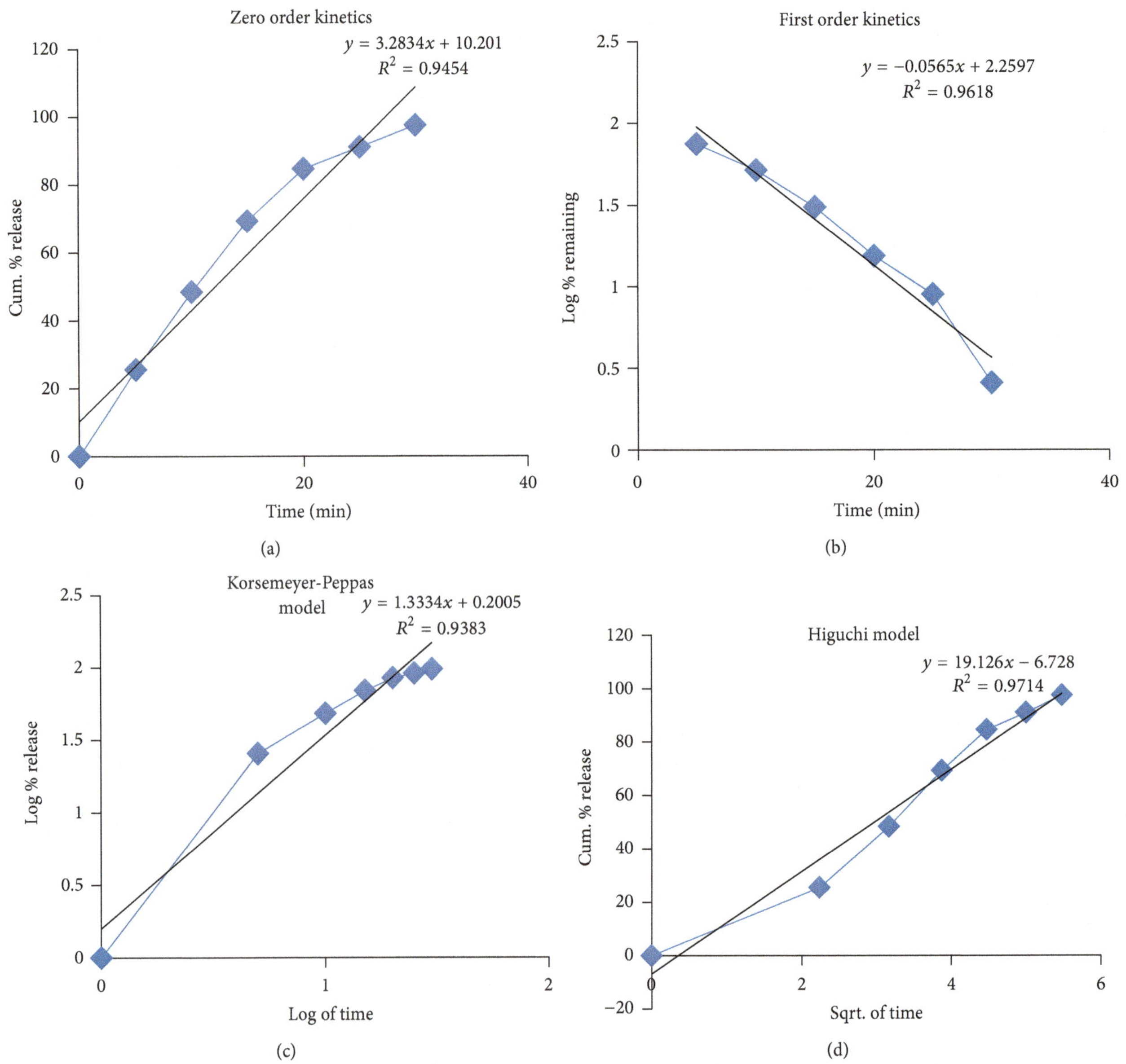

FIGURE 10: Drug release kinetics of Nebivolol (immediate release) layer in bilayer tablet.

TABLE 16: Evaluation parameters of bilayer tablet.

Name	Weight variation (%)	Hardness (kg/cm^2)	Thickness (mm)	Friability (%)
Bilayer tablet	0.54	6.5	5.36	0.48

added in NBL8 and NBL9 and both formulations had shown good drug release 96-97% at the end of 30 minutes. From that above data formulation NBL8 was optimized for bilayer tablet as it reflects good disintegration and dissolution characters with lesser amount of superdisintegrant (5%). These results are represented in Table 13 and Figure 7.

Nateglinide sustained release layer of bilayer tablet was prepared by wet granulation method using common granulating agent and diluent for all the formulations, that is, 5% PVP +IPA and MCC, respectively, having varying concentrations of polymers and gums which were used either individually or in combination, with N13 as an exception in which combination of diluents such as Mannitol and MCC was used. Postcompression parameters were evaluated for all the formulations and results were found to be within the limits as mentioned in above section and were shown in Table 14. *In vitro* drug release studies were carried out in 900 mL of 0.01 N HCl with 0.5% w/v SLS for 12 hours at 50 rpm and 37 ± 0.5°C using USP dissolution apparatus type II. The formulations N1–N8 in which either polymer or gum

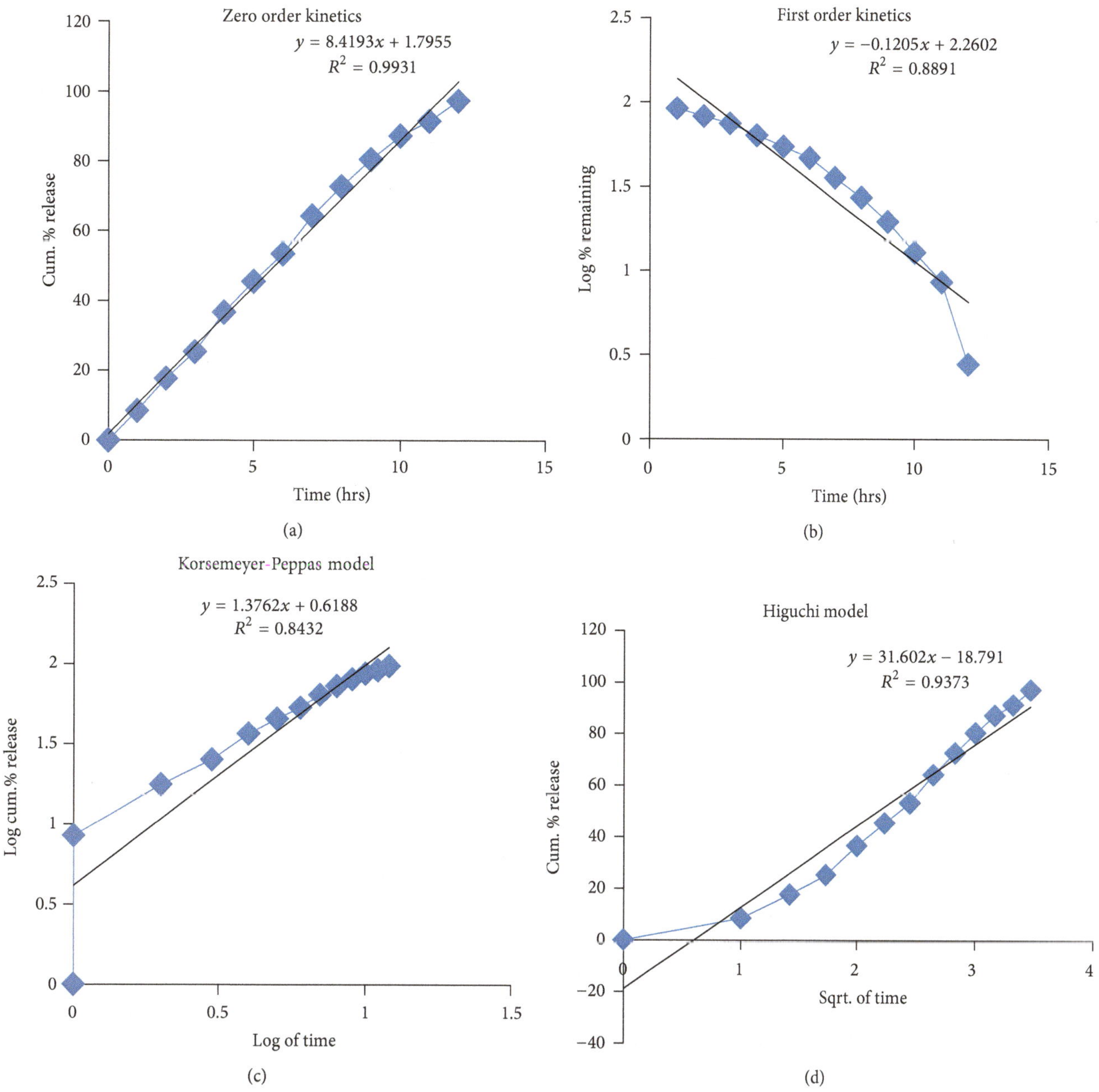

FIGURE 11: Drug release kinetics of Nateglinide (sustain release) layer in bilayer tablet.

was used individually in the range of 10–25% had shown drug release in the range of 10–98% in 10 hours. In the above formulations as the single retarding agent was used and even its amount was less, release was not controlled up to 12 hours; hence formulations N9–N13 were prepared with different combinations of polymers and gums. In the formulations N11 and N12 containing same amount of guar gum (20%) and increasing amount of ethyl cellulose, respectively (5% and 10%), drug release was not sustained up to 12 hours because of less amount of ethyl cellulose. Similar effect was observed for N13 which contain same material as N11 with an exception in diluent where combination of diluents MCC and Mannitol was used. Here it implies that the change in diluent has no effect on drug release. For the formulation N10 containing two natural gums, that is, Guar gum (20%) and Xanthan gum (15%) in combination, drug release was found to be less in 12 hours when compared to the formulation N9 in which HPMC (20%) and Xanthan gum (15%) were used in combination. Here it can be understood that more retardation of drug release was observed when two natural gums were used in combination (N10) compared to combination of a polymer and natural gum (N11, N12, N13, and N9). But here N9 formulation was optimized as it achieves the objective by showing maximum drug release (97%) in 12 hours and all the results are represented in Table 15 and Figure 8.

3.4. Evaluation of Bilayer Tablets. Bilayer tablets were prepared successfully after selecting the optimized formulations

Table 17: *In vitro* drug release data of Nebivolol and Nateglinide bilayer tablet.

	Nebivolol (NBL8)	Nateglinide (N9)
Time (min)	% drug release	
	0.1 N HCl	
0	0	0
5	25 ± 3.45	1.8 ± 1.01
10	48 ± 3.37	2.4 ± 1.23
15	69 ± 4.28	3.1 ± 1.21
20	84 ± 4.61	3.6 ± 1.34
25	91 ± 4.02	4.1 ± 1.28
30	97 ± 3.43	4.9 ± 1.46
Time (hrs)	% drug release	
	0.01 N HCl with 0.5% w/v SLS	
1		8 ± 3.46
2		17 ± 3.69
3	—	25 ± 4.29
4	—	36 ± 3.66
5	—	45 ± 3.46
6	—	53 ± 4.32
7	—	64 ± 4.23
8	—	72 ± 3.70
9		80 ± 3.42
10	—	87 ± 4.18
11		91 ± 3.42
12	—	97 ± 3.22

of immediate release layer (NBL8) and sustain release layer (N9) using 10 mm punches (Mini Press I, Karnavati, Gujarat, India). The prepared bilayer tablets were evaluated for post-compression parameters and results were found to be within the limits mentioned in the above section and were shown in Table 16. *In vitro* drug release studies of bilayer tablets were carried out using USP dissolution apparatus type II in 500 mL of 0.1 N HCl for first 30 minutes and in 900 mL of 0.01 N HCl with 0.5% SLS up to 12 hours. From the results, drug release of Nebivolol immediate release layer was found to be 97.43% in 30 minutes and that of the Nateglinide sustain release layer was 97.22% at the end of 12 hours and % drug release of Nateglinide in first half hour was found to be 4.9%. It implies that the release of sustain release drug in the medium preferred for immediate release layer was found to be negligible and thus shows no irregularities in the drug release of bilayer tablet and values are represented in the Table 17 and Figure 9.

3.5. Kinetic Data Analysis. The drug release kinetic data of Nebivolol layer is shown in Table 18 and graphs are represented in Figure 10. From the graphical representation it can be understood that this layer is best fit in to Higuchi model which had shown a regression coefficient (R^2) of 0.9714. The results of the *in vitro* release data of this layer were fitted to the Korsemeyer-Peppas equation given in Table 4 to analyze the release pattern of the drug from the polymeric system. The value of "n" was found to be more than 0.89, indicating the drug release follows super case-II transport.

The drug release kinetic data of Nateglinide layer is shown in Table 19 and graphs are represented in Figure 11. From the graphical representation it can be understood that this layer is best fit in to zero order kinetics which had shown a regression coefficient (R^2) of 0.9931. The results of the *in vitro* release data of this layer were fitted to the Korsemeyer-Peppas equation to analyze the release pattern of the drug from the polymeric system. The value of "n" was found to be more than 0.89, indicating the drug release follows super case-II transport.

3.6. Stability Studies

3.6.1. Condition: 40°C/75% RH. See Table 20.

3.6.2. Test Frequency: 0 Months, 1 Month, 2 Months, and 3 Months

(i) All physical and chemical parameters were found to be satisfactory based on the stability data.

(ii) Photostability studies have shown that the medicinal product is non-light sensitive.

4. Conclusion

The present study demonstrated the successful formulation and evaluation of an antidiabetic and antihypertensive in a single dosage form as bilayer tablet. In the bilayer tablet, immediate release layer of Nebivolol was prepared by direct compression method using various super disintegrants in which optimized formula (NBL8) contains sodium starch glycolate as super disintegrant and sustain release layer of Nateglinide was prepared by wet granulation method using different release retarding agents in which optimized formula (N8) contains combination of HPMC and Xanthan gum as release retardants. The drug excipient compatibility studies carried out using FTIR revealed that there was no interaction found between drugs and excipients. All the pre- and postcompression studies revealed that the results were found to be within the official limits. *In vitro* release studies reveal that Nebivolol immediate release layer in bilayer tablet was found to be 97.43% within 30 minutes and Nateglinide sustained release layer was 97.22% at the end of 12 hrs. Release kinetics showed good linearity by best fitting in to Higuchi model for IR layer and zero order kinetics for SR layer and stability studies showed no changes after exposing to accelerated conditions for a period of 3 months with respect to physical characteristics and *in vitro* drug release studies.

From the above study, it can be concluded that the prepared bilayer tablets achieve the objective of the research work in treating the diabetes and hypertension with the sequential release of two drugs. As these tablets are supposed to be given twice a day which reduces the dosage frequency and are cost effective, it can be best alternative to conventional dosage forms having more frequency of administration.

Table 18: Kinetic data analysis of Nebivolol (immediate release) layer in bilayer tablet.

Zero order		First order		Higuchi		Korsemeyer	
Time (min)	Cum. %release	Time (min)	Log cum. %remaining	Sqrt. of time	Cum. %drug release	Log of time	Log cum. %release
0	0	0	0	0	0	0	0
5	25.45	5	1.872447648	2.236067977	25.45	0.698970004	1.405687787
10	48.37	10	1.712902125	3.16227766	48.37	1	1.684576087
15	69.28	15	1.487421211	3.872983346	69.28	1.176091259	1.840607879
20	84.61	20	1.18723862	4.472135955	84.61	1.301029996	1.927421695
25	91.02	25	0.953276337	5	91.02	1.397940009	1.959136831
30	97.43	30	0.409933123	5.477225575	97.43	1.477121255	1.988692703

Table 19: Kinetic data analysis of Nateglinide (sustain release) layer in bilayer tablet.

Zero order		First order		Higuchi		Korsemeyer	
Time (hr)	Cum. %release	Time (hr)	Log cum. %remaining	Sqrt. of time	Cum. %drug release	Log of time	Log cum. %release
0	0	0	0	0	0	0	0
1	9.9	1	0	1	8.46	0	0.927370363
2	15.68	2	1.96161091	1.4142136	17.69	0.301029996	1.247727833
3	26.42	3	1.9154526	1.7320508	25.29	0.477121255	1.402948829
4	32.2	4	1.87337874	2	36.66	0.602059991	1.564192461
5	39.63	5	1.80167806	2.236068	45.46	0.698970004	1.657629431
6	47.06	6	1.73671513	2.4494897	53.32	0.77815125	1.726890141
7	53.67	7	1.66913085	2.6457513	64.23	0.84509804	1.807737922
8	60.27	8	1.55351894	2.8284271	72.7	0.903089987	1.861534411
9	75.14	9	1.43616265	3	80.42	0.954242509	1.905364069
10	81.74	10	1.29181269	3.1622777	87.18	1	1.940416865
11	92.48	11	1.10788803	3.3166248	91.42	1.041392685	1.961041217
12	96.92	12	0.93348729	3.4641016	97.22	1.079181246	1.987755617

Table 20: Stability studies.

S. number	Parameters	Conditions			
		Initial	40°C/75%RH		
		0 days	1 month	2 months	3 months
		Nebivolol and Nateglinide bilayer tablet			
1	Average weight (mg)	450 ± 5.0	450 ± 5.0	450 ± 5.0	450 ± 5.0
2	Hardness (kg/cm^2)	6.5 ± 0.5	6.5 ± 0.5	6.3 ± 0.5	6.0 ± 0.5
3	Thickness (mm)	5.36 ± 0.04	5.34 ± 0.05	5.34 ± 0.08	5.34 ± 0.08
	Dissolution (cum.% drug release)				
4	Nebivolol (30 min)	97 ± 3.43	97 ± 3.15	96 ± 3.24	96 ± 3.65
	Nateglinide (12 hrs)	97 ± 3.22	97 ± 3.83	96 ± 3.67	96 ± 3.48

Conflict of Interests

The authors declare that there is no conflict of interests regarding the publication of this paper.

References

[1] R. A. King, J. I. Rotter, and A. G. Motulsky, *The Genetic Basis of Common Diseases*, Oxford University Press, Oxford, UK, 1992.

[2] M. Epstein and J. R. Sowers, "Diabetes mellitus and hypertension," *Hypertension*, vol. 19, no. 5, pp. 403–418, 1992.

[3] I. Hasan and S. Khatoon, "Prevalence of diabetes mellitus and obesity among population of Sultanpur kunhari and its surrounding area, Haridwar Uttarakhand," *International Research Journal of Pharmacy*, vol. 3, pp. 226–229, 2012.

[4] A. H. Zargar, A. A. Wani, B. A. Laway et al., "Prevalence of diabetes mellitus and other abnormalities of glucose tolerance in young adults aged 20-40 years in North India (Kashmir Valley)," *Diabetes Research and Clinical Practice*, vol. 82, no. 2, pp. 276–281, 2008.

[5] G. F. H. Ehud, E. Z. Messerlib, and A. Tenenbaum, "Hypertension and diabetes," in *Cardiovascular Diabetologyclinical , Metabolic and Inflammatory Facets*, vol. 45 of *Advances in Cardiology*, pp. 82–106, Karger, Basel, Switzerland, 2008.

[6] R. A. de Boer, A. A. Voors, and D. J. van Veldhuisen, "Nebivolol: third-generation β-blockade," *Expert Opinion on Pharmacotherapy*, vol. 8, no. 10, pp. 1539–1550, 2007.

[7] A. Veverka, D. S. Nuzum, and J. L. Jolly, "Nebivolol: a third-generation β-adrenergic blocker," *Annals of Pharmacotherapy*, vol. 40, no. 7-8, pp. 1353–1360, 2006.

[8] O. Kamp, G. T. Sieswerda, and C. A. Visser, "Comparison of effects on systolic and diastolic left ventricular function of Nebivolol versus Atenolol in patients with uncomplicated essential hypertension," *American Journal of Cardiology*, vol. 92, no. 3, pp. 344–348, 2003.

[9] A. C. Pessina, "Metabolic effects and safety profile of nebivolol," *Journal of Cardiovascular Pharmacology*, vol. 38, no. 3, pp. S33–S35, 2002.

[10] C. J. Dunn and D. Faulds, "Nateglinide," *Drugs*, vol. 60, no. 3, pp. 607–615, 2000.

[11] P. Norman and X. Rabasseda, "Nateglinide: a structurally novel, short-acting, hypoglycemic agent," *Drugs of Today*, vol. 37, no. 6, pp. 411–426, 2001.

[12] J. Cooper and C. Gunn, "Powder flow and compaction," in *Tutorial Pharmacy*, S. J. Carter, Ed., pp. 211–233, CBS Publishers and Distributors, Delhi, India, 1986.

[13] J. R. Patel, B. A. Patel, D. G. Patel, D. S. Patel, and V. B. Patel, "Formulation and evaluation of oral controlled drug delivery system for a model anti diabetic drug metformin," *International Journal of Current Pharmaceutical Research*, vol. 3, pp. 37–39, 2011.

[14] M. Rangapriya, V. Manigandan, R. Natarajan, and K. Mohan Kumar, "Formulation and evaluation of floating tablets of Pioglitazone hydrochloride," *International Journal of Pharmaceutical and Chemical Sciences*, vol. 1, pp. 1048–1054, 2012.

[15] V. Thanda, S. Firoz, C. Yerram, A. Vikram, S. K. Divya, and K. T. Murali, "Design and characterisation sustained release matrix tablets of Repaglinide using natural polymers," *International Journal of Pharmacy*, vol. 2, pp. 73–83, 2012.

[16] D. Vamshi, P. Laxmi Madhuri, and G. Tuljarani, "Method development and validation of indapamide and nebivolol hydrochloride by rp-hplc method," *International Journal of Research In Pharmaceutical and Nano Sciences*, vol. 2, no. 6, pp. 798–810, 2013.

[17] Indian Pharmacopoeia, *Indian Pharmacopoeia*, vol. 3, World-wide Book Service, 2014.

[18] United States Pharmacopoeia 34, vol. 3, pp. 3611–3614, 2011.

[19] G. H. Kumar, K. Jaganathan, R. S. Kumar, and P. Peruma, "Formulation and *in-vitro* evaluation of bilayer floating tablets of Metformin hydrochloride and Sitagliptin phosphate," *International Journal of Advanced Pharmaceutics*, vol. 2, no. 2, pp. 64–81, 2012.

[20] D. Rohini, S. Alexandar, and M. J. N. Chandrasekar, "Preparation and in vitro evaluation of sustained release tablet formulations of metformin HCL," *Asian Journal of Pharmaceutical and Clinical Research*, vol. 5, no. 1, pp. 45–48, 2012.

[21] K. Venkateswarlu and A. Shanthi, "Formulation and evaluation of sustained release glipizide matrix," *IOSR Journal of Pharmacy and Biological Sciences (IOSRJPBS)*, vol. 2, no. 5, pp. 17–23, 2012.

[22] P. Shirse, "Formulation and evaluation of bilayered tablets of HP-β-cyclodextrin complexed glimepiride with metformin hydrochloride for immediate and sustain release," *International Journal of Pharmacy and Biological Sciences*, vol. 3, no. 3, pp. 148–160, 2012.

[23] C. H. Harika, Y. R. J. Rao, S. K. Gousia Parvin, and S. S. Sastry, "Formulation and evaluation of immediate release tablets of Nebivolol Hydrochloride," *International Journal of Pharmaceutical Archives*, vol. 2, no. 11, pp. 251–258, 2013.

[24] L. Preethi, B. Sree Giri Prasad, and R. Pranitha, "Formulation and evaluation of immediate release tablets of Nebivolol hydrochloride," *Journal of Global Trends in Pharmaceutical Sciences*, vol. 5, no. 3, pp. 1790–1796, 2014.

[25] M. Sudhakar, V. Umesh Rao, and N. Samalla, "Development and optimization of paracetamol immediate release and aceclofenac control release bilayer tablet," *American Journal of Advanced Drug Delivery*, vol. 2, pp. 98–103, 2013.

4

Poly(lactic-co-glycolic) Acid-Chitosan Dual Loaded Nanoparticles for Antiretroviral Nanoformulations

Faithful Makita-Chingombe,[1] Hilliard L. Kutscher,[2,3] Sara L. DiTursi,[4] Gene D. Morse,[3,4] and Charles C. Maponga[1,3,4]

[1]*School of Pharmacy, University of Zimbabwe, P.O. Box MP167, Mount Pleasant, Harare, Zimbabwe*
[2]*The Institute of Lasers, Photonics and Biophotonics, University at Buffalo, Buffalo, NY 14260, USA*
[3]*Center for Integrated Global Health Sciences, Translational Pharmacology Research Core, New York State Center of Excellence in Bioinformatics and Life Sciences, University at Buffalo, Buffalo, NY 14203, USA*
[4]*School of Pharmacy and Pharmaceutical Sciences, University at Buffalo, Buffalo, NY 14214, USA*

Correspondence should be addressed to Faithful Makita-Chingombe; faithmakita@gmail.com

Academic Editor: Philippe Maincent

Poly(lactic-co-glycolic acid) (PLGA) chitosan (CS) coated nanoparticles (NPs) were loaded with two antiretrovirals (ARVs) either lamivudine (LMV) which is hydrophilic or nevirapine (NVP) which is hydrophobic or both LMV and NVP. These ARVs are of importance in resource-limited settings, where they are commonly used in human immunodeficiency virus (HIV-1) treatment due to affordability and accessibility. NPs prepared by a water-oil-water emulsion and reduced pressure solvent evaporation technique were determined to have a positive zeta potential, a capsule-like morphology, and an average hydrodynamic diameter of 240 nm. Entrapment of NVP as a single ARV had a notable increase in NP size compared to LMV alone or in combination with LMV. NPs stored at room temperature in distilled water maintained size, polydispersity (PDI), and zeta potential for one year. No changes in size, PDI, and zeta potential were observed for NPs in 10% sucrose in lyophilized or nonlyophilized states stored at 4°C and −20°C, respectively. Freezing NPs in the absence of sucrose increased NP size. Drug loading, encapsulation efficiency, and kinetic release profiles were quantified by high performance liquid chromatography (HPLC). Our novel nanoformulations have the potential to improve patient outcomes and expand drug access in resource-limited countries for the treatment of HIV-1.

1. Introduction

HIV infection is one of the deadliest diseases worldwide, particularly in resource-limited settings. Antiretrovirals (ARVs) have offered life-sustaining treatment for people living with HIV infection and acquired immunodeficiency syndrome (AIDS). As of March 2015, ARV access remains limited with only 15 million (~40%) of the 36.9 million individuals infected worldwide receiving treatment [1, 2]. Combination antiretroviral therapy (cART) is highly effective because it targets multiple stages of the HIV lifecycle. While patient access to ARVs is increasing, adverse effects, large pill burden, and frequent administration of many first generation ARVs have led to their reduced use. This provides an opportunity to reformulate currently approved cART therapies.

The World Health Organization (WHO) guidelines for the use of ARVs in treating HIV infection in adults recommend NVP in combination with zidovudine/lamivudine or tenofovir/lamivudine when combination therapy with tenofovir/lamivudine/efavirenz is contraindicated or not available [3]. NVP and LMV are still utilized as first-line ARVs particularly in resource-limited settings due to their availability and lower cost. Although more efficacious regimens have been recommended by the WHO, their availability has been largely delayed in resource-limited settings. Additional barriers also exist that make adherence to the prescribed regimen a challenge for patients being treated for HIV such as stigma, complexity of regimens, pill burden/fatigue, food requirements, adverse effects, nondisclosure, failure to fill prescriptions, and cost-related issues [4]. Therefore, long-acting, cell-targeted ARVs have become a major area of research.

NPs have revolutionized sustained drug delivery and cell specific targeting approaches and have been developed to deliver conventional drugs, recombinant proteins, vaccines, and nucleotides. Modifying plasma exposure through sustained release profiles and/or cell targeting can further reduce the toxicities associated with these therapeutics. Therapeutic agents that are efficacious but have serious adverse effects and/or toxicities have the potential to be reinvestigated and reformulated as NPs in order to diminish or eliminate these unfavorable properties. For example, doxorubicin is an FDA approved chemotherapeutic agent that was reformulated into PEGylated liposomes (Doxil®). Doxil demonstrated enhanced antitumor efficacy compared to doxorubicin alone and had a lower incidence of toxicities, most notably cardiotoxicity [5]. Paclitaxel, an FDA approved chemotherapeutic, was reformulated into albumin-based NPs (Abraxane®). Abraxane greatly reduced adverse effects associated with the former formulation [6].

A major concern with reformulation of a drug is maintaining its stability during manufacturing and storage. Biodegradable and biocompatible polymers such as poly(lactic-co-glycolic acid) (PLGA) have been shown to protect drug molecules from enzymatic degradation and provide physicochemical stability [7].

NPs can be optimized by size and shape or functionalized with protein and lipid coatings to facilitate their drug release, cellular uptake, and ability to cross physiologic barriers, for example, the blood-brain barrier [8–10]. Furthermore, NPs can be functionalized with ligands such as those with immune system modulating effects, concurrently modifying the cellular immune response and enhancing intracellular drug delivery [11]. Chitosan (CS) has gained attention in the nanomedicine field because it carries a positive charge that can be utilized for cellular and anatomic targeting of NPs [12]. The electrostatic interactions between positively charged CS NPs and the negatively charged cell surface have been shown to enhance nanoparticle uptake [13–18]. By using a PLGA core in conjunction with a CS shell, both hydrophobic and hydrophilic drugs can be encapsulated within NP.

The objective of this study was to prepare and characterize NVP- and LMV-NPs both as single ARVs and in combination and to assess their physicochemical stability.

2. Materials and Methods

2.1. Materials. Poly(lactic-co-glycolic acid) (PLGA) (lactide : glycolide = 50 : 50, molecular weight (MW) = 38–54 kDa), poly(vinyl alcohol) (PVA) (Mowiol® 4-88, MW = 31 kDa), and chitosan (CS) oligosaccharide lactate (MW = 5 kDa) were purchased from Sigma Aldrich (St. Louis, MO). Nevirapine (NVP) and lamivudine (LMV) were purchased from TCI America (Portland, OR). All other reagents were used as received without further purification.

2.2. Preparation of NPs. NPs were prepared using a modified water-oil-water (w/o/w) double emulsion and solvent evaporation technique [19]. LMV, NVP, or both (4 mg) were added to a microcentrifuge tube containing 200 μL water with 90 μg of CS and 500 μL of 10 mg/mL PLGA dissolved in dichloromethane (DCM). The microcentrifuge tube was probe sonicated (750-watt probe sonicator, 1/4-inch probe tip, Cole-Parmer Vernon Hills, IL) at 21% amplitude for 30 seconds in a 4°C water bath. The resulting emulsion was quickly added to 2 mL of 2.5% (w/v) PVA in water in a 5 mL centrifuge tube and probe sonicated again for 90 seconds in a 4°C water bath to obtain the w/o/w emulsion. The resulting w/o/w emulsion was quickly added dropwise to 10.25 mL of 0.025% PVA in a 100 mL round bottom flask with a stir bar. Under constant stirring, DCM was evaporated under vacuum. The NP suspension was washed once with water followed by centrifugation at 14,000 ×g for 15 minutes. NPs were resuspended in water or 10% (w/v) sucrose prior to storage or characterization.

2.3. Characterization of NPs. NP size and polydispersity index (PDI) were determined by 3 ways: (1) dynamic light scattering (DLS) (Brookhaven 90 plus Particle Analyzer, Brookhaven Instruments, Holtsville, NY) at an angle of 90°; (2) nanoparticle tracking analysis (NTA) (LM-10, Malvern Instruments, Westborough, MA); and (3) transmission electron microscopy (TEM). Surface morphology was analyzed by TEM. TEM samples were prepared by staining with 0.1% w/v phosphotungstic acid. Zeta potential was determined by Zeta PALS (Brookhaven Instruments). ARV loading and *in vitro* release were characterized by high performance liquid chromatography (HPLC) (Alliance 2795, Waters Corporation, Milford, MA).

2.4. Chromatographic Separation. Detection of NVP and LMV was adapted from Rezk et al. [20]. ARVs were separated by reverse phase chromatography on an Atlantis dC_{18} column (3.9 × 150 mm, 5 μm, Waters Corporation) with an Atlantis dC_{18} guard column (3.9 × 20 mm, 5 μm, Waters Corporation) and detected using a photodiode array detector (PDA 996, Waters Corporation) collecting at 270 nm for LMV and 282 nm for NVP. Zalcitabine (ddC) was used as the internal standard (IS) and detected at both 270 and 282 nm. Chromatographic separation was performed with gradient elution. LMV, NVP, and IS eluted at 6.1, 14.1, and 7.7 minutes, respectively. The two mobile phase components were as follows: mobile phase A: 10 mM ammonium acetate; mobile phase B: 200 mL mobile phase A, 500 mL acetonitrile, and 300 mL methanol. Both mobile phases were filtered through a 0.22 μm membrane filter (Millipore, Milford, MA). A linear gradient was programmed in which the initial percentages of mobile phases A and B were 96% and 4%, respectively. Mobile phase B changed to 10% at 8 minutes, 30% at 9.5 minutes, 43% at 13 minutes, and then to the initial 4% at 16.5 minutes up to 20 minutes. The mobile phase flow rate was 1 mL/minute, column temperature was set to 40°C, and injection volume was 100 μL. Data were collected and processed using Waters Empower Chromatography Software. The calibration curve was linear from 200 ng/mL to 10,000 ng/mL for NVP and 50 ng/mL to 10,000 ng/mL for LMV.

2.5. ARV Loading and Encapsulation Efficiency. The amounts of NVP and LMV entrapped in the nanoparticles were determined using the HPLC method described above. A 1 mL aliquot of PLGA-CS NPs was centrifuged for 15 minutes at 14,000 ×g. The supernatant was removed and 0.5 mL acetonitrile and 0.5 mL water were added to dissolve the PLGA-CS NPs. Each sample was bath sonicated for 5 minutes followed by drying under nitrogen gas (Zymark TurboVap LV, Hopkinton, MA). Samples were then reconstituted with HPLC grade water before measuring ARV content by the HPLC method described above. The percentage of drug loading and encapsulation efficiency were calculated using the following equations:

$$\begin{aligned}&\text{Drug loading efficiency}\\&\quad=\left(\frac{\text{amount of drug loaded}}{\text{amount of PLGA}}\right)\times 100\%,\\&\text{Encapsulation efficiency}\\&\quad=\left(\frac{\text{amount of drug loaded}}{\text{total drug amount}}\right)\times 100\%.\end{aligned} \tag{1}$$

2.6. ARV Release Kinetics. Release kinetics of dual and singly loaded ARV PLGA-CS NPs were evaluated by taking 1 mL aliquots of PLGA-CS NPs. Each aliquot was washed twice with distilled water by centrifuging the sample for 15 minutes at 14,000 ×g and removing the supernatant. The pellet was resuspended in 1 mL of 10 mM phosphate buffer, pH 7.2 or pH 5, and added to a microcentrifuge tube. Microcentrifuge tubes were stored at 37°C or 4°C. At predetermined time points, a microcentrifuge tube was removed from the storage condition and centrifuged for 15 minutes at 14,000 ×g. From the microcentrifuge tube, 250 μL of supernatant was aliquoted, spiked with IS, and analyzed for ARV using the HPLC method described above. Data were fit using GraphPad Prism 6.0 (La Jolla, CA) to several drug release models including zero order, first order, Higuchi, Korsmeyer-Peppas, and Hixson-Crowell to determine the release mechanism.

2.7. Stability of NPs. Size, PDI, surface morphology, surface charge (zeta potential), and drug encapsulation were determined at time of fabrication, two weeks, one month, and one year for single ARV or dual ARV-loaded NPs stored at room temperature, 4°C, −20°C, and −70°C. The stability of NPs lyophilized with and without 10% sucrose was also evaluated.

3. Results and Discussion

Recently, a paradigm shift in HIV research from drug discovery to drug delivery has occurred [21]. Novel ARV nanoformulations have shown improvements in pharmacokinetics which have the potential to simplify dosing strategies, increase patient adherence, and maximize antiviral efficacy [22, 23]. Rilpivirine (TMC-278, Edurant®) and cabotegravir (GSK1265744) are two ARVs currently in phase II/III trials as once monthly, long-acting injectables. Clinical trials have shown promise for these agents as long-acting NP injections for the treatment of HIV-1 infection. These novel formulations have been shown to maintain plasma concentrations significantly above the target plasma inhibitory concentration, reducing the likelihood of subtherapeutic plasma concentrations and thus reducing the potential for viral resistance. These formulations are administered monthly or even quarterly as opposed to once daily dosing, which can greatly improve patient adherence to ARVs.

We used an existing encapsulation method to load ARVs into polymeric NPs. The emulsion-solvent-evaporation technique is a proven method for encapsulating hydrophobic therapeutics but has poor results in encapsulating hydrophilic therapeutics. This study utilized a modification of this technique by adding an additional emulsification step which provides an opportunity to encapsulate hydrophilic agents [24, 25]. By fabricating NP with both PLGA and CS, we are able to successfully incorporate two ARVs that have markedly different aqueous solubilities and hydrophobicities (NVP: 0.1 mg/mL, $\log P = 2.5$; LMV: 70 mg/mL, $\log P = -1.4$).

3.1. Morphology and Size of Single and Dual Loaded NPs. Figure 1 illustrates the capsule morphology of ARV-loaded NPs confirming the existence of an inner core and an outer shell. We postulate that NVP is encapsulated within the hydrophobic inner core of PLGA while LMV is encapsulated within the hydrophilic CS outer shell.

Small-sized NPs are associated with higher uptake by cells, offering an efficient delivery system. However, drug loading efficiency of passively entrapped therapeutics decreases with particle size [16]. To enable sufficient drug loading, we targeted NPs that are 250 nm in diameter. In this study, NPs had an average diameter of 242 nm (Table 1) measured by DLS. In DLS, the intensity weighted function of the hydrodynamic diameter is biased to larger NPs [26]. However, when comparing the number-weighted DLS result to NTA and TEM, they are comparable (Table 2). The low polydispersity and size distribution of Sample 3.4 is shown in Figure 2.

NP size was influenced by the hydrophobicity of the encapsulated ARV. PLGA-CS-LMV NPs had an average diameter of 237 nm, whereas PLGA-CS-NVP NPs had an average diameter of 282 nm. The increase in size of the NVP-loaded NPs can be attributed to encapsulation of the hydrophobic drug entrapped in the core leading to changes in the packing structure of the polymer upon NP fabrication. In addition, the physicochemical interactions between PLGA and NVP influenced the increased PDI of the PLGA-CS-NVP NPs compared to PLGA-CS-LMV NPs (Table 1). However, PDI remained below 0.2, which is considered a monodisperse system [27]. Monodisperse NPs are ideal in drug delivery as they tend to yield more consistent pharmacokinetic properties as a function of their size, for example, release kinetics and biodistribution [28, 29].

NPs formulated with CS exhibited a positive zeta potential suggesting successful coating with CS (Table 1). This

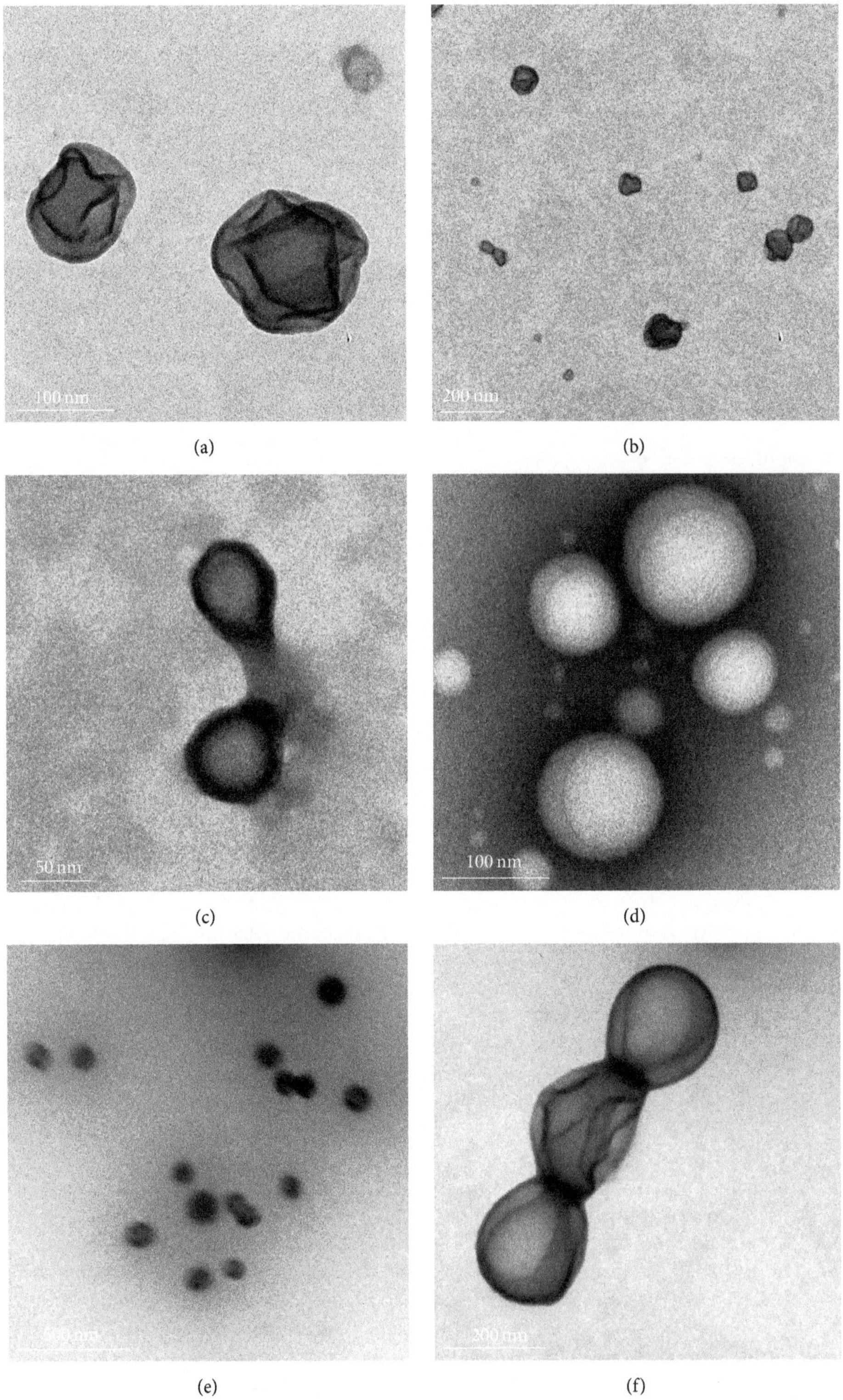

FIGURE 1: TEM image of PLGA-CS-NVP-LMV NPs. NPs following fabrication (a, b); after 1 year, stored at room temperature (c); after 1 year, stored at −70°C (d); lyophilized with 10% sucrose, stored at 4°C (e); and stored at −20°C in 10% sucrose but nonlyophilized (f).

TABLE 1: Average size, PDI, zeta potential, and encapsulation efficiency of single and dual drug loaded NPs.

Sample	Components	Size (nm)	Polydispersity index (PDI)	Zeta potential (mV)
1.1	PLGA-CS-LMV	233	0.084	+25
1.2	PLGA-CS-LMV	231	0.072	+19
1.3	PLGA-CS-LMV	240	0.127	+28
1.4	PLGA-CS-LMV	244	0.148	+25
Mean		237	0.108	+24
Std. Dev.		6	0.04	3.9
Average EE%		7.5%		
2.1	PLGA-CS-NVP	317	0.314	+18
2.2	PLGA-CS-NVP	250	0.245	+22
2.3	PLGA-CS-NVP	293	0.272	+20
2.4	PLGA-CS-NVP	273	0.206	+22
Mean		283	0.259	+20.4
Std. Dev.		29	0.05	2.0
Average EE%		7.5%		
3.1	PLGA-CS-NVP-LMV	246	0.176	+23
3.2	PLGA-CS-NVP-LMV	242	0.131	+25
3.3	PLGA-CS-NVP-LMV	261	0.151	+15
3.4	PLGA-CS-NVP-LMV	220	0.122	+21
Mean		242	0.145	+21
Std. Dev.		17	0.02	4.2
Average EE%		13%		
4.1	PLGA-CS	227	0.010	+21
4.2	PLGA-CS	242	0.118	+18
Mean		235	0.064	+20
Std. Dev.		11	0.08	1.8
5.1	PLGA-LMV	278	0.125	−21
6.1	PLGA-NVP	306	0.305	−9

TABLE 2: Comparison of NPs size determinations by DLS and NTA.

Formulation	Dynamic light scattering (DLS)		Nanoparticle size tracking analysis (NTA)
	By intensity	By number	By number
PLGA-LMV	279	169	169
PLGA-CS-LMV	234	130	170
PLGA-CS	227	147	156

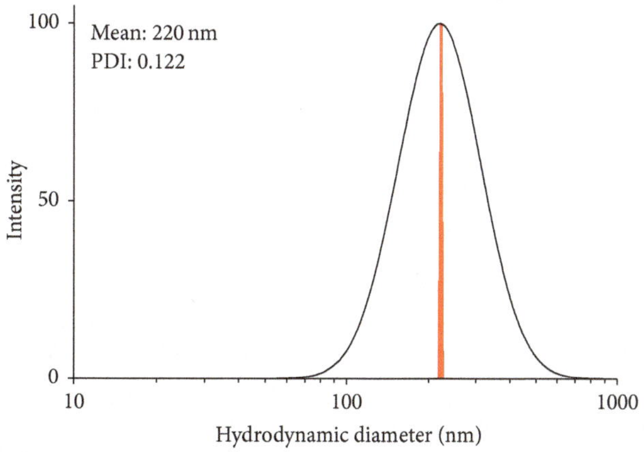

FIGURE 2: Log-normal distribution for PLGA-CS-NVP-LMV NPs (Sample 3.4). MSD histogram in red.

overall positive charge is a direct result of the electrostatic interactions between the negatively charged PLGA and positively charged CS, indicating adsorption of CS onto the surface of the PLGA NP [11]. PLGA NPs formulated without CS (Table 1, Samples 5.1 and 6.1) were negatively charged, as consistent with the literature [15].

3.2. Stability Evaluation

3.2.1. Stability of Prepared Single and Dual Loaded NPs. A major area of concern for NPs is their long-term physical and chemical stability [30]. Long-term stability is generally defined to be at least 12 months [31]. To advance an ARV NP formulation towards clinical usage, the NP and incorporated ARV must be stable. Furthermore, given the limited resources available in developing countries, storage at room temperature is highly desirable. In this study, dual loaded NPs stored at room temperature showed little to no change in morphology (Figure 1(c)), size, PDI (Figure 3(a)), or zeta potential after one year. This stability was also observed for both PLGA-CS-NVP NPs (Figure 3(b)) and PLGA-CS-LMV NPs (data not shown).

This stability of NPs may be due in part to using PVA as a surfactant. Stabilizers such as PVA have been shown to enhance short-term and long-term stability of NP formulations [32]. PVA can act as a stabilizer, providing sufficient steric hindrance between NPs, allowing them to overcome colloidal instabilities. Moreover, PVA may act as a stabilizer by adsorbing to the NP surface, forming an outer layer that is not easily removed during washing.

In this study, NPs stored at −70°C for one year were larger in size with a mean of 500 nm using DLS and 200 nm using TEM (Figure 1(e)). However, PDI and zeta potential showed no marked differences upon storage at −70°C for one year (not shown). Between −70°C and 0°C, freezing and nonfreezing water molecules bind to polymer molecules through hydrogen bonds [33]. Hydrogen bond interactions between the OH and NH_2 groups of chitosan and the OH groups of PVA may cause the NPs to aggregate, resulting in an apparent increase in NP size [34].

3.2.2. Stability of Lyophilized NPs. Lyophilization has been shown to enhance long-term stability of colloidal NPs [30]. It has been reported that NPs prepared with 2.5–5% PVA may be lyophilized without the use of a cryoprotectant [30]. However, following washing to remove excess ARV, CS, and PVA, the addition of a cryoprotectant such as sucrose may be required to ensure stability. NPs lyophilized with 10% sucrose readily dispersed in water upon reconstitution both immediately after lyophilization and following storage at 4°C for one year. The presence of an easily dispersible lyophilized powder and conservation of NP size (Figures 3(g) and 3(h)) indicate successful lyophilization of the NPs [30]. At one year, the capsule morphology (Figure 1(e)), size, PDI (Figure 3(c)), and surface charge of NPs lyophilized with sucrose were preserved. These results are similar to changes in size when PLGA NPs lyophilized with 1–3% sucrose were stored at 4°C and 25°C for 3 months [35]. However, the size and PDI of dual loaded NPs lyophilized in the absence of sucrose increased when stored at 4°C for one year (Figure 3(d)). This change in size and PDI was also observed for single loaded PLGA-CS-LMV NPs lyophilized in the absence of sucrose (Figure 3(e)). These results demonstrate the importance of using sucrose as a cryoprotectant. Finally, nonlyophilized NPs in 10% sucrose stored at −20°C for one year had no notable differences in morphology (Figure 1(f)), size, or PDI (Figure 3(f)) when compared to NPs directly following their fabrication.

3.3. *In Vitro* ARV Release Kinetics and Mechanism.

Prolonged release of ARVs from polymeric NPs has been reported [36]. However, *in vivo* ARV release and drug pharmacokinetics may differ from *in vitro* results [37]. In particular, lysosomes and proteasomes play an important role in the destruction of HIV-1 during endocytosis of the virus. Apart from HIV being internalized by fusion to the cell membrane, HIV can also enter the cell via endocytosis if spared from degradation in late endosomes and lysosomes [38]. If the HIV pathogen remains intact and viable in the endosome, the cell becomes prone to viral infection [39]. Although the internalization of HIV by endocytosis does not result in productive infection [38], it has been reported that infectivity of HIV-1 is enhanced by the inhibition of lysosomal function [39]. In order to predict future biological efficacy, this study sought to determine the drug release kinetics and possible mechanism of LMV and NVP from single or dual loaded NPs. Release studies were performed in phosphate buffer at 37°C at pH 7.2 and pH 5 in order to mimic physiologic and late stage lysosomal pH, respectively [40]. At 37°C in pH 7.2 (Figure 4), both LMV and NVP in the dual loaded NPs exhibited a biphasic release profile. An initial burst in the first 20 hours was observed for LMV followed by a slow and almost stable release over the remaining 100 hours. Concurrently, within the first 20 hours, NVP was slowly released initially but gradually surpassed LMV levels over the remaining 100 hours.

ARV release in various storage conditions was determined (Figures 4–7). At 4°C, there was no significant initial burst release of LMV. For both ARVs, consistent but lower drug amounts were released (Figure 5) compared to that at 37°C. At 4°C, water absorption and hydration of PLGA and/or chitosan within the NP may have decreased. This resulted in reduced NP degradation and subsequently less LMV being released.

During NP fabrication, ARVs may be adsorbed to the NP surface, entrapped within the NP, or chemically conjugated to the NP [41], or the NP may be a nanocrystal of the ARV itself [42]. Release of ARVs from PLGA NPs is initially controlled by diffusion, whereas in the final stages ARV release is controlled by dissolution/erosion [43, 44]. The release of NVP is primarily dependent on the degradation of the PLGA core and NVP's poor water solubility. Additionally, ionic interactions between NVP and PLGA may result in shielding PLGA's terminal carboxyl group. This shielding reduces the hydrophilicity of the polymer, thereby lessening the PLGA erosion and its concomitant NVP release [45]. The observed initial burst release of LMV suggests that once the

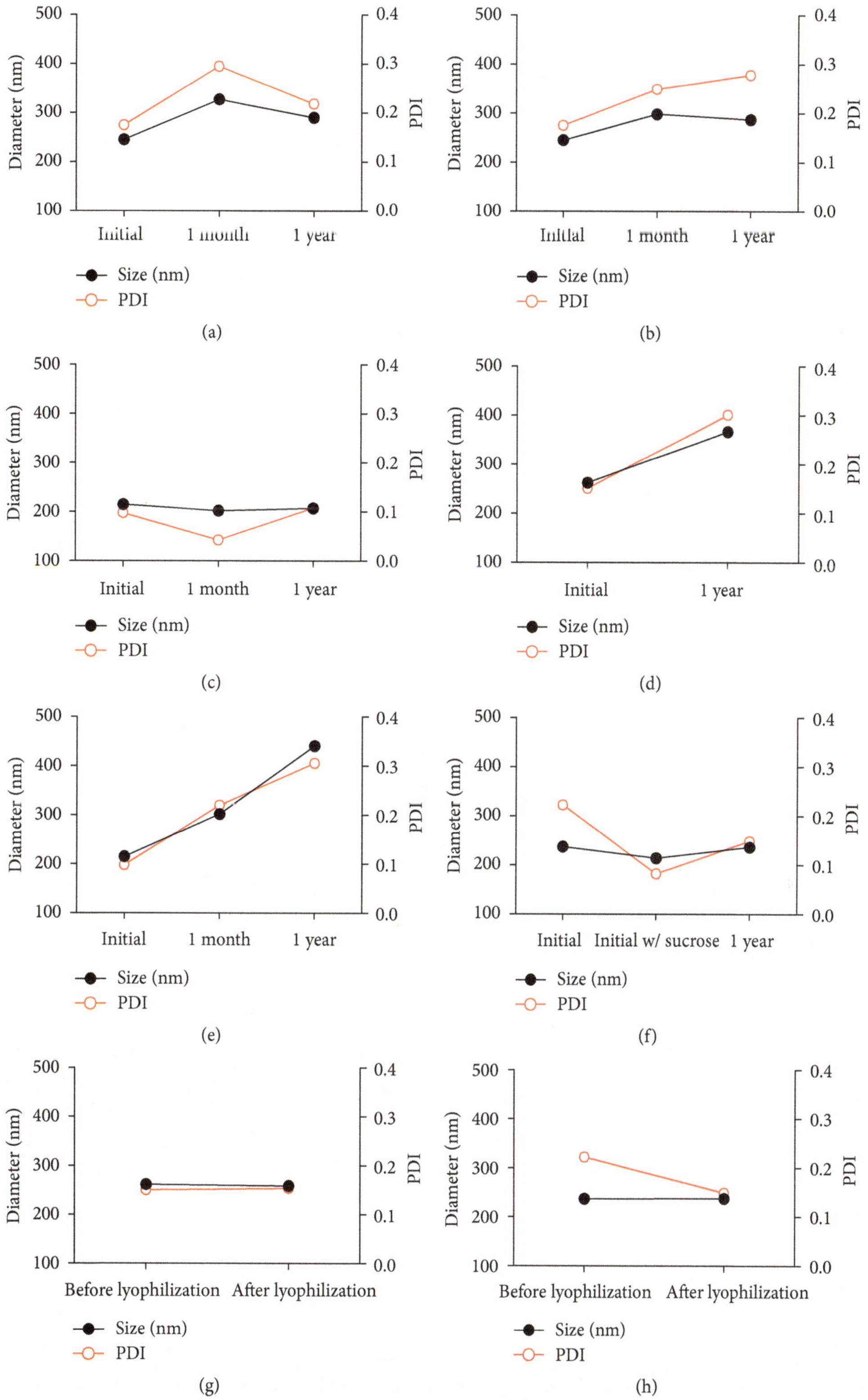

FIGURE 3: Size and PDI stability of NPs at different storage conditions; (a), (b), (c), and (f) were stable while (d) and (e) were unstable. Size is maintained after lyophilization (g and h). (a) PLGA-CS-NVP-LMV NPs stored at room temperature; (b) PLGA-CS-NVP NPs stored at room temperature; (c) PLGA-CS-LMV NPs lyophilized with 10% sucrose and stored at 4°C; (d) PLGA-CS-NVP-LMV NPs lyophilized without sucrose and stored at 4°C; (e) PLGA-CS-LMV NPs lyophilized without sucrose and stored at 4°C; (f) PLGA-CS-NVP NPs in 10% sucrose stored at −20°C; (g) PLGA-CS-NVP-LMV NPs lyophilized in 10% sucrose; (h) PLGA-CS-NVP NPs lyophilized in 10% sucrose.

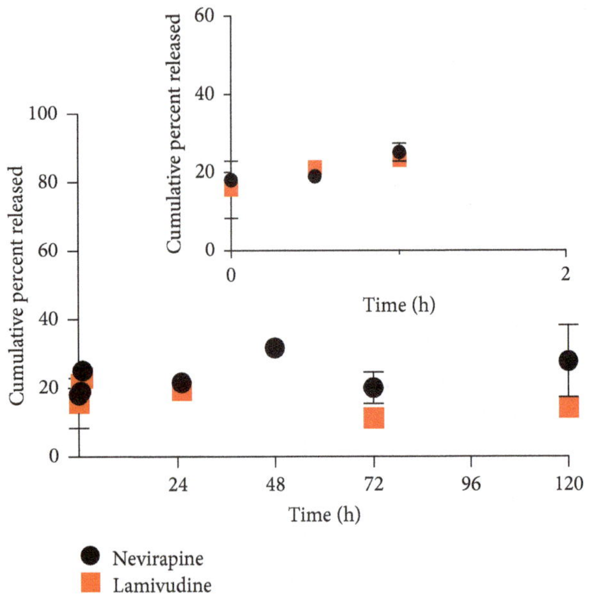

FIGURE 4: Release of LMV and NVP from PLGA-CS-NVP-LMV NPs at 37°C in PBS pH 7.2 (mean $n = 3$).

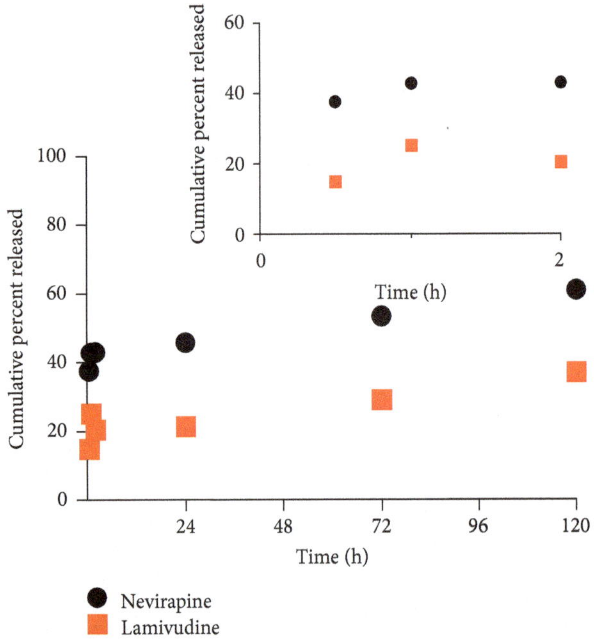

FIGURE 5: Release of LMV and NVP from PLGA-CS-NVP-LMV NPs at 4°C in PBS pH 7.2 (mean $n = 3$).

hydrophobic PLGA core is exposed and perhaps partially disrupted, a portion of the LMV is immediately physically released and quickly diffuses through the outer, hydrophilic CS shell, although some LMV may eventually be adsorbed on the outer surface [46]. The slower, later release of LMV could result from the rest of the LMV that is entrapped within the PLGA core being more slowly released as the PLGA core undergoes less rapid dissolution.

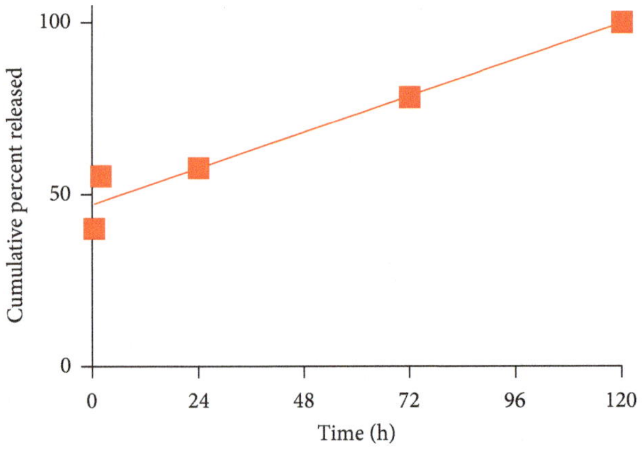

FIGURE 6: Release kinetics of PLGA-CS-LMV NPs in pH 5 at 37°C. Data are fit using the zero-order model.

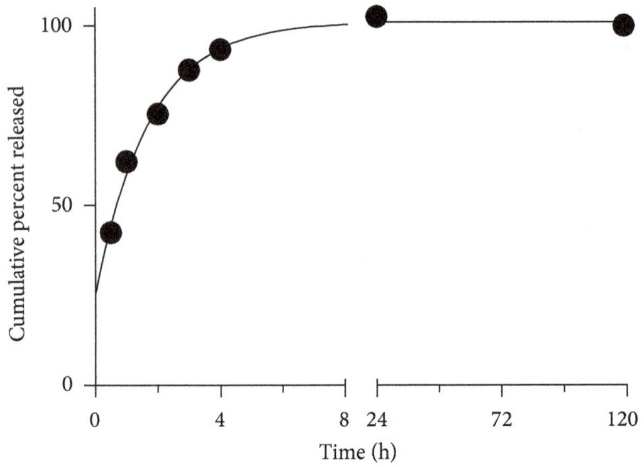

FIGURE 7: Release kinetics of PLGA-CS-NVP NPs in pH 7.2 at 37°C. Data are fit using the first-order model.

Based on the best fit regression model, NVP exhibited a first-order release mechanism in pH 7.2 (Figure 7). The release of LMV in pH 5 was determined to be zero order (Figure 6). At this pH, late lysosomes and endosomes play an important role in the degradation of foreign matter in the endocytotic pathway [38]. In the presence of lysosomotropic agents in HIV patients, the release profile of LMV may play an important role in derailing HIV infectivity.

4. Conclusion

We have successfully fabricated positively charged, biodegradable PLGA-CS NPs that integrate both a hydrophobic and a hydrophilic ARV using a reproducible method. ARV release from a dual loaded NP, where one drug is released as a burst before the other, can be of therapeutic significance in HIV management. The initial LMV burst followed by a decrease that is paralleled by an increase in NVP observed in PBS pH 7.2 at 37°C may entail efficacy in inhibiting enzymes targeted by these ARVs at different times. This phenomenon may go a long way in managing viral load in the plasma and possibly prolong the ability of the HIV virus to develop resistance. The stability of these core-shell NPs demonstrates the ability to reformulate two first-generation ARVs into a nanoformulation with more favorable properties. In resource-limited settings, the stability of ARV-loaded NPs at room temperature would reduce expenses associated with cold-chain logistics and distribution, allowing for increased access to these medications. The observed stability of non-lyophilized NPs with 10% sucrose may be another storage strategy where lyophilization equipment may not be readily available. Our approach to fabricating dual loaded NPs, with stable physicochemical properties, offers the potential of further developing novel nanoformulations for use in HIV-1 infection. Further investigation of these core-shell ARV nanomedicines, using cellular and animal models of HIV-1 infection, will provide information critical to their clinical advancement.

Disclosure

Part of the work in this paper was presented under "posters category" at the Conference on Retroviruses and Opportunistic Infections (CROI) 2015, Seattle, Washington. The content presented in this paper is solely the responsibility of the authors and does not necessarily represent the official views of the Fogarty International Center, National Institute of Allergy and Infectious Diseases, or the National Institutes of Health.

Competing Interests

The authors report no competing interests in this work.

Authors' Contributions

Faithful Makita-Chingombe and Hilliard L. Kutscher contributed equally.

Acknowledgments

This project was supported in part by Grants U01AI068636 and HHSN272201500006C from the National Institutes of Health and National Institute of Allergy and Infectious Diseases (NIAID); Grant D43TW007991 from the National Institutes of Health and Fogarty International Center AIDS International Training and Research and Grant (AITRP); and the University of Rochester Center for AIDS Research Grant P30AI078498 (NIH/NIAID) and the University of Rochester School of Medicine and Dentistry. Hilliard L. Kutscher is supported by Ruth L. Kirschstein National Research Service Award (NRSA) Institutional Research Training Grant 1T32GM099607. The collaborative contributions and dedication of the research staff from the Translational Pharmacology Research Core at the University at Buffalo are appreciated. The authors would also like to express their appreciation to Waters Corporation for their generous donation of an HPLC.

References

[1] World Health Organization, "HIV/AIDS Fact Sheet," http://www.who.int/mediacentre/factsheets/fs360/en/.

[2] UNAIDS, "How AIDS changed everything—MDG6: 15 years, 15 lessons of hope from the AIDS response," http://www.unaids.org/en/resources/documents/2015/MDG6_15years-15lessonsfrom-theAIDSresponse.

[3] World Health Organization, *Consolidated Guidelines on the Use of Antiretroviral Drugs for Treating and Preventing HIV Infection*, World Health Organization, Geneva, Switzerland, 2013, http://www.who.int/hiv/pub/guidelines/arv2013/download/en/.

[4] National Institutes of Health, "Guidelines for the use of antiretroviral agents in HIV-1-infected adults and adolescents," https://aidsinfo.nih.gov/guidelines/html/1/adult-and-adolescent-treatment-guidelines/0.

[5] S. Mitra, U. Gaur, P. C. Ghosh, and A. N. Maitra, "Tumour targeted delivery of encapsulated dextran-doxorubicin conjugate using chitosan nanoparticles as carrier," *Journal of Controlled Release*, vol. 74, no. 1–3, pp. 317–323, 2001.

[6] E. Miele, G. P. Spinelli, E. Miele, F. Tomao, and S. Tomao, "Albumin-bound formulation of paclitaxel (Abraxane ABI-007) in the treatment of breast cancer," *International Journal of Nanomedicine*, vol. 4, pp. 99–105, 2009.

[7] F. Danhier, E. Ansorena, J. M. Silva, R. Coco, A. Le Breton, and V. Préat, "PLGA-based nanoparticles: an overview of biomedical applications," *Journal of Controlled Release*, vol. 161, no. 2, pp. 505–522, 2012.

[8] S. D. Mahajan, I. Roy, G. Xu et al., "Enhancing the delivery of anti retroviral drug 'saquinavir' across the blood brain barrier using nanoparticles," *Current HIV Research*, vol. 8, no. 5, pp. 396–404, 2010.

[9] M. I. Alam, S. Beg, A. Samad et al., "Strategy for effective brain drug delivery," *European Journal of Pharmaceutical Sciences*, vol. 40, no. 5, pp. 385–403, 2010.

[10] K. Nagpal, S. K. Singh, and D. N. Mishra, "Drug targeting to brain: a systematic approach to study the factors, parameters and approaches for prediction of permeability of drugs across BBB," *Expert Opinion on Drug Delivery*, vol. 10, no. 7, pp. 927–955, 2013.

[11] A. Dube, J. L. Reynolds, W.-C. Law, C. C. Maponga, P. N. Prasad, and G. D. Morse, "Multimodal nanoparticles that provide immunomodulation and intracellular drug delivery for infectious diseases," *Nanomedicine*, vol. 10, no. 4, pp. 831–838, 2014.

[12] H. Dai, X. Jiang, G. C. Y. Tan et al., "Chitosan-DNA nanoparticles delivered by intrabiliary infusion enhance liver-targeted gene delivery," *International Journal of Nanomedicine*, vol. 1, no. 4, pp. 507–522, 2006.

[13] M. Wang, Y. Zhang, J. Feng et al., "Preparation, characterization, and in vitro and in vivo investigation of chitosan-coated poly (d,l-lactide-co-glycolide) nanoparticles for intestinal delivery of exendin-4," *International Journal of Nanomedicine*, vol. 8, pp. 1141–1154, 2013.

[14] S. H. Bakhru, E. Altiok, C. Highley et al., "Enhanced cellular uptake and long-term retention of chitosan-modified iron-oxide nanoparticles for MRI-based cell tracking," *International Journal of Nanomedicine*, vol. 7, pp. 4613–4623, 2012.

[15] L. Chronopoulou, M. Massimi, M. F. Giardi et al., "Chitosan-coated PLGA nanoparticles: a sustained drug release strategy for cell cultures," *Colloids and Surfaces B: Biointerfaces*, vol. 103, pp. 310–317, 2013.

[16] Y. Luo, Z. Teng, Y. Li, and Q. Wang, "Solid lipid nanoparticles for oral drug delivery: chitosan coating improves stability, controlled delivery, mucoadhesion and cellular uptake," *Carbohydrate Polymers*, vol. 122, pp. 221–229, 2015.

[17] P. N. Prasad, *Introduction to Nanomedicine and Nanobioengineering*, John Wiley & Sons, New York, NY, USA, 2012.

[18] H. L. Kutscher, F. Makita-Chingombe, S. DiTursi et al., "Macrophage targeted nanoparticles for antiretroviral (ARV) delivery," *Journal of Personalized NanoMedicine*, vol. 1, no. 2, pp. 40–48, 2015.

[19] C. Stigliano, S. Aryal, M. D. de Tullio et al., "siRNA-chitosan complexes in poly(lactic-co-glycolic acid) nanoparticles for the silencing of aquaporin-1 in cancer cells," *Molecular Pharmaceutics*, vol. 10, no. 8, pp. 3186–3194, 2013.

[20] N. L. Rezk, R. R. Tidwell, and A. D. M. Kashuba, "Simultaneous determination of six HIV nucleoside analogue reverse transcriptase inhibitors and nevirapine by liquid chromatography with ultraviolet absorbance detection," *Journal of Chromatography B*, vol. 791, no. 1-2, pp. 137–147, 2003.

[21] A. G. Nelson, X. Zhang, U. Ganapathi et al., "Drug delivery strategies and systems for HIV/AIDS pre-exposure prophylaxis and treatment," *Journal of Controlled Release*, vol. 219, pp. 669–680, 2015.

[22] H. L. Kutscher, P. N. Prasad, G. D. Morse, and J. L. Reynolds, "Emerging nanomedicine approaches to targeting HIV-1 and antiretroviral therapy," *Future Virology*, vol. 11, no. 2, pp. 101–104, 2016.

[23] B. J. Edagwa, T. Zhou, J. M. McMillan, X.-M. Liu, and H. E. Gendelman, "Development of HIV reservoir targeted long acting nanoformulated antiretroviral therapies," *Current Medicinal Chemistry*, vol. 21, no. 36, pp. 4186–4198, 2014.

[24] A. Lamprecht, N. Ubrich, M. Hombreiro Pérez, C.-M. Lehr, M. Hoffman, and P. Maincent, "Biodegradable monodispersed nanoparticles prepared by pressure homogenization-emulsification," *International Journal of Pharmaceutics*, vol. 184, no. 1, pp. 97–105, 1999.

[25] E. Piñón-Segundo, M. G. Nava-Arzaluz, and D. Lechuga-Ballesteros, "Pharmaceutical polymeric nanoparticles prepared by the double emulsion-solvent evaporation technique," *Recent Patents on Drug Delivery and Formulation*, vol. 6, no. 3, pp. 224–235, 2012.

[26] nanoComposix, "nanoComposix' guide to dynamic light scattering measurement and analysis," 2015, https://cdn.shopify.com/s/files/1/0257/8237/files/nanoComposix_Guidelines_for_DLS_Measurements_and_Analysis.pdf.

[27] http://www.nbip.dcu.ie/papers/DLS.pdf.

[28] H. Cui, Y. Feng, W. Ren, T. Zeng, H. Lv, and Y. Pan, "Strategies of large scale synthesis of monodisperse nanoparticles," *Recent Patents on Nanotechnology*, vol. 3, no. 1, pp. 32–41, 2009.

[29] T. Sugimoto, *Monodispersed Particles*, 2001.

[30] W. Abdelwahed, G. Degobert, S. Stainmesse, and H. Fessi, "Freeze-drying of nanoparticles: formulation, process and storage considerations," *Advanced Drug Delivery Reviews*, vol. 58, no. 15, pp. 1688–1713, 2006.

[31] M. H. Golden, D. C. Cooper, M. T. Riebe, and K. E. Carswell, "A matrixed approach to long-term stability testing of pharmaceutical products," *Journal of Pharmaceutical Sciences*, vol. 85, no. 2, pp. 240–245, 1996.

[32] L. Wu, J. Zhang, and W. Watanabe, "Physical and chemical stability of drug nanoparticles," *Advanced Drug Delivery Reviews*, vol. 63, no. 6, pp. 456–469, 2011.

[33] S. J. Kim, S. J. Park, and S. I. Kim, "Swelling behavior of interpenetrating polymer network hydrogels composed of poly(vinyl alcohol) and chitosan," *Reactive and Functional Polymers*, vol. 55, no. 1, pp. 53–59, 2003.

[34] K. Yao, J. Li, F. Yao, and Y. Yin, *Chitosan-Based Hydrogels: Functions and Applications*, CRC Press, 2011.

[35] M. Holzer, V. Vogel, W. Mäntele, D. Schwartz, W. Haase, and K. Langer, "Physico-chemical characterisation of PLGA nanoparticles after freeze-drying and storage," *European Journal of Pharmaceutics and Biopharmaceutics*, vol. 72, no. 2, pp. 428–437, 2009.

[36] N. M. Khalil, E. Carraro, L. F. Cótica, and R. M. Mainardes, "Potential of polymeric nanoparticles in AIDS treatment and prevention," *Expert Opinion on Drug Delivery*, vol. 8, no. 1, pp. 95–112, 2011.

[37] S. Dash, P. N. Murthy, L. Nath, and P. Chowdhury, "Kinetic modeling on drug release from controlled drug delivery systems," *Acta Poloniae Pharmaceutica*, vol. 67, no. 3, pp. 217–223, 2010.

[38] B. L. Fredericksen, B. L. Wei, J. Yao, T. Luo, and J. V. Garcia, "Inhibition of endosomal/lysosomal degradation increases the infectivity of human immunodeficiency virus," *Journal of Virology*, vol. 76, no. 22, pp. 11440–11446, 2002.

[39] B. L. Wei, P. W. Denton, E. O'Neill, T. Luo, J. L. Foster, and J. V. Garcia, "Inhibition of lysosome and proteasome function enhances human immunodeficiency virus type 1 infection," *Journal of Virology*, vol. 79, no. 9, pp. 5705–5712, 2005.

[40] A. Sorkin and M. von Zastrow, "Signal transduction and endocytosis: close encounters of many kinds," *Nature Reviews Molecular Cell Biology*, vol. 3, no. 8, pp. 600–614, 2002.

[41] K. S. Soppimath, T. M. Aminabhavi, A. R. Kulkarni, and W. E. Rudzinski, "Biodegradable polymeric nanoparticles as drug delivery devices," *Journal of Controlled Release*, vol. 70, no. 1-2, pp. 1–20, 2001.

[42] S. Balkundi, A. S. Nowacek, R. S. Veerubhotla et al., "Comparative manufacture and cell-based delivery of antiretroviral nanoformulations," *International Journal of Nanomedicine*, vol. 6, pp. 3393–3404, 2011.

[43] S. Fredenberg, M. Wahlgren, M. Reslow, and A. Axelsson, "The mechanisms of drug release in poly(lactic-co-glycolic acid)-based drug delivery systems—a review," *International Journal of Pharmaceutics*, vol. 415, no. 1-2, pp. 34–52, 2011.

[44] M. Körber, "PLGA erosion: solubility- or diffusion-controlled?" *Pharmaceutical Research*, vol. 27, no. 11, pp. 2414–2420, 2010.

[45] M. Miyajima, A. Koshika, J. I. Okada, A. Kusai, and M. Ikeda, "The effects of drug physico-chemical properties on release from copoly (lactic/glycolic acid) matrix," *International Journal of Pharmaceutics*, vol. 169, no. 2, pp. 255–263, 1998.

[46] B. Wang, G. Chen, Z. Mao, Y. Zhang, D. Yu, and C. Gao, "Preparation and cellular uptake of PLGA particles loaded with lamivudine," *Chinese Science Bulletin*, vol. 57, no. 31, pp. 3985–3993, 2012.

5

Development of Oral Dissolvable Films of Diclofenac Sodium for Osteoarthritis Using *Albizia* and *Khaya* Gums as Hydrophilic Film Formers

Martina Aduenimaa Bonsu, Kwabena Ofori-Kwakye, Samuel Lugrie Kipo, Mariam El Boakye-Gyasi, and Mary-Ann Fosu

Department of Pharmaceutics, Faculty of Pharmacy and Pharmaceutical Sciences, College of Health Sciences, Kwame Nkrumah University of Science and Technology (KNUST), Kumasi, Ghana

Correspondence should be addressed to Kwabena Ofori-Kwakye; koforikwakye@yahoo.com

Academic Editor: Ali Nokhodchi

Oral dissolvable films (ODFs) of diclofenac sodium intended for osteoarthritis were prepared using *Albizia* and *Khaya* gums as hydrophilic film formers. The physicochemical properties of the gums were characterized and the gums were used to prepare diclofenac sodium ODFs (~50 mg/4 cm^2 film) by solvent casting. The two gums showed satisfactory film forming properties. The physicomechanical properties, drug-excipient compatibility, and *in vitro* drug release of the films in phosphate buffer pH 6.8 were studied. *Khaya* gum had higher extraction yield, moisture content, insoluble matter and true density while *Albizia* gum showed greater swelling capacity, solubility, and minerals content. The ODFs were thin, soft, and flexible with smooth glossy surfaces and possessed satisfactory physicomechanical properties. FTIR studies showed that no interaction occurred between the drug and the gums. The ODFs disintegrated in <45 s achieved >75% drug release within 7 min with dissolution efficiencies of ~83–96%. Drug releases from F2, F3, F4, F5, and F6 were similar to F1 ($p > 0.05$; $f1 < 15$ and $f2 \geq 50$) while F7 differed markedly from F1 ($p < 0.001$; $f1 > 15$ and $f2 < 50$). Drug release followed the Higuchi kinetic model which is indicative of Fickian drug diffusion.

1. Introduction

Fast dissolving drug delivery systems like oral dissolvable films (ODFs) and fast disintegrating tablets (FDTs) were introduced in the late 1970s as alternative dosage forms for paediatric and geriatric patients who have difficulties in swallowing conventional oral solid dosage forms such as tablets and capsules [1]. ODFs are presented as thin flexible solid dosage forms and come in different sizes and shapes [2]. ODFs are administered by placing the dosage form on the tongue where they hydrate and break up releasing the active agent into the buccal cavity for oromucosal absorption or swallowing [3]. ODFs emerged from the confectionery and oral care department in the form of breath strips and soon grew into a contemporary and widely accepted dosage form by end users for delivering vitamins and personal care products [1]. They are composed basically of the active pharmaceutical ingredient (API), hydrophilic polymers, plasticizers, sweeteners, flavours, colours, surfactants, saliva stimulating agents, and so forth [4, 5].

ODFs are easy to transport and offer fast, safe, and accurate dosing without the need for water or any measuring device. Also, dysphagic, schizophrenic, and dementia patients are able to use ODFs with little or no difficulty [6]. In addition, they exhibit enhanced bioavailability as they bypass the hepatic first pass metabolism [7]. The main disadvantages of ODFs are the difficulty in attaining uniform dosage and achieving high drug loadings in the films. Also, there is a challenge with packaging of the films which may demand the use of special packaging machines [8]. Many drugs have been formulated as ODFs; these include NSAIDs, antihistamines, antiulcer drugs, nicotine replacements, antiemetics, antipsychotics, anti-Alzheimer drugs, antiepileptic drugs, and drugs for sleeping disorders [9–11].

Gums are pathological compounds produced by certain plants as a result of mechanical injury or due to undesirable climatic conditions, such as drought [12]. Examples include *Acacia*, tragacanth, *Albizia*, *Khaya*, xanthan, and guar gums. Gums find wide applications in the pharmaceutical industry where they are used as viscosity enhancers in some suspensions, as emulsifying agents in stabilizing emulsions, as binding agents in tablets and capsules, and so forth [13]. Gums have also shown great potential as gelling agents, film forming agents in ODF technology, coating agents in tablet cores intended for colonic drug delivery [14, 15], and also vehicles in the fabrication of modified release dosage forms [16].

Albizia gum is obtained as natural exudates from the incised trunk of *Albizia zygia* (DC.) J. F. Macbr., family Leguminosae. The plant is widely distributed in tropical Africa, and it is found in Senegal through to Kenya, northern Angola, and Tanzania [17]. *Khaya* gum is obtained from the incised trunk of *Khaya grandifoliola* CDC, family Meliaceae. The tree is found in Benin, Democratic Republic of Congo, Côte D'Ivoire, Ghana, Togo, Nigeria, Sudan, Guinea, and Uganda [18]. *Albizia* and *Khaya* gums have been evaluated as binding agents [13], thickening agents [16], nonfunctional film coatings [19, 20], and compression coatings for colonic drug delivery [14].

Osteoarthritis is the third leading diagnosis in the aged population [21] and causes substantial amount of pain leading to impairment and reduction in the quality of life of patients above 65 years [22]. NSAIDs such as diclofenac, aceclofenac, ibuprofen, and celecoxib are widely used to alleviate the pain of osteoarthritis. These drugs relieve inflammatory pain and slow down the inflammatory process and its associated tenderness and joint constraints. One of the challenges facing geriatric patients is the difficulty in swallowing conventional tablets which affects medication compliance and hinders good therapeutic outcomes. The formulation of active pharmaceutical ingredients (APIs) as ODF formats can help to resolve medication noncompliance in the elderly [1].

This study was aimed at developing oral dissolvable films of diclofenac sodium using *Albizia* and *Khaya* gums as natural hydrophilic film forming polymers. The developed ODFs are intended for the management of osteoarthritis in the elderly.

2. Materials and Methods

2.1. Materials. Diclofenac sodium was received as a gift from Trade Winds Chemists (Kumasi, Ghana). Hydroxypropyl methylcellulose (HPMC) E15 (viscosity of 2% solution at 15 cPs) was obtained as a gift from UK Chemicals Ltd. (Kumasi, Ghana). Aspartame was a gift from Aspee Pharmaceuticals Ltd. (Kumasi, Ghana). Pineapple flavour and titanium dioxide were supplied by Kinapharma Ltd. (Accra, Ghana). Glycerol, Tween 80, and citric acid were obtained from the chemical stores of the Departments of Pharmaceutics and Pharmaceutical Chemistry, KNUST (Kumasi, Ghana). All other reagents used were of analytical grade. Crude *Albizia* and *Khaya* gums were obtained from forest areas around Kwahu in the Eastern Region of Ghana, as natural exudates from the incised trunks of the trees *Albizia zygia* (DC.) J. F. Macbr., family Leguminosae, and *Khaya grandifoliola* CDC, family Meliaceae, respectively. The gums were authenticated, collected, and supplied by a technician at the Department of Herbal Medicine, Faculty of Pharmacy and Pharmaceutical Sciences, KNUST, Ghana.

2.2. Methods

2.2.1. Purification of Gums. Crude *Albizia* and *Khaya* gums were freed from extraneous materials and purified using methods described elsewhere [23, 24], with minor modifications. Gums were oven-dried at 50°C for 48 h and sorted into light and dark coloured grades. Eight hundred grams of the light coloured grades was separately milled and hydrated with 2 L double strength chloroform for 48 h, with occasional stirring. The gum mucilage substances were filtered with calico and the filtrates were precipitated with three times their volumes of ethanol, refiltered, and washed with diethyl ether. The resultant gums were oven-dried at 40°C for 24 h, milled, and screened through 250 μm sieves, packed in airtight plastic pouches, and stored in a desiccator ready for use.

2.2.2. Moisture Content and Insoluble Matter. The moisture content and insoluble matter in the gums were determined using British Pharmacopoeia methods [25].

2.2.3. pH and Ash Values Determination. One gram of the gum was dispersed in sufficient distilled water, with occasional agitation, to form 1% w/v gum mucilage. The pH of the resultant mucilage was determined with a calibrated Eutech pH meter (pH 510, pH/mV/°C meter, Singapore) at 25°C. The total ash, acid insoluble ash, and water soluble ash of the gums were determined using official methods [25].

2.2.4. True Density and Solubility Determination. The true density of the gums was determined by liquid displacement method at 25°C [26] and calculated as the weight of gum divided by the weight of the liquid it displaces. Chloroform was used as the displacement liquid as the gums are practically insoluble in the solvent. The solubility of the purified gums was determined in cold and warm water, acetone, chloroform, and ethanol (96%). One gram of the gum was added to 50 mL of the solvent and left overnight at 25°C. Twenty-five-milliliter portions of the clear supernatant were placed in preweighed glass petri dishes and evaporated to dryness over a water bath. The mass of the residues was weighed with an analytical balance (Adam Equipment, UK) and expressed as the percentage solubility of the gum in the solvent.

2.2.5. Swelling Index. One gram of the gum powder was weighed into a 10 mL measuring cylinder. The initial volume

TABLE 1: Composition of diclofenac sodium ODF formulations.

Code	*Diclofenac sodium (g)	HPMC (g)	*Albizia* (g)	*Khaya* (g)	Gly (g)	Tw (g)	Fla (g)	Asp (g)	Tit (g)	CA (g)	Water (mL)
F1	4	3	—	—	5	1	5	1	1	1	100
F2	4	2	2	—	5	1	5	1	1	1	100
F3	4	2	—	5	5	1	5	1	1	1	100
F4	4	—	5	—	5	1	5	1	1	1	100
F5	4	—	2	5	5	1	5	1	1	1	100
F6	4	—		10	5	1	5	1	1	1	100
F7	4	1	2	5	5	1	5	1	1	1	100

*Each 4 cm^2 film contains ~50 mg diclofenac sodium; Gly = glycerol; Tw = Tween 80; Fla = pineapple flavour; Asp = aspartame; Tit = titanium dioxide; and CA = citric acid.

of the gum was noted after which distilled water was added to the 10 mL mark. The cylinder was stoppered, mixed lightly, and allowed to stand for 24 h and the final volume occupied by the gum sediment was noted. The swelling index was calculated as follows: Swelling Index = $(X_t - X_o/X_o) \times 100$, where X_t is volume of gum after 24 h and X_o = initial volume of gum.

2.2.6. Charring Temperature. The charring temperature was determined by the open capillary method using the Stuart melting point apparatus (Bibby Scientific Ltd., UK). An open capillary tube was sealed using a Bunsen burner. The tube was packed by pressing the open end gently into a sample of the dry powder gum. The gum was transferred from the open end to the bottom of the tube by gently tapping the bottom on the bench. The sample tube was then inserted into the melting point apparatus and the temperature at which the gum sample changed colour was determined.

2.2.7. Viscosity Measurements. The viscosity of 5, 10, 20, 30, and 40% gum mucilage was measured with a Brookfield viscometer (Brookfield Engineering Laboratories, Inc., Middleboro, USA) at 25°C and shear rate of 30 rpm. The effect of temperature on the viscosity of 40% gum mucilage was also studied at 25, 50, 65, 75, and 85°C with the Brookfield viscometer at a shear rate of 30 rpm.

2.2.8. Determination of Mineral and Toxic Ion Content. The mineral and toxic ion contents of the gums, namely, iron (Fe), copper (Cu), zinc (Zn), manganese (Mn), cadmium (Cd), lead (Pb), mercury (Hg), and arsenic (As), were determined with an atomic absorption spectrophotometer (AAS) (Buck Scientific Model 210V GP). The gums were subjected to dry ash digestion and the clear supernatant digest after centrifugation was used for the analysis. The file for the AAS analysis and hollow cathode lamps were set as follows: Fe at 248.3 nm, Cu at 324.8 nm, Zn at 213.9 nm, Mn at 279.5 nm, Cd at 228.9 nm, Pb at 283.3 nm, Hg at 253.7 nm, and Ar at 193.7 nm. A calibration curve was plotted for each of the elements to be analyzed from the stock standards. The stock standard followed by the sample solutions was analyzed for the elements. The determinations were done in triplicate for each supernatant digest. The contents of potassium and sodium in the gums were determined by flame photometry (Jenway flame photometer PFP7) at wavelengths of 766 nm and 589 nm, respectively. The content of phosphorus was evaluated using the phosphovanadomolybdate method [27] for colour development and absorbance was determined spectrophotometrically (Jenway 6051 colorimeter) at 430 nm. The nitrogen and organic carbon contents of the gums were determined by the Kjeldahl method and the modified Walkley-Black wet oxidation method, respectively [28].

2.3. Preparation of Diclofenac Sodium ODFs. Diclofenac sodium ODFs were prepared using the solvent casting method [7, 29], with minor modifications. Table 1 shows the composition of the seven ODF formulations prepared. The polymers were immersed in half the volume of distilled water overnight to obtain a homogeneous dispersion. The specified amount of glycerol was added to the aqueous dispersion and mixed until being homogeneous. The aqueous solution was allowed to stand for 1 h to take out all entrapped air bubbles. Another aqueous solution was made by dissolving the specified amounts of diclofenac sodium, aspartame, titanium dioxide, flavour, Tween 80, and citric acid in the remainder of the distilled water. Both aqueous solutions were put together, stirred, and sonicated for 30 min. Twenty-milliliter portions of the resultant aqueous dispersion were cast onto glass petri dishes of diameter 90 mm and oven-dried at 60°C for 24. The dried films were meticulously taken out of the petri dishes, inspected for any imperfections, and cut into 2 cm × 2 cm sizes with a scalpel. The cut films were packaged singly in aluminium foils and kept in a desiccator pending assessment.

2.4. Evaluation of Films

2.4.1. Appearance and Uniformity of Thickness. All prepared films were checked for their appearances, whether uniform or not, and for the presence or absence of air bubbles, and so forth. The thickness of five randomly selected 2 cm × 2 cm films from each ODF formulation was determined using a digital caliper (Powerfix, Milomex Ltd., UK). The measurements were taken along various planes of the films and the mean and standard deviation were calculated [30].

2.4.2. Determination of Mean Weight and pH. The individual weights of ten randomly selected 2 cm × 2 cm films were determined using an analytical balance (Adam Equipment, UK). The average weight and standard deviations were calculated. The pH of the films was determined by dissolving a 2 cm × 2 cm film in 10 mL of distilled water. The pH of the resulting solution was measured using a standardized Eutech pH meter (pH 510, pH/mV/°C meter, Singapore). The mean of five determinations of each film was calculated.

2.4.3. Drug-Excipient Compatibility Studies Using FTIR Spectroscopy. A Bruker FTIR spectrophotometer (Alpha-Platinum ATR, Jos Hansen & Soehne GmbH, Hamburg, Germany) run by the Opus software (Version 7.2 Build 7.2. 139. 1294) was set to baseline to format previous entries that may interfere with the determination. About 0.1 g of diclofenac sodium was loaded onto the stage directly on top of the platinum. The force gauge was pulled closer to the sample to compress the sample. When the setup was ready, the Opus software generated the spectrum of the loaded sample on the monitor of a computer. The FTIR spectra of both *Albizia* (F4) and *Khaya* (F6) films (each containing diclofenac sodium as API) were also determined to assess possible interaction between diclofenac sodium and the excipients in the formulation [3]. The spectra of all three samples were superimposed using the Opus software to make comparison of the spectra easier. The spectra were compared on the basis of whether or not the principal bands present in the pure diclofenac sodium were still present in the formulated diclofenac sodium ODFs.

2.4.4. Disintegration Time of Films. The petri dish method was employed in the determination of the disintegration time of the ODFs. Five randomly selected 2 cm × 2 cm films were placed into 25 mL distilled water in a petri dish at 37 ± 0.5°C. The petri dish and its contents were swirled gently every 10 seconds till the film started to break up. The time taken by the film to break up completely was recorded as the disintegration time [4].

2.4.5. Assay of ODFs. Five randomly selected 2 cm × 2 cm diclofenac sodium ODFs each containing ~50 mg diclofenac sodium were placed in separate conical flasks containing 70 mL of 0.1 M sodium hydroxide. The flasks were shaken for 15 min using a shaker. Sufficient quantities of 0.1 M NaOH were added to produce 100 mL in each flask. The resultant solutions were filtered and 2 mL of each filtrate was diluted to 100 mL with 0.1 M NaOH. The drug concentrations were evaluated spectrophotometrically (T90 UV/VIS spectrometer, PG Instruments Ltd., UK) at a wavelength of 276 nm using the regression data of the calibration curve ($y = 336.9x - 0.0715$, $R^2 = 0.9971$) [31].

2.4.6. Evaluation of Mechanical Properties. The mechanical properties of 2 cm × 2 cm ODFs were evaluated using a Brookfield Texture Analyzer CT3-100 with TexturePro CT Software (Brookfield Engineering Lab. Inc., Middleboro, MA, USA), fitted with TA-DE and TA-DGA probes and equipped with a 10 kg load cell. The required test parameters were entered into the Texture Loader Software and the appropriate mode was chosen. In the measurement of tensile strength and elastic modulus, a randomly selected film was held between two clamps of probe TA-DGA using low pressure clips, allowing a distance of 3 cm between the sample surface and the base of the probe. For the elongation at break, a film was clamped between the accessory fixtures of probe TA-DE. During measurement, the film was pulled at a rate of 2 mm/s. The force at break and elongation were shown on the CT3 display when the film broke. With an attached computer and TexturePro CT software, the mechanical parameters, namely, tensile strength, elastic modulus, and percentage elongation, were obtained. The experiment was carried out in triplicate for each ODF formulation and the average and standard deviations were calculated [32]. The folding endurance of 2 cm × 2 cm films was determined by folding the film of uniform cross-sectional area and thickness in the same place until it broke. The number of times the film was folded in the same plane (before breaking) was recorded as the folding endurance of that film. Ten randomly sampled 2 cm × 2 cm films of uniform thickness per formulation were used and the average of the determinations was recorded as the folding endurance.

2.4.7. In Vitro Release Studies. In vitro drug release studies on the ODFs were conducted with an Erweka dissolution apparatus (Type DT6, GmbH, Heusenstamm, Germany). Six 2 cm × 2 cm films of each formulation were evaluated. A film was placed with the help of forceps into a vessel containing 300 mL phosphate buffer pH 6.8, maintained at 37 ± 0.5°C with a stirring rate of 100 rpm. At 0, 7, 14, 21, and 28 min, 10 mL aliquots of the dissolution medium were withdrawn and replaced with an equal volume of fresh medium maintained at 37 ± 0.5°C. The withdrawn samples were filtered using Whatman filter paper (number. 5) and 5 mL of the filtrates was diluted ten times with phosphate buffer pH 6.8. The absorbance of the diluted filtrates was determined with a UV-visible spectrophotometer (T90 UV/VIS spectrometer, PG Instruments Ltd., UK) at a wavelength of 276 nm. Using the regression data obtained from the calibration curve ($y = 333.97x - 0.0686$, $R^2 = 0.9981$), the amount of diclofenac sodium in the samples was calculated. The percentage of diclofenac sodium released with reference to the expected content in each film was then calculated. A graph of cumulative mean percentage content of drug dissolved against the respective time points was plotted for each formulation to obtain the release profiles using GraphPad Prism Version 5.00 (GraphPad Software, Inc., USA).

2.5. Data Analysis

2.5.1. Model Independent Approaches. Dissolution efficiency (DE), difference ($f1$), and similarity ($f2$) factors and one-way analysis of variance (ANOVA) were used to analyze the drug release data.

The dissolution efficiency was calculated using the equation

$$\mathrm{DE} = \left\{ \frac{\left(0 \int tY\, dt\right)}{Y100} \cdot \left(t_2 - t_1\right) \right\} \times 100, \tag{1}$$

where $(0 \int tY\, dt)$ is area under the dissolution curve (AUC); Y is the percentage dissolved at t_2; t_2 is time for all active ingredient to dissolve; t_1 is time at which first sample was withdrawn.

The difference and similarity factors were calculated using the following equations:

$$f1 = \left\{ \frac{\left[S_t = \ln \left|R_t - T_t\right|\right]}{\left[S_t = \ln R_t\right]} \right\} \times 100$$

$$f2 = 50 \times \log \left\{ \left[1 + \left(\frac{1}{n}\right) S_t = \ln \left(R_t - T_t\right) 2 \right] - 0.5 \times 100 \right\}, \tag{2}$$

where n is time points; R_t is cumulative percentage dissolved at time t for the reference; and T_t is cumulative percentage dissolved at time t for the test.

The drug release data were also subjected to one-way ANOVA followed by Dunnett's multiple comparison test using GraphPad Prism Version 5.00 (GraphPad Software, Inc., USA). Paired samples with $P < 0.05$ were considered to be significantly different.

2.5.2. Model Dependent Approach. The drug release data were fitted into the zero-order, first-order, Higuchi, and Hixson-Crowell kinetic models to determine the release mechanism [33]. The model that produced good linearity indicated by a high R^2 value was considered the best model to describe the release kinetics of the formulated films.

3. Results and Discussion

Albizia and *Khaya* gums were collected, purified, and employed in the preparation of the diclofenac sodium ODFs.

3.1. Physicochemical Properties of Gums. The physicochemical properties of the purified *Albizia* and *Khaya* gums studied are presented in Table 2. *Khaya* gum gave a higher purification yield, true density, moisture content, and insoluble matter compared to *Albizia* gum. *Albizia* gum also exhibited higher ash values and greater solubility in four of the solvents tested than *Khaya* gum. In addition, *Albizia* gum produced greater swelling capacity and charring temperature than *Khaya* gum. The moisture content and insoluble matter of the two gums were less than 15% and 0.5%, respectively, and hence complied with the official specifications for natural gums [25]. The moisture content affects the flow properties and microbiological stability of gum powders. This is because high moisture content enhances microbial growth and causes some powders to clump and form hard aggregates. The

TABLE 2: Comparative physicochemical properties of purified *Albizia* and *Khaya* gums (mean ± SD, $n = 3$).

Parameter	Type of gum	
	Albizia	*Khaya*
Extraction yield (%)	39.38 ± 2.35	67.50 ± 2.98
Moisture content (%)	12.42 ± 2.10	13.92 ± 1.51
Insoluble matter (%)	0.275 ± 0.041	0.282 ± 0.013
pH (1% w/v @ 25°C)	5.00 ± 0.12	3.84 ± 0.09
Total ash (% w/w)	7.853 ± 0.064	5.603 ± 0.023
Water soluble ash (% w/w)	1.303 ± 0.023	1.200 ± 0.017
Acid insoluble ash (% w/w)	0.600 ± 0.017	0.607 ± 0.012
Solubility (%)		
Cold water	1.273 ± 0.064	0.380 ± 0.020
Warm water	1.747 ± 0.083	0.527 ± 0.064
Acetone	0.110 ± 0.044	0.127 ± 0.031
Chloroform	0.070 ± 0.062	0.020 ± 0.020
Ethanol	0.093 ± 0.023	0.087 ± 0.042
Swelling index (%)	611.29 ± 4.07	477.97 ± 8.67
True density (g/mL)	1.363 ± 0.012	1.412 ± 0.073
Temperature of charring (°C)	258.33 ± 2.89	242.67 ± 2.52

insoluble matter in gums is the result of the mode of gum collection or the foreign materials collected in the gum exudates as they remain on the bark [34].

Khaya gum mucilage was more acidic than *Albizia* mucilage and confirms previous findings about the acidity of the two gums [19]. The pH of the gums determines whether they can cause oromucosal irritation when administered as ODFs. Also, the pharmaceutical applications of natural gums such as thickening and suspending agents which are dependent on their viscosity also tend to be pH-dependent. The ash values provide valuable information about the presence of inorganic and other extraneous materials in a natural product and are helpful in aiding the detection of product adulteration. The acid insoluble ash values of <1% indicate that the gums contain insignificant amount of earthly materials due possibly to the proper processing and cleaning of the gum exudates after collection. The gums exhibited high solubility in water at low temperatures and the solubility was enhanced in warm water due to the acquisition of more kinetic energy at elevated temperatures which makes them more mobile to interact with the solvent molecules. On the other hand, the gums were practically insoluble in acetone, ethanol, and chloroform.

The swelling capacity is an important characteristic of ODFs as the dosage form will have to absorb water, increase in size, and disintegrate in order to release the drug for dissolution and subsequent oromucosal absorption [1]. The two gums being hydrocolloids demonstrated excellent swelling capacities. In aqueous media, the gums will absorb water and swell to varying sizes depending on the pH, ionic strength, and the presence of salts in the medium. The true density of a solid is defined as the mass per unit volume exclusive of all voids that are not part of the molecular packing arrangement [26] and is employed in the identification of solid

TABLE 3: The mineral and toxic metal ion content of *Albizia* and *Khaya* gums (mean ± SD, $n = 3$).

Parameter	Type of gum	
	Albizia	*Khaya*
Mineral ions		
Iron (mg/100 g)	16.450 ± 0.087	9.640 ± 0.069
Copper (mg/100 g)	3.240 ± 0.069	2.087 ± 0.023
Manganese (mg/100 g)	18.933 ± 0.058	2.637 ± 0.064
Zinc (mg/100 g)	7.883 ± 0.029	6.633 ± 0.058
Calcium (g/100 g)	0.413 ± 0.012	0.870 ± 0.035
Magnesium (g/100 g)	0.633 ± 0.029	0.847 ± 0.046
Potassium (g/100 g)	2.777 ± 0.064	0.193 ± 0.006
Sodium (g/100 g)	0.133 ± 0.012	0.070 ± 0.000
Phosphorus (g/100 g)	0.070 ± 0.000	0.103 ± 0.006
Other elements		
Nitrogen (g/100 g)	1.137 ± 0.012	0.560 ± 0.017
Carbon (g/100 g)	45.903 ± 0.023	47.303 ± 0.040
Toxic metal ions		
Lead (μg/g)	0.010 ± 0.000	Nil
Mercury (μg/g)	0.005 ± 0.007	Nil
Cadmium (μg/g)	0.015 ± 0.007	0.005 ± 0.007
Arsenic (μg/g)	Nil	0.012 ± 0.002
Cyanide (μg/g)	Nil	Nil

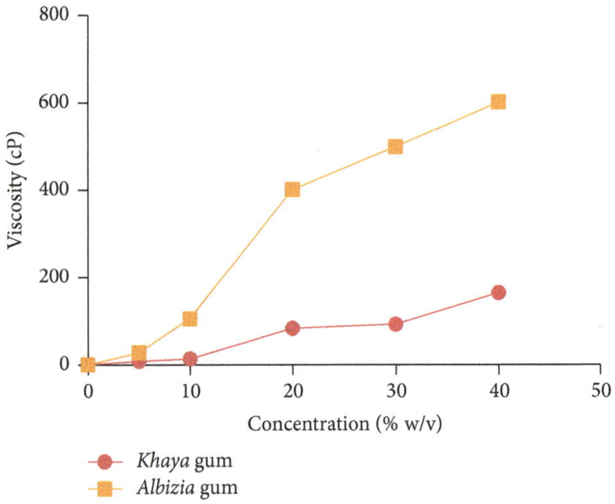

FIGURE 1: Effect of concentration on the viscosity of *Albizia* and *Khaya* gums.

materials. The temperature at which *Albizia* and *Khaya* gums changed appearance (charring temperature) without melting was 258°C and 243°C, respectively. The charring temperature is partly affected by the density and moisture content of the gum. It can be applied in product development to set limits for important parameters like formulation procedures and storage conditions that can affect the appearance of the gum.

Elemental analysis of the two gums showed the presence of the macrominerals calcium, magnesium, sodium, phosphorus, and potassium and the microminerals iron, copper, zinc, and manganese (Table 3). *Albizia* gum was found to contain comparatively higher amounts of iron, copper, manganese, potassium, and zinc than *Khaya* gum. On the other hand, *Khaya* gum had higher levels of calcium and magnesium than *Albizia* gum. The minerals with the highest concentration in *Albizia* and *Khaya* gums were potassium (2.78 g/100 g) and calcium (0.87 g/100 g), respectively. The mineral content affects the properties of the gums in aqueous media such as viscosity and solubility and also determines the nutritional quality of the gums. The macrominerals and microminerals present in the gums are needed for various metabolic activities in the body. The two gums being organic compounds were found to contain high amounts of carbon with *Khaya* gum having relatively higher levels than *Albizia* gum. As organic compounds the gums require proper storage conditions as they are suitable substrates for microbial growth and contamination.

The elemental analysis showed negligible amounts of the toxic metals cadmium, lead, mercury, cyanide, and arsenic in the two gums. These toxic metals have no known function in the body but are very harmful to the proper functioning and metabolic activities of the human body. The near absence of these toxic metals gives a good indication of the possible safety of the gums when used as pharmaceutical excipients. *Albizia* and *Khaya* gums being naturally occurring are readily available and relatively inexpensive and are generally considered to be nontoxic and nonirritant. Characterization of the gums has shown that the two gums also possess the requisite physicochemical properties to be employed as vehicles for the fabrication of diclofenac sodium ODFs.

Figure 1 shows the effect of concentration on the viscosities of the gums. The viscosities of both gums increased with an increase in concentration with *Albizia* gum demonstrating higher viscosities at all concentrations. The effect of temperature on the viscosity of the two gums is shown in Figure 2. The viscosities of both gums decreased with increasing temperature. The higher kinetic energies attained at elevated temperatures possibly facilitate the cleavage of intermolecular bonds between contiguous layers causing a reduction in viscosity of the gum mucilage.

3.2. Preparation and Characterization of Diclofenac Sodium ODFs. In the preparation of diclofenac sodium ODFs, HMPC, *Albizia*, and *Khaya* gums were employed as hydrophilic film forming vehicles while glycerol was used as a plasticizer to improve the flexibility of the films. Aspartame and citric acid were used as sweetening and saliva stimulating agents, respectively. Pineapple flavour was meant to impart the needed flavour to the dosage form. Titanium dioxide (1%) was used to mask the unpleasant appearance of the natural gums while Tween 80 was incorporated as a wetting agent. The films were prepared using the solvent casting method which is simple and economical. All the film ingredients used are safe and are commonly used in the pharmaceutical industry. The formulated ODFs were opaque and whitish because of the titanium dioxide used as colouring agent. The films were thin, soft, and flexible (except F7) with smooth and glossy surfaces.

TABLE 4: Physicochemical properties of diclofenac sodium ODF formulations.

Code	*Weight (g), $n = 10$	Thickness (mm), $n = 5$	pH, $n = 5$	Disintegration time (s), $n = 5$	Assay (%), $n = 5$
F1	0.186 ± 0.019	0.128 ± 0.013	4.66 ± 0.452	43.19 ± 0.077	98.74 ± 0.448
F2	0.250 ± 0.016	0.128 ± 0.015	5.08 ± 0.181	37.16 ± 0.043	99.46 ± 0.337
F3	0.194 ± 0.023	0.142 ± 0.008	4.82 ± 0.084	41.23 ± 0.070	99.94 ± 0.388
F4	0.208 ± 0.019	0.138 ± 0.023	3.80 ± 0.035	40.32 ± 0.081	100.41 ± 0.212
F5	0.254 ± 0.011	0.126 ± 0.013	3.09 ± 0.026	38.33 ± 0.053	99.68 ± 0.542
F6	0.116 ± 0.011	0.108 ± 0.008	3.62 ± 0.060	43.13 ± 0.058	97.58 ± 0.231
F7	0.298 ± 0.095	0.174 ± 0.011	5.23 ± 0.043	47.45 ± 0.050	98.82 ± 0.734

*2 × 2 cm film.

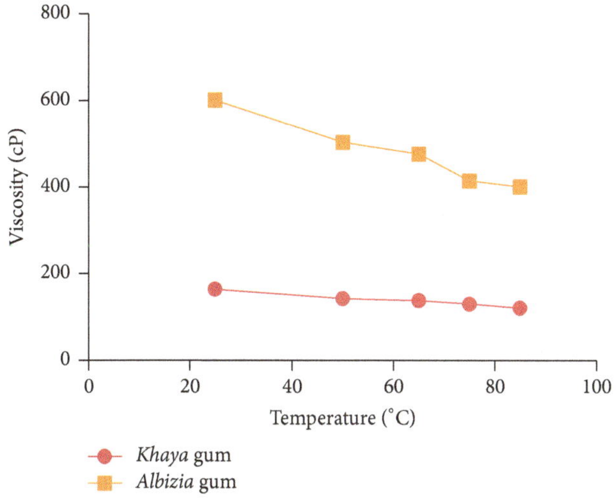

FIGURE 2: Effect of temperature on the viscosity of *Albizia* and *Khaya* gums.

Table 4 presents the physicochemical properties of the films. All pharmaceutical dosage forms are required to exhibit constant dosage and variations in weight within a batch should fall within specified limits [25]. The individual weights of films within the same ODF formulation varied only slightly as shown by the low standard deviations. The average weight of the films increased as the number of polymers used in producing the films was increased, as per the order: F1, F4, F6 (only one polymer) < F2, F3, F5 (two polymers) < F7 (three polymers). Uniformity of thickness is a key physical parameter in the evaluation of ODFs as it has direct correlation with the precision of dose of the films. The films were generally of uniform thickness with the order of thickness of the various formulations as follows: F6 < F5 < F2 < F1, F2 < F4 < F3 < F7.

The pH of the films was determined to understand their possible effect on the mucous membrane of the mouth upon usage of the dosage form. The pH of a product is determined by the drug and the excipients used in the formulation [35]. Generally, acidic and basic oral formulations can cause inflammation of the oral mucosa [36]; hence formulations of neutral pH are preferred. However, the formulations in the current study were acidic due probably to the diclofenac sodium and the excipients, especially *Albizia* and *Khaya* gum and citric acid used. The final pH of the polymeric solution needs to be adjusted to an almost neutral pH before casting into films to prevent any irritation to the oral mucosal lining when administered.

ODFs are required to release the drug in a controlled and reproducible manner and the primary step towards drug release is through disintegration of the films. The average disintegration time for the formulations was 37.16 to 47.45 s. Although no official specifications and guidelines for the disintegration time of ODFs exist [30], they are expected to have short disintegration times. In the current study, formulations F2 and F7 had the lowest and highest disintegration times, respectively. It was observed that combining the polymers in the ODF formulation slightly prolonged the disintegration time due to possible cross-linking of the polymer molecules and/or increased film thickness which makes them less penetrable to water. The limit of content uniformity of ODFs is 85–115% [5, 10]. The average content of diclofenac sodium in the formulations ranged from 97.58 to 100.41%, meaning all the formulations complied with the assay test.

Figure 3 shows the FTIR spectra of pure diclofenac sodium and *Albizia* (F4) and *Khaya* (F6) containing ODFs. The spectrum for pure diclofenac sodium shows a very broad band at 3225.26 cm^{-1} sloping into the aliphatic –CH region around 3000 cm^{-1}. This denotes the presence of a carboxylic acid –OH which overlaps, causing the disappearance of the –CH group in the aromatic system. In addition, medium intensity bands at 1603.42 cm^{-1}, 1572.03 cm^{-1}, and 1547.76 cm^{-1} indicate the presence of aromatic groups and this is confirmed by bending vibrations around 700–900 cm^{-1}. All the above principal bands present in the spectrum of diclofenac sodium were present in the ODF formulations produced with *Albizia* and *Khaya* gums. It can therefore be inferred that no interaction occurred between the excipients and diclofenac sodium in the ODFs.

Pharmaceutical ODFs are required to exhibit good mechanical properties in order to maintain their integrity during handling, packaging, and transportation. The mechanical properties can be influenced by the film forming polymer, the technique of film fabrication, and the type and amount of plasticizer used. Plasticizers confer pliability to films and greatly improve their mechanical properties [5]. Tensile strength provides an indication of the mechanical strength and hardness of films [19] and high tensile strength

TABLE 5: Mechanical properties of diclofenac sodium ODF formulations (mean ± SD, $n = 3$).

Code	Tensile strength (MPa)	Elastic modulus (MPa)	Elongation at break (%)	Folding endurance
F1	5.95 ± 0.976	4.20 ± 0.786	17.87 ± 0.432	85 ± 1.57
F2	6.32 ± 0.542	3.89 ± 0.321	17.64 ± 0.156	103 ± 2.06
F3	6.51 ± 0.985	4.39 ± 0.465	13.49 ± 0.768	54 ± 1.56
F4	5.67 ± 0.231	4.05 ± 0.654	15.91 ± 0.563	67 ± 1.45
F5	6.14 ± 0.331	4.46 ± 0.943	10.73 ± 0.105	79 ± 2.15
F6	7.32 ± 0.432	4.86 ± 0.543	8.20 ± 0.445	39 ± 0.98
F7	7.19 ± 0.652	5.11 ± 0.213	7.65 ± 0.154	46 ± 1.57

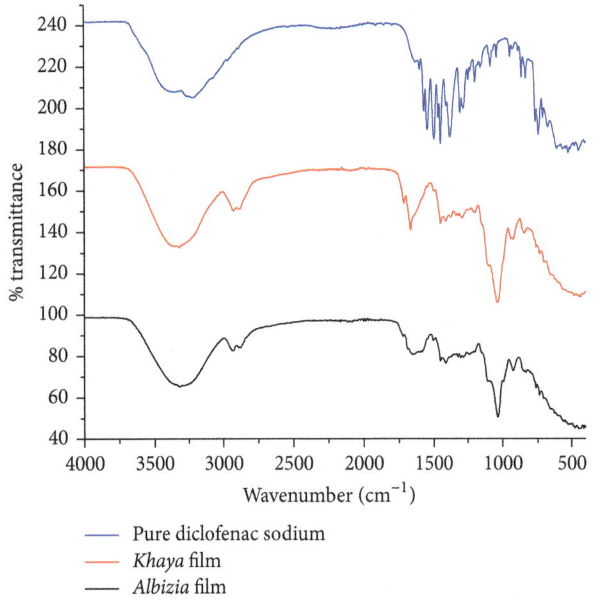

FIGURE 3: FTIR spectra of pure diclofenac sodium and *Albizia* and *Khaya* gum containing ODFs.

values are desirable. Table 5 presents the mechanical properties of the diclofenac sodium ODFs. The tensile strength of the formulations ranged from 5.67 to 7.32 MPa. The use of *Khaya* gum alone (F6) produced hard films while *Albizia* gum alone (F4) produced soft films. Addition of HPMC to *Albizia* gum increased the tensile strength of the films (F2) but the inclusion of HPMC to *Khaya* gum rather reduced the hardness of the films (F3).

Elastic modulus describes the stiffness of films [5] and also provides information about how well the film can resist mechanical deformation. Films with low elastic modulus have low rigidity which translates into high elasticity, and vice versa [19]. The range of elastic modulus recorded for the formulations was 3.89 MPa to 5.11 MPa. Generally, a film with high tensile strength and elasticity (low elastic modulus) is preferred because it can withstand stress better and can also resist changes due to mechanical deformation. In the current study, addition of HPMC to both *Albizia* and *Khaya* gums increased their elasticity by decreasing their elastic modulus (F2 and F3). HPMC thus confers flexibility to *Albizia* and *Khaya* films while *Khaya* gum increased the rigidity of *Albizia* films (F5). The highest elastic modulus was observed in the combination of all three polymers (F7) possibly due to the effect of *Khaya* gum as *Albizia*/HPMC combination (F2) showed moderate elastic modulus.

The exertion of stress on a film causes the film to stretch. This effect called strain is expressed as the change in length of a film divided by its initial length before the applied strain [1]. It describes the pliability of films. A low elongation at break signifies a low capacity of the film to resist deformation and hence the film will be easily breakable. A high elongation at break means that the film has a high capacity to withstand mechanical strain. In the current study, the percentage elongation of the formulations ranged from 7.65% to 17.87%. It was observed that HPMC increases the flexibility of both *Albizia* (F2) and *Khaya* (F3) by increasing their respective percentage elongations. A combination of *Albizia* and *Khaya* gum (F5) showed a decrease in flexibility compared to *Albizia* films alone (F4). It can therefore be deduced that *Khaya* gum produces brittle films and its combination with other polymers increases their inelasticity.

Folding endurance expresses the capacity of the film to resist breaking when folded repeatedly along the same plane. High folding endurance values portray considerable mechanical strength of the film. It is directly regulated by the type and amount of plasticizer used in the formulation. The folding endurance of the films was in the order, F6 < F7 < F3 < F4 < F5 < F1 < F2. Folding endurance of 00 is considered satisfactory for oral films [37]; hence the plasticizer concentration could be increased to improve the folding endurance of the films.

Figure 4 shows the drug release profiles of the ODF formulations in phosphate buffer pH 6.8 at various time intervals. Although there is no official specification, the dissolving time of ODFs has been defined as the time at which not less than 80% of the film under testing dissolves in aqueous media [38]. Formulations F1 and F4 showed over 80% drug release within the first 7 min and the rest of the formulations (except F7) showed over 80% release in the next 7 min. The release of diclofenac sodium from formulation F7 was slowest due to possible polymer cross-linking between the three polymers used. In general, an increase in the number of polymers used resulted in increased dissolution time of the films.

Table 6 presents the dissolution efficiency and difference and similarity factors of the film formulations. Dissolution efficiency describes how competent a dosage form is in releasing its API for pharmacological effect [39]. The higher

TABLE 6: The difference factor ($f1$), similarity factor ($f2$), and dissolution efficiency (DE) of the diclofenac sodium ODF formulations.

Code	Difference factor ($f1$)	Similarity factor ($f2$)	Dissolution efficiency (DE) [%]
*F1	—	—	95.85
F2	7	61	91.88
F3	7	55	89.27
F4	2	89	89.37
F5	5	66	91.84
F6	4	70	93.01
F7	27	33	82.85

*Reference sample.

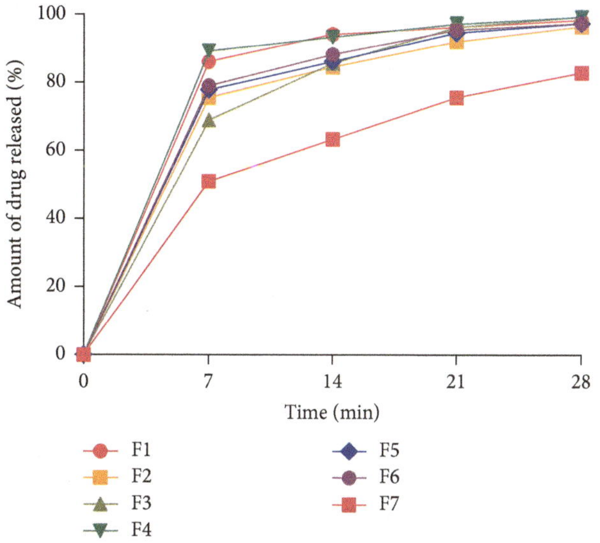

FIGURE 4: Drug release profiles of diclofenac sodium ODF formulations in phosphate buffer pH 6.8 at 37°C (mean ± SD, $n = 3$).

the dissolution efficiency, the more capable the dosage form at releasing its deep-seated API. The order of dissolution efficiencies of the formulations was F7 < F3 < F4 < F5 < F2 < F6 < F1. Thus, F1 can be said to be the superior film formulation in terms of drug release. This trend supports the findings from the drug release studies.

The difference factor ($f1$) estimates the percentage difference between two dissolution profiles at every point and is a measure of the relative error between the dissolution profiles of both the test and reference drug. Usually, $f1$ values in the range of 0–15 indicate insignificant difference between the two batches [40]. From the results, all formulations (except F7) had $f1$ values within the desirable range of 0–15. This means that in terms of drug release F2, F3, F4, F5, and F6 were not different from F1, the reference formulation. Formulation F7 however differed from F1 because of its high $f1$ value of 27. In terms of similarity ($f2$), a test formulation is considered similar to the reference if the $f2$ value is in the range of 50–100 [41]. All the formulations (except F7) had $f2$ values within the 50–100 range. Thus, it can be inferred that F2, F3, F4, F5, and F6 are similar to F1 (reference) in terms of their dissolution characteristics and can be used as alternatives. Table 7 presents the results of one-way ANOVA followed by Dunnett's multiple comparison test on the dissolution profiles of the ODF formulations. No significant difference ($P > 0.05$) was observed in the comparisons of the reference formulation (F1) and formulations F2, F3, F4, F5, and F6. However, there was a significant difference ($P < 0.001$) between F1 and F7.

TABLE 7: Data of one-way ANOVA followed by Dunnett's multiple comparison test on drug release profiles of different ODF formulations.

Code	Statistical significance
F1 versus F2	NS
F1 versus F3	NS
F1 versus F4	NS
F1 versus F5	NS
F1 versus F6	NS
F1 versus F7	SD

NS = no significant difference between the two formulations ($P > 0.05$); SD = significant difference between the two formulations ($P < 0.001$).

The kinetic data for the diclofenac sodium ODFs are shown in Table 8. In drug release studies, mathematical models are currently employed to better understand the mechanism of drug release from dosage forms. Advancement in this area has made it possible to predict the release kinetics of drugs based on which mathematical model the dissolution data best fits [33]. The kinetic models employed in the present study were zero-order, first-order, Higuchi, and Hixson-Crowell models. The data from the dissolution studies conducted were fitted into the individual kinetic models to determine their linearity using the coefficient of regressions. In all the film formulations the highest R^2 values were recorded for the Higuchi model which describes drug release by Fickian diffusion. The Higuchi model is mostly applied to describe drug dissolution from various modified release pharmaceutical dosage forms especially in transdermal systems and matrix tablets with water soluble drugs [42].

4. Conclusion

In can be concluded from the study that *Albizia* and *Khaya* gums possess the requisite physicochemical properties for use as film formers for the development of oral dissolvable films. Diclofenac sodium ODFs were successfully formulated using the gums through the solvent casting technique. The ODFs produced generally exhibited satisfactory physicomechanical properties with most of the formulations attaining over 75% drug release in phosphate buffer pH 6.8 within 7 min. The study has demonstrated the potential of *Albizia* and *Khaya* gums as vehicles for the fabrication of diclofenac sodium ODFs and with film properties enhanced through addition of HPMC in the formulation.

TABLE 8: Drug release kinetic models of diclofenac sodium ODF formulations.

Code	Zero-order model		First-order model		Higuchi model		Hixson-Crowell model	
	K_0	R^2	K_1	R^2	K_H	R^2	K_{HC}	R^2
F1	32.54	0.8685	0.163	0.8580	34.46	0.9250	0.505	0.8615
F2	60.09	0.9834	0.979	0.9736	63.04	0.9989	0.865	0.9651
F3	87.18	0.9097	0.428	0.8860	85.29	0.9575	1.497	0.8942
F4	29.08	0.9793	0.146	0.9755	30.11	0.9938	0.976	0.9770
F5	57.79	0.9464	0.946	0.9400	58.80	0.9722	0.955	0.9601
F6	51.60	0.9144	0.266	0.9059	55.71	0.9554	0.893	0.9089
F7	92.40	0.9853	0.874	0.9704	96.24	0.9941	1.896	0.9753

K_0, K_1, K_H, and K_{HC} are kinetic constants for zero-order, first-order, Higuchi, and Hixson-Crowell models, respectively; R^2 = correlation coefficient.

Competing Interests

The authors declare that there is no conflict of interests regarding the publication of this paper.

Acknowledgments

The authors gratefully acknowledge the technical assistance of the technicians in the Departments of Pharmaceutics and Pharmaceutical Chemistry, KNUST, Kumasi, Ghana.

References

[1] A. Arya, A. Chandra, V. Sharma, and K. Pathak, "Fast dissolving oral films: an innovative drug delivery system and dosage form," *International Journal of ChemTech Research*, vol. 2, no. 1, pp. 576–583, 2010.

[2] U. Vollmer and P. Galfetti, "Rapid film: oral thin films as an innovative drug delivery system and dosage," Drug Development Report, 2006.

[3] S. Barnhart and B. Vondrak, "Dissolvable films: dissolvable films for flexible product format in drug delivery," 2008, http://www.pharmtech.com/dissolvable-films-dissolvable-films-flexible-product-format-drug-delivery.

[4] M. J. Chien, G. Tirol, C. Chien, and R. Schmitt, "Film forming polymers in oral films," in *Proceedings of the Annual Meeting and Exposition of the American Association of Pharmaceutical Scientists*, pp. 1–5, AAPS, October-November 2006.

[5] M. Irfan, S. Rabel, Q. Bukhtar, M. I. Qadir, F. Jabeen, and A. Khan, "Orally disintegrating films: a modern expansionin drug delivery system," *Saudi Pharmaceutical Journal*, 2015.

[6] S. B. Borsadia, D. O'Halloran, and J. L. Osborne, "Quick dissolving films: a novel approach to drug delivery," *Drug Development & Delivery*, vol. 3, no. 3, pp. 1–7, 2003.

[7] D. R. Choudhary, V. A. Patel, U. K. Chhalotiya, H. V. Patel, and A. J. Kundawala, "Development and characterization of pharmacokinetic parameters of fast-dissolving films containing levocetirizine," *Scientia Pharmaceutica*, vol. 80, no. 3, pp. 779–787, 2012.

[8] R. Bala, P. Pawar, S. Khanna, and S. Arora, "Orally dissolving strips: a new approach to oral drug delivery system," *International Journal of Pharmaceutical Investigation*, vol. 3, no. 2, pp. 67–76, 2013.

[9] R. C. Mashru, V. B. Sutariya, M. G. Sankalia, and P. P. Parikh, "Development and evaluation of fast-dissolving film of salbutamol suplhate," *Drug Development and Industrial Pharmacy*, vol. 31, no. 1, pp. 25–34, 2005.

[10] R. Sharma, R. Parikh, M. Gohel, and M. Soniwala, "Development of taste masked film of valdecoxib for oral use," *Indian Journal of Pharmaceutical Sciences*, vol. 69, no. 2, pp. 320–323, 2007.

[11] M. Nishimura, K. Matsuura, T. Tsukioka et al., "In vitro and in vivo characteristics of prochlorperazine oral disintegrating film," *International Journal of Pharmaceutics*, vol. 368, no. 1-2, pp. 98–102, 2009.

[12] C. S. Shah, J. S. Quadry, and B. S. Shah Prakashan, *Quadry's Pharmacognosy*, 2008.

[13] M. E. Aulton, *Pharmaceutics: The Design and Manufacture of Medicines*, Churchill Livingstone, London, UK, 3rd edition, 2007.

[14] O. A. Odeku and J. T. Fell, "In-vitro evaluation of khaya and albizia gums as compression coatings for drug targeting to the colon," *Journal of Pharmacy and Pharmacology*, vol. 57, no. 2, pp. 163–168, 2005.

[15] A. Jain, Y. Gupta, and S. K. Jain, "Perspectives of biodegradable natural polysaccharides for site-specific drug delivery to the colon," *Journal of Pharmacy and Pharmaceutical Sciences*, vol. 10, no. 1, pp. 86–128, 2007.

[16] G. K. Jani, D. P. Shah, V. D. Prajapatia, and V. C. Jain, "Gums and mucilages: versatile excipients for pharmaceutical formulations," *Asian Journal of Pharmaceutical Sciences*, vol. 4, no. 5, pp. 309–323, 2009.

[17] K. Fern and R. Morris, "Albizia zygia—Useful Tropical Plants Database," 2014.

[18] W. Hawthorne, *Khaya grandifoliola*, The IUCN Red List of Threatened Species, 1998.

[19] K. Ofori-Kwakye and E. N. N. Adom, "Mechanical properties of khaya and albizia films intended for pharmaceutical coating," *Journal of the Ghana Science Association*, vol. 9, no. 2, pp. 43–53, 2007.

[20] K. Ofori-Kwakye, E. N. N. Adom, and S. L. Kipo, "Preparation and in vitro characteristics of tablet cores coated with albizia, albizia/khaya and albizia/HPMC films," *International Journal of Applied Pharmaceutics*, vol. 1, no. 1, pp. 22–29, 2009.

[21] D. T. Felson, R. C. Lawrence, P. A. Dieppe et al., "Osteoarthritis: New insights—part 1: the disease and its risk factors," *Annals of Internal Medicine*, vol. 133, no. 8, pp. 635–646, 2000.

[22] F. Mili, C. G. Helmick, and D. G. Moriarty, "Health related quality of life among adults reporting arthritis: analysis of data

from the Behavioral Risk Factor Surveillance System, US, 1996–99," *The Journal of Rheumatology*, vol. 30, no. 1, pp. 160–166, 2003.

[23] M. N. Femi-Oyewo, M. O. Adedokun, and T. O. Olusoga, "Evaluation of the suspending properties of *Albizia zygia* gum on sulphadimidine suspension," *Tropical Journal of Pharmaceutical Research*, vol. 3, no. 1, pp. 279–284, 2004.

[24] O. A. Odeku, "Assessment of *Albizia zygia* gum as a binding agent in tablet formulations," *Acta Pharmaceutica*, vol. 55, no. 3, pp. 263–276, 2005.

[25] *British Pharmacopoeia, Volume II*, Her Majesty's Stationery Office, London, UK, 2013.

[26] T. K. Ghosh and B. R. Jasti, *Theory and Practice of Contemporary Pharmaceutics*, CRC Press, Boca Raton, Fla, USA, 2005.

[27] A. O. Oyewale, "Estimation of the essential inorganic constituents of commercial toothpastes," *Journal of Scientific & Industrial Research*, vol. 64, no. 2, pp. 101–107, 2005.

[28] D. W. Nelson and L. E. Sommers, "Total carbon, organic carbon, and organic matter," in *Methods of Soil Analysis Part 2*, A. L. Page, R. H. Miller, and D. R. Keeney, Eds., vol. 9 of *Agronomy Monograph*, pp. 539–579, ASA and SSSA, Madison, Wis, USA, 2nd edition, 1982.

[29] R. Mishra and A. Amin, "Manufacturing techniques of orally dissolving films," *Pharmaceutical Technology*, vol. 35, no. 1, pp. 70–73, 2011.

[30] B. Bhyan, S. Jangra, M. Kaur, and H. Singh, "Orally fast dissolving films: innovations in formulation and technology," *International Journal of Pharmaceutical Sciences Review and Research*, vol. 9, no. 2, pp. 50–57, 2011.

[31] S. Bansal, M. Bansal, and G. Garg, "Formulation and evaluation of fast dissolving film of an antihypertensive drug," *International Journal of Pharmaceutical, Chemical and Biological Sciences*, vol. 3, no. 4, pp. 1097–1108, 2013.

[32] K. K. Peh and C. F. Wong, "Polymeric films as vehicle for buccal delivery: swelling, mechanical, and bioadhesive properties," *Journal of Pharmacy and Pharmaceutical Sciences*, vol. 2, no. 2, pp. 53–61, 1999.

[33] G. Singhvi and M. Singh, "Review: in-vitro drug release characterization models," *International Journal of Pharmaceutical Studies and Research*, vol. 2, no. 1, pp. 77–84, 2011.

[34] F. N. Howes, *Vegetable Gums and Resins*, Chronica Botanica, Waltham, Mass, USA, 1949.

[35] D. P. Elder and P. J. Crowley, *Antimicrobial Preservatives Part Two: Choosing a Preservative*, 2012, http://www.americanpharmaceuticalreview.com/Featured-Articles/38885-Antimicrobial-Preservatives-Part-Two-Choosing-a-Preservative/.

[36] R. S. Patel and S. S. Poddar, "Development and characterization of mucoadhesive buccal patches of salbutamol sulphate," *Current Drug Delivery*, vol. 6, no. 1, pp. 140–144, 2009.

[37] N. A. Nafee, N. A. Boraie, F. A. Ismail, and L. M. Mortada, "Design and characterization of mucoadhesive buccal patches containing cetylpyridinium chloride," *Acta Pharmaceutica*, vol. 53, no. 3, pp. 199–212, 2003.

[38] B. P. Panda, N. S. Dey, and M. E. B. Rao, "Development of innovative orally fast disintegrating film dosage forms: a review," *International Journal of Pharmaceutical Sciences and Nanotechnology*, vol. 5, no. 2, pp. 1666–1674, 2012.

[39] N. H. Anderson, M. Bauer, N. Boussac, R. Khan-Malek, P. Munden, and M. Sardaro, "An evaluation of fit factors and dissolution efficiency for the comparison of in vitro dissolution profiles," *Journal of Pharmaceutical and Biomedical Analysis*, vol. 17, no. 4-5, pp. 811–822, 1998.

[40] FDA, *Guidance for Industry: Immediate Release Solid Oral Dosage Forms, Scale-Up and Post-Approval Changes: Chemistry, Manufacturing and Controls, In-Vitro Dissolution Testing and In-Vivo Bioequivalence Documentation*, Center for Drug Evaluation and Research, Rockville, Md, USA, 1995.

[41] M. C. Gohel, K. G. Sarvaiya, N. R. Mehta, C. D. Soni, V. U. Vyas, and R. K. Dave, "Assessment of similarity factor using different weighting approaches," *Dissolution Technology*, vol. 1, no. 1, pp. 22–27, 2005.

[42] T. Higuchi, "Mechanism of sustained-action medication. Theoretical analysis of rate of release of solid drugs dispersed in solid matrices," *Journal of Pharmaceutical Science*, vol. 52, no. 12, pp. 1145–1149, 1963.

6

High-Resolution Imaging of Polyethylene Glycol Coated Dendrimers via Combined Atomic Force and Scanning Tunneling Microscopy

Shawn Riechers,[1] Qian Zhong,[2] Nai-Ning Yin,[1] Arpad Karsai,[1] Sandro R. P. da Rocha,[2] and Gang-yu Liu[1]

[1] *Department of Chemistry, University of California, Davis, CA 95616, USA*
[2] *Department of Chemical Engineering & Materials Science, Wayne State University, Detroit, MI 48202, USA*

Correspondence should be addressed to Gang-yu Liu; gyliu@ucdavis.edu

Academic Editor: Kang Choon Lee

Dendrimers have shown great promise as drug delivery vehicles in recent years because they can be synthesized with designed size and functionalities for optimal transportation, targeting, and biocompatibility. One of the most well-known termini used for biocompatibility is polyethylene glycol (PEG), whose performance is affected by its actual conformation. However, the conformation of individual PEG bound to soft materials such as dendrimers has not been directly observed. Using atomic force microscopy (AFM) and scanning tunneling microscopy (STM), this work characterizes the structure adopted by PEGylated dendrimers with the highest resolution reported to date. AFM imaging enables visualization of the individual dendrimers, as well as the differentiation and characterization of the dendrimer core and PEG shell. STM provides direct imaging of the PEG extensions with high-resolution. Collectively, this investigation provides important insight into the structure of coated dendrimers, which is crucial for the design and development of better drug delivery vehicles.

1. Introduction

Dendrimers provide an alternative and potent means for drug delivery due to their nanometer size and the ability to incorporate various functionalities on their interior and exterior. Modern chemical synthesis capabilities allow various functionalities to be incorporated on the dendrimer exterior in order to optimize performance in terms of drug binding, transport, targeting, delivery, and biocompatibility [1–3]. Polyamidoamine (PAMAM) dendrimers, for example, have been tailored for enhanced drug solubility, retention time, targeting, and efficacy [1–3]. In addition to optimizing delivery, another issue is the reduction or elimination of cytotoxicity, which has been addressed by masking the terminal functional groups and charge [4]. This can be accomplished by adding biologically compatible terminal groups such as carboxylate, hydroxyl, acetamide, lipid, or polyethylene glycol (PEG) [2]. Among these, PEG is the most widely used due to its minimal or nontoxicity, nonimmunogenicity, and nonantigenicity and has been approved by the FDA in oral intravenous and pulmonary pharmaceutical formulations [5–8]. It is known that PEG chains adopt a variety of conformations, lengths, and packing density and that these structural presentations directly affect biocompatibility [9–11]. In some cases, PEG alters dendrimer's drug loading capacity, retention time, and thus their delivery performance [8, 12, 13]. Therefore, the characterization of PEG coating prior to animal testing is of great importance. While computational studies have been carried out to probe PEG conformation on dendrimers surfaces, experimental studies are lacking due to the difficulties in obtaining high-resolution structural characterization of PEG when bound to soft materials, such as dendrimers [11, 14]. Our prior work shows that high-resolution structural characterization of simple dendrimers such as PAMAM can be achieved by advanced sample preparation and combined atomic force and scanning tunneling microscopy (AFM and STM) imaging [15, 16]. Encouraged by this initial success, this work reports extending our approach to PEGylated PAMAM dendrimers. From the high-resolution images, the molecular conformation, packing density, and distribution of PEG on the surface of individual dendrimers can be obtained. This knowledge of the PEG presentation on dendrimers provides important insights for understanding structure-delivery performance correlation, which could guide the design, optimization, and development of the next generation of dendrimers and reduce usage of animal tests.

2. Materials and Methods

2.1. Materials. The following materials were used as received: methoxy polyethylene glycol 1000 Da (PEG_{1000}) (Sigma-Aldrich), triethylamine (TEA) (99.5%, Sigma-Aldrich), pyridine (99.8%, Sigma-Aldrich) p-nitrophenyl chloroformate (pNPCF) (98%, Sigma-Aldrich), 2,5-dihydroxybenzoic acid (2,5-DHB) (Sigma-Aldrich), anhydrous dichloromethane (DCM) (Sigma-Aldrich), dimethyl sulfoxide (DMSO) (Acros Geel), K_2PtCl_4 (min. 42.4% Pt, Alfa Aesar), n-octanethiol (C8) (98%, Sigma-Aldrich), deuterium oxide (D, 99.96%, Cambridge Isotope Laboratories), and phosphate buffer (10x, Lief Technologies). Fourth generation amine terminated PAMAM dendrimers were purchased as 10% by weight solutions in methanol (Sigma-Aldrich, St. Louis, MO). Silica gel 60 A 230–400 mesh ATSM (Whatman Inc) and silica gel 60 F_{254} plastic sheets (TLC) (Merck KGaA) were used for column and thin layer chromatography, respectively. Ultrapure water (≥18 MΩ·cm, Millipore Milli-Q) and 200 proof ethanol (Gold Shield Chemical Co.) were used for dilution and washing. Ultrapure N_2 (98%, Air Gas Co.) and H_2 (99.99%, Praxair, Inc.) were used for drying and flaming, respectively. Tungsten wire (d = 0.010 in., 99.95%, California Fine Wire Co.) was used to make STM tips. Au slugs (99.99%, Alpha Aesar Premion Co.) and mica (clear ruby muscovite, Mica New York Corp.) were used for Au thin film preparation.

2.2. Methods

2.2.1. Preparation of Gold Thin Films. The following materials were used as received: methoxy polyethylene glycol 1000 Da (PEG1000) (Sigma-Aldrich, St. Louis, MO), triethylamine (TEA) (99.5%, Sigma-Aldrich, St. Louis, MO), pyridine (99.8%, Sigma-Aldrich, St. Louis, MO) p-nitrophenyl chloroformate (pNPCF) (98%, Sigma-Aldrich, St. Louis, MO), 2,5-dihydroxybenzoic acid (2,5-DHB) (Sigma-Aldrich, St. Louis, MO), anhydrous dichloromethane (DCM) (Sigma-Aldrich, St. Louis, MO), dimethyl sulfoxide (DMSO) (99.7%, Acros, Geel, Belgium), K2PtCl4 (min. 42.4% Pt, Alfa Aesar, Ward Hill, Massachusetts), n-octanethiol (C8) (98%, Sigma-Aldrich, St. Louis, MO), deuterium oxide (D, 99.96%, Cambridge Isotope Laboratories, Tewksbury, MA), and phosphate buffer (10x, Lief Technologies, Grand Island, NY). Fourth generation amine terminated PAMAM dendrimers were purchased as 10% by weight solutions in methanol (Sigma-Aldrich, St. Louis, MO). Silica gel 60A 230-400 mesh ATSM (Whatman Inc, Pittsburgh, PA) and silica gel 60 F254 plastic sheets (TLC) (Merck KGaA, Darmstadt, Germany) were used for column and thin layer chromatography, respectively. Ultrapure water (≥18MΩ · cm, MilliporeMilli-Q, Billerica, MA) and 200 proof ethanol (Gold Shield Chemical Co., Hayward, CA) were used for dilution and washing. Ultrapure N2 (98%, Air Gas Co., Woodland, CA) and H2 (99.99%, Praxair Inc., Sacramento, CA) were used for drying and flaming, respectively. Tungsten wire (d = 0.010 in., 99.95%, California Fine Wire Co., Grover Beach, CA) was used to make STM tips. Au slugs (99.99%, Alpha Aesar Premion Co., Ward Hill MA) and mica (clear ruby muscovite, Mica New York Corp., New York, NY) were used for Au thin film preparation.

2.2.2. PEGylation of G4-PAMAM-NH_2 Dendrimers. G4-PAMAM-NH_2 dendrimers were PEGylated according to previous reports with some modifications [13]. Briefly, PEG_{1000} was first modified by reaction with TEA and a catalyst amount of pyridine in anhydrous DCM with PEG_{1000}. To the organic solution was added pNPCF dropwise. The organic solvent was then removed under reduced pressure. To remove unreacted pNPCF, the resultant product was purified by column chromatography.

The G4-PAMAM-$nPEG_{1000}$ was synthesized by adding an anhydrous DMSO solution of G4-PAMAM-NH_2 dropwise to a solution of PEG_{1000} carbonate in anhydrous DMSO. The reaction system was then stirred 24 hours for G4-PAMAM-6PEG_{1000}, or 72 hours for G4-PAMAM-50PEG_{1000}. The resulting G4-PAMAM-$n$$PEG_{1000}$ was purified by centrifugal filter (MWCO = 10 kDa) until thin layer chromatography (DCM/methanol = 80/20, v/v) showed no unreacted PEG_{1000} carbonate or byproduct p-nitrophenol.

2.2.3. G4-PAMAM-$nPEG_{1000}$ Characterization. The molecular weight of the modified and unmodified dendrimers was determined by matrix assisted laser desorption ionization time-of-flight mass spectrometry (MALDI-TOF-MS) (Ultraflex, Bruker). Spectra were acquired under positive ion reflector mode. The conjugates were dissolved in deionized water at a concentration of 1.0 mg/mL. 10 mg/mL of 2,5-DHB in methanol was used as matrix. 10 μL of the conjugate solution was mixed with 10 μL of the DHB solution. 2 μL of the sample was spotted on a MALDI target plate (MTP 384, Bruker Daltonics, Inc.). The spotted sample was dried gently by air flow. The G4-PAMAM-NH_2, G4-PAMAM-6PEG_{1000}, and G4-PAMAM-50PEG_{1000} dendrimers were found to have a molecular weight of 14,579, 22,080, and 75,929 Da, respectively.

The number of PEG chains per dendrimer was determined by ^{1}H NMR spectroscopy (MR-400, Agilent) using deuterated solvent. The deuterated solvent peak (DMSO_d6: 2.483; D_2O: 4.577) in ^{1}H NMR was set as a reference peak. The PEGylation resulted in 5.9 PEG per dendrimer, referred to as G4-PAMAM-6PEG_{1000}, and 50.5 PEG per dendrimer, referred to as G4-PAMAM-50PEG_{1000}.

The hydrodynamic diameter (HD) of samples was measured using dynamic light scattering (DLS) (Zetasizer Nano ZS, Melvern Instruments). The sample (1.0 mg/mL) was dissolved in phosphate buffer solution (0.1 M, pH 7.4) to maintain the pH during the measurement. HD and standard deviations were automatically calculated by built-in software. G4-PAMAM-NH_2, G4-PAMAM-6PEG_{1000}, and G4-PAMAM-50PEG_{1000} dendrimers were found to have a HD of 4.4 ± 1.4, 5.8 ± 2.1, and 12.2 ± 4.4 nm, respectively.

2.2.4. AFM and STM Imaging. Dendrimers were immobilized on gold surfaces for AFM and STM imaging. The solutions were prepared following previously established procedures, including metal ion doping to facilitate STM imaging [15–17]. In short, dendrimer solutions were diluted to 1 μM in pure water. K_2PtCl_4 was then added to obtain molar ratios of 1 : 70, or 1 : 700 dendrimer : Pt^{2+}. Solutions were kept at room temperature for 48 hours in order to allow for sufficient Pt^{2+}-amine coordination within dendrimers. For the surface deposition of dendrimers, 1 cm^2 pieces of gold films were H_2-flamed and allowed to cool for 10 minutes under clean ambient conditions. Then, a 60–100 μL drop of the dendrimer solution was deposited resulting in a droplet with a contact diameter of 0.7–0.9 cm. After 1.25 minutes the surface was washed with 2 mL of pure water, dried with N_2, washed with 2 mL of ethanol, and dried again with N_2. A 60–100 μL drop of 1.0 mM C8 solution was then applied to the substrate for 4 minutes, washed with 2 mL of ethanol, and dried with N_2. C8 SAMs are incorporated in order to replace weakly adsorbed molecules, confine dendrimers laterally, and prevent mobility during scanning. This process results in a clean, high coverage submonolayer of dendrimers on the surface.

AFM images were acquired using a MFP3D-SA system (Asylum Research), which includes a closed loop capability. A silicon cantilever (AC-240, Olympus) was used for imaging and nanoshaving. The probe has a typical force constant of $k = 1.0$ N/m as measured by the thermal noise method [16, 18, 20, 21]. During tapping mode imaging, the cantilever was modulated by a driving frequency of 74 kHz and amplitude of 87 nm (1.0 V). During nanoshaving to displace adsorbates such as dendrimers or alkanethiolates, tips were placed in contact with the surface with increasing load beyond threshold [22, 23]. Image processing and data analysis were performed using Gwyddion (Version 2.33, http://gwyddion.net/).

STM images were taken using a walker-type scanner (UHV 300, RHK Technologies, Inc.), under ambient pressure and temperature [18, 19]. STM tips were prepared by etching tungsten wires electrochemically at 2.0 V in 3.0 M NaOH solutions using a homemade potentiostat to monitor the etching process [18, 19]. All STM images were acquired in constant current mode with typical bias voltages ranging from 0.4 to 0.9 V and tunneling currents from 10 to 40 pA. The scanner was calibrated laterally using an octanethiol SAM lattice constant of 0.50 nm and vertically using Au(111) single atomic step (0.235 nm). Image processing and data analysis were performed using XPMPro (Version 2.0.0.8, RHK Technologies, Inc.). Surface contact area measurements were carried out using ImageJ (Version 1.47v, Wayne Rasband, NIH, http://imagej.nih.gov/ij/index.html).

3. Results and Discussion

3.1. AFM Imaging of the PEGylated G4 Dendrimers. The characteristic AFM tapping mode images of G4-PAMAM-50PEG_{1000}, are shown in Figures 1(a) and 1(b). The two images are of the same area but under two different damping set points during tapping mode AFM imaging. In the case of G4-PAMAM-50PEG_{1000}, the topographic images were found to vary with the set point values. In Figure 1(a), at 42% damping, each dendrimer appears as a ring. Reducing the damping to 23%, that is, gentler tapping, an ellipsoidal cap morphology is observed, as shown in Figure 1(b). We have varied damping (from 0% to 100%) and found that dendrimers appear as either rings as shown in Figure 1(a) or ellipsoidal caps as shown in Figure 1(b). We assigned the two features to PAMAM core and PEG shell (or coating), respectively. The assignment is based on three observations. First, the damping-dependence was not present for non-PEGylated dendrimers, such as G4-PAMAM-NH_2, as revealed in Figures 1(c) and 1(d). Regardless of tapping conditions, the G4-PAMAM-NH_2 dendrimers always appear as ellipsoidal caps, consistent with prior studies [16]. Secondly, the core region of the G4-PAMAM-50PEG_{1000} ring structures is commensurate in size with that of the G4-PAMAM-NH_2 core, as shown in cursor 1 of Figure 1. Thirdly, damping dependence in tapping mode AFM imaging typically indicates variation in materials' viscoelastic property, for example, how materials respond to periodical tapping of the AFM tip [24–27]. The distinct differences in the case of G4-PAMAM-50PEG_{1000} dendrimers are consistent with a tight and elastic dendrimer core and a relatively loose and viscoelastic PEG coating. The PEG regions could exhibit high responses at specific damping conditions, revealing rings more evidently.

The width of the rings, measured as full width at half of the maximum height, varies from 5.0 to 12.4 nm, with an average value of 6.9 ± 2.3 nm. The measured ring width provides an approximate view regarding the extension, or conformation, of the PEG molecules suggesting a variation in the PEG conformation. According to AFM imaging, the thickness of the PEG coating surrounding individual dendrimers is asymmetric. The difference between the thickest and thinnest regions of the PEG coating on a single dendrimer varies by 3.4% up to 47.6%. This preliminary assessment of dendrimer morphology indicates that the PEG density and extension are not uniform at the outer shell of individual dendrimers. To determine the fine structure of the PEG coating, STM imaging is performed and provides a more accurate visualization of the PEG presentation, as will be discussed in detail in Section 3.2.

To verify that the features are not due to deformation upon surface immobilization, we have also imaged dendrimers at various surface coverages. At high surface coverage, as shown in Figure 2, AFM topographs are again found to depend on tapping conditions. Overall, the trend is similar to that at low coverage, that is, solid ellipsoidal caps are observed under most tapping conditions, while rings are observed at greater dampening. This indicates that the ring-like features are intrinsic to the dendrimer structure instead of surface deformation.

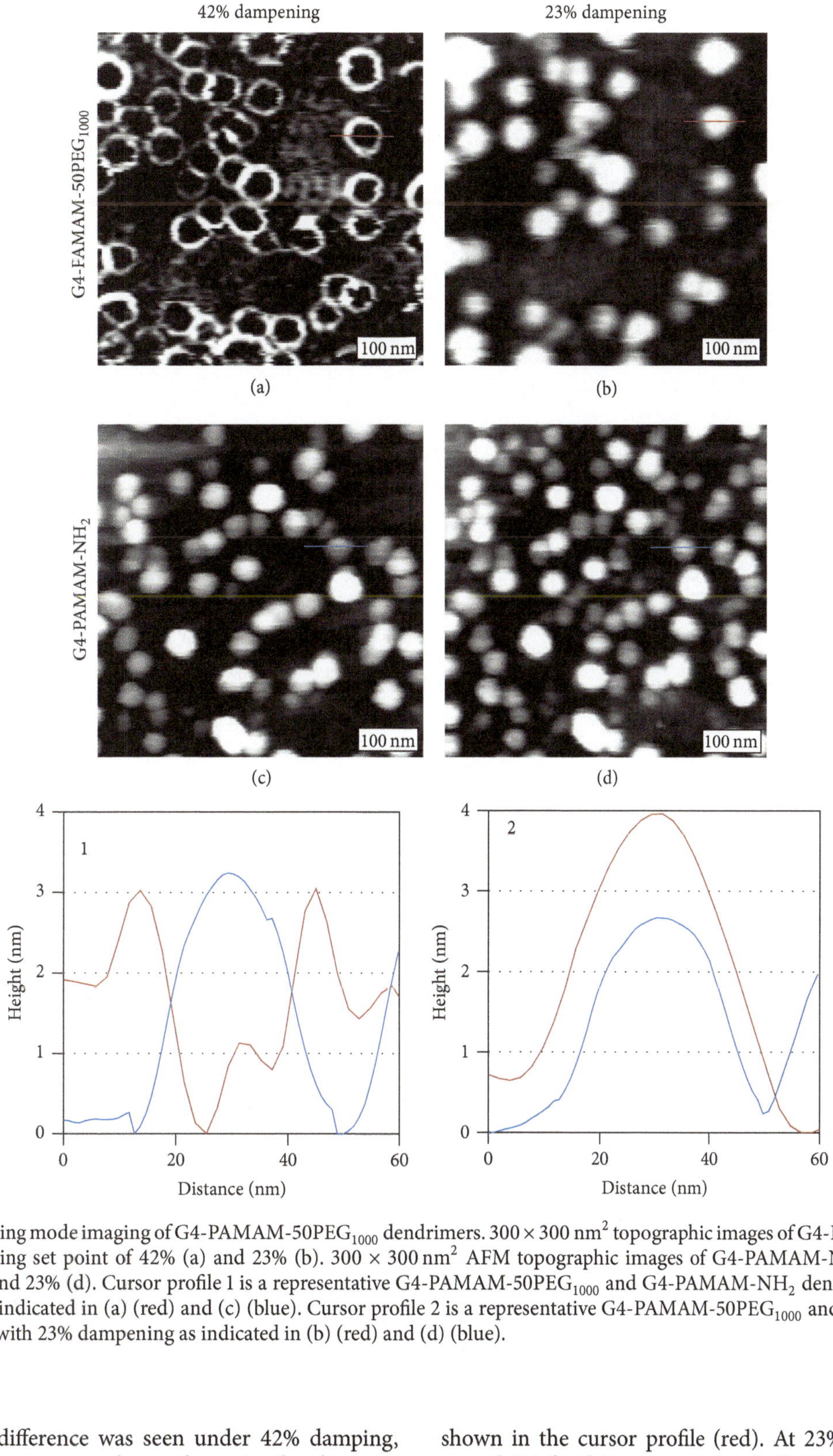

FIGURE 1: AFM tapping mode imaging of G4-PAMAM-50PEG$_{1000}$ dendrimers. 300 × 300 nm^2 topographic images of G4-PAMAM-50PEG$_{1000}$ acquired at a damping set point of 42% (a) and 23% (b). 300 × 300 nm^2 AFM topographic images of G4-PAMAM-NH$_2$ at damping set points of 42% (c), and 23% (d). Cursor profile 1 is a representative G4-PAMAM-50PEG$_{1000}$ and G4-PAMAM-NH$_2$ dendrimer imaged with 42% dampening as indicated in (a) (red) and (c) (blue). Cursor profile 2 is a representative G4-PAMAM-50PEG$_{1000}$ and G4-PAMAM-NH$_2$ dendrimer imaged with 23% dampening as indicated in (b) (red) and (d) (blue).

One specific difference was seen under 42% damping, at which ring contrast was observed previously; the morphology appears fragmented, analogous to flower pedals, as shown in Figure 2(a). The brighter lobes correspond to overlapping PEG regions between two neighboring dendrimers. This overlapping region can extend the entire thickness of the PEG coating up to the PAMAM core as shown in the cursor profile (red). At 23% damping, PEG-coated G4 dendrimers appear as individual ellipsoidal caps with a clear depression between adjacent dendrimers, as shown in Figure 2(b) and the cursor (blue) of Figure 2. In the case of G4-PAMAM-NH$_2$ dendrimers, no overlap among dendrimers was ever observed, regardless of imaging conditions. These observations suggest that the PEG chains

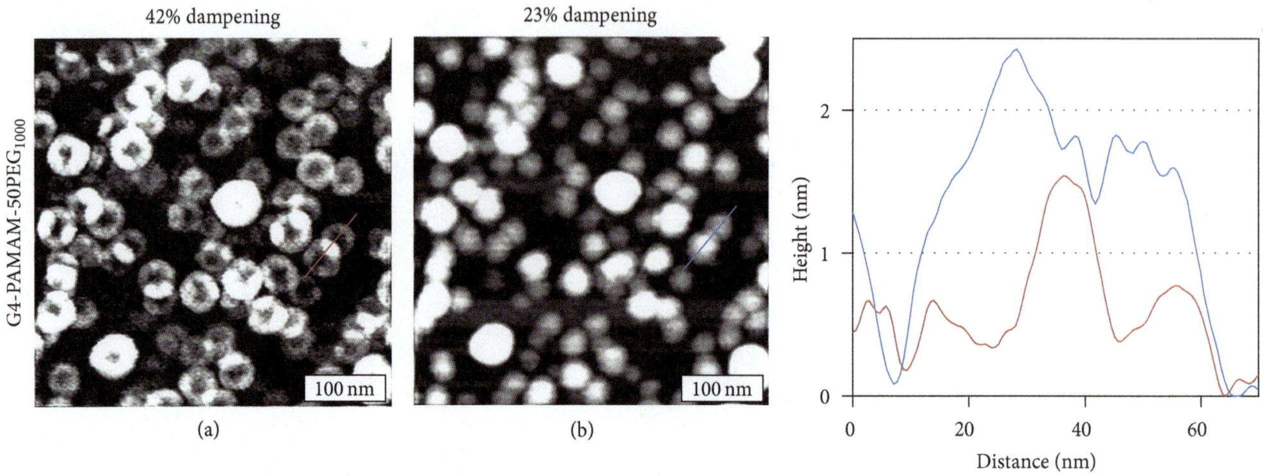

Figure 2: 300 × 300 nm^2 AFM topographic images of G4-PAMAM-50PEG$_{1000}$ imaged with 42% (a) and 23% (b) dampening. Cursor profile is taken from representative G4-PAMAM-50PEG$_{1000}$ dendrimers in images (a) (red) and (b) (blue).

could be interdigitated at close proximity, which could lead to stacking, interspersion, and merging among neighboring dendrimers. This behavior is in sharp contrast to the PAMAM cores, where no overlapping or coalescing was seen. These observations are important in the context of drug delivery in vivo, as aggregation due to high accumulations of dendrimers is of concern.

Our previous work has demonstrated that the physical height of surface immobilized dendrimers can be measured using nanoshaving, an AFM based technique, in conjunction with topographic imaging [15–17]. The surface was first surveyed to select a relatively flat 1.5 μm × 1.5 μm region. Higher force was then applied during scanning of a central 0.5 μm × 0.5 μm region to remove the dendrimer monolayer. Finally the entire area was imaged again in tapping mode to reveal both the freshly exposed surface region and the surrounding dendrimer monolayer in a single frame, shown in Figure 3(a) inset. The physical height of individual G4-PAMAM-NH$_2$ dendrimers relative to the bare substrate can be directly obtained from the cursor profile. As shown in Figure 3(a), cursor 1 reveals the height of five individual dendrimers. The height taken from multiple experiments and a large number of G4-PAMAM-NH$_2$ dendrimers was found to be 2.2 ± 0.3 nm, which is identical to 3 previous measurements of surface immobilized G4-PAMAM dendrimers [15–17]. This value is lower than 4.4 nm determined by DLS which probes hydrodynamic diameter. This is not uncommon due to the deformation of the dendrimer upon surface immobilization under ambient conditions [15–17, 28–30]. G4-PAMAM-50PEG$_{1000}$ dendrimers appear taller than the G4-PAMAM-NH$_2$ core. Figure 3(b) is a topographical AFM image containing G4-PAMAM-50PEG$_{1000}$. The dendrimers were displaced in the upper left region, enabling accurate height measurements, as shown for two representative G4-PAMAM-50PEG$_{1000}$ in cursor 2. The average height of G4-PAMAM-50PEG$_{1000}$ measured from two experiments and multiple images is 3.4 ± 1.2 nm, which is 1.2 nm taller than the core, G4-PAMAM-NH$_2$. As indicated by the increased standard deviation relative to G4-PAMAM-NH$_2$, the PEGylated dendrimers have a far greater distribution of height, indicating a greater range of size and/or conformation upon surface immobilization.

3.2. High-Resolution STM Imaging of PEGylated G4 Dendrimers. STM provides submolecular resolution characterization of PEGylated dendrimers, revealing the morphology and structure of the PEG chains. With the overall morphology of dendrimers established by AFM, we could use STM to provide a more detailed look at the intramolecular structure especially at PEG region. Although dendrimers are not sufficiently conductive for direct STM imaging, our prior work has indicated that STM conductivity may be enhanced by coordinating metal ions into the dendrimer [15–17]. This work demonstrates that the same approach is effective to enable STM imaging of PEGylated dendrimers.

The G4-PAMAM-NH$_2$ structure was first characterized without PEGylation. Figure 4(a) is a STM topographic image of G4-PAMAM-NH$_2$. Individual dendrimers are clearly resolved, at the coverage of submonolayer with sufficient interparticle separation. At higher resolution shown in Figure 4(b), it is apparent that the geometry of surface immobilized G4-PAMAM-NH$_2$ adopts a very similar shape to the most commonly known PAMAM dendrimers, G4-PAMAM-OH, which are ellipsoidal caps [15–17]. While these dendrimers are considered to be nearly spherical in solution, the flattening and deformation from spherical geometry are due to dendrimer-surface interaction. The dendrimer-surface contact areas, as highlighted in red, of the three dendrimers were measured as 7.7, 12.0, and 13.4 nm^2. Intraparticular features are also visible, such as the bright protrusions on the surface of each dendrimer, which likely correspond to individual NH$_2$ termini, analogous to OH termini visualized previously [16].

Upon PEGylation, the STM images reveal significant structural changes from that of core particles. Figure 4(c) is a typical high-resolution STM image for G4-PAMAM-50PEG$_{1000}$. The PAMAM cores of individual dendrimers are

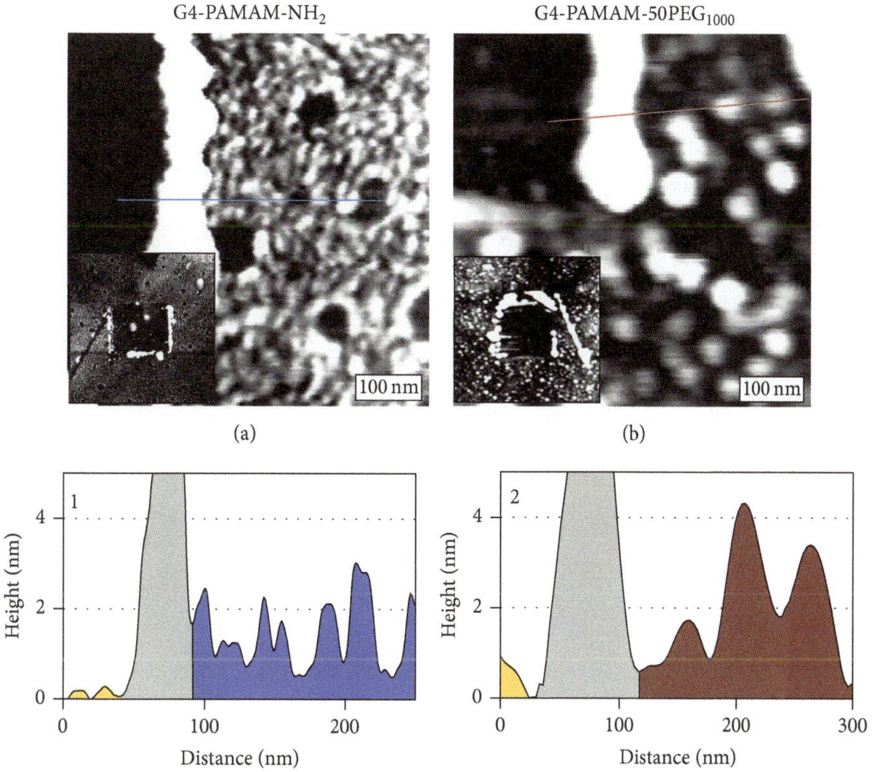

FIGURE 3: Height characterization of dendrimers without and with PEGylation via nanoshaving. (a) A $300 \times 300\,nm^2$ AFM topographic image of a nanoshaved monolayer of G4-PAMAM-NH_2. The (a) inset is a $1.5 \times 1.5\,\mu m$ AFM topographic image of the G4-PAMAM-NH_2 surface where a $0.5 \times 0.5\,\mu m$ area was removed during nanoshaving to reveal the Au substrate. (b) A $400 \times 400\,nm^2$ AFM topographic image of a nanoshaved monolayer of G4-PAMAM-50PEG_{1000}. The (b) inset is a $1.5 \times 1.5\,\mu m$ AFM topographic image of the G4-PAMAM-50PEG_{1000} surface where a $0.5 \times 0.5\,\mu m$ area was removed during nanoshaving to reveal the Au substrate. Cursor 1 reveals the height of individual G4-PAMAM-NH_2 from image (a). From left to right, the gold substrate (gold), dendrimers displaced during nanoshaving (grey), and the dendrimer monolayer (blue). Cursor 2 reveals the height of individual G4-PAMAM-50PEG_{1000} from image (b). From left to right, the gold substrate (gold), dendrimers displaced during nanoshaving (grey), and the dendrimer monolayer (red).

still visible, but the footprint or dendrimer-surface contact area is interspersed with PEG chains spreading out and filling the space between dendrimers. At higher resolution the PEG are visualized more clearly, as shown in Figure 4(d). Unlike G4-PAMAM-NH_2, the dendrimers are no longer ellipsoidal, as the contact area adopts a more irregular geometry (see red lines tracing the boundaries). The periphery of these dendrimers was determined using multiple cursor profiles to accurately determine the boundaries of each dendrimer. The contact area of the two PEGylated dendrimers is much greater than the corresponding core particles, measuring 41.8 and $29.1\,nm^2$, respectively. These high-resolution images reveal that the PEG presentation varies from dendrimer to dendrimer, which leads to a large variation in contact upon surface immobilization. As shown in Figure 4(d), the majority of the PEG chains extend as groups to form PEG "podia." The PEG podia tend to fan out in regions of bare substrate and bunch up near adjacent dendrimer PEG extensions. These PEG podia extend from 0.5 to 4.5 nm from the core contact region, which indicate variations in PEG conformation. Previous work indicated several conformations adopted by PEG chains attached to solid substrates [9, 10]. To our knowledge, results shown in Figure 4 represent the first observation of the PEG conformational variations in the context of dendrimers.

In order to determine the effect of the packing density of the PEG at the dendrimer surfaces, various PEG : core ratios were prepared. Figure 4(e) shows a STM topograph of a low PEGylation, G4-PAMAM-6PEG_{1000}. The overall morphology of G4-PAMAM-6PEG_{1000} closely resembles that of G4-PAMAM-NH_2, as clearly defined ellipsoidal caps with intraparticular features and protrusions visible. The degree of spreading observed is shown in Figure 4(f), which falls in between G4-PAMAM-50PEG_{1000} and G4-PAMAM-NH_2. The dendrimer-surface contact area of the two representative G4-PAMAM-6PEG_{1000} shown in Figure 4(f) measures 24.5 and $21.1\,nm^2$, from left to right. The majority of the PEG chains are located close to the core. PEG podia appear shorter than that in high PEG : core ratio cases with their extension 0.5–2.0 nm from the PAMAM core. It is known that the packing density of PEG chains on flat surfaces greatly impacts their conformation [9, 13]. Our investigations indicate that this concept appears to be valid in the context of PEG chains at the surface of PAMAM dendrimers.

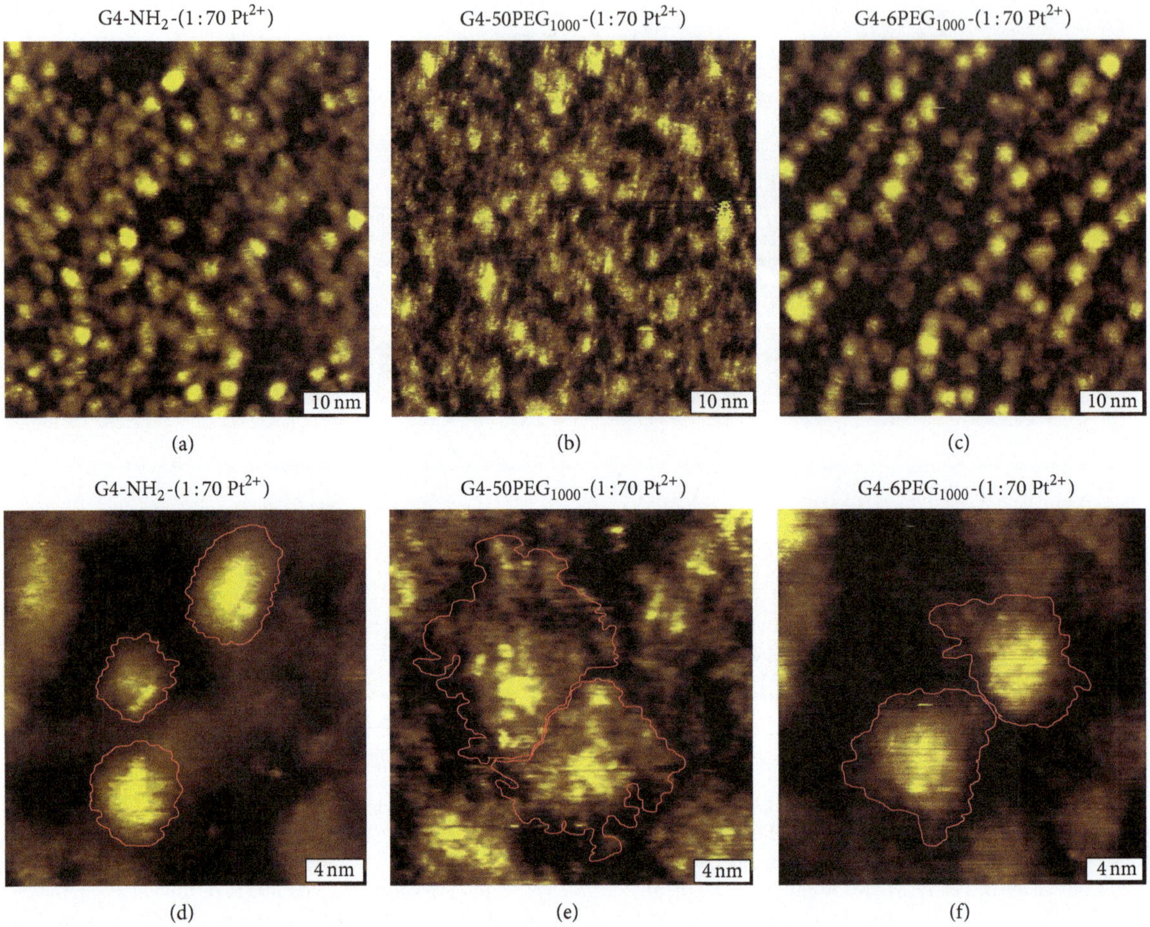

Figure 4: High-resolution characterization of dendrimers with varying degrees of PEGylation. (a) A $60 \times 60\,nm^2$ STM topographic image of G4-PAMAM-NH_2. (b) A $15 \times 15\,nm^2$ STM topographic image of G4-PAMAM-NH_2 with three representative dendrimer contact areas highlighted in red. (c) $60 \times 60\,nm^2$ image of G4-PAMAM-50PEG_{1000}. (d) $15 \times 15\,nm^2$ image of G4-PAMAM-50PEG_{1000} with two representative dendrimer/PEG contact areas highlighted in red. (e) $60 \times 60\,nm^2$ image of G4-PAMAM-6PEG_{1000}. (f) $15 \times 15\,nm^2$ image of G4-PAMAM-6PEG_{1000} with two representative dendrimer/PEG contact areas highlighted in red. All images were acquired at 0.7–0.9 V and 20–30 pA.

The observed coverage dependence of PEG conformation may be understood by taking into account PEG-PEG, PEG-solution, and PEG-surface interactions. On solid flat surfaces PEG_{1000} chains adopt various conformations depending on the interplay between these interactions. Three characteristic conformations have been described previously, known as pancake, mushroom, and brush, with the extension length of 0.5, 1.0, and 2.5 nm, respectively [8–10]. PEG chains on the dendrimer exterior differ from those on flat surfaces due to the curvature and mechanical flexibility of the core. The curvature allows more space than that on flat surfaces under the same coverage, while the relatively soft core allows for greater deformation and flexibility upon surface immobilization. Computational studies on G3-PAMAM-8PEG_{1000} indicate that PEG chains fold in close contact with the dendrimer core in solution, due primarily to interactions between the ether groups of PEG and the protonated amine termini of the dendrimers extending approximately 1 nm in solution [11, 31]. In the case of dendrimers with lower coverage PEG, such as in G4-PAMAM-6PEG_{1000}, the PEG chains seem to follow this theoretical prediction and exhibit tightly bound podia. The extension is larger than predicted, extending from 0.5 to 2.5 nm, which indicates the presence of all three conformations described previously. At higher coverage, G4-PAMAM-50PEG_{1000}, the PEG podia extension ranges from 0.5 to 4.5 nm. The longest extensions exceed the brush conformation, which we attribute to the effect of dendrimer support and interchain interactions. Considering that PEG-surface interactions could offset the intramolecular interactions in solution phase, local structural characterization is critical to reveal individual dendrimers' structures. The observation of heterogeneity should also be considered when designing dendrimers for drug delivery.

3.3. Impact of PEGylation on STM Imaging. Results from STM investigations indicate that the incorporation of Pt^{2+} ions leads to sufficient conductivity for high-resolution STM imaging, despite PEGylation, which in principle should

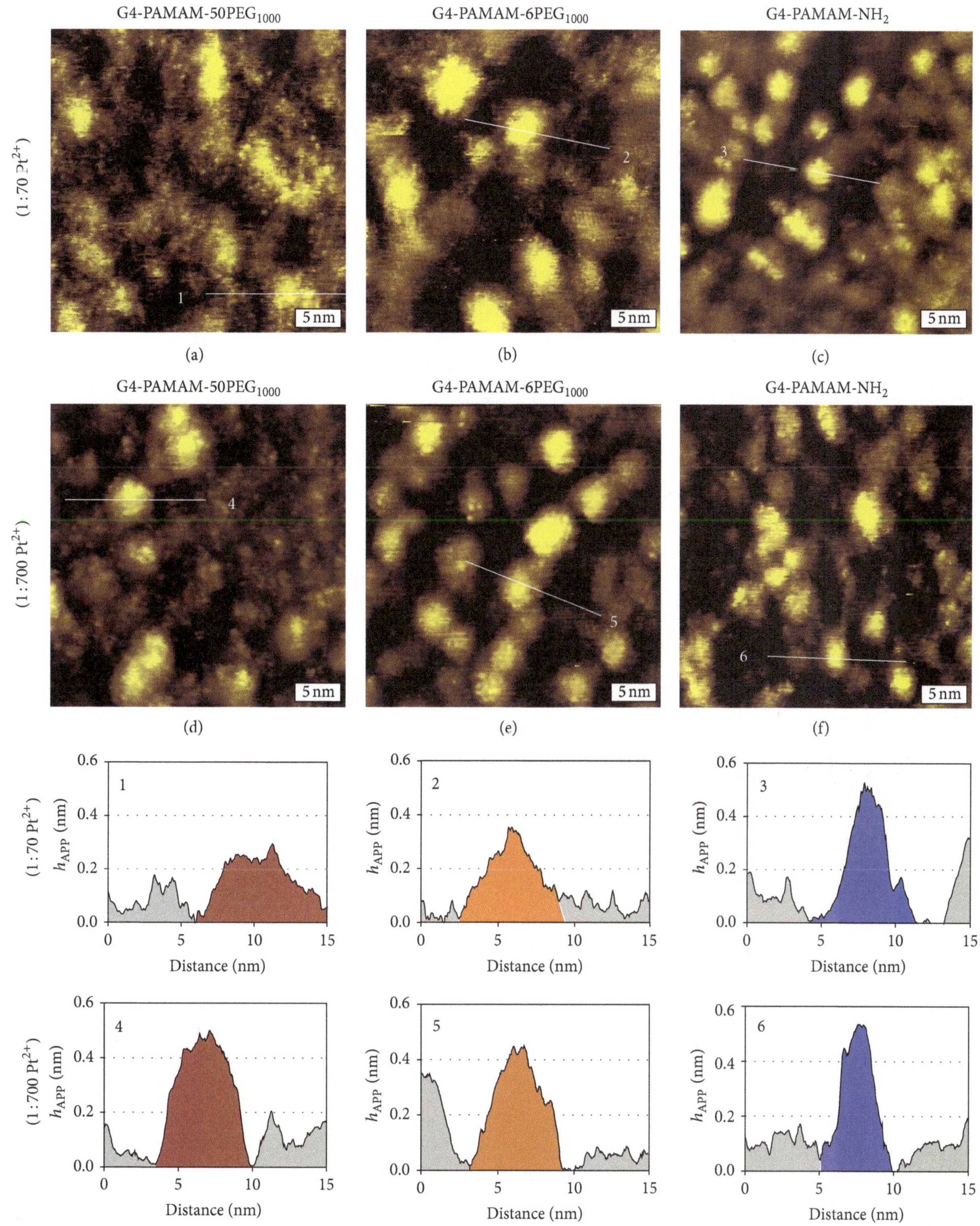

FIGURE 5: High-resolution characterization of dendrimers doped at 1:70 and 1:700 dendrimer to Pt^{2+} molar ratios. (a–c) $15 \times 15\,nm^2$ STM topographic images of G4-PAMAM-50PEG_{1000}, G4-PAMAM-6PEG_{1000}, and G4-PAMAM-NH_2 doped in a solution containing a 1:70 molar ratio of dendrimer to Pt^{2+}. (d–f) $15 \times 15\,nm^2$ STM topographic images of G4-PAMAM-50PEG_{1000}, G4-PAMAM-6PEG_{1000}, and G4-PAMAM-NH_2 doped in a solution containing a 1:700 molar ratio of dendrimer to Pt^2. Cursors 1–3 provide the lateral and apparent height dimensions of individual representative G4-PAMAM-50PEG_{1000}, G4-PAMAM-6PEG_{1000}, and G4-PAMAM-NH_2 dendrimers doped at a 1:70 Pt^{2+} ratio. Cursors 4–6 provide the lateral and apparent height dimensions of individual representative G4-PAMAM-50PEG_{1000}, G4-PAMAM-6PEG_{1000}, and G4-PAMAM-NH_2 dendrimers doped at a 1:700 Pt^{2+} ratio. All images were acquired at 0.7–0.9 V and 20–30 pA.

hinder metal ion doping. In comparison to PAMAM dendrimers, the incorporation of metal ions follows slower kinetics. In the case of G4-PAMAM-OH, for example, each dendrimer was saturated by Pt^{2+} within 48 hrs, under 1:70 dendrimer : Pt^{2+} molar ratio, at a 1 μM concentration [16]. The resulting increase in tunneling probability allowed for high-resolution STM imaging, which could resolve individual dendrimer termini [15–17]. Under identical conditions, G4-PAMAM-NH_2 also yielded high-resolution STM images, as shown in Figures 4(b) and 5(c). In the presence of a PEG coating high-resolution is still provided; however, the apparent height, or h_{APP}, is lower, as shown in Figures 5(a)–5(c) and cursors 1–3. The average h_{APP} of G4-PAMAM-NH_2 is 0.42 ± 0.11 nm, whereas the h_{APP} for G4-PAMAM-6PEG_{1000} and G4-PAMAM-50PEG_{1000} is 0.38 ± 0.13 nm and 0.32 ± 0.07 nm, respectively. We infer that the metal ion concentration inside G4-PAMAM-50PEG_{1000} and G4-PAMAM-6PEG_{1000} dendrimers is lower than G4-PAMAM-NH_2, leading to a lower local density of states and therefore h_{APP}. To increase the metal ion coordination within the dendrimers, the dendrimer : Pt^{2+} molar ratio was increased from 1:70 to 1:700, and the results are shown in Figures 5(d)–5(f) and cursors 4–6. At a higher Pt^{2+} ratio, the average h_{APP} of G4-PAMAM-NH_2, G4-PAMAM-6PEG_{1000}, and G4-PAMAM-50PEG_{1000} increased to 0.51 ± 0.07 nm, 0.45 ± 0.12 nm, and 0.56 ± 0.04 nm, respectively. In the case of G4-PAMAM-NH_2, the average h_{APP} increases only 17%, indicating that the intraparticulate Pt^{2+} concentration is very similar under the two concentrations. This is in contrast to G4-PAMAM-50PEG_{1000}, where the h_{APP} increases by 43%. It is important to note here that a height increase was not observed, as measured by AFM, for any of the dendrimers when the Pt^{2+} ratio was increased. Thus, by increasing the Pt^{2+} concentration, the metal ions were able to penetrate the PEG coating and coordinate with the amines within the dendrimer core to a greater extent. Since the G4-PAMAM-NH_2 dendrimer is already nearly saturated at the lower Pt^{2+} concentration the effect on h_{APP} is relatively small as compared to the highly PEGylated dendrimer. These observations should shed light when using dendrimers as drug delivery vehicles, as the coating may change the pharmacokinetic behavior.

4. Conclusions

Using AFM and STM, we have characterized the morphology and structure of PEGylated dendrimers. AFM investigation allows for the visualization of individual dendrimers on surfaces and provides accurate height measurements. In addition, AFM studies reveal that the PAMAM core and PEG shell can be visualized under tapping mode imaging to ascertain the uniformity and distribution of PEGylation on individual dendrimers. Further, the results indicate that PEG chains among adjacent dendrimers could interdigitate, in contrast to the dendrimer cores. STM imaging enables direct visualization of the PEG extensions with high-resolution. The PEG chains at the exterior PAMAM cores adopt various conformations including pancake, mushroom, and brush, similar to that at the solid and flat surfaces. Unique to high coverage PEGylated dendrimers, a greater variation in PEG structure and degree of extension is observed with the PEG podia, up to 4.5 nm from the core. To the best of our knowledge, this work is among the first to reveal high-resolution information on the local structure of PEGylated dendrimers. Collectively, this investigation provides important insight into the structure of coated dendrimers, which shall be important to guide the design and development of better drug delivery vehicles. Work is in progress to correlate structural information with the efficacy of drug delivery.

Conflict of Interests

All the authors of this paper declare that there is no conflict of interests with any financial organization regarding the material discussed in this paper.

Acknowledgments

This work is supported by NSF (CHE-0809977, DMR-1104260, and CBET-0933144), W. M. Keck Foundation, and Nano@WSU Incubator. The authors thank Dr. Chris Fleming of BST NanoCarbon, Ms. Susan Stagner, and Drs. Ming Zhang and Jianli Zhao of UC Davis for helpful discussion and assistance in paper preparation.

References

[1] U. Gupta, H. B. Agashe, A. Asthana, and N. K. Jain, "Dendrimers: novel polymeric nanoarchitectures for solubility enhancement," *Biomacromolecules*, vol. 7, no. 3, pp. 649–658, 2006.

[2] A. R. Menjoge, R. M. Kannan, and D. A. Tomalia, "Dendrimer-based drug and imaging conjugates: design considerations for nanomedical applications," *Drug Discovery Today*, vol. 15, no. 5-6, pp. 171–185, 2010.

[3] S. Svenson and D. A. Tomalia, "Dendrimers in biomedical applications—reflections on the field," *Advanced Drug Delivery Reviews*, vol. 57, no. 15, pp. 2106–2129, 2005.

[4] R. Jevprasesphant, J. Penny, R. Jalal, D. Attwood, N. B. McKeown, and A. D'Emanuele, "The influence of surface modification on the cytotoxicity of PAMAM dendrimers," *International Journal of Pharmaceutics*, vol. 252, no. 1-2, pp. 263–266, 2003.

[5] S. Brocchini, A. Godwin, S. Balan, J.-W. Choi, M. Zloh, and S. Shaunak, "Disulfide bridge based PEGylation of proteins," *Advanced Drug Delivery Reviews*, vol. 60, no. 1, pp. 3–12, 2008.

[6] B. A. Luxon, M. Grace, D. Brassard, and R. Bordens, "Pegylated interferons for the treatment of chronic hepatitis C infection," *Clinical Therapeutics*, vol. 24, no. 9, pp. 1363–1383, 2002.

[7] C. D. Walkey, J. B. Olsen, H. Guo, A. Emili, and W. C. W. Chan, "Nanoparticle size and surface chemistry determine serum protein adsorption and macrophage uptake," *Journal of the American Chemical Society*, vol. 134, no. 4, pp. 2139–2147, 2012.

[8] W. Li, P. Zhan, E. De Clercq, H. Lou, and X. Liu, "Current drug research on PEGylation with small molecular agents," *Progress in Polymer Science*, vol. 38, no. 3-4, pp. 421–444, 2013.

[9] V. B. Damodaran, C. J. Fee, T. Ruckh, and K. C. Popat, "Conformational studies of covalently grafted poly(ethylene glycol) on modified solid matrices using X-ray photoelectron spectroscopy," *Langmuir*, vol. 26, no. 10, pp. 7299–7306, 2010.

[10] Y. Hu, J. Jin, Y. Han, J. Yin, W. Jiang, and H. Liang, "Study of fibrinogen adsorption on poly(ethylene glycol)-modified surfaces using a quartz crystal microbalance with dissipation and a dual polarization interferometry," *RSC Advances*, vol. 4, no. 15, pp. 7716–7724, 2014.

[11] L. Yang and S. R. P. da Rocha, "PEGylated, NH_2-terminated PAMAM dendrimers: a microscopic view from atomistic computer simulations," *Molecular Pharmaceutics*, vol. 11, no. 5, pp. 1459–1470, 2014.

[12] C. Kojima, K. Kono, K. Maruyama, and T. Takagishi, "Synthesis of polyamidoamine dendrimers having poly(ethylene glycol) grafts and their ability to encapsulate anticancer drugs," *Bioconjugate Chemistry*, vol. 11, no. 6, pp. 910–917, 2000.

[13] Y. Kim, A. M. Klutz, and K. A. Jacobson, "Systematic investigation of polyamidoamine dendrimers surface-modified with poly(ethylene glycol) for drug delivery applications: synthesis, characterization, and evaluation of cytotoxicity," *Bioconjugate Chemistry*, vol. 19, no. 8, pp. 1660–1672, 2008.

[14] H. Lee and R. G. Larson, "Molecular dynamics study of the structure and interparticle interactions of polyethylene glycol-conjugated PAMAM dendrimers," *The Journal of Physical Chemistry B*, vol. 113, no. 40, pp. 13202–13207, 2009.

[15] C. J. Fleming, N.-N. Yin, S. L. Riechers, G. Chu, and G.-Y. Liu, "High-resolution imaging of the intramolecular structure of indomethacin-carrying dendrimers by scanning tunneling microscopy," *ACS Nano*, vol. 5, no. 3, pp. 1685–1692, 2011.

[16] C. J. Fleming, Y. X. Liu, Z. Deng, and G.-Y. Liu, "Deformation and hyperfine structures of dendrimers investigated by scanning tunneling microscopy," *The Journal of Physical Chemistry A*, vol. 113, no. 16, pp. 4168–4174, 2009.

[17] L. Shi, C. J. Fleming, S. L. Riechers et al., "High-resolution imaging of dendrimers used in drug delivery via scanning probe microscopy," *Journal of Drug Delivery*, vol. 2011, Article ID 254095, 12 pages, 2011.

[18] A. Riposan, Y. Li, Y. H. Tan, G. Galli, and G.-Y. Liu, "Structural characterization of aldehyde-terminated self-assembled monolayers," *Journal of Physical Chemistry A*, vol. 111, no. 49, pp. 12727–12739, 2007.

[19] G. Yang and G.-Y. Liu, "New insights for self-assembled monolayers of organothiols on Au(111) revealed by scanning tunneling microscopy," *The Journal of Physical Chemistry B*, vol. 107, no. 34, pp. 8746–8759, 2003.

[20] J. P. Cleveland, S. Manne, D. Bocek, and P. K. Hansma, "A nondestructive method for determining the spring constant of cantilevers for scanning force microscopy," *Review of Scientific Instruments*, vol. 64, no. 2, pp. 403–405, 1993.

[21] V. Lulevich, T. Zink, H.-Y. Chen, F.-T. Liu, and G.-Y. Liu, "Cell mechanics using atomic force microscopy-based single-cell compression," *Langmuir*, vol. 22, no. 19, pp. 8151–8155, 2006.

[22] S. Xu and G.-Y. Liu, "Nanometer-scale fabrication by simultaneous nanoshaving and molecular self-assembly," *Langmuir*, vol. 13, no. 2, pp. 127–129, 1997.

[23] X.-D. Xiao, G.-Y. Liu, D. H. Charych, and M. Salmeron, "Preparation, structure, and mechanical stability of alkylsilane monolayers on mica," *Langmuir*, vol. 11, no. 5, pp. 1600–1604, 1995.

[24] G. Bar, Y. Thomann, R. Brandsch, H.-J. Cantow, and M.-H. Whangbo, "Factors affecting the height and phase images in tapping mode atomic force microscopy. Study of phase-separated polymer blends of poly(ethene-co-styrene) and poly(2,6-dimethyl-1,4-phenylene oxide)," *Langmuir*, vol. 13, no. 14, pp. 3807–3812, 1997.

[25] R. Brandsch, G. Bar, and M.-H. Whangbo, "On the factors affecting the contrast of height and phase images in tapping mode atomic force microscopy," *Langmuir*, vol. 13, no. 24, pp. 6349–6353, 1997.

[26] R. García and R. Pérez, "Dynamic atomic force microscopy methods," *Surface Science Reports*, vol. 47, no. 6–8, pp. 197–301, 2002.

[27] S. N. Magonov and D. H. Reneker, "Characterization of polymer surfaces with atomic force microscopy," *Annual Review of Materials Science*, vol. 27, no. 1, pp. 175–222, 1997.

[28] A. Mecke, I. Lee, J. R. Baker Jr., M. M. B. Holl, and B. G. Orr, "Deformability of poly(amidoamine) dendrimers," *The European Physical Journal E*, vol. 14, no. 1, pp. 7–16, 2004.

[29] Y. Gu, H. Xie, J. Gao et al., "AFM characterization of dendrimer-stabilized platinum nanoparticles," *Langmuir*, vol. 21, no. 7, pp. 3122–3131, 2005.

[30] R. W. J. Scott, O. M. Wilson, and R. M. Crooks, "Synthesis, characterization, and applications of dendrimer-encapsulated nanoparticles," *The Journal of Physical Chemistry B*, vol. 109, no. 2, pp. 692–704, 2005.

[31] I. Lee, B. D. Athey, A. W. Wetzel, W. Meixner, and J. R. Baker Jr., "Structural molecular dynamics studies on polyamidoamine dendrimers for a therapeutic application: effects of pH and generation," *Macromolecules*, vol. 35, no. 11, pp. 4510–4520, 2002.

7

PEG-Immobilized Keratin for Protein Drug Sequestration and pH-Mediated Delivery

Roche C. de Guzman and Sina Y. Rabbany

Bioengineering Program, Department of Engineering, Hofstra University, Hempstead, NY 11549, USA

Correspondence should be addressed to Roche C. de Guzman; roche.c.deguzman@hofstra.edu

Academic Editor: Subbu S. Venkatraman

Protein drugs like growth factors are promising therapeutics for damaged-tissue repair. Their local delivery often requires biomaterial carriers for achieving the therapeutic dose range while extending efficacy. In this study, polyethylene glycol (PEG) and keratin were crosslinked and used as sponge-like scaffolds (KTN-PEG) to absorb test proteins with different isoelectric points (pI): albumin (~5), hemoglobin (~7), and lysozyme (~11). The protein release kinetics was influenced by charge at physiological pH 7.4. The keratin network, with pI 5.3, electrostatically attracted lysozyme and repulsed albumin generating the release rate profile: albumin > hemoglobin > lysozyme. However, under acidic conditions (pH 4), all proteins including keratins were positively charged and consequently intermolecular repulsion altered the release hierarchy, now determined by size (MW) diffusion: lysozyme (14 kDa) > hemoglobin (64 kDa) > albumin (66 kDa). Vascular endothelial growth factor C (VEGF-C), with properties comparable to lysozyme, was absorbed into the KTN-PEG scaffold. Endothelial cells cultured on this substrate had significantly larger numbers than on scaffolds without VEGF-C suggesting that the ionically bound and retained growth factor at neutral pH indirectly increased acute cell attachment and viability. PEG and keratin based sequestrations of proteins with basic pIs are therefore a feasible strategy with potential applications for selective biologics delivery.

1. Introduction

Protein drugs, also called protein therapeutics and protein biologics, are proteins that provide healing, repair, and regenerative functionalities to injured and damaged cells and tissues. These include cell-secreted extracellular growth factors (GFs) and signaling proteins for induction of cell growth, cell division (proliferation), movement, changes in shape, survival and inhibition of apoptosis, differentiation, and tissue morphogenesis [1–4]. GFs bind to target enzyme-linked cell-surface receptors and activate intracellular signaling pathways leading to expression of genes involved in macromolecular synthesis, metabolism, and alteration of cellular behaviors. Effective levels of GFs are usually in the pico- to nanomolar ranges, acting in the order of hours [5]. To extend this range and regulate the spatiotemporal dose release for treatment applications, drug-delivery systems or biomaterial carriers are utilized [6–8]. A charge-based sequestration strategy can be employed wherein the protein drug load and the carrier matrix have opposing electrical charges to provide electrostatic or coulombic attraction. Proteins and peptides are zwitterions; that is, they can alter their net charges depending on the aqueous environmental pH; those with isoelectric points (pIs) lower than the pH of the medium will have negative molecular electrical charges, while those with higher pIs will be positively charged [9, 10]. Accordingly, proteins with acidic and basic pIs in phosphate-buffered saline (PBS, pH 7.4) carry negative and positive net charges, respectively, and can potentially associate together.

Polyethylene glycol (PEG) and hair keratin (KTN) biomaterials have been shown to be safe, biocompatible (with minimal fibrous encapsulation), and appropriate drug-delivery vehicles for tissue engineering purposes [11–19]. Diacrylates of linear PEG (PEGDA) can be photopolymerized for PEG chain growth to form scaffolds [20, 21]. Reduced KTN proteins containing free thiols (–SH) can be gelled by reforming of disulfide bonds (–S–S–) [22, 23]. PEGDA and KTN can also be combined and crosslinked via a photopolymerization

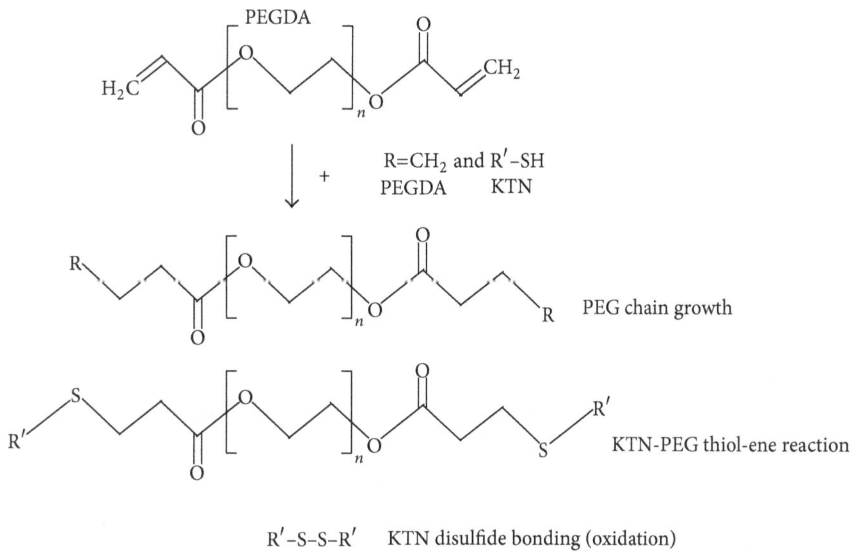

FIGURE 1: Crosslinking reactions of polyethylene glycol diacrylate (PEGDA) and keratin (KTN) mixture.

TABLE 1: Charge-based protein interaction.

Role	Protein	pI	Medium condition			
			pH 7.4		pH 4	
			Net charge	KTN interaction	Net charge	KTN interaction
Scaffold	Keratin (KTN)	5.3	−	Repulsion	+	Repulsion
Drug load	Albumin	~5	−	Repulsion	+	Repulsion
Drug load	Hemoglobin	~7	0	None	+	Repulsion
Drug load	Lysozyme	~11	+	Attraction	+	Repulsion

thiol-ene reaction [24, 25]. We capitalized on these reactions (Figure 1) to form stable KTN-PEG scaffolds. KTN, having a pI of 5.3, is negatively charged in PBS, pH 7.4 (Table 1) [22]. Moreover, the reactions do not target any of the ionizable amino acid groups [9] and should not significantly alter the crosslinked keratin pI. The KTN network of KTN-PEG, hence, can theoretically hold onto positively charged proteins with basic pIs. Several GFs, including vascular endothelial growth factor C (VEGF-C), exhibit pIs greater than 7.4 [26, 27]. As a result, they are likely to ionically associate with the KTN-PEG bulk material. In this study, we investigated the diffusion release profiles of KTN-PEG scaffold-absorbed soluble proteins with varying pIs (charges) and sizes in physiological pH and, additionally, in acidic PBS, pH 4 (Table 1). At a pH level lower than the KTN's pI, the biomaterial scaffold is expected to gain positive charges, thereby inducing repulsion and quick release of sequestered positively charged proteins. The functional bioactivity of a bound-protein, represented by VEGF-C, was tested through endothelial cell culture onto the KTN-PEG substrate with absorbed VEGF-C.

2. Materials and Methods

2.1. Materials. The following reagents and proteins were purchased from Sigma-Aldrich (St. Louis, MO): polyethylene glycol diacrylate (PEGDA; $M_n = 700$ g/mol; $n \sim 13$), glycerol, methanol (MeOH), NaOH, HCl, phosphate-buffered saline (PBS; pH = 7.4), Na_2CO_3, $NaHCO_3$, Tween 20 (Polysorbate 20), 3,3′,5,5′-tetramethylbenzidine (TMB substrate), calcein AM, propidium iodide, bovine serum albumin (BSA; pI ~ 5, MW = 66 kDa), human hemoglobin (pI ~ 7, MW = 64 kDa), and chicken egg white lysozyme (pI ~ 11, MW = 14 kDa) [28]. Antibodies, goat anti-BSA (sc-50710), goat anti-human hemoglobin (sc-31110), goat anti-hen egg lysozyme (sc-325025), and anti-goat IgG-HRP (sc-2020), were bought from Santa Cruz Biotechnology (Dallas, TX). The test growth factor, human vascular endothelial growth factor C (VEGF-C), was obtained from ACROBiosystems (Newark, DE). Acidic PBS (pH = 4) was prepared by dropwise addition of HCl. Irgacure® 2959 (I2959), provided by BASF (Ludwigshafen, Germany), was dissolved at a stock solution of 10% (m/V) in MeOH. Reduced keratin biomaterial (KTN; MW = 98 kDa) was extracted [22] and obtained from Mark Van Dyke's Lab at the School of Biomedical Engineering and Sciences, Virginia Tech (Blacksburg, VA). Distilled deionized water (at 18.2 MΩ·cm electrical resistivity) was used as the default aqueous solvent, unless otherwise indicated.

2.2. Scaffold Fabrication. KTN-PEG scaffolds were prepared for prereaction concentration of 20% (V/V) PEGDA,

FIGURE 2: Preparation of scaffolds: (a) keratin gelation via disulfide bond formation of intermolecular chains, (b) photopolymerization reaction to increase polyethylene glycol molecular weight and to crosslink to keratin, (c) freezing, and (d) lyophilization to remove unbound water, finally producing PEG and KTN-PEG constructs.

10% (V/V) glycerol, 1% I2959 (m/V), and 5% (m/V) KTN in 10 mM NaOH solution at 3 mL per well in 6-well plates. The mixture was thoroughly stirred until being homogenous while minimizing air bubbles. Using DC Protein Assay (Bio-Rad, Hercules, CA), the initial keratin concentration was verified to be 48.7 ± 9.8 mg/mL, within the expected 50 mg/mL (or 5%) KTN. Disulfide bond formation (via oxidation of thiols and direct thiol-thiol interaction) of keratin chains was ensured by overnight incubation at 4°C (Figure 2(a)) [22, 23]. Polyethylene glycol (PEG) network formation (PEGDA-PEGDA; PEG chain growth) and thiol-ene reaction for crosslinking keratins to PEG were made via exposure to UV light at 254 nm for 20 min (Figure 2(b)). The energy to polymerize was computed to be (9 W/bulb) · (4 bulbs) · (1200 s) = 43200 J = 43.2 kJ. After freezing at −80°C (Figure 2(c)), samples were then lyophilized using FreeZone 2.5 Plus (Labconco, Kansas City, MO) for 24 hr (Figure 2(d)). Control PEG constructs were fabricated similarly except for the absence of KTN. Excess glycerol plasticizer [29] that did not integrate into the network was blotted out.

2.3. Liquid Absorption and Stability. PEG and KTN-PEG scaffolds were tested for their ability to absorb PBS. Samples were immersed in PBS and weighed at time points: 10 and 30 min and 1, 2, 14, 24, 48, and 72 hr. The ratio of absorbed liquid (absorbate) to scaffold mass ($m_{\text{absorbate}}/m_{\text{scaffold}}$) was plotted as a function of time. Caliper measurements of radius $= r$ and thickness $= h$ of scaffold discs were employed to approximate the bulk cylindrical volume, $V = \pi r^2 h$.

2.4. Crosslinked Network Properties. The following properties of PEG and KTN-PEG scaffolds were quantified [23, 30–32]: Q, ν_e, and M_c. Consider

$$Q = \frac{V_{\text{swollen}}}{V_{\text{dry}}}, \tag{1}$$

where Q is equilibrium volume swelling ratio, V_{swollen} is volume of absorbate and scaffold, and V_{dry} is volume of scaffold. Consider

$$\nu_e = \frac{E_c}{RTQ^{1/3}}, \tag{2}$$

where ν_e is effective crosslink density (mol/mL), E_c is compressive modulus of elasticity (MPa), R is gas constant = 8.314 mL·MPa·K^{-1}·mol^{-1}, and T is temperature (K). E_c values were obtained from the slope of the linear elastic region of true stress versus true stain curve of equilibrated PBS-soaked scaffolds compressed at 0.1 mm/s using the Instron 3345 mechanical tester (Norwood, MA). Consider

$$M_c = \frac{\rho_{\text{polymer}}}{\nu_e}, \tag{3}$$

where M_c is molecular weight between crosslinks (g/mol) and ρ_{polymer} is polymer density (g/mL).

2.5. Release of Uncrosslinked Network Proteins. Representative KTN-PEG discs were cut into smaller pieces of known volume, placed into 1.5 mL flip-top tubes with 1 mL PBS, and incubated at 37°C. Aliquots of the PBS medium were collected at 2, 4, 14, and 24 hr and 2, 4, and 7 d. At each time point, fresh PBS was added at equal volume to replenish the sampled liquid. DC Protein Assay was used to quantify the KTN concentration ([KTN]) of the collected samples.

2.6. Loading and Release of Test Proteins. KTN-PEG scaffolds were extensively washed to remove uncrosslinked materials including "free" keratins. Samples were immersed in PBS, incubated with shaking for 2 hours, and spent PBS removed and replaced with fresh PBS. Washing was performed trice and the final wash subjected to overnight incubation. Model globular proteins, albumin (Alb), hemoglobin (Hem), and lysozyme (Lys), were diluted with PBS to a stock concentration of 2 mg/mL. Approximately 0.3 cm^3 (=0.3 mL) scaffolds were individually placed in microfuge tubes and 1 mL of 200 μg/mL Alb, Hem, or Lys in PBS was added. Proteins were allowed to be absorbed into the gel matrix overnight at 4°C. The following day, excess protein solutions were removed by aspiration and scaffolds were quickly rinsed with either PBS or acidic PBS, ×3 at 1 mL each. Gels were left in 1 mL of either PBS or acidic PBS. Protein release samples were collected at time points: 2, 6, and 24 hr and 2, 4, and 6 d. Fresh medium at equal volume was added after each collection. Total protein concentrations were measured through the DC Protein Assay, while specific protein release profiles were assessed using enzyme-linked immunosorbent assay (ELISA).

2.7. ELISA Detection. Experimental samples and protein standards were neutralized (for acidic samples) and diluted in carbonate coating buffer (3.03 g Na_2CO_3 and 6 g $NaHCO_3$ per 1 L; pH 9.6), placed in NUNC MaxiSorp™ (Fisher Scientific, Hampton, NH) 96-well plates at 100 μL per well, and incubated overnight at 4°C. After washing with PBS twice, wells were blocked (300 μL) with blocking buffer (1% (m/V) nonfat dry milk in PBS) for 2.5 hr and then washed twice with PBS-T (0.05% (V/V) Tween 20 in PBS). Samples were hybridized with primary antibody (100 μL; anti-BSA at 1 : 100, anti-human hemoglobin at 1 : 200, or anti-hen egg lysozyme at 1 : 200 in blocking buffer) for 2 hr, washed ×4 with PBS-T, hybridized again with secondary antibody conjugate (100 μL; anti-goat IgG-HRP at 1 : 1000 for Alb or 1 : 5000 for Hem and Lys in blocking buffer) for 1 hr, and then washed ×4 with PBS-T. Color was developed by adding 100 μL of TMB substrate and the reaction was stopped after 15 min with 0.5 N HCl (100 μL). Light absorbance at 450 nm was read using iMark™ (Bio-Rad) spectrophotometer.

2.8. Bioactivity of Sequestered Growth Factor. KTN-PEG scaffolds were fabricated on a 24-well tissue culture plate (600 μL per well) and then washed with PBS overnight. VEGF-C (1 mL at 2.5 μg/mL in PBS) was absorbed overnight and scaffolds subsequently were washed with PBS followed by culture medium (CM) composed of Dulbecco's Modified Eagle Medium (DMEM), 20% (V/V) fetal bovine serum, and antibiotics. Control groups without keratin and/or VEGF-C were also included. Human umbilical artery endothelial cells (HUAECs; Sigma-Aldrich) in CM were seeded at 10^4 cells per well and cultured at 37°C, 5% CO_2, and 90% relative humidity. CM was removed and replenished after 2 days. At day 5, CM was aspirated out, scaffolds were rinsed with PBS and overlaid with 4 μM calcein AM and 5 μM propidium iodide in PBS for 10 min. After rinsing in PBS, cells were imaged and counted using an inverted fluorescence microscope at both green and red filters (for live and dead cells, resp.) under a ×4 objective field-of-view.

Table 2: KTN-PEG scaffold properties.

	Lyophilized	Swollen (in PBS)	Unit
Density	1.09 ± 0.04	1.02 ± 0.15	g/mL
Water content	36 ± 2	82 ± 12	% (V/V)
[PEG]	59 ± 3	17 ± 3	% (m/V)
[KTN]	10 ± 1	3 ± 0	% (m/V)

2.9. Sample Management and Statistical Analyses. Experimental replicates were conducted with sample sizes of $n \geq 3$. Computed values, plots, and bar graphs were reported as average ±1 standard deviation. Charts including scatterplots and trendlines were generated using MATLAB (MathWorks, Natick, MA) scripts with LaTeX symbolics. Excel Solver (Microsoft, Redmond, WA) and Prism (GraphPad, San Diego, CA) were employed for the nonlinear curve fitting to coefficient of determination (r^2) approaching 1. Student's t-test and one-way analysis of variance (ANOVA) combined with Tukey's post hoc multiple comparison analyses were done with Prism at 95% confidence intervals and 5% probability of type I error (α).

3. Results and Discussion

3.1. Equilibrium Swelling and Crosslinking Properties. Control PEG scaffolds (without keratins) reached liquid absorption equilibrium at half an hour in PBS (Figure 3: PEG). ANOVA and Tukey's test showed no significant differences ($p > 0.05$) among groups from the 30 min time point and later. KTN-PEG, on the other hand, had an almost instantaneous equilibration time (Figure 3: KTN-PEG). All of the experimental time groups for KTN-PEG generated statistically similar ($p = 0.0625$) liquid absorbate-to-scaffold mass ratio. At the 10 min time point, KTN-PEG yielded a higher ratio ($p = 0.0036$) compared to PEG (1.86 ± 0.17 versus 0.89 ± 0.22, resp.), indicating that the presence of keratin led to a twofold (1.86/0.89 = 2.08) mass increase in hydrophilicity of the material. Keratins bound to the PEG matrix therefore facilitated more water absorption. The volumetric increase from lyophilized to PBS-wetted KTN-PEG scaffolds after 24 hours was found to be 304 ± 1% or a 3-fold size increase. From the initial prereaction mix volume of 3 mL (Figure 2(a): KTN-PEG), the soaked scaffold swelled to 3.99 mL or a volumetric ratio increase of 133 ± 2%. Conservation of mass principles enabled the computation of several KTN-PEG properties displayed in Table 2.

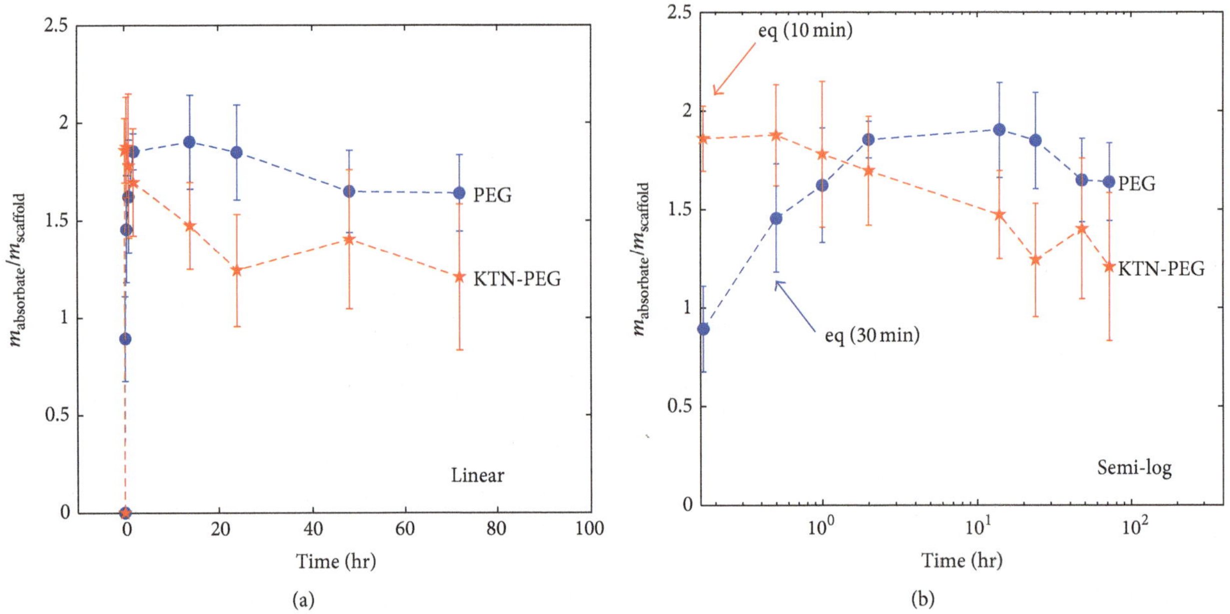

FIGURE 3: Swelling behavior of PEG and KTN-PEG scaffolds with time at linear (a) and semilog (b) scales. Equilibrium (eq) was attained at 30 min for PEG and at 10 min for KTN-PEG. KTN-PEG samples absorbed water faster due to network-associated hydrophilic keratin proteins.

TABLE 3: Scaffold network properties.

	Q	E_c (MPa)	ν_e (μmol/mL)	M_c (kDa)
PEG scaffold	2.6 ± 0.3	0.88 ± 0.35	257 ± 103	5.0 ± 2.4
KTN-PEG scaffold	3.0 ± 0.2	0.15 ± 0.01	42 ± 3	25.9 ± 1.7

Table 3 summarizes the results obtained from measurement of scaffold network properties. It was found that the molecular weight between crosslinks (M_c) in KTN-PEG scaffolds immersed in PBS was 25.9 kDa. A 5% KTN gel only was determined to have M_c = 183 kDa. Since M_c was reduced in the presence of PEG additive, this suggests successful photocrosslinking of keratin-to-PEG via thiol-ene reaction. The average molecular weight (MW) of the KTN biomaterial was reported to be 98 kDa [22]. Accordingly, there were about 3.8 (=98 kDa/25.9 kDa) crosslinks per KTN molecule in the fabricated KTN-PEG scaffold. In the KTN-PEG scaffold, any of the possible reactions illustrated in Figure 1 can occur: PEG-PEG chain growth, KTN-KTN disulfide oxidation, and KTN-PEG thiol-ene reaction [33].

3.2. Release of Unbound Keratins. Despite statistical similarities in the $m_{absorbate}/m_{scaffold}$ ratio among KTN-PEG time groups, there was a downward plateauing trend over time (Figure 3), suggesting that some of the water-absorbing keratins were initially being released into the PBS medium. Total protein assay showed that uncrosslinked keratin proteins were indeed leaving the bulk of the scaffolds (Figure 4) in

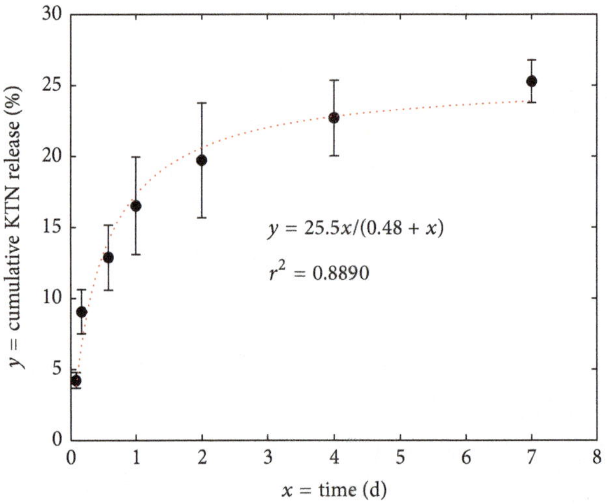

FIGURE 4: Rectangular hyperbolic release of uncrosslinked keratin (KTN) out of KTN-PEG scaffolds in PBS. The fitted equation predicted the maximum KTN release at 25.5%, half of which was released in just 0.48 days.

a rectangular hyperbolic fashion (r^2 = 0.8890) following Michaelis-Menten kinetics,

$$y = \frac{V_{max} \cdot x}{K_M + x}, \quad (4)$$

where x is time (d), y is release concentration ratio, V_{max} is maximum release, and K_M is time at half V_{max}. V_{max} was found to be 25.5%, implying that 74.5% of keratins were stably

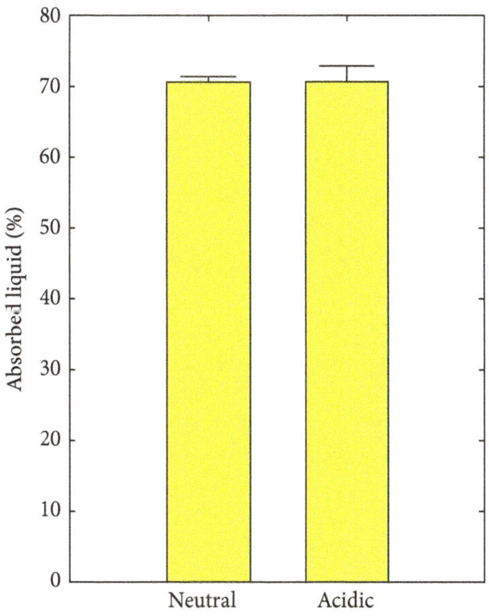

FIGURE 5: Liquid absorption at different pH levels: neutral (pH 7.4) and acidic (pH 4).

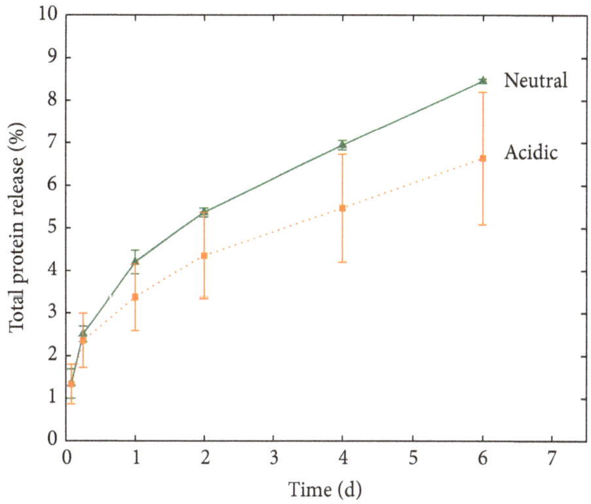

FIGURE 6: Release of crosslinked KTN (keratin degradation) in neutral and acidic PBS. Degradation in acidic pH 4 generated more variability among samples but at a slower trend relative to those in neutral pH 7.4.

integrated into the KTN-PEG scaffold network. At 0.48 days or about 11.5 hours (K_M), half of the unbound keratins were released in a static PBS environment at 37°C. Overall, washing and rinsing of the scaffolds in PBS on a shaker accelerated the removal of "free" or nonnetwork keratins.

3.3. Absorption and Then Release of Proteins in Neutral and Acidic pH. KTN-PEG scaffolds absorbed 70.7 ± 1.4% liquid ($V_{\text{liquid}}/(V_{\text{liquid}}+V_{\text{scaffold}})$) containing 200 μg/mL of test globular proteins (Alb, Hem, or Lys). This value can also be interpreted as the gel water content, determined to be less than reported 82% in Table 2. The discrepancy can be accounted for by the loss of uncrosslinked keratins, thereby slightly decreasing the capacity to hold water into the scaffold matrix. No significant difference (p = 0.9627) was observed between the liquid absorption behavior in neutral (pH 7.4) and in acidic (pH 4) PBS (Figure 5; 70.6 ± 0.7% versus 70.7 ± 2.2%, resp.).

Keratins covalently linked into the scaffold network degraded and released proteinaceous materials into the surrounding liquid medium at a relatively slow pace, 8.46 ± 0.05% in neutral PBS versus 6.64 ± 1.56% in acidic PBS for 6 days (Figure 6), although there was no significant difference between them (p = 0.1139). The keratin degradation profile was relatively slower with higher variability (standard deviation) at the pH of 4, suggesting that the scaffold has more stability in acidic pH. This was consistent with our previous findings in experiments of keratin gel degradation at varying pH [22], possibly because disulfide bonds were more protected during hydrolysis in acidic pH levels [34].

Proteins absorbed into the bulk gel matrix were released into the surrounding PBS through the processes of diffusion and osmosis: movement of mobile masses from higher to lower concentration gradients. The experimental setup allowed for high volume of PBS to scaffold ratio; hence the movement of molecules was not hindered by the saturation effect of the supernatant. In PBS pH 7.4, albumin was released the fastest, followed by hemoglobin and then lysozyme (Figure 7(a)). At this pH level, scaffolding keratin matrix proteins (with pI = 5.3) [22] are negatively charged (pI < pH; Table 1), dictating the overall charge density of the KTN-PEG sponge-like material. While albumin (pI ~ 5) is also negatively charged, hemoglobin (pI ~ 7) is almost neutral (though slightly negative) and lysozyme (pI ~ 11) is positively charged. The observed protein release rates can be explained by electrostatic interactions between charged species; that is, negative-negative repulsion drove albumin diffusion out the fastest. At day six, 28.5% of the original albumin load had been released into the medium. Conversely, the positively charged lysozyme electrostatically bound to the negative keratin backbone which consequently registered minimal release kinetics, at about the same rate as keratin degradation (4.9% for 6 days).

In an acidic environment, the amine groups of amino acids in proteins are more conducive to protonation ($-NH_3^+$), inducing net positive charges. Specifically at pH 4, the keratin matrix charge shifts to positive (Table 1). All loaded proteins, with pIs > 4, also now carry positive charges. Accordingly, repulsive forces dominate between the scaffold matrix and the absorbed globular proteins, thereby inducing even faster release of mobile proteins and the order dictated by size diffusion (the smaller the faster the release). The porous nature of the scaffold enables repulsion to force like-charged molecules out of the bulk material [35, 36]. Experimental results (Figure 7(b)) concurred with the projected kinetics wherein the smallest protein, lysozyme (14 kDa), had the highest rate of 48.4% in 6 days. Next in the order of release was hemoglobin (64 kDa) at 29.6% and finally albumin (66 kDa) at 9.8% in the 6-day period. Both lysozyme and hemoglobin were released at a higher rate in pH 4 than in physiological pH (Figure 7(b) versus

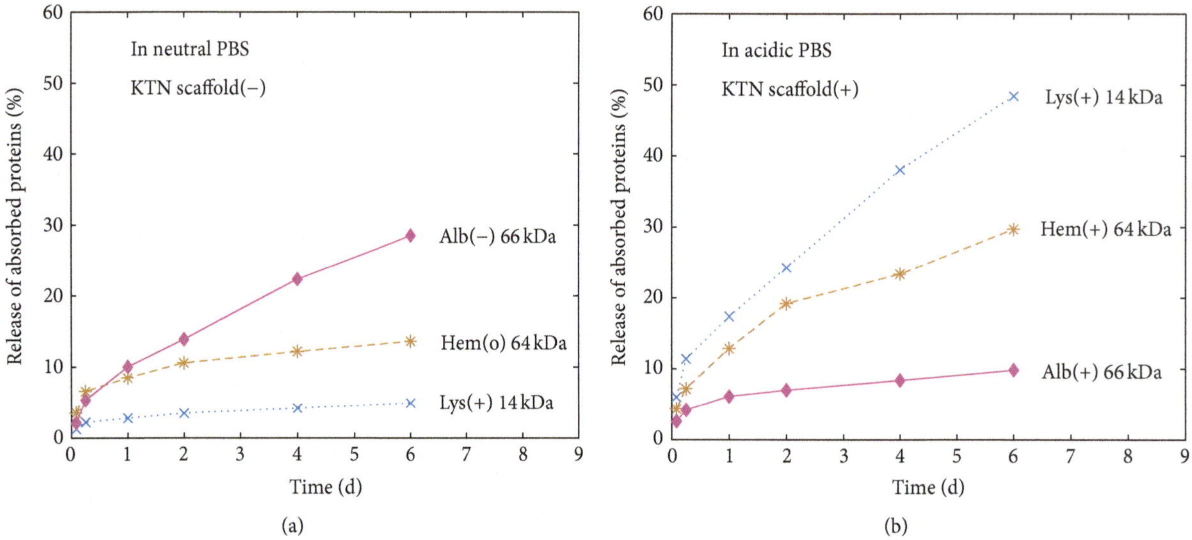

FIGURE 7: Release of absorbed proteins out of KTN-PEG scaffolds in (a) neutral (pH 7.4) and (b) acidic (pH 4) PBS media.

Figure 7(a)). Albumin, on the other hand, had a lower rate of release in acidic medium, suggesting that the positive-positive repulsive force ($^{+}$KTN and $^{+}$Alb) is relatively weaker than the negative-negative interaction ($^{-}$KTN and $^{-}$Alb). Another possible explanation is that the low pH condition enabled the exposure of hydrophobic regions in both keratin [37] and albumin [38] resulting in hydrophobic attraction and slower albumin release.

Growth factors (GFs) are proteins secreted by cells targeting recipient cells via binding and interaction to cell-surface growth factor receptors leading to a variety of downstream effects [2–4] including local recruitment of repair stem cells for tissue engineering and regenerative medicine applications [39]. They can be held into the scaffold matrix through affinity-based methods [6] for sustained delivery and extension of efficacy [40]. Lysozyme can act as an inexpensive model for studying the kinetics of GF release since its size and isoelectric point (charge) properties are close to clinically relevant GFs [3] such as bone morphogenetic protein 2 (BMP-2; MW = 18 kDa (monomer); pI = 9) [41, 42] and brain-derived neurotrophic factor (BDNF; MW = 14 kDa (monomer); pI = 9) [43]. At neutral pH, lysozyme was sequestered tightly within the scaffold but was extensively released in an acidic condition (Figure 7) when the KTN charge flipped from negative to positive. GFs loaded into the KTN-PEG construct are thus anticipated to behave similarly to lysozyme. For evaluation, vascular endothelial growth factor C (VEGF-C; MW ~ 15 kDa (monomer); pI = 8.3) [26, 27] solution was utilized as an absorbent and its retention and activity were assessed indirectly on the survival of endothelial cells.

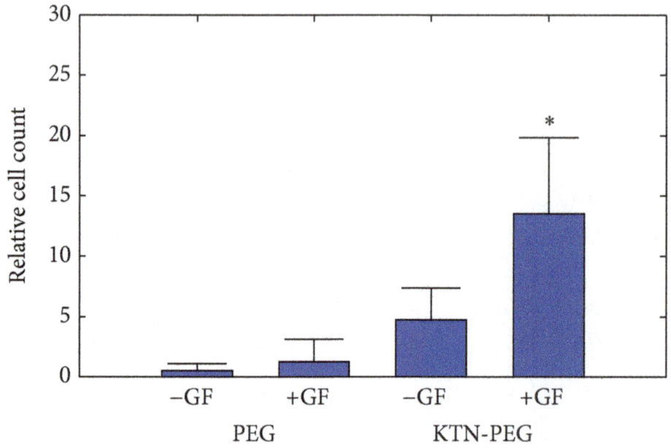

FIGURE 8: Endothelial cell culture on scaffolds, with (KTN-PEG) and without (PEG) keratins, in the presence (+GF) and absence (−GF) of absorbed VEGF-C. $^{*}p < 0.05$ compared to the other groups.

3.4. Interaction of Endothelial Cells on VEGF-C-Absorbed KTN-PEG Scaffold. Fluorescence microscopy revealed no dead cells (no propidium iodide, red fluorescence staining) for any of the adherent cells. Endothelial cells (calcein AM for living cells, green fluorescence signals) cultured on KTN-PEG scaffold with electrostatically bound VEGF-C showed statistically more ($p < 0.05$) cell attachment and survival relative to the other three groups: KTN-PEG without VEGF-C, PEG with VEGF-C, and PEG without VEGF-C (Figure 8). The bar graph trend indicated that the presence of keratin as a network material generally increased cell growth, likely because of cell-interaction with the inherent cell-binding domains of keratins [44]. Addition of the growth factor VEGF-C further increased the number of cells on the scaffold surface suggesting that VEGF-C bound to the immobilized keratin network allowed cells to interact via their growth factor receptors facilitating attachment and promoted viability. Despite the outcome, the number of cells that anchored onto the substrate material was still relatively low. Application of cyclic sinusoidal pressure may induce endothelial cell proliferation with VEGF-C exposure [45]. Cultured lymphatic endothelial cells may respond better to the sequestered VEGF-C due to VEGF-C's importance in lymphangiogenesis or the formation of lymphatic vessels [46–48]. Future experiments may also require addition of surface-incorporated integrin-binding molecules such as laminin and its cell-binding peptides, RGD, YIGSR, and IKVAV, to improve the initial endothelial cell attachment [49].

4. Conclusions

Keratin (KTN) proteins in the recent years are gaining interest as appealing biocompatible biomaterial carriers of potent therapeutics which include growth factors. We have integrated and immobilized KTN with polyethylene glycol (PEG) diacrylate (PEGDA) through photoactivated linkage of KTN free thiols with PEGDA acrylate ends forming a stable KTN-PEG scaffold. KTN in the scaffold matrix enabled increased water uptake along with solubilized proteins. Its water-absorption capacity was found to be similar in physiological phosphate-buffered saline (PBS) pH 7.4 and in PBS pH 4. This network-bound KTN provided low hydrolytic degradation rate over the 7-day period with trend suggesting an even slower KTN release in acidic pH. Scaffold-absorbed proteins interacted with the KTN bulk following the First Law of Electrostatics: like charges repel and opposite charges attract. At pH 7.4, the negatively charged KTN tightly held onto proteins with basic isoelectric points (pIs) while preserving bioactivity. Lowering the pH to 4, below KTN's pI of 5.3, induced the fast release of a sequestered protein. The fabricated KTN-PEG construct can potentially be used as a slowly degradable sponge-like material for burst-release of high quantities of growth factors in acidic environment but also attract endogenous positively charged growth factors in neutral to basic pH states.

Conflict of Interests

The authors declare that there is no conflict of interests regarding the publication of this paper.

Acknowledgments

Support for this study was provided by Hofstra University Internal Research Funds. The authors would like to thank Mark Van Dyke at Virginia Tech for the use of his lab to extract keratin biomaterial samples. They also appreciate the help and support of Hofstra University Bioengineering students and staff, Jennifer Miller, Nathaniel Vaduthala, Ariel Golshan, and Daniel Foyt for proofreading and discussion, Jacqueline Scarola for reagents purchasing, and Andrew Wong for sharing the initial cell culture batch.

References

[1] S. K. Karathanasis, "Regenerative medicine: transforming the drug discovery and development paradigm," *Cold Spring Harbor Perspectives in Medicine*, vol. 4, no. 8, Article ID a014084, 2014.

[2] S. Barrientos, H. Brem, O. Stojadinovic, and M. Tomic-Canic, "Clinical application of growth factors and cytokines in wound healing," *Wound Repair and Regeneration*, vol. 22, no. 5, pp. 569–578, 2014.

[3] P. Koria, "Delivery of growth factors for tissue regeneration and wound healing," *BioDrugs*, vol. 26, no. 3, pp. 163–175, 2012.

[4] K. Lee, E. A. Silva, and D. J. Mooney, "Growth factor delivery-based tissue engineering: general approaches and a review of recent developments," *Journal of the Royal Society Interface*, vol. 8, no. 55, pp. 153–170, 2011.

[5] B. Alberts, *Molecular Biology of the Cell*, Garland Science, New York, NY, USA, 5th edition, 2008.

[6] K. Vulic and M. S. Shoichet, "Affinity-based drug delivery systems for tissue repair and regeneration," *Biomacromolecules*, vol. 15, no. 11, pp. 3867–3880, 2014.

[7] G. Gainza, S. Villullas, J. L. Pedraz, R. M. Hernandez, and M. Igartua, "Advances in drug delivery systems (DDSs) to release growth factors for wound healing and skin regeneration," *Nanomedicine*, vol. 11, no. 6, pp. 1551–1573, 2015.

[8] Y. Liang and K. L. Kiick, "Heparin-functionalized polymeric biomaterials in tissue engineering and drug delivery applications," *Acta Biomaterialia*, vol. 10, no. 4, pp. 1588–1600, 2014.

[9] F. M. A. H. Schuurmans Stekhoven, M. H. A. G. Gorissen, and G. Flik, "The isoelectric point, a key to understanding a variety of biochemical problems: a minireview," *Fish Physiology and Biochemistry*, vol. 34, no. 1, pp. 1–8, 2008.

[10] A. Wittemann and M. Ballauff, "Interaction of proteins with linear polyelectrolytes and spherical polyelectrolyte brushes in aqueous solution," *Physical Chemistry Chemical Physics*, vol. 8, no. 45, pp. 5269–5275, 2006.

[11] K. Knop, R. Hoogenboom, D. Fischer, and U. S. Schubert, "Poly(ethylene glycol) in drug delivery: pros and cons as well as potential alternatives," *Angewandte Chemie—International Edition*, vol. 49, no. 36, pp. 6288–6308, 2010.

[12] B. Engebretson and V. I. Sikavitsas, "Long-term in vivo effect of peg bone tissue engineering scaffolds," *Journal of Long-Term Effects of Medical Implants*, vol. 22, no. 3, pp. 211–218, 2012.

[13] G. M. Bonora and S. Drioli, "Recent advances on patents in poly(ethylene glycol)-based drug delivery," *Recent Patents on Drug Delivery and Formulation*, vol. 2, no. 2, pp. 189–195, 2008.

[14] A. Kolate, D. Baradia, S. Patil, I. Vhora, G. Kore, and A. Misra, "PEG—a versatile conjugating ligand for drugs and drug delivery systems," *Journal of Controlled Release*, vol. 192, pp. 67–81, 2014.

[15] J. K. Tessmar and A. M. Göpferich, "Customized PEG-derived copolymers for tissue-engineering applications," *Macromolecular Bioscience*, vol. 7, no. 1, pp. 23–39, 2007.

[16] H. Takahashi, Y. Wang, and D. W. Grainger, "Device-based local delivery of siRNA against mammalian target of rapamycin (mTOR) in a murine subcutaneous implant model to inhibit fibrous encapsulation," *Journal of Controlled Release*, vol. 147, no. 3, pp. 400–407, 2010.

[17] G. D. Mogoşanu, A. M. Grumezescu, and M. C. Chifiriuc, "Keratin-based biomaterials for biomedical applications," *Current Drug Targets*, vol. 15, no. 5, pp. 518–530, 2014.

[18] P. Hill, H. Brantley, and M. Van Dyke, "Some properties of keratin biomaterials: kerateines," *Biomaterials*, vol. 31, no. 4, pp. 585–593, 2010.

[19] A. Vasconcelos and A. Cavaco-Paulo, "The use of keratin in biomedical applications," *Current Drug Targets*, vol. 14, no. 5, pp. 612–619, 2013.

[20] K. T. Nguyen and J. L. West, "Photopolymerizable hydrogels for tissue engineering applications," *Biomaterials*, vol. 23, no. 22, pp. 4307–4314, 2002.

[21] S. Sokic, M. Christenson, J. Larson, and G. Papavasiliou, "In situ generation of cell-laden porous MMP-sensitive PEGDA hydrogels by gelatin leaching," *Macromolecular Bioscience*, vol. 14, no. 5, pp. 731–739, 2014.

[22] R. C. de Guzman, S. M. Tsuda, M.-T. N. Ton et al., "Binding interactions of keratin-based hair fiber extract to gold, keratin, and BMP-2," *PLoS ONE*, vol. 10, no. 8, Article ID e0137233, 2015.

[23] J. R. Richter, R. C. de Guzman, O. K. Greengauz-Roberts, and M. Van Dyke, "Structure-property relationships of meta-kerateine biomaterials derived from human hair," *Acta Biomaterialia*, vol. 8, no. 1, pp. 274–281, 2012.

[24] K. Xu, Y. Fu, W. Chung et al., "Thiol-ene-based biological/synthetic hybrid biomatrix for 3-D living cell culture," *Acta Biomaterialia*, vol. 8, no. 7, pp. 2504–2516, 2012.

[25] C.-C. Lin, A. Raza, and H. Shih, "PEG hydrogels formed by thiol-ene photo-click chemistry and their effect on the formation and recovery of insulin-secreting cell spheroids," *Biomaterials*, vol. 32, no. 36, pp. 9685–9695, 2011.

[26] V. Joukov, K. Pajusola, A. Kaipainen et al., "A novel vascular endothelial growth factor, VEGF-C, is a ligand for the Flt4 (VEGFR-3) and KDR (VEGFR-2) receptor tyrosine kinases," *The EMBO Journal*, vol. 15, no. 2, pp. 290–298, 1996.

[27] T. Klaus, M. Kulesza, M. Bzowska, B. Wyroba, W. W. Kilarski, and J. Bereta, "Overcoming inefficient secretion of recombinant VEGF-C in baculovirus expression vector system by simple purification of the protein from cell lysate," *Protein Expression and Purification*, vol. 110, pp. 151–158, 2015.

[28] R. Pethig, "Dielectric properties of biological materials: biophysical and medical applications," *IEEE Transactions on Electrical Insulation*, vol. 19, no. 5, pp. 453–474, 1984.

[29] V. M. Hernandez-Izquierdo and J. M. Krochta, "Thermoplastic processing of proteins for film formation—a review," *Journal of Food Science*, vol. 73, no. 2, pp. R30–R39, 2008.

[30] J. H. Lee and D. G. Bucknall, "Swelling behavior and network structure of hydrogels synthesized using controlled UV-initiated free radical polymerization," *Journal of Polymer Science Part B: Polymer Physics*, vol. 46, no. 14, pp. 1450–1462, 2008.

[31] S. J. Bryant and K. S. Anseth, "Photopolymerization of hydrogel scaffolds," in *Scaffolding in Tissue Engineering*, P. X. Ma and J. H. Elisseeff, Eds., pp. 71–90, Taylor & Francis, Boca Raton, Fla, USA, 2006.

[32] A.-A. A. Abdel-Azim, A. M. Abdul-Raheim, A. M. Atta, W. Brostow, and T. Datashvili, "Swelling and network parameters of crosslinked porous octadecyl acrylate copolymers as oil spill sorbers," *e-Polymers*, vol. 9, no. 1, pp. 1592–1605, 2009.

[33] G. Colucci, A. Aluigi, C. Tonin, and R. Bongiovanni, "Photopolymerization of keratin-based thiol-ene coatings," *Progress in Organic Coatings*, vol. 77, no. 6, pp. 1104–1110, 2014.

[34] T. M. Florence, "Degradation of protein disulphide bonds in dilute alkali," *Biochemical Journal*, vol. 189, no. 3, pp. 507–520, 1980.

[35] J. E. Glasgow, M. A. Asensio, C. M. Jakobson, M. B. Francis, and D. Tullman-Ercek, "Influence of electrostatics on small molecule flux through a protein nanoreactor," *ACS Synthetic Biology*, vol. 4, no. 9, pp. 1011–1019, 2015.

[36] D. V. Volodkin, N. I. Larionova, and G. B. Sukhorukov, "Protein encapsulation via porous $CaCO_3$ microparticles templating," *Biomacromolecules*, vol. 5, no. 5, pp. 1962–1972, 2004.

[37] K. M. Bernot, C.-H. Lee, and P. A. Coulombe, "A small surface hydrophobic stripe in the coiled-coil domain of type I keratins mediates tetramer stability," *Journal of Cell Biology*, vol. 168, no. 6, pp. 965–974, 2005.

[38] U. Kragh-Hansen, "Structure and ligand binding properties of human serum albumin," *Danish Medical Bulletin*, vol. 37, no. 1, pp. 57–84, 1990.

[39] K. Andreas, M. Sittinger, and J. Ringe, "Toward in situ tissue engineering: chemokine-guided stem cell recruitment," *Trends in Biotechnology*, vol. 32, no. 9, pp. 483–492, 2014.

[40] S. Reed and B. Wu, "Sustained growth factor delivery in tissue engineering applications," *Annals of Biomedical Engineering*, vol. 42, no. 7, pp. 1528–1536, 2014.

[41] H. Uludag, W. Friess, D. Williams et al., "rhBMP-collagen sponges as osteoinductive devices: effects of in vitro sponge characteristics and protein pI on in vivo rhBMP pharmacokinetics," *Annals of the New York Academy of Sciences*, vol. 875, pp. 369–378, 1999.

[42] J. M. Wozney, V. Rosen, A. J. Celeste et al., "Novel regulators of bone formation: molecular clones and activities," *Science*, vol. 242, no. 4885, pp. 1528–1534, 1988.

[43] A. L. Mandel, H. Ozdener, and V. Utermohlen, "Identification of pro- and mature brain-derived neurotrophic factor in human saliva," *Archives of Oral Biology*, vol. 54, no. 7, pp. 689–695, 2009.

[44] J. R. Richter, R. C. de Guzman, and M. E. Van Dyke, "Mechanisms of hepatocyte attachment to keratin biomaterials," *Biomaterials*, vol. 32, no. 30, pp. 7555–7561, 2011.

[45] H. Y. Shin, M. L. Smith, K. J. Toy, P. M. Williams, R. Bizios, and M. E. Gerritsen, "VEGF-C mediates cyclic pressure-induced endothelial cell proliferation," *Physiological Genomics*, vol. 11, no. 3, pp. 245–251, 2002.

[46] J. W. Breslin, S. Y. Yuan, and M. H. Wu, "VEGF-C alters barrier function of cultured lymphatic endothelial cells through a VEGFR-3-dependent mechanism," *Lymphatic Research and Biology*, vol. 5, no. 2, pp. 105–113, 2007.

[47] H. Shimoda and S. Kato, "A model for lymphatic regeneration in tissue repair of the intestinal muscle coat," *International Review of Cytology*, vol. 250, pp. 73–108, 2006.

[48] A. Yan, T. Avraham, J. C. Zampell, S. Z. Aschen, and B. J. Mehrara, "Mechanisms of lymphatic regeneration after tissue transfer," *PLoS ONE*, vol. 6, no. 2, Article ID e17201, 2011.

[49] H. W. Schnaper, H. K. Kleinman, and D. S. Grant, "Role of laminin in endothelial cell recognition and differentiation," *Kidney International*, vol. 43, no. 1, pp. 20–25, 1993.

8

Thermochemical Properties of Hydrophilic Polymers from Cashew and Khaya Exudates and Their Implications on Drug Delivery

Emmanuel O. Olorunsola,[1,2] Partap G. Bhatia,[3]
Babajide A. Tytler,[2] and Michael U. Adikwu[4]

[1]*Department of Pharmaceutics and Pharmaceutical Technology, University of Uyo, Uyo, Nigeria*
[2]*Department of Pharmaceutics and Pharmaceutical Microbiology, Ahmadu Bello University, Zaria, Nigeria*
[3]*Department of Pharmaceutics and Pharmaceutical Microbiology, Usmanu Danfodiyo University, Sokoto, Nigeria*
[4]*University of Abuja, Abuja, Nigeria*

Correspondence should be addressed to Emmanuel O. Olorunsola; olorunsolaeo@yahoo.com

Academic Editor: Ali Nokhodchi

Characterization of a polymer is essential for determining its suitability for a particular purpose. Thermochemical properties of cashew gum (CSG) extracted from exudates of *Anacardium occidentale L.* and khaya gum (KYG) extracted from exudates of *Khaya senegalensis* were determined and compared with those of acacia gum BP (ACG). The polymers were subjected to different thermal and chemical analyses. Exudates of CSG contained higher amount of hydrophilic polymer. The pH of 2% w/v gum dispersions was in the order KYG < CSG < ACG. Calcium was the predominant ion in CSG while potassium was predominant in KYG. The FTIR spectra of CSG and KYG were similar and slightly different from that of ACG. Acacia and khaya gums exhibited the same thermal behaviour which is different from that of CSG. X-ray diffraction revealed that the three gums are the same type of polymer, the major difference being the concentration of metal ions. This work suggests the application of cashew gum for formulation of basic and oxidizable drugs while using khaya gum for acidic drugs.

1. Introduction

Plant gums are produced either as exudates, seed gums, seaweed gums, or pectin [1]. Many tropical plants produce gum as exudates, and these include *Acacia senegal, Anacardium occidentale* L., and *Khaya senegalensis* [1, 2]. Gummy exudates are produced by a process called gummosis which is the secretion of gluey substances from plant stem and trunk. The sticky substance, on exposure to air, solidify to form amorphous translucent solid called gum [3].

Cashew, *Anacardium occidentale* L., belongs to the family Anacardiaceae [2]. It is native to Brazil and grows in many tropical and subtropical countries including Nigeria. It can grow on soils that are considered too poor or too stony for other crops to grow. However, it prefers a well drained sandy-loamy soil. The tree tolerates a wide range of soil acidity [4]. Cashew gum is light to dark brown in colour. It has a pH range of 3.80 to 5.22 depending on the source and duration of storage. The gum contains 9.8–13.2% moisture, 1.9–4.8% insoluble matter, 0.5–1.2% total ash, 1.27–1.80% protein, 9.6–21.0% sugar, and 0.21–2.26% phenol [5]. In terms of sugar composition, it is composed of 61% galactose, 14% arabinose, 7% rhamnose, 8% glucose, 5% glucuronic acid, and <2% other sugar residues. The gum has a highly branched galactan framework made up of chains of 1,3-linked β-D-galactopyranosyl units interspersed with β- 1, 6-linked bonds [6].

Khaya senegalensis (commonly called African mahogany) belongs to the Family Meliaceae. The plant is widely distributed in the rain forest and scattered within the higher rainfall savannah regions. It is characterized and recognized by its evergreen crown [7]. Khaya gum occurs in long thin glass-like translucent fragments. It is colourless to light brown and its mucilage has an acidic pH of about 4.2. It is insoluble in ethanol and acetone and only slightly soluble in water [7]. It is a hydrophilic polymer with a galactan core in which the 1,3-linked β-D-galactopyranosyl residues are concentrated in the inner chains. According to Edmund [8], the gum shares a lot of similarities with acacia gum.

Cashew gum has been evaluated and subsequently suggested for use as a binder in tablet formulations [9], as an agglutinant for capsules and pills in place of gum Arabic [6], as a gelling agent in topical gel formulation [10], and as a suspending and emulsifying agent [11]. Similarly, khaya gum has been evaluated and subsequently suggested for use as a binder in tablet formulation [12] and as a suspending agent in liquid formulation [13]. Therefore, cashew gum and khaya gum have been recommended in several instances for use as alternatives to standard acacia gum.

Cashew gum, khaya gum, and acacia gum are related in that they are all hydrophilic polymers with galactan core and are all obtained from plant exudates [6–8]. Acacia gum is well characterized and it is the official standard. In contrast, most of the information obtained from literature on work carried out till date on characterization of the other two polymers concentrated on the physical properties and carbohydrate monomer composition of the polymers. This work was aimed at evaluating the thermal and chemical properties of cashew and khaya gums and comparing them with those of standard acacia gum. It provides information about the suitability of these hydrophilic polymers as pharmaceutical excipients.

2. Materials and Methods

2.1. Materials. Crude cashew exudates were collected from *Anacardium occidentale* L. trees in Abuja, Nigeria, authenticated by the taxonomist in the Department of Biological Sciences, University of Abuja, Abuja, Nigeria, and issued with voucher number UNIABUJA 150. Crude khaya exudates were collected from *Khaya senegalensis* trees in Abuja, Nigeria, authenticated by the same taxonomist and issued with voucher number UNIABUJA 152. Standard *Acacia senegal* gum (BDH Chemicals, Poole, England) was used as obtained. Ethanol (BDH Chemicals, Poole, England), acetone (Merck, Germany), and diethyl ether (Sigma-Aldrich, Germany) were used as obtained.

2.2. Extraction and Purification of the Polymers. The cashew tree exudates were cleaned by removing the particles of the bark and other extraneous materials by hand and then purified using the modified form of the method described by Ofori-Kwakye et al. [2]. A 500 g quantity of the exudates was added to 1 L of distilled water. The mixture was homogenized using a laboratory blender and then left for 24 h to ensure complete dissolution. The mucilage was screened with muslin cloth to obtain particulate-free slurry. The gum was precipitated using absolute ethanol and defatted using diethyl ether. The precipitated gum was air-dried for 3 h then at 50°C in a hot air oven (Gallenkamp, Germany) for 24 h. It was pulverized using laboratory blender (Model 38BL40, Christison, United Kingdom).

The khaya tree exudates were cleaned by removing extraneous materials by hand. A 500 g quantity of the exudates was purified using the method described for cashew gum. However, 2 L of distilled water was used and time period of 48 h was allowed for gum dissolution. The mucilage was screened with muslin cloth and the gum was precipitated using twice the volume of acetone and defatted using 500 mL of diethyl ether. The gum was dried and then pulverized.

2.3. Determination of Percentage Yield of the Purified Gums. The dried, precipitated, and purified gums obtained from the exudates were weighed and the percentage yields were expressed relative to the initial weight of the crude exudates.

2.4. Determination of Moisture Content. The percentage of moisture content of 2 g sample of each polymer was analysed using electronic moisture analyser (Type MB 35, OHAUS, Switzerland).

2.5. Determination of pH. A 2 g sample of each polymer was dispersed in sufficient deionized water and the volume was made to 100 mL with more of the deionized water to produce a 2% w/v dispersion of the polymer. The pH of the dispersion was determined 24 h after preparation using a pH meter.

2.6. Atomic Absorption Spectrophotometry (AAS). The AAS was carried out using the method described by Ofori-Kwakye et al. [2]. One mL of the digest was used to determine the amount of lead, magnesium, copper, and calcium at wavelengths of 283.30 nm, 285.21 nm, 324.75 nm, and 422.67 nm, respectively, using an Atomic Absorption Spectrophotometer (Perkin Elmer Analyst 400, Perkin Elmer, USA) fitted with an acetylene flame. Also, 2 mL of the digest was used for the determination of sodium and potassium using a flame photometer (Jenway Model PFP7, United Kingdom) operated on methane gas.

2.7. Differential Scanning Calorimetry (DSC). DSC analysis was carried out on 3 mg sample in a 40 μL Al crucible using a DSC-204FI machine (NETZSCH Co., Germany). The scanning was done at 20°C/min heating rate over a temperature range of 0–500°C under nitrogen environment.

2.8. Fourier Transform Infrared (FTIR) Spectrophotometry. Samples of the polymers were prepared in KBr disks in a hydrostatic press at 6–8-ton pressure. FTIR spectra of these prepared samples were recorded at scanning range of 350 to 5000 cm^{-1} using a spectrophotometer (model 8400S, Shimadzu Corporation, Koyto, Japan).

2.9. X-Ray Diffraction (XRD). Powder X-ray diffraction pattern of the samples was recorded on an X-ray diffractometer (PANalytical Spectris Pvt. Ltd., Singapore) using a copper

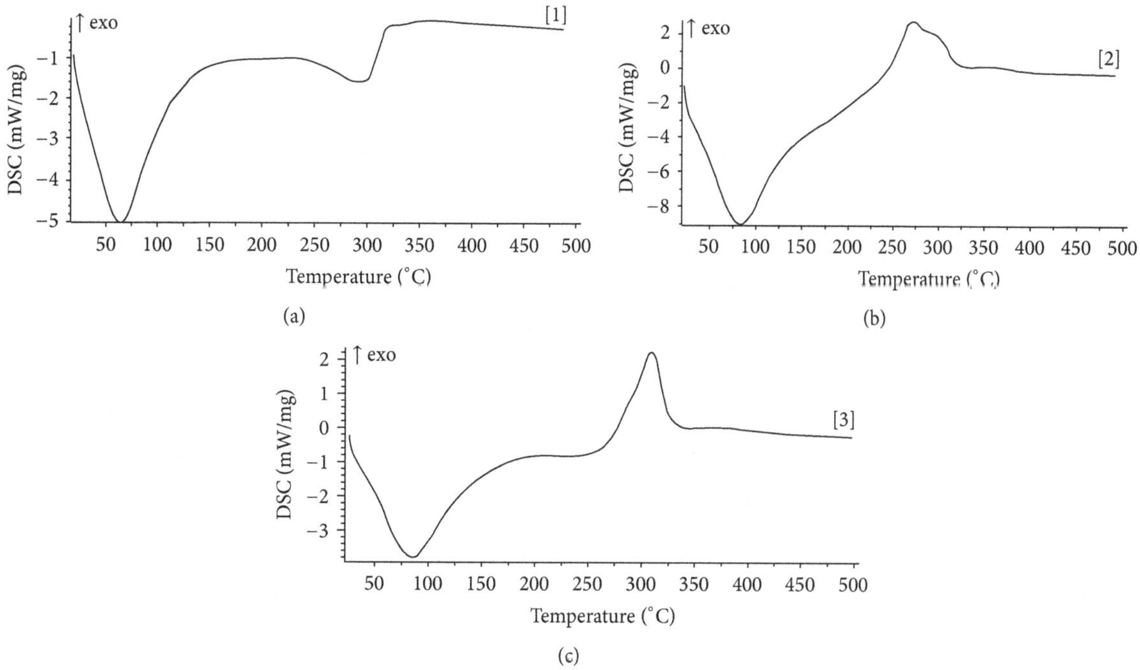

FIGURE 1: DSC thermograms of (a) cashew gum, (b) khaya gum, and (c) acacia gum.

TABLE 1: Some physicochemical properties of the polymers.

Parameter	CSG	KYG	ACG
Yield (%)	48.0	25.0	ND
Moisture content (%)	6.59 ± 0.26	6.62 ± 0.41	6.52 ± 1.38
pH	4.04 ± 0.01	3.38 ± 0.00	4.61 ± 0.01

ND: not determined, CSG: cashew gum, KYG: khaya gum, and ACG: acacia gum.

TABLE 2: Metal ion content of the polymers.

Ion	Concentration (mg/kg)		
	CSG	KYG	ACG
Na^+	1,500 ± 0.20	300 ± 0.11	900 ± 0.32
K^+	550 ± 0.25	1,600 ± 0.50	140 ± 0.17
Mg^{2+}	1,375 ± 0.19	2.85 ± 0.15	441 ± 0.15
Ca^{2+}	2,397 ± 0.26	18 ± 0.22	705 ± 0.15
Cu^{2+}	3.1 ± 0.04	9.0 ± 0.09	0.00 ± 0.00
Pb^{2+}	0.00 ± 0.00	0.00 ± 0.00	0.00 ± 0.00

CSG: cashew gum, KYG: khaya gum, and ACG: acacia gum.

target at voltage of 40 KV and a current of 30 mA over scanning range of 10 to 120°2 Theta.

2.10. Data Analysis. Data obtained were expressed as mean ± standard error of the mean. Statistical analysis was done using one-way analysis of variance followed by Turkey-Kramer multiple comparison test using GraphPad Instat-3 software. Significance of difference was taken at *p values* < 0.05.

3. Results

3.1. Some Physicochemical Properties. Some physicochemical properties of the three hydrophilic polymers are shown in Table 1. The cashew plant exudates gave a higher yield of gum compared to the khaya plant exudates. There was no significant difference in the moisture content of the three polymers. The pH of the 2% w/v dispersion of the gums was in the order KYG < CSG < ACG and the differences were significant.

3.2. Metal Ion Content. The metal ion contents of the different polymers are illustrated in Table 2. Cashew gum had the highest concentration of sodium ion while KYG had the lowest concentration. Khaya gum had the highest potassium ion concentration while ACG had the lowest value. Potassium was observed to be the predominant monovalent ion in khaya gum while sodium was observed to be the predominant in acacia gum. Cashew gum had the highest magnesium ion concentration while khaya gum had the lowest value. Calcium ion was observed to be the predominant ion in CSG. There was a significant difference in the concentration of calcium ion in the different polymers. Khaya gum had a significantly higher concentration of copper ion compared to cashew gum. All the polymers were observed to be free of lead ion.

3.3. Differential Scanning Thermograms. The DSC thermograms of the polymers are shown in Figure 1. The thermogram of CSG showed a sharp endothermic transition between 20 and 100°C with a peak at 70°C followed by

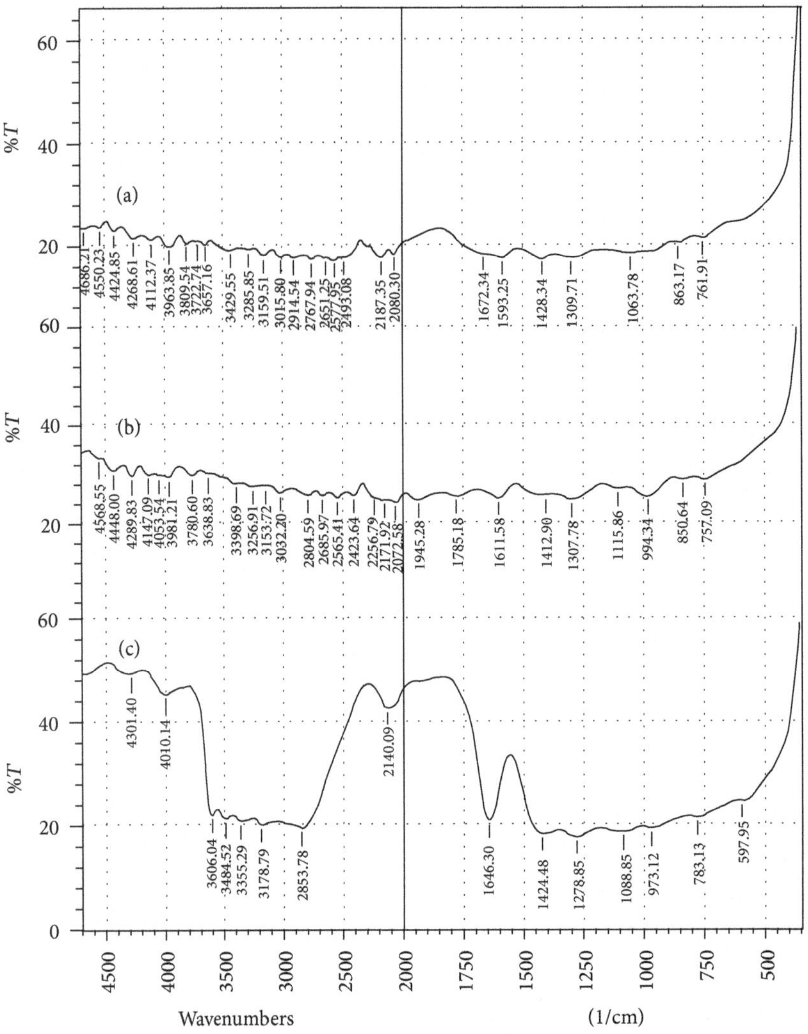

FIGURE 2: FTIR spectra of (a) cashew gum, (b) khaya gum, and (c) acacia gum.

TABLE 3: Enthalpy changes in the thermograms of the polymers.

Polymer	Enthalpy of first transition	Enthalpy of second transition
CSG	909.09 J/g (endotherm)	286.36 J/g (endotherm)
KYG	2833.30 J/g (endotherm)	−454.50 J/g (exotherm)
ACG	1060.61 J/g (endotherm)	−363.63 J/g (exotherm)

CSG: cashew gum, KYG: khaya gum, and ACG: acacia gum.

a diffuse endotherm which peaked at 305°C. There was an endothermic transition having peak at 90°C followed by a diffuse exotherm which peaked at 275°C in the thermogram of KYG. In the thermogram of ACG, an endotherm which peaked at 85°C was observed between 20 and 200°C. This was immediately followed by a sharp exotherm between 275 and 335°C. The enthalpy changes in the thermograms of the three polymers are shown in Table 3.

3.4. Fourier Transform Infrared (FTIR) Spectra. The FTIR spectra of the different polymers are shown in Figure 2. The spectra of cashew gum and khaya gum were similar, the peak of highest intensity being 4,550.23 cm^{-1} for cashew gum and 4,568.55 cm^{-1} for khaya gum. The first absorption peak was 761.91 cm^{-1} for CSG while it was 757.09 cm^{-1} for KYG. The absorption pattern for CSG and KYG was different from that of ACG. The first peak for ACG was noticed at 597.95 cm^{-1} and the peak at 4,301.4 cm^{-1} had the highest intensity.

3.5. X-Ray Diffraction (XRD) Spectra. The XRD spectra of the different polymers are shown in Figure 3. The three polymers had major peak of height > 6400 counts lying between 20 and 22 °2 Theta. Cashew gum had two other peaks at 26.50 and 42.34 °2 Theta corresponding to calcium pantoate. The major peak of KG spectrum is shorter and more flattened.

4. Discussion

The exudates of *Anacardium occidentale* L. contains higher amount of gum compared to that of *Khaya senegalensis* (Table 1). The yield of 48.0% of cashew gum is lower than

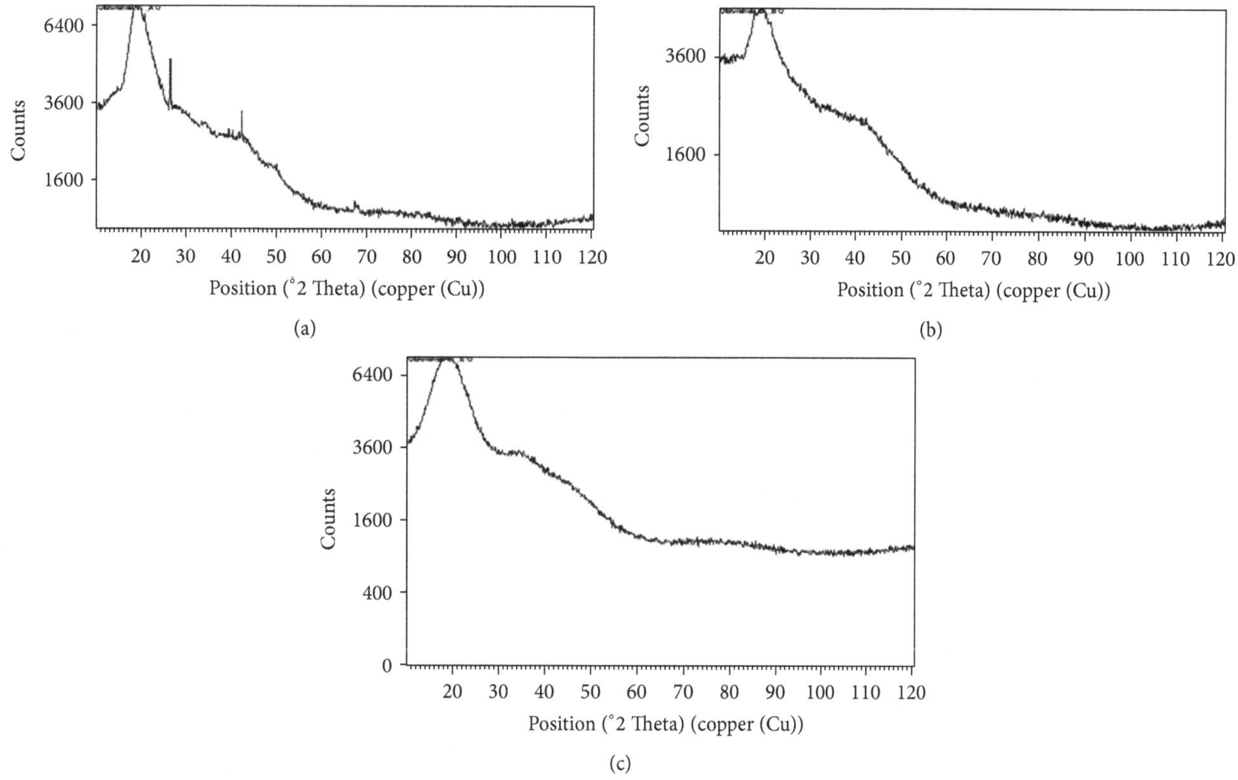

FIGURE 3: XRD spectra of (a) cashew gum, (b) khaya gum, and (c) acacia gum.

the value reported (78.5%) by Ofori-Kwakye et al. [2]. It was claimed that the high yield was due to the nature of the precipitating solvent (ethanol) used. Ethanol was used in this present work, yet the yield is not higher than that obtained by Kumar et al. [10] who used acetone as precipitating solvent. Therefore, the difference in yield could not be due to solvent alone but also due to other factors such as the source of the exudates.

The moisture content was in the order ACG < CSG < KYG, though the difference was not significant. Water is known to catalyze many degradative processes including hydrolysis and microbial attack. The higher the moisture content, the more liable the polymer to degradation [14]. Therefore, the difference in their stability in the dry state might not be significant.

The three polymers have pH in the acidic range showing their commercial and pharmaceutical importance. Basic excipients promote oxidation of susceptible drugs when used for their formulations [15]. Therefore, acidic and neutral hydrocolloids are more widely used for pharmaceutical formulations [7]. Interactions between acidic drugs and basic excipients and vice versa have also been reported by many researchers [16]. Hence, CSG might possess better drug/excipient compatibility as the pH is closer to neutrality.

Calcium ion being the predominant ion in cashew gum is in agreement with the work of Ofori-Kwakye et al. [2]. The concentration of potassium and calcium ions might be a good distinguishing factor between khaya and cashew gums. While potassium was the predominant ion (1600 mg/kg) in khaya gum, calcium was the most predominant (2397 mg/kg) in cashew gum (Table 2). Interactions between drugs and pharmaceutical excipients based on their ionic composition were also reported by Zhou [16]. According to him, indomethacin is incompatible with sodium bicarbonate and ibuprofen is incompatible with magnesium oxide while norfloxacin is incompatible with magnesium stearate. Cashew gum having significantly higher concentration of sodium and magnesium ions might interact with these drugs.

Copper (II) ion is a strong oxidizing agent and catalyzes oxidation of susceptible substances [15]. Khaya gum has a significantly higher concentration of copper (II) ion and might be more vulnerable to autooxidation. It is also less suitable for formulation of drugs that are susceptible to oxidation. Lead is a highly toxic metal and it is absent in all the polymers. This factor and the low concentration of copper ion in all the polymers support the statement that gums are safe pharmaceutical excipients [3].

The first endotherm of the thermogram of CSG (illustrated in Figure 1) can be ascribed to the enthalpy relaxation of the polymer [17]. No exothermic transition was observed. Therefore, there was no clear degradation of the polymer by heating up to 500°C. The second endotherm can be ascribed to melting of the polymer [18] and the peak of the endotherm (305°C) represents its melting point. The latent heat of melting of the polymer was 286.36 J/g (Table 3). This is the amount of energy required to melt a unit gram of the polymer [19]. The observed polymer melting instead of polysaccharide degradation might be due to high inorganic composition of the polymer as revealed by the atomic absorption spectrophotometry. Melting transition is characteristic of crystalline domain [20].

The endotherm of the thermogram of KYG (also illustrated in Figure 1) can be ascribed to the enthalpy relaxation of the polymer [17]. Therefore, it could be said that the polymer experienced enthalpy relaxation between 20 and 250°C. The diffuse exotherm represents polysaccharide degradation [21] and the observed enthalpy change of −454.50 J/g shows that 454.50 J of heat was lost as 1 g of the polymer degraded.

The enthalpy relaxation of acacia gum was illustrated by the endothermic transition between 20 and 200°C [17]. Just like in khaya gum, the exotherm can be ascribed to polysaccharide degradation [21]. The enthalpy change of −363.63 J/g shows that 363.63 of heat was lost as 1 g of the polymer degraded. Relating this to the thermogram of khaya gum, it shows that a smaller amount of heat was lost as acacia gum degraded.

Enthalpy relaxation is an endothermic process as it involves heat flow to the system. It is associated with increase in temperature and hence involves change in heat capacity. It is, therefore, a second-order reaction. In some instances, when the right temperature is reached after relaxation, particles attain an orderly arrangement forming crystals in the process referred to as crystallization. Crystallization involves heat loss. Hence, it is an exothermic transition [18]. Since it takes place at a constant temperature, it is a first-order reaction [19]. As heating continues beyond crystallization, a temperature is reached when the crystals move out of the orderly arrangement in a process called melting. Unlike most polysaccharides, cashew gum experienced endothermic transition of melting instead exothermic transition of degradation. Just like crystallization, melting takes place at a constant temperature. It is thus a first-order transition [18].

The enthalpy relaxation of both KYG and ACG that were accompanied by exothermic transition of degradation reflects their polymeric nature [21]. It can be concluded that when these polymers were heated, they were converted from the amorphous to pseudoamorphous form in the process of enthalpy relaxation. Further heating resulted in polysaccharide breakdown reflected by the exothermic transition.

The Fourier transform infrared spectra of cashew gum and khaya gum are similar (Figure 2). The first absorption peak of 761.91 cm^{-1} in cashew gum and 757.09 cm^{-1} in khaya gum correspond to the presence of aromatic nuclei in the two polymers [22]. The two spectra have similar peak pattern and may contain similar functional groups.

The prominent peak of cashew gum at 761.91 cm^{-1} could be assigned to C-H bending vibration of substituted aromatic hydrocarbon while those at 2914.54–3265.65 cm^{-1} could be attributed to stretching vibration of the aromatic C-H. The peaks at 1063.78 and 1309.71 cm^{-1} could be assigned to O-H bending and C-O stretching of ether and alcohol. The peaks at 2577.95 and 2651.25 cm^{-1} could be assigned to stretching vibration of intramolecularly bonded O-H group, while 3657.16 cm^{-1} peak could be assigned to stretching vibration of free O-H based on infrared spectrophotometry bands of selected functional groups given by Coutts [22].

In the FTIR spectrum of khaya gum, the peak at 757.09 cm^{-1} could be assigned to aromatic C-H bending vibration while those at 3032.20–3256.91 cm^{-1} could be attributed to stretching vibration of C-H in the substituted aromatic hydrocarbon. The peaks at 1115.86 and 1307.78 cm^{-1} could be assigned to O-H bending and C-O stretching of ether and alcohol. The peaks at 2561.41 and 2685.97 cm^{-1} could be assigned to stretching vibration of bonded hydroxyl group while 3638.83 cm^{-1} could be assigned to stretching vibration of free O-H [22].

The absorption at 597.95 cm^{-1} ($<600\ cm^{-1}$) found in acacia gum was not found in cashew nor khaya gum. However, peaks below 600 cm^{-1} are not used in characterization. In the FTIR spectrum of acacia gum, the peak at 783.13 cm^{-1} could be assigned to aromatic C-H bending vibration while those at 2853.78 and 3178.79 cm^{-1} could be assigned to C-H stretching vibration of the aromatic hydrocarbon. The peaks at 1088.85 and 1278.85 cm^{-1} could be assigned to O-H bending and C-O stretching of ether and alcohol. The peak at 3484.52 cm^{-1} could be assigned to the stretching of bonded O-H group while 3606.04 cm^{-1} could be assigned to stretching vibration of free O-H group (Figure 2) based on specifications of Coutts [22].

From the X-ray diffraction patterns (Figure 3), the major peaks of CSG, KYG, and ACG lying at the same point are an indication that the three gums are the same type of polymer. The abundance of calcium in cashew gum was confirmed by the two additional peaks at 26.49 and 42.34 °2 Theta which correspond to the presence of calcium pantoate. The shorter and more flattened peak of KYG indicates the presence of impurities [23]. Organic molecules are large and their crystals have large unit cells. Their interplanar spacings are, therefore, large. The large spacing gives rise to diffraction peaks at small values of °2 Theta. This is particularly true for amorphous materials [24]. All the polymers have single major peak below 25 °2 Theta which is on the low side. They are, therefore, amorphous organic materials.

5. Conclusion

Exudate of cashew plant contains higher amount of gum compared to that of khaya plant. The polymers are good and safe pharmaceutical excipients with pH in the acidic range. They are free of lead ion and are distinguishable by the level of different metal ions present. Khaya gum and acacia gum have similar thermal behaviour which is different from that of cashew gum. The three gums are the same type of polymer, the only significant difference being the concentration of the different metal ions. This work suggests the application of cashew gum for formulation of basic drugs while using khaya gum for acidic drugs. Cashew gum might also be better as excipient for formulation of drugs that are susceptible to oxidation. The suitability of each polymer can be verified by utilizing and investigating them for delivery of the different drugs.

Competing Interests

The authors declare that there are no competing interests regarding the publication of this paper.

References

[1] I. S. Ogaji, E. I. Nep, and J. D. Audu-Peters, "Advances in natural polymers as excipients," *Pharmaceutica Analytica Acta*, vol. 3, article 146, 2012.

[2] K. Ofori-Kwakye, Y. Asantewaa, and S. L. Kipo, "Physicochemical and binding properties of cashew tree gum in metronidazole tablet formulations," *International Journal of Pharmacy and Pharmaceutical Sciences*, vol. 2, no. 4, pp. 105–109, 2010.

[3] J. Muñoz, F. Rincón, M. Carmen Alfaro et al., "Rheological properties and surface tension of *Acacia tortuosa* gum exudate aqueous dispersions," *Carbohydrate Polymers*, vol. 70, no. 2, pp. 198–205, 2007.

[4] D. J. Udoh, B. A. Ndon, P. E. Asuquo, and N. U. Ndaeyo, *Crop Production Techniques for the Tropics*, Concept, Lagos, Nigeria, 2005.

[5] E. Gyedu-Akolo, I. Oduro, E. M. Amoah et al., "Physicochemical properties of cashew tree gum," *African Journal of Food Science*, vol. 2, pp. 60–64, 2008.

[6] R. D. S. N. Lima, J. R. Lima, C. R. De Salis, and R. D. A. Moreira, "Cashew-tree (*Anacardium occidentale* L.) exudate gum: a novel bioligand tool," *Biotechnology and Applied Biochemistry*, vol. 35, no. 1, pp. 45–53, 2002.

[7] H. S. Mahmud, A. R. Oyi, and T. S. Allagh, "Studies on some physicochemical properties of *Khaya senegalensis* gum," *Nigerian Journal of Pharmaceutical Sciences*, vol. 7, no. 1, pp. 146–152, 2008.

[8] L. H. Edmund, "Extensive studies on gum," *Biographical Memoirs of Fellows of the Royal Society*, vol. 22, no. 147, 1976.

[9] E. I. Okoye, A. O. Onyekweli, F. O. Ohwoavworhua, and O. O. Kunle, "Comparative study of some mechanical and release properties of paracetamol tablets formulated with cashew tree gum, povidone and gelatin as binders," *African Journal of Biotechnology*, vol. 8, no. 16, pp. 3970–3973, 2009.

[10] R. Kumar, M. B. Patil, S. R. Patil, and M. S. Paschapur, "Evaluation of *Anacardium occidentale* gum as gelling agent in aceclofenac gel," *International Journal of Pharmaceutical Technology Research*, vol. 1, no. 3, pp. 695–704, 2009.

[11] A. Abdulsamad, P. G. Bhatia, and J. E. Ojile, "Emulsifying and suspending properties of cashew gum," *Nigerian Journal of Pharmaceutical Research*, vol. 5, no. 1, pp. 40–47, 2006.

[12] A. Mgbahurike and C. Igwilo, "Binding properties of gums from *Khaya senegalensis* in granules," *Nigerian Journal of Pharmacy*, vol. 22, pp. 41–43, 1991.

[13] H. S. Mahmud, A. R. Oyi, and T. S. Allagh, "Evaluation of the suspending property of *Khaya senegalensis* gum in formulation of paracetamol suspension," *Nigerian Journal of Pharmaceutical Sciences*, vol. 8, no. 1, pp. 128–134, 2009.

[14] A. B. Isah, E. O. Olorunsola, and Y. E. Zaman, "Physicochemical properties of *Borassus aethiopum* starch," *Asian Journal of Pharmaceutical and Clinical Research*, vol. 5, supplement 3, pp. 132–134, 2012.

[15] A. R. Barnes, "Product stability and stability testing," in *The Design and Manufacture of Medicine*, M. E. Aulton, Ed., pp. 650–665, Churchill Livingstone, Philadelphia, Pa, USA, 2007.

[16] D. Zhou, "Understanding physicochemical properties for pharmaceutical product development and manufacturing II: physical and chemical stability and excipient compatibility," *Journal of Validation Technology*, pp. 36–47, 2009.

[17] H.-J. Chung, E.-J. Lee, and S.-T. Lim, "Comparison in glass transition and enthalpy relaxation between native and gelatinized rice starches," *Carbohydrate Polymers*, vol. 48, no. 3, pp. 287–298, 2002.

[18] M. Horvat, E. Meštrović, A. Danilovski, and D. Q. M. Craig, "An investigation into the thermal behaviour of a model drug mixture with amorphous trehalose," *International Journal of Pharmaceutics*, vol. 294, no. 1-2, pp. 1–10, 2005.

[19] P. F. Builders, C. Chukwu, I. Obidike, M. I. Builders, A. A. Attama, and M. U. Adikwu, "A novel xyloglucan gum from seeds of *Afzelia africana* Se. Pers.: some functional and physicochemical properties," *International Journal of Green Pharmacy*, vol. 3, no. 2, pp. 112–118, 2009.

[20] P. F. Builders, O. O. Kunle, and M. U. Adikwu, "Preparation and characterization of mucinated agarose: a mucin-agarose physical crosslink," *International Journal of Pharmaceutics*, vol. 356, no. 1-2, pp. 174–180, 2008.

[21] M. S. Iqbal, S. Massey, J. Akbar, C. M. Ashraf, and R. Masih, "Thermal analysis of some natural polysaccharide materials by isoconversional method," *Food Chemistry*, vol. 140, no. 1-2, pp. 178–182, 2013.

[22] R. T. Coutts, "Infrared spectroscopy," in *Pharmaceutical Chemistry—Instrumental Techniques*, L. G. Chatten, Ed., pp. 59–125, CBS Publishers and Distributors PVT Ltd, New Delhi, India, 2008.

[23] M. T. H. Nutan, M. S. Soliman, E. I. Taha, and M. A. Khan, "Optimization and characterization of controlled release multiparticulate beads coated with starch acetate," *International Journal of Pharmaceutics*, vol. 294, no. 1-2, pp. 89–101, 2005.

[24] J. W. Shell, "X-ray analysis," in *Pharmaceutical Chemistry—Instrumental Techniques*, L. G. Chatten, Ed., pp. 371–406, CBS Publishers and Distributors PVT Ltd, New Delhi, India, 2008.

9

Investigation of Diffusion Characteristics through Microfluidic Channels for Passive Drug Delivery Applications

Marcus J. Goudie, Alyssa P. Ghuman, Stephanie B. Collins, Ramana M. Pidaparti, and Hitesh Handa

College of Engineering, University of Georgia, Athens, GA 30602, USA

Correspondence should be addressed to Ramana M. Pidaparti; rmparti@uga.edu and Hitesh Handa; hhanda@uga.edu

Academic Editor: Viness Pillay

Microfluidics has many drug delivery applications due to the ability to easily create complex device designs with feature sizes reaching down to the 10s of microns. In this work, three different microchannel designs for an implantable device are investigated for treatment of ocular diseases such as glaucoma, age-related macular degeneration (AMD), and diabetic retinopathy. Devices were fabricated using polydimethylsiloxane (PDMS) and soft lithography techniques, where surface chemistry of the channels was altered using 2-[methoxy(polyethyleneoxy)propyl]trimethoxysilane (PEG-silane). An estimated delivery rate for a number of common drugs was approximated for each device through the ratio of the diffusion coefficients for the dye and the respective drug. The delivery rate of the model drugs was maintained at a physiological condition and the effects of channel design and surface chemistry on the delivery rate of the model drugs were recorded over a two-week period. Results showed that the surface chemistry of the device had no significant effect on the delivery rate of the model drugs. All designs were successful in delivering a constant daily dose for each model drug.

1. Introduction

Various ocular diseases such as age-related macular degeneration (AMD), glaucoma, diabetic retinopathy, and retinitis pigmentosa require lifelong treatment through daily eye drops or monthly injections into the eye to avoid blindness [1]. Due to the cost and frequency of doctor visits, many patients opt to only get injections every 6 months. Decreasing the frequency of injections is detrimental to the patient's eyesight. Monthly injections are required to maintain vision at a constant level or to have any chance of improvement. Ocular diseases are prevalent throughout society, especially affecting adults over the age of 50. An estimated 1.6 million adults suffer from AMD in the US alone, with approximately 500,000 cases diagnosed annually worldwide [2].

Age-related macular degeneration is caused by a buildup of waste in the retina, resulting in blurred central vision and eventual loss of vision. There are two types of AMD: dry and wet. Dry AMD is caused by improper nourishment of the retina, resulting in a buildup of waste in the eye known as drusen. Wet AMD is more threatening, where 90% of cases result in severe vision loss. Breakages in the inner membrane of the retina cause new blood vessels to leak blood and lipid materials into the eye, progressively blurring vision until all sight is lost [3].

Treatment of these ocular diseases is typically done through monthly ocular injections, costing time and money in doctor visits. In addition, the repeated ocular injections run the risks of intraocular infections, hemorrhages, and retinal detachment [4]. While daily eye drops are an alternative to injections, only 5% of the administered drug may reach the anterior intraocular tissues through the cornea [2]. Orally delivered medications may be most convenient for the patient but come with serious systemic side effects due to the high dosages [5]. These high dosages are required for therapeutic levels to be reached in the eye through the blood-retina barrier [6]. Developing an implantable drug delivery device would provide controlled delivery and effective use of drugs, while avoiding required doctor visits and complications from frequent injections. The controlled delivery of drugs will maximize efficiency and allow the patients to experience improvements in their eyesight.

Both biodegradable and nonbiodegradable ocular devices have been approved, each with their own pros and cons. The advantage of biodegradable devices is their ability to degrade after all of the drug has been released. Once they degrade, the device can be replaced to continue delivery of the drug. However, the drug-release lifetime of biodegradable devices can be much shorter than that of nonbiodegradable devices [7]. Nonbiodegradable devices allow for more precise drug release over a longer period of time but remain in the eye after all of the drug has been released and must be replaced.

Currently, there are several options for ocular drug delivery microdevices. Some of the top known devices are from pSivida Corp including Retisert, Iluvien, and Vitrasert. Other top devices in the market include Ozurdex, Surodex, and I-Vation. A biodegradable device example is Ozurdex, whereas Retisert and Iluvien are examples of nonbiodegradable devices. Some of these devices can be inserted into the eye through the use of a needle and others must be surgically implanted in the eye [8]. However, none of the current devices on the market are refillable and must be replaced once the entire drug load has been dispensed.

The field of microfluidics has become a promising tool for drug delivery applications. One of the most common techniques for creating these devices is through the use of soft lithography, where a polymer is poured over a master mold to create the required channels [9, 10]. Polydimethylsiloxane (PDMS) has become the most popular material for these devices due to its inherent biocompatibility and ease of use. Due to the hydrophobic nature of PDMS, methods to alter its surface chemistry have been studied extensively. One of the most common techniques is through the use of oxygen plasma exposure, which provides a dense covering of hydroxyl (–OH) groups on the surface. However, this surface has been shown to recover with time due to migrating uncured oligomers forming the material bulk and rearranging the functional groups away from the surface [11]. It has been shown that these surfaces can be reacted with methoxy-silane or other alkyl-silane groups, by applying a grafted silane to the surface [12, 13]. With PDMS being used for a wide variety of biomedical applications, investigations in altering the surface chemistry of PDMS through grafting of polymer chains or bioactive molecules such as heparin have been studied extensively [14–19].

This study investigates three designs for a refillable microfluidic device for intraocular drug delivery. Various channel configurations were used to demonstrate the effect of surface modification over a range of diffusion lengths, as well as an attempt to limit the burst release kinetics that are associated with reservoir based drug delivery systems. Surface modification of PDMS channels was done through exposure to a silanized polyethylene glycol after exposure to air plasma. Hydrophobic and hydrophilic devices were examined to determine if surface chemistry would alter the drug delivery rate. The release kinetics were studied using two model dyes in various channel geometries over a two-week period.

2. Materials and Methods

2.1. Materials. For silicon wafer mold fabrication, SU-8 2025 permanent epoxy negative photoresist and SU-8 developer were purchased from MicroChem (Newton, MA). Four-inch silicon wafers were purchased from University Wafer (Boston, MA). Custom laminated masks for patterning of photoresist were designed in AutoCad and sent for printing from CAD/Art Services, Inc. (Bandon, OR). Sylgard 184 silicone elastomer base and curing agent (Dow Corning, Midland, MI) were purchased from Krayden Inc. (Denver, CO). Extra dry acetone, sodium chloride, potassium chloride, sodium phosphate dibasic, potassium phosphate monobasic, Rhodamine B (RB), and Toluidine Blue (TB) were purchased from Sigma Aldrich (St. Louis, MO). Glass slides and cuvettes were purchased from Fisher Scientific. 2-[Methoxy(polyethyleneoxy)propyl]trimethoxysilane (PEG-silane) was purchased from Gelest (Morrisville, PA). Phosphate buffered saline (PBS), pH 7.4, containing 138 mM NaCl, 2.7 mM KCl, 10 mM sodium phosphate, and 100 mM EDTA was used for all experiments.

2.2. Design Considerations. Three channel configurations, with varying diffusive resistances, are proposed as novel designs for ocular drug delivery and are shown in Figure 1. The large range in resistances was selected to examine if the surface chemistry would have more considerable effects with increasing channel length. The dye is stored in the square reservoir region of the device, where delivery of the drug is done through Fick's second law. The use of the passive devices for drug delivery requires customization for the specific drug as diffusion coefficients of drugs vary and can range within $1.25–3 \times 10^{-7}\,cm^2\,s^{-1}$ [21, 23, 24, 26]. Using model dyes with increased diffusion coefficients is beneficial, as measuring extremely dilute solutions can be challenging. A list of drugs and their diffusion characteristics as compared to the model dyes used are shown in Table 1. A number of features of the final device for implantable use were identified including the following:

(i) Refillable through injection.

(ii) Requiring only minor surgical procedures for implantation.

(iii) Diffusion period between 1 and 2 years.

(iv) Diffusion rate within 2% of the dosing rate.

(v) Overall volume of less than 280 mm^3.

The diffusion rates of the three designs were investigated using two dyes as model drugs. The reservoir for each design is identical, totaling 112.5 mm^3 (3 mm × 5 mm × 7.5 mm, $H \times L \times W$). As the dosage requirement and diffusion characteristics vary from drug to drug, the proposed designs are investigated to determine if they are suitable for a variety of deliverable drugs.

2.3. Diffusion Modeling. Steady-state diffusion rates were calculated for the three device designs to confirm the experimental measurements. The following assumptions were made

Table 1: Dosing and diffusion characteristics of common drugs to treat ocular diseases. Diffusion coefficient of Toluidine Blue calculated using Stokes-Einstein approximation.

Drug name (type)	Diffusion coefficient (cm^2/s)	Average dosage (nL/min)	Injection amounts/periods	Molecular weight	Molar delivery (nmol/day)	References
Macugen (pegaptanib sodium)	3×10^{-7}	0.2083	3 mg/10 days	400 kDa	6.00	[20]
Lucentis (ranibizumab)	2.08×10^{-7}	0.0124	0.5 mg/month	500 kDa	0.35	[21]
Intravitreal Avastin (bevacizumab)	1.25×10^{-7}	0.0289	1.25 mg/month	100 kDa	0.28	[22]
Fluocinolone Acetonide	2.3×10^{-7}	0.0744	15 mg/20 weeks	400 Da	237.04	[23, 24]
Toluidine Blue	1.42×10^{-5}					
Rhodamine B	4.2×10^{-6}					[25]

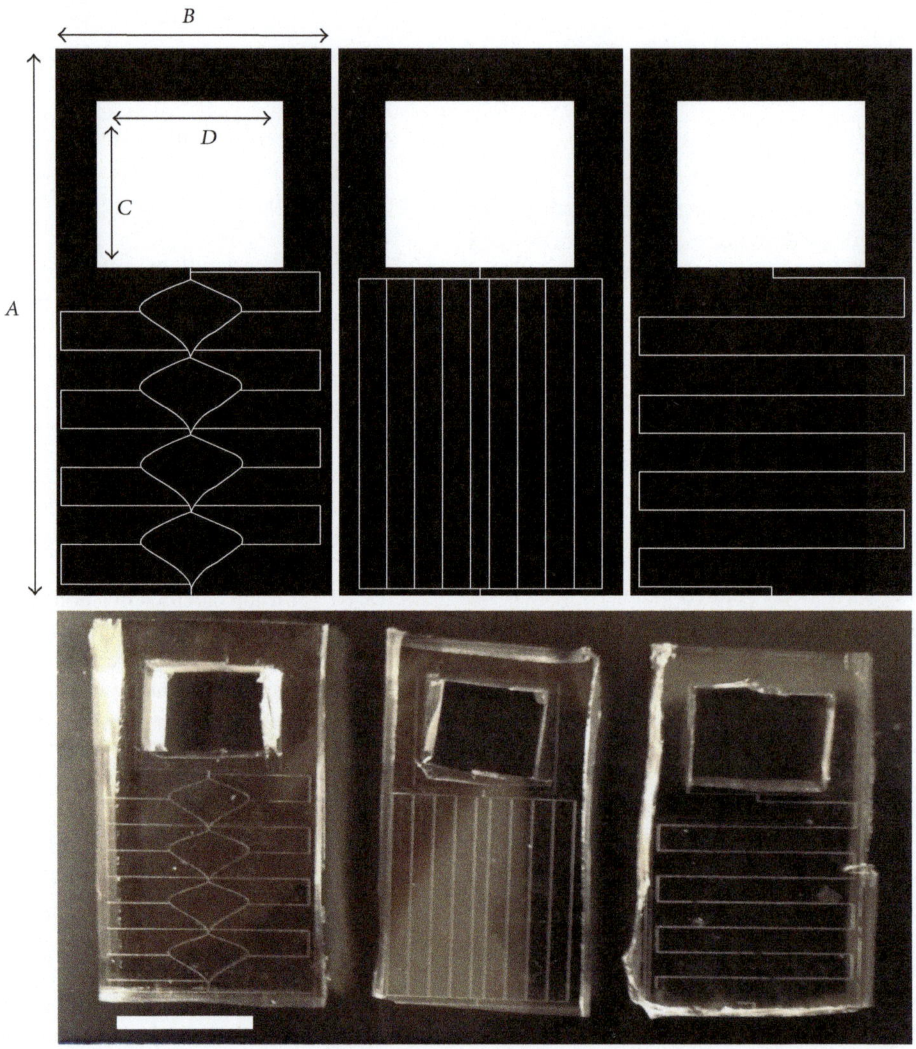

Figure 1: Leaf, Straight, and Snake (left to right) microchannel designs for a range of diffusive characteristics. All channels are 50 μm wide and 50 μm tall. Device length (A) 2.5 cm. Width (B) 1.5 cm. Reservoir length (C) 0.5 cm. Reservoir width (D) 0.75 cm. Reservoir height was kept constant at 3 mm. Representative devices for each design are shown below the corresponding graphic (scale bar represents 1 cm).

for the steady-state analysis: concentration of the dye at the outlet = 0, concentration of the dye in the reservoir is constant, and the delivery of the dye is solely from diffusion governed by Fick's Law (1).

For diffusion-based devices with reservoirs much larger than the channel volumes, along with delivery over a long period of time, diffusion can be approximated using Fick's first law, relating the diffusive flux to the concentration gradient:

$$J = -D\frac{\partial C}{\partial x}, \qquad (1)$$

where J is the diffusive flux (mol m^{-2} s^{-1}), D is the diffusion coefficient (m^2 s^{-1}), and C is the concentration of drug in the reservoir (mol m^{-3}). The molar delivery of the drug (M) into the eye is then

$$M = JA, \tag{2}$$

where A is the cross sectional area of the microfluidic channel (m^2).

For steady-state, the flux can be simplified to the change in concentration times the diffusive resistance. For the Snake design, the resistance was taken to be the inverse of the channel length (m^{-1}), whereas the resistance for the Straight and Leaf designs was calculated using the analogous method for parallel resistors in a circuit:

$$R_{\text{eq}} = \sum_i \frac{1}{L_i}. \tag{3}$$

Desired molar delivery rates for the example drugs were calculated (nmol/day) and are shown in Table 1. To correlate the model drug dyes to a predicted delivery rate of the proposed drug, the flux is multiplied by the ratio of the diffusion coefficients between the two compounds and the ratios of the concentrations to be used in the reservoirs:

$$M_{\text{drug}} = \frac{D_{\text{drug}}}{D_{\text{dye}}} J_{\text{dye}} A. \tag{4}$$

The diffusion coefficient used for Rhodamine B has been reported previously through experimental testing [25], while the coefficient for Toluidine Blue was approximated using the Stokes-Einstein approximation.

2.4. Device Fabrication. Devices were created using soft lithography techniques. Negative photoresist SU-8 2025 was spin coated on silicon wafers to achieve a layer of 50 microns. Wafers were exposed to UV light (365 nm) using a Karl Suss MA6 mask aligner with soft contact. Preexposure bake, exposure time, and postexposure bake were all determined from the MicroChem datasheet. A 10 : 1 ratio of PDMS base and a curing agent was mixed thoroughly, poured over the silicon wafer, and degassed in a vacuum for 1 hour. The PDMS was then left in an oven at 90°C for 60 minutes. After curing, the PDMS was peeled away from the molds forming the channels. The individual devices were cut out and the reservoir region was removed.

Bonding of the devices was done through exposure to air plasma (Harrick Plasma Cleaner) in a two-step process (Figure 2): (1) a top section of PDMS was bonded to the PDMS block with the channels and (2) channel side of PDMS was bonded to a glass base. The side to be bonded was exposed to oxygen plasma (700 mTorr air) for 5 minutes and subsequently brought into contact with the glass slide or PDMS in order to form an irreversible seal [27]. After plasma treatment, hydrophobic devices were left on a hot plate at 80°C for 30 minutes. Devices were left to sit for one week to ensure hydrophobic recovery of the channel walls prior to testing [11]. For devices to have hydrophilic surfaces, channels were

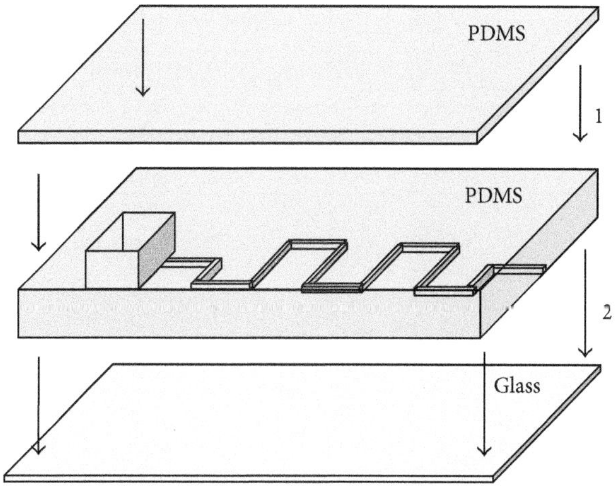

FIGURE 2: Bonding procedure for device fabrication. (1) Top PDMS is bonded to seal top of the reservoir. (2) PDMS channel design is bonded to glass slide. Devices for hydrophilic surface chemistry were filled immediately after step (2).

filled with a 50 : 50 solution of PEG-silane and extra dry acetone and allowed to react for 1 hour at room temperature after exposure to oxygen plasma [12, 13]. Hydrophilic devices were then rinsed thoroughly with PBS and flushed with air to dry.

2.5. Confirmation of PEG Attachment. Contact angles of untreated PDMS and PEG treated PDMS were measured to validate the method used to change the surface chemistry for the devices. Films of PDMS (10 : 1 base to curing agent) were poured, degassed for 1 hour, and cured at 80°C for 1 hour. Films to be plasma treated were then exposed to air plasma for 5 min in the Harrick Plasma Cleaner. Following plasma treatment, films to be exposed to the PEG-silane were immediately submerged in the 50 : 50 PEG-silane: extra dry acetone solution for one hour. After one hour, films were rinsed thoroughly with deionized water and left to dry for 24 hours. Contact angle was measured at three randomly selected areas for each sample ($N = 3$) using a Kruss Drop Shape Analyzer.

2.6. UV Spectra of Rhodamine B and Toluidine Blue. Full spectra of both RB and TB were measured to confirm adsorption peaks as found in the literature using a Cary Bio Spectrophotometer (Varian). Scans were recorded from 900 to 200 nm. Baseline measurements were measured with 0.1 M PBS.

2.7. In Vitro Testing. The three channel configurations were tested using the two dyes as model drugs, where concentration of the dye in the external reservoir was measured. Smallest diffusion path was varied between the device designs from 15 mm to 115 mm. Height and width of the microfluidic channels were kept constant between the devices at 50 μm.

Diffusion characteristics of the devices were measured by filling the reservoirs of the devices with either 5 mM Rhodamine B or 32 mM Toluidine Blue using a 1 mL syringe with 27 gauge needle. These concentrations were selected as they are near the saturation limit of the model drugs. After devices

TABLE 2: Steady-state delivery rates for the various channel geometries as compared to the desired dosing rate.

Drug	Design	Flux mol m^{-2} s^{-1}	nmol/day	Desired dosing rate (nmol/day)	Lifetime (years)
Macugen	Snake	$2.68E-06$	0.579	6	1.042
	Leaf	$1.71E-05$	3.703		0.163
	Straight	$6.11E-05$	13.207		0.046
Lucentis	Snake	$1.86E-06$	0.401	0.3472	1.503
	Leaf	$1.19E-05$	2.567		0.235
	Straight	$4.24E-05$	9.157		0.066
Intravitreal Avastin	Snake	$1.12E-06$	0.241	0.279	2.500
	Leaf	$7.14E-06$	1.543		0.391
	Straight	$2.55E-05$	5.503		0.110
Fluocinolone acetonide	Snake	$2.05E-06$	0.444	237	1.359
	Leaf	$1.31E-05$	2.839		0.212
	Straight	$4.69E-05$	10.125		0.060

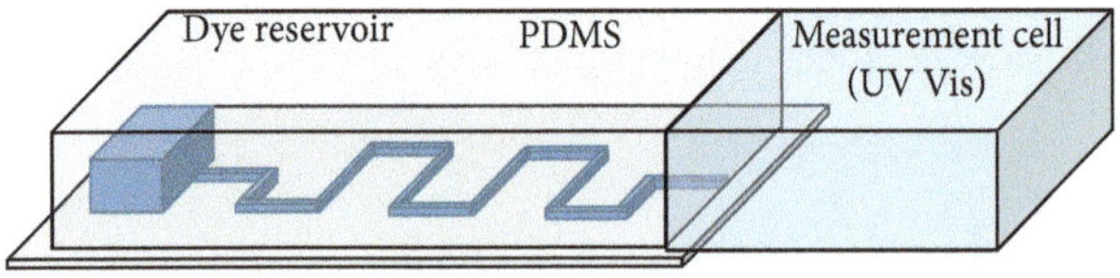

FIGURE 3: Representation of experimental setup for measurement of total dye diffused from the microchannel device.

were filled, they were placed in a sealed plastic centrifuge tube with 4 mL of (PBS) and placed in a Series 2 Water Jacketed Incubator (Thermo Scientific) at 37°C to simulate the vitreous humor of the eye. Absorbance values of the solution of PBS and dye for each device were measured using Genesys 10S UV-Vis Spectrophotometer (Thermo Scientific) every 24 hours at 550 nm [28] and 640 nm [29] for Rhodamine B (RB) and Toluidine Blue (TB), respectively. The device was taken out of the centrifuge tube and the liquid was mixed in a vortex mixer before each measurement. Concentration of the model drug in the PBS was calculated using a calibration curve for the corresponding dye, which was created using five known concentrations. A representation of the test configuration is shown in Figure 3.

3. Results and Discussion

3.1. Steady-State Analysis. Delivery rate of each dye for each design was calculated as a way to assess the validity of each experimental data set. While the burst release of these devices is important to consider for patient safety, it is also important to consider the clinically relevant concentration for the drugs to be active at the delivery site. Likewise, if the release rate is high for one day when devices are to be used on the order of years, this increased release rate can be insignificant in the overall effectiveness of the device. Resistance to diffusion was calculated for each design using (3), using the sum of the inverse of the path lengths, along with the theoretical delivery rate of each dye (Table 2). The steady-state delivery rates for the drugs listed in Table 1 are also shown. The target lifetime for these devices is between 1 and 2 years.

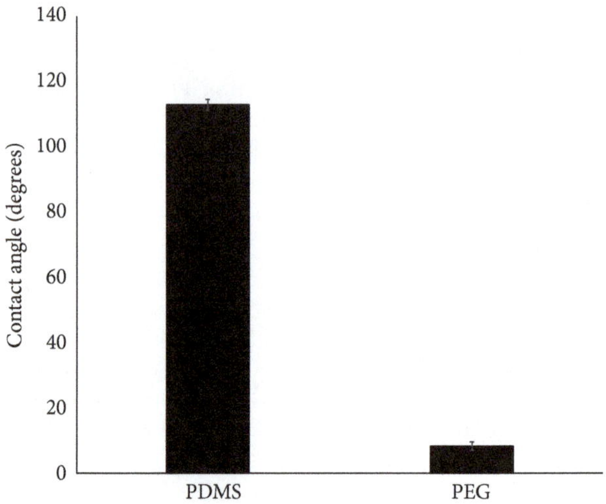

FIGURE 4: Confirmation of PEG attachment to PDMS as measured through contact angle. Measurement was conducted 24 hours after air plasma exposure.

3.2. Confirmation of PEG Attachment. The method to modify the PDMS surface was confirmed through contact angle measurements. After air plasma exposure, PDMS to be treated were submerged in 50 : 50 PEG-silane:extra dry acetone for one hour. After thoroughly rinsing with deionized water, films were left to sit 24 hours prior to measurement due to the recovery of PDMS after plasma exposure. Contact angle was observed to decrease from $113 \pm 1.63°$ (PDMS) to $8.33 \pm 1.24°$ (PEG) and is shown in Figure 4. This significant decrease in contact angle confirms not only the attachment of the PEG-silane to the surface, but also the fact that the attachment is highly uniform as very little deviations are seen throughout the surface, but between samples as well.

3.3. UV Spectra of Rhodamine B and Toluidine Blue. Full UV spectra of both RB and TB were shown to have peaks similar to those reported in the literature [28, 29]. Rhodamine B was found to have a peak at 550 nm, where TB has two peaks in the 600 region (596 nm and 640 nm). Full spectra of both RB and TB are shown in Figure 5.

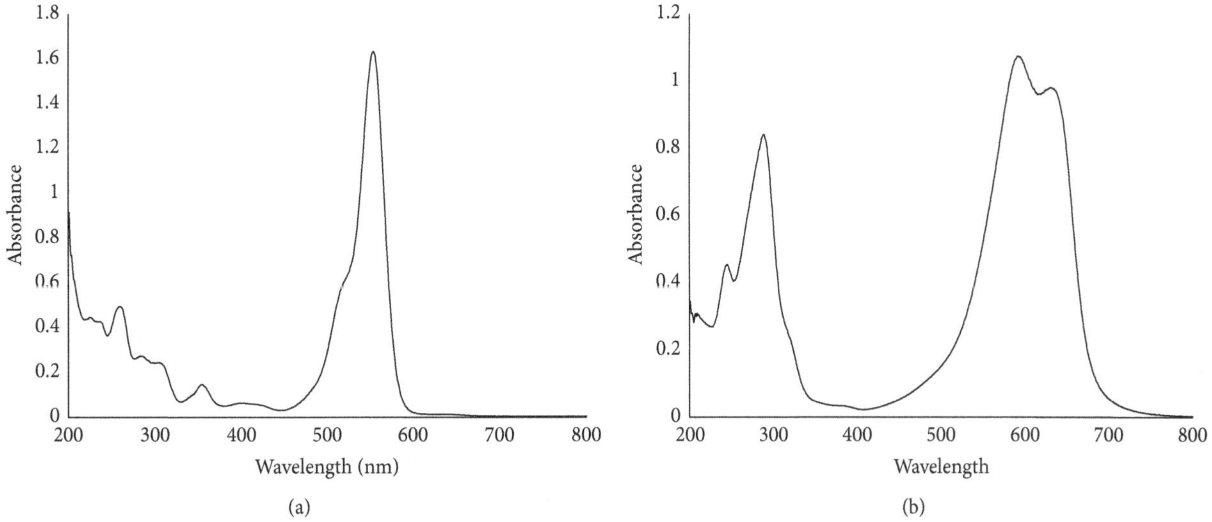

FIGURE 5: Full UV spectra for (a) Rhodamine B and (b) Toluidine Blue.

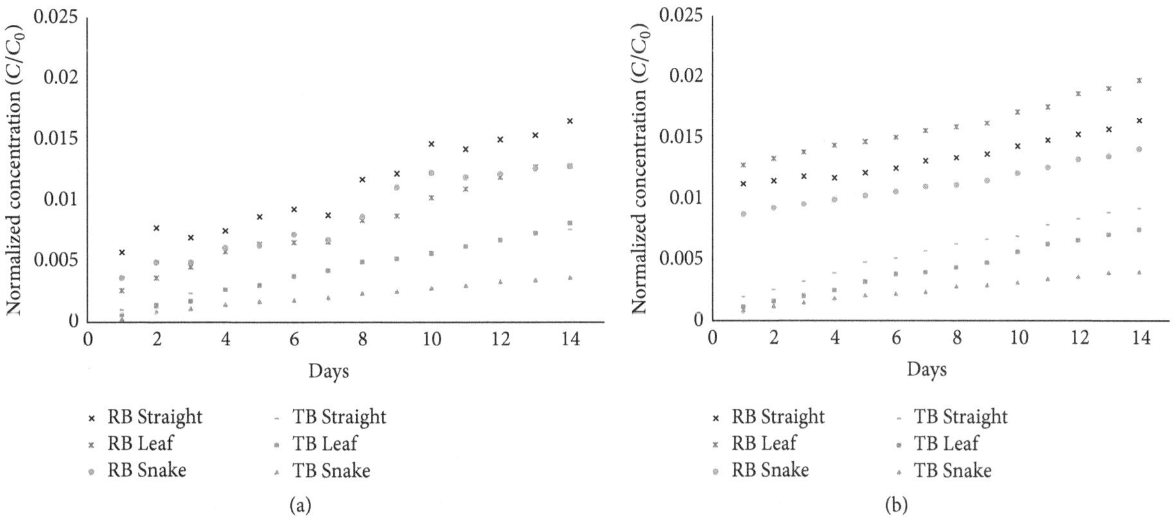

FIGURE 6: Normalized outlet concentration of Rhodamine B and Toluidine Blue as measured by UV-Vis spectrophotometer. (a) Release from hydrophilic devices. (b) Release from hydrophobic devices.

3.4. In Vitro Testing. The three channel geometries (Straight, Snake, and Leaf) were tested *in vitro* over a two-week period. While the PBS in the measurement cell of the device may not replicate the ocular fluid directly, the rate limiting step in consumption of the drug stems from the diffusion of the drug from the devices from the channel design, and not the diffusion of the drug from exit of the device to the final treatable area. Therefore, we feel that the measurement technique is valid for measuring cumulative delivery of the drug from each design. As with diffusion-limited delivery methods, a burst release was seen in the first 24 hours. After 24 hours, the devices reached steady-state delivery. The normalized amount of delivered model drugs for each design with each surface chemistry is shown in Figure 6, where C_0 denotes the initial concentration of the model drug in the device reservoir. As the diffusion of the dyes reached steady-state after 24 hours, the diffusion rates were calculated for both stages of the device (first 24 hours, after 24 hours). Delivery rates for the two stages of delivery are summarized in Table 3. Normalized release rates for both model drugs were examined for both hydrophilic and hydrophobic channels. While there are higher initial releases for all designs, release rates are on the same order of magnitude for three of the four device conditions. Hydrophilic devices as measured with RB showed considerable burst and may be from excess pressure in the reservoir when priming the devices, as the PDMS top layer is thin. The deformation of the top layer can provide an active pumping stage, which may be beneficial for applications requiring immediate relief. As the primary focus of this paper is to observe passive delivery, the ability for these devices to provide active pumping is outside of the scope of this paper and is being further investigated.

The steady-state delivery of each model drug was compared to the theoretical steady-state value for each design

Table 3: Normalized delivery rates for first 24 hours and following 13 days for each design and surface chemistry.

Device	Design	Day 1 (C/C_0 per day)	13-day average (C/C_0 per day)
TB	Straight	$1.25E-01$	$3.56E-02$
	Leaf	$7.22E-02$	$3.16E-02$
	Snake	$5.62E-02$	$1.52E-02$
TB-PEG	Straight	$6.44E-02$	$3.22E-02$
	Leaf	$4.00E-02$	$3.52E-02$
	Snake	$1.80E-02$	$1.56E-02$
RB	Straight	$8.98E-05$	$1.25E-05$
	Leaf	$4.06E-05$	$1.25E-05$
	Snake	$5.67E-05$	$1.25E-05$
RB-PEG	Straight	$1.76E-04$	$6.25E-06$
	Leaf	$1.99E-04$	$6.25E-06$
	Snake	$1.36E-04$	$6.25E-06$

Table 4: Comparison of measured *in vitro* rates to theoretical delivery rates for all geometries.

Device	Design	13 day measured average (C/C_0 per day)	Theoretical steady state approximation (SSA)	Average/SSA
TB	Straight	0.0713	0.7742	0.0921
	Leaf	0.0622	0.6636	0.0938
	Snake	0.0307	0.1037	0.2962
TB-PEG	Straight	0.0649	0.7742	0.0838
	Leaf	0.0735	0.6636	0.1108
	Snake	0.0334	0.1037	0.3217
RB	Straight	0.0012	0.003	0.3939
	Leaf	0.0014	0.0026	0.5385
	Snake	0.0018	0.0004	4.5263
RB-PEG	Straight	0.0009	0.003	0.2934
	Leaf	0.0011	0.0026	0.4129
	Snake	0.0008	0.0004	2.0449

(Table 4). The decreased delivery rate for the experimental testing can be attributed to the permeable nature of PDMS, as the channel walls were not solid boundaries as assumed in the steady-state analysis. This can be confirmed through the observation that the effective Toluidine Blue delivery was a lower percentage than the Rhodamine B delivery rate, as the smaller TB dye can diffuse through the PDMS more easily. While this effect will be minimized when using large molecule drugs, some treatments such as the fluocinolone acetonide (MW 452 g/mol) are small enough that these diffusion rates in the PDMS devices are not negligible. Controlling the delivery rate in future designs for diffusion-based drug delivery systems utilizing PDMS should primarily utilize decreasing channel dimensions as opposed to increasing channel lengths to limit drug release.

To correlate the delivery rates seen by the model dyes, rates of the proposed drugs were estimated by multiplying the delivery rate by the ratio of the diffusion coefficients. A table of the estimated drug delivery values is shown in Table 5. Hydrophobic Straight and Leaf designs were best suited for Lucentis and Intravitreal Avastin but did not meet the dosing accuracy of ±2% of the target dose. Currently, scaling of these devices is being explored for implantable devices and will be tested in the future.

4. Conclusions

Three microfluidic device designs were tested *in vitro* using two model drugs and compared to theoretical delivery rates. Three channel configurations were proposed to provide a wide range of drug delivery rates, while also examining the effect of surface wettability on delivery of these drugs. The devices were fabricated using soft lithography techniques and tested over a two-week period using Rhodamine B and Toluidine Blue as model drugs. Confirmation of PEG surface modification was observed through the decrease in contact angle from 113 ± 1.63° (PDMS) to 8.33 ± 1.24° (PEG). As observed previously from diffusion-controlled drug delivery systems, delivery rates from all designs provided a burst release during the first 24 hours and then reached a steady-state for the following 13 days. It was observed that altering the surface chemistry of these channels had no significant effect on the release kinetics of the model drugs from the devices, as well as not limiting the adsorption of the model drugs into the bulk device. An estimated delivery rate for a number of common drugs was approximated for each device through the ratio of the diffusion coefficients for the dye and the respective drug. The Straight and Leaf designs most closely matched the required dosages of Lucentis and

TABLE 5: Fraction of estimated delivered drug to required dosing rate for each design for commonly used drugs. Ratio is given by delivery drug/recommended dose.

Device	Design	Macugen	Lucentis	Intravitreal Avastin	Fluocinolone acetonide
TB	Straight	0.108	1.292	0.964	0.002
	Leaf	0.096	1.146	0.855	0.002
	Snake	0.046	0.551	0.411	0.001
TB-PEG	Straight	0.098	1.168	0.872	0.002
	Leaf	0.107	1.277	0.953	0.002
	Snake	0.047	0.566	0.422	0.001
RB	Straight	23.81	285.00	212.00	0.462
	Leaf	23.81	285.26	212.86	0.462
	Snake	23.81	285.26	212.86	0.462
RB-PEG	Straight	23.81	285.26	212.86	0.462
	Leaf	23.81	285.26	212.86	0.462
	Snake	23.81	285.26	212.86	0.462

Intravitreal Avastin. However, all three designs provided a constant delivery of the model drugs after 24 hours. Based on these results, scaling of these devices for an implantable model is currently under investigation.

Competing Interests

The authors declare that there is no conflict of interests regarding the publication of this paper.

Acknowledgments

The authors thank the NSF for funding this work through Grant NSF-1430374.

References

[1] R. Gaudana, J. Jwala, S. H. S. Boddu, and A. K. Mitra, "Recent perspectives in ocular drug delivery," *Pharmaceutical Research*, vol. 26, no. 5, pp. 1197–1216, 2009.

[2] D. H. Geroski and H. F. Edelhauser, "Drug delivery for posterior segment eye disease," *Investigative Ophthalmology & Visual Science*, vol. 41, no. 5, pp. 961–964, 2000.

[3] N. M. Bressler, S. B. Bressler, and S. L. Fine, "Age-related macular degeneration," *Survey of Ophthalmology*, vol. 32, no. 6, pp. 375–413, 1988.

[4] J.-H. Lee and R. M. Pidaparti, "An implantable device design concept for ocular drug delivery," in *Proceedings of the ASME Summer Bioengineering Conference: American Society of Mechanical Engineers*, pp. 1169–1170, Fajardo, Puerto Rico, June 2012.

[5] F. W. Fraunfelder and F. T. Fraunfelder, "Adverse ocular drug reactions recently identified by the National Registry of Drug-Induced Ocular Side Effects," *Ophthalmology*, vol. 111, no. 7, pp. 1275–1279, 2004.

[6] R. Lo, P.-Y. Li, S. Saati, R. N. Agrawal, M. S. Humayun, and E. Meng, "A passive MEMS drug delivery pump for treatment of ocular diseases," *Biomedical Microdevices*, vol. 11, no. 5, pp. 959–970, 2009.

[7] A. Patel, K. Cholkar, V. Agrahari, and A. K. Mitra, "Ocular drug delivery systems: an overview," *World Journal of Pharmacology*, vol. 2, no. 2, pp. 47–64, 2013.

[8] N. Haghjou, M. Soheilian, and M. J. Abdekhodaie, "Sustained release intraocular drug delivery devices for treatment of uveitis," *Journal of Ophthalmic & Vision Research*, vol. 6, no. 4, pp. 317–319, 2011.

[9] D. C. Duffy, J. C. McDonald, O. J. A. Schueller, and G. M. Whitesides, "Rapid prototyping of microfluidic systems in poly(dimethylsiloxane)," *Analytical Chemistry*, vol. 70, no. 23, pp. 4974–4984, 1998.

[10] S. K. Sia and G. M. Whitesides, "Microfluidic devices fabricated in poly(dimethylsiloxane) for biological studies," *Electrophoresis*, vol. 24, no. 21, pp. 3563–3576, 2003.

[11] D. Bodas and C. Khan-Malek, "Hydrophilization and hydrophobic recovery of PDMS by oxygen plasma and chemical treatment—an SEM investigation," *Sensors and Actuators B: Chemical*, vol. 123, no. 1, pp. 368–373, 2007.

[12] C.-C. Wu, C.-Y. Yuan, and S.-J. Ding, "Effect of polydimethylsiloxane surfaces silanized with different nitrogen-containing groups on the adhesion progress of epithelial cells," *Surface and Coatings Technology*, vol. 205, no. 10, pp. 3182–3189, 2011.

[13] A.-J. Wang, J.-J. Feng, and J. Fan, "Covalent modified hydrophilic polymer brushes onto poly(dimethylsiloxane) microchannel surface for electrophoresis separation of amino acids," *Journal of Chromatography A*, vol. 1192, no. 1, pp. 173–179, 2008.

[14] I. Wong and C.-M. Ho, "Surface molecular property modifications for poly(dimethylsiloxane) (PDMS) based microfluidic devices," *Microfluidics and Nanofluidics*, vol. 7, no. 3, pp. 291–306, 2009.

[15] S. Thorslund, J. Sanchez, R. Larsson, F. Nikolajeff, and J. Bergquist, "Bioactive heparin immobilized onto microfluidic channels in poly(dimethylsiloxane) results in hydrophilic surface properties," *Colloids and Surfaces B: Biointerfaces*, vol. 46, no. 4, pp. 240–247, 2005.

[16] K. M. Kovach, M. A. LaBarbera, M. C. Moyer et al., "*In vitro* evaluation and *in vivo* demonstration of a biomimetic, hemocompatible, microfluidic artificial lung," *Lab on a Chip*, vol. 15, no. 5, pp. 1366–1375, 2015.

[17] K. M. Kovach, J. R. Capadona, A. S. Gupta, and J. A. Potkay, "The effects of PEG-based surface modification of PDMS

microchannels on long-term hemocompatibility," *Journal of Biomedical Materials Research—Part A*, vol. 102, no. 12, pp. 4195–4205, 2014.

[18] V. Sharma, M. Dhayal, Govind, S. M. Shivaprasad, and S. C. Jain, "Surface characterization of plasma-treated and PEG-grafted PDMS for micro fluidic applications," *Vacuum*, vol. 81, no. 9, pp. 1094–1100, 2007.

[19] Z. Zhang, J. Borenstein, L. Guiney, R. Miller, S. Sukavaneshvar, and C. Loose, "Polybetaine modification of PDMS microfluidic devices to resist thrombus formation in whole blood," *Lab on a Chip*, vol. 13, no. 10, pp. 1963–1968, 2013.

[20] S. Swanson, "Selective MRI and MRS of PEGylated compounds," in *Proceedings of the 14th Scientific Meeting International Society for Magnetic Resonance in Medicine*, p. 1848, 2006.

[21] S. A. Molokhia, H. Sant, J. Simonis et al., "The capsule drug device: novel approach for drug delivery to the eye," *Vision Research*, vol. 50, no. 7, pp. 680–685, 2010.

[22] R. M. Pidaparti, J.-H. Lee, and H. Yang, "Micro-channel diffusion characteristics of an implantable drug delivery device for age-related macular degeneration," *Microsystem Technologies*, vol. 21, no. 9, pp. 1967–1974, 2015.

[23] T. Li, D. O. Kildsig, and K. Park, "Computer simulation of molecular diffusion in amorphous polymers," *Journal of Controlled Release*, vol. 48, no. 1, pp. 57–66, 1997.

[24] G. J. Jaffe, C. H. Yang, H. Guo, J. P. Denny, C. Lima, and P. Ashton, "Safety and pharmacokinetics of an intraocular fluocinolone acetonide sustained delivery device," *Investigative Ophthalmology and Visual Science*, vol. 41, no. 11, pp. 3569–3575, 2000.

[25] P.-O. Gendron, F. Avaltroni, and K. J. Wilkinson, "Diffusion coefficients of several rhodamine derivatives as determined by pulsed field gradient-nuclear magnetic resonance and fluorescence correlation spectroscopy," *Journal of Fluorescence*, vol. 18, no. 6, pp. 1093–1101, 2008.

[26] S. Swanson, "Selective MRI and MRS of PEGylated compounds," in *Proceedings of the 14th Scientific Meeting of the International Society for Magnetic Resonance in Medicine*, May 2006.

[27] S. Bhattacharya, A. Datta, J. M. Berg, and S. Gangopadhyay, "Studies on surface wettability of poly(dimethyl) siloxane (PDMS) and glass under oxygen-plasma treatment and correlation with bond strength," *Journal of Microelectromechanical Systems*, vol. 14, no. 3, pp. 590–597, 2005.

[28] P. Bartasun, H. Cieśliński, A. Bujacz, A. Wierzbicka-Woś, and J. Kur, "A study on the interaction of rhodamine B with methylthioadenosine phosphorylase protein sourced from an antarctic soil metagenomic library," *PLoS ONE*, vol. 8, no. 1, Article ID e55697, 2013.

[29] C. F. H. Allen, G. F. Frame, and C. V. Wilson, "The structure of the so-called Toluidine Blue," *Journal of Organic Chemistry*, vol. 6, no. 5, pp. 732–749, 1941.

10

Solid Lipid Nanoparticles Improve the Diclofenac Availability in Vitreous after Intraocular Injection

Mojtaba Abrishami,[1,2] Majid Abrishami,[1] Asma Mahmoudi,[3] Navid Mosallaei,[3] Mohammad Vakili Ahrari Roodi,[3] and Bizhan Malaekeh-Nikouei[4]

[1] *Retina Research Center, School of Medicine, Mashhad University of Medical Sciences, Mashhad, Iran*
[2] *Eye Research Center, Farabi Eye Hospital, Tehran University of Medical Sciences, Tehran, Iran*
[3] *School of Pharmacy, Mashhad University of Medical Sciences, Mashhad, Iran*
[4] *Nanotechnology Research Center, School of Pharmacy, Mashhad University of Medical Sciences, Mashhad, Iran*

Correspondence should be addressed to Bizhan Malaekeh-Nikouei; malaekehb@mums.ac.ir

Academic Editor: Roberta Cavalli

Purpose. In order to improve the drug availability after intravitreal administration, solid lipid nanoparticles (SLNs) containing diclofenac were prepared. *Methods.* In this experimental study, 18 albino rabbits were included. In right and left eyes of all rabbits, SLNs containing diclofenac and commercial form of diclofenac (0.3 mg drug) were intravitreally injected, respectively. One, four, twelve, twenty-four, and forty-eight hours after injection, vitreous and aqueous humor samples were obtained in all cases. Then, the concentration of diclofenac sodium was evaluated in all samples. *Results.* Size of nanoparticles was around 170 nm after preparation. Drug concentration in eyes injected with SLNs was significantly higher than left eyes injected with commercial formulation up to 4 hours after intravitreal injection ($p < 0.05$). Diclofenac was quantified in samples up to 48 hours after intraocular injection. Four hours after intravitreal injection, the concentration of diclofenac in vitreous and aqueous humor of eyes receiving SLNs was, respectively, 2.5 and 6.5 times higher than eyes injected with commercial form of drug. *Conclusions.* Here, we demonstrate the potential of SLNs as a carrier of diclofenac for intraocular injection in order to prevent the systemic effects of the drug, increase the injection intervals, and improve the patient compliance.

1. Introduction

Diclofenac sodium is an analgesic and anti-inflammatory drug administrable through various dosage forms such as oral, topical, parenteral, suppositories, and eye drops. Recently, diclofenac is used as an intravitreal injection in order to maintain a high intravitreal dose of the drug in naive diabetic macular edema [1], refractory uveitic cystoid macular edema [2], and uveitic cystoid macular edema [3]. Because of restricted half-life of drug after intravitreal administration, achievement of novel drug delivery systems containing this drug for intraocular injection could be a big help in the prevention of local and systemic effects of the drug. Also any increase in the injection intervals improves the patient compliance.

Solid lipid nanoparticles (SLNs) are made of solid lipids with size ranging from 50 to 1000 nm [4]. These nanoparticles have high loading capacity for lipophilic molecules. Chemical protection of labile drug against degradation, high physical stability, easy scaling of the production, and sustained drug release profile are some of the advantages of these colloidal carrier systems [5, 6].

Solid lipid nanoparticles as carrier of diclofenac sodium were used in the study of Attama et al. [7]. These nanoparticles were prepared in order to increase the permeation of ketorolac and diclofenac sodium through cornea. The results of permeation studies showed that the amount of permeated drug was higher at higher drug loading. Efficacy and pharmacokinetics of ketorolac and diclofenac after intraocular injection of the commercial formulation were evaluated in the study of Barañano et al. [8]. The potent anti-inflammatory effect of these drugs after intraocular injection was reported in this study. Also, good penetration of ketorolac and diclofenac into the retina/choroid and rapid clearance of them by 48 h after intravitreal injection were demonstrated.

Intraocular injections have been developed as a method of drug delivery in the treatment of diseases of the retina and macula. Recently, intraocular injection of diclofenac has been considered in these cases. Some studies have shown that this drug is safe for injection into the eye, and fewer complications have reported after intraocular injections compared to corticosteroids such as triamcinolone [3, 9, 10]. The aim of the present study was to prepare SLNs containing diclofenac in order to increase drug residence time after intraocular injection. So, these nanoparticles were prepared and characterized and the kinetics of drug after intraocular injection was evaluated.

2. Materials and Methods

2.1. Materials. Compritol 888 ATO and Precirol 5 ATO were kindly offered by Gattefosse (France). Hydrogenated soy PC (H-SPC) was purchased from Lipoid (Germany). Poloxamer 188 was provided by Sigma (Germany). Diclofenac sodium injection was from Exir Pharmaceutical Company (Borujerd, Iran), and diclofenac sodium powder was kindly offered by Sobhan Pharmaceutical Company (Rasht, Iran).

2.2. Preparation of SLNs Containing Diclofenac. In the first step, diclofenac base (diclofenac acid) was prepared by acidification of an aqueous solution of diclofenac sodium and extraction by chloroform [11]. SLNs containing diclofenac were produced using microemulsion method [12]. Lipid phase was composed of Compritol : Precirol : H-SPC (3 : 5.5 : 1). Diclofenac was added to lipid phase. This phase was melted in 90°C and homogenized using high-speed homogenizer (Ultra-Turrax, IKA, Germany) (20000 rpm, 10 min). Then, isothermal aqueous phase containing 5% w/v Poloxamer 188 as nonionic polymeric stabilizer was added to melted lipid phase. The resulted preemulsion was kept in 25°C for 2 hr and then in 4°C for 24 hr. The preemulsion was heated to 40°C and ultrasonicated in 5 and 10 cycles of 1 min on –1 min off using probe sonicator (MSE, UK).

2.3. Characterization of SLNs Containing Diclofenac. The mean size, polydispersity index (PDI), and zeta potential of the prepared SLNs were measured by Zetasizer Nano ZS (Malvern, Worcestershire, UK) after suitable dilution of samples. Size and zeta potential were measured on the basis of Dynamic Light Scattering and Laser Doppler Velocimetry, respectively.

HPLC was used for quantitation of diclofenac base or diclofenac sodium in samples. Calibration curve was plotted in concentration range of 0.02–50 μg/mL. The HPLC condition was as below:

> column (4.6 mm × 250 mm reverse phase stainless steel C18 column), mobile phase (Acetonitrile : Acetic Acid, 60 : 40), flow rate (1 mL/min), and measurement wavelength (270 nm) (retention time of drug in the mentioned condition was 8 min).

To determine the encapsulation efficacy (EE) of drug, desired amount of lyophilized SLNs was weighed and dissolved in chloroform : methanol (1 : 1 v/v) to produce concentration of 0.1 mg/mL if EE was 100%. Twenty μL of clear solution was injected to HPLC, and the real concentration of diclofenac in sample was detected using calibration curve. EE was determined using following formula:

$$\mathrm{EE\%} = \frac{\text{actual diclofenac concentration in sample}}{\text{input diclofenac concentration}} \times 100. \quad (1)$$

2.4. Animal Studies. New Zealand albino rabbits weighing 1.8 to 2.0 kg were used in the study. Rabbits were sedated with 60 mg/kg of intramuscular ketamine hydrochloride and 6 mg/mL of intramuscular xylazine hydrochloride. Eyes were anesthetized with topical administration of 1% tetracaine ophthalmic drop. Before the injection, povidone iodine 5% was applied on the surface of the eye for 2 minutes. After washing with balanced salt solution, the eyes of each rabbit received an intravitreal injection of 0.3 mg diclofenac, 2.5 mm behind the limbus in the superotemporal quadrant using a 30-gauge needle. The left eyes were injected with diclofenac sodium (commercial formulation) injection, and right eyes received SLNs containing diclofenac. Eyes were repeatedly monitored for signs of inflammation. Rabbits (3 in each group) were sacrificed at 1, 4, 12, 24, and 48 hours after the intravitreal injection by CO_2 inhalation. Three animals were used as control (no treatment).

In both eyes, aqueous humor was aspirated with a 30-gauge needle via an anterior limbal paracentesis. Then, the whole of the vitreous was aspirated through incision 4 mm from the limbus. The aqueous humor and vitreous were then immediately frozen at −80°C. Before analysis, the frozen aqueous humor and vitreous were defrosted overnight at 4°C. The next day, samples were centrifuged at 14000 rpm for 30 minutes. Diclofenac sodium concentrations were measured in whole vitreous and aqueous fluid by HPLC. The animal protocol was approved by the Ethical Committee of Mashhad University of Medical Sciences (Mashhad, Iran).

2.5. Statistical Analysis. All statistical analysis was done by one-way ANOVA test. Mean ± SD was compared using InStat software (version 3.1). The p value less than 0.05 considered to be statistically significant.

3. Results

Table 1 shows the characteristics of SLNs containing diclofenac. Size of nanoparticles was around 170 nm after preparation. Zeta potential of prepared nanoparticles was neutral and almost all diclofenac was encapsulated in SLNs. After storage of nanoparticles at 2–8°C, size of nanoparticles was increased, but zeta potential remained unchanged. Loading efficiency

Table 1: Mean size, polydispersity index (PDI), zeta potential, and encapsulation efficiency of solid lipid nanoparticles containing diclofenac after preparation and two-month storage at 2–8°C (mMean ± SD, $n = 3$).

	After preparation	After one month	After two months
Mean size (nm)	172.7 ± 6.3	216.4 ± 10.2	269.5 ± 2.8
PDI	0.254 ± 0.001	0.184 ± 0.044	0.150 ± 0.083
Zeta potential (mV)	−0.9 ± 2.0	−1.5 ± 0.5	0.5 ± 1.3
Encapsulation efficiency (%)	95.1 ± 4.2	98.2 ± 0.8	98.0 ± 2.4

Table 2: Concentration of diclofenac (μg/mL) in vitreous and aqueous humor samples after intravitreal injection of solid lipid nanoparticles containing diclofenac (mean ± SD, $n = 3$). Right eyes and left eyes were injected with solid lipid nanoparticles containing diclofenac and diclofenac commercial injection, respectively (dose = 0.3 mg).

Time (hour)	Vitreous samples		Aqueous humor samples	
	Right eyes	Left eyes	Right eyes	Left eyes
1	88.94 ± 13.03	33.47 ± 22.45	10.220 ± 4.943	1.564 ± 0.547
4	58.93 ± 17.86	3.87 ± 2.11	8.661 ± 3.419	1.988 ± 1.469
12	1.94 ± 1.31	0.30 ± 0.22	0.200 ± 0.102	0.181 ± 0.109
24	0.24 ± 0.14	0.12 ± 0.07	0.133 ± 0.041	0.113 ± 0.084
48	0.14 ± 0.01	0.09 ± 0.06	0.076 ± 0.023	0.008 ± 0.007

of drug in prepared SLNs was almost unchanged after two months of storage.

Variation of drug concentration in vitreous and aqueous humor samples after intravitreal injection of SLNs containing diclofenac was summarized in Table 2. Drug concentration in eyes injected with SLNs was significantly higher than left eyes injected with commercial product up to 4 hours after intravitreal injection ($p < 0.05$). Diclofenac was quantified in samples up to 48 hours after intraocular injection. Four hours after intravitreal injection, concentration of diclofenac in vitreous and aqueous humor of eyes that received SLNs was, respectively, 2.5 and 6.5 times higher than the eyes injected with commercial form of drug.

4. Discussion

In the present study, SLNs as carrier of diclofenac have been prepared and characterized. SLNs were used as carrier of this drug due to some advantages such as maintaining drug concentration in therapeutic range for a long time, reduction of ocular toxicity, and slow and controlled drug release. In order to increase the drug residence time in vitreous, application of colloidal carrier system has been evaluated in previous studies [13–15]. Different drug carriers such as liposomes [16], microspheres [17], thermogel [18], and insert [19] have been used. For example, Abrishami and his colleagues [16] have evaluated *in vitro* and *in vivo* characteristics of bevacizumab nanoliposomes. After the intraocular injection of liposomal formulation, vitreal concentration of drug was higher compared to the injection of commercial form in different times even 42 days after injection. Nanoliposomal formulation provided more stable concentration for a longer time.

SLNs have been used as a suitable carrier for encapsulation of hydrophobic drugs, but most of hydrophilic drugs had low encapsulation efficiency due to hydrophobic nature of SLNs matrix [20]. Encapsulation efficiency of nanoformulations is affected by different factors including preparation method, nature of drug, and other formulation ingredients. To solve the problem of poor encapsulation of drugs in SLNs, different strategies have been used to improve the liposolubility of drugs. In the present study, we used diclofenac base instead of diclofenac sodium. Almost all of feed diclofenac was loaded into SLNs matrix.

In the study of Barañano et al. [8], pharmacokinetic evaluation of diclofenac sodium commercial formulation showed the rapid clearance of this drug after intravitreal injection. No drug was detected 24 and 48 hours after intraocular injection of 0.3 mg diclofenac sodium. But, in the present study, concentration of diclofenac sodium after intraocular injection of both commercial and SLN formulation was determined in vitreous and aqueous humor samples until 48 hours after intraocular administration. This difference can be related to the sensitivity of analysis method.

On the other hand, differences observed between SLN and commercial formulation showed that SLN could be a choice of slow-release formulation for ocular drug delivery. This kind of formulation provided longer appropriate therapeutic concentration in eye. In addition, drug concentration in vitreous and aqueous humor was evaluated in the present study, but the concentration in other parts of eye (e.g., cornea, iris, ciliary body, conjunctiva, sclera, and retina) was not determined. So, the reported concentration may be lower than the real concentration in eye. It has been shown that basic and lipophilic drugs could attach to melanin [21]. This attachment significantly reduces pharmacological activity of drugs [22]. So, melanin in the iris and ciliary body may change drug concentration in posterior [23] and inferior parts of eyes [24]. Determination of drug concentration in the other parts of eye is suggested for future studies.

5. Conclusion

Results showed that SLN formulation could provide higher vitreous and aqueous humor concentration for a longer time in rabbit eye compared to commercial formulation. SLN formulation can increase intraocular injection intervals and decrease the drug toxicity due to multiple drug administration.

Disclosure

The results described in this paper were part of a PharmD student thesis.

Competing Interests

The authors declare that there is no conflict of interests regarding this study.

Acknowledgments

This work was supported financially by a research grant from the Vice Chancellor for Research of Mashhad University of Medical Sciences, Mashhad, Iran.

References

[1] M. Soheilian, S. Karimi, A. Ramezani et al., "Intravitreal diclofenac versus intravitreal bevacizumab in naive diabetic macular edema: a randomized double-masked clinical trial," *International Ophthalmology*, vol. 35, no. 3, pp. 421–428, 2015.

[2] A. Ramezani, N. F. Esmaeilpour, A. Eskandari, Z. Rabbanikhah, R. Soheilian, and M. Soheilian, "Intravitreal diclofenac for refractory uveitic cystoid macular edema," *Journal of Ophthalmic and Vision Research*, vol. 8, no. 1, pp. 47–52, 2013.

[3] M. Soheilian, A. Eskandari, A. Ramezani, Z. Rabbanikhah, and R. Soheilian, "A pilot study of intravitreal diclofenac versus intravitreal triamcinolone for uveitic cystoid macular edema," *Ocular Immunology and Inflammation*, vol. 21, no. 2, pp. 124–129, 2013.

[4] R. H. Müller, K. Mäder, and S. Gohla, "Solid lipid nanoparticles (SLN) for controlled drug delivery—a review of the state of the art," *European Journal of Pharmaceutics and Biopharmaceutics*, vol. 50, no. 1, pp. 161–177, 2000.

[5] S. Mukherjee, S. Ray, and R. S. Thakur, "Solid lipid nanoparticles: a modern formulation approach in drug delivery system," *Indian Journal of Pharmaceutical Sciences*, vol. 71, no. 4, pp. 349–358, 2009.

[6] W. Mehnert and K. Mäder, "Solid lipid nanoparticles: production, characterization and applications," *Advanced Drug Delivery Reviews*, vol. 47, no. 2-3, pp. 165–196, 2001.

[7] A. A. Attama, S. Reichl, and C. C. Müller-Goymann, "Diclofenac sodium delivery to the eye: in vitro evaluation of novel solid lipid nanoparticle formulation using human cornea construct," *International Journal of Pharmaceutics*, vol. 355, no. 1-2, pp. 307–313, 2008.

[8] D. E. Barañano, S. J. Kim, H. F. Edelhauser, C. Durairaj, U. B. Kompella, and J. T. Handa, "Efficacy and pharmacokinetics of intravitreal nonsteroidal anti-inflammatory drugs for intraocular inflammation," *British Journal of Ophthalmology*, vol. 93, no. 10, pp. 1387–1390, 2009.

[9] M. Soheilian, A. Eskandari, A. Ramezani, Z. Rabbanikhah, and R. Soheilian, "A pilot study of intravitreal diclofenac versus intravitreal triamcinolone for uveitic cystoid macular edema," *Ocular Immunology and Inflammation*, vol. 21, no. 2, pp. 124–129, 2013.

[10] S. J. Kim, N. A. Adams, H. S. Toma et al., "Safety of intravitreal ketorolac and diclofenac: an electroretinographic and histopathologic study," *Retina*, vol. 28, no. 4, pp. 595–605, 2008.

[11] S. A. Mohajeri, B. Malaekeh-Nikouei, and H. Sadegh, "Development of a pH-responsive drug delivery system for diclofenac using molecularly imprinted polymers," *Drug Development and Industrial Pharmacy*, vol. 38, pp. 616–622, 2012.

[12] N. Mosallaei, M. R. Jaafari, M. Y. Hanafi-Bojd, S. Golmohammadzadeh, and B. Malaekeh-Nikouei, "Docetaxel-loaded solid lipid nanoparticles: preparation, characterization, in vitro, and in vivo evaluations," *Journal of Pharmaceutical Sciences*, vol. 102, no. 6, pp. 1994–2004, 2013.

[13] A. Bochot and E. Fattal, "Liposomes for intravitreal drug delivery: a state of the art," *Journal of Controlled Release*, vol. 161, no. 2, pp. 628–634, 2012.

[14] S. G. Schwartz, I. U. Scott, H. W. Flynn Jr., and M. W. Stewart, "Drug delivery techniques for treating age-related macular degeneration," *Expert Opinion on Drug Delivery*, vol. 11, no. 1, pp. 61–68, 2014.

[15] B. Guidetti, J. Azéma, M. Malet-Martino, and R. Martino, "Delivery systems for the treatment of proliferative vitreoretinopathy: materials, devices and colloidal carriers," *Current Drug Delivery*, vol. 5, no. 1, pp. 7–19, 2008.

[16] M. Abrishami, S. Zarei-Ghanavati, D. Soroush, M. Rouhbakhsh, M. R. Jaafari, and B. Malaekeh-Nikouei, "Preparation, characterization, and in vivo evaluation of nanoliposomes-encapsulated bevacizumab (avastin) for intravitreal administration," *Retina*, vol. 29, no. 5, pp. 699–703, 2009.

[17] S. Zarei-Ghanavati, B. Malaekeh-Nikouei, R. Pourmazar, and S. Seyedi, "Preparation, characterization, and in vivo evaluation of triamcinolone acetonide microspheres after intravitreal administration," *Journal of Ocular Pharmacology and Therapeutics*, vol. 28, no. 5, pp. 502–506, 2012.

[18] L. Zhang, W. Shen, J. Luan et al., "Sustained intravitreal delivery of dexamethasone using an injectable and biodegradable thermogel," *Acta Biomaterialia*, vol. 23, pp. 271–281, 2015.

[19] M. A. Sadiq, A. Agarwal, M. K. Soliman et al., "Sustained-release fluocinolone acetonide intravitreal insert for macular edema: clinical pharmacology and safety evaluation," *Expert Opinion on Drug Safety*, vol. 14, no. 7, pp. 1147–1156, 2015.

[20] D. Liu, L. Chen, S. Jiang et al., "Formulation and characterization of hydrophilic drug diclofenac sodium-loaded solid lipid nanoparticles based on phospholipid complexes technology," *Journal of Liposome Research*, vol. 24, no. 1, pp. 17–26, 2014.

[21] B. Leblanc, S. Jezequel, T. Davies, G. Hanton, and C. Taradach, "Binding of drugs to eye melanin is not predictive of ocular toxicity," *Regulatory Toxicology and Pharmacology*, vol. 28, no. 2, pp. 124–132, 1998.

[22] R. D. Schoenwald, V. Tandon, D. E. Wurster, and C. F. Barfknecht, "Significance of melanin binding and metabolism in the activity of 5-acetoxyacetylimino-4-methyl-Δ^2-1,3,4,-thiadiazoline-2-sulfonamide," *European Journal of Pharmaceutics and Biopharmaceutics*, vol. 46, no. 1, pp. 39–50, 1998.

[23] M. J. Koeberle, P. M. Hughes, G. G. Skellern, and C. G. Wilson, "Pharmacokinetics and disposition of memantine in the arterially perfused bovine eye," *Pharmaceutical Research*, vol. 23, no. 12, pp. 2781–2798, 2006.

[24] L. Pitkänen, V.-P. Ranta, H. Moilanen, and A. Urtti, "Binding of betaxolol, metoprolol and oligonucleotides to synthetic and bovine ocular melanin, and prediction of drug binding to melanin in human choroid-retinal pigment epithelium," *Pharmaceutical Research*, vol. 24, no. 11, pp. 2063–2070, 2007.

11

Characterization and Compatibility Studies of Different Rate Retardant Polymer Loaded Microspheres by Solvent Evaporation Technique: *In Vitro-In Vivo* Study of Vildagliptin as a Model Drug

Irin Dewan,[1,2] Swarnali Islam,[2] and Md. Sohel Rana[1]

[1]*Department of Pharmacy, Jahangirnagar University, Savar 1342, Dhaka, Bangladesh*
[2]*Department of Pharmacy, University of Asia Pacific, Dhanmondi, Dhaka 1209, Bangladesh*

Correspondence should be addressed to Irin Dewan; irin_d@yahoo.com

Academic Editor: Carla Caramella

The present study has been performed to microencapsulate the antidiabetic drug of Vildagliptin to get sustained release of drug. The attempt of this study was to formulate and evaluate the Vildagliptin loaded microspheres by emulsion solvent evaporation technique using different polymers like Eudragit RL100, Eudragit RS100, Ethyl cellulose, and Methocel K100M. *In vitro* dissolution studies were carried out in 0.1 N HCl for 8 hours according to USP paddle method. The maximum and minimum drug release were observed as 92.5% and 68.5% from microspheres, respectively, after 8 hours. Release kinetics were studied in different mathematical release models to find out the linear relationship and release rate of drug. The SEM, DSC, and FTIR studies have been done to confirm good spheres and smooth surface as well as interaction along with drug and polymer. In this experiment, it is difficult to explain the exact mechanism of drug release. But the drug might be released by both diffusion and erosion as the correlation coefficient (R^2) best fitted with Korsmeyer model and release exponent (n) was 0.45–0.89. At last it can be concluded that all *in vitro* and *in vivo* experiments exhibited promising result to treat type II diabetes mellitus with Vildagliptin microspheres.

1. Introduction

Vildagliptin is a potent, selective, and orally active dipeptidyl peptidase-4 (DPP-4) inhibitor, which prevents inactivation of incretion hormones by inhibiting DPP-4. It has been shown to be an effective and safe option for better glycemic control in a wide range of T2DM patients and has demonstrated HbA1C lowering potential when given as monotherapy or in combination with other OADs, without weight gain and minimal hypoglycemia [1]. Drugs like sulfonylureas, meglitinides, and insulin are associated with weight gain and hypoglycemia; thiazolidinediones (TZDs) cause weight gain and possibly peripheral edema. Metformin and a-glucosidase inhibitors are associated with gut-related side effects. Additionally, the impact of different drugs, even within a single class, on the risk of long-term vascular complications has recently come under scrutiny [2]. Its biological half-life is 1 to 3 hrs as a consequence; it requires repeated administration to keep plasma concentration. This causes bother to the patient and also leads to fluctuations in plasma drug concentration so that it might reduce the therapeutic effect. But advanced controlled release forms enhance patient compliance by reducing frequency of dosing. Therefore, development of Vildagliptin sustained release dosage forms is desirable to achieve a more effective therapy avoiding the large fluctuations in drug concentration and consequently reduction in adverse effects and to reduce the need of several administrations.

Microspheres constitute an important part of this particulate drug delivery system by virtue of their small size and efficient carrier characteristics. However, the success of this novel drug delivery system is limited due to their short residence time at the site of absorption. It would therefore be advantageous to have means for providing intimate contact of the drug delivery system with absorbing gastric mucosal membranes. Along with a range of methods developed designed for formulation of microspheres, emulsion solvent evaporation technique is one of the typically extensively used ones because of its simplicity of fabrication devoid of compromising the action of drug [3]. This method facilitates altering the liquids to solids, by considering the colloidal and surface properties, as long as there is environmental protection, and controlling the liberate distinctiveness of unlikely coated materials. This has been made by developing the new drug entities, discovering of new polymeric materials that are appropriate for prolonging the drug release and safety and improvement in therapeutic efficacy. In general the size of the microencapsulated products is considered as larger than 1 micrometer and up to 1000 micrometers in diameter [4].

Ethyl cellulose, a nonbiodegradable and biocompatible polymer, one of the extensively studied encapsulating materials for the controlled release of pharmaceuticals, was preferred as the retardant material. Methacrylate copolymers (Eudragits) have recently received increased consideration for modified dosage forms because of their inertness, solubility in relatively nontoxic solvents, and availability of resins with different properties. In the present investigation Eudragit RL is used as a rate retardant polymer. Eudragit RL is a water insoluble polymer which is widely used as a wall material for controlled release microparticles. The permeability of Eudragit RS and Eudragit RL in aqueous media is due to the presence of quaternary ammonium groups in their structure; Eudragit RL has a greater proportion of these groups and as such is more permeable than Eudragit RS [5].

The primary view of the present effort was to prepare and estimate oral controlled release microparticulate drug delivery system of Vildagliptin using different polymers by water-in-oil emulsion solvent diffusion method by means of high entrapment capacity and extended release. Moreover, such small single units enable more reproducible dispersion throughout the gastrointestinal tract leading to reduction of drug release variations and improved bioavailability. Multiple-unit system generally disperses freely in the gastrointestinal fluids, maximizes absorption, minimizes side effects, and reduces inter- and intrapatient variability.

2. Materials and Methods

2.1. Materials. Materials were Vildagliptin as donation sample from Eskayef Bangladesh Limited, Ethyl cellulose (Colorcon Asia Pvt. Limited, India), Eudragit RS100 (Evonik, Germany), Eudragit RL100 (Evonik, Germany), magnesium stearate (Merck, Germany), Ethanol (Merck, Germany), Dichloromethane (Merck, Germany), light liquid paraffin, Tween 80 (Merck, Germany), cyclohexane (Merck, Germany), sodium hydroxide (Merck, Germany), potassium dihydrogen phosphate (Merck, Germany), *n*-hexane (Merck, Germany), and so forth.

2.2. Method

2.2.1. Preparation of Vildagliptin Microspheres by Emulsion Solvent Evaporation Technique. The microspheres were prepared according to Table 1 by solvent evaporation method. The process was initiated from dispersion of Vildagliptin in 70 mL of light liquid paraffin (LLP) using 1% Tween 80. At first, LLP was emulsified in plastic beaker with Tween 80 for few minutes with the help of stirrer at 500 rpm. By this time the polymer solution (internal phase) was prepared by dissolving properly weighed polymer(s) in combination of Ethanol and Dichloromethane at a ratio of 5 : 5 in volumetric flask. Then appropriately weighed drug was added in the internal phase slowly and stirred for 20–30 minutes. After proper mixing prepared polymeric phase was added dropwise to the external phase. Stirring was performed for 2.5 hours. After stirring, the microspheres were decanted and washed by *n*-hexane and allowed to dry in natural air. The microspheres were transferred to glass vials and placed in the desiccators for further experiment as shown in Figure 1.

2.3. Preparation of Standard Curve of Pure Vildagliptin. At first 20 mg of Vildagliptin was taken in 100 mL volumetric flask and dissolved in 100 mL 0.1 N HCl and taken into sonicator for 10 minutes. Then 10 mL of the previous solution was taken in another 100 mL volumetric flask and diluted up to 100 mL with 0.1 N HCl and kept as stock solution. Then 1 mL, 2 mL, 3 mL, 4 mL, 5 mL, 6 mL, 7 mL, 8 mL, 9 mL, and 10 mL of stock solution were taken in ten different 10 mL volumetric flasks and diluted all up to 10 mL with 0.1 N HCl. Thus the concentrations of solution ranging from 2 μg/mL to 20 μg/mL were obtained. Finally different concentrations solutions were analyzed by spectrophotometry at 210 nm.

2.4. Assay Methods of Prepared Microspheres by Emulsion Solvent Evaporation Technique. Approximately 50 mg of Vildagliptin microspheres was taken in 100 mL volumetric flask and dissolved with minimum quantity of Ethanol. After that 25 mL of 0.1 N HCl was added and sonicated for 30 minutes to make clear solution. Then the solution was finally filtered. Absorbance value was determined using UV spectrophotometer at wavelength of 210 nm. Using the absorbance value, the amount of Vildagliptin entrapped was determined with the help of standard curve. Percent drug loading and drug entrapment efficiency were calculated by using the following equation:

$$\begin{aligned} &\%\text{ drug loading} \\ &\quad = \left(\frac{\text{Actual drug loading}}{\text{Weighed quantity of microspheres}}\right) \times 100, \\ &\text{Drug entrapment efficiency (\%)} \\ &\quad = \left(\frac{\text{Actual drug loading}}{\text{Theoretical drug loading}}\right) \times 100. \end{aligned} \tag{1}$$

2.5. In Vitro Release Study of Vildagliptin Microspheres Prepared by Emulsion Solvent Evaporation Technique. In vitro dissolution study was performed in paddle type dissolution apparatus. At first 900 mL of 0.1 N HCl was used as dissolution media, paddle speed was 100 rpm, and temperature was maintained fixed at 37°C. Approximately 20 mg equivalent amount of Vildagliptin microspheres from each batch was taken into size 2 capsule shell and transferred in each dissolution basket. The dissolution process was carried out

TABLE 1: Formulation of Vildagliptin microspheres prepared by emulsion solvent evaporation technique.

Formulation code	Polymers (mg)			
	D : EURS100 : EC	D : EURL100 : EC	D : EURS100 : MK100M	D : EURL100 : MK100M
VF1	1 : 1 : 1	—	—	—
VF2	1 : 1 : 2	—	—	—
VF3	1 : 1 : 3	—	—	—
VF4	—	1 : 1 : 1	—	—
VF5	—	1 : 1 : 2	—	—
VF6	—	1 : 1 : 3	—	—
VF10	—	—	1 : 1 : 1	—
VF11	—	—	1 : 1 : 2	—
VF12	—	—	1 : 1 : 3	—
VF13	—	—	—	1 : 1 : 1
VF14	—	—	—	1 : 1 : 2
VF15	—	—	—	1 : 1 : 3

D = drug, EC = Ethyl cellulose, EU = Eudragit, and M = Methocel.

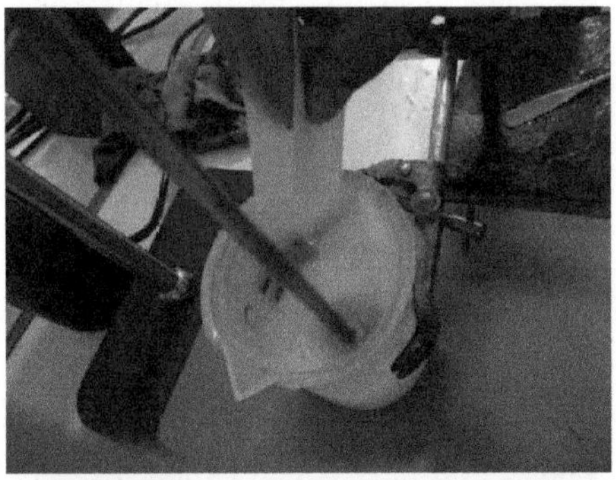

Addition of drug to mixture of LLP and 1% Tween 80

Addition of reared polymer mixture (internal phase)

Filtration of microspheres after washing

Storage in airtight container after drying

FIGURE 1: Schematically presenting the steps of microspheres prepared by emulsion solvent evaporation method.

for 8 hours and 10 mL dissolution sample was withdrawn at predetermined different time intervals and replaced with the same volume of test medium to maintain sink conditions. Each and every time 10 mL dissolution sample was compensated by fresh 10 mL of 0.1 N HCl. Dissolution samples were withdrawn with the help of 10 mL syringe and kept in test tube. The withdrawn samples were diluted, where necessary, filtered through 0.45μ membrane filter, and analyzed in UV-VIS spectrophotometer at wavelength of 210 nm.

2.6. Kinetic Analysis of Dissolution Data. To study the mechanism of drug release from the microspheres, the release data were fitted to zero order, first order, and Higuchi equation. Therefore, the dissolution data was fitted to the well-known exponential equation (Korsmeyer equation), which was often used to describe the drug release behavior from polymeric system [5]:

$$\log\left(\frac{Mt}{mf}\right) = \log K + \log t, \quad (2)$$

where Mt is the amount of drug release after infinite time and K is release rate constant incorporating structural and geometric characteristics of the mechanism of drug release.

To clarify the release exponent batches of microspheres, the log value of percentage drug dissolved was plotted against log time for each batch according to the above equation. A value of $n = 0.45$ indicates Fickian (case I) release; a value of >0.45 but <0.89 indicates non-Fickian (anomalous) release; and >0.89 indicates super case II type of release. Case II generally refers to the erosion of the polymeric chain and anomalous transport (non-Fickian) refers to combination of both diffusion and erosion controlled drug release.

2.7. Successive Fractional Dissolution Time. To characterize the drug release rate in different experimental conditionals like $T_{25\%}$, $T_{50\%}$, and $T_{80\%}$ they were calculated from dissolution data according to the following equations:

$$T_{25\%} = \left(\frac{0.25}{k}\right)^{1/n},$$
$$T_{50\%} = \left(\frac{0.50}{k}\right)^{1/n}, \quad (3)$$
$$T_{80\%} = \left(\frac{0.80}{k}\right)^{1/n}.$$

Another fractional tool MDT (mean dissolution time) can be calculated by the following equation:

$$\text{MDT} = \left(\frac{n}{n+1}\right) \cdot K^{-1/n}. \quad (4)$$

MDT value is used to characterize the drug release rate from the microspheres and the retarding efficiency of the polymer. A higher value of MDT indicates higher drug retarding ability of the polymer and vice versa. The MDT value is also considered to be a function of polymer loading, polymer nature, and physico-chemical properties of the drug molecule [6].

2.8. Surface Morphology Study with the Help of Scanning Electron Microscope (SEM). Surface nature of microspheres was examined with the help of Scanning Electron Microscope (JEOL, JSM-6490 LA, Japan). The microspheres were dried completely before examination and SEM was done at different magnifications of 20.0 kv × 75, 20.0 kv × 90, 20.0 kv × 95, 20.0 kv × 140, 20.0 kv × 300, 20.0 kv × 600, and 20.0 kv × 1000.

2.9. Fourier Transform Infrared (FTIR) Spectroscopy Studies. The FTIR technique is used to measure the absorption of various infrared radiations by the target material, to produce an IR spectrum that can be used to identify functional groups and molecular structure in the sample. FTIR spectra of pure Vildagliptin and formulated microspheres were recorded by using FTIR 8400S (SHIMADZU, Japan). Appropriate quantity of KBr and microspheres (in the ratio 100 : 2) was mixed by grinding in agate mortar. Disk was made with about 100 mg mixture under hydraulic pressure of 600 kg. Then the FTIR spectra were recorded between 4000 and 400 cm^{-1}. The resolution was 2 cm^{-1}.

2.10. Drug-Polymer Compatibility Study by Differential Scanning Calorimetry (DSC) Study of Microspheres. The DSC measurements were performed on DSC-60 (SHIMADZU) differential scanning calorimeter with thermal analyzer (TA-60WS). Pure Vildagliptin microsphere sample of 7.8 mg was placed in aluminum pan and sealed before heating under nitrogen flow (300 mL/min) at a scanning rate of 10°C min^{-1} from 30°C to 550°C. An empty aluminum pan was used as reference.

2.11. In Vivo Study

2.11.1. Experimental Animals. At first Albino rats were taken (about 165 to 200 gm) and collected from the animal house of Jahangirnagor University and kept back in an area with a 12-hour day-night cycle, at even temperature of 22°C and humidity of 45–64%. During the investigational study rats were fed on pellets (Rat Feed, Bangladesh) with free access to distilled water.

2.11.2. Induction of Experimental Diabetes. Rats were turned into diabetic ones via single intraperitoneal injection of freshly ready Streptozotocin (STZ-65 mg/kg body weight) in 0.1 M citrate buffer (pH 4.5) in volume of 1 mL/kg body weight. Standard rats received 1 mL citrate buffer as vehicle. After 48 hrs of Streptozotocin administration, blood glucose levels were estimated in rats following overnight fasting. Rats with blood glucose ranging between 200 and 300 mg/dL were considered diabetic and used for the experiments.

2.11.3. Drugs and Chemicals. Streptozotocin was procured from Sigma Aldrich Co., St. Louis, MO, USA; 0.1 M citrate buffer (pH 4.5) was procured from Merck, Germany. All other biochemicals and chemicals used for the experiment were of analytical grade.

2.11.4. Experimental Design. The rats were divided into 4 groups comprising 6 animals in each group as follows.

Group I (Negative Control). Normal rats were treated with saline daily and served as the negative control.

Group II (Positive Control). Animals were treated with single dose of Streptozotocin (65 mg/kg) by the intraperitoneal route to induce diabetes and served as a positive control.

Group III (Pure Vildagliptin). Diabetic rats were treated with 2.5 mg/kg body weight of pure Vildagliptin.

Group IV (Formulation VF13). Diabetic rats were treated with 2.5 mg/kg body weight of Vildagliptin containing microsphere.

2.11.5. Collection of Blood from the Rats. After the experimental course of therapy, the rats were sacrificed by cervical dislocation under mild chloroform anesthesia. Blood was collected on decapitation and serum was separated by centrifugation (for 20 min at 2000 rpm).

2.11.6. Estimation of Biochemical Parameters in Serum or Plasma. Serum glucose, cholesterol, triglycerides, urea,

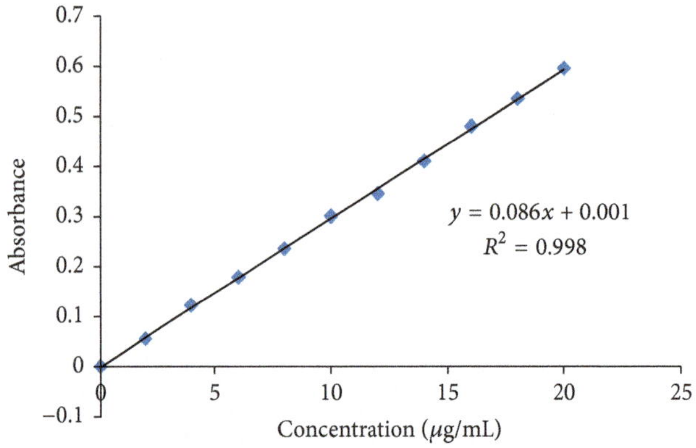

FIGURE 2: Standard curve of Vildagliptin.

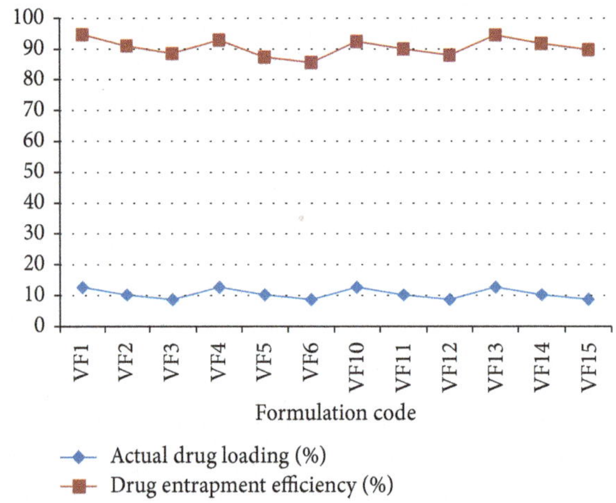

FIGURE 3: Comparative percent release study of actual drug loading and drug entrapment efficiency of different formulations.

creatinine, bilirubin, and glycohemoglobin were assayed using diagnostic reagent kit manufactured by Crescent Diagnostics Ltd., Atlas Medical Diagnostics Ltd., and Stanbio Diagnostics Ltd.

3. Results and Discussions

3.1. Standard Curve Analysis. Absorbance was taken at 210 nm with the help of UV-Visible spectrophotometer and the data were plotted in graph which has $y = 0.086x + 0.001$ and $R^2 = 0.998$ shown in Figure 2.

3.2. Actual Drug Loaded and Drug Entrapment Efficiency (DEE) of Prepared Microspheres by Emulsion Solvent Evaporation Technique. Drug loading and the drug entrapment efficiency (DEE) of the prepared microspheres were carried out and the graphical presentations are given in Figure 3. The actual drug loaded and the drug entrapment efficiency were found to be in the range of 8.5% to 12.5% and 82.56% to 94.59%, respectively.

3.3. In Vitro Dissolution Study of Vildagliptin Microspheres Prepared by Emulsion Solvent Evaporation Technique. To find out the mechanism of drug release, the controlled release Vildagliptin microspheres were treated in different mathematical models like zero order (cumulative percentage of drug release versus time), first order (log percentage of drug remaining versus time), Higuchi model (cumulative percentage of drug release versus square root of time), and Korsmeyer model (log cumulative percentage of drug release versus log time). The release data was plotted. From the linear portions of the curve slope correlation coefficients (R^2) were calculated. With the Korsmeyer plot, linearity was noted highest in all formulations using all data points. The data yielded apparently straight line with Korsmeyer plot ($R^2 > 0.99$) but a bit with zero order, first order kinetics, and Higuchi plot. It is observed that drug released from sustained release microsphere followed Korsmeyer release log cumulative percentage of drug release versus log time. The mechanism of drug release was calculated according to Peppas equation. The calculated "n" values along with the correlation coefficients (R^2) have been shown in Table 2. The values of n depend upon the polymer concentration. The calculated "n" values suggest that the mechanism of drug release followed non-Fickian transport.

3.4. Effect of Different Polymers on the Release of Vildagliptin from Microspheres Prepared by Emulsion Solvent Evaporation Technique. Vildagliptin microspheres were prepared

TABLE 2: Release rate constants and correlation coefficient (r^2) values of different formulations of Vildagliptin microspheres using different polymers by emulsion solvent evaporation technique, respectively.

Formulation code	Rate constants and R-squared values							
	Zero order		First order		Higuchi		Korsmeyer-Peppas	
	K_0	R^2	K_1	R^2	K_H	R^2	n	R^2
VF1	9.83	0.983	−0.218	0.919	29.81	0.96	0.62	0.991
VF2	9.73	0.979	−0.211	0.951	29.7	0.974	0.61	0.995
VF3	9.8	0.981	−0.209	0.969	30.06	0.98	0.64	0.994
VF4	9.97	0.979	−0.221	0.929	30.57	0.98	0.63	0.994
VF5	10.35	0.988	−0.211	0.957	31.33	0.963	0.67	0.991
VF6	10.67	0.984	−0.204	0.964	32.54	0.973	0.66	0.993
VF10	10.4	0.989	−0.225	0.925	31.51	0.966	0.75	0.991
VF11	9.39	0.951	−0.221	0.944	29.16	0.976	0.67	0.995
VF12	8.48	0.988	−0.218	0.965	25.54	0.959	0.7	0.994
VF13	11.13	0.993	−0.222	0.945	33.51	0.958	0.78	0.995
VF14	10.6	0.981	−0.225	0.954	32.37	0.973	0.77	0.995
VF15	9.86	0.987	−0.231	0.924	29.05	0.912	0.76	0.992

by polymeric concentration variation to study the effect of combination of polymers on the release of drug from microspheres. Formulations VF1 to VF3 were prepared by using Eudragit RS100 and Ethyl cellulose. After the end of 8 hours of dissolution, the release drug from microspheres was 87.5%, 85.7%, and 84.5%, respectively, which is shown in Figure 4(a). Formulations VF4 to VF6 were prepared by using Eudragit RL100 and Ethyl cellulose. After the end of 8 hours of dissolution, the release drug from microspheres was 86.6%, 88.2%, and 90.2%, respectively, which is shown in Figure 4(b). Formulations VF10 to VF12 were prepared by using Eudragit RS100 and Methocel K100M. After the end of 8 hours of dissolution, the release drug from microspheres was 88.0%, 81.1%, and 68.5%, respectively, which is shown in Figure 4(c). Formulations VF13 to VF15 were prepared by using Eudragit RL100 and Methocel K100M. After the end of 8 hours of dissolution, the release drug from microspheres was 92.4%, 85.5%, and 81.23%, respectively, which is shown in Figure 4(d).

It is noticeable that the entrapment efficiency of Eudragit RL100 microspheres was higher than that of the Eudragit RS100 microspheres. Eudragit RL100 contains higher amount of quaternary ammonium groups, which facilitates the diffusion of a part of entrapped drug to the surrounding medium during preparation of microspheres. Eudragit RS100 has thick polymeric surfaces due to the presence of lower amount of quaternary ammonium groups, which restrict the migration of drug particles to the surrounding medium. This suggested that the release of Vildagliptin from Eudragit RS100 microsphere exhibits diffusional characteristics, closely following Higuchi model, and is highly correlated with Korsmeyer-Peppas model release kinetics. This difference in drug release behavior suggested structural differences of the wall materials, and it is dependent on the content of the quaternary ammonium groups. Ethyl cellulose has given good retardant effect due to its hydrophobic nature, less permeability in dissolution medium by decreasing the drug diffusion. Methocel, on the other hand, due to its high water absorption ability and fast hydration and swelling might form an outer pseudo-gel layer to control drug release from the inner to the outer side of the microspheres. Thus the results showed that the release rate of drug from the microspheres can be modulated with adjusting the ratios of polymer/drug in the formulation.

All the formulations were best fitted with Korsmeyer model as shown in Table 2. The data obtained were also put in Korsmeyer-Peppas model in order to find out n value, which describes the drug release mechanism. The n value of microspheres of different drug to polymer ratio was ranged between 0.45 and 0.83, indicating that the mechanism of the drug release was diffusion controlled and erosion.

3.5. Comparative Study of Percent Release of Vildagliptin after 8 Hours of Different Formulations Prepared by Emulsion Solvent Evaporation Technique. From Figure 5 it has been seen that drug entrapment efficiency of different formulations was in range of 82.56% to 94.59%. It has been seen that when percent of drug loading increased the percent of drug entrapment also increased for all formulations containing Eudragit RS100 and Ethyl cellulose (94.59%, 90.89%, and 88.43%). This tendency was found for other formulations containing Eudragit RL100 and Ethyl cellulose; Eudragit RS100 and Methocel K100M; Eudragit RL100 and Methocel K100M.

3.6. Successive Fractional Dissolution Time. To characterize the drug release rate in different experimental conditionals they were calculated from dissolution data. MDT of formulations VF1, VF2, and VF3 were found 4.78 hours, 4.67 hours, and 4.58 hours, respectively. MDT of formulations VF4, VF5, and VF6 were found 4.36 hours, 4.28 hours, and 4.35 hours, MDT of formulations VF10, VF11, and VF12 were found 4.99 hours, 4.76 hours, and 3.98 hours, and MDT of formulations VF13, VF14, and VF15 were found 5.39 hours, 4.62 hours, and 5.18 hours, respectively, which is shown in Figure 6. The figure

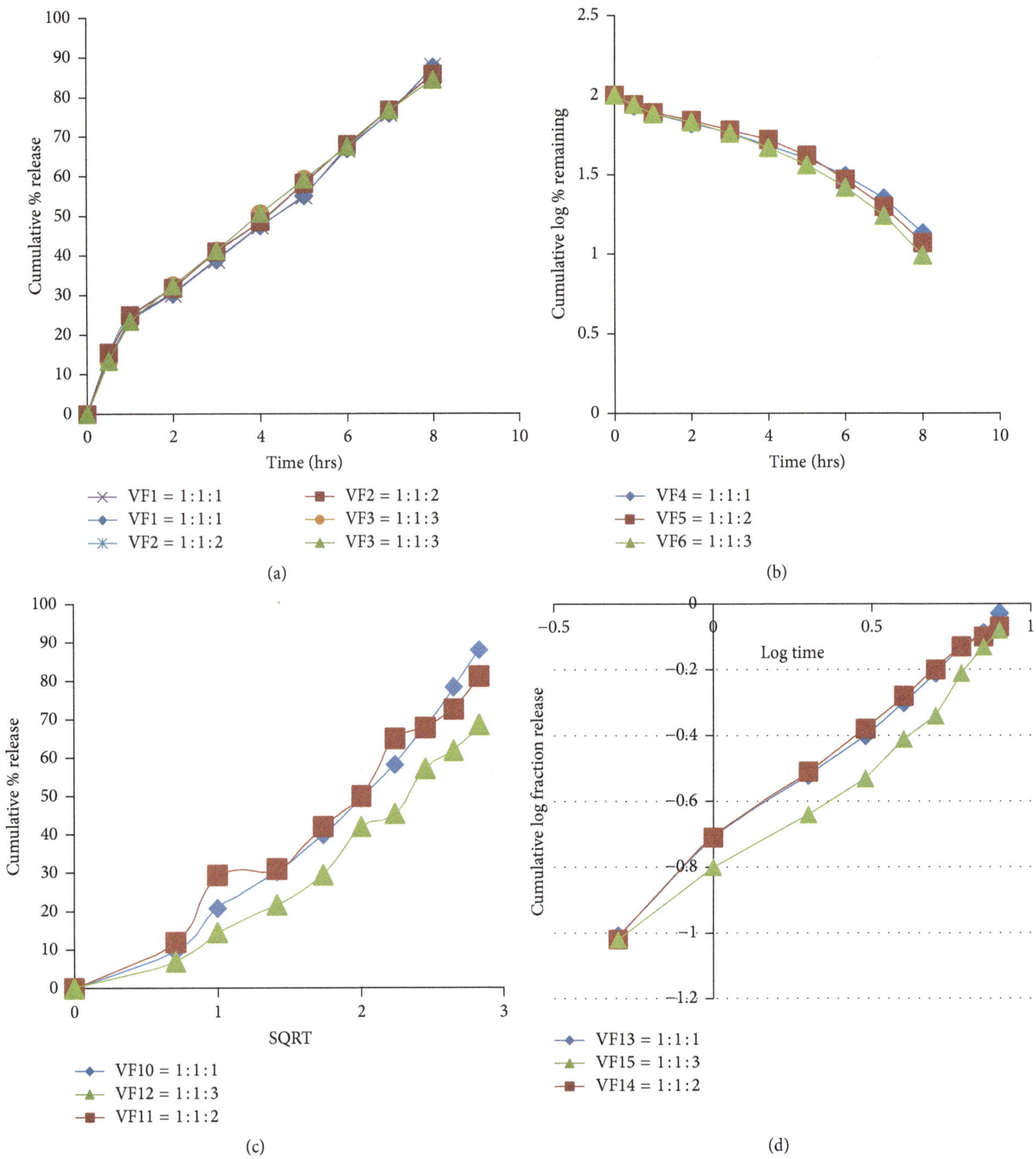

FIGURE 4: Release of Vildagliptin from microspheres prepared by emulsion solvent evaporation technique, respectively, where (a) zero order is from VF1 to VF3, (b) first order is from VF4 to VF6, (c) Higuchi model is from VF10 to VF12, and (d) Korsmeyer model is from VF13 to VF5.

indicates that the higher the polymer level, the lower the value of $T_{25\%}$, $T_{50\%}$, MDT, and $T_{80\%}$, and they behave according to their properties.

3.7. Effect of Polymers Concentration on the Surface Morphology of Vildagliptin Microspheres Prepared by Emulsion Solvent Evaporation Technique. SEM study showed that microspheres VF13 made of Eudragit RL100 and Methocel K100M were spherical and aggregated shown in Figure 7. The SEM of drug-polymer loaded microspheres had uneven shell owing to elevated application of drug in the microspheres. Surface analysis of the microspheres following liberate study showed larger pores signifying that the drug was unconfined from side to side pores and the means of drug release was diffusion controlled.

3.8. Drug-Polymer Compatibility Study by Fourier Transform Infrared (FTIR) Spectroscopy. The FTIR spectrum of pure

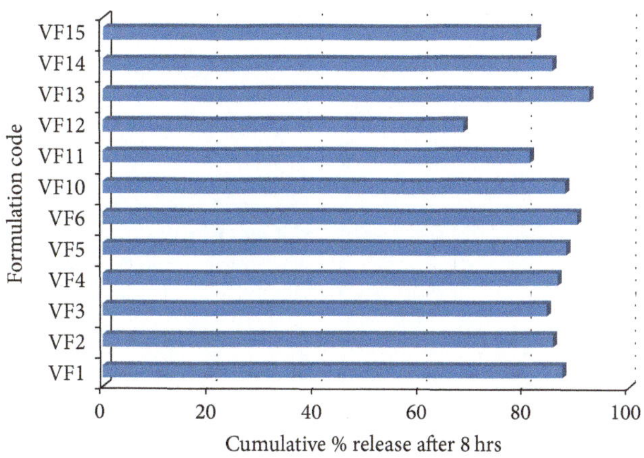

FIGURE 5: Comparative release studies of Vildagliptin microspheres after 8 hrs.

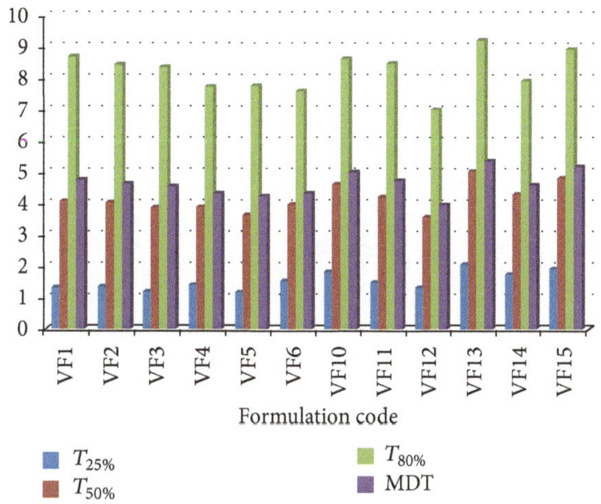

FIGURE 6: Successive fractional dissolution time ($T_{25\%}$, $T_{50\%}$, MDT, and $T_{80\%}$) of different formulations, respectively.

drug showed characteristic amide peaks at 3367.5, 3314.3, and 1713.5 per cm, urea carbonyl stretching (urea N-H stretching) vibrations at 1618.4 and 1526.5 per cm, and SO_2 stretching vibration at 1158 and 1341.5 per cm that are shown in Figure 8. There were no new bands observed in the spectrum, which confirms that no new chemical bonds were formed between the drug and the polymer.

3.9. Drug-Polymer Compatibility Study by Differentiate Scanning Calorimetry (DSC) Study of Microspheres. DSC is a fast and reliable method for understanding polymorphic transitions when screening drugs and polymers for compatibility, obtaining information about possible interactions. It was evident from the DSC profile (Figure 9) that Vildagliptin exhibited a sharp endothermic peak at 172.99°C, which corresponds to the drug crystallinity whereas formulation VF13 is thrashing its sharpness at its endothermic peak at 118.33°C. It appears that there is a significant reduction of drug crystallinity in the microspheres. The absence of detectable crystalline domains in drug loaded microspheres clearly indicates that drug was dispersed completely in the formulation, thus modifying the microspheres to an amorphous, disordered-crystalline phase.

3.10. Study of In Vivo Antihyperglycemic and Different Biochemical Effects on Albino Rats. From Table 3 it was observed that Streptozotocin could induce diabetics greatly in rats. On the other hand pure drug reduced the blood glucose level in an irregular manner up to 7 hours and then blood glucose level increased to the top, because it could not give sustained release of drug. It might be due to the fact that, here, Vildagliptin rapidly inhibited DPP-4 activity which increased fasting and postprandial endogenous levels of the incretin hormones GLP-1 (glucagon-like peptide 1) and GIP for short time and reduces blood glucose level rapidly. But the drug release was not sustained for a long time uniformly due to the absence of sustained release polymers.

For the formulation VF13 it was observed that it provided sustained release of drug up to 08 hours and that was proved by the data of reduction of blood glucose level in Table 3. Here administration of sustained release formulation of Vildagliptin resulted in a rapid and complete inhibition of DPP-4 activity, resulting in increased fasting and postprandial endogenous levels of the incretin hormones GLP-1 (glucagon-like peptide 1) and GIP. As a result blood glucose level reduced rapidly and reduced glucose level maintained for 08 hours smoothly. It was due to the uniform sustained

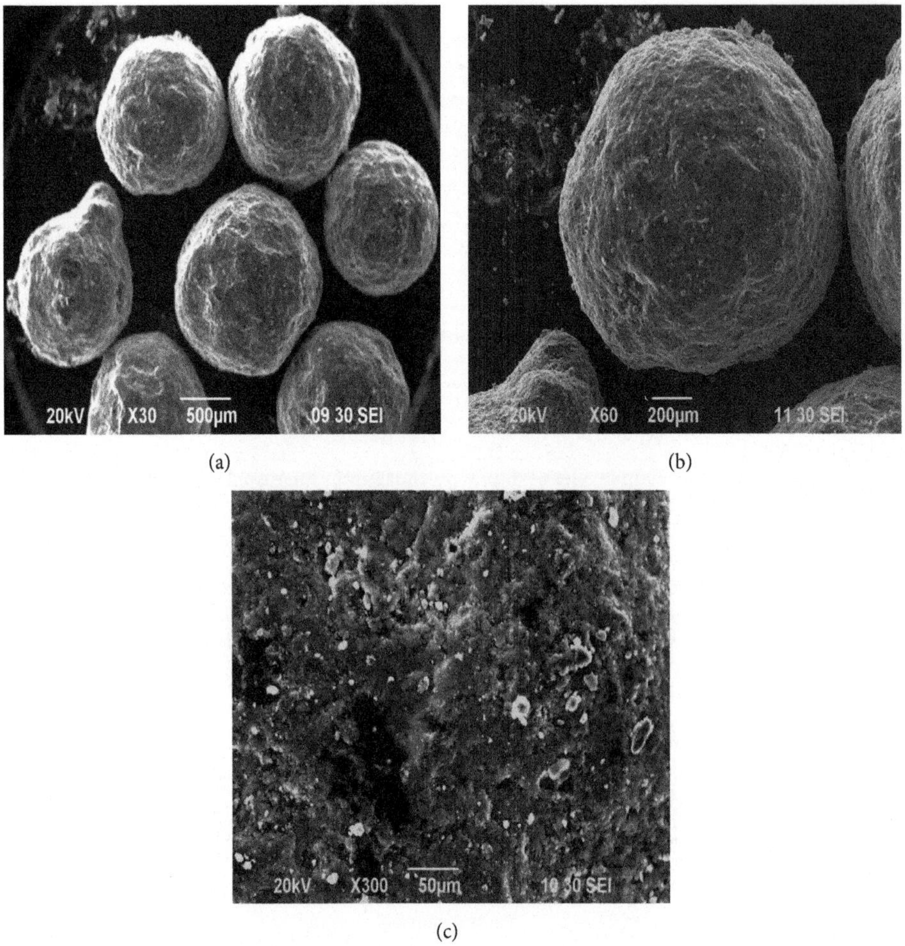

FIGURE 7: SEM studies of Vildagliptin microspheres of formulation VF13 prepared by emulsion solvent evaporation technique with different magnification (a) at ×30 SEI, (b) at ×60 SEI, and (c) at ×300 SEI, respectively.

release of drug from formulations containing sustained release polymers Methocel K100M and Eudragit RL100.

STZ diabetic rats were found to have significantly elevated serum creatinine and urea levels as compared to nondiabetic control rats. This is because STZ diabetic rats have diminished ability to filter urea and creatinine from blood and excrete them in urine. This is another characteristic change in diabetes. Whereas after treatment both the values were comparable to those which received Vildagliptin treatment, there was no significant difference in values obtained for group I and group IV shown in Figure 10. Various parameters of blood lipid profiles were tested in the normal and diabetic rats. The levels of TC and TG were significantly elevated and level of serum HDL was decreased in diabetic control group as compared to normal control rats. In case of insulin deficiency, there is increased lipolysis leading to hyperlipidemia. In insulin deficient diabetes, the concentration of free fatty acids is elevated as a result of free fatty acid outflow from fat depots, where the balance of free fatty acid esterification-triglyceride lipolysis cycle is displaced in favor of lipolysis. It has been shown from Figure 11 that, after being treated with formulation VF13, the alteration in lipid metabolism was partially attenuated as evidenced by decreased serum TG and TC levels in diabetic rats.

4. Conclusion

The present study was conducted to design Vildagliptin sustained release microspheres by emulsion solvent evaporation technique. *In vitro* dissolution study showed the sustained release of Vildagliptin from the microsphere for about 8 hours. From the *in vitro* dissolution data it has been established that the drug dissolution profile could be slowed down by increasing the amount of retardant polymers in the formulations and 5 : 5 solvent ratios ensured the better sustained release. Scanning electron microscopy showed the smooth and slightly porous surface of microspheres. From differential scanning calorimetric test it can be concluded that there was no significant change in melting point and glass transition temperature and no significant crystallinity. FTIR data showed absence of any new functional group and any other interaction in between drugs and polymers. In addition formulated microspheres can be chosen for *in vivo* antidiabetic study and another biomedical study exhibited satisfactory results.

So from the results it can be concluded that drug retardant polymers and their concentration affect all the evaluation parameters significantly. Hence the prepared polymeric microspheres of Vildagliptin might be proved to be potential

Table 3: Average reduction in glucose level (mg/dL) in negative control, positive control, pure drug Vildagliptin, and formulation VF13.

Time (hour)	Average glucose level reduction (mg/dL)			
	Negative control (group I)	Positive control (group II)	Pure drug (group III)	Formulation VF13 (group IV)
0	70 ± 5.329	311.9 ± 5.92	361.44 ± 5.44	344.17 ± 7.49
1	70 ± 5.556	312.3 ± 4.36	205.82 ± 13.25	233.17 ± 8.68
2	70.1 ± 5.663	316.16 ± 7.77	157.7 ± 11.26	214.87 ± 7.71
3	70.2 ± 3.445	318.77 ± 8.67	137.4 + 9.89	202.75 + 8.21
4	70.25 ± 3.687	325.53 ± 11.26	110.08 ± 10.94	174.75 ± 5.94
5	70.29 ± 3.567	329.33 ± 3.77	119.98 ± 8.90	140.07 ± 4.67
6	70.3 ± 2.478	329.83 ± 4.78	139.96 ± 7.37	118.92 ± 3.32
7	70.3 ± 3.568	335.57 ± 10.57	162.32 ± 10.81	108.32 ± 3.70
8	70.31 ± 3.598	338.9 ± 11.93	186.14 ± 11.03	102.37 ± 4.68
12	71 ± 2.456	351.77 ± 12.06	237.56 ± 9.66	132.72 ± 5.19
24	71 ± 1.456	362.77 ± 7.39	307.68 ± 7.97	279.82 ± 6.05
48	71.2 ± 2.786	392.77 ± 7.40	317.68 ± 9.98	309.82 ± 8.06

Values are given as mean ± standard deviation for group of six rats.

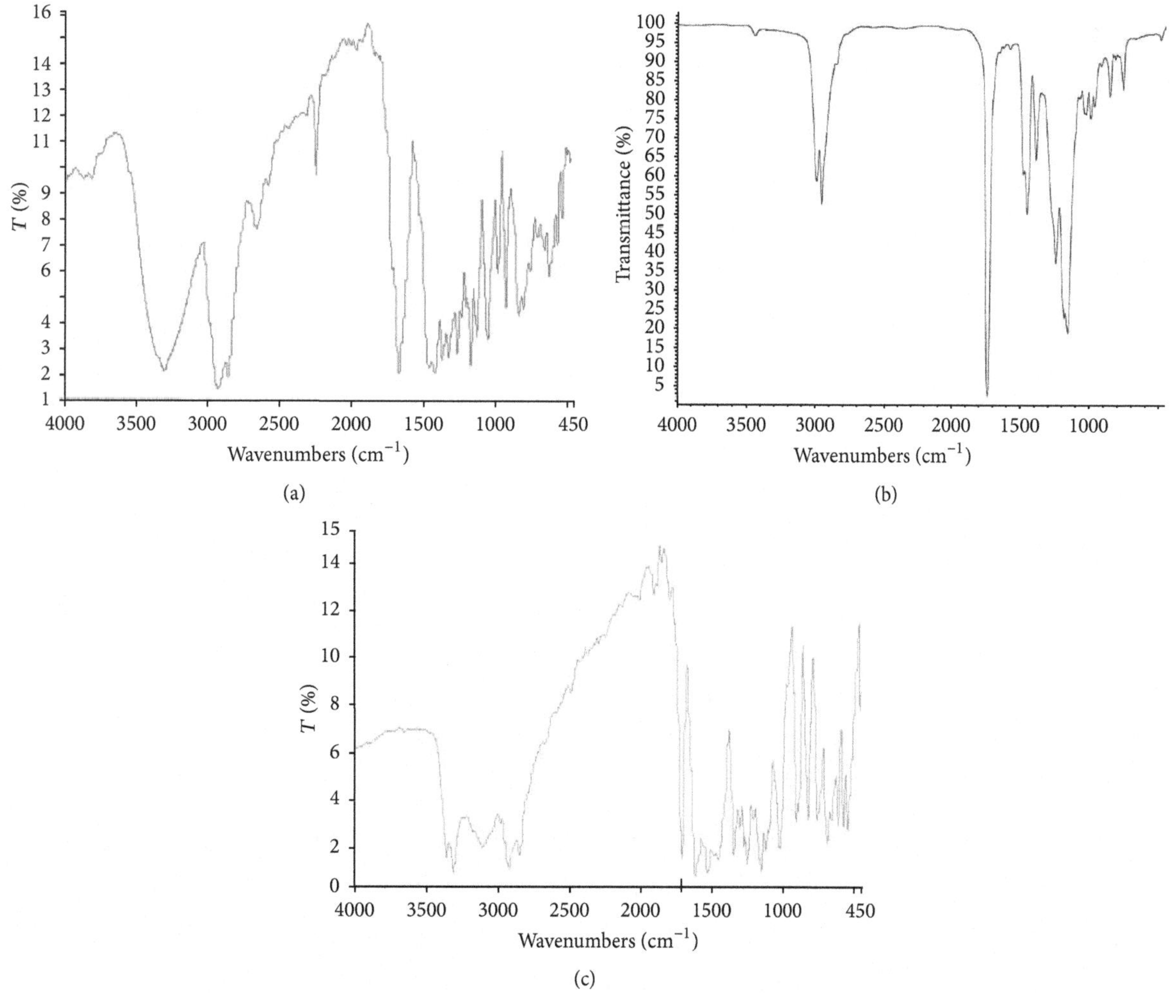

Figure 8: FTIR spectrum of (a) pure drug Vildagliptin, (b) Eudragit RL, and (c) formulation VF13, respectively.

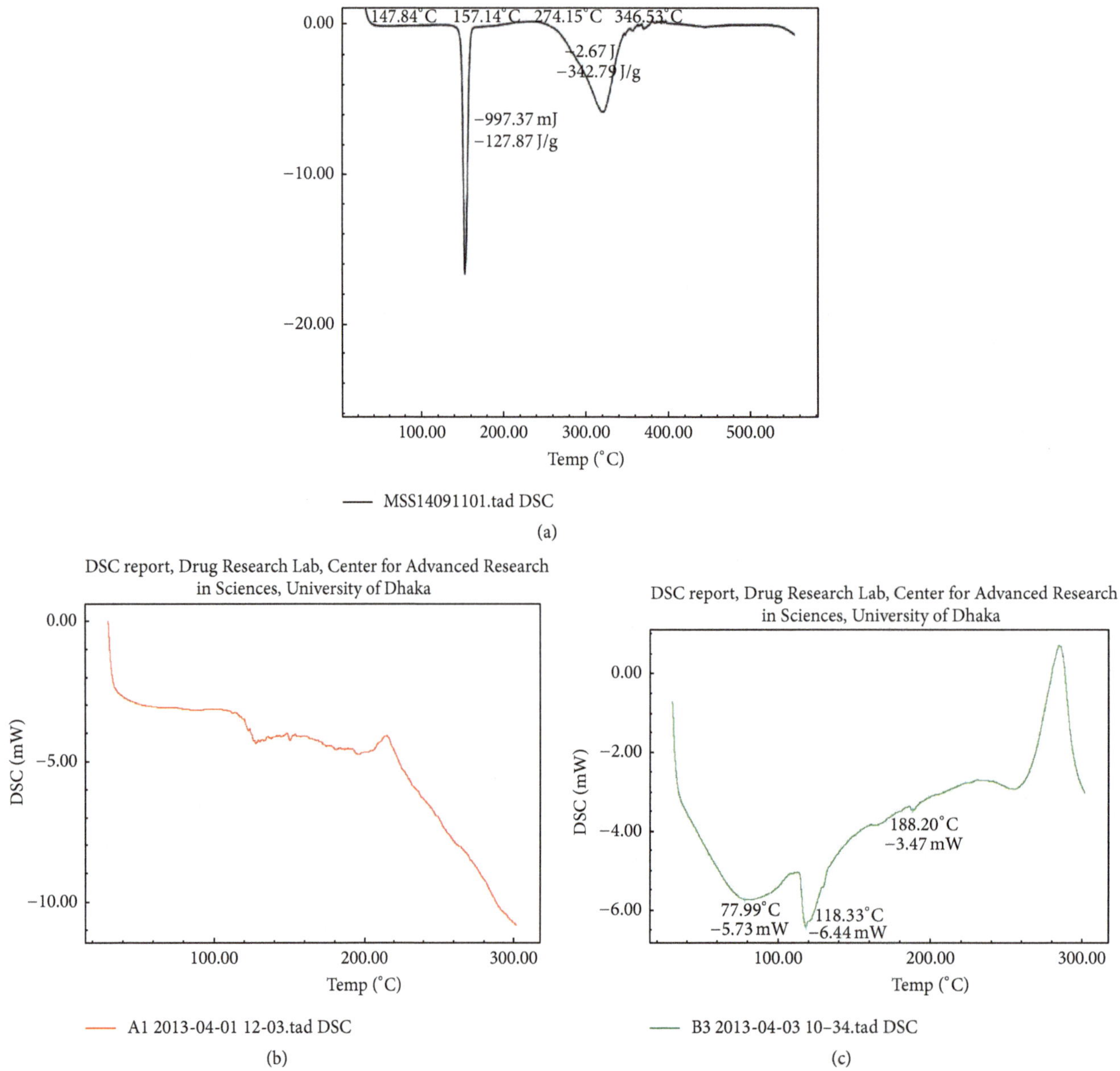

FIGURE 9: DSC of (a) pure Vildagliptin, (b) Eudragit RL100, and (c) formulation VF13.

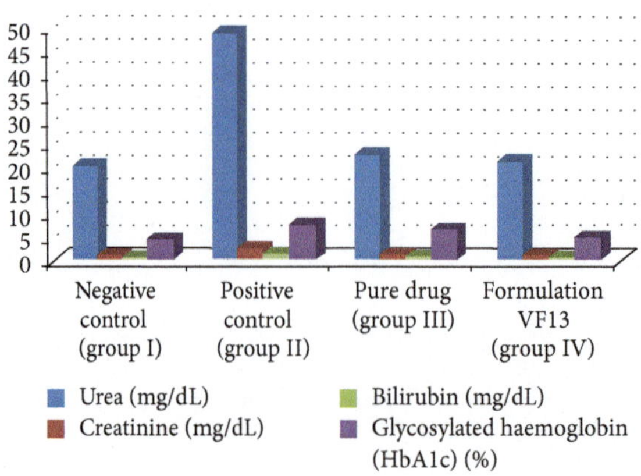

FIGURE 10: Effect of different formulation on urea, creatinine, bilirubin, and glycosylated haemoglobin (HbA1c) in serum or plasma of control and experimental groups.

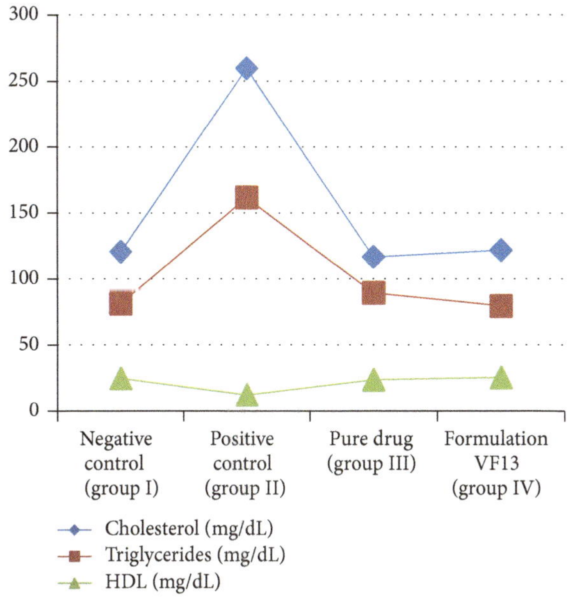

FIGURE 11: Effect of drug on lipid profile of control and experimental groups.

candidate for safe and effective sustained drug delivery from microspheres for the treatment of type II diabetes.

Conflict of Interests

The authors affirm that there is no conflict of interests concerning the publication of this paper.

Acknowledgments

The authors are grateful to the Eskayef Bangladesh Limited for giving active ingredients as a gift and University of Asia Pacific for providing facilities to carry out this research work.

References

[1] B. Satish, L. M. Bikash, and Z. Tomal, "Design and evaluation of sustained release microspheres," *Indian Journal of Clinical Practice*, vol. 22, pp. 125–128, 2012.

[2] D. J. Drucker, "Modeling of drug release from sustained release polymers," *Europian Journal of Pharmaceutical Technology*, vol. 36, pp. 1696–1705, 2006.

[3] S. P. Vyas and R. K. Khar, *Targeted and Controlled Drug Delivery: Novel Carrier System*, edited by: M. K. Jain, CBS Publishers & Distributors, New Delhi, India, 2002.

[4] P. Srivastava and S. Visht, "Application and advancement of microsphere as controlled delivery system: a review," *International Journal of Pharmacy & Life Sciences*, vol. 4, no. 4, pp. 2583–2594, 2013.

[5] T. Mohima, I. Dewan, S. M. A. Islam, S. Rana, and A. Hossain, "Encapsulation of zidovudine in different cellulosic acrylic and methacrylic polymers loaded microspheres: *in vitro* characterization and compatibility studies," *International Journal of Pharmacy and Pharmaceutical Sciences*, vol. 7, no. 1, pp. 486–495, 2015.

[6] J. E. Mockel and B. C. Lippold, "Zero-order drug release from hydrocolloid matrices," *Pharmaceutical Research*, vol. 10, no. 7, pp. 1066–1070, 1993.

12

Stabilized Polymer Micelles for the Development of IT-147, an Epothilone D Drug-Loaded Formulation

Adam Carie, Bradford Sullivan, Tyler Ellis, J. Edward Semple, Taylor Buley, Tara Lee Costich, Richard Crouse, Suzanne Bakewell, and Kevin Sill

Intezyne Technologies, 3720 Spectrum Blvd. Ste. 104, Tampa, FL, USA

Correspondence should be addressed to Adam Carie; adam.carie@intezyne.com

Academic Editor: Jia You Fang

Epothilones have demonstrated promising potential for oncology applications but suffer from a narrow therapeutic window. Epothilone D stabilizes microtubules leading to apoptosis, is active against multidrug-resistant cells, and is efficacious in animal tumor models despite lack of stability in rodent plasma. Clinical development was terminated in phase II due to dose limiting toxicities near the efficacious dose. Taken together, this made epothilone D attractive for encapsulation in a stabilized polymer micelle for improved safety and efficacy. We have designed a library of triblock copolymers to develop IT-147, a lead formulation of epothilone D that extends plasma circulation for accumulation in the tumor environment, and potentially decrease systemic exposure to reduce dose limiting toxicities. The drug loading efficiency for IT-147 exceeds 90%, is 75 nm in diameter, and demonstrates pH-dependent release of epothilone D without chemical conjugation or enzymatic activation. Administration of IT-147 at 20 mg/kg increases exposure of epothilone D to the plasma compartment over 6-fold compared to free drug. At the same dose, 20 mg/kg epothilone D from IT-147 is considered the no observed adverse effect level (NOAEL) but is the maximum tolerated dose for free drug. Consequently, IT-147 is positioned to be a safer, more effective means to deliver epothilone D.

1. Introduction

Systemic administration of cytotoxic drugs, accompanied by their severe dose limiting toxicities, is standard practice in oncology. The expansive search for new drugs through natural product discovery and rationally designed chemical libraries have identified an abundance of therapeutic agents with new mechanisms of action and potential for difficult-to-treat diseases such as cancer. Epothilones are a class of cytotoxic macrocyclic compounds originally discovered in the mid-1980s isolated from myxobacteria *Sorangium cellulosum* [1–3]. Epothilones A and B were isolated and determined to have taxane-like activity in 1993 [4]. Epothilone B was found to be a potent inhibitor of tubulin polymerization and was shown to displace bound paclitaxel on microtubules [4, 5]. Total synthesis of epothilones A and B was published by 1997, and family members C–F, along with libraries of analogues, were subsequently investigated for antitumor activity [6–11]. The epothilones demonstrated potent in vitro inhibition of cancer cell growth with low nanomolar IC_{50} values and maintained activity against cell lines that demonstrate multidrug resistance, including paclitaxel cross-resistance [8, 12–16]. Epothilone B demonstrated the highest potency of the family of epothilones. In vivo, epothilone B dosed by intraperitoneal bolus in mouse tumor models demonstrated a maximum tolerated dose of 0.3 mg/kg, with an LD_{50} of 0.6 mg/kg, compared to epothilone D which demonstrated a maximum tolerated dose of 25 mg/kg on the same dosing schedule [13]. Although epothilone D was better-tolerated, clinical development was halted after phase II studies demonstrated a poor response rate at the maximum tolerated dose [17–19]. An analogue of epothilone B, ixabepilone, was approved by FDA for treatment of refractory breast cancer, although some clinical studies have indicated that ixabepilone is not superior to paclitaxel in treating refractory solid tumors [20–22]. The epothilones have demonstrated promise as potential anticancer treatments but suffer from a narrow therapeutic window. Therefore, formulations of epothilones that improve tolerability while maintaining efficacy should demonstrate clinical utility.

Many different drug delivery technologies, including liposomes, degradable polyester particles, and polymer micelles, have been investigated both preclinically and clinically, but few have achieved FDA approval [23]. There are many factors to consider when designing chemotherapeutic nanoparticles, including size, shape, payload capacity, targeted drug release, and stability [24]. We have hypothesized that stability of the nanoparticle after administration is the most important aspect in the clinical success of this class of drug delivery technologies. In our investigation of polymer micelle delivery systems, we have designed a library of triblock copolymers to encapsulate hydrophobic chemotherapeutic agents in micelles that are stabilized to dilution in the circulatory system. The amphiphilic block of the polymer is composed of 12 kDa poly(ethylene glycol) (PEG), and the hydrophobic core-forming block is composed of mixture of amino acids, as shown in Figure 2. The stabilizing block incorporated between the PEG block and core block differentiates this approach from the abundance of polymer micelle formulations reported previously. The stabilizing block in the polymers investigated for epothilone encapsulation is based either on iron-hydroxamate bonds formed among hydroxamic acid (NHOH) residues on polymer chains or on disulfide bonds formed between cysteine (Cys) moieties in the polymer chains (Figure 2). The ability to stabilize a drug-encapsulated micelle for systemic administration without the need to chemically conjugate the drug to the polymer allows for extended circulation time in the plasma compartment, time to accumulate in the tumor environment, and the ability to release payload without reliance upon enzymatic activity for cleavage. Stabilizing the drug-loaded polymer micelles by forming iron-hydroxamate dative bonds allows for a pH-dependent release of the dug payload. The iron chelated hydroxamic acid forms a stable bond at physiological pH, which subsequently becomes unstable as the pH decreases. This allows for a triggered release mechanism in the acidified tumor microenvironment, as well as in endosomal/lysosomal compartments upon intracellular transport [25, 26]. Stabilizing polymer micelles with disulfide bonds allow for targeted release of the drug payload upon cellular entry based on the oxidative potential in tumor cells [27]. These release mechanisms are represented graphically in Figure 3. Formation of drug-loaded micelles with these triblock copolymers typically represents a 70–90% efficient process, and results in nanoparticles with average diameters between 60 and 100 nm. Herein we discuss formulation and lead optimization of epothilone D in stabilized triblock copolymer micelles and physiochemical characterization of a small library of formulations.

2. Materials and Methods

2.1. Materials. Epothilone B was purchased from Toronto Research Chemical (Toronto, Ontario, Canada) and epothilone D was purchased from Austin Chemical (Buffalo Grove, Illinois). Dichloromethane, ferric chloride, phenylmethylsulfonyl fluoride (PMSF), cremaphor, dithiothreitol (DTT), anhydrous dichloromethane (DCM), anhydrous *N,N*-dimethylformamide (DMF), *N*-methylmorpholine (NMM), 4-dimethylaminopyridine (DMAP), and lithium hydroxide monohydrate ($LiOH{\cdot}H_2O$) were purchased from Sigma-Aldrich (St. Louis, Missouri). Trehalose was purchased from Carbosynth (Berkshire, United Kingdom). Dialysis tubing with 3500 molecular weight cut-off (MWC) and tangential flow filtration filters with 10 kDa pore size were purchased from Spectrum Labs (Rancho Dominguez, California). Pass-through sterile 0.22 micron filters were purchased from Sartorious (Goettingen, Germany). Thermo Syncronis C18 HPLC column (97105 251630), HPLC grade methanol, HPLC grade acetonitrile, *n*-butyl chloride, absolute ethanol, K_2EDTA tubes, black wall, clear bottom 96-well plates, tetrahydrofuran (THF), isopropyl alcohol, methyl *tert*-butyl ether (MTBE), acetic anhydride (Ac_2O), acetone, and acetic acid were purchased from Fisher Scientific (Waltham, Massachusetts). Absolute ethanol was purchased from Decon Labs. Hydroxylamine (50% aqueous solution) was obtained from Alfa Aesar (Haverhill, Massachusetts).

2.2. Triblock Copolymer Synthesis. All NHOH or Cys triblock polymers were synthesized from in-house prepared mPEG-NH_2 and α-amino acid *N*-carboxyanhydrides (NCAs) using previously published procedures and as a demonstrated in Figure 1 [28, 29]. As a specific example, the synthesis of ITP-103 mPEG12K-NH-*b*-*p*-[D-Glu(NHOH)$_5$-*co*-L-Glu(NHOH)$_5$]-*b*-*p*-[D-Phe$_{15}$-*co*-L-Tyr$_{15}$-*co*-D-Leu$_{10}$]-Ac is as follows: synthesis of mPEG12K-NH-*b*-*p*-[D-Glu(OBn)$_5$-*co*-L-Glu(OBn)$_5$]-*b*-*p*-[D-Phe$_{15}$-*co*-L-Tyr(OAc)$_{15}$-*co*-D-Leu$_{10}$]-Ac (ITP-103 precursor): mPEG12.7K-NH_2 was dried via azeotropic vacuum distillation with toluene to remove trace amounts of moisture. The dry PEG was dissolved 0.1 g/mL in a mixture of 2 : 1 v/v anhydrous DCM and DMF. D-Glu(OBn) NCA (5 eq.) and L-Glu(OBn) NCA (5 eq.) were added and the reaction was stirred at room temperature. After ~16 hrs, gel permeation chromatography (GPC) analysis indicated complete consumption of the NCAs. D-Phe NCA (15 eq.), L-Tyr(OAc) NCA (15 eq.), and D-Leu NCA (10 eq.) were added and the reaction was stirred for ~21 hrs, at which point the reaction was complete (GPC analysis). Ac_2O (10 eq.), NMM (11 eq.), and DMAP (1 eq.) were added and the reaction was stirred overnight before diluting with DCM and filtering through a glass microfibre filter. The reaction mixture was concentrated under reduced pressure to remove the DCM, transferred to a large polypropylene bucket, and precipitated by the addition of isopropyl alcohol (~8–10 volume equivalents) with vigorous mixing. The solids were collected and washed with MTBE (6–8 volume eq.) and then dried *in vacuo* to yield the title compound as a fine cream-colored powder (yield typically > 95%). Synthesis of mPEG12K-NH-*b*-*p*-[D-Glu(NHOH)$_5$-*co*-L-Glu(NHOH)$_5$]-*b*-*p*-[D-Phe$_{15}$-*co*-L-Tyr$_{15}$-*co*-D-Leu$_{10}$]-Ac (ITP-103): mPEG12K-NH-*b*-*p*-[D-Glu(OBn)$_5$-*co*-L-Glu(OBn)$_5$]-*b*-*p*-[D-Phe$_{15}$-*co*-L-Tyr(OAc)$_{15}$-*co*-D-Leu$_{10}$]-Ac (ITP-precursor) was dissolved 0.1 g/mL in anhydrous THF with the assistance of gentle heating. Once cooled to ambient temperature, $LiOH{\cdot}H_2O$ (25 eq.) and NH_2OH (50 wt.% in H_2O, 125 eq.) were added. The reaction was monitored via ^1H NMR (400 MHz, DMSO-d_6) for the disappearance of the -$C\underline{H_2}$OBn and -OAc protons and was typically complete after

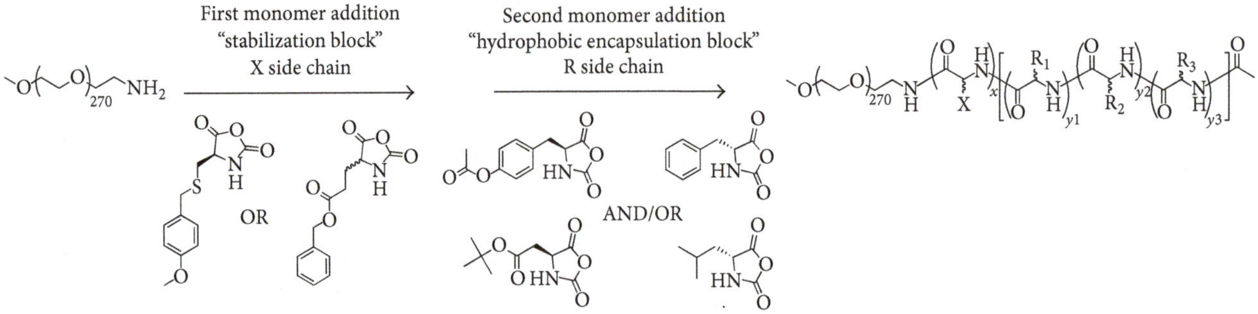

FIGURE 1: General polymerization scheme for triblock copolymers. Monomer addition by living polymerization followed by sequential functional group manipulations yields triblock copolymers for formulation of drug-encapsulated polymer micelles.

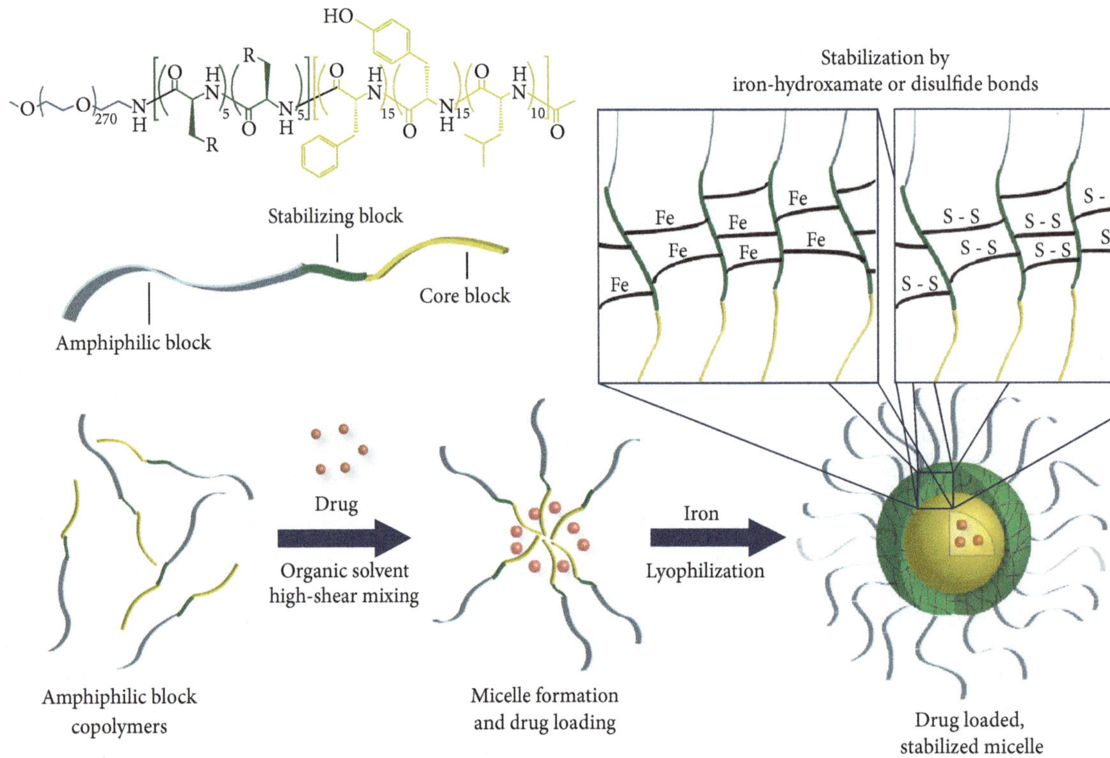

FIGURE 2: Formulation of epothilone D drug-loaded, stabilized micelles with triblock copolymers. The general formulation method includes formation of a polymer drug emulsion under high shear conditions, stabilization by iron-hydroxamate or disulfide bond formation, and lyophilization.

24–36 hrs. Acetic acid (125 eq.) and acetone (1250 eq.) were added and the reaction mixture was heated until reflux and then left to stir and cool to ambient temperature overnight. The reaction mixture was filtered through a glass microfibre filter and transferred to a large polypropylene bucket. The product was precipitated by the addition of MTBE (~8–10 volume eq.) with vigorous mechanical stirring. The solids were collected, washed with absolute ethanol (~5 volume eq.) and then isopropyl alcohol (~1 volume eq.), and dried *in vacuo* to yield the title compound as a fine light cream-colored granular solid (yield typically > 90%).

2.3. General Method for Formulation of Epothilone D Loaded Micelles (Hydroxamate). Formulation of epothilone-loaded micelles was performed using an oil in water emulsion technique. Polymer was dissolved in water, and epothilone D was dissolved in a solution of 20% methanol in dichloromethane. The feed ratio for epothilone to polymer was 5% (w/w). The organic solution containing epothilone D was added to the aqueous polymer solution while stirring under high shear using a Silverson L4RT rotor/stator mixer with a fine emulsor screen. The resulting emulsions were stirred in a fume hood for 12 hours to allow the evaporation of the organic phase. Ferric chloride solution (10 mM final concentration) was added to form iron-hydroxamate bonds between polymer strands for micelle stabilization for formulations with polymers containing a hydroxamic acid stabilizing block and was then purified and concentrated by tangential flow

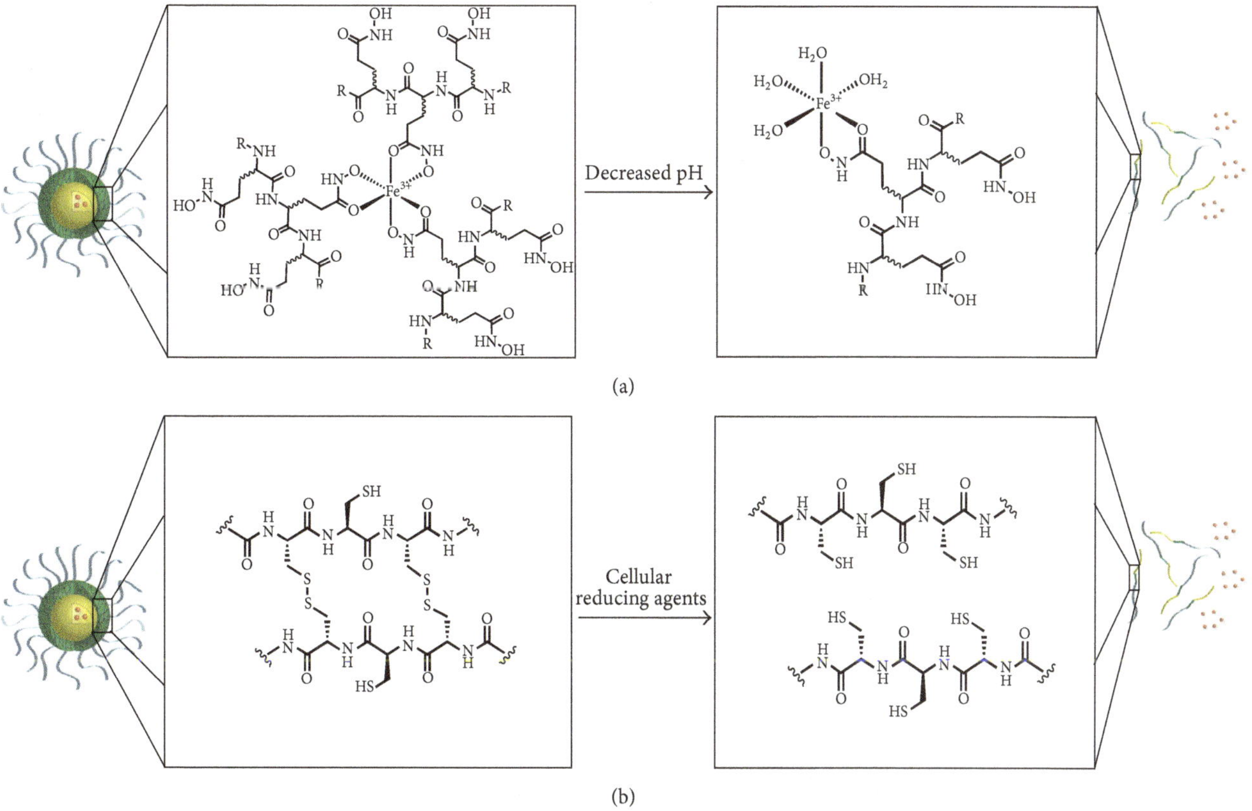

FIGURE 3: Mechanism of drug payload release from the polymer micelle formulations. (a) Stabilization by iron-hydroxamate bonds between polymer chains is reversed by a decrease in pH. (b) Stabilization by disulfide bonds between polymer chains is reversed by intracellular reducing agents.

filtration (TFF). Trehalose (50% w/w polymer) was added as a cryoprotectant, and the solution was filtered through a 0.2 μm filter and lyophilized.

2.4. General Method for Formulation of Epothilone D Loaded Micelles (Disulfide). Formulation of epothilone-loaded micelles was performed using an oil in water emulsion technique. Polymer was dissolved in water containing dithiothreitol (DTT, 20 mM), and epothilone D was dissolved in a solution of 20% methanol in dichloromethane. The feed ratio for epothilone to polymer was 5% (w/w). The organic solution containing epothilone D was added to the aqueous polymer solution while stirring under high shear using a Silverson L4RT rotor/stator mixer with a fine emulsor screen. The resulting emulsions were stirred in a fume hood for 12 hours to allow the evaporation of the organic phase. The solution was then subjected to diafiltration by TFF to remove dithiothreitol for stabilization of the micelles by interstrand disulfide bond formation and then concentrated. Trehalose (50% w/w polymer) was added as a cryoprotectant, and the solution was filtered through a 0.2 μm filter and lyophilized.

2.5. Assay for Epothilone D Drug Loading. Drug loading of epothilone micelle formulations was performed by HPLC/UV using an Waters Alliance 2695 HPLC separations module equipped with a 2998 photodiode array detector (Milford, Massachusetts). Separation was performed using a Synchronis C18, 5 μm, 250 × 4.6 mm HPLC column. Mobile phase A consisted of water with 0.2% acetic acid, and mobile phase B consisted of methanol. Flow was isocratic at 1.2 mL/minute and consisted of 15% mobile phase A and 85% mobile phase B. Injection volume was 10 μL. Analyte was monitored at 249 nm with retention time at 7.0 minutes and a total run time of 10 minutes. Formulations were dissolved in methanol at a concentration of 2 mg/mL, and epothilone peak area was compared to epothilone standards in a range of 20–100 μg/mL in methanol. Epothilone concentration in the formulations was then converted to percentage of epothilone content to polymer content on a weight-to-weight basis.

2.6. Particle Size by Dynamic Light Scattering. Average particle diameter for the formulations was determined by dynamic light scattering (DLS) using a Wyatt DynaPro 96-well plate reader (Santa Barbara, California). Formulations were dissolved in 0.9% saline at a concentration of 1 mg/mL, and 200 μL of each sample was added to the wells of a 96-well plate. Average particle diameter was determined using 10 acquisitions per well with a 30-second acquisition time at 37°C for each sample.

2.7. Dialysis Stability Assays. Retention of the epothilone drug substance within the micelle formulation and the release profile of the drug substance over time, concentration, and pH were investigated using dialysis. Formulations were reconstituted at concentrations of 20 mg/mL and 0.2 mg/mL and placed in dialysis tubing with 3500 MWC pore size, which allows for retention of the micelles within the bag and release of the free drug from the bag into the reservoir. A volume of 3 mL of reconstituted formulation was placed into dialysis bags and then placed in a 300 mL reservoir containing 10 mM phosphate buffer and stirred for 6 hours at room temperature. HPLC assay for epothilone concentration of the formulation inside the bag was done before and after dialysis to determine the percentage of epothilone retained inside the dialysis bag over 6 hours. pH-dependent release was performed using 10 mM phosphate buffer at pH 3, 4, 5, 6, 7, 7.4, and 8 in the reservoirs during dialysis.

2.8. Epothilone D Rat Plasma Pharmacokinetics. The lead hydroxamic acid and cysteine containing formulations were compared to free epothilone D using a cannulated rat model by administering a 10 mg/kg dose by fast bolus to the jugular vein catheter. Female, Sprague-Dawley rats surgically modified with jugular vein catheters exteriorized posteriorly were purchased from Harlan Labs. Catheters were flushed and maintained with heparinized saline to ensure patency over the study period. The catheter port was used for both test article administration and blood collection. IT-147 pharmacokinetics at 20, 30, and 40 mg/kg were compared to epothilone D free drug at 20 mg/kg in the cannulated rat model. IT-147 was reconstituted in saline, while epothilone D free drug was reconstituted in cremaphor : ethanol : saline at 1 : 1 : 4 ratio. Dosing summaries for the rat pharmacokinetic studies are shown in Table 2. All in vivo studies were conducted under Institutional Guidelines. The Institutional Animal Care and Use Committee (IACUC), at the University of South Florida (USF), approved all rat in vivo study protocols. Animals were maintained and evaluated under pathogen-free conditions in accordance with USF College of Medicine IACUC standards of care. Approximately 300 μL of blood was collected into K_2EDTA tubes containing PMSF (final concentration 2.5 mM) at time points of 1, 5, 15, and 60 minutes after test article administration. Samples were centrifuged at 2000 RPM for 5 minutes to isolate plasma. Plasma was aliquoted into microcentrifuge tubes and frozen at −20°C until processed for HPLC/UV analysis. The following bioanalytical method is a modification of the procedure originally developed by Yuan et al. [30]. Bioanalytical sample preparation was performed by liquid : liquid extraction. 50 μL of plasma sample was added to 600 μL of *n*-butyl chloride and vortexed for 10 minutes. Samples were centrifuged at 10,000 RPM for 10 minutes and the organic supernatant was aliquoted into microcentrifuge tubes. The *n*-butyl chloride supernatant was evaporated to dryness using a turbovap with nitrogen flow at room temperature, and 75 μL of a 40% acetonitrile in water solution was added to each tube. Samples were then vortexed for 5 minutes, aliquoted into HPLC vials, and processed using HPLC methodology as described in Section 2.3. Blank rat plasma containing PMSF was used to spike in epothilone D for standard curve preparation and processed as described for the plasma samples to determine concentration of epothilone D isolated from the samples collected from the cannulated rats. Noncompartmental analysis of the pharmacokinetic data was done using Phoenix WinNonlin version 6.3.

3. Results

3.1. Synthesis of Triblock Copolymers. All of the hydroxamate and cysteine triblock polymers used in this study were prepared by the ring-opening polymerization of α-amino acid *N*-carboxyanhydrides (NCAs) by a 12 kDa α-methoxy-ω-amine polyethylene glycol (mPEG12K-NH_2) initiator followed by sequential functional group manipulations as shown in Figure 1. The quality of the triblock polymers is essential to the formulation of epothilone D. For this reason, the NCA monomers and hemitelechelic PEG were synthesized in-house. The NCAs were prepared by reacting the appropriate α-amino acid (side chain protected as necessary) with diphosgene in THF, filtration through celite, and precipitated from heptane. The PEG was prepared from the *N,N*-dibenzylethanolamine initiated polymerization of ethylene oxide followed by a methyl iodide quench. Heterogeneous hydrogenation with Pearlman's catalyst ($Pd(OH)_2/C$) furnished the PEG as its free base. Polymerization of the protected cysteine or glutamate NCAs is performed first to install the stabilizing block; this free amine terminus serves as the initiator for the second NCA polymerization to equip the hydrophobic core block. The appropriate basic or acidic conditions are used to deprotect the amino acid side chains, while treatment of the D/L-glutamic acid γ-benzyl esters with hydroxylamine and LiOH facilitates the formation of the hydroxamic acid moiety (Figure 1). Aqueous GPC and ^{1}H NMR of the final triblock polymers was used to confirm the desired degree of polymerization and purity.

3.2. Pilot Formulation and Physiochemical Characterization. Epothilones B and D were selected for encapsulation using triblock copolymers. Initial analysis of pilot formulations demonstrated low drug loading and lack of stability of the epothilone B drug substance. Upon further investigation utilizing mass spectrometry, it was determined that the epoxide ring of epothilone B was unstable to all experimental formulation conditions. This was not completely surprising as stability of epothilone B both in vitro and in vivo has been addressed in the literature [31, 32]. Epothilone D, the alkene derivative of epothilone B (also known as desoxy-epothilone B), was selected as the preferred drug substance for encapsulation due to increased stability in aqueous environments and pH fluctuations. A small library of triblock copolymers was used to conduct pilot formulations of epothilone D drug-loaded micelles, with the ultimate goal to select IT-147, the lead for development of an epothilone D encapsulated polymer micelle formulation. Five of the polymers chosen for the library contained stabilizing blocks comprised of hydroxamic acid functionalized poly(glutamic acid), and five of the polymers contained poly(cysteine) amino acid moieties as stabilizing blocks (Figure 2, Table 1). All polymers contained a 12 kDa PEG and a mixture of hydrophobic

Table 1: Physiochemical characterization of epothilone D pilot formulations with iron-hydroxamate or disulfide bond stabilization. Formulations were performed with each polymer listed as an entry number and characterized by drug weight loading, efficiency, particle size, and dialysis above and below the critical micelle concentration. Entry numbers 1 and 7 represent the leads selected for screening, and entry number 2 represents the scaled-up lead formulation.

Entry number	Polymer core block	Polymer stabilizing block	Weight loading (% w/w)	Efficiency (%)	Average diameter (nm)	Dialysis > CMC (% remaining)	Dialysis < CMC (% remaining)
1	D-Phe_{15}/ L-Tyr_{15}/ D-Leu_{10}	NHOH	3.4	66	70	90	60
2	D-Phe_{15}/ L-Tyr_{15}/ D-Leu_{10}	NHOH	4.4	91	75	94	68
3	D-Phe_{15}/ L-Tyr_{25}	NHOH	3.3	64	70	80	25
4	D-Phe_{15}/ L-Tyr_{20}/ D-Leu_{5}	NHOH	3.0	58	91	91	28
5	D-Phe_{15}/ L-Tyr_{20}/ D-Asp_{5}	NHOH	1.7	33	97	82	28
6	D-Phe_{10}/ L-Tyr_{20}/ D-Asp_{10}	NHOH	0.9	17	>200	55	<10
7	L-Tyr_{20}/ D-Leu_{20}	Cysteine	3.7	72	68	94	38
8	D-Phe_{15}/ L-Tyr_{25}	Cysteine	2.9	56	86	87	11
9	D-Phe_{15}/ L-Asp_{25}	Cysteine	0.1	<1	35	ND	ND
10	L-Tyr_{20}/ D-Asp_{20}	Cysteine	0.1	<1	>200	47	<10
11	D-Leu_{15}/ L-Tyr_{20}/ D-Asp_{20}	Cysteine	0.5	1	>200	ND	ND

amino acids with D and L isomers in the core block. Pilot formulations were characterized by determining formulation efficiency, epothilone D drug loading (% w/w), average particle diameter, and retention of epothilone D following dialysis above and below the critical micelle concentration (Table 1).

Epothilone D formulations containing polymer core blocks with a combination of phenylalanine, tyrosine, and leucine with hydroxamic acid (NHOH) stabilizing blocks demonstrated successful encapsulation of epothilone D based on greater than 80% retention of the API upon dialysis above the CMC, formulation efficiency above 50%, and average particle diameter between 70 and 100 nm. However, only the formulation utilizing a polymer with a core-forming block consisting of a mixture of phenylalanine/tyrosine/leucine (Table 1, entry number 1) demonstrated stability upon dilution when cross-linked with iron, which resulted in 60% retention of the drug after dialysis below the CMC. Epothilone D formulations containing polymer core blocks with aspartic acid resulted in low drug weight loading leading to inefficient formulations.

Polymers containing cysteine stabilizing blocks with leucine/tyrosine or phenylalanine/tyrosine core blocks demonstrated successful encapsulation of epothilone D with formulation efficiencies of 72% and 56%, average particle diameter of 68 and 86 nm, and API retention of 94% and 87% after dialysis above the CMC. The formulation with polymer core block D-Leu_{20}/L-Tyr_{20} (this nomenclature represents a random copolymer comprised of 20 leucine and 20 tyrosine monomer units) demonstrated the greatest stability upon dilution for the cysteine-containing polymers with 38% retention when dialyzed below the CMC (Table 1, entry number 7). Cysteine-containing polymers with aspartic acid in the core did not result in the successful encapsulation of epothilone D. Based on the data presented in Table 1 formulations with NHOH-block-D-Phe_{15}/L-Tyr_{15}/D-Leu_{10} and Cysteine-block-D-Leu_{20}/L-Tyr_{20} were chosen as the top candidates for lead selection of IT-147.

3.3. Selection of IT-147 Lead Formulation by Rat Pharmacokinetics. Stability of polymer micelles to dilution is one of the

TABLE 2: Plasma pharmacokinetic screening of pilot epothilone D formulations compared to free drug. A cannulated rat model was used to determine the AUC, C_{max}, and Clast of epothilone D in plasma for the first hour after administration.

Test article	Animals per group	Dose (mg/kg)	$AUC_{(0\text{-}1\,h)}$ (h∗μg/mL)	C_{max} (μg/mL)	Clast (μg/mL)
NHOH micelle	3	10	18.9	42.7 ± 4.9	7.7 ± 0.2
Cys micelle	3	10	10.6	34.0 ± 11.0	4.8 ± 1.1
Free drug	3	10	5.2	19.7 ± 4.1	1.6 ± 0.8

most important physiochemical characteristics for a formulation to be successful in vivo. Dialysis assays and other in vitro stability experiments provide important information and a cost effective means for screening formulations. However, the true measure of stability is the ability of the micelle to remain intact and circulate once injected into the bloodstream. It has been our experience that for screening purposes C_{max} and first hour of the distribution phase in plasma are highly predictive of the performance of the polymer micelle formulations. This allows for rapid assessment of the effectiveness of the encapsulation by comparing the micelle formulations to the free drug, while minimizing the total number of animals and samples needed for the study. This approach is beneficial for screening purposes for lead selection prior to full characterization of the pharmacokinetic properties of the lead formulation. The top two candidates from the pilot epothilone D formulations were evaluated, along with epothilone D free drug, using a cannulated rat model for pharmacokinetics. Selection of the lead epothilone D formulation, termed IT-147, was determined from the exposure of epothilone D to the plasma compartment by calculating the area under the concentration versus time curve (AUC) and maximum concentration (C_{max}). To determine the elimination of the drug from the plasma compartment over the first hour, 10 mg/kg epothilone D was administered by fast bolus to the rat jugular vein catheter (Table 2). Plasma was isolated from blood collected at time points of 1, 5, 15, and 60 minutes and processed for epothilone D concentration by HPLC/UV, as shown in Figure 4. The dose of 10 mg/kg epothilone D equivalent was chosen to screen the formulations against the free drug due to toxicities that occur when dosing the free drug above 10 mg/kg, as noted in the toxicokinetic results described in Table 4. Epothilone D from the NHOH micelle formulation demonstrated a C_{max} of 42.7 μg/mL at the 1 minute time point and an $AUC_{(0\text{-}1\,h)}$ of 18.9 h∗μg/mL. Epothilone D from the Cys micelle formulation demonstrated a C_{max} of 34 μg/mL at the 1-minute time point and an $AUC_{(0\text{-}1\,h)}$ of 10.6 h∗μg/mL. Epothilone D free drug demonstrated a C_{max} of 19.7 μg/mL at the 1 minute time point and an $AUC_{(0\text{-}1\,h)}$ of 5.2 h∗μg/mL. The pharmacokinetics of epothilone D from the NHOH micelle formulation showed an increased C_{max} and AUC based on plasma circulation after 1 hour compared to the Cys formulation and epothilone D free drug in the distribution phase (Figure 4, Table 2). Based on this data the NHOH micelle was selected as IT-147, the lead formulation for scale up and development. The polymer used in IT-147, mPEG12K-NH-*b*-*p*-[D-Glu(NHOH)$_5$-*co*-L-Glu(NHOH)$_5$]-*b*-*p*-[D-Phe$_{15}$-*co*-L-Tyr$_{15}$-*co*-D-Leu$_{10}$]-Ac, was termed ITP-103.

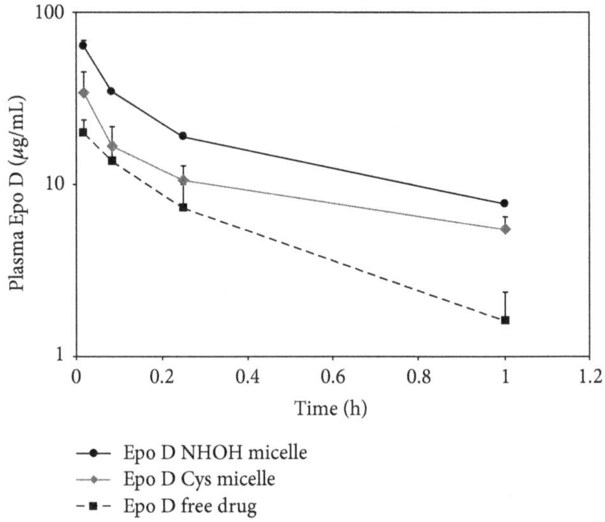

FIGURE 4: Plasma pharmacokinetics of epothilone D from lead pilot formulations and free drug doses at 10 mg/kg. Screening of the first hour of plasma circulation demonstrates increased C_{max} and AUC for the NHOH micelle formulation.

3.4. Scale-Up and Physiochemical Characterization of IT-147. With lead selection complete for the IT-147 formulation the next step was to scale the batch size from a pilot scale of 5 grams to a larger scale of 200 grams. This scale allowed for further physiochemical characterization, assessment of scalability for future larger scale batches, and further in vivo testing. Formulation of IT-147 on the 200 gram scale led to an 91% efficient process, with a drug loading of 4.4% on a 5% feed based on polymer weight. The average particle diameter was 75 nm as measured by DLS, displaying a narrow particle size distribution with *D*10/*D*50/*D*90 measurements of 29.7 nm, 34.5 nm, and 39.5 nm, respectively (Figure 5). Stability of the IT-147 formulation was tested by dialysis above the CMC and below the CMC and compared to the unstabilized NHOH formulation and epothilone D free drug (Figure 6). Dialysis of IT-147 above the CMC (20 mg/mL) demonstrated successful encapsulation with 90% of epothilone D remaining after dialysis, compared to 15% of epothilone D free dug retained after 6 hours of dialysis. Likewise, dialysis of IT-147 below the CMC (0.2 mg/mL) led to 60% retention of epothilone D, compared to 10% of epothilone D remaining from the unstabilized formulation. The release of epothilone D from IT-147 below the CMC based on pH-dependence was tested by dialysis in phosphate buffer between pH 3 and 8 over 6 hours (Figure 6). IT-147 demonstrated a pH-dependent

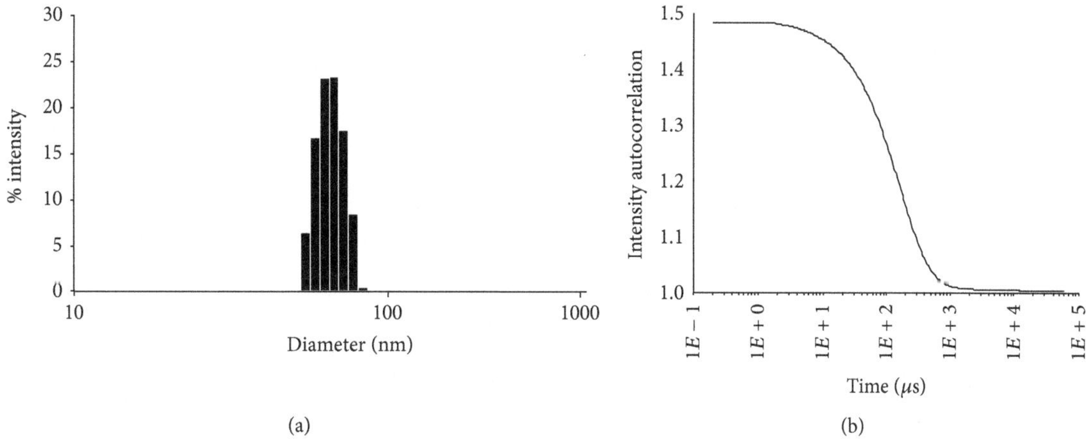

FIGURE 5: Particle size analysis of IT-147 by dynamic light scattering. Particle size distribution histogram (a) and correlation function (b) for particle size analysis demonstrates a monomodal particle size distribution at 75 nm in diameter.

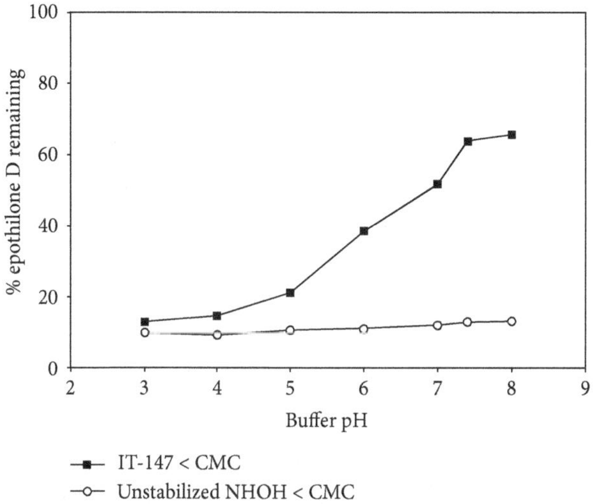

FIGURE 6: pH-dependent release of IT-147 by dialysis. The iron-stabilized IT-147 formulation demonstrates stability at physiological pH and a pH-dependent release of epothilone D as the pH decreases, whereas the unstabilized formulation releases the drug payload at all pH levels tested within the 6-hour dialysis assay.

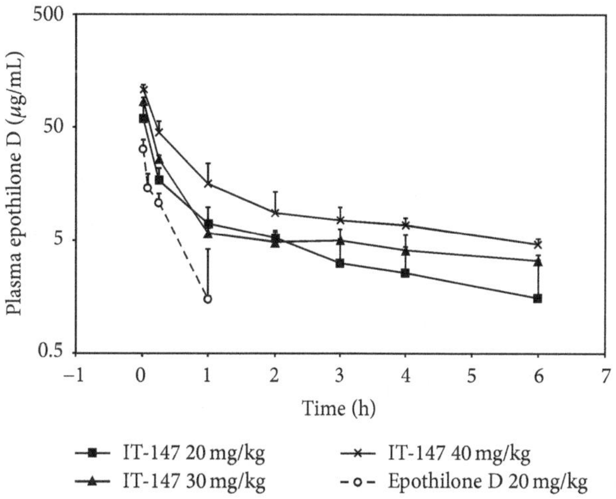

FIGURE 7: Plasma pharmacokinetics from the pilot toxicokinetic dose range-finding screen of IT-147. Plasma samples were isolated and assayed for epothilone D content during the pilot toxicokinetic screen to support full toxicokinetic and pharmacokinetic studies. IT-147 demonstrated superior pharmacokinetics compared to free drug at 20 mg/kg, and a linear increase in C_{max} and AUC in dosing from 20 to 40 mg/kg.

release of epothilone D with 13, 15, 21, 39, 52, 64, and 66% remaining at pH 3, 4, 5, 6, 7, 7.4, and 8, respectively. Dialysis of the unstabilized NHOH formulation resulted in 10–15% epothilone D remaining over the pH ranging 3–8.

3.5. Pilot Toxicokinetics in a Cannulated Rat Model. A pilot dose range-finding toxicokinetic study in a cannulated rat model was performed to support future full scale toxicokinetic studies of IT-147. Doses of IT-147 at 20, 30 and 40 mg/kg were compared to epothilone D free drug at 20 mg/kg (Table 3, Figure 7) followed by monitoring of animal weight change, gross signs of clinical toxicity, and limited plasma sampling for pharmacokinetic analysis (Table 4). IT-147 was reconstituted in saline while epothilone D free drug was administered in a cremaphor : ethanol : saline mixture. Test articles were given by fast bolus to the rat jugular vein, and blood was collected at time points of 1 minute, 5 minutes, 15 minutes, 1 hour, 2 hours, 4 hours, and 6 hours. Epothilone D from IT-147 demonstrated a linear increase in maximum concentration and exposure to plasma compartment by area under the curve analysis (Table 4). IT-147 administered at 20 mg/kg epothilone D equivalent resulted in a C_{max} of 59.1 μg/mL, an AUC of 53.5 h∗μg/mL, a clearance rate of 373.7 mL/h/kg, and a terminal half-life of 4.3 hours. Animals were monitored for one week after test article administration and demonstrated no signs of gross clinical toxicity or significant weight fluctuation. In contrast, Epothilone D free drug administered at 20 mg/kg resulted in a C_{max} of 32.2 μg/mL, an AUC of 8.3 h∗μg/mL, a clearance rate of 2414.7 mL/h/kg, and a terminal half-life of 0.3 hours. Samples collected after the 1-hour time point were below the limit of quantitation for

TABLE 3: Dosing summary for rat pharmacokinetic studies. Epothilone D free drug was dosed at 10 and 20 mg/kg. IT-147 was dosed at 10, 20, 30, and 40 mg/kg epothilone D equivalent or 500, 1000, 1500, and 2000 mg/kg formulation, respectively.

Test article	Dose epothilone D (mg/kg)	Dose IT-147 (mg/kg)	Epothilone D concentration (mg/mL)	IT-147 concentration (mg/mL)	Test article volume (mL)
Epo D	10	0	1.15	0	2
Epo D	20	0	2.3	0	2
IT-147	10	500	1.15	57.5	2
IT-147	20	1000	2.30	115	2
IT-147	30	1500	3.45	173	2
IT-147	40	2000	4.60	230	2

TABLE 4: Pilot toxicokinetic dose range-finding study for IT-147 formulation. IT-147 was administered at 20, 30, and 40 mg/kg epothilone D equivalent compared to free drug at 20 mg/kg. Limited pharmacokinetic sampling was used to determine C_{max}, AUC, clearance, and half-life data for each animal up to 6 hours after test article administration.

Test article	Dose (mg/kg)	Animals per group	C_{max} (μg/mL)	$AUC_{(0-6\,h)}$ (h$*\mu$g/mL)	Clearance (mL/h/kg)	Half-life (h)	Dose limiting Toxicities
Epo D	20	6	32.2	8.3	2414.7	0.3	>10% w.l. lethargy impaired gait orbital-bleeding
IT-147	20	4	59.1	53.5	373.7	4.3	None
IT-147	30	4	85.4	82.9	361.8	5.1	10% w.l. slight-lethargy
IT-147	40	4	107.6	110.8	361.0	4.4	>10% w.l. lethargy impaired gait orbital-bleeding

analysis. Animals were monitored for four days before test article administration and were euthanized on the fourth day due to welfare concerns. Animals demonstrated weight loss on average of 12% and clinical signs of dose limiting toxicities such as lethargy, impaired gait, orbital bleeding, porphyrin accumulation around the face, and disheveled fur. It was concluded that 20 mg/kg epothilone D free drug was above the maximum tolerated dose for these animals. IT-147 administered at 30 mg/kg epothilone D equivalent resulted in a C_{max} of 85.4 μg/mL, an AUC of 82.9 h$*\mu$g/mL, a clearance rate of 361.8 mL/h/kg, and a terminal half-life of 5.1 hours. Animals were monitored for one week following test article administration. They demonstrated an average weight loss of 10% over the first four days, which started to recover between days five and seven. Animals in this dosing group demonstrated slight lethargy unless prompted to move about their cage. No orbital bleeding or gait impairment was noted for these animals. IT-147 administered at 40 mg/kg epothilone D equivalent resulted in a C_{max} of 107.6 μg/mL, an AUC of 110.8 h$*\mu$g/mL, a clearance rate of 361.0 mL/h/kg, and a terminal half-life of 4.4 hours. Animals were monitored for four days after test article administration and were euthanized on the fourth day due to welfare concerns. Animals demonstrated weight loss on average of 14%, and clinical signs of dose limiting toxicities such as lethargy, impaired gait, orbital bleeding, porphyrin accumulation around the face, and disheveled fur. It was concluded that 40 mg/kg epothilone D from IT-147 was above the maximum tolerated dose for these animals. Taken together, this data demonstrated that the maximum tolerated dose for IT-147 was greater than 30 mg/kg but below 40 mg/kg. This data will be used to support full toxicokinetic studies with complete pharmacokinetic analysis in order to determine the NOAEL and maximum tolerated dose for IT-147.

4. Discussion

Enabling technologies for drug delivery have the potential to expand the utility of drug substances, especially cytotoxic chemotherapeutics. Polymer micelles have long been studied for these purposes; however they have demonstrated limited success in providing safer and more effective formulations. We hypothesized that parameters such as stability to dilution below the critical micelle concentration, particle size, and targeted drug release without the need for chemical conjugation or enzymatic activation are paramount to the success of micellar formulations. Encapsulation of epothilone D provided an opportunity to investigate stabilizing technologies for triblock copolymers using iron-hydroxamate or disulfide bonds in the stabilizing middle block. A small library of polymers that incorporate a mixture of D and L isomer amino acids in the core block for sequestration of epothilone D was used for pilot formulations. The D/L mix strategy is critical for forming a micelle core that is less rigid by breaking up the α-helix secondary structure.

Traditional polymer micelles inherently suffer from instability due to dilution and exposure to surfactant proteins and salt gradients when administered systemically. Instability leads to premature release of the drug substance that abrogates the benefits imparted by encapsulation in the micelle. To address the instability issue Intezyne has incorporated a stabilizing block between the amphiphilic PEG block and encapsulation core block. Two strategies were employed to investigate cross-linking stability for the micelle formulations. The first strategy was to functionalize a middle block by converting glutamic acid to hydroxamic acid (NHOH) moieties such that iron molecules form dative bonds between polymer strands effectively cross-linking the micelle and stabilizing the structure. The second strategy was to incorporate cysteine (Cys) amino acids in the middle block so that formulation could be performed in the presence of a reducing agent (DTT), and upon removal of the agent disulfide bonds could form between the cysteine molecules. Physiochemical parameters such as drug loading efficiency, particle size, and stability to dilution were used to screen the pilot formulations to determine the leads. Successful encapsulation was demonstrated with both NHOH and Cys polymers as determined by dialysis of the formulations when reconstituted above the critical micelle concentration (20 mg/mL). Polymers with leucine in the core block led to more efficient encapsulation of epothilone D, as well as the most stable formulations to dilution after cross-linking. When reconstituted at 0.2 mg/mL the lead formulations retained 60% (NHOH) and 38% (Cys) of the epothilone D inside the dialysis bag compared to less than 15% remaining for the same formulations without iron (NHOH) or DTT (Cys) present in the formulation. Ultimately, the lead NHOH polymer with the core of D-Phe_{15}/L-Tyr_{15}/D-Leu_{10}, and the lead Cys polymer with the core L-Tyr_{20}/D-Leu_{20} were selected for screening using a cannulated rat model for pharmacokinetics to determine the optimized lead for further characterization and development. The iron-hydroxamate stabilized formulation outperformed in the cannulated rat model and was chosen to scale up for further characterization.

The ability to scale up production of materials and drug product is critical to the development of nanoparticle formulations. Preclinical animal models and studies necessary for enabling Investigational New Drug (IND) applications can require hundreds of grams to kilograms of material. Therefore, we demonstrated production of IT-147 drug product on the 200 gram scale for complete physiochemical characterization and preliminary dose range-finding toxicokinetic studies, with future studies focused on determining antitumor efficacy and toxicokinetics with full pharmacokinetics in dose range-finding studies. When produced on scale the formulation efficiency increased to over 90 percent, likely due to a decrease in loss during transfer, tangential flow filtration, and sterile filtration. Particle size analysis demonstrated an average hydrodynamic diameter of 75 nm, with a narrow particle size distribution. Particle size has been shown to play a key role in influencing nanoparticle circulation time, accumulation in the tumor environment by the enhanced permeability and retention (EPR) effect, depth of penetration into the tumor, and cellular entry mechanism. This was taken into account when tuning the block lengths of the polymer monomers such that the self-assembly of the micelle around the drug substance would yield a nanoparticle with optimal size characteristics.

In addition to the size and stability of the nanoparticle formulation, the release of the drug substance is critical to providing an efficacious drug product. A distinct advantage of using iron to chelate hydroxamic acid moieties for micelle stability is the reversibility of this interaction based on pH, as depicted graphically in Figure 3. A pH-dependent targeted release of drug substance payload for oncology applications is hypothesized to lead to increased efficacy with a greater exposure to the tumor compartment, while keeping the drug exposure low to other critical compartments should lead to decreased toxicity. In vitro we have demonstrated the pH-dependent release of epothilone D from the micelle using dialysis in buffers with a range of pH from 3 to 8. IT-147 formulation was reconstituted at 0.2 mg/mL and dialyzed for 6 hours in the corresponding buffers. This release profile serves as proof of concept for targeted release. It has been well documented that the pH of most tumor microenvironments is in the range of 5.5 to 7 [25, 33–37]. In addition, cellular uptake by endocytosis can lead to the formation of lysosomes, which can have an internal pH of 4 to 5 [26]. It is of great interest to determine the precise location and mechanism for release of the drug payload from the micelle, whether it is intracellular or extracellular. However, this is a highly complex question that despite ongoing experimentation has not been adequately addressed at this time.

An important mechanism for nanoparticles to accumulate in the tumor compartment is prolonged circulation in the blood/plasma compartment. A dose-dependent pharmacokinetic study in cannulated rats was done to assess the plasma pharmacokinetics of epothilone D from IT-147. A dose of 20 mg/kg epothilone D from IT-147 was well tolerated with no observed adverse events and resulted in greater than 6-fold increase in plasma exposure compared to free drug. Administration of epothilone D free drug at 20 mg/kg was determined to be above the maximum tolerated dose in these animals and resulted in weight loss greater than 10%, with clinical signs of toxicity such as lethargy, gait impairment, and retro-orbital bleeding. Pharmacokinetic analysis of the dose dependency from IT-147 showed near linearity for AUC and C_{max}, with increased half-life and decreased clearance compared to epothilone D free drug. The extended circulation in the plasma compartment can be directly attributed to the increased stability of the micelle from iron-mediated cross-linking. In addition to imparting stability, the geometrical arrangement of iron atoms around the core of the micelle also provides superparamagnetic properties that allow for positive contrast using T_1-weighted magnetic resonance imaging. This theranostic strategy could provide a potential imaging biomarker for clinical applications.

Taken together, formulation of IT-147 presents a significant improvement in delivery of epothilone D and is positioned for development for oncology applications. Future preclinical studies will focus on determining the full toxicokinetic profile, antitumor efficacy, and tissue biodistribution of epothilone D delivered by IT-147.

Competing Interests

The authors declare that they have no competing interests.

Acknowledgments

This work was supported by the National Cancer Institute of the National Institute of Health Small Business Innovative Research (SBIR) Program [Contract no. HHSN2612201400018C].

References

[1] H. Reichenbach and G. Höfle, "Biologically active secondary metabolites from myxobacteria," *Biotechnology Advances*, vol. 11, no. 2, pp. 219–277, 1993.

[2] G. Hofle, "Epothilone A and B—novel 16-membered macrolides with cytotoxic activity: isolation, crystal structure, and conformation in solution," *Angewandte Chemie*, vol. 35, pp. 1567–1569, 1996.

[3] K. Gerth, N. Bedorf, G. Höfle, H. Irschik, and H. Reichenbach, "Epothilons A and B: antifungal and cytotoxic compounds from Sorangium cellulosum (Myxobacteria) production, physico-chemical and biological properties," *The Journal of Antibiotics*, vol. 49, no. 6, pp. 560–563, 1996.

[4] D. M. Bollag, P. A. McQueney, J. Zhu et al., "Epothilones, a new class of microtubule-stabilizing agents with a taxol- like mechanism of action," *Cancer Research*, vol. 55, no. 11, pp. 2325–2333, 1995.

[5] R. J. Kowalski, P. Giannakakou, and E. Hamel, "Activities of the microtubule-stabilizing agents epothilones A and B with purified tubulin and in cells resistant to paclitaxel (Taxol®)," *The Journal of Biological Chemistry*, vol. 272, no. 4, pp. 2534–2541, 1997.

[6] K. C. Nicolaou, N. Winssinger, J. Pastor et al., "Synthesis of epothilones A and B in solid and solution phase," *Nature*, vol. 387, no. 6630, pp. 268–272, 1997.

[7] F. Y. F. Lee, R. Borzilleri, C. R. Fairchild et al., "BMS-247550: a novel epothilone analog with a mode of action similar to paclitaxel but possessing superior antitumor efficacy," *Clinical Cancer Research*, vol. 7, no. 5, pp. 1429–1437, 2001.

[8] T.-C. Chou, H. Dong, A. Rivkin et al., "Design and total synthesis of a superior family of epothilone analogues, which eliminate xenograft tumors to a nonrelapsable state," *Angewandte Chemie*, vol. 42, no. 39, pp. 4761–4767, 2003.

[9] S. Goodin, M. P. Kane, and E. H. Rubin, "Epothilones: mechanism of action and biologic activity," *Journal of Clinical Oncology*, vol. 22, no. 10, pp. 2015–2025, 2004.

[10] T. O'Reilly, P. M. J. McSheehy, F. Wenger et al., "Patupilone (epothilone B, EPO906) inhibits growth and metastasis of experimental prostate tumors in vivo," *Prostate*, vol. 65, no. 3, pp. 231–240, 2005.

[11] P. Fumoleau, B. Coudert, N. Isambert, and E. Ferrant, "Novel tubulin-targeting agents: anticancer activity and pharmacologic profile of epothilones and related analogues," *Annals of Oncology*, vol. 18, supplement 5, pp. v9–v15, 2007.

[12] D.-S. Su, A. Balog, D. Meng et al., "Structure-activity relationship of the epothilones and the first in vivo comparison with paclitaxel," *Angewandte Chemie*, vol. 36, no. 19, pp. 2093–2096, 1997.

[13] T.-C. Chou, X.-G. Zhang, A. Balog et al., "Desoxyepothilone B: an efficacious microtubule-targeted antitumor agent with a promising in vivo profile relative to epothilone B," *Proceedings of the National Academy of Sciences of the United States of America*, vol. 95, no. 16, pp. 9642–9647, 1998.

[14] T.-C. Chou, X.-G. Zhang, C. R. Harris et al., "Desoxyepothilone B is curative against human tumor xenografts that are refractory to paclitaxel," *Proceedings of the National Academy of Sciences of the United States of America*, vol. 95, no. 26, pp. 15798–15802, 1998.

[15] W. Blum, R. Aichholz, P. Ramstein et al., "In vivo metabolism of epothilone B in tumor-bearing nude mice: identification of three new epothilone B metabolites by capillary high-pressure liquid chromatography/mass spectrometry/tandem mass spectrometry," *Rapid Communications in Mass Spectrometry*, vol. 15, no. 1, pp. 41–49, 2001.

[16] T.-C. Chou, O. A. O'Connor, W. P. Tong et al., "The synthesis, discovery, and development of a highly promising class of microtubule stabilization agents: curative effects of desoxyepothilones B and F against human tumor xenografts in nude mice," *Proceedings of the National Academy of Sciences of the United States of America*, vol. 98, no. 14, pp. 8113–8118, 2001.

[17] J. M. G. Larkin and S. B. Kaye, "Potential clinical applications of epothilones: a review of phase II studies," *Annals of Oncology*, vol. 18, no. 5, pp. v28–v34, 2007.

[18] S. W. B. Overmoyer, P. A. Kaufman, T. Doyle et al., "Phase II trial of KOS-862 (epothilone D) in anthracycline and taxane pretreated metastatic breast cancer," *Journal of Clinical Oncology*, vol. 23, article 778, 2005.

[19] T. L. L. Yee, M. Villalona-Calero, N. Rizvi et al., "A phase II study of KOS-862 (epothilone D) as second-line therapy in non-small cell lung cancer," *Journal of Clinical Oncology*, vol. 23, p. 7127, 2005.

[20] D. R. Feldman, G. V. Kondagunta, M. S. Ginsberg et al., "Phase II Trial of ixabepilone in patients with cisplatin-refractory germ cell tumors," *Investigational New Drugs*, vol. 25, no. 5, pp. 487–490, 2007.

[21] S. McMeekin, D. Dizon, J. Barter et al., "Phase III randomized trial of second-line ixabepilone versus paclitaxel or doxorubicin in women with advanced endometrial cancer," *Gynecologic Oncology*, vol. 138, no. 1, pp. 18–23, 2015.

[22] H. S. Rugo, W. T. Barry, A. Moreno-Aspitia et al., "Randomized phase III trial of paclitaxel once per week compared with nanoparticle albumin-bound nab-paclitaxel once per week or ixabepilone with bevacizumab as first-line chemotherapy for locally recurrent or metastatic breast cancer: CALGB 40502/NCCTG N063H (Alliance)," *Journal of Clinical Oncology*, vol. 33, no. 21, pp. 2361–2369, 2015.

[23] V. J. Venditto and F. C. Szoka Jr., "Cancer nanomedicines: so many papers and so few drugs!," *Advanced Drug Delivery Reviews*, vol. 65, no. 1, pp. 80–88, 2013.

[24] T. Stylianopoulos and R. K. Jain, "Design considerations for nanotherapeutics in oncology," *Nanomedicine: Nanotechnology, Biology, and Medicine*, vol. 11, no. 8, pp. 1893–1907, 2015.

[25] X. Zhang, Y. Lin, and R. J. Gillies, "Tumor pH and its measurement," *Journal of Nuclear Medicine*, vol. 51, no. 8, pp. 1167–1170, 2010.

[26] J. A. Mindell, "Lysosomal acidification mechanisms," *Annual Review of Physiology*, vol. 74, pp. 69–86, 2012.

[27] J. Wang, S. Li, T. Luo, C. Wang, and J. Zhao, "Disulfide linkage: a potent strategy in tumor-targeting drug discovery," *Current Medicinal Chemistry*, vol. 19, no. 18, pp. 2976–2983, 2012.

[28] (K.T. Sill, FL, US), Vojkovsky, Tomas (Palm Beach Gardens, FL, US), Carie, Adam (Ruskin, FL, US), Block copolymers for stable micelles, in, Intezyne Technologies, Inc. (Tampa, FL, US), United States, 2015.

[29] T. L. C. Costich, A. Semple, J. E. Sullivan et al., "IT-143, a polymer micelle nanoparticle, widens therapeutic window of daunorubicin," *Pharmaceutical Nanotechnology*, vol. 4, no. 1, pp. 3–15, 2016.

[30] L. Yuan, Y. Fu, D. Zhang et al., "Use of a carboxylesterase inhibitor of phenylmethanesulfonyl fluoride to stabilize epothilone D in rat plasma for a validated UHPLC-MS/MS assay," *Journal of Chromatography B: Analytical Technologies in the Biomedical and Life Sciences*, vol. 969, pp. 60–68, 2014.

[31] K. C. Nicolaou, P. K. Sasmal, G. Rassias et al., "Design, synthesis, and biological properties of highly potent epothilone B analogues," *Angewandte Chemie*, vol. 42, no. 30, pp. 3515–3520, 2003.

[32] G. H. K.-H. Altman, R. Muller, J. Mulzer, and K. Prantz, *The Epothilones: An Outstanding Family of Anti-Tumor Agents*, Springer, New York, NY, USA, 2009.

[33] I. F. Tannock and D. Rotin, "Acid pH in tumors and its potential for therapeutic exploitation," *Cancer Research*, vol. 49, no. 16, pp. 4373–4384, 1989.

[34] D. B. Leeper, K. Engin, A. J. Thistlethwaite et al., "Human tumor extracellular pH as a function of blood glucose concentration," *International Journal of Radiation Oncology, Biology, Physics*, vol. 28, no. 4, pp. 935–943, 1994.

[35] K. Engin, D. B. Leeper, J. R. Cater, A. J. Thistlethwaite, L. Tupchong, and J. D. Mcfarlane, "Extracellular pH distribution in human tumours," *International Journal of Hyperthermia*, vol. 11, no. 2, pp. 211–216, 1995.

[36] A. S. E. Ojugo, P. M. J. McSheehy, D. J. O. McIntyre et al., "Measurement of the extracellular pH of solid tumours in mice by magnetic resonance spectroscopy: a comparison of exogenous 19F and 31P probes," *NMR in Biomedicine*, vol. 12, no. 8, pp. 495–504, 1999.

[37] R. van Sluis, Z. M. Bhujwalla, N. Raghunand et al., "In vivo imaging of extracellular pH using 1H MRSI," *Magnetic Resonance in Medicine*, vol. 41, no. 4, pp. 743–750, 1999.

13

Sustained Release of Protein Therapeutics from Subcutaneous Thermosensitive Biocompatible and Biodegradable Pentablock Copolymers (PTS*gels*)

Elizabeth Schaefer,[1] Santhi Abbaraju,[2] Mary Walsh,[1] Donna Newman,[1] Jacklyn Salmon,[1] Rasidul Amin,[2] Sidney Weiss,[3] Ulrich Grau,[3] Poonam Velagaleti,[3] and Brian Gilger[1]

[1]*North Carolina State University, Raleigh, NC, USA*
[2]*Symmetry Biosciences, Research Triangle Park, NC, USA*
[3]*i-novion, Inc., Randolph, NJ, USA*

Correspondence should be addressed to Brian Gilger; bgilger@ncsu.edu

Academic Editor: Kang Choon Lee

Objective. To evaluate thermosensitive, biodegradable pentablock copolymers (PTS*gel*) for sustained release and integrity of a therapeutic protein when injected subcutaneously. *Materials and Methods.* Five PTS*gels* with PEG-PCL-PLA-PCL-PEG block arrangements were synthesized. *In vitro* release of IgG from PTS*gels* and concentrations was evaluated at 37°C. Released IgG integrity was characterized by SDS-PAGE. *In vitro* disintegration for 10GH PTS*gel* in PBS was monitored at 37°C over 72 days using gravimetric loss and GPC analysis. Near-infrared IgG in PTS*gel* was injected subcutaneously and examined by *in vivo* imaging and histopathology for up to 42 days. *Results.* IgG release was modulated from approximately 7 days to more than 63 days in both *in vitro* and *in vivo* testing by varying polymer composition, concentration of PTS*gel* aqueous solution, and concentration of IgG. Released IgG *in vitro* maintained structural integrity by SDS-PAGE. Subcutaneous PTS*gels* were highly biocompatible and *in vitro* IgG release occurred in parallel with the disappearance of subcutaneous gel *in vivo*. *Conclusions.* Modulation of release of biologics to fit the therapeutic need can be achieved by varying the biocompatible and biodegradable PTS*gel* composition. Release of IgG parallels disappearance of the polymeric gel; hence, little or no PTS*gel* remains after drug release is complete.

1. Introduction

Increase in the use of biologics has occurred over the past decade for the treatment, prevention, or cure of a variety of diseases in humans. Biological products include blood-derived products, vaccines, immunoglobulins, cells or microorganisms, and other proteins [1–4]. These have led to major therapeutic advances in several prevalent diseases, including immune-mediated arthritis and cancer immunotherapy [5]. Many biologics are administered to the patient, usually by daily or weekly subcutaneous injection. A controlled, sustained release therapeutic would decrease the frequency of injections, leading to increased patient compliance and therapeutic efficacy.

Sustained release subcutaneous therapeutics have been available for several decades, but recent advances in polymer science have led to development of hydrogels that provide sustained drug release, have high tissue biocompatibility, and allow self-administration by the patient [6]. Hydrogels provide a deformable drug depot that slowly elutes a high concentration of drug to surrounding tissue for an extended period of time [6]. However, because most hydrogels only physically incorporate, instead of forming covalent bonds to the drugs, a rapid drug release occurs over a few hours to days, limiting their value for sustained drug delivery [6].

Triblock copolymers of poly(ethylene oxide)-poly(propylene oxide)-poly(ethylene oxide) (PEO-PPO-PEO, poloxamers/pluronics) are the most widely used reverse thermal gelation polymers [7]. Other types of multiblock amphiphiles (i.e., polymers with both hydrophilic and hydrophobic domains) have been synthesized using a wide range of polymers. Some of these hydrogels are sufficiently deformable to be injectable, but many are not, necessitating surgical implantation for drug delivery. In either case, a high initial burst and lack of sustained drug release limit the clinical utility of these hydrogels [6, 8].

Polylactic-co-glycolic acid (PLGA) based hydrogels exhibit better biodegradability, higher gelation temperatures (permitting easier handling before injection), and longer periods of sustained drug release compared to poloxamer systems [9]. However, degradation of PLGA and PLGA copolymers produces lactic acid and glycolic acid, which reduces local pH substantially and may degrade protein therapeutics [10]. Furthermore, local tissue reaction to the PLGA may reduce tolerability and biocompatibility [11]. Therefore, an injectable and biocompatible hydrogel that provides a sustained release of biologically active protein therapeutic remains to be developed.

Pentablock copolymers are thermosensitive gels (*PTSgel*) composed of biodegradable or biocompatible polymer blocks, such as polyethylene glycol (PEG), polycaprolactone (PCL), polyglycolide (PGA), and polylactic acid (PLA). The relative block arrangement and molecular weight of PTS*gel* polymers affect the solution-gelation (sol-gel) transition behavior, degradation, and *in vitro* release characteristics of the hydrogel [12]. PTS*gels* may act as a drug delivery vehicle by entrapping the drug in the core of a micelle of PTS*gel* [12]. PTS*gels* can be injected through a small-gauge needle to form a firm, *in situ*, hydrogel depot [12]. PTS*gels* have been demonstrated to be biocompatible *in vitro* and *in vivo* and provide sustained release of immunoglobulin G (IgG) [12, 13]. Furthermore, enhanced stability of biologic proteins (IgG and bevacizumab) delivered from PTS*gels* *in vitro* was recently shown [13]. The amounts of PLA used in the described polymers ranged from 28 to 37% of the total molar mass. Compared to PLGA, the lower molar mass of PLA or PGA blocks in the PTS*gel* produces much lower amounts of lactic acid or glycolic acid on degradation, thereby improving protein stability of the delivered biologic. Therefore, the potential advantages of PTS*gels* as carriers for subcutaneous sustained delivery of protein biologic therapeutics include biodegradation, their high biocompatibility, long-term release kinetics, ease of injectability, and stability of the protein therapeutic being delivered.

The objective of this work was to further evaluate the sustained release properties of promising thermosensitive PTS*gels* for the controlled release of a model full-length therapeutic protein (IgG; mw 150 kDal) for subcutaneous injection. This study investigated the *in vitro* modulated release of IgG, the structural integrity of released IgG, and the *in vivo* duration of IgG release from PTS*gel* after subcutaneous injection. *In vitro*/*in vivo* correlation has been established and presented for selected PTS*gel* polymers. The study also investigated *in vitro* disintegration of 10GH PTS*gel* in PBS (pH 7.4) at 37°C over a period of several weeks.

2. Materials and Methods

2.1. PTSgel Synthesis. Monomethoxy PEG (550), L-lactide, tin octoate, hexamethylenediisocynate (HMDI), ethylene glycol-bis(2-aminoethylether)-N,N,N′,N′-tetraacetic acid (EGTA), sodium sulfate, dichloromethane, heptanes, and endotoxin free water were purchased from Sigma-Aldrich (St. Louis, MO). ε-Caprolactone was purchased from Alfa Aesar (Ward Hill, MA). PTS*gels* with PEG-PCL-PLA-PCL-PEG block arrangements were synthesized as previously described [12, 13]. Briefly, the diblock copolymer was synthesized by ring-opening copolymerization of ε-caprolactone with monomethoxy PEG using tin octoate as a catalyst. The resulting diblock copolymer was similarly converted to triblock by adding L-lactide. The resulting triblock copolymer was coupled utilizing hexamethylenediisocynate (HMDI) as a linker to prepare PEG-PCL-PLA-PCL-PEG pentablock copolymers. The purified pentablock was stored at −20°C until being used.

2.2. PTSgel Characterization

2.2.1. Fourier Transform Infrared Spectroscopy (FTIR) Analysis. Fourier transform infrared spectroscopy (FTIR) spectra were recorded with a Perkin Elmer Spectrum Version 10.03.09 infrared spectrophotometer. FTIR scan of neat polymer was carried out in a range of 4000–400 cm^{-1}.

2.2.2. ^{1}H-NMR Analysis. Purity, molecular structure, and molecular weight (Mn) of the PTS*gel* were analyzed utilizing a Mercury 300 MHz NMR spectrometer. ^{1}H-NMR spectrograms were recorded by dissolving the polymers in deuterated chloroform ($CDCl_3$).

2.2.3. Gel Permeation Chromatography (GPC) Analysis. Molecular weights (Mn and Mw) and polydispersity of polymers were examined by GPC analysis. Briefly, 20 mg of polymer was dissolved in 1 mL of tetrahydrofuran (THF). Polymer samples were separated on two OligoPore columns (Agilent, Santa Clara, CA) connected in series and maintained at 40°C. Solvent THF at the rate of 0.6 mL/min was utilized as eluting solvent. Samples were analyzed on Wyatt technologies MINI DAWN instrument (S. number 528-T) connected to OPTILAB DSP interferometric refractometer, using ASTRA 6 software.

2.2.4. Determination of Tin, Organic Solvents, and Endotoxin Levels in the Polymers. Amount of stannous (Tin) present was determined on 5% aqueous polymer solution using ICP-OES method on a Thermo iCAP 6100 instrument. Residual dichloromethane and heptane in the PTS*gel* were determined by head space GC-MS using an Agilent 5890 GC and an Agilent 5972 mass spectrometer. The column employed was Restek Rtx-5MS, 30 m × 0.25 mm, 0.1 μm film. The endotoxin levels were determined using Pierce Chromogenic Endotoxin Quantification Kit (Thermo Fisher Scientific, Waltham, MA).

2.3. Sol-Gel Transition Testing at 37°C. The sol (flow)-gel (no flow) transition of PTS*gel* was examined by following a previously published protocol [14]. Briefly, the polymers were dissolved in PBS buffer (pH 7.4) at 25 wt% concentration. 0.5 mL of aqueous polymeric solution was transferred into 2.5 mL glass vial and placed in water bath maintained at 37°C. Vials were kept for 5 min at 37°C. Gel formation was observed visually by inverting the tubes, immediately after pulling out of the water bath.

2.4. In Vitro PTSgel Disintegration (Incubation in PBS Buffer, pH 7.4 at 37°C)

2.4.1. Gravimetric Measurement of the Residual Gelling Polymer. Three concentrations (12.5, 18.75, and 25%) of PTS*gel* 10GH were evaluated for disintegration/degradation *in vitro*. Each individual PTS*gel* (500 μL of 10GH in triplicate) was pipetted into an 8 mL glass vial, weighed, and placed into a 37°C water bath for gelling for 30 minutes. 4 mL of PBS (37°C) with 0.02% sodium azide as preservative was placed over each PTS*gel*. The vials were placed into a 37°C shaker water bath, maintained at 60 rpm. Every 5 days, vials were centrifuged (2000 rpm for 5 minutes at 37°C), the PBS buffer was removed and replaced with fresh PBS, and the vials returned to the 37°C shaker water bath. Samples of gel were withdrawn after 0, 5, 15, 30, and 45 days and every 15 days thereafter until polymer completely disintegrated. At each time point, vials with residual gel were stored at −80°C until being lyophilized. Vials containing lyophilized gels were weighed and the dry gel weight was determined by subtracting the empty vial weight from the final dry weight.

2.4.2. GPC Analysis of the Residual Gelling Polymer and the Supernatant. The residual gelling polymer (PTS*gel* 10GH) and the supernatant collected during the gravimetric studies were analyzed using GPC. The gels were lyophilized using a Labconco Model 5 lyophilizer (Kansas City, MO) and 10–50 mL of the buffer samples were dried using a Genevac EZ-2 evaporator overnight. The lyophilized and dried samples were dissolved in 1 mL of tetrahydrofuran and further dried using 0.3–0.5 g of sodium sulfate. Samples were then vortexed and filtered using 0.2 μm PTFE ISO disc filters. Selected samples were analyzed by GPC as described in Section 2.2.3.

2.5. In Vitro Release of IgG from PTSgel. In vitro drug release experiments were conducted by adding 500 μL of 22.5% aqueous gelling polymeric solution containing 10 mg of IgG (Human IgG, Lee Biosolutions, Maryland Heights, MO) into an 8 mL silanized glass vial (Thermo Scientific, Waltham, MA) in triplicate. Vials were incubated in a 37°C water bath for ~5 minutes until polymer gelled. Release buffer, 4 mL of phosphate buffer saline (PBS, pH 7.4) with 0.02% (wt/vol) sodium azide, was gently layered over the solidified gel in each vial. Vials were sealed with parafilm and maintained at 60 rpm in a 37°C water bath to replicate physiologic conditions. 2 mL out of the 4 mL of overlaid buffer solution was removed from each vial on days 1, 2, 3, 4, 5, 7, 10, and 14 and then weekly thereafter until no more IgG was released. Following collection, 2 mL PBS release buffer with 0.02% sodium azide (maintained at 37°C) was layered back into the test vials which were returned to the shaker bath until the next sampling period. The concentration of released IgG samples was evaluated by comparing the released samples to a standard IgG calibration curve. Calibrators and release samples (200 μL) were pipetted into a 96-well, UV-free microplate (Greiner Bio-One, Monroe, NC) in triplicate and the absorbance was measured at 280 nm (Synergy 2 Microplate Reader, BioTek, Winooski, VT). All experiments were set up in triplicate and absorbance of a blank control (0% IgG in 22.5% PTS*gel*) was subtracted from the released samples for estimation of protein concentration. Similar experiments were set up using three different concentrations of 10GH PTS*gel* to evaluate further modulation of the release profiles.

2.6. After Releasing IgG Integrity

2.6.1. Sodium Dodecyl Sulfate Polyacrylamide Gel Electrophoresis (SDS-PAGE) Analysis: Reducing and Nonreducing. Collected buffer samples from the *in vitro* release assays were evaluated for IgG integrity by SDS-PAGE analysis. The IgG samples included were standards and the samples released in PBS buffer (pH 7.4, 37°C) after incorporation into a selected PTS*gel*. Samples were evaluated within 7 days of collection and stored at 4°C until analysis. IgG standards, diluted in PBS, or sample eluates were combined with 4x Laemmli dye, with (reducing) or without (nonreducing) β-mercaptoethanol, to achieve a 1x dye concentration. Reduced samples were heated to 95°C for 10 minutes, cooled, and loaded on 4–12% Bis-Tris NuPAGE gels (Life Technologies, Carlsbad, CA). Prestained markers (cat. number LC5925, Life Technologies) and nonreduced samples were loaded without heating. Gels were run in MOPS buffer (Life Technologies), with antioxidants for reduced samples only, at 180 V for 60 minutes. Electrophoresed gels were fixed in 50% methanol, 10% acetic acid for 30 minutes, stained in Coomassie Brilliant Blue R250 Staining Solution (Bio-Rad Laboratories, Inc., Hercules, CA) for 30 minutes, and destained in 5% methanol, 7.5% acetic acid until clearance. Gels were scanned on a Canon CanoScan 9000F at 600 dpi and images saved as TIFFs in Adobe Photoshop.

2.6.2. Size Exclusion HPLC Analysis (Shodex Column). Collected buffer samples from the *in vitro* release assays were evaluated for IgG integrity by SE-HPLC analysis. The IgG samples included were standards and the samples released in PBS buffer (pH 7.4, 37°C) after incorporation into a selected PTS*gel* for up to 28 days. Samples were stored at −20°C until analysis. Twenty microliters of IgG standards, diluted in PBS, or sample eluates were analyzed on a Shodex column (KW403-4F, 4.6 mm ID × 300 mm L) using a UV absorption detector with the wavelength selected at 214 nm. The mobile phase was 100 mM sodium phosphate, 250 mM NaCl, pH 7.0, used under isocratic conditions at 0.35 mL/min.

2.7. In Vivo Subcutaneous Release of IgG in Mice. Use of animals in this study was approved and monitored by the North Carolina State University Institutional Animal Care and Use Committee (IACUC). IgG was labeled with a near-infrared (NIR) dye (IRDye 800CW by LICOR Biosciences, Lincoln, NE). NIR-labeled IgG in PTS*gel* gelling solution or in PBS was made by adding 1 mL of cold PTS*gel* (25% polymer solution in PBS, pH 7.4) or PBS to 1 mg of lyophilized NIR-labeled IgG. After gentle vortexing, the solutions were stored at 4°C until being used within 24 hours. Insulin syringes with 31 G needles were used to inject 200 μL of solution subcutaneously over the dorsum of a female CD-1 mouse (10 weeks of age) (Charles River, Morrisville, NC) that was maintained on an alfalfa-free diet. Mice ($n = 3$) were injected with PBS, PTS*gel*, or a combination of NIR-IgG in PBS or NIR-IgG in PTS*gel*. Mice were anesthetized with 2.5% isoflurane in oxygen and imaged using an *in vivo* imager (IVIS, Xenogen, Alameda, CA) using Indocyanine Green (ICG) settings. Quantification of fluorescence was measured using the imaging software automatic region of interest (ROI) setting to calculate the radiant efficiency of the injection site. Mice were imaged prior to injection, immediately after injection, and then on days 1–5, 7, 10, and 14 after injection and then weekly using the same imager settings and protocol as used for day 0 imaging.

2.8. In Vivo Safety Assessment. Assessment of the injection site was done at each imaging time to evaluate for signs of inflammation or swelling. Once the injection site was negative for dye detection on IVIS imaging, the mice were euthanized and the skin at the injection site was collected, the inverted skin exposing the injection site/PTS*gel* depot was imaged *ex vivo* using IVIS imaging to detect residual IgG, and the skin section was fixed in 10% formalin. The formalin-fixed skin was then processed for histopathology, stained with hematoxylin and eosin, and examined using light microscopy.

3. Results

3.1. PTSgel Synthesis. For the purposes of this study, five thermosensitive PTS*gel* polymers were synthesized. The five polymers developed for this study were designated 101GH, 10GH, 103GH, 113GH, and 122GH. The polymers were constructed with different block sizes of m-PEG, PCL, and PLA with PLA in the center of the molecule (m-PEG_x-PCL_y-PLA_z-PCL_y-PEG_x-m). The molecular weight (Mw) ranged between 3000 and 4000 Da with gradual increase in the hydrophobicity of molecules. The objective was to vary molecular weights and hydrophobic-hydrophilic block ratios in the polymers to achieve modulation of drug release. In the described polymers, the PEG blocks were Mw of 500 or 550 Da, the PCL block Mw ranged from 400 to 800 Da, and the PLA block was of constant size at Mw 1100 across all polymers. All polymers were characterized by NMR, FTIR for structural confirmation, and GPC for PDI determination and ability to transition from liquid phase to gel at 37°C. All five polymers were compared for *in vitro* release profiles. Two polymers, 10GH and 113GH, were used for *in vivo* subcutaneous release, polymer disappearance, and safety investigations. 10GH at various concentrations was also analyzed for *in vitro* degradation analyses.

3.2. PTSgel Characterization

FTIR Spectrum. FTIR spectrum of 10GH polymer is reported in Figure 1(a). Absorption band at 1726 cm^{-1} and multiple bands ranging from 1000 to 1300 cm^{-1} established the presence of ester linkages in pentablock copolymer. Existence of terminal hydroxyl group was confirmed by C-O stretching band at 1092 cm^{-1} and O-H band (stretch) in the range of 3300–3400 cm^{-1}. C-H stretching bands at 2938 and 2866 cm^{-1} depicted presence of PCL blocks. The presence of N-H (stretch) in the urethane group may be overlapped in the area of O-H band (stretch) 3300–3400 cm^{-1}. Similarly, the C=O in urethane group might have been overlapped with other C=O (stretch) peaks from ester linkages in pentablock copolymer. Absorption band at 1529 cm^{-1} (N-H bending) also exhibited the presence of urethane group in pentablock copolymer.

^{1}H-NMR Spectrum. A Mercury 300 MHz NMR spectrometer was employed to characterize the pentablock copolymers. Figure 1(b) depicts ^{1}H-NMR spectra of 10GH in deuterated chloroform. As described in Figure 1(b), typical ^{1}H-NMR characteristic peaks were observed at 1.55, 2.30, and 4.04 δ ppm representing methylene protons of $-(CH_2)_3-$, $-OCOCH_2-$, and $-CH_2OOC-$ of PCL units, respectively. A sharp peak at 3.64 δ ppm was attributed to methylene protons ($-CH_2CH_2O-$) of PEG. Typical signals at 1.50 ($-CH_3$) and 5.17 (-CH-) δ ppm were assigned for PLA blocks, whereas a peak at 3.36 δ ppm was denoted to terminal methyl ($-OCH_3-$) of PEG. The [EO]-[CL]-[LA] molar ratios of final products were calculated from integrations of PEG signal at 3.36 δ ppm, PCL signal at 4.04 δ ppm, and PLA signal at 5.17 δ ppm. PEG signal at 3.36 δ ppm was applied for the calculation of molar ratio of various blocks within the pentablock copolymer. Estimated molecular weight, calculated using NMR, was close to theoretical feed ratio (Table 1).

Molecular Weight (Mw and Mn) and Polydispersity Determination. Molecular weight (Mw and Mn) and polydispersity of polymers were determined by GPC. Retention time for the three components used for PTS*gel* synthesis is depicted in Figure 1(c). A typical GPC chromatogram of 10GH pentablock copolymer is shown in Figure 1(d). A single peak for the polymer was observed describing unimodal distribution of molecular weight and absence of any other homopolymer block such as PEG, PCL, or PLA. Polydispersity (PDI) for the five analyzed polymers ranged from 1.08 to 1.28 indicating narrow distribution of molecular weights. Estimated molecular weights of synthesized PTS*gel* were close to the feed ratio (Table 1).

Residual Tin, Organic Solvents, and Endotoxin Evaluation. Each polymer was tested for tin levels, organic solvents,

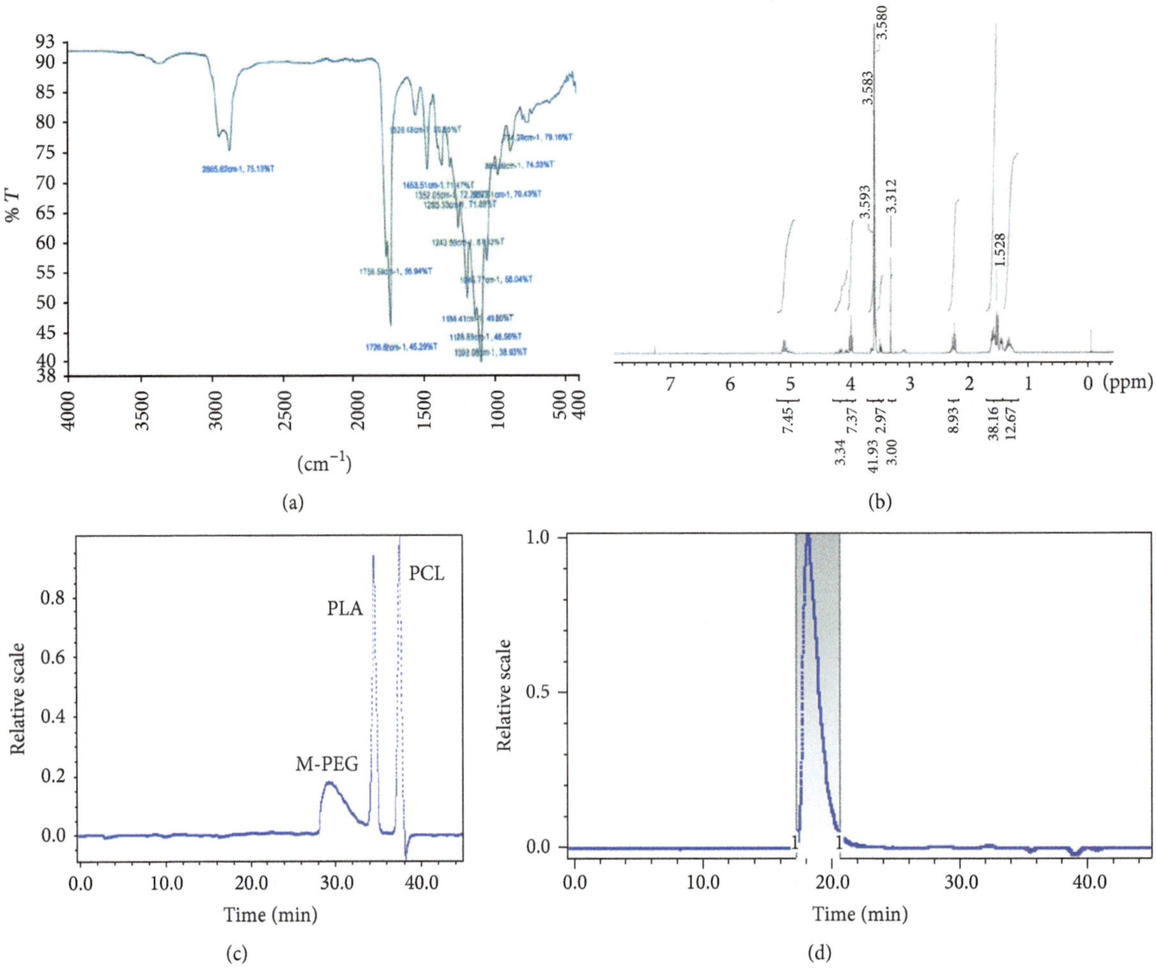

FIGURE 1: (a) FTIR spectrum of 10GH PTS*gel*. (b) ^{1}H NMR spectrum of PEG$_x$-PCL$_y$-PLA$_z$-PCL$_y$-PEG$_x$. (c) GPC chromatogram for reference standards (m-PEG, PCL, and PLA). (d) GPC chromatogram for 10GH PTS*gel*. PD of the 10GH polymer = 1.08.

and endotoxin levels. Sample analysis for the determination of residual dichloromethane (DCM) and heptane was performed by GC-MS. In all samples, no residual heptane was detected. Residual DCM was 0.2 ppm (10GH), 124 ppm (101GH), 74 ppm (103GH), 170 ppm (113GH), and 278 ppm (122GH). Stannous (tin) levels were less than 2 ppm. Endotoxin levels were determined to be less than 0.1 EU/mL.

3.3. PTSgel Gelling Evaluation. All polymers were free flowing liquids at 4°C. Sol-gel transition for the five polymers is as shown in Figure 2. The PTS*gels* 10GH and 103GH were clear liquids, whereas the PTS*gels* 113GH and 122GH were slightly turbid liquid at 4°C (Figure 2). Immediately after removal of the vials from the 37°C water bath, the PTS*gels* were a solid, slightly opaque white gel. On inversion of gel tubes at room temperature, the PTS*gels* remained a solid gel for 15 to 60 seconds (Figure 2). Eventually, all gels slowly transitioned back to liquid form at room temperature. All five polymers could be injected through a 31-gauge needle and form a solid gel in PBS at 37°C (see videos in Supplementary Material available online at http://dx.doi.org/10.1155/2016/2407459).

TABLE 1: Mw, Mn, and PDI determination of PTS*gels*.

PTS*gel* ID	Total Mn[a] (theoretical)	Total Mn[b] (calculated)	Total Mn[c] (calculated)	Mw[c] (GPC)	PDI[c]
101GH	3000	3898	4784	5132	1.07
10GH	3100	3534	4855	5264	1.08
103GH	3600	4271	3404	4347	1.28
113GH	3500	3542	4615	5078	1.1
122GH	3700	3941	4349	4941	1.14

[a]Theoretical value, calculated according to the feed ratio.
[b]Calculated from ^{1}H NMR.
[c]Determined by GPC analysis.

3.4. In Vitro PTSgel Disintegration (Gravimetric Measurement). The gravimetric dry weight loss over time of PTS*gel* 10GH (12.5, 18.75, and 25%) in PBS was evaluated at 37°C. There was a large difference in dry weight between the *PTSgel* concentrations at time 0, with 25% polymeric gel having a mean weight of 120.8 mg, 18.75% polymer of 79.1 mg, and 12.5% polymer of 41.8 mg. The lowest concentration

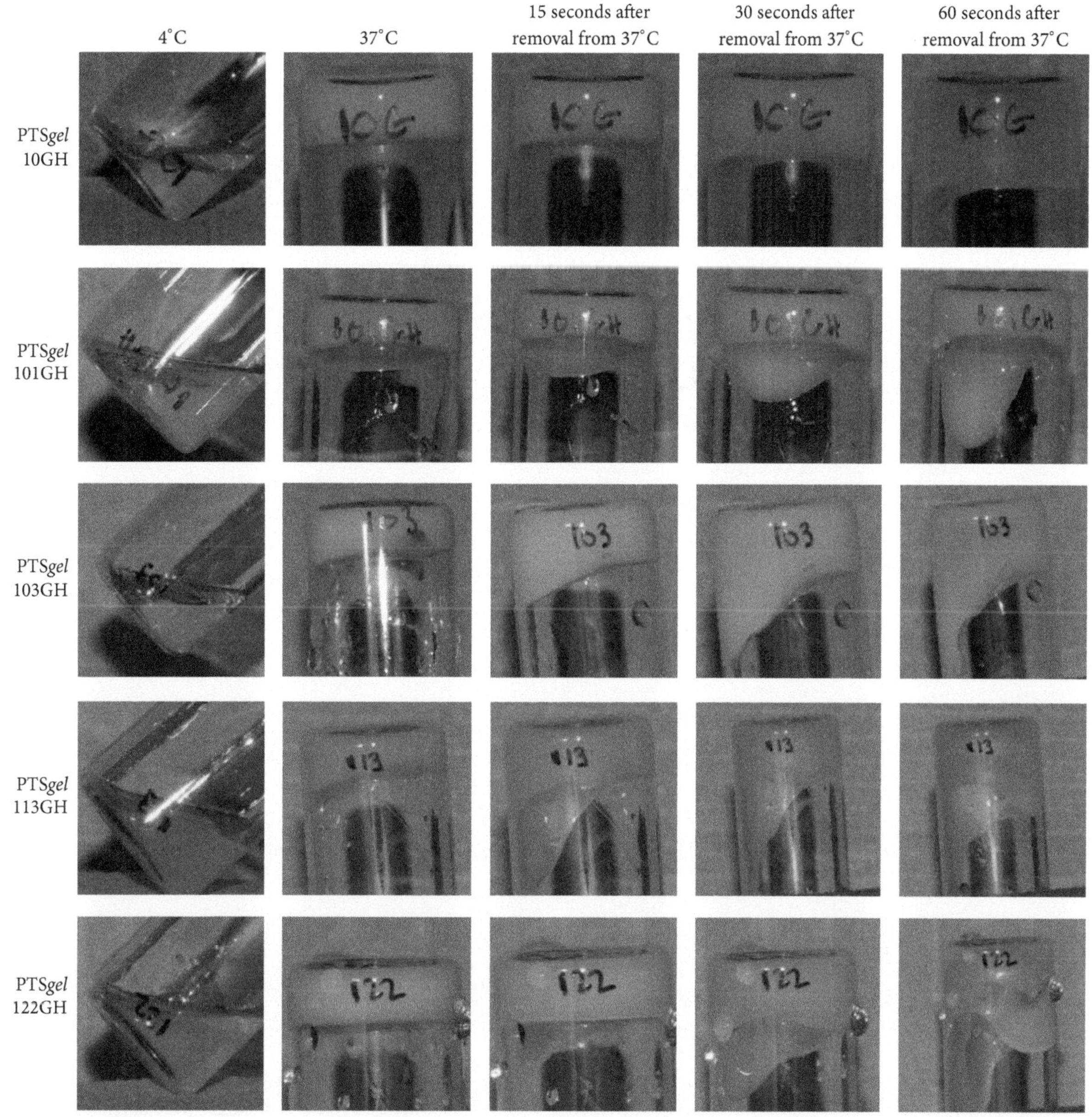

FIGURE 2: Sol-gel transition of 10GH, 101GH, 103GH, 113GH, and 122GH. At 4°C temperature the PTS*gels* are in liquid form and transition into solid gels at 37°C. The gels slowly transition back to liquid form at room temperature.

of 10GH (12.5% gelling polymer) nearly completely disintegrated by 30 days (92.7%), while 18.75 and 25% 10GH PTS*gel* demonstrated disappearance of polymer with 74.2 and 76% dissolved, respectively, by day 75 (Figure 3(a)).

Residual polymer and supernatant collected at various time points were analyzed by GPC (Figure 3(b)). It is visually clear that the polymer peaks eluted as a symmetrical peak at day 0 and at days 30 and 60. However, the peak at days 30 and 60 is wider than that observed at day 0 suggesting degradation of the polymer. The supernatant shows a small amount of dissolved polymers on day 0; however, there is no polymer present on day 30 and the disintegrated fragments are much smaller than the polymer but larger than the monomers used for the synthesis. The individual peaks have not yet been further characterized.

3.5. Modulation of In Vitro IgG Release from PTSgels. The solid gel PTS*gel* was maintained at 37°C and half of PBS buffer was removed and replaced on days 1, 2, 3, 4, 5, 7, 10, and 14 and then weekly thereafter until no additional release was observed. Extensive modulation of *in vitro* release was achieved by using five different PTS*gels*, 101GH, 10GH, 103GH, 113GH, and 122GH, with increasing hydrophobicity of the polymers in the order, respectively. In most polymers, there was a low initial burst of drug release at 20 mg/mL IgG (11–24% release on day 1) and an almost negligible release

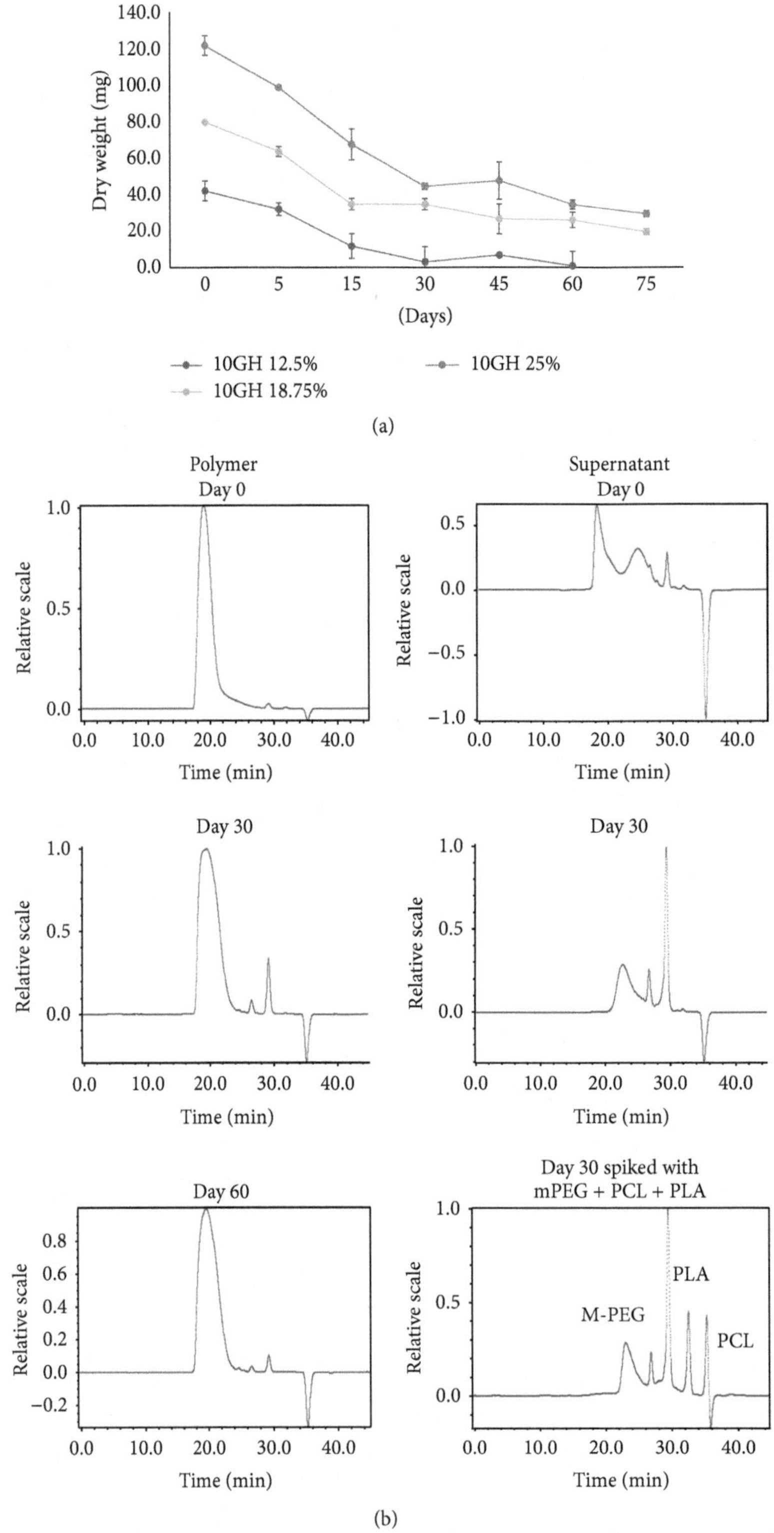

FIGURE 3: (a) *In vitro* dissolution/disintegration of 10GH PTS*gel*. Three concentrations (12.5, 18.75, and 25%) of PTS*gel* 10GH (500 μL in triplicate) were evaluated for disintegration in phosphate buffered saline (pH 7.4) *in vitro* at 37°C. On day 0 and after 5, 15, 30, and 45 days and every 15 days thereafter, overlaid buffer was removed and the remaining PTS*gels* were lyophilized and weighed to determine PTS*gel* dry weight over time. (b) GPC analysis of residual polymer (10GH, 25%) and supernatant collected on various days for *in vitro* disintegration in PBS buffer, pH 7.4 at 37°C.

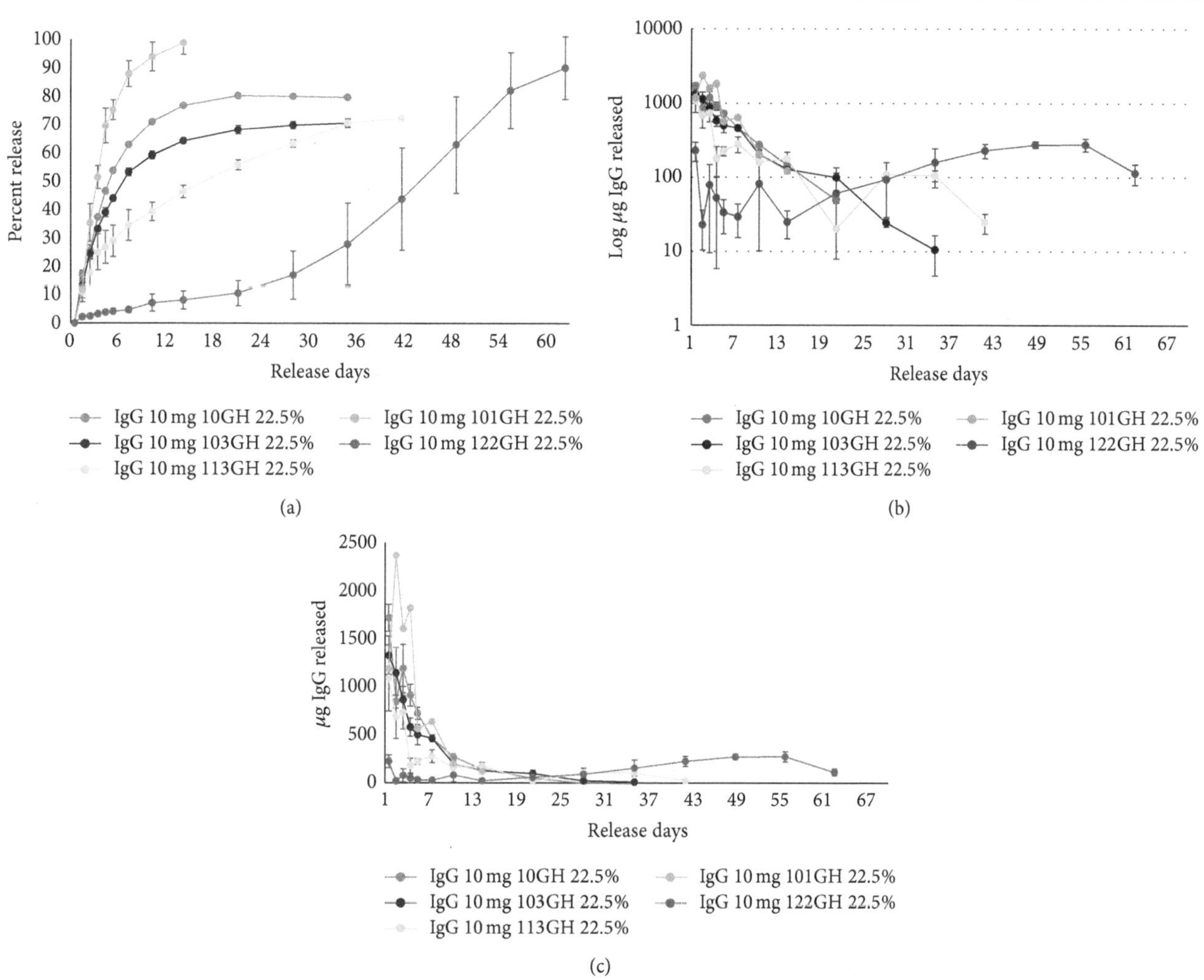

FIGURE 4: *In vitro* release of IgG from pentablock copolymers (PTS*gel*). Mean ± SD of cumulative release (a) and daily release of IgG from PTS*gel* on a log scale (b) and on a linear scale (c). Using 20 mg/mL IgG in 22.5% PTS*gel* maintained at 37°C, half of overlaid PBS buffer was removed and replaced at days 1, 2, 3, 4, 5, 7, 10, and 14 and then weekly thereafter.

with 122GH (~2%), the most hydrophobic polymer. Initial release is followed by a controlled release over extended period of several days to weeks as shown in Figure 4. Using 22.5% of each PTS*gel*, the quickest release rate was observed with the most hydrophilic polymer in the group (101GH) with 100% of the IgG load released in 14 days. The PTS*gels* 10GH and 103GH had a slower release with 80% and 69% of the IgG released in 21 days, respectively. Both the PTS*gels* 113GH and 122GH had a much slower rate of release with 73% and only 44% by day 42, respectively. From 122GH, 91% of IgG release was achieved by day 63 (Figure 4(a)). A significant decrease in initial burst release related to increase in hydrophobicity demonstrates that the capacity to hold drugs possibly increases with increase in hydrophobicity of these PTS*gels*. Also, modulation of drug release at different rates can be achieved for long periods by changing the hydrophobicity of the polymers, as shown in Figures 4(b) and 4(c). As the polymer became more hydrophobic, the drug was released at a slower rate and the drug release had a much longer duration. The initial burst is also reduced considerably when lower IgG concentrations (2 mg/mL) were loaded into the polymer, as is shown in Figure 5 for PTS*gel* 10GH, suggesting that the polymer's capacity to hold the drug may dictate initial burst release.

In addition, *in vitro* release of IgG was also demonstrated to be modulated by varying the concentration of PTS*gel* polymer. Using 2 mg/mL IgG in 10GH PTS*gel*, 9.6% PTS*gel* resulted in a faster release of IgG, accompanied by a higher (40%) initial release on day 1 and 80% cumulative release by day 7, compared to a gradual and more sustained release achieved with 14.4 and 24% of 10GH PTS*gel* and less initial burst (Figure 5), again strongly suggesting that the drug release is a function of polymer capacity which increases with higher polymer concentration. Optimal loading for each therapeutic at different gelling polymer concentration will need to be determined during development.

3.6. Structural Integrity of IgG Released from PTSgel

(A) Using SDS-PAGE Analysis. Reduced (using beta-mercaptoethanol) and nonreduced sodium dodecyl sulfate-polyacrylamide gel electrophoresis (SDS-PAGE) were used

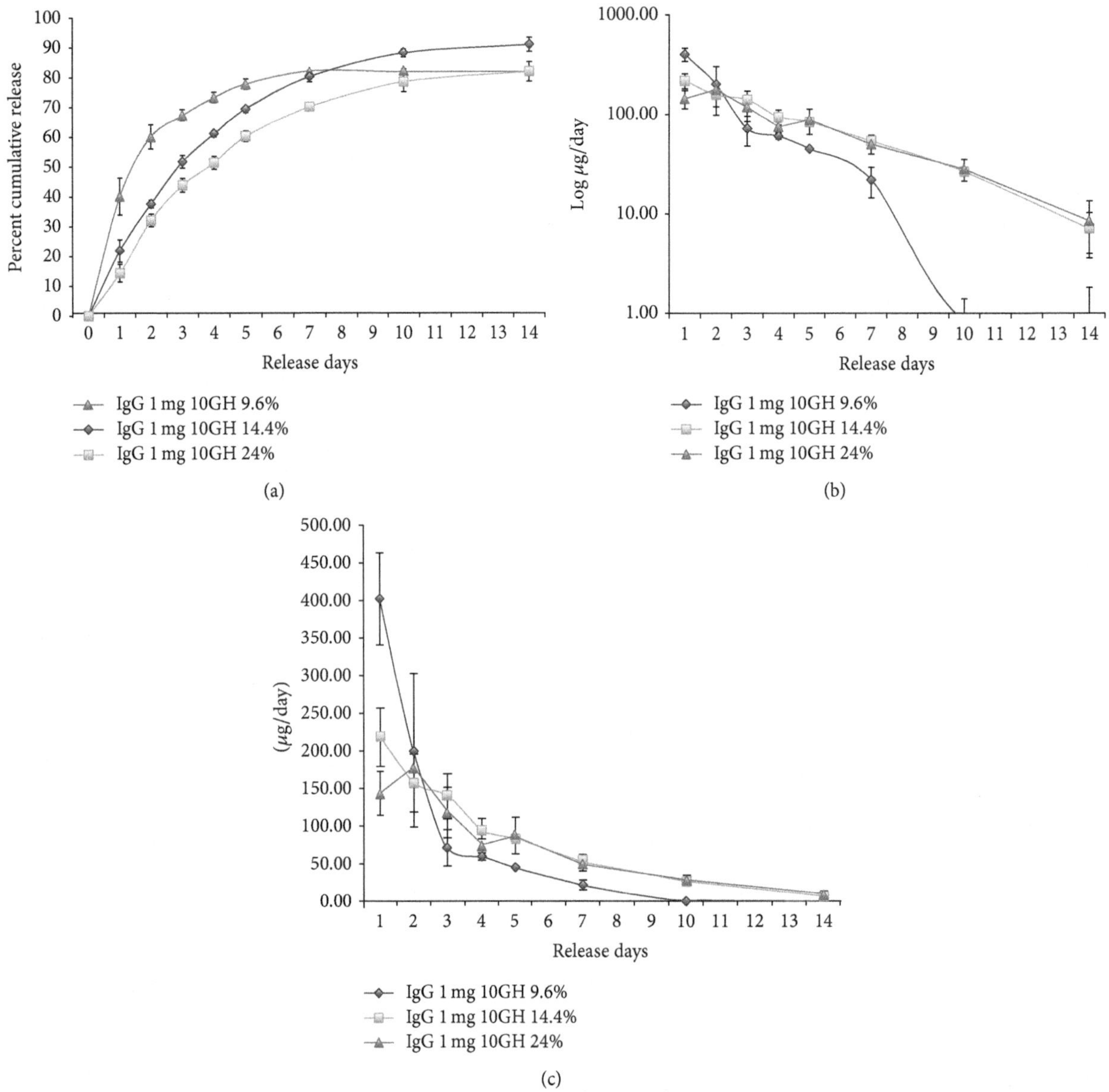

FIGURE 5: Effect of polymeric gel concentration on *in vitro* release of IgG from pentablock copolymers (PTS*gel*). Mean ± SD of cumulative release (a) and log (b) and linear (c) daily release of IgG from PTS*gel*.

for size-based separations of the IgG for determining IgG integrity in the *in vitro* samples released from PTS*gel* over a period of seven days. Reducing conditions disrupt disulphide bonds separating IgG light and heavy chains. The IgG released from 10GH had the same bands of approximately 150 kDa for the nonreduced and 28 and 51 kDa for the reduced SDS-PAGE at days 1 and 7, which appeared identical to the IgG standards (Figure 6(a)). These results suggest that the IgG molecules were intact and no degradation of IgG had occurred during incubation with PTS*gel* and after release into the buffer. Similarly, there appeared to be excellent integrity for the IgG released from the 103GH polymer through 14 days (Figure 6(b)) and the 113GH polymer through 28 days (Figure 6(c)), suggesting that the PTS*gel* polymer did not affect the integrity of the IgG protein. Low amounts of PLA utilized in the synthesis of PTS*gel* polymers do not result in lowering local pH upon polymer degradation and hence offer safe environment to drugs, especially biologics, for sustained release.

(B) SE-HPLC Analysis. Figures 6(d) and 6(e) compare chromatograms of SE-HPLC analysis conducted on a reference standard IgG and on an *in vitro* sample released after incubation with 10GH for 28 days at 37°C. IgG maintained its structural integrity as is clearly demonstrated in Figures 6(d) and 6(e).

3.7. In Vivo Studies for IgG Release. Following subcutaneous injection of 200 μL of PTS*gel* (either 10GH or 113GH) containing 200 μg of near-infrared dye labeled IgG (NIR-IgG) or

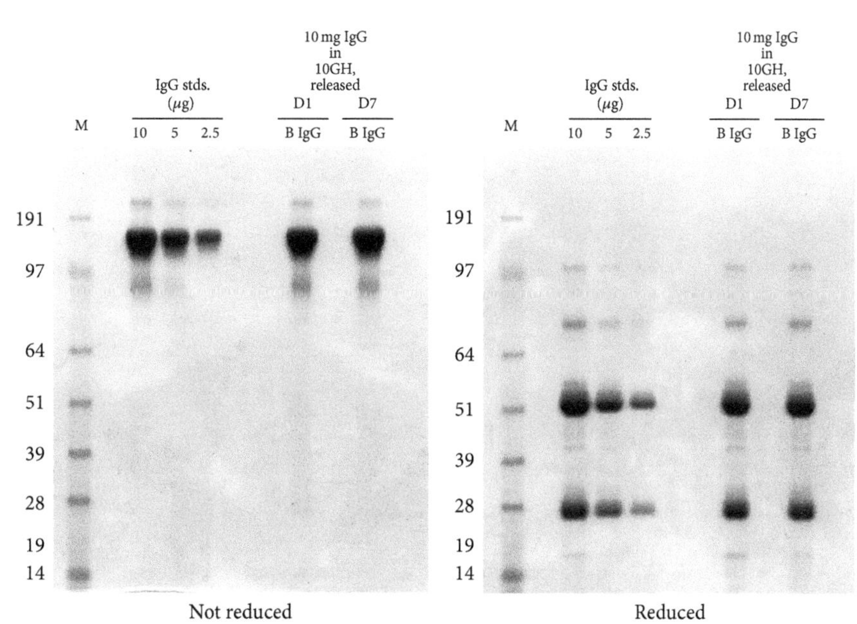

(a)

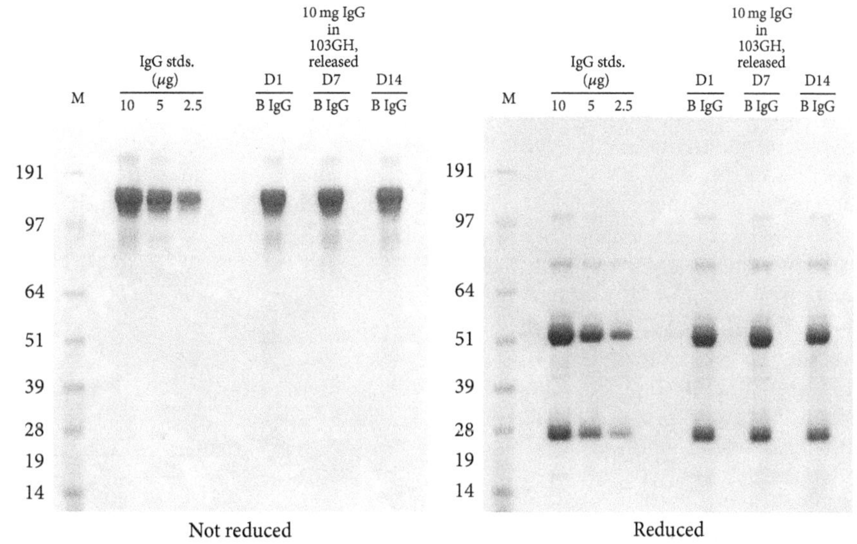

(b)

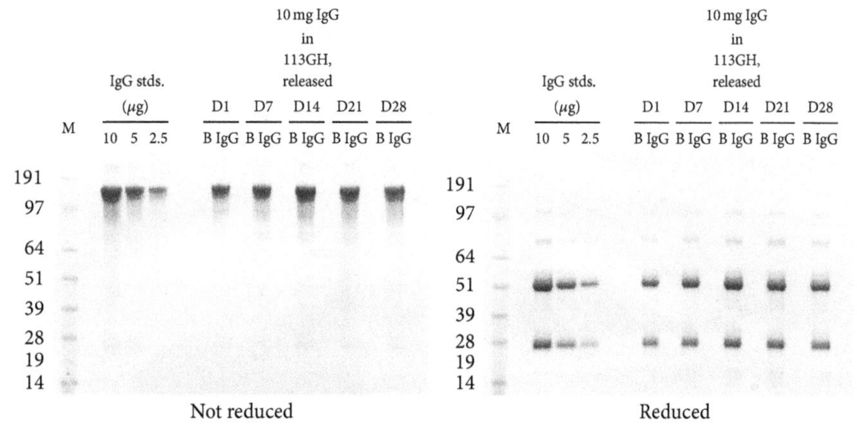

(c)

Figure 6: Continued.

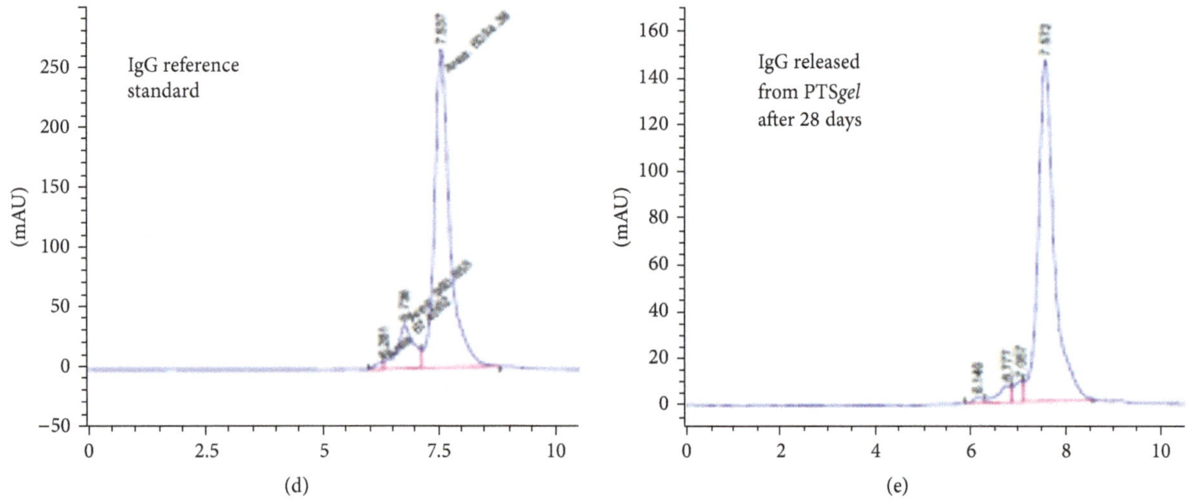

FIGURE 6: IgG integrity evaluated by SDS-PAGE. Reduced (using beta-mercaptoethanol) and nonreduced sodium dodecyl sulfate-polyacrylamide gel electrophoresis (SDS-PAGE) were used for size-based separations of the IgG for determining IgG integrity in the PTS*gel* *in vitro* release rate samples over time. The IgG released from 10GH (a), 103GH (b), and 113GH (c) had the same bands of approximately 150 kDa for the nonreduced and 28 and 51 kDa for the reduced SDS-PAGE at each time point tested, which appeared identical to the IgG standards. D, release day; B, blank lanes; M, molecular size marker; IgG stds., IgG standards. (d) and (e) SE-HPLC analysis of IgG reference standard (d) and of released sample (e) after incubation with PTS*gel* 10GH for 28 days in PBS at 37°C.

NIR-IgG in PBS in mice, no adverse reaction, swelling, or redness was observed at the injection site for the duration of the study. NIR-IgG in PBS was visible on IVIS imaging immediately after injection but was no longer visible 24 hours after injection (Figures 7(a)–7(d)). Fluorescence of NIR-IgG in the PTS*gel* *in vivo* paralleled the *in vitro* release rates for 10GH and 113GH presented in Figure 4. Mice injected with 10% 10GH had fluorescence through approximately day 4, while those injected with 20% 10GH fluoresced through approximately day 14 (Figures 7(a) and 7(b)). Mice injected with 10% 113GH fluoresced through approximately 7 days, and those injected with 20% 113GH fluoresced through approximately 35 days (Figures 7(c) and 7(d)).

Once negative for fluorescence on IVIS imaging, mice were euthanized; the skin at the site of the injection was excised and imaged *ex vivo*. In all animals, there was a very small deposit of gel visible in the subcutaneous tissue, indicating the nearly complete dissolution/disintegration of the PTS*gel* (Figure 8). On imaging, there was a small signal of fluorescence that corresponded to approximately the size of the gel deposit, suggesting that IgG was tightly held by the PTS*gel* and that IgG release and gel dissolution/disintegration occurred in parallel and that an "empty shell" of undissolved PTS*gel* did not remain.

3.8. In Vivo Safety Assessment after Subcutaneous Injection of NIR-IgG with PTSgel. Following imaging, skin samples were fixed and processed for histopathology. When examined using light microscopy, the subcutaneous depot of PTS*gel* could be visualized and was mildly infiltrated with mononuclear cells. At the 6-day examination of the 10% PTS*gel* 10GH, there were a few scattered neutrophils and macrophages surrounding and infiltrating the site of the injection. At 14 days with the 20% PTS*gel*, there were only a few macrophages associated with the gel deposit. At 42 days with the 113GH PTS*gel*, there were macrophages surrounding the depot but no epidermal or dermal inflammation or swelling was observed (Figure 9).

4. Discussion

We have demonstrated, both *in vitro* and *in vivo*, that PTS*gels* can modulate the release of IgG, a model therapeutic protein, from less than 7 days to greater than 63 days and possibly much longer by altering block composition for change in hydrophobicity and/or aqueous polymer solution concentration as well as amount of drug loaded in the polymer. These polymers seem to exhibit a very high capacity to hold IgG and thus result in minimal initial burst. The exact capacity for each polymer is currently undergoing investigation in our laboratory. We also demonstrated that the IgG was associated with the PTS*gel* as *in vitro* release and *in vivo* degradation of polymers occurred in parallel. In addition, we demonstrated that the PTS*gel* provides a safe environment for the protein as evidenced by the intact IgG structure when tested on day 28 of *in vitro* release from the PTS*gel*. Since IgG structure remained intact after release from PTS*gel* and based on work in progress in our laboratory, we anticipate that the functional proteins would also maintain their bioactivity when incubated with PTS*gel*. The PTS*gel* composition and concentration determined timing of gel dissipation *in vivo*. Only small remnants of PTS*gel* were present *ex vivo* in subcutaneous tissues of mice at the time of euthanasia and these gel remnants had NIR-labeled IgG visible on IVIS imaging, suggesting that the rate of IgG release and gel disappearance occurred in parallel. In a separate study, a similar phenomenon was observed

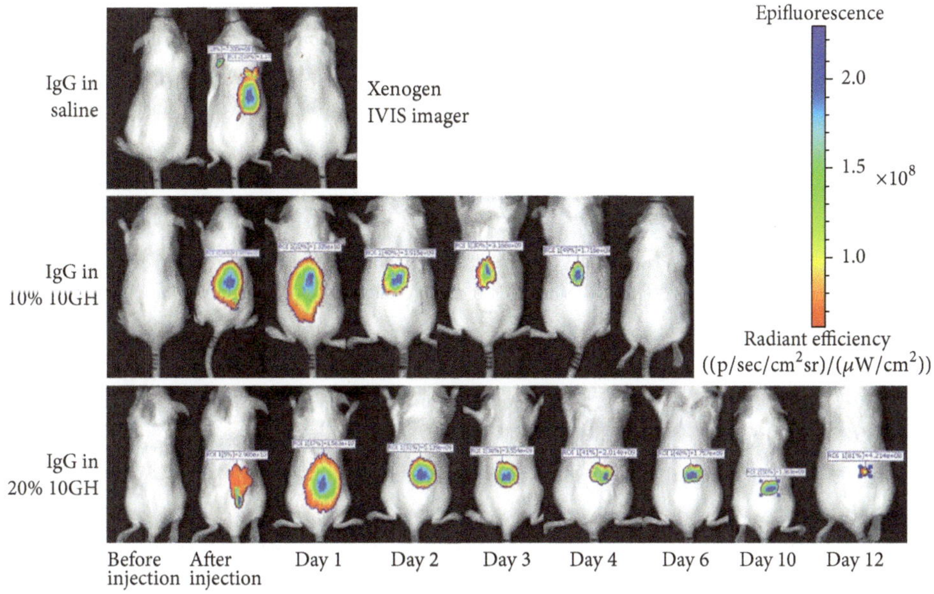

(a)

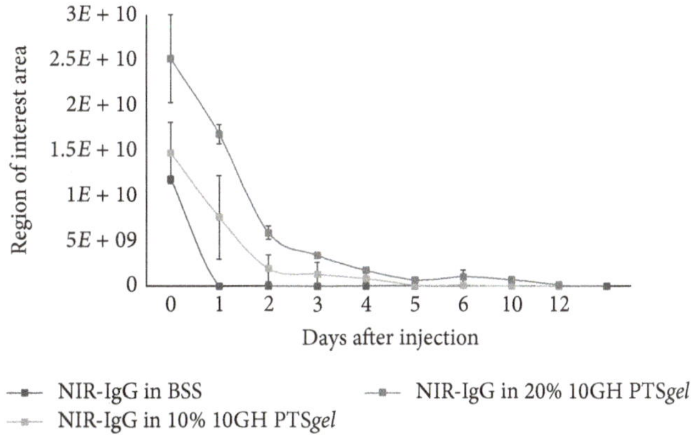

(b)

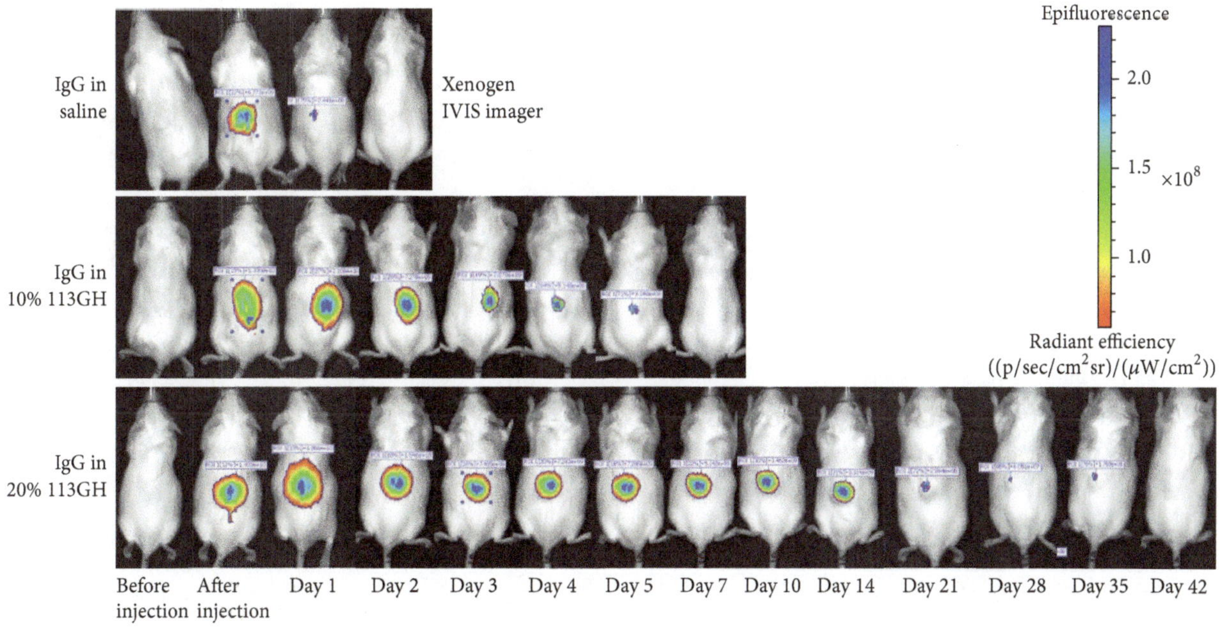

(c)

Figure 7: Continued.

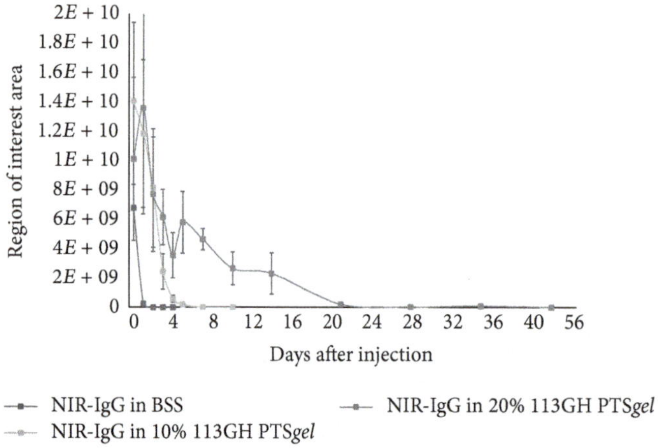

(d)

FIGURE 7: *In vivo* imaging of mice after subcutaneous injection of PTS*gel*. Mice were injected with PBS, PTS*gel* (10% and 20% 10GH or 113GH), or a combination of NIR-IgG PBS or NIR-IgG PTS*gel* in triplicate. Mice were anesthetized and imaged prior to injection, immediately after injection, and then on days 1–5, 7, 10, and 14 after injection and then weekly thereafter using an *in vivo* imager (IVIS, Xenogen, Alameda, CA) ((a) and (c)). Quantification of fluorescence was measured using the imaging software automatic region of interest (ROI) setting to calculate the radiant efficiency of the injection site ((b) and (d)).

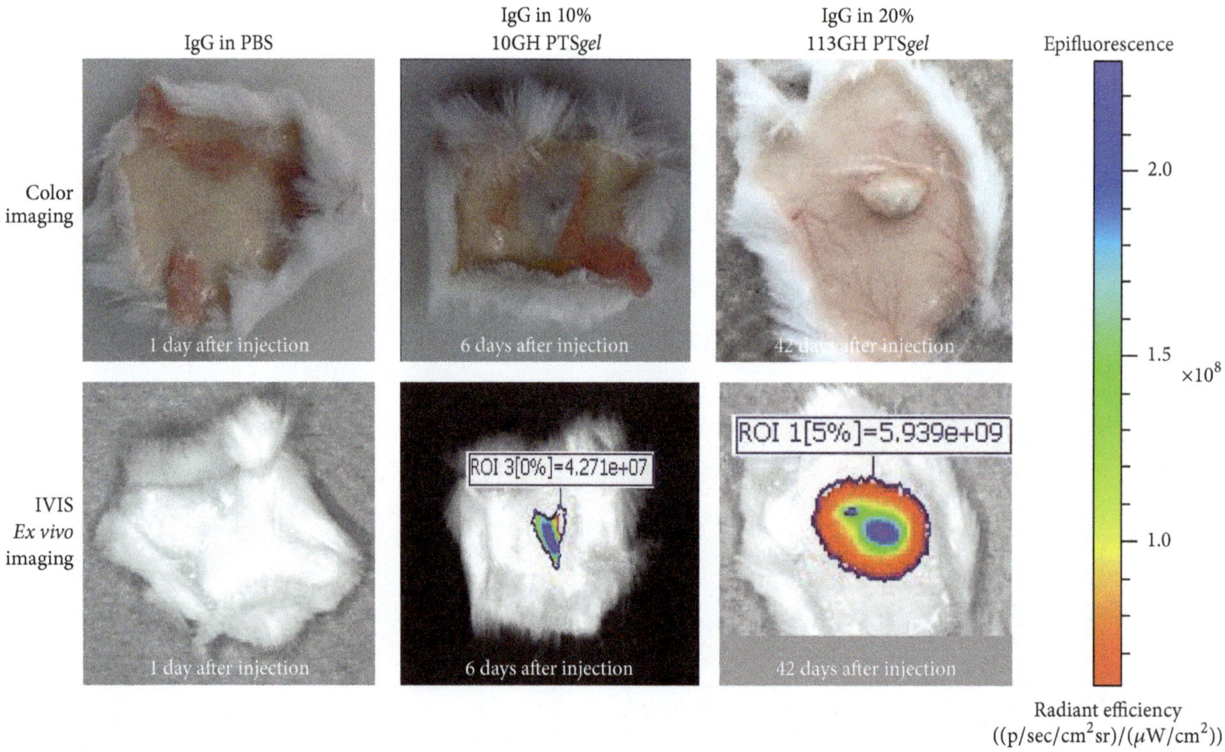

FIGURE 8: *Ex vivo* imaging of mice skin after subcutaneous injection of PTS*gel*. Once the mice were negative for fluorescence on IVIS imaging, they were euthanized; the skin at the site of the injection was excised and imaged *ex vivo*.

for NIR-labeled IgG when injected intracamerally [15]. The 25% PTS*gel* (10GH) gradually dissolved/disintegrated over the course of 30 days in the anterior chamber of the eye and the PTS*gel* had a strong signal of NIR-IgG in small remnants of PTS*gel* until the gel was completely dissolved or disintegrated [15].

When evaluating the *in vitro* IgG release, an initial 1-day to 2-day higher release (burst effect) was observed with lower concentrations of PTS*gel* (9.6% polymer), while in the higher concentrations of PTS*gel* (22 or 24% polymer), reduced burst effects were observed (see Figures 4–6) and they exhibited sustained release of IgG which paralleled the

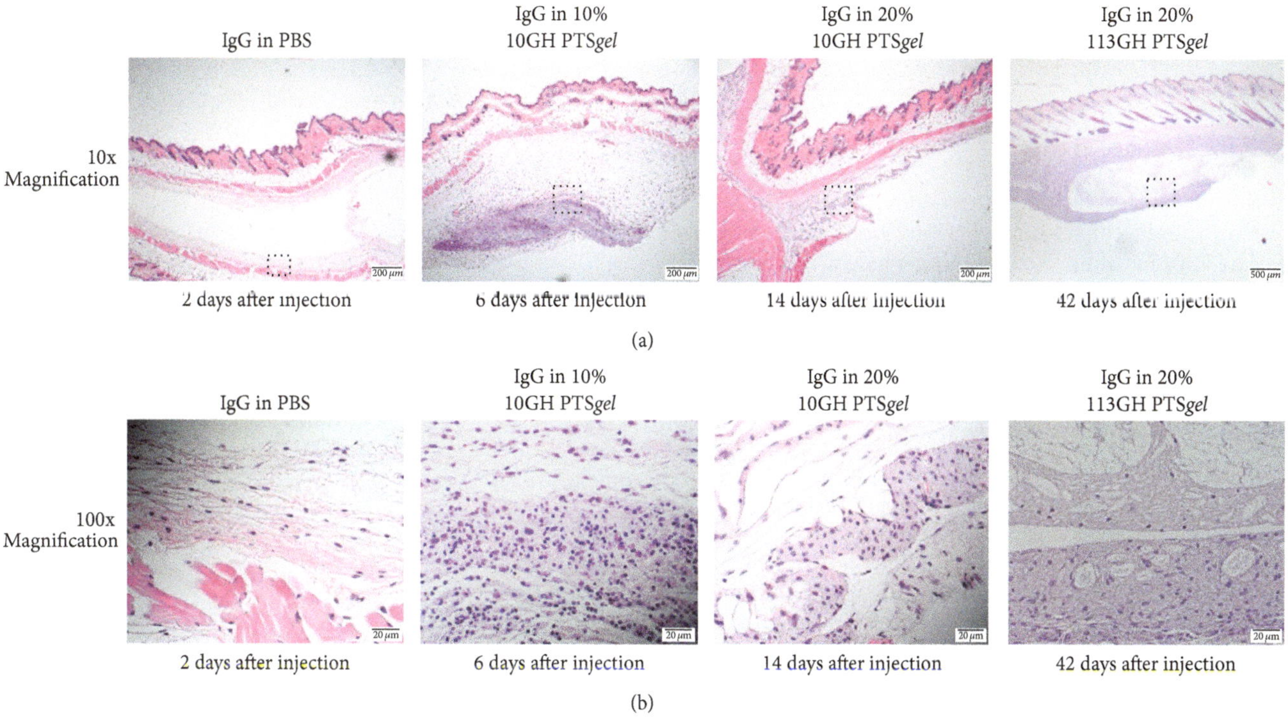

FIGURE 9: Dermal histopathology after subcutaneous injection of PTS*gel*. Using lower magnification light microscopy (a), the subcutaneous depot of PTS*gel* could be visualized in the 10 and 20% 10GH- and 113GH-injected tissue. Dotted box in (a) was the site of higher magnification represented in (b).

polymer dissolution/disintegration (see Figure 3), suggesting that the IgG was not just physically entrapped in the gel but perhaps a large portion of IgG is likely entrapped in the micellar structure of the polymer [12] which is released as the polymer dissolves or disintegrates. We have also observed this phenomenon with proteins other than IgG (data not shown). This suggests that initial burst effect likely occurs when added drug exceeds the capacity of the PTS*gel* to hold the drug for sustained release. As stated earlier, the dose capacity, though it has not been measured quantitatively, is likely dependent on a combination of factors such as polymer composition and percentage of the PTS*gel*.

In this study we achieved extensive modulation of IgG release from 7 days to longer than 63 days by varying the Mw size of PCL block comprising the PTS*gel*. Release rates of IgG from the fastest to the slowest (i.e., 101GH (fastest release) to 122GH (slowest release)) correlated with higher hydrophobicity created by increasing the PCL block size (from Mw 400 to 800). As shown in Figure 4, the PTS*gel* 122GH shows a continuing IgG release at 63 days, suggesting an expected duration of *in vitro* IgG release of 70 to 80 days. The PTS*gel* 113GH achieved sustained IgG release for at least 42 days (mean 278 μg (day 7) to 25 μg released on day 42), PTS*gel* 103GH for at least 21 days, and PTS*gel* 10GH for at least 14 days (each from a 22.5% polymer and total loading of 10 mg IgG) (see Figure 4). Patel et al. [13] demonstrated similar release of IgG with PTS*gel* 113GH but required the use of polymer-IgG nanoparticles to achieve a 45-day release profile, which is far shorter duration than what we have been able to obtain with PTS*gel* 122GH alone.

Although we demonstrated *in vivo* that IgG remained in the gel until the polymer was nearly completely dissolved, further studies are needed to confirm drug bioactivity after delivery and to evaluate pharmacokinetics and pharmacodynamics for each route of therapy. However, a steady release *in vitro* which correlated well to the decrease in NIR-IgG *in vivo* was observed; hence one can hypothesize that *in vivo* drug release may be similar to that observed *in vitro*. Further studies are ongoing in our laboratory to evaluate drug bioactivity and to demonstrate pharmacokinetics and pharmacodynamics from protein and small molecule drug release of both hydrophobic and hydrophilic nature from a variety of PTS*gels*.

5. Conclusions

PTS*gels* create biocompatible/biodegradable thermosensitive formulations which can provide sustained release of biologics without chemical modification of the therapeutic molecule. Modulation of release and control of initial burst of IgG, a model therapeutic protein, was achieved by varying block composition and aqueous solution concentration of the PTS*gels*. When injected subcutaneously, PTS*gels* provided a safe environment for the protein and were well tolerated.

Importantly, disintegration of the polymer paralleled IgG release *in vivo*, leaving little or no remnant of PTS*gel* after drug release was complete.

Competing Interests

Elizabeth Schaefer, Santhi Abbaraju, Mary Walsh, Donna Newman, and Jacklyn Salmon have no competing interests to declare. Rasidul Amin and Brian Gilger have financial interest in i-novion, Inc., and Ulrich Grau, Sidney Weiss, and Poonam Velagaleti are cofounders of i-novion, Inc.

References

[1] D. Chandler and A. Bewley, "Biologics in dermatology," *Pharmaceuticals*, vol. 6, no. 4, pp. 557–558, 2013.

[2] L. Kobrynski, "Subcutaneous immunoglobulin therapy: a new option for patients with primary immunodeficiency diseases," *Biologics: Targets and Therapy*, vol. 6, pp. 277-287, 2012.

[3] M. A. A. Siddiqui, "The efficacy and tolerability of newer biologics in rheumatoid arthritis: best current evidence," *Current Opinion in Rheumatology*, vol. 19, no. 3, pp. 308–313, 2007.

[4] J. G. Sathish, S. Sethu, M.-C. Bielsky et al., "Challenges and approaches for the development of safer immunomodulatory biologics," *Nature Reviews Drug Discovery*, vol. 12, no. 4, pp. 306–324, 2013.

[5] M. B. Atkins and M. Sznol, "Cancer immunotherapy: past progress and future directions," *Seminars in Oncology*, vol. 42, no. 4, pp. 518–522, 2015.

[6] T. R. Hoare and D. S. Kohane, "Hydrogels in drug delivery: progress and challenges," *Polymer*, vol. 49, no. 8, pp. 1993–2007, 2008.

[7] R. Vaishya, V. Khurana, S. Patel, and A. K. Mitra, "Long-term delivery of protein therapeutics," *Expert Opinion on Drug Delivery*, vol. 12, no. 3, pp. 415–440, 2015.

[8] P. Agarwal and I. D. Rupenthal, "Injectable implants for the sustained release of protein and peptide drugs," *Drug Discovery Today*, vol. 18, no. 7-8, pp. 337–349, 2013.

[9] M. Qiao, D. Chen, X. Ma, and Y. Liu, "Injectable biodegradable temperature-responsive PLGA-PEG-PLGA copolymers: synthesis and effect of copolymer composition on the drug release from the copolymer-based hydrogels," *International Journal of Pharmaceutics*, vol. 294, no. 1-2, pp. 103–112, 2005.

[10] M. L. Houchin and E. M. Topp, "Chemical degradation of peptides and proteins in PLGA: a review of reactions and mechanisms," *Journal of Pharmaceutical Sciences*, vol. 97, no. 7, pp. 2395–2404, 2008.

[11] H. K. Makadia and S. J. Siegel, "Poly Lactic-co-Glycolic Acid (PLGA) as biodegradable controlled drug delivery carrier," *Polymers*, vol. 3, no. 3, pp. 1377–1397, 2011.

[12] S. P. Patel, R. Vaishya, X. Yang, D. Pal, and A. K. Mitra, "Novel thermosensitive pentablock copolymers for sustained delivery of proteins in the treatment of posterior segment diseases," *Protein and Peptide Letters*, vol. 21, no. 11, pp. 1185–1200, 2014.

[13] S. P. Patel, R. Vaishya, G. P. Mishra, V. Tamboli, D. Pal, and A. K. Mitra, "Tailor-made pentablock copolymer based formulation for sustained ocular delivery of protein therapeutics," *Journal of Drug Delivery*, vol. 2014, Article ID 401747, 15 pages, 2014.

[14] M. J. Hwang, J. M. Suh, Y. H. Bae, S. W. Kim, and B. Jeong, "Caprolactonic poloxamer analog: PEG-PCL-PEG," *Biomacromolecules*, vol. 6, no. 2, pp. 885–890, 2005.

[15] E. Schaefer, J. H. Salmon, S. Abbaraju et al., *Sustained IgG Delivery to the Anterior Chamber of Rabbits Using Pentablock Co-polymers*, ARVO Abstract, Association for Research in Vision and Ophthalmology, Seattle, Wash, USA, 2016.

14

Formulation Development and Evaluation of Fast Disintegrating Tablets of Salbutamol Sulphate, Cetirizine Hydrochloride in Combined Pharmaceutical Dosage Form: A New Era in Novel Drug Delivery for Pediatrics and Geriatrics

Deepak Sharma,[1] Gurmeet Singh,[2] Dinesh Kumar,[3] and Mankaran Singh[4]

[1] *Department of Pharmaceutics, Rayat Bahra Institute of Pharmacy, Hoshiarpur, Punjab 146001, India*
[2] *ISF College of Pharmacy, Ghal Kalan, Moga, Punjab 142001, India*
[3] *Institute of Microbial Technology, Sector 39-A, Chandigarh 160036, India*
[4] *Quantum Solutions, Chandigarh 160101, India*

Correspondence should be addressed to Deepak Sharma; deepakpharmacist89@yahoo.com

Academic Editor: Ali Nokhodchi

The objective of the present study was to prepare the fast disintegrating tablet of Salbutamol Sulphate, Cetirizine Hydrochloride in combined tablet dosage form for respiratory disorders such as bronchitis, asthma, and coughing for pediatrics and geriatrics. The tablets were prepared by direct compression technique. Superdisintegrant such as Sodium Starch Glycolate was optimized as 4% on the basis of least disintegration time. Different binders such as MCC and PVP K-30 were optimized along with optimized superdisintegrant concentration. 1% MCC was selected as optimum binder concentration on the basis of least disintegration time. The tablets were evaluated for hardness, friability, weight variation, wetting time, disintegration time, and drug content uniformity. Optimized formulation was further evaluated by in vitro dissolution test, drug-excipient compatibility, and accelerated stability study. Percent weight variation and content uniformity were within the acceptable limit. The friability was less than 1%. The wetting time and disintegration time were practically good for all formulations. FTIR studies and accelerated stability study showed that there was no interaction between the drug and excipients. It was concluded that, by employing commonly available pharmaceutical excipients such as superdisintegrants, hydrophilic and swellable excipients and proper filler, a fast disintegrating tablet of Salbutamol Sulphate, Cetirizine Hydrochloride in combined tablet dosage form, were formulated successfully with desired characteristics.

1. Introduction

Fast disintegrating tablets (FDTs) have received ever-increasing demand during the last decade, and the field has become a rapidly growing area in the pharmaceutical industry. Recent advancements in novel drug delivery system (NDDS) aim to enhance safety and efficacy of drug molecule by formulating a convenient dosage form for administration in order to achieve better patient compliance. One such approach is "fast disintegrating tablet." Many patients find it difficult to swallow tablets and hard gelatin capsules that results in high incidence of noncompliance and ineffective therapy [1, 2]. Fast disintegrating drug delivery systems (FDDDS) are a new generation of formulations which combine the advantages of both liquid and conventional tablet formulations and, at the same time, offer added advantages over both traditional dosage forms. They provide the convenience of a tablet formulation and also allow the ease of swallowing provided by a liquid formulation [3]. The concept of fast dissolving/disintegrating tablets emerged from the desire to provide patients with more conventional means of taking their medication when drinking water is not available and in certain cases such as motion sickness, sudden episodes of allergic attacks, or coughing. Particularly these types of difficulty are faced by pediatric and geriatric patients [4]. Recent developments in technology have presented viable dosage alternatives for pediatric, geriatric, bedridden, nauseous, or noncompliant patients [5].

Recent developments in the technology have prompted scientists to develop FDTs with improved patient compliance and convenience. Upon introduction into the mouth, these tablets dissolve or disintegrate in the mouth in the absence of additional water for easy administration of active pharmaceutical ingredients. The popularity and usefulness of the formulation resulted in development of several FDT technologies. FDTs are solid unit dosage forms, which disintegrate or dissolve rapidly in the mouth without chewing and water [6]. Fast disintegrating tablets (FDTs) are also known as "fast dissolving," "mouth dissolving," "quick disintegrating," "orally disintegrating," "orodispersible," "melt-in-mouth," "quick dissolving," "porous tablets" and "effervescent drug absorption system" [7]. Drug dissolution and absorption as well as onset of clinical effect and drug bioavailability may be significantly greater than those observed from conventional dosage forms. The amount of drug that is subjected to first pass metabolism is reduced as compared to standard tablet [8]. The target populations for these new fast dissolving/disintegrating dosage forms have generally been pediatric, geriatric, and bedridden or mentally disabled patients. Patients with diarrhea, persistent nausea, or vomiting, who are traveling or who have little or no access to water, are also good candidates for FDTs [9].

Formulations of the drugs chosen in combination for the treatment of asthmatic cough and other respiratory disorders are available in the market in conventional tablet and liquid dosage forms. Liquid dosage forms are having their own limitation from stability and dose measurement perspectives. Tablets to be swallowed are resisted by children patients and patient compliance is an issue with such dosage forms. Hence they do not comply with the prescription, which results in high incidence of noncompliance and ineffective therapy. Salbutamol sulphate is a β_2 receptor agonist widely used as bronchodilator to relieve acute asthma. A fast dissolving tablet form would thus be advantageous, as salbutamol sulphate is water soluble and its preparation into a fast dissolving form would render it to dissolve rapidly and thereby result in rapid absorption without any lag time [10]. Cetirizine hydrochloride (CTZ) is an orally active white, crystalline water soluble drug and selective second generation nonsedative H1-receptor antagonist indicated in upper respiratory allergies, pollinosis, urticaria, and atopic dermatitis and is also used as adjuvant in seasonal asthma. Due to sore throat conditions, the patient experiences difficulty in swallowing a tablet type of dosage form [11]. Hence the present investigation was undertaken for preparation of fast disintegrating tablet of Salbutamol Sulphate, Cetirizine Hydrochloride in combined dosage form with an aim of improving/enhancing patient convenience and compliance, reducing the lag time, and providing faster onset of action to relieve the respiratory disorders immediately.

2. Materials and Methods

2.1. Materials. Salbutamol sulphate and cetirizine hydrochloride were obtained as gift samples from Trojan Pharma, Baddi, India. Microcrystalline Cellulose (Avicel PH-102) was received as gift sample from NB Entrepreneurs, Nagpur, India. Sodium Starch Glycolate (Primojel) and directly compressible mannitol (D-mannitol) were obtained from Qualikems Fine Chem Pvt. Ltd. Sodium Stearyl Fumarate was purchased from HiMedia. Sodium Saccharin was obtained from Loba Chemie, Mumbai, and talc from Nice Chemicals Private Limited, Hyderabad, India. PVP K-30 was obtained from HiMedia. All the chemicals and reagents used in research work were of analytical grade.

2.2. Methods

2.2.1. Selection of Excipients and Optimization of Their Concentration. In the development of fast disintegrating tablets, the most important parameter that needs to be optimized is the disintegration time. Fast disintegrating tablets were prepared firstly using different excipients (binders and superdisintegrants) and then evaluated for various parameters like friability, hardness, and disintegration time to select the best combination for formulation of fast disintegrating tablets. The combination with the lowest disintegration time, optimum hardness, and friability was selected for further study.

2.2.2. Optimization of Superdisintegrant Sodium Starch Glycolate (Primojel). Total six formulations (F1–F6) were manufactured to study the effect of type and concentration of superdisintegrants shown in Table 1. Tablets were manufactured by the technique of direct compression. Required quantity of each ingredient was taken for each specified formulation. The superdisintegrant in (1%, 2%, 4%, 6%, 8%, and 10%) concentration was used to develop the tablets. All the ingredients were passed through mesh number 60. All the ingredients were cogrind in a pestle motor. Finally talc and Sodium Stearyl Fumarate were added and mixed for 5 minutes. The mixed blend of excipients was compressed into tablets using 8 mm punch in multipunch tablet compression machine (Dhiman Industries, India).

2.2.3. Optimization of Polyvinylpyrrolidone (PVP K-30) or Microcrystalline Cellulose (Avicel PH-102) as Binder along with Optimized Concentration of Superdisintegrant. Total 14 formulations (F1–F14) were manufactured to study the effect of type of binder with optimized concentration of superdisintegrants shown in Table 2. Tablets were manufactured by the technique of direct compression. Required quantity of each ingredient was taken for each specified formulation. Optimized concentration of Sodium Starch Glycolate along with different concentration of binders (PVP K-30, MCC) was used to develop the tablets. All the ingredients were passed through mesh number 60. All the ingredients were cogrind in a pestle motor. Finally talc and Sodium Stearyl Fumarate were added and mixed for 5 minutes. The mixed blend of excipients was compressed into tablets using 8 mm punch in multipunch tablet compression machine (Dhiman Industries, India).

2.2.4. Final Formulation of Salbutamol Sulphate, Cetirizine Hydrochloride Fast Disintegrating Tablets. Fast disintegrating tablets of Salbutamol Sulphate, Cetirizine Hydrochloridein

TABLE 1: Formula for 1 tablet (200 mg) of different concentration of SSG (data in mg).

Serial number	Ingredients	F1	F2	F3	F4	F5	F6
1	Salbutamol Sulphate	2	2	2	2	2	2
2	Cetirizine Hydrochloride	5	5	5	5	5	5
3	Sodium Starch Glycolate	2 (1%)	4 (2%)	8 (4%)	12 (6%)	16 (8%)	20 (10%)
4	Polyvinylpyrrolidone K-30	4	4	4	4	4	4
5	Sodium Stearyl Fumarate	3	3	3	3	3	3
6	Talc	3	3	3	3	3	3
7	Sodium Saccharin	5	5	5	5	5	5
8	Mannitol	176	174	170	166	162	158

TABLE 2: Formula for 1 tablet (200 mg) for the optimization of PVP K-30 or MCC with optimized concentration of SSG.

Serial number	Ingredients	F1	F2	F3	F4	F5	F6	F7	F8	F9	F10	F11	F12	F13	F14
1	Salbutamol Sulphate	2	2	2	2	2	2	2	2	2	2	2	2	2	2
2	Cetirizine Hydrochloride	5	5	5	5	5	5	5	5	5	5	5	5	5	5
3	Sodium Starch Glycolate	8	8	8	8	8	8	8	8	8	8	8	8	8	8
4	Polyvinylpyrrolidone K-30	2	4	6	8	10	12	14	—	—	—	—	—	—	—
5	Microcrystalline Cellulose	—	—	—	—	—	—	—	2	4	6	8	10	12	14
6	Sodium Stearyl Fumarate	2	2	2	2	2	2	2	2	2	2	2	2	2	2
7	Talc	2	2	2	2	2	2	2	2	2	2	2	2	2	2
8	Sodium Saccharin	5	5	5	5	5	5	5	5	5	5	5	5	5	5
9	Mannitol	174	172	170	168	166	164	162	174	172	170	168	166	164	162

combined form were manufactured by direct compression technique, the formula of which is shown in Table 3. Required quantity of each ingredient was taken for specified formulation. Accurately weighed quantities of Salbutamol Sulphate, Cetirizine Hydrochloride taken with optimized concentration of superdisintegrant and binder with excipients were cogrind in geometric progression in a dry and clean mortar. All the ingredients were passed through mesh number 60. Finally talc and Sodium Stearyl Fumarate were added and mixed for 5 minutes. The mixed blend of excipients was compressed into tablets using 8 mm punch in multipunch tablet compression machine (Dhiman Industries, India).

TABLE 3: Formula of albutamol Sulphate, Cetirizine Hydrochloride FDT (data in mg).

Serial number	Ingredients	Formula for 1 tablet (200 mg)	Formula for 200 tablets (200 mg)
1	Cetirizine Hydrochloride	5	1000
2	Salbutamol Sulphate	2	400
3	Sodium Starch Glycolate	8	1600
4	Microcrystalline Cellulose	2	400
5	Sodium Stearyl Fumarate	4	800
6	Talc	2	400
7	Sodium Saccharin	8	1600
8	Mint Flavor	8	1600
9	Mannitol	161	32200

2.3. Evaluation Parameters

2.3.1. Weight Variation Test. Weight variation test was done by weighing 20 tablets individually by using digital weighting balance (Ohaus, USA). Calculate the average weight and compare the individual tablet weight to the average weight of 20 tablets (Table 4) [12].

TABLE 4: Weight variation limit as per IP.

Average weight of tablet	Deviation %
80 mg or less	±10
More than 80 mg but less than 250 mg	±7.5
250 mg or more	±5

2.3.2. Thickness. The thickness of tablets was measured by placing tablet between two arms of the vernier caliper (Indian caliper industries, Ambala, India). Three tablets from each batch were taken and an average thickness was measured [12].

2.3.3. Hardness. The strength of tablet is expressed as tensile strength (Kg/cm^2). The tablet crushing load is the force required to break a tablet into halves by compression. It was measured using a Monsanto Hardness Tester (Perfit). Three tablets from each formulation batch were taken randomly and the average reading was noted [13].

2.3.4. Friability. The friability of the tablets was measured in a Roche friabilator (Camp-bell Electronics, Mumbai). Tablets of a known weight (W_0) or sample 10 tablets are dedusted in a drum for a fixed time (100 revolutions) and weighed (W) again. Percentage friability was calculated from the loss in weight as given in the equation as below. The weight loss should not be more than 1% [14]:

$$\text{Percentage friability} = \frac{\text{Initial weight}(W_0) - \text{Final weight}(W)}{\text{Initial weight}(W_0)} \times 100. \quad (1)$$

2.3.5. In Vitro Disintegration Test. The disintegration time of the tablet was measured in water (37 ± 2°C) according to using Digital Tablet Disintegration Tester (Veego, India). The time in seconds taken for the complete disintegration of the tablet with no palpable mass in the apparatus was measured in seconds. Six tablets from each batch (formulation) were tested for the disintegration time calculations [15].

2.3.6. Wetting Time. A piece of tissue paper folded twice was placed in a small Petri dish (ID6.5 cm) containing 6 mL of distilled water being taken. A tablet containing a small quantity of amaranth color was placed on this being put on the paper and the time for the upper surface of the tablet to become complete red was measured. Three trials for each were performed [16].

2.3.7. Drug Content Uniformity. Ten tablets were powdered and the blend equivalent to 2 mg of salbutamol sulphate and 5 mg of cetirizine hydrochloride was weighed and dissolved in suitable quantity of 6.8 pH phosphate buffer. The solution was sonicated, filtered, and suitably diluted and the drug content was determined from simultaneous equation method by using Double Beam UV Spectrophotometer (UV-1800 Shimadzu) at 276 nm and 230 nm wavelengths corresponding to salbutamol sulphate and cetirizine hydrochloride, respectively. Each sample was analyzed in triplicate [17, 18].

2.3.8. In Vitro Dissolution Study. In vitro dissolution studies for all the fabricated tablets were carried out using USP eight-stage dissolution testing apparatus-2 (paddle method) (Lab, India), at 50 rpm in 500 mL of phosphate buffer solution, pH 6.8 at 37 ± 0.5°C. 5 mL of aliquot was withdrawn at the specified time intervals, filtered through Whatman filter paper and assayed spectrophotometrically at 276 nm and 230 nm. An equal volume of fresh medium was replaced into the dissolution medium after each sampling, to maintain the constant volume throughout the test. Dissolution studies were performed in triplicate. Absorbance of these solutions was measured at their respective λ_{max} using a Double Beam UV Spectrophotometer (UV-1800 Shimadzu) [17]. Cumulative percentage (%) drug release was calculated from simultaneous equation method which is given as

$$\text{At 276 nm} \quad A_1 = 0.0066\text{C}_s + 0.0050\text{C}_c, \quad (2)$$

$$\text{At 230 nm} \quad A_2 = 0.023\text{C}_s + 0.0338\text{C}_c, \quad (3)$$

where C_s is concentration of salbutamol sulphate and C_c is concentration of cetirizine hydrochloride.

By putting the values of absorbances A_1 and A_2 at their respective λ_{max}, the concentrations of salbutamol sulphate and cetirizine hydrochloride were obtained in sample solutions [18].

2.3.9. Drug-Excipient Compatibility Studies. FTIR spectra of pure drugs and formulated FDT containing drugs were recorded on FTIR Spectrophotometer (Bruker, USA). This study generally includes FTIR spectroscopy and these are generally performed to confirm the drug-excipient compatibility. FTIR spectra of samples were recorded in scanning range of 4000 to 600 cm^{-1} and the resolution was 1 cm^{-1}. FTIR scans were then evaluated for shifting and masking and appearance of new peaks due to drug-excipient incompatibility [19].

2.3.10. Accelerated Stability Studies. Accelerated stability studies were performed out on formulated FDTs (formulated in three primary batches) which were wrapped in aluminium foil and then stored in air-tight containers that is impermeable to solid, liquid, and gases, for a period of one month as prescribed by ICH guidelines at temperature of 40±2°C and at ambient humidity and at room temperature. The tablets were withdrawn on 15th, 30th day and analyzed for drug content, friability, hardness, and in vitro disintegration time [20].

3. Results and Discussion

An attempt was made in the present investigation to make a fast disintegrating tablet of Salbutamol Sulphate, Cetirizine Hydrochloride in combination by direct compression method by employing superdisintegrant such as Sodium Starch Glycolate and mannitol as directly compressible diluent and Sodium Saccharin was used to enhance palatability. MCC (Avicel PH 102) was used in the formulation as a disintegrant and a binder. To impart pleasant taste and improve mouth feel, Sodium Saccharin was included as sweetening agent which is 400 times sweeter than sucrose. Sodium Stearyl Fumarate was used as a lubricant because of its water soluble nature and directly compressible features.

3.1. Optimization of Superdisintegrant Sodium Starch Glycolate (Primojel). For optimal bioavailability and rapid absorption, the selection of the optimum concentration of superdisintegrant is necessary for rapid disintegration of tablets. Superdisintegrant decreases the disintegration time, resulting in the enhancement of dissolution rate of the drug. Therefore, for the formulation of rapidly disintegrating dosage forms, the proper selection of optimum concentration of superdisintegrant is of vital importance in dosage form development of FDTs. The results for optimization of superdisintegrant concentration in FDTs by direct compression method are shown in Table 5.

From the evaluation parameters, it was observed that 4% *Sodium Starch Glycolate* was the optimum concentration for rapid tablet disintegration on the basis of the least disintegration time observed with F3 formulation.

TABLE 5: Evaluation parameters for the optimization of Sodium Starch Glycolate.

Serial number	Evaluation parameters	F1 (1%)	F2 (2%)	F3 (4%)	F4 (6%)	F5 (8%)	F6 (10%)
1	Weight variation (IP)	Passed	Passed	Passed	Passed	Passed	Passed
2	Friability (%)	0.8	0.8	0.1	0.3	0.1	0.1
3	Hardness* (Kg/cm^2) ± S.D	2.2 ± 0.57	1.6 ± 0.28	1.5 ± 0.28	1.5 ± 0.32	2.0 ± 0.57	1.8 ± 0.28
4	Disintegration time** (Sec) ± S.D	80 ± 2.34	59 ± 6.67	**42 ± 3.56**	49 ± 6.38	78 ± 7.39	95 ± 6.97

*Average of three determinations.
**Average of six determinations.

TABLE 6: Evaluation parameters for the optimization of PVP K-30 or MCC with optimized concentration of SSG.

Formula number	Evaluation parameters			
	Weight variation (IP)	Friability (%)	Hardness* (Kg/cm^2) ± S.D	Disintegration time** (Sec) ± S.D
F1	Passed	0.1	2.2 ± 0.28	60 ± 1.78
F2	Passed	0.2	1.8 ± 0.28	**47 ± 2.45**
F3	Passed	0.5	2.0 ± 0.00	69 ± 2.89
F4	Passed	0.3	3.2 ± 0.76	83 ± 2.40
F5	Passed	0.3	1.6 ± 0.50	90 ± 5.16
F6	Passed	0.8	2.5 ± 0.50	120 ± 5.77
F7	Passed	0.8	2.0 ± 0.00	145 ± 5.43
F8	Passed	0.1	1.5 ± 0.50	**38 ± 4.34**
F9	Passed	0.1	1.5 ± 0.28	47 ± 2.34
F10	Passed	0.2	1.5 ± 0.28	62 ± 3.10
F11	Passed	0.1	1.8 ± 0.28	75 ± 1.32
F12	Passed	0.1	1.5 ± 0.28	82 ± 2.08
F13	Passed	0.1	1.8 ± 0.28	94 ± 3.67
F14	Passed	0.1	1.8 ± 0.28	110 ± 2.78

*Average of three determinations.
**Average of six determinations.

The superdisintegrant action of SSG is exhibited by swelling and capillary action which causes rapid disintegration of tablets. Due to its hydrophilic nature, it rapidly absorbs water and swells up to 200–300% of their own weight. It is used in concentration range of 4–8%. Disintegration time increases above 8% due to gelling effect of the SSG [21].

3.2. Optimization of Polyvinylpyrrolidone (PVP K-30) or Microcrystalline Cellulose (Avicel PH-102) as Binder along with Optimized Concentration of Superdisintegrant. To study the effect of binders with the optimized concentration of SSG on the disintegration time, hardness, and friability of tablets, total 14 formulations (F1–F14) were prepared using different concentration of polyvinylpyrrolidone (PVP K-30) or Microcrystalline Cellulose. The results for optimization of different binder in FDTs are given in Table 6.

It was observed from the evaluation parameters that the disintegration time of the formulation F8 was further decreased and friability and hardness of tablets comply with the IP limits. The least disintegration time was observed in *F8* formulation that is 1% *MCC* as compared to *F2* formulation that is 2% *PVP K-30*. The probable reason was that MCC has porous morphology, due to which water is "wicked" through the capillary action which causes the tablet to break apart rapidly. On the other hand, water soluble materials such as PVP K-30 dissolving faster rather than disintegrating. Therefore 1% *Microcrystalline Cellulose* was selected as optimum binder concentration selected for final formulation of Salbutamol Sulphate, Cetirizine Hydrochloride FDT.

3.3. Evaluation Parameters for Salbutamol Sulphate, Cetirizine Hydrochloride FDT. Tablets were prepared using direct compression technique. The drug content was found in the range of 85–115% of the label claim (acceptable limit) and friability of the tablets was found below 1% indicating a good mechanical resistance of tablets. The in vitro disintegration time (DT) of the tablets was found to be less than 60 sec as shown in Table 7. Since mechanical integrity is of paramount importance in successful formulation of FDTs, hence the hardness of tablets was determined. The wetting time was practically good for formulation. The formulated FDTs had shown low DT indicating suitability of formulation for mouth dissolving tablet.

3.4. In Vitro Dissolution Study. From the in vitro dissolution data it was observed that 94.70 ± 2.24% of salbutamol sulphatereleased in 10 minutes and 95.59±2.34% of cetirizine hydrochloride released in 16 minutes indicate that the tablet

Table 7: Evaluation parameters for Salbutamol Sulphate, Cetirizine Hydrochloride FDT.

Serial number	Evaluation parameters	Results
1	Weight variation (IP)	Passed
2	Thickness* (mm) ± S.D	3.63 ± 0.06
3	Hardness* (Kg/cm^2) ± S.D	1.8 ± 0.29
4	Friability (%)	0.3
5	Disintegration time** (sec) ± S.D	45 ± 2.34
6	Wetting time* (sec) ± S.D	28 ± 1.53
7	Drug content uniformity* (mg) ± S.D	SAL-100.8 ± 3.36, CET-104.7 ± 1.97

*Average of three determinations.
**Average of six determinations.

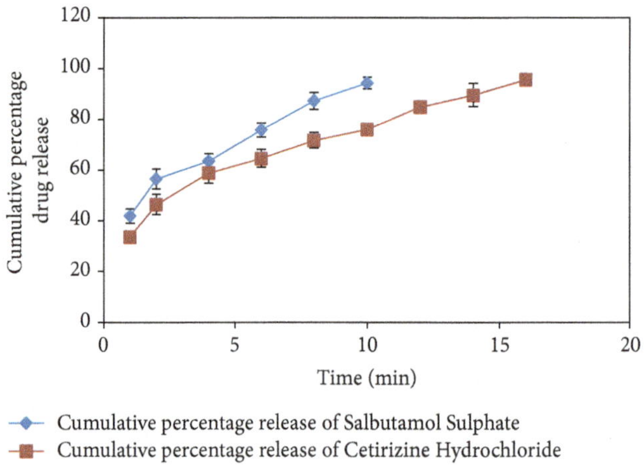

Figure 1: In vitro dissolution profile of Salbutamol Sulphate, Cetirizine Hydrochloride FDT.

complies as per IP specifications that is 85%–110% shown in Figure 1.

3.5. Drug-Excipient Compatibility Studies. The results obtained with FTIIR studies showed that there was no interaction between the drug and other excipients used in the formulation. The FTIR spectra of Salbutamol Sulphate, Cetirizine Hydrochloride had shown intense absorption band at 1384.70 cm^{-1}, 1613.03 cm^{-1}, and 1384.70 cm^{-1} corresponding to the presence of functional groups such as Tri-methyl group, secondary amine group, and phenol group in salbutamol sulphate and at 756.96 cm^{-1}, 1318.89 cm^{-1}, 1024.90 cm^{-1}, and 1191.03 cm^{-1} corresponding to the presence of functional groups such as aliphatic chloro compound, carboxylic acid, alkyl substituted ether, and tertiary amine in cetirizine hydrochloride. The FTIR of salbutamol sulphate, cetirizine hydrochloride FDT formulation showing intense absorption bands at 1388.28 cm^{-1}, 1610.83 cm^{-1}, and 1388.28 cm^{-1} and at 757.55 cm^{-1}, 1312.78 cm^{-1}, 1019.73 cm^{-1}, and 1194.89 cm^{-1} indicates no change in the functional groups confirmed undisturbed structure of Salbutamol Sulphate, Cetirizine Hydrochloride, which indicates no drug-excipient incompatibility as shown in Figures 2 and 3.

3.6. Accelerated Stability Studies. Accelerated stability studies were carried out on formulated FDTs (formulated in three primary batches) as prescribed by ICH guidelines, wrapped in aluminium foil to prevent the formulation from exposure to light to simulate the aluminum packaging that is Alu Alu packing of drug products, and stored in air-tight containers which is impermeable to solid, liquid, and gases, for one-month period. The product is exposed to normal and extreme condition of temperature and humidity. The stability data of formulation was given in Tables 8 and 9.

The result of the stability study indicated that there were not much differences observed in hardness, disintegration time, drug content uniformity, and friability before and after the storage period at room temperature and at ambient humidity but at temperature of 40°C ± 2°C and at ambient humidity hardness was increasing with time, prolonging the DT of the tablet [22]; the probable reason was loss of moisture from tablets but in all cases DT is within the specified IP limit (within 3 min.). This indicates that formulation is fairly stable at both storage conditions.

4. Conclusion

Fast disintegrating tablets of Salbutamol Sulphate, Cetirizine Hydrochloride in combination were prepared by direct compression method using Sodium Starch Glycolate as a superdisintegrant and commonly available excipient. The tablets disintegrated rapidly in oral cavity and had acceptable hardness and friability. In vitro drug release from the tablets shows rapid drug dissolution. From the above study, it was concluded that, by employing commonly available pharmaceutical excipients such as superdisintegrants, hydrophilic and swellable excipients and proper filler, a fast disintegrating tablet of Salbutamol Sulphate, Cetirizine Hydrochloride FDT used in respiratory disorders, were formulated successfully with desired characteristics in combined pharmaceutical dosage form which disintegrated rapidly, providing rapid onset of action and enhancing the patient convenience and compliance. The technique adopted was found to be economical and industrially feasible.

Conflict of Interests

The authors declare that they do not have any financial and personal relationships with other people or any other organizations that could inappropriately influence this research work.

Acknowledgments

All authors are highly acknowledged to NB Entrepreneurs, Nagpur, and Trojan Pharma, Baddi, India, for providing gift samples of Avicel PH-102 and drug and CT Institute

Table 8: Stability data of Salbutamol Sulphate, Cetirizine Hydrochloride FDT at room temperature and at ambient humidity.

Evaluation parameters	Time interval Data of three primary batches on								
	0 day			15th day			30th day		
	B-1	B-2	B-3	B-1	B-2	B-3	B-1	B-2	B-3
Hardness* (Kg/cm^2) ± S.D	1.5 ± 0.29	1.8 ± 0.29	1.5 ± 0.29	1.5 ± 0.00	1.5 ± 0.00	1.7 ± 0.29	1.5 ± 0.00	1.5 ± 0.29	1.5 ± 0.29
Friability (%)	1	0.6	1	0.2	0.3	0.2	0.1	0.1	0.1
Drug content uniformity* (mg) ± S.D	SAL-100.8 ± 3.36, CET-104.7 ± 1.97	SAL-95.6 ± 2.34, CET-95.4 ± 2.86	SAL-93.8 ± 1.24, CET-97.7 ± 3.97	SAL-99.5 ± 2.14, CET-103 ± 1.76	SAL-94.5 ± 2.67, CET-98.6 ± 2.07	SAL-94.8 ± 1.23, CET-93.4 ± 1.77	SAL-98.3 ± 1.98, CET-97.8 ± 2.97	SAL-95.4 ± 1.65, CET-97.7 ± 2.75	SAL-95.7 ± 3.63, CET-94.2 ± 2.43
Disintegration time** (sec) ± S.D	39 ± 2.28	47 ± 1.80	42 ± 3.01	42 ± 3.97	50 ± 4.52	47 ± 1.66	46 ± 2.83	49 ± 2.52	48 ± 3.75

*Average of three determinations/batches.
**Average of six determinations/batches.

Table 9: Stability data of Salbutamol Sulphate, Cetirizine Hydrochloride FDT at temperature (40°± 2°C) and at ambient humidity.

Evaluation parameters	Time interval Data of three primary batches on								
	0 day			15th day			30th day		
	B-1	B-2	B-3	B-1	B-2	B-3	B-1	B-2	B-3
Hardness* (Kg/cm^2) ± S.D	1.5 ± 0.29	1.8 ± 0.29	1.5 ± 0.29	2.5 ± 0.00	2.2 ± 0.29	2.5 ± 0.00	2.5 ± 0.00	2.5 ± 0.29	3.2 ± 0.29
Friability (%)	1	0.6	1	0.1	0.2	0.9	0.6	0.5	0.1
Drug content uniformity* (mg) ± S.D	SAL-100.8 ± 3.36, CET-104.7 ± 1.97	SAL-95.6 ± 2.34, CET-95.4 ± 2.86	SAL-93.8 ± 1.24, CET-97.7 ± 3.97	SAL-98.5 ± 2.14, CET-100 ± 1.78	SAL-99.4 ± 2.67, CET-96.3 ± 2.07	SAL-90.42 ± 3.64, CET-95.7 ± 2.78	SAL-92.8 ± 1.98, CET-95.5 ± 1.97	SAL-99 ± 1.65, CET-98.1 ± 1.97	SAL-97.6 ± 3.63, CET-94.2 ± 1.63
Disintegration time** (sec) ± S.D	39 ± 2.28	47 ± 1.80	42 ± 3.01	49 ± 2.38	55 ± 3.08	51 ± 1.76	55 ± 2.09	61 ± 1.89	58 ± 2.96

*Average of three determinations/batches.

**Average of six determinations/batches.

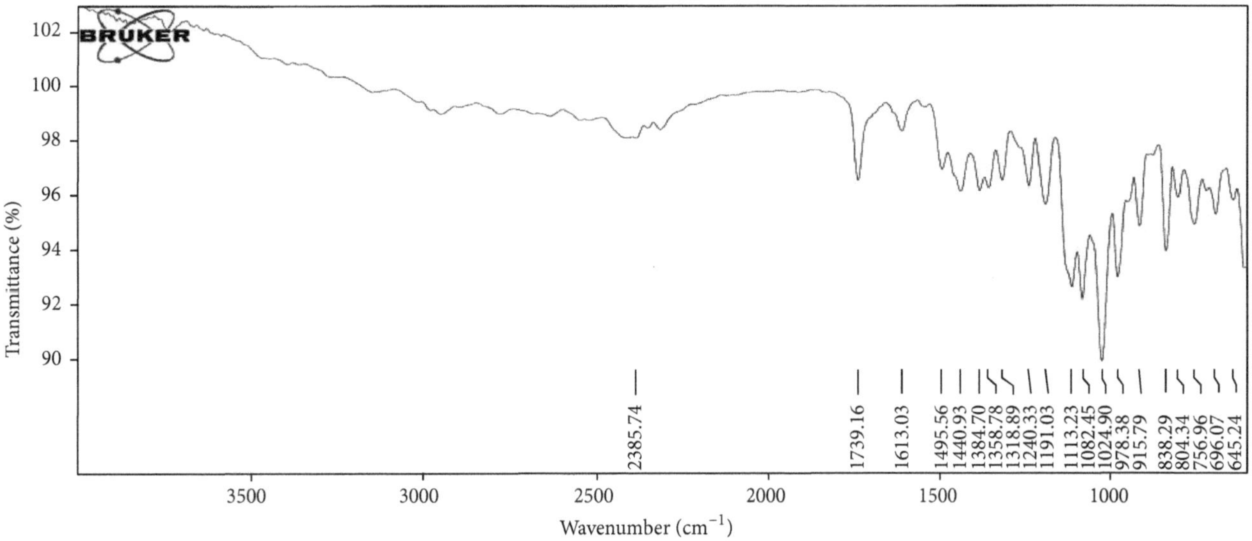

FIGURE 2: FTIR spectra of physical mixture of Salbutamol Sulphate, Cetirizine Hydrochloride.

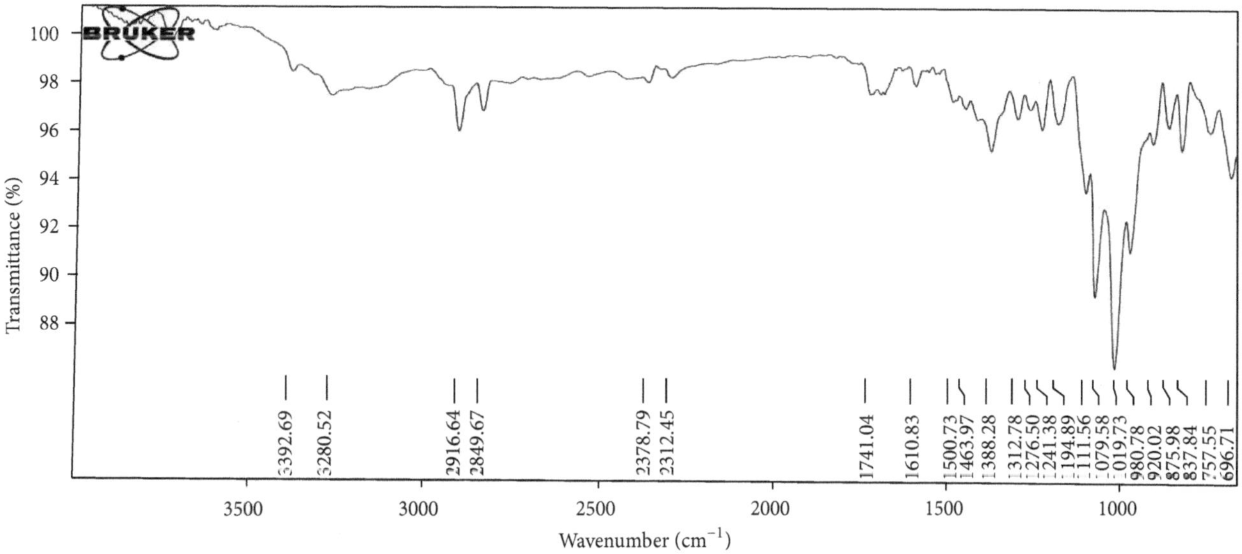

FIGURE 3: FTIR spectra of Salbutamol Sulphate, Cetirizine Hydrochloride FDT.

of Pharmaceutical Sciences, Jalandhar, for their efforts to facilitate the use of the necessary instruments and materials required during the entire course of this research work.

References

[1] R. Pahwa, M. Piplani, P. C. Sharma, D. Kaushik, and S. Nanda, "Orally disintegrating tablets—friendly to pediatrics and geriatrics," *Archives of Applied Science Research*, vol. 2, no. 2, pp. 35–48, 2010.

[2] S. Divate, K. Kavitha, and G. N. Sockan, "Fast disintegrating tablets—an emerging trend," *International Journal of Pharmaceutical Sciences Review and Research*, vol. 6, no. 2, pp. 18–22, 2011.

[3] R. Panigrahi and S. A. Behera, "Review on fast dissolving tablets," *Webmed Central Quality and Patient*, vol. 1, no. 9, pp. 1-17, 2010.

[4] M. Slowson and S. Slowson, "What to do when patients cannot swallow their medications," *Pharma Times*, vol. 51, pp. 90–96, 1985.

[5] S. Corveleyn and J. P. Remon, "Formulation and production of rapidly disintegrating tablets by lyophilisation using hydrochlorothiazide as a model drug," *International Journal of Pharmaceutics*, vol. 152, no. 2, pp. 215–225, 1997.

[6] A. K. Nayak and K. Manna, "Current developments in orally disintegrating tablet technology," *Journal of Pharmaceutical Education and Research*, vol. 2, no. 1, pp. 21–34, 2011.

[7] S. A. Sreenivas, P. M. Dandagi, A. P. Gadad et al., "Orodispersible tablet: new-fanged drug delivery system—a review," *Indian Journal of Pharmaceutical Education and Research*, vol. 39, no. 4, pp. 177–181, 2005.

[8] D. Bhowmik, B. Chiranjib, K. Pankaj, and M. R. Chandira, "Fast dissolving tablet: an overview," *Journal of Chemical and Pharmaceutical Research*, vol. 1, no. 1, pp. 163–177, 2009.

[9] B. G. Prajapati and N. Ratnakar, "A review on recent patents on fast dissolving drug delivery system," *International Journal of PharmTech Research*, vol. 1, no. 3, pp. 790–798, 2009.

[10] S. Nayak, B. Das, D. K. Tarai, D. Panda, and J. Sahoo, "Formulation and evaluation of salbutamol sulphate fast dissolving tablet," *Journal of Pharmacy Research*, vol. 3, no. 4, pp. 824–827, 2010.

[11] K. D. Tripathi, *Essential of Medical Pharmacology*, Jaypee Brothers Medical Publisher, New Delhi, India, 6th edition, 2008.

[12] S. B. Jadhav, D. R. Kaudewar, G. S. Kaminwar, A. B. Jadhav, R. V. Kshirsagar, and D. M. Sakarkar, "Formulation and evaluation of dispersible tablets of diltiazem hydrochloride," *International Journal of PharmTech Research*, vol. 3, no. 3, pp. 1314–1321, 2011.

[13] M. Vishal, K. Anuj, P. Naveen, P. Kumud, and S. Sangram, "Formulation and evaluation of orodispersible tablets of lornoxicam," *International Journal of Drug Development and Research*, vol. 3, no. 1, pp. 281–285, 2011.

[14] D. Sharma, "Formulation development and evaluation of fast disintegrating tablets of salbutamol sulphate for respiratory disorders," *ISRN Pharmaceutics*, vol. 2013, Article ID 674507, 8 pages, 2013.

[15] R. B. Parmar, A. H. Baria, H. M. Tank, and S. D. Faldu, "Formulation and evaluation of domperidone fast dissolving tablets," *International Journal of PharmTech Research*, vol. 1, no. 3, pp. 483–487, 2009.

[16] B. Senthilnathan and A. Rupenagunta, "Formulation development and evaluation of venlafaxine hydrochloride orodispersible tablets," *International Journal of Pharmaceutical Sciences and Research*, vol. 2, no. 4, pp. 913–921, 2011.

[17] S. H. Rasheed, M. Arief, S. R. Gajavalli et al., "Comparison of different superdisintegrants in designing of fast dissolving tablets of salbutamol sulphate," *Research Journal of Pharmaceutical, Biological and Chemical Sciences*, vol. 2, no. 2, pp. 155–163, 2011.

[18] D. Sharma, G. Singh, M. Singh, D. Kumar, and M. S. Rathore, "Development and validation of spectrophotometric method for the simultaneous estimation of salbutamol sulphate and cetirizine hydrochloride in combined dosage form," *International Research Journal of Pharmacy*, vol. 3, no. 7, pp. 292–296, 2012.

[19] D. Sharma, M. Singh, D. Kumar, and G. Singh, "Formulation development and evaluation of fast disintegrating tablet of cetirizine hydrochloride: a novel drug delivery for pediatrics and geriatrics ," *Journal of Pharmaceutics*, vol. 2014, Article ID 808167, 8 pages, 2014.

[20] ICH Harmonised Tripartite Guideline. Cover Note for Revision of Q1A(R) Stability Testing of New Drug Substances and Products. Q1A (R2): pp. 9.

[21] M. Mangal, S. Thakral, M. Goswami, and P. Ghai, "Superdisintegrants: an updated review," *International Journal of Pharmacy and Pharmaceutical Science Research*, vol. 2, no. 2, pp. 26–35, 2012.

[22] I. Ahmad and R. H. Shaikh, "Effect of temperature and humidity on the disintegration time of packaged paracetamol tablet formulations," *Pakistan Journal of Pharmaceutical Sciences*, vol. 7, no. 1, pp. 1–7, 1994.

15

Design and Evaluation of Voriconazole Loaded Solid Lipid Nanoparticles for Ophthalmic Application

Anubha Khare,[1] Inderbir Singh,[1] Pravin Pawar,[2] and Kanchan Grover[1]

[1] *Chitkara College of Pharmacy, Chitkara University, Chandigarh-Patiala National Highway, Rajpura, Patiala, Punjab 140401, India*
[2] *Gourishankar Institute of Pharmaceutical Education & Research, Limb, Satara, Survey No. 990, Near NH-4, Satara 415020, India*

Correspondence should be addressed to Pravin Pawar; pkpawar80@yahoo.com

Academic Editor: Jaleh Varshosaz

Voriconazole is a second-generation antifungal agent with excellent broad spectrum of antifungal activity commercially available for oral and intravenous administration. Systemic administration of voriconazole is associated with side effects including visual and hepatic abnormalities. This study assessed the feasibility of using solid lipid nanoparticles for ocular delivery of voriconazole adopting stearic acid as lipidic material, tween 80 as a stabilizer, and Carbopol 934 as controlled release agent and for increasing the precorneal residence time in eye. The systems were prepared using two different methods, that is, ultrasonication method and microemulsion technique. The results indicated that the larger particle size of SLNs was found with microemulsion technique (308 ± 3.52 nm to 343 ± 3.51) compared to SLN prepared with ultrasonication method (234 ± 3.52 nm to 288 ± 4.58 nm). The polydispersity index values were less than 0.3 for all formulations and zeta potential of the prepared formulations by these two methods varied from -22.71 ± 0.63 mV to -28.86 ± 0.58 mV. Powder X-ray diffraction and differential scanning calorimetry indicated decrease in crystallinity of drug. The *in vitro* release study and the SLN formulations prepared with ultrasonication method demonstrated sustained release up to 12 hours. This study demonstrated that SLN prepared by ultrasonication method is more suitable than microemulsion technique without causing any significant effect on corneal hydration level.

1. Introduction

Eye is the most simply accessible site for topical administration of a medication. Drugs are commonly applied to the ocular system for a localized action on the surface or in the interior of the eye [1]. The major challenge to the formulator is to outwit these barriers without causing any tissue damage [2]. The cornea is the anterior layer of the eye, comprised of epithelium, stroma, and endothelium. However, this layer represents a mechanical barrier restraining the delivery of drug molecules. Due to their high lipid content, the epithelium and the endothelium are considered as an obstruction to the passage of hydrophilic molecules. The stroma is characterized by a high water content that makes this layer impermeable to lipophilic molecules [3]. Corneal barrier also plays a considerable role in low ocular bioavailability due to which only <5% of the applied drugs are able to penetrate through the cornea into the intraocular tissues [4].

As a result to optimize ocular drug delivery, different strategies were developed to increase the bioavailability of drugs in the front of eye to prolong time. An ideal ophthalmic drug delivery must be able to release the drug in sustained manner and remain in the front of eye to prolong period of the time. As a result various attempts have been made to prolong the residence time of drug on the ocular surface and also to slow down the drug elimination [5, 6].

To overcome the above problems related to ocular delivery, novel drug delivery systems (NDDS) consisting mainly of nanoemulsions, liposomes, microemulsions, microspheres, and solid lipid nanoparticles (SLNs) have been projected newly for oral, topical, and parental administration of drugs [6, 7]. SLN represented an exceptional carrier system to conventional colloidal carriers, such as emulsions, lipid emulsion, liposomes, and polymeric microparticles, and so forth. SLNs are submicron colloidal carriers ranging from 50 to 1000 nm, which are composed of physiological lipid,

Table 1: Composition of voriconazole loaded solid lipid nanoparticles.

Batches	Drug (% w/v)	Stearic acid (% w/v)	Tween 80 (mL)	Carbopol 934 (gm)	Dichloromethane (mL)	Distilled water (mL)
VUSLN-1	0.02	0.3	2	25	2	q.s
VUSLN-2	0.02	0.3	2	50	2	q.s
VUSLN-3	0.02	0.3	2	75	2	q.s
VUSLN-4	0.02	0.3	2	100	2	q.s
VUSLN-5	0.02	0.3	2	150	2	q.s
VMSLN-6	0.02	0.3	2	25	2	q.s
VMSLN-7	0.02	0.3	2	50	2	q.s
VMSLN-8	0.02	0.3	2	75	2	q.s
VMSLN-9	0.02	0.3	2	100	2	q.s
VMSLN-10	0.02	0.3	2	150	2	q.s

dispersed in water or in aqueous surfactant solution [8]. They are appropriate for the incorporation of lipophilic, hydrophilic, and poorly water soluble drugs [9]. Various researchers have been working in the area of ocular drug delivery; that is, formulated meloxicam solid lipid nanoparticles were formulated and it was concluded that SLNs have excellent physical stability, high entrapment efficiency, and sustained drug release and also represent a promising carrier for topical delivery of meloxicam [10]. Some researchers describe the preparation and characterization of solid lipid nanoparticles (SLNs) prepared with stearic acid (SLN-A) and a mixture of stearic acid and Compritol (SLN-B) as lipid matrix and poloxamer-188 as surfactant, using sodium taurocholate and ethanol as cosurfactant mixture, which proves SLN to be a good ocular drug delivery system considering the smaller particle size, particle size stability, physiologically tolerable components, and so forth [9]. Amphotericin B and natamycin fungal ulcers tend to have very poor outcomes. Since 1960 no new medications have been permitted by the FDA and there has been only a randomized trial of antifungal therapy for fungal ulcers [11]. There are studies that indicate the newer triazoles; that is, voriconazole is a novel second-generation triazole derivative of fluconazole with exceptional broad spectrum activity commercially available for oral and intravenous administration. Voriconazole has broad *in vitro* antifungal activity against yeasts and moulds, including a broad range of less common pathogens. Voriconazole possesses fungicidal *in vitro* activity against all *Aspergillus* species, moulds such as *Scedosporium* species and *Fusarium* species, and is highly potent against fluconazole-resistant *Candida* species including *Candida krusei*, *Candida glabrata*, and *Candida albicans*. The minimum inhibitory concentrations (MIC90) of voriconazole are considerably less than that of fluconazole. It inhibits cytochrome P450-dependent 14α sterol demethylase enzyme which is responsible for inhibiting and disrupting fungal cell membrane synthesis, resulting in depletion of ergosterol [12]. Voriconazole marketed formulations are also present; namely, Vozole is a lyophilized powder (VCZ eye drops 1% w/v and VCZ injection 1 mg/vial).

Voriconazole is a lipophilic drug with a low pH dependent aqueous solubility (maximum 2.7 mg/mL at pH 1.2). To improve the accessibility of voriconazole at the intraocular level, voriconazole loaded solid lipid formulations were prepared. Stearic acid is a saturated, wax-like, fatty acid commonly used in the production of SLNs. In addition to this, it has excellent biodegradability and has low toxicity and also incorporates both hydrophilic and lipophilic drugs [13]. Tween 80 is a nonionic surfactant derived from sorbitan esters and acting as stabilizer in the preparation [14]. Carbopol 934 is a polyacrylic polymer which has inherent mucoadhesiveness, acts as controlled release agent, and also prolongs the precorneal residence time and avoids systemic side effects [15].

The purpose of the study was to formulate voriconazole loaded-SLN formulations as sustained ocular drug delivery systems with the aim of improving availability of voriconazole at the intraocular level. It was proposed to prepare the SLN of voriconazole by both ultrasonication and microemulsion techniques so that the best suitable method out of these two can be projected and to determine the effect of formulation factors on the transcorneal permeation of voriconazole through freshly excised goat corneas.

2. Materials and Methods

2.1. Materials. Voriconazole was received as gift samples from Matrix Laboratories, Hyderabad (India), and stearic acid and Carbopol 934 were purchased from Sigma-Aldrich Pvt. Ltd. (India). All other chemicals used were of analytical reagent grade. Fresh whole eyeballs of goat were obtained from local butcher's shop (Zirakpur, Punjab, India) within one hour of slaughtering of animal.

2.2. Methods

2.2.1. Ultrasonication Method. Firstly, stearic acid was melted in porcelain dish (for relaxation of lipid side chain) and then required quantity of tween 80 was added. Secondly, drug was soluble in dichloromethane and this drug solution was added in the above lipid phase. The detailed formulae of VCZ loaded SLNs with their percentage (w/w or w/v) are given in Table 1. An aqueous phase containing different concentrations of Carbopol 934 was prepared in 20 mL of distilled water with constant stirring and heating at approximately 70°C in which lipid phase is added slowly. The prepared solution was stirred at 2000 rpm for 3 min and instantly ultrasonicated by probe sonicator (PCI analytics, Mumbai, India). Ultrasonication was done by adjusting frequency 0.5 for 30 min at 45% amplitude. After sonication, the dispersion was diluted with 80 mL of distilled cold water under continuous stirring for 15 min. A stable SLN suspension of voriconazole by ultrasonication (VUSLN) was obtained [16].

2.2.2. Microemulsion Technique. In this technique, stearic acid was melted in porcelain dish (for relaxation of lipid side chain) and then required quantity of tween 80 was added. Then, drug was soluble in dichloromethane and this drug solution was added in the above lipid phase. The detailed formulae of VCZ loaded SLNs with their percentage (w/w or w/v) are given in Table 1. An aqueous phase containing different concentrations of Carbopol 934 was prepared in 20 mL of distilled water in which lipid phase is added slowly with constant stirring and heating at approximately 70°C for 15 minutes. The solid lipid nanoparticles were obtained by dispersing warm o/w microemulsion dropwise into cold water (2-3°C) in a beaker under continuous stirring at 2000 rpm for 4 hr. After completion of stirring, SLN dispersion was instantly ultrasonicated by probe sonicator (PCI analytics, Mumbai, India). Ultrasonication was done by adjusting frequency 0.5 for 30 min at 45% amplitude. A stable SLN suspension of voriconazole by microemulsion (VMSLN) technique was obtained [17].

2.2.3. Lyophilization. To these above prepared aqueous dispersions, 2.5% w/v mannitol was dissolved as a cryoprotectant and then lyophilization was carried out for 24 hr to verify physical stability and redispersibility. Firstly, prefreezing was done by freezing the mixture at −74°C, at 0.02 mm Hg pressure, and then vials were kept in adapter. The adapter was then fit into freeze-dryer (Lyophilizer FD-5-3, Allied Frost, New Delhi, India) and dispersion was lyophilized in a laboratory to get free flowing powder of voriconazole SLN [18, 19].

3. Physicochemical Characterization of VCZ-SLN

3.1. Particle Size, Polydispersity Index, and Zeta Potential Measurements. The particle size and polydispersity index (PDI) of the SLN were determined by photon correlation spectroscopy (PCS) with a Zetasizer Nano ZS-90 (Malvern Instruments Ltd., Worcestershire, UK). Prior to analysis, samples of all SLN formulations were diluted with double distilled water. The zeta potential measurements were done by laser-doppler-anemometer coupled with Zetasizer Nano ZS-90 (Malvern Instruments Ltd., Worcestershire, UK) to validate the electrophoretic mobility of particles. All the analysis were repeated in triplicate.

3.2. Determination of Entrapped VCZ. It is the percentage of the actual mass of drug that was entrapped in the polymeric carrier, relative to the initial amount of loaded drug, and was calculated using the following equation:

$$\text{Entrapment efficiency\%} = \frac{\text{Actual loading}}{\text{Theoretical loading}} \times 100. \quad (1)$$

Theoretical drug loading was calculated from the amount of drug taken relative to the amount of total drug and excipients used in the preparation of nanoparticles as follows:

$$\text{Theoretical loading (\%)} = \frac{\text{Total drug}}{\text{Total drug} + \text{Total excipients}}. \quad (2)$$

For actual drug loading, the SLN dispersion prepared by dispersing 25 mg of the lyophilized SLN powder in 5 mL mixture of methanol : distilled water (1 : 4) was centrifuged at 13000 rpm for 20 min. The clear supernatant was analyzed for free voriconazole content by measuring absorbance at 255 nm in an UV-visible spectrophotometer (Systronics, Mumbai). The total amount of drug present in the SLN was determined by dispersing 25 mg of the lyophilized SLN powder in 10 mL dichloromethane by sonication and filtering through a microsyringe filter (0.2 μm) and analyzing the filtrate for voriconazole by measuring absorbance at 255 nm using UV-visible spectrophotometer [18]. The following formula was used to calculate actual loading:

$$\text{Actual loading (\%)} = \frac{\text{Total drug} - \text{Free drug}}{\text{mg of lyophilized powder}} \times 100. \quad (3)$$

3.3. Fourier Transform Infrared Spectroscopy (FTIR) Analysis. FTIR spectra of prepared SLN were recorded by Bruker spectrophotometer (Bruker IFS 66/S, Germany), using the potassium bromide (KBr) disk technique (5 mg samples for 100 mg dry KBr). KBr discs of the lyophilized formulations were prepared and analyzed at the wavelength range of 4000–400 cm^{-1}.

3.4. Electron Microscope Examination. The morphological observation of the VCZ loaded SLN was performed by transmission electron microscope (TEM). The samples of nanoparticles were stained with 2% (w/v) phosphotungstic acid. The nanoparticle suspension (5–10 μL) was placed on the copper grids with films for viewing by TEM (Hitachi H-7500, Tokyo, Japan). Digital micrograph and imaging viewer software was used to capture the image.

3.5. Powder X-Ray Diffraction (PXRD) Analysis. PXRD was done to examine the crystalline state of the formulated SLN. The X-ray powder diffraction patterns of the samples were recorded with the XPERT-PRO multipurpose X-ray diffractometer (PAN analytical, Netherlands) using the PRS measurement program using Ni-filtered, CuKα radiation generated at 45 kV, and a current intensity of 40 mA. The diffraction angle range of the instrument was operated over a range of 2θ angles from 5° to 40°.

3.6. Differential Scanning Calorimetry (DSC) Analysis. Thermograms of the different samples were obtained using a DSC TA-60 (Shimadzu, Tokyo, Japan) 208 calorimeter. Samples (3–5 mg) were heated in crimped aluminum pans from 40°C to 200°C at a scanning rate of 10°C/min. Analyses were carried out under an inert nitrogen purge (35 mL/min) and an empty pan of alumina was used as reference in every case.

3.7. In Vitro Drug Release from VCZ-SLN. The *in vitro* drug release studies were carried out in the modified USP dissolution apparatus 1 (37 ± 0.5°C) containing a two-sided open glass cylinder for 12 hr. The diffusion barrier was dialysis membrane, and molecular weight cut-off 12000–14000 A (Himedia, Mumbai) was a release barrier. A presoaked dialysis membrane was adapted to the terminal portion of the glass cylinder. In each case, solid lipid nanosuspension (5 mL) was accurately introduced into the glass cylinder from the open side and this cylinder was fixed on the stirrer. The stirrer was suspended in 100 mL dissolution of simulated tear fluid (pH 7.4) medium maintained at 37°C ± 0.5°C at 100 rpm. Aliquots of samples were withdrawn at predetermined time intervals with volume replacement. The withdrawn samples were analyzed for drug content, by measuring absorbance at 255 nm in the UV-visible spectrophotometer (Systronics, Mumbai, India). Sink conditions were maintained throughout the release period. Data obtained in triplicate were analyzed graphically; that is, percent drug release versus time graph was plotted [14].

3.8. Release Kinetics. The kinetics of voriconazole release from solid lipid nanoparticles was determined using the release kinetics method of drug release into various kinetic equations: zero-order release kinetics, first-order release kinetics, and Higuchi model. The release data obtained was calculated using various parameters. The parameters "n" and time component "k," the release rate constant, and "R" the regression coefficient were determined by Korsmeyer-Peppas equation to understand the release mechanism [20].

3.9. Corneal Permeation Studies. Drug permeation studies were carried out by putting the voriconazole solid lipid nanoparticles (5 mL) on a freshly excised goat cornea. The fresh, whole eyeballs of goats were obtained from a local butcher's shop and transported to the laboratory chilled in normal saline (4°C). The cornea was then carefully excised along with 2 to 4 mm of surrounding scleral tissue and was washed with normal saline until the washing was free from protein. The excised cornea was fixed between the clamped donor and receptor compartments of an all-glass modified Franz diffusion cell in such a way that its epithelial surface faced the donor compartment at a temperature of 37 ± 0.5°C. The corneal area available for diffusion was 0.75 cm^2. The receptor compartment was filled with 10 mL freshly prepared simulated tear fluid (pH 7.4), and all air bubbles were expelled from the compartment. The whole corneal preparation procedure was completed within 1 hr after the sacrifice of goat. The aliquots (1 mL) of the formulated nanoparticles were placed on the excised cornea and the opening of the donor cell was sealed with a glass cover slip to prevent evaporation. The acceptor solution was kept at 37°C with constant stirring using a Teflon-coated magnetic stir bead. The permeation study was carried out for 120 min, and samples were withdrawn from the receptor at predetermined time intervals. The withdrawn samples were analyzed for drug content by measuring absorbance at 255 nm in a UV/Visible spectrophotometer (Systronics, Mumbai, India) [21, 22].

3.9.1. Corneal Hydration Studies. At the end of the experiment, each cornea (freed from adhering sclera) was weighed, soaked in 1 mL methanol, dried overnight at 80°C, and reweighed. From the difference in weights, corneal hydration was calculated [21]:

$$\text{Corneal hydration} = \frac{(\text{Initial weight} - \text{Final weight})}{(\text{Initial weight})} \times 100. \tag{4}$$

3.10. Stability Assessment. Stability studies were performed on voriconazole loaded solid lipid nanoparticles according to ICH guidelines. All prepared formulations were stored in closed amber glass at room temperature conditions. Samples were withdrawn at time intervals 0 days, 3 weeks, 6 weeks, and 3 months. The samples were evaluated for their drug content, entrapment efficiency, and particle size. The degradation rate constant (K_{cal}), shelf life, t_{90}, and initial concentrations were also calculated.

3.11. Data Analysis. All values presented in the study are average of triplicate experiments for the same time points. Particle size, zeta potential, polydispersity index (PDI) entrapment efficiency, *in vitro* drug release, and *ex vivo* permeation profile of voriconazole SLN were tested statistically using one-way analysis of variance (ANOVA) followed by Dunnett's test using graph pad prism 5 software (GraphPad Software Inc., San Diego, CA) at different level of significance (†statistically significant difference at $p < 0.05$; ††statistically significant difference at $p < 0.01$; †††statistically significant). The results were expressed as mean values ± SD.

4. Results and Discussion

The SLNs of voriconazole were projected to prepare by two different techniques, in order to check the influence of these techniques on physiochemical characteristics. SLN prepared by ultrasonication method relies on the dispersing technique in which sufficient high-energy input was necessary to break down the droplets into the nanometre range. It is predominantly effective in breaking up aggregates and in reducing the size and decreasing the polydispersity of nanoparticles which offers advantages, that is, easy handling, no critical parameters, and fast production process [23, 24]. Another method for formulating SLN, that is, microemulsion technique in which there is addition of a microemulsion to water, leads to precipitation of the lipid phase forming finer particles [25]. Low mechanical energy input, easy handling, and so forth are certain advantages of microemulsion method [23].

TABLE 2: Physiochemical characterization of VCZ loaded solid lipid nanoparticles.

S. number	Batches	Particle size (nm ± SD)	Zeta potential (mV ± SD)	*PDI (±SD)	Entrapment efficiency (% ± SD)
1	*VUSLN-1	234 ± 1.52	−22.71 ± 0.63	0.327 ± 0.01	70.26 ± 0.09
2	*VUSLN-2	247 ± 2.08††	−27.10 ± 0.55††	0.192 ± 0.02††	72.08 ± 0.02††
3	*VUSLN-3	265 ± 1.50††	−25.23 ± 0.56††	0.261 ± 0.07†	76.64 ± 0.04††
4	*VUSLN-4	274 ± 4.04††	−24.73 ± 0.61††	0.291 ± 0.03†	84.25 ± 0.11††
5	*VUSLN-5	288 ± 4.58††	−28.86 ± 0.58††	0.232 ± 0.05†	61.91 ± 0.04††
6	*VUSLN-6	308 ± 3.51	−26.46 ± 0.30	0.248 ± 0.04	59.13 ± 0.07††
7	*VUSLN-7	319 ± 2.64†	−27.96 ± 0.41††	0.188 ± 0.02†	63.23 ± 0.12††
8	*VUSLN-8	325 ± 4.16††	−24.83 ± 0.65††	0.337 ± 0.06†	65.13 ± 0.05††
9	*VUSLN-9	335 ± 4.50††	−23.46 ± 0.40††	0.219 ± 0.02†	72.50 ± 0.05††
10	*VUSLN-10	343 ± 3.51††	−28.6 ± 0.36††	0.263 ± 0.02†	60.17 ± 0.05††

*VUSLN: voriconazole loaded solid lipid nanoparticle prepared with ultrasonication method. *VMSLN: voriconazole loaded solid lipid nanoparticle prepared with microemulsion technique.*PDI : polydispersity index. *Values are mean ± SD ($n = 3$).

†Statistically significant difference at $p < 0.05$; ††statistically significant difference at $p < 0.01$, from control (VUSLN-4 and VMSLN-9) as determined by one-way ANOVA followed by Dunnett's test.

4.1. Particle Size, Polydispersity Index, and Zeta Potential Analysis

4.1.1. Particle Size and Polydispersity Index Analysis. The results of particle size of freshly prepared lyophilized VCZ loaded formulations are depicted in Table 2 which are formulated with 2 different techniques. All SLN formulations showed a mean particle size below 400 nm which is an optimum size for ophthalmic delivery as the human eye can tolerate particles smaller than 10 μm [14]. The particle size of formulations, that is, VUSLN-1 to VUSLN-5 ranges from 234 ± 3.52 nm to 288 ± 4.58 nm with ultrasonication method and VMSLN-6 to VMSLN-10 ranges from 308 ± 3.52 nm to 343 ± 3.51 nm with microemulsion technique respectively. The particle size increases with increase in polymer concentration were basically due to increased viscosity of dispersed phase resulting in larger nanodroplets formation. Similar findings were observed in earlier studies on Eudragit RL 100 based nanoparticulate system [20]. The particle size of SLNs prepared with microemulsion technique (VMSLN-6 to VMSLN-10) was significantly $p < 0.01$ higher as compared to mean particle size of formulations (VUSLN-1 to VUSLN-5) prepared with the ultrasonication method. This was explained by the fact that ultrasonication method generally leads to the breakdown of particles into smaller droplets during the preparation process.

4.1.2. Polydispersity Index. The polydispersity index (PDI) is a marker of particle size distribution. Its value in case of submicron particles ranges from 0.15 to 0.3 indicates size homogeneity, while PDI greater than 0.3 results in heterogeneity [26]. The polydispersity index of all SLNs was significantly $p < 0.05$ varying from 0.188 ± 0.013 to 0.337 ± 0.015 as depicted in Table 2 indicating narrow size distribution which reveals the higher stability of solid lipid nanoparticles. Similar findings were reported in earlier studies on cyclosporine A incorporated cationic solid lipid nanoparticles for ocular drug delivery [27].

4.1.3. Zeta Potential Analysis. Zeta potential is an important surface characterization technique which helps in determining the potential stability and surface charge of nanoparticulate system. Usually absolute large negative or positive zeta potential value required for colloidal dispersion stability as electrostatic repulsion between particles with same charges avoids aggregation [28]. All formulations of exhibited negative zeta potential values because of the presence of stearic acid (0.3% w/v), which were significantly $p < 0.01$, vary from −22.71 ± 0.63 mV to −28.86 ± 0.58 mV as depicted in Table 2 which is closer to −30 mV ensuring physical stability. Similar results have been reported in earlier studies on lopinavir solid lipid nanoparticles prepared by microemulsion technique [29].

4.2. Entrapment Efficiency (EE%). The corresponding percent entrapment efficiency of SLN was found to be satisfactory high which is ranging from 61.91 ± 2.04% to 84.25 ± 1.11% (VUSLNs) prepared by ultrasonication method and 59.13 ± 1.97% to 72.50 ± 2.05% (VMSLNs) prepared by microemulsion technique, respectively, as depicted in Table 2. The results suggested that as the polymer concentration increases, the drug entrapment efficiency increased significantly ($p < 0.01$) due to its higher viscosity. But further increase in polymer concentration (VUSLN-5 and VMSLN-10 containing higher concentration of polymer as compared to others) showed decrease in entrapment efficiency which is basically due to decrease in drug loading, as entrapment efficiency is the ratio of actual drug loading and theoretical drug loading [14]. Higher entrapment efficiency of SLNs prepared with ultrasonication method is due to lesser particle size as compared to microemulsion technique.

4.3. Fourier Transform Infrared Spectroscopy (FTIR) Analysis. FTIR is the backup analysis for the authentication of stability of crystalline shield of SLNs. Figure 1 shows stacked IR spectra of pure drug, lipid, polymer, and physical mixtures and the prepared lyophilized VCZ loaded SLNs. The

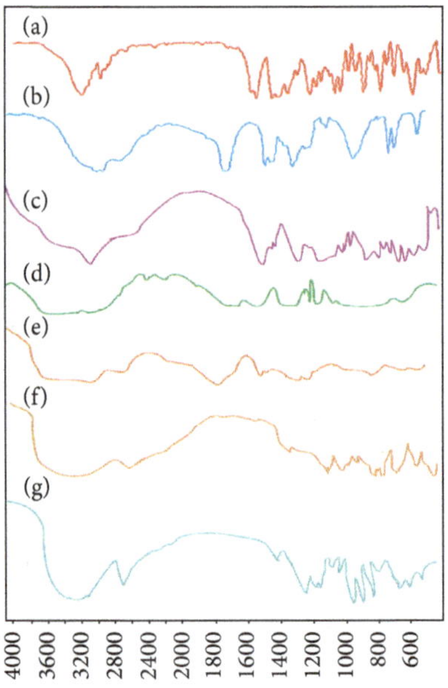

Figure 1: FTIR spectrum of (a) voriconazole, (b) stearic acid, (c) voriconazole, stearic acid, and Carbopol physical mixture, (d) Carbopol 934, (e) mannitol, (f) VUSLN-4, and (g) VMSLN-9.

voriconazole FTIR spectrum showed OH stretching at 3200.09–3046.04 cm^{-1}, C-N stretching at 1510.28–1451.28 cm^{-1}, and C-F stretching at 1587.44–1451.28 cm^{-1}, respectively. Stearic acid showed IR absorption band of C=O stretching at 1.700 cm^{-1}. Spectrum of Carbopol 934 exhibited OH stretching at 3000–2950 cm^{-1} and the prominent peak between 1750–1700 cm^{-1} corresponds to carbonyl C=O stretching band. The spectrum of mannitol exhibited OH stretching at 3400 cm^{-1}, OH in plane bending at 1420 cm^{-1}, C-O stretching at 1081 cm^{-1}, and OH out of plane bending for alcohol at 701 cm^{-1}. The physical mixture of voriconazole, Carbopol 934, and stearic acid showed no major shifting of any functional peaks between the spectra of drug, lipids, polymer, and its physical mixtures. Hence, it was indicated that there was no interaction between the drug, lipids, and polymer used. The IR spectra of lyophilized nanoparticles (VUSLN-4) showed the characteristic peaks of stearic acid at 1702 cm^{-1}, Carbopol 934 at 2935 cm^{-1}, and mannitol at 3389 cm^{-1} and 1086 cm^{-1} correspond to OH stretching and C-O stretching, respectively, prepared with ultrasonication method. The same results were observed in case of lyophilized nanoparticles of voriconazole prepared by microemulsion technique. The characteristics peaks of drug in both the methods of SLN were diminished when compared with pure drug peak at same wave number (3197.80 cm^{-1}). This indicated that the drug is dispersed in lipid matrix in a microcrystalline form and also the prominent peak of polymer in both methods of SLN could not be located due to dilution effect of lipids. Similar findings were observed in earlier studies on gatifloxacin solid lipid nanoparticles for ocular drug delivery [9].

4.4. Electron Microscope Examination. Morphological examination of VCZ-SLN formulations was performed using transmission electron microscopy (TEM). TEM images of SLN formulations prepared by both methods are shown in (Figures 2(a) and 2(b)). This revealed that all prepared formulations were found to be spherical in shape with a smooth surface and suggesting possible stabilization of nanoparticles. These nanoparticles possibly do not cause any irritation to the ocular surface, as it is already reported that isometric particles with obtuse angles and edges cause less irritation than particles with sharp angles and edges [30]. There were minor differences observed in the general structure of the voriconazole SLN prepared by both methods. It may be confirmed by the fact that the shape of solid lipid nanoparticles is mainly decided by the property of lipid including solubility and film forming capability [31].

4.5. Powder X-Ray Diffraction (PXRD) Analysis. X-ray diffraction was carried out to evaluate the crystalline character of lipid matrices and VCZ-SLN prepared by both methods as shown in Figure 3 and displays the X-ray diffractograms of drug, lipids, polymer, physical mixture, mannitol, and lyophilized SLNs. Voriconazole exhibited the distinctive peaks at 12.13°, 13.45°, 14.20°, 19.30°, 21.14°, 27.15°, and 34.15° 2θ. The presence of sharp peaks in the diffractogram of voriconazole indicated its crystalline nature. From the XRD patterns of Carbopol 934, it is clear that the polymer is completely amorphous as there are no sharp peaks observed. The physical mixture of voriconazole, Carbopol 934, and stearic acid resulted in a relatively less crystalline form and exhibited peaks at 5.2°, 14.52°, and 20.28° 2θ. Mannitol showed crystalline nature and manifested several distinct peaks at 10.55°, 15.35°, 18.78°, 19.89°, 23.39°, 24.22°, 29.43°, 33.29°, 34.98°, and 39.53° 2θ which correspond to its β polymorphic form (mannitol exists in α, β, and δ polymorphic forms) [32]. The freeze-dried SLNs containing VCZ exhibited peaks at 8.94°, 9.76°, 15.98°, 19.70°, 20.42°, 20.54°, 21.44°, and 24.60° 2θ which appears to be contributed by mannitol and stearic acid. The intensity of peaks was sharpening and it may reveal that the SLN product is crystalline in nature [14, 18].

4.6. Differential Scanning Colorimetry (DSC) Analysis. DSC is the technique to investigate the melting and recrystallization behaviour of the substance. The DSC thermograms of samples are represented in Figure 4. The thermogram of voriconazole is characterized by a sharp melting endotherm at 132.04°C and heat of fusion of 95.08 J/g. The thermal curve of stearic acid is characterized by a sharp melting endotherm at 56.18°C with heat of fusion of 157.19 J/g. The physical mixture of voriconazole, stearic acid, and Carbopol 934 showed characteristic peak at 140.52°C, 56.48°C, and 83.32°C, respectively with no depression in the melting point. A broad endothermic peak was observed at 78°C in the DSC scan of Carbopol 934. The thermal behaviour of mannitol is characterized by an endothermic peak at 165.96°C with heat of fusion of 291.31 J/g. The DSC curve of lyophilized SLNs showed a small endotherm at 81.02°C which corresponds to the melting point of Carbopol 934 followed by a sharp endotherm at 164.64°C which appears to be the depressed endothermic peak of β polymorph of mannitol. The thermograms did not show any melting peak of drug.

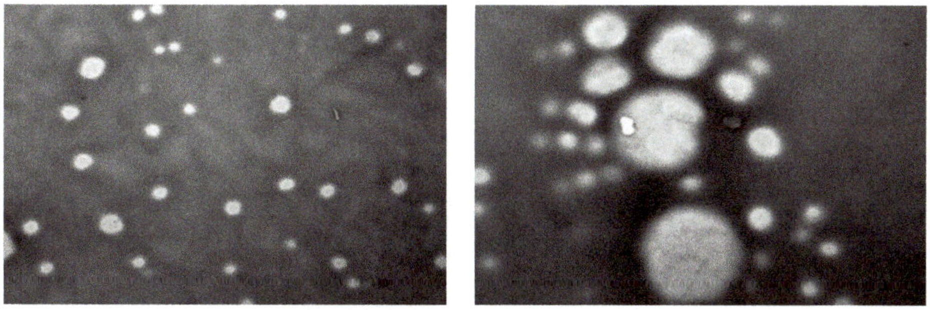

(a) (b)

FIGURE 2: TEM images of (a) VUSLN-4 and (b) VMSLN-9.

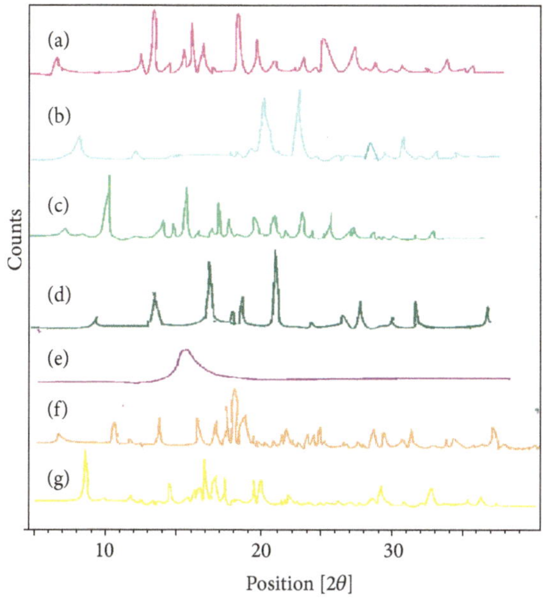

FIGURE 3: PXRD spectra of (a) voriconazole, (b) stearic acid, (c) voriconazole, stearic acid, and Carbopol physical mixture, (d) Carbopol 934, (e) mannitol, (f) VUSLN-4, and (g) VMSLN-9.

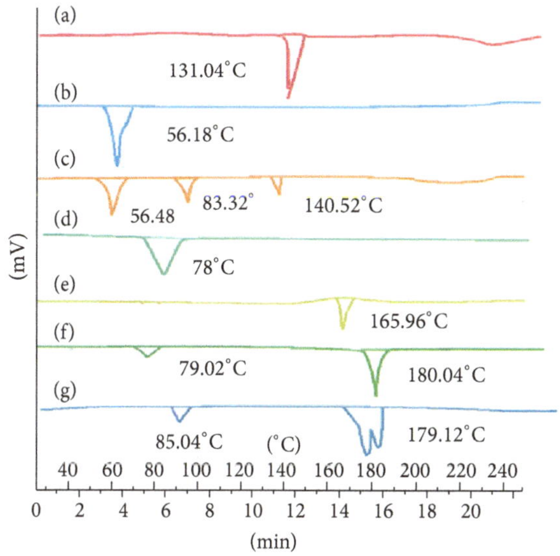

FIGURE 4: DSC of (a) voriconazole, (b) stearic acid, (c) voriconazole, stearic acid, and Carbopol physical mixture, (d) Carbopol 934, (e) mannitol, (f) VUSLN-4, and (g) VMSLN-9.

This suggests that VCZ was present in amorphous state and drug is entirely entrapped in lipid matrix. As reported earlier, rapid quenching of microemulsion and presence of surfactant do not allow the drug to crystallize [33].

4.7. In Vitro Drug Release from VCZ-SLN. In vitro release of VCZ from solid lipid nanoparticles prepared by both methods is represented in Figures 5(a) and 5(b). The drug release from SLN was assessed by dialysis membrane, using simulated tear fluid (pH 7.4) as the release medium. The solid nanoparticles made with ultrasonication method (VUSLN-4) showed 17.19 ± 0.09% drug release in 1 hr and 86.76 ± 0.78% drug release in 12 hr, while solid lipid nanoparticles prepared by microemulsion technique (VMSLN-9) demonstrated 13.86 ± 0.9% and 84.27 ± 1.01% drug release in 1 hr and 10 hr. There was statistically significant difference ($p < 0.01$) among both methods in drug release aspect. The results demonstrated that ultrasonication method caused a sustained drug release up to 12 h as indicated by the percentage drug release versus time profile (Figure 5(a)). The results suggested that entrapment of drug in solid lipid nanoparticles hinders the drug release, that is, initial burst release followed by slow release phase in case of ultrasonication method. This might be explained by the fact that smaller particle size formed by ultrasonication was responsible for increased surface area which increases the diffusional path length. Moreover, in case of microemulsion technique, the entrapment efficiency was lesser which ultimately affects the drug release. The polymer concentration increases the drug release more sustained, but in VUSLN-5 and VMSLN-10 the drug release is lesser due to improper drug loading [18]. SLNs prepared with ultrasonication method (VUSLN-4) were able to control the drug release till 12 hr, while solid lipid nanoparticles with microemulsion technique observed controlled drug release till 10 hr. Therefore, ultrasonication method was better as compared to microemulsion technique as it increases the precorneal residence time for longer period and provides sustained drug release.

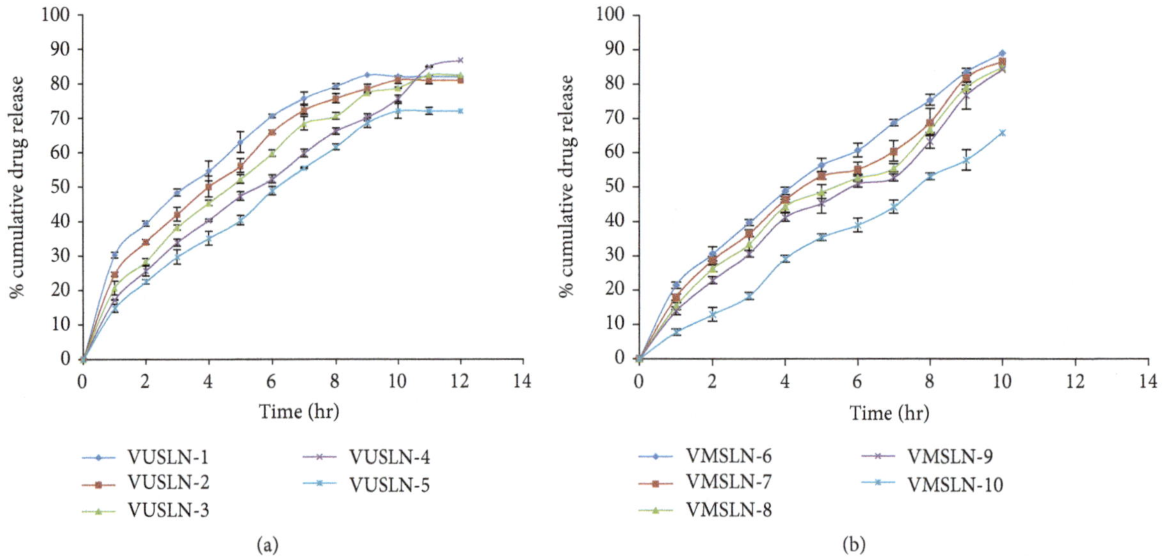

FIGURE 5: (a) *In vitro* release profile of voriconazole from SLN formulations prepared by ultrasonication method through dialysis membrane. (b) *In vitro* release profile of voriconazole from SLN formulations prepared by microemulsion technique through dialysis membrane.

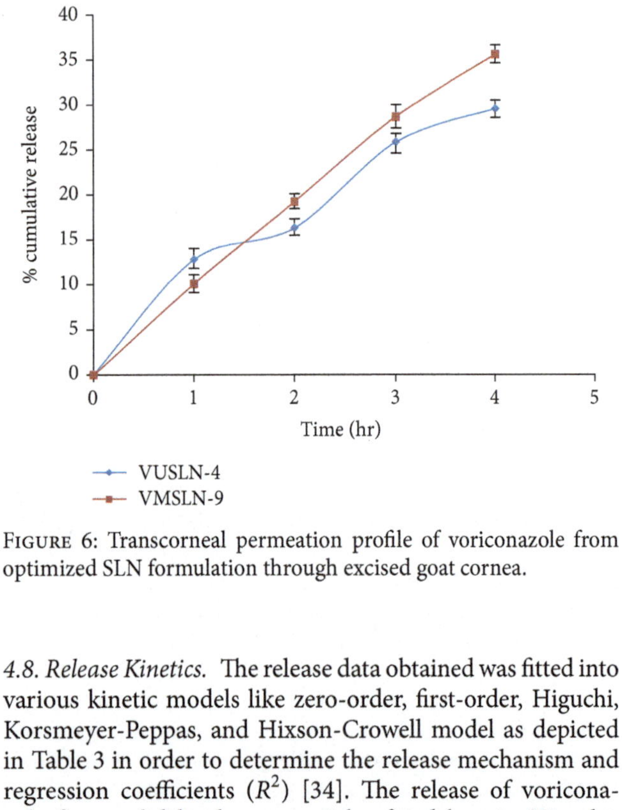

FIGURE 6: Transcorneal permeation profile of voriconazole from optimized SLN formulation through excised goat cornea.

4.8. Release Kinetics. The release data obtained was fitted into various kinetic models like zero-order, first-order, Higuchi, Korsmeyer-Peppas, and Hixson-Crowell model as depicted in Table 3 in order to determine the release mechanism and regression coefficients (R^2) [34]. The release of voriconazole from solid lipid nanoparticles fitted best in Higuchi-square-root release kinetics, which can be confirmed by comparing values for the regression coefficients of zero-order, first-order, Higuchi, Korsmeyer-Peppas, and Hixson-Crowell model (Table 3). The value of "n" (>0.45 to <0.89) and the diffusion exponent of Korsmeyer-Peppas equation confirmed that release of voriconazole from solid lipid nanoparticles is anomalous, that is, contributed by combination of dissolution and diffusion. Similar findings were observed in earlier studies on Eudragit RL 100 based nanoparticulate system of aceclofenac [18].

4.9. Corneal Permeation Studies. Ex vivo transcorneal permeation studies compared the corneal permeation characteristics of the solid lipid nanoparticle formulation. The optimized batches (VUSLN-4 and VMSLN-9) prepared by 2 different methods according to *in vitro* release profile were selected for corneal permeation studies. The *in vitro* drug permeation studies of solid lipid nanoparticles of voriconazole through excised goat corneas were depicted in Figure 6. To imitate the real life conditions, excised goat corneas were used for permeation studies and the experiment was conducted for 4 hr considering cornea viability. The drug permeation from SLN prepared by ultrasonication method (VMSLN-4) was 29.56 ± 0.9%, which was less than the permeation observed with the (VMSLN-9) which was 35.65 ± 0.75% at the end of 4 h. The results suggested that SLN prepared by ultrasonication method demonstrated more sustained drug release which was possibly due to high entrapment efficiency in comparison to microemulsion technique.

Cornea (made of epithelium (lipophilic), stroma (hydrophilic), and endothelium (less lipophilic than epithelium)) acts as a lipophilic-hydrophilic barrier and the drug will have to partition through the barrier for corneal permeation while dialysis membrane filter acts as a mechanical barrier to drug diffusion. Accordingly, penetration through the excised goat cornea would be lower compared to that across the dialysis membrane.

4.10. Corneal Hydration Studies. The corneal hydration level of normal mammalian cornea is between 75% and 80% [32]. The increase in polymer concentration, in solid lipid nanoparticles, did not show any corneal damage. Corneal hydration value of the formulations prepared by both

TABLE 3: Kinetic profiles of *in vitro* drug release from solid lipid nanoparticles through dialysis membrane prepared by different techniques.

Batches	Zero-order model		First-order model		Higuchi model		Korsmeyer-Peppas model			Hixson-Crowell model	
	R^2	K_0	R^2	K_1	R^2	K_H	R^2	n	K_{KP}	R^2	K_{HC}
VUSLN-1	0.8875	0.1075	0.9882	−0.0011	0.9925	3.0573	0.9957	0.4559	0.6995	0.9871	−0.0026
VUSLN-2	0.9276	0.1092	0.9891	−0.001	0.9917	3.2493	0.9944	0.5081	0.4820	0.9909	−0.0026
VUSLN-3	0.9526	0.1044	0.9852	−0.001	0.9919	3.3457	0.9949	0.5718	0.2854	0.9922	−0.0026
VUSLN-4	0.9773	0.1013	0.9323	−0.001	0.9793	3.4423	0.9923	0.6257	0.110	0.9678	−0.0027
VUSLN-5	0.9789	0.1004	0.9650	−0.0008	0.9720	3.1781	0.9885	0.6537	0.0072	0.9786	−0.0022
VMSLN-6	0.9632	0.1189	0.9245	−0.0013	0.9285	3.6661	0.9992	0.5843	0.2800	0.9640	−0.0032
VMSLN-7	0.9589	0.1145	0.8832	−0.0011	0.9581	3.5647	0.9824	0.6181	0.1620	0.9279	−0.0029
VMSLN-8	0.9601	0.1127	0.8738	−0.0011	0.9449	3.5609	0.9762	0.6635	0.020	0.9171	−0.0028
VMSLN-9	0.9653	0.1119	0.8609	−0.0010	0.9371	3.5845	0.9778	0.7037	0.1072	0.9078	−0.0028
VMSLN-10	0.9908	0.0945	0.960	−0.0007	0.9667	3.1574	0.9906	0.8909	0.7185	0.9744	−0.002

TABLE 4: Degradation rate constant and shelf life of SLN formulations after 3-month storage.

Batches	Degradation constant (K) in day^{-1}	t_{90} (days)	Shelf life (years)
VUSLN-1	1.37×10^{-4}	763.25	2.09
VUSLN-2	1.59×10^{-4}	659.88	1.80
VUSLN-3	1.33×10^{-4}	783.99	2.14
VUSLN-4	1.08×10^{-4}	963.81	2.64
VUSLN-5	1.29×10^{-4}	811.54	2.22
VMSLN-6	1.32×10^{-4}	789.91	2.16
VMSLN-7	1.30×10^{-4}	803.77	2.20
VMSLN-8	1.42×10^{-4}	737.14	2.01
VMSLN-9	1.26×10^{-4}	826.98	2.26
VMSLN-10	1.63×10^{-4}	644.11	1.76

methods was between 76 and 79%, which indicated that the formulations did not cause any damage to the corneal tissue.

4.11. Stability Assessment. All the SLN formulations were kept on storage for three months at 25°C ± 2°C and 60% RH ±5% resulted in increase in particle size (Figure 7(a)). Increase in particle size ranges from 234 ± 1.5 nm to 301 ± 2.06 nm with batches prepared with ultrasonication method and from 308.66 ± 3.5 nm to 363.4 ± 1.25 nm with microemulsion technique. Entrapment efficiencies of SLN formulations were lowered by 6%–10% prepared by both methods after 3-month storage at room temp as shown in Figure 7(b) [17]. All the formulations showed slight increase in zeta potential ranging from 3.2% to 4.4% during room temperature storage conditions as depicted in Figure 7(c) [9]. The degradation of voriconazole loaded SLNs followed first-order kinetics. The degradation constant (K), t_{90} values, and shelf life of all the formulations at room temperature are shown in Table 4. The degradation rate constants (K) and shelf life (t_{90}) at room temperature for all SLN formulations range from 1.08 $\times 10^{-4}$ day^{-1} to 1.62 $\times 10^{-4}$ day^{-1} and 644.11 to 963.8 days, respectively, as depicted in Table 4. The calculated t_{90} of optimized formulation (VUSLN-4) at room temperature was found to be 963.81 days confirming that the SLN would provide more than 2-year shelf life at room temperature [18].

5. Conclusion

The present investigation finally concluded that the lipophilic drugs like voriconazole can also be effectively incorporated in solid lipid (stearic acid) using tween 80 as stabilizer. The study was also able to explore the potential of both methods of preparation of voriconazole loaded solid lipid nanoparticles, that is, ultrasonication method and microemulsion technique. During the preparation of SLN, Carbopol 934 was used as controlled release agent. Increasing the concentration of the polymer (Carbopol 934) results in more sustained drug release of SLN due to formation of strong matrices due to its highly cross-linked structure. In determination of particle size study, the SLNs were obtained below 400 nm for all formulations with good PDI and negative zeta potential with optimum physiochemical characteristics. The negative zeta potential and fine particle size help to prolong precorneal residence time. The PXRD and DSC indicated decrease of drug crystallinity in the nanoparticles. *In vitro* release and *ex vivo* corneal permeation of drug from SLNs were found promising without causing any significant effect on the corneal hydration level. The nanoparticle was found to provide biphasic release pattern initial burst release followed by sustained release which fitted best into Higuchi-square-root release kinetics. The results demonstrated that SLN (VUSLN-4) prepared by ultrasonication method was able to sustain the drug release for up to 12 hours as compared to microemulsion technique. The optimized formulation (VUSLN-4) would provide more than 2-year shelf life at room temperature. However, the resulting solid lipid nanoparticles seem to be promising for providing a solution to the challenge caused by unsuccessful ocular delivery.

Competing Interests

The authors declare that they have no competing interests.

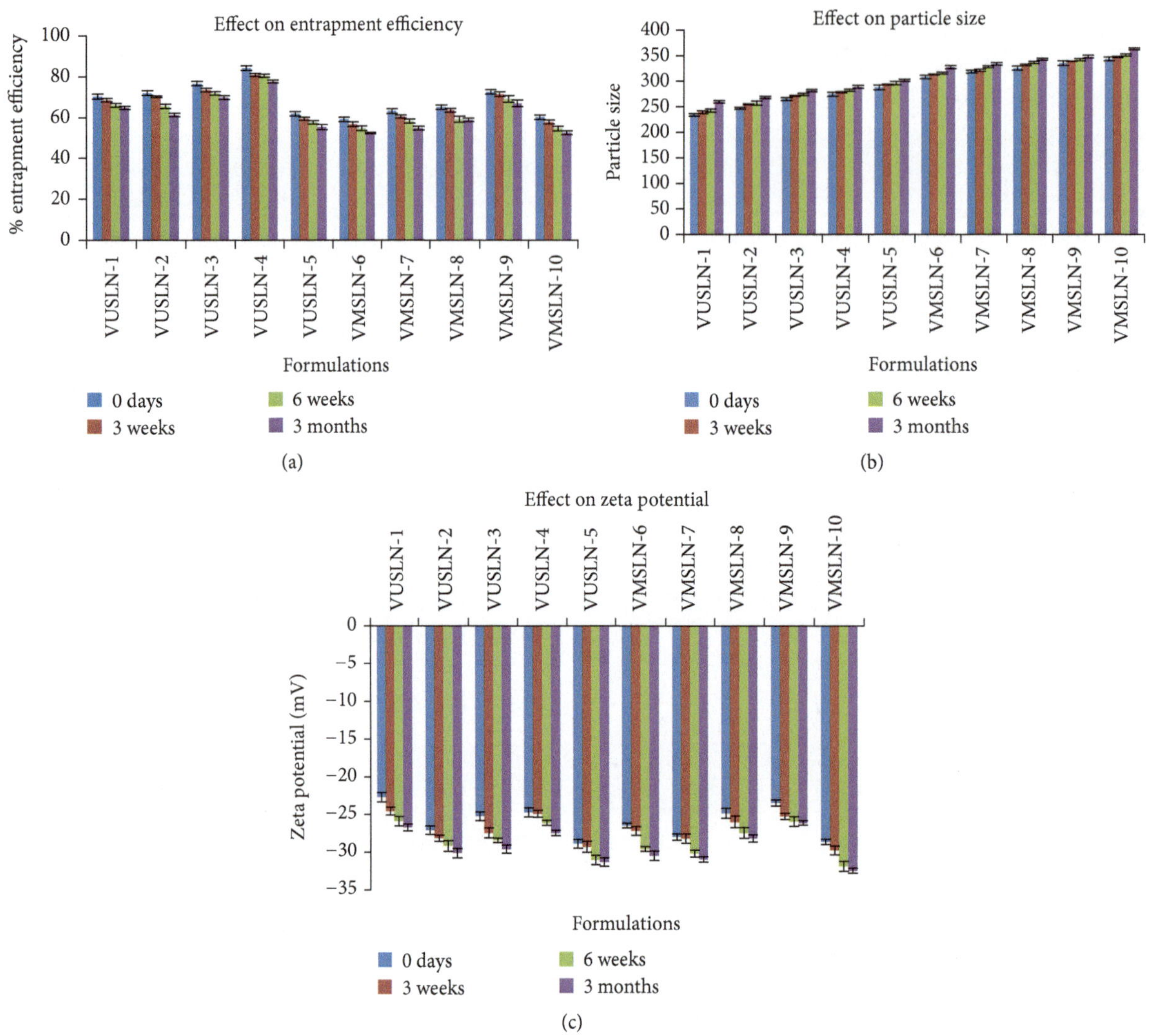

FIGURE 7: Stability profile of voriconazole loaded SLNs under room temperature. (a) Effect on particle size. (b) Effect on entrapment efficiency. (c) Effect on zeta potential. Mean ± SD ($n = 3$).

Acknowledgments

The authors are grateful to M Chitkara, Vice Chancellor, Chitkara University, for providing excellent infrastructure facility for literature review.

References

[1] R. Malviya, A. Kumar, and P. K. Sharma, "Recent trends in ocular drug delivery: a short review," *Europian Journal of Applied Science*, vol. 3, no. 3, pp. 86–92, 2011.

[2] P. Tangri and S. Khurana, "Basics of ocular drug delivery systems," *International Journal of Pharmaceutical Biomedical Research*, vol. 2, no. 4, pp. 1541–1552, 2011.

[3] D. Achouri, K. Alhanout, P. Piccerelle, and V. Andrieu, "Recent advances in ocular drug delivery," *Drug Development and Industrial Pharmacy*, vol. 39, no. 11, pp. 1599–1617, 2013.

[4] D. M. Maurice and S. Mishima, "Ocular pharmacokinetics," in *Handbook of Experimental Pharmacology*, M. L. Sears, Ed., Springer, Berlin, Germany, 1984.

[5] S. Ding, "Recent developments in ophthalmic drug delivery," *Pharmaceutical Science and Technology Today*, vol. 1, no. 8, pp. 328–335, 1998.

[6] M. Kumar and G. T. Kulkarni, "Recent advances in ophthalmic drug delivery system," *International Journal of Pharmacy and Pharmaceutics Sciences*, vol. 4, no. 1, pp. 387–394, 2012.

[7] H. A. Patel, J. K. Patel, N. K. Patel, and R. R. Patel, "Ophthalmic drug delivery system-a review," *Der Pharmacia Lettre*, vol. 2, no. 4, pp. 100–115, 2010.

[8] M. Mudgil and P. K. Pawar, "Preparation and in Vitro/Ex Vivo evaluation of moxifloxacin-loaded PLGA nanosuspensions for ophthalmic application," *Scientia Pharmaceutica*, vol. 81, no. 2, pp. 591–606, 2013.

[9] M. A. Kalam, Y. Sultana, A. Ali, M. Aqil, A. K. Mishra, and K. Chuttani, "Preparation, characterization, and evaluation of gatifloxacin loaded solid lipid nanoparticles as colloidal ocular drug delivery system," *Journal of Drug Targeting*, vol. 18, no. 3, pp. 191–204, 2010.

[10] R. M. Khalil, A. Abd-Elbary, M. A. Kassem, M. M. Ghorab, and M. Basha, "Nanostructured lipid carriers (NLCs) versus solid

lipid nanoparticles (SLNs) for topical delivery of meloxicam," *Pharmaceutical Development and Technology*, vol. 19, no. 3, pp. 304–314, 2014.

[11] N. V. Prajna, J. Mascarenhas, T. Krishnan et al., "Comparison of natamycin and voriconazole for the treatment of fungal keratitis," *Archives of Ophthalmology*, vol. 128, no. 6, pp. 672–678, 2010.

[12] L. B. Johnson and C. A. Kauffman, "Voriconazole: a new triazole antifungal agent," *Clinical Infectious Diseases*, vol. 36, no. 5, pp. 630–637, 2003.

[13] K. Ruckmani, M. Sivakumar, and P. A. Ganeshkumar, "Methotrexate loaded Solid Lipid Nanoparticles (SLN) for effective treatment of carcinoma," *Journal of Nanoscience and Nanotechnology*, vol. 6, no. 9-10, pp. 2991–2995, 2006.

[14] J. Youshia, A. O. Kamel, A. E. Shamy, and S. Mansour, "Design of cationic nanostructured heterolipid matrices for ocular delivery of methazolamide," *International Journal of Nanomedicine*, vol. 2012, article 7, pp. 2483–2496, 2012.

[15] C. Wu, H. Qi, W. Chen et al., "Preparation and evaluation of a Carbopol®/HPMC-based *in situ* gelling ophthalmic system for puerarin," *Yakugaku Zasshi*, vol. 127, no. 1, pp. 183–191, 2007.

[16] A. Sharma, M. Jindal, G. Aggarwal, and S. Jain, "Development of a novel method for fabrication of solid lipid nanoparticles: using high shear homogenization and ultrasonication," *Research Journal of Pharmaceutical, Biological and Chemical Sciences*, vol. 1, no. 2, pp. 265–274, 2010.

[17] S. Sood, N. Jawahar, K. Jain, K. Gowthamarajan, and S. N. Meyyanathan, "Olanzapine loaded cationic solid lipid nanoparticles for improved oral bioavailability," *Current Nanoscience*, vol. 9, no. 1, pp. 26–34, 2013.

[18] R. Katara and D. K. Majumdar, "Eudragit RL 100-based nanoparticulate system of aceclofenac for ocular delivery," *Colloids and Surfaces B: Biointerfaces*, vol. 103, pp. 455–462, 2013.

[19] U. Ghanshyam, P. Patel, and J. Patel, "Formulation and characterization of solid lipid nanoparticles dry powder inhaler containing triamcinolone acetonide," *International Journal of Research in Pharmacy and Chemistry*, vol. 1, no. 3, pp. 662–673, 2011.

[20] S. Das, P. K. Suresh, and R. Desmukh, "Design of Eudragit RL 100 nanoparticles by nanoprecipitation method for ocular drug delivery," *Nanomedicine: Nanotechnology, Biology, and Medicine*, vol. 6, no. 2, pp. 318–323, 2010.

[21] M. Yadav and M. Ahuja, "Preparation and evaluation of nanoparticles of gum cordia, an anionic polysaccharide for ophthalmic delivery," *Carbohydrate Polymers*, vol. 81, no. 4, pp. 871–877, 2010.

[22] S. K. Motwani, S. Chopra, S. Talegaonkar, K. Kohli, F. J. Ahmad, and R. K. Khar, "Chitosan-sodium alginate nanoparticles as submicroscopic reservoirs for ocular delivery: formulation, optimisation and in vitro characterisation," *European Journal of Pharmaceutics and Biopharmaceutics*, vol. 68, no. 3, pp. 513–525, 2008.

[23] A. Garud, D. Singh, and N. Garud, "Solid Lipid Nanoparticles (SLN): method, characterization and applications," *International Current Pharmaceutical Journal*, vol. 1, no. 11, pp. 384–393, 2012.

[24] P. Pawar, H. Kashyap, S. Malhotra, and R. Sindhu, "Hp-β-CD-voriconazole *in situ* gelling system for ocular drug delivery: *in vitro*, stability, and antifungal activities assessment," *BioMed Research International*, vol. 2013, Article ID 341218, 9 pages, 2013.

[25] R. H. Müller, K. Mäder, and S. Gohla, "Solid lipid nanoparticles (SLN) for controlled drug delivery—a review of the state of the art," *European Journal of Pharmaceutics and Biopharmaceutics*, vol. 50, no. 1, pp. 161–177, 2000.

[26] M. Cegnar, J. Kos, and J. Kristl, "Cystatin incorporated in poly(lactide-co-glycolide) nanoparticles: development and fundamental studies on preservation of its activity," *European Journal of Pharmaceutical Sciences*, vol. 22, no. 5, pp. 357–364, 2004.

[27] E. Basaran, M. Demirel, and B. Sirmagul, "Cyclosporine-a incorporated cationic solid lipid nanoparticles for ocular delivery," *Journal of Microencapsul*, vol. 27, no. 1, pp. 37–47, 2010.

[28] K. Manjunath, J. S. Ready, and V. Venkateswarlu, "Solid lipid nanoparticles as drug delivery systems," *Methods and Findings in Experimental and Clinical Pharmacology*, vol. 27, no. 2, pp. 127–144, 2005.

[29] J. S. Negi, P. Chattopadhyay, A. K. Sharma, and V. Ram, "Development of solid lipid nanoparticles (SLNs) of lopinavir using hot self nano-emulsification (SNE) technique," *European Journal of Pharmaceutical Sciences*, vol. 48, no. 1-2, pp. 231–239, 2013.

[30] M. Malhotra and D. K. Majumdar, "*In vivo* ocular availability of ketorolac following ocular instillations of aqueous, oil, and ointment formulations to normal corneas of rabbits: a technical note," *AAPS PharmSciTech*, vol. 6, no. 3, pp. E523–E526, 2005.

[31] F.-Q. Hu, S.-P. Jiang, Y.-Z. Du, H. Yuan, Y.-Q. Ye, and S. Zeng, "Preparation and characterization of stearic acid nanostructured lipid carriers by solvent diffusion method in an aqueous system," *Colloids and Surfaces B: Biointerfaces*, vol. 45, no. 3-4, pp. 167–173, 2005.

[32] W. L. Hulse, R. T. Forbes, M. C. Bonner, and M. Getrost, "The characterisation and comparison of spray dried mannitol," *Drug Development and Indusutrail Pharmaacy*, vol. 35, no. 6, pp. 7121–7718, 2009.

[33] R. Cavalli, O. Caputo, M. E. Carlotti, M. Trotta, C. Scarnecchia, and M. R. Gasco, "Sterilization and freeze-drying of drug-free and drug-loaded solid lipid nanoparticles," *International Journal of Pharmaceutics*, vol. 148, no. 1, pp. 47–54, 1997.

[34] P. Costa and J. M. S. Lobo, "Modeling and comparison of dissolution profiles," *European Journal of Pharmaceutical Sciences*, vol. 13, no. 2, pp. 123–133, 2001.

16

Calcium Alginate-Neusilin US2 Nanocomposite Microbeads for Oral Sustained Drug Delivery of Poor Water Soluble Drug Aceclofenac Sodium

Manjanna Kolammanahalli Mallappa,[1] Rajesh Kesarla,[2] and Shivakumar Banakar[3]

[1]*Department of Pharmaceutics, TVM College of Pharmacy, Bellary, Karnataka, India*
[2]*Department of Pharmaceutics, Parul Institute of Pharmacy, Limda, Gujarat, India*
[3]*Department of Pharmaceutical Chemistry, B.L.D.E College of Pharmacy, Bijapur, Karnataka, India*

Correspondence should be addressed to Manjanna Kolammanahalli Mallappa; kmhuruli@rediffmail.com

Academic Editor: Jaleh Varshosaz

The aim of the present study was to formulate and investigate the calcium alginate- (CA-) Neusilin US2 nanocomposite microbeads containing preconcentrate of aceclofenac sodium (ACF-Na) liquid microemulsion (L-ME) for enhancement of oral bioavailability. The preconcentrate L-ME is prepared by using Labrafac PG, Labrasol, and Span 80 as oil, surfactant, and cosurfactant, respectively. The solid CA nanocomposite microbeads of L-ME prepared by microemulsification internal gelation technique using sodium alginate (SA) gelling agent, Neusilin US2 as adsorbent, and calcium chloride as crosslinking agent. L-ME has good thermodynamic stability; globule size was found to be 32.4 nm with polydispersity index 0.219 and −6.32 mV zeta potential. No significant interactions of excipients, drug in the formulations observed by FT-IR, DSC and XPRD. The concentration of SA and Neusilin US2 influences the flow properties, mean particle size, mechanical strength, drug entrapment efficiency, and percentage of drug release. All the formulations show minimum drug release in simulated gastric fluid (SGF) pH 1.2 for initial 2 h, maximum drug release in pH 6.8 phosphate buffer solution (PBS) at 6 h, followed by sustaining in simulated intestinal fluid (SIF) of pH 7.4 up to 12 h. The interaction of SA with Neusilin US2 creates a thick thixotropic gel network structure which acts as barrier to control the release of drug in the alkaline pH environment. Neusilin US2 is a novel filler used to convert L-ME into solid nanocomposite microbeads to enhance dissolution rate of poor water soluble drugs sustaining the drug release for prolonged period of time.

1. Introduction

Aceclofenac sodium (ACF-Na) is a nonsteroidal anti-inflammatory drug (NSAID) used extensively in the treatment of rheumatoid arthritis, osteoarthritis, and ankylosing spondylitis. It is rapidly and completely absorbed after oral administration, the biological half-life is 1.8–3.5 h, and dosing frequency is 2-3 times daily with dose range 100–200 mg [1]. However, ACF-Na is a water insoluble lipophilic drug coming under biopharmaceutical classification system (BCS) class II (low solubility and high permeability) which suffers limited oral bioavailability, high intra- and intersubject variability and lack of dose related adverse effects [2]. In recent years, liquid microemulsifying system (L-MES) is being investigated as potential new colloidal carrier for lipophilic drugs and has excellent thermodynamic stability, high drug solubilization capacity, nanosize (<200 nm), ease of scale-up and manufacturing, long shelf life, ability to improve dissolution rate and lymphatic transport of hydrophobic drugs, improved oral bioavailability, and protection against enzymatic hydrolysis [3]. Conventionally, L-MES is filled in hard or soft gelatin capsules for ease of administration. However, there exist a few limitations associated with this delivery system, including stability, manufacturing methods, leaking, leaching of components from the capsule shell, interaction of the fill with the capsule shell, and storage temperature [4]. To minimize the above-mentioned issues with L-MES, there is a growing trend to formulate solid microemulsifying system (S-MES) by adsorbing onto suitable carriers like lactose, natural gums, microcrystalline cellulose, and silicates to obtain dry powders

[5]. Many literature reports conclude blending liquid systems with selected powder excipients to produce free flowing by using spray drying, solvent evaporation, and extrusion spheronization techniques [6]. But, in all these studies, to obtain solids with suitable processing properties, the required ratio of solidifying excipients to L-MES was very high and it seems to be practically infeasible for drugs having limited solubility in oil phase showing less drug content uniformity. Moreover, the powder formulations are primarily designed for filling into hard gelatin capsules; there is a limitation of how much powders may be filled into a capsule, especially by considering that most of the silicates have low bulk densities [7]. Therefore, better alternative for delivering L-MES can be modified into CA spheres or nanosized particles and easily filled in hard gelatin capsules and they readily form microemulsion gel layer due to swelling nature of sodium alginate which acts as barrier to diffuse the dissolved drug into bulk of the solution in a sustained manner [8]. Recently, microencapsulation has been employed to convert L-MES into solid spheres using dextran 40 as a water soluble solid carrier by spray drying method [9]. Microencapsulation is well accepted technique for development of homogeneous, monolithic particles in the range of about 0.1–1000 μm and is employed to sustain the drug release [10]. Sodium alginate (SA) is a natural polysaccharide found in all species of brown algae and certain species of bacteria. It is a linear polymer of β (1–4) mannuronic acid (M) and α (1–4) guluronic acid (G) residue in varying proportions and arrangements [11]. SA can be ionically cross-linked with various types of cations like Ca^{2+}, Ba^{2+}, and Al^{3+} to form a viscous gel [12]. Among all that calcium ions interacting with alginates even small concentrations will produce very viscous gel compared to alginate alone. The gelation of alginic acid forms high viscous acid gel by intermolecular binding with calcium ion. During the cross-linking process, the water molecules will entrap inside the polymeric gel and are free to migrate throughout the gel layer [13]. This phenomenon has been applied to the preparation of CA beads for use as a drug delivery system, by dropping the drug-containing SA dispersion into a calcium chloride bath. CA microbeads have the advantages of being unable to reswell in acidic environment, whereas they easily reswell in an alkaline environment. So acid sensitive drugs incorporated into the CA beads would be protected from gastric juice [14].

Neusilin US2 is a synthetic, amorphous form of magnesium aluminometasilicate. It is a multifunctional excipient that can be used in both direct compression and wet granulation of solid dosage forms. It has good flow and compressibility properties and high specific surface area and adsorbs high loads of oils or water and can be mechanically compacted into high quality solid dosage forms [15]. Several literature reports explain that Neusilin US2 is a very good filler to convert the L-MES into solid microemulsifying drug delivery system (SMEDDS) [16].

The objectives of the present study were therefore (1) to develop ACF-Na microemulsion using the nonionic Labrasol (as surfactant HLB 16), Span 80 (as cosurfactant, HLB 4.6), and Labrafac PG, a lipophilic liquid, and water. Pseudoternary phase diagrams were constructed to find out the zone of microemulsion at different ratios of surfactant to cosurfactant (e.g., 1 : 1, 2 : 1, and 3 : 1). The effect of formulation variables on different physicochemical characteristics such as dispersibility tests, globule size, and zeta potential was studied and (2) to formulate ACF-Na preconcentrate L-ME loaded solid CA nanocomposite microbeads using SA and Neusilin US2 as carriers and calcium chloride as cross-linking agent. To study the effects of various formulation and process variables. In this research work we investigate the effect of various concentrations of SA, calcium chloride, and Neusilin US2 on mean particle size, actual drug content, drug entrapment efficiency, mechanical strength, and *in vitro* drug release potential of the formulated nanocomposite microbeads.

2. Material and Methods

Materials. ACF-Na was obtained as a gift sample from Microlabs, Bengaluru, Karnataka, India. SA was gift sample from F.M.C. International biopolymers, Willington, Ireland, to Signet Chemical Corporation Pvt. Ltd., Mumbai, India. Labrafac PG (propylene glycol dicaprylocaprate EP/NF), Labrafil 2125 CS (Linoleoyl macrogolglycerides), and Labrasol (Caprylocaproyl macrogol-8 glycerides EP) are gift samples from Gattefosse groups, Saint Priest Cedex, France. Neusilin US2 (magnesium aluminometasilicate) was gift sample from Fuji Chemical Industry Co., Burlington, NJ, USA, to Gangwal Chemicals Ltd., Mumbai, India. All other reagents and solvents used were of analytical grade satisfying pharmacopoeias specifications.

2.1. Preformulation Studies

2.1.1. Saturation Solubility Study. Solubility studies were conducted by placing an excess amount of ACF-Na (approximately 1 g) in a 50 mL volumetric flask containing 10 mL of different oils, surfactants, and cosurfactants (Table 1). Then, the mixture was vortexes for 30 min and was kept for 48 h at room temperature in a water bath by shaking with mechanical shaker to facilitate the solubilisation. The samples were centrifuged at 3000 g for 15 min to remove the undissolved ACF-Na. The supernatant was taken and diluted with methanol for quantification of ACF-Na at 275 nm using Shimadzu 1201 UV-visible spectrophotometer (Shimadzu 1201, Japan) [17].

2.1.2. Fourier Transform Infrared (FT-IR) Spectroscopic Analysis. The drug polymer interactions were studied by using FT-IR spectrophotometer (Shimadzu 1700S). The samples were prepared by adopting KBr pellet technique and scanned from 4000 to 450 cm^{-1} taking air as the reference.

2.1.3. Differential Scanning Calorimetry (DSC). Differential scanning calorimetry (DSC) was performed using DSC-60 (Shimadzu, Tokyo, Japan) calorimeter to study the thermal behaviours of ACF-Na alone and mixture of ACF-Na and polymer. The instrument comprised calorimeter (DSC-60), flow controller (FCL-60), thermal analyser (TA-60), and operating software (TA-60). The samples were heated in

Table 1: Saturation solubility of ACF-Na in different vehicles.

Vehicles	Solubility of ACF-Na (mg/mL)
Surfactants	
Tween 20	>1000 mg
Tween 80	>1000 mg
Labrasol	>1000 mg
Oils	
Castor oil	095.22 ± 08.66
Cotton seed oil	112.65 ± 43.03
Sesame oil	136.42 ± 33.04
Peanut oil	148.25 ± 22.17
Labrafil M 1944 CS	192.78 ± 44.15
Labrafac PG	308.12 ± 12.08

Data are the mean ± S.D. $n = 3$.

sealed aluminium pans under nitrogen flow (30 mL/min) at a scanning rate of 5°C/min from 24 ± 1 to 250°C. Empty aluminium pan was used as reference. The heat flow as a function of temperature was measured for the drug and drug polymer mixture.

2.1.4. X-Ray Powder Diffractometry (XRPD). The crystalline nature of ACF-Na and polymers in the manufacturing process was performed by using Philips X-ray powder diffractometry (model; PW 1710) with copper target. The X-ray diffraction patterns of pure drug and the optimized drug loaded formulations were recorded using the radiation at 30 kv and 25 mA^0, scanning speed at 20/min^{-1}, and 40 to 400 diffraction angle (2θ) ranges.

2.1.5. Constructing Pseudoternary Phase Diagram. From solubility study, Labrafac PG, Labrasol, and Span 80 were selected as oil, surfactant, and cosurfactant, respectively. The stable microemulsion region was identified by constructing pseudoternary phase diagram containing different proportion of surfactant:cosurfactant (Km value 1 : 1, 2 : 1, and 3 : 1), oil, and water. In brief, the different concentration of surfactant and oil was mixed at ratio of 1 : 9, 2 : 8, 3 : 7, 4 : 6, 5 : 5, 6 : 4, 7 : 3, 8 : 2, and 9 : 1 in preweighed test tube. To the resultant mixtures, double distilled water was added dropwise till the first sign of turbidity in order to identify the end point and after equilibrium. After complete equilibrium was reached, the mixtures were checked visually for transparency and by visualizing through optical polarizer (Nikkon, Japan). The systems which appeared to be black when visualized through the crossed polarizers were deemed to be within the microemulsion region. The amount of each of the components (% w/w) for a particular composition was determined with the help of pseudoternary phase diagram [18].

2.1.6. Preparation of Liquid Microemulsion of ACF-Na. The phase diagrams were constructed at different Km values and which Km values ratio gives high microemulsion region obtained was selected for formulation of L-MES. For 200 mg of ACF-Na and Labrafac PG (10% w/w) was placed in glass vial, warmed on water bath. The mixture of Labrasol and Span 80 in the proportion 2 : 1 (40% w/w) was added into the oily dispersion. Then, the components were mixed gently by using microhomogenizer and vortexes at 37°C until drug was completely dissolved to form clear homogeneous mixture. Then, the mixture was sealed in glass vial and stored at room temperature until use [19].

2.1.7. Preparation of Solid CA-Neusilin US2 Nanocomposite Microbeads. The ACF-Na preconcentrate L-MES was saturated with 20 mL of SA solution (0.5, 1.0, 1.5, and 2% w/v) and by adding Neusilin US2 (0.4, 0.6, 1.0, and 1.5% w/w) as adsorbent stirred 500 rpm for 30 min at 40°C. The bubble-free dispersion was dropped through a 10 mL glass syringe fitted with 24-gauge hypodermic needle into 50 mL (0.5, 2.0, 4.0, and 6.0% w/v) of calcium chloride solution and was stirred at 200 rpm for 30 min. The droplets from the dispersion instantaneously gelled into discrete matrices upon contact with the solution of calcium chloride. After specified stirring time and stirring speed, gelled beads were separated by filtration, washed with isopropyl alcohol and further 3 × 50 mL volumes of deionized water, and finally dried at 60°C for 4 h in a hot air oven. The various concentrations of SA, Neusilin US2, and calcium chloride were evaluated on physicochemical and drug release characteristics of nanocomposite microbeads.

2.2. Characterization and Evaluation of L-ME, Solid Nanocomposite Microbeads

2.2.1. Visual Assessment Test (Dilution Effect). L-ME was diluted with 1-, 25-, 50-, 100-, 150-, and 200-fold with pH 4.5 mixed PBS. The contents were then mixed gently with magnetic stirrer at room temperature. The tendency to form emulsion spontaneously and also the arrangement of emulsion droplets were observed. When droplets spread easily in the medium and formed a fine milky emulsion, this indicates very good tendency. When there was poor or no emulsion formation with immediate coalescence of oil droplets, especially when stirring, being stopped, this indicates less tendency.

2.2.2. Globule Size, Polydispersity Index (PDI), and Zeta Potential. The L-MES was diluted to 10 times with distilled water and globule size, PDI, and zeta potential were determined using Malvern Zetasizer (Nano ZS90) by dynamic light scattering (DLS) by monitoring at 25°C at a scattering angle 173° in which measure size ranges between 6 nm and 0.6 μm. The nanometric size range of the particle was retained even after 100 times dilution with water which proves the compatibility of the system with excess water [20, 21].

2.2.3. Measurement of Micromeritic Properties of Nanocomposite Microbeads. The flow properties were investigated by measuring the angle of repose of drug loaded microbeads using fixed-base cone method [22]. The angle of repose was calculated by using the following formula. Each experiment was carried out in triplicate ($n = 3$). Consider

$$\text{Angle of repose } (\theta) = \tan^{-1}\left(\frac{h}{r}\right), \tag{1}$$

where h is cone height and r is radius of circular base formed by the microbeads on the ground.

The bulk and tapped densities of the formulated microbeads were evaluated by using the bulk density apparatus. The experiment was repeated in triplicate ($n = 3$). The respective densities were calculated by using the following formulas:

$$\text{Bulk density [gm/cc]} = \frac{\text{Mass of the sample (g)}}{\text{Bulk volume (mL)}}. \quad (2)$$

Compressibility index or Carr's index value of microbeads was computed according to the following equation:

$$\text{Carr's index (\%)} = \left[\frac{(\text{Tapped density} - \text{Bulk density})}{\text{Tapped density}}\right] \times 100. \quad (3)$$

Hausner's ratio of microbeads was determined by comparing the tapped density to the bulk density by using the following equation:

$$\text{Hausner's ratio} = \frac{\text{Tapped density}}{\text{Bulk density}}. \quad (4)$$

2.2.4. Mechanical Property of Nanocomposite Microbeads. Mechanical strength of the CA and CA-Neusilin US2 nanocomposite microbeads was carried out using a texture analyser (TA.XT plus, Stable Micro Systems, UK) with a 50 kg load cell equipped with a cylindrical probe of 6 mm in diameter. Large beads were prepared with SA alone and SA/Neusilin US2 dispersion dropped through 1 mL pipette into calcium chloride solution. The fully formed beads were collected, washed with distilled water, and subsequently dried at 60°C for 4 h. One bead was placed on the platform and probe was positioned to touch the bead, recorded as the initial position, and then crosshead speed and probe diameter were set at a constant speed of 1.0 mms^{-1}. The probe was removed when the bead was broken or reduced to 50% of its original height [23]. The force and percent displacement were plotted, and the maximum force at 50% displacement, which represents the strength of the beads, was reported.

2.2.5. Particle Size Analysis. The particle sizes of drug loaded CA nanocomposite microbeads were measured by an optical microscope fitted with an ocular and stage micrometer and particle size distribution was calculated. The Olympus model (SZX-12) having resolution of 30 xs was used for this purpose. The instrument was calibrated at 1 unit of eyepiece micrometer which was equal to 1/30 mm (33.33 μm). In all measurements, at least 100 particles in five different fields were examined [24]. Each experiment was carried out in triplicate ($n = 3$).

2.2.6. Scanning Electron Microscopy (SEM) Analysis. The shape and surface characteristics of drug loaded CA nanocomposite microbeads were determined by scanning electron microscopy (model-JSM, 35CF, Jeol, Japan) using gold sputter technique. A working distance of 20 nm, a tilt of zero degree, and accelerating voltage of 15 kv were the operating parameters. Photographs were taken within a range of 50–5000 magnifications.

2.2.7. Drug Entrapment Efficiency (DEE). Accurately weighed 50 mg of CA nanocomposite microbeads was ground using a mortar and pestle and was dispersed in 100 mL of PBS pH 6.8±0.1. The mixture was sonicated for 30 min and incubated at 37°C for 24 h. Next day, it was stirred for 15 min. The solution was filtered, after suitable dilution, ACF-Na content in the filtrate was analysed at 275 nm using Shimadzu 1201 UV-visible spectrophotometer. The obtained absorbance was plotted on the standard curve to get the exact concentration of the entrapped drug. Calculate the concentration of drug and determine the percentage of actual drug encapsulated in nanocomposite microbeads with dilution factor. The percentage of drug entrapment efficiency was determined using the following relationship:

$$\text{DEE (\%)} = \left[\frac{\text{Actual drug content}}{\text{Theoretical drug content}}\right] \times 100. \quad (5)$$

2.2.8. In Vitro Drug Release Studies. The release profiles of ACF-Na from nanocomposite microbeads were examined in three different buffer solutions to mimic various physiological GI-tracts. The media SGF of pH 1.2 was representing the gastric condition; pH 6.8 PBS was a compromise condition between pH of the gastric and small intestine and pH 7.4 is simulated intestinal fluid. The dissolution process was carried out by using USP XIII rotating basket apparatus (Microlabs, Mumbai, India). The drug loaded microbeads (equivalent to 200 mg of ACF-Na) filled in empty capsule shells were put into the basket and rotated at a constant speed at 75 rpm/min and maintained temperature 37°C. The 900 mL SGF of pH1.2 dissolution medium was used in dissolution process for initial 2 h and the test was continued with changing the dissolution media with pH 6.8 PBS up to 6 h and SIF of pH 7.4 at the end of 12 h. At scheduled time intervals, the sample (5 mL) was withdrawn and replaced with the same volume of fresh medium. The withdrawn samples were filtered through a 0.45 μm membrane filter and after appropriate dilution and then estimated for aceclofenac sodium concentration at 275 nm by using UV-visible spectroscopy (Shimadzu 1201, Japan). Finally, corresponding drug content in the samples was calculated from the calibration curve to determine the drug release pattern [25].

2.2.9. Kinetics of Drug Release. In order to understand the mechanism and kinetics of drug release and best fit model for the formulations by using PCP-Disso-V2 software, the drug release data of the *in vitro* dissolution study was analysed with various kinetic equations like zero-order (% release v/s time), first-order (Log % retained v/s time), and Korsmeyer and Peppas equations ($Mt/M\infty = Ktn$). Where Mt is the amount of drug released at time t, $M\infty$ is the amount of drug released at infinite time, K is the kinetic constant incorporating the structural and geometric characteristics of the beads, and n is the diffusional exponent indicative of the release mechanism. Where $n = 0.5$ represents Fickian diffusion, <1.0 represents non-Fickian diffusion, $n = 1.0$ case-II transport, and $n > 1.0$ super case-II transport [26]. Coefficient of correlation (r) values were calculated for the linear curves obtained by regression analysis of the above plots.

3. Results and Discussions

3.1. Preformulation Studies

3.1.1. Solubility Studies. The microemulsion is a clear monophasic liquid formulation consisting of oils, surfactants, cosurfactants, and drug at ambient temperature when introduced to aqueous phase. They have very good solvent properties to solubilize the insoluble solids. The solubility of poor water soluble aceclofenac sodium in various vehicles is presented in Table 1. All the surfactants showed good solubility of the drug. Among all the surfactants tested in this study, Labrasol a medium-length alkyl chain surfactant with HLB 14 was selected as a surfactant because it was reported for its enhanced intestinal absorption of drugs [27]. The solubility of ACF-Na with Labrasol is higher than other surfactants. Moreover, the miscibility of these oils with Labrasol at 2 : 1 volume ratio was investigated by clarity of oil/surfactant mixture. Castor oil, cotton seed oil, sesame oil, peanut oil, and Labrafil 2125 CS were poorly miscible with Labrasol, whereas Labrafac PG was well miscible and formed clear solution. Labrafac PG showed higher drug solubility than other oils. Thus, Labrafac PG was selected as an oily vehicle due to its good solubility and good emulsion forming with surfactant and cosurfactant. Furthermore, Span 80 (HLB 6) was selected as a cosurfactant for its good solubility and for preparing homogenous polymeric dispersion resulting in the improvement of drug loading in the solid microbeads.

3.1.2. FT-IR Spectroscopic Analysis. The molecular interactions of ACF-Na, SA, and Neusilin US2 in the CA nanocomposite microbeads were investigated using FTIR spectroscopy. The characteristic absorption peaks of pure ACF-Na were obtained 3276.5, 2915.5, 1716.5, 1589.3, 1279.6, and 749.4 cm^{-1} corresponding to NH-stretching, C=O stretching of -COO, and -COOH group, respectively (Figure 1(a)). The characteristic absorption peaks SA showed peaks around 3077.15, 2914.98, 1615.34, 1359.60, and 754.05 cm^{-1} reflective of O–H, C–H, COO– (asymmetric), COO– (symmetric), and C–O–C stretching, respectively (Figure 1(b)). The cross-linking process of SA with calcium caused an obvious shift to higher wave numbers and a decrease in the intensity of COO– stretching peaks. Additionally, a change to lower wave numbers and a decrease in the intensity of the C–O–C stretching peak of SA was observed. This indicated the presence of an ionic bond between the calcium ion and the carboxyl groups of SA and partial covalent bonding between the calcium and oxygen atoms of the ether groups [28]. The physical mixture SA and ACF-Na characteristic peaks were obtained at 2820.28, 1591.72, 1384.91, 1102.03, and 766.4 cm^{-1} causing a shift in the O–H, COO– (asymmetric), and COO– (symmetric) stretching peaks to lower wave numbers (Figure 1(c)), suggesting that a molecular interaction between SA and ACF-Na was formed due to hydrogen bonding and electrostatic force. The addition of Neusilin US2 in the aceclofenac sodium-loaded CA nanocomposite microbeads caused a change in the carboxylate peaks of SA. The Si–O–Si stretching peak of Neusilin US2 at 1115.24 cm^{-1} (Figure 1(d)) became narrower and moved to a lower wave number 996.15 cm^{-1} (Figure 1(e)), suggesting that Neusilin US2 could interact with SA and ACF-Na in the microbeads. These results suggested no considerable changes in the IR peaks of ACF-Na in the physical mixture thereby indicating the absence of any interactions. Moreover, ACF-Na-Neusilin US2 complex-loaded CA nanocomposite microbeads might have higher drug entrapment efficiency due to being molecularly dispersed in the SA-Neusilin US2 matrix. The peaks shown at 2916.5, 1589.3, 1279.6, and 749.4 cm^{-1} as major peaks for ACF-Na are present in all physical mixtures of drug and polymer which confirms that the drug was molecularly dispersed in the polymer without any interaction.

3.1.3. Differential Scanning Calorimetry (DSC). DSC is a well-established method often used as a qualitative technique to characterize physical and chemical changes in either enthalpy or heat capacity of a crystalline drug in the polymer matrix during the manufacturing process. The thermal behavior of the pure ACF-Na, drug loaded CA, and CA-Neusilin US2 nanocomposite microbeads were characterized using DSC, as shown in Figure 2. The thermograms of pure ACF-Na showed a sharp endothermic peak at 158.50°C followed by corresponding melting point (Figure 2(a)). However, the DSC thermograms of drug loaded CA-Neusilin US2 microbeads were observed at 189.5°C and 195.6°C, respectively. It can clearly suggest that the CA nanocomposite microbeads containing SA and SA-Neusilin US2 showed an increase in the exothermic peak temperature (Figures 2(b) and 2(c)) and improved the thermal stability. The extra obvious peak of the ACF-Na (158.5°C) was not observed in any type of prepared nanocomposite microbeads and no appreciable change in the melting endothermic peak of the physical mixture as compared to pure ACF-Na. It may indicate that there were no changes in thermal behavior of drug and also the drug was molecularly dispersed in hydrogel matrix.

3.1.4. X-Ray Powder Diffractometry (X-RPD). The X-ray powder diffraction patterns of pure drug are compared with drug loaded CA and CA-Neusilin US2 nanocomposite microbeads. The XRPD scan of plain ACF-Na showed sharp intense peaks of crystallinity (Figure 3(a)), whereas the XRPD pattern of the drug loaded CA and CA-Neusilin US2 nanocomposite microbeads exhibited halo pattern with less intense and denser peaks compared to plain ACF-Na indicating the decrease in crystallinity or partial amorphization of the drug in the microbeads (Figure 3(b)). The intensity of the ACF-Na peaks at 14.47, 24.87, 26.26, 29.95, and 36.55°C (2θ), CA microbeads (AF3) at 16.29, 39.23, and 43.76°C (2θ), and CA-Neusilin US2 nanocomposite microbeads (AF7) shown at 14.06, 26.65, and 55.65°C (2θ) was calculated

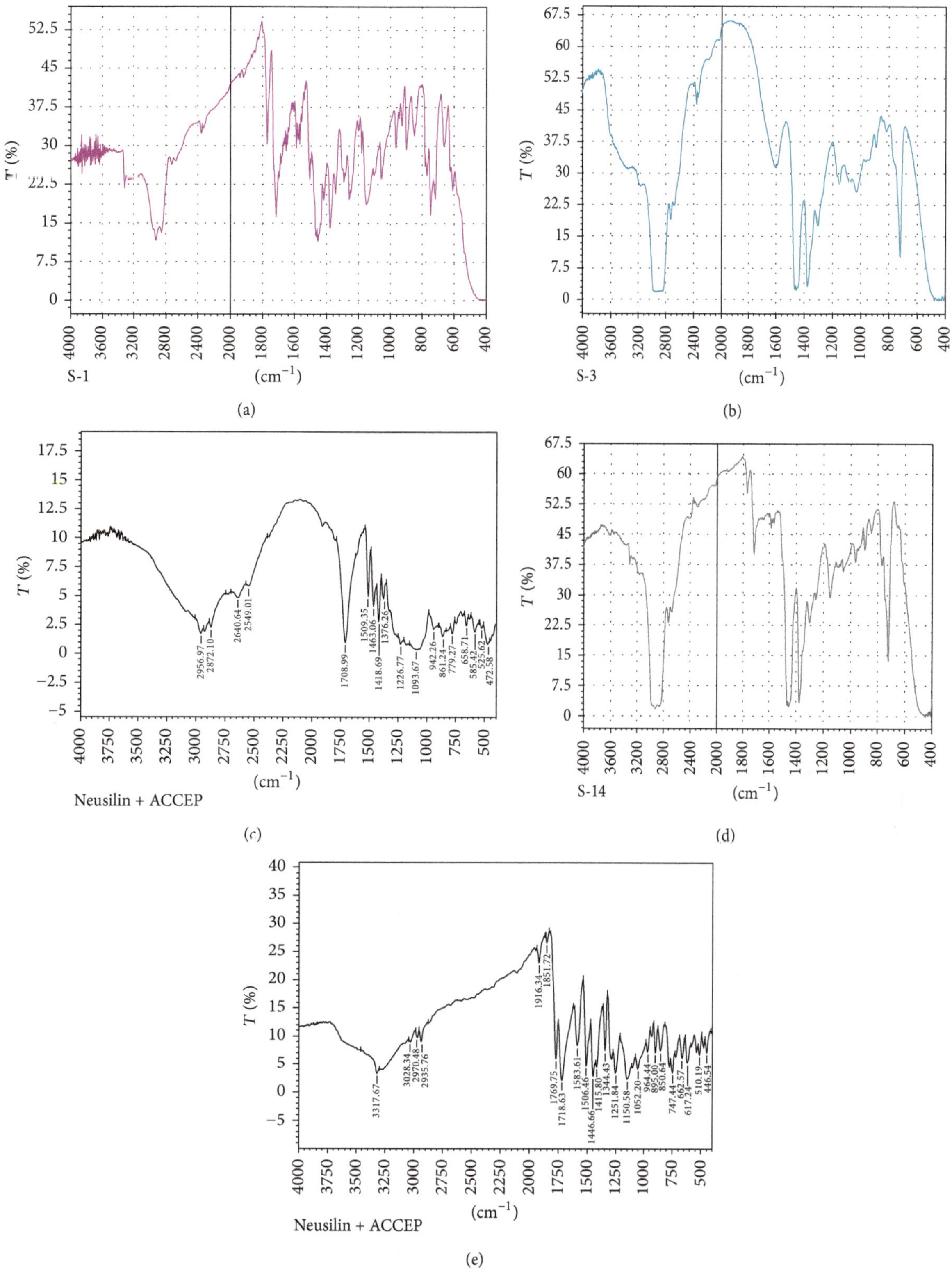

FIGURE 1: FT-IR spectra: (a) pure aceclofenac sodium, (b) sodium alginate, (c) Neusilin US2, (d) physical mixture of aceclofenac sodium and sodium alginate, and (e) physical mixture of aceclofenac sodium and Neusilin US2.

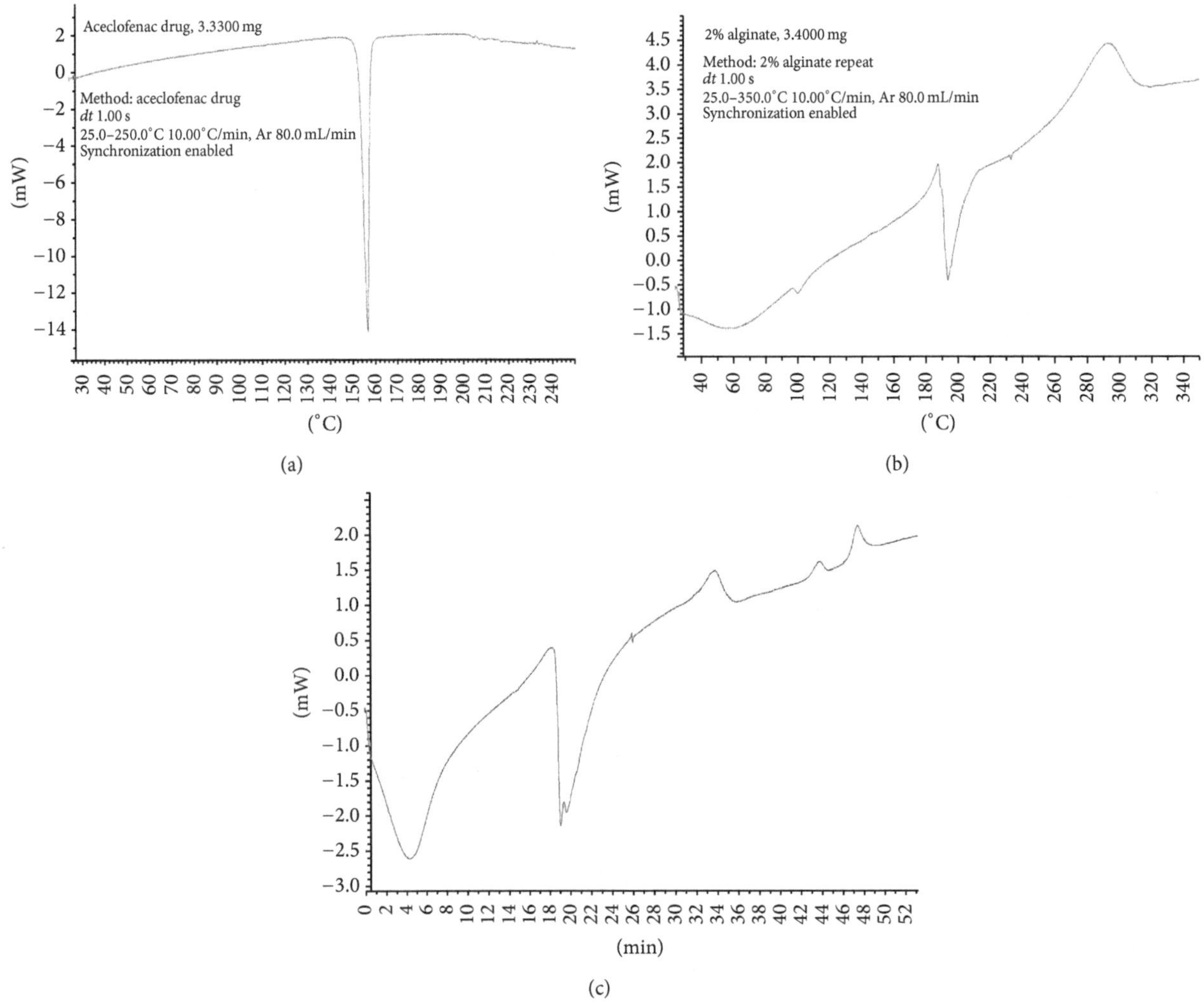

FIGURE 2: DSC thermograms: (a) pure aceclofenac sodium, (b) CA drug loaded nanocomposite microbeads (AF-3), and (c) CA-Neusilin US2 drug loaded nanocomposite microbeads (AF-7).

using D8 TOOLS software. The calculated percentage relative crystallinity value for pure ACF-Na was 92.40% and those of formulations containing SA (AF-3) and SA-Neusilin US2 (AF-7) were 89.25 and 80.09, respectively (Figures 3(b) and 3(c)). This is possibly due to the decrease in the degree of crystallinity of the drug following dispersal in the polymer matrix.

3.1.5. Pseudoternary Phase Diagram. This is the first stage to determine the ratio of surfactant:cosurfactant to formulation development of spontaneous microemulsion formation. The boundaries of the microemulsion domains were determined by plotting pseudoternary phase diagrams for the selected components based on solubility studies. Nine different potential combinations of surfactant and cosurfactant mixture to oil at different Km values (1 : 1, 2 : 1) were used for construction of pseudoternary phase diagram. The shaded area in phase diagram shows a stable microemulsion region (Figures 4(a) and 4(b)). The nature of phase behavior of the system was proven to determine concentration of oil, surfactant:cosurfactant and water. Phase diagram at Km value 2 : 1 showed maximum microemulsion region.

3.2. Evaluation of Liquid Microemulsion System

3.2.1. Globule Size, PDI, and Zeta Potential. The efficiency of L-ME could be estimated by determining the rate of emulsification and droplet size distribution. The droplet size is a crucial factor in microemulsification performance because it determines the rate and extent of drug release as well as absorption [29]. Globule size was found to be 32.4 nm with polydispersity index 0.219 and zeta potential was found to be −6.32 mV (Figures 5(a) and 5(b)). An increase in the ratio of the oil phase (Labrafac PG) resulted in a proportional increase in droplet size. It is well known that the addition of surfactants to the L-ME causes the interfacial film to stabilize and condense, while the addition of cosurfactant causes the film to expand; thus, the relative proportion of surfactant to cosurfactant has varying effects on the droplet size. The decrease in surfactant concentration leads to decreased viscosity of the formulation.

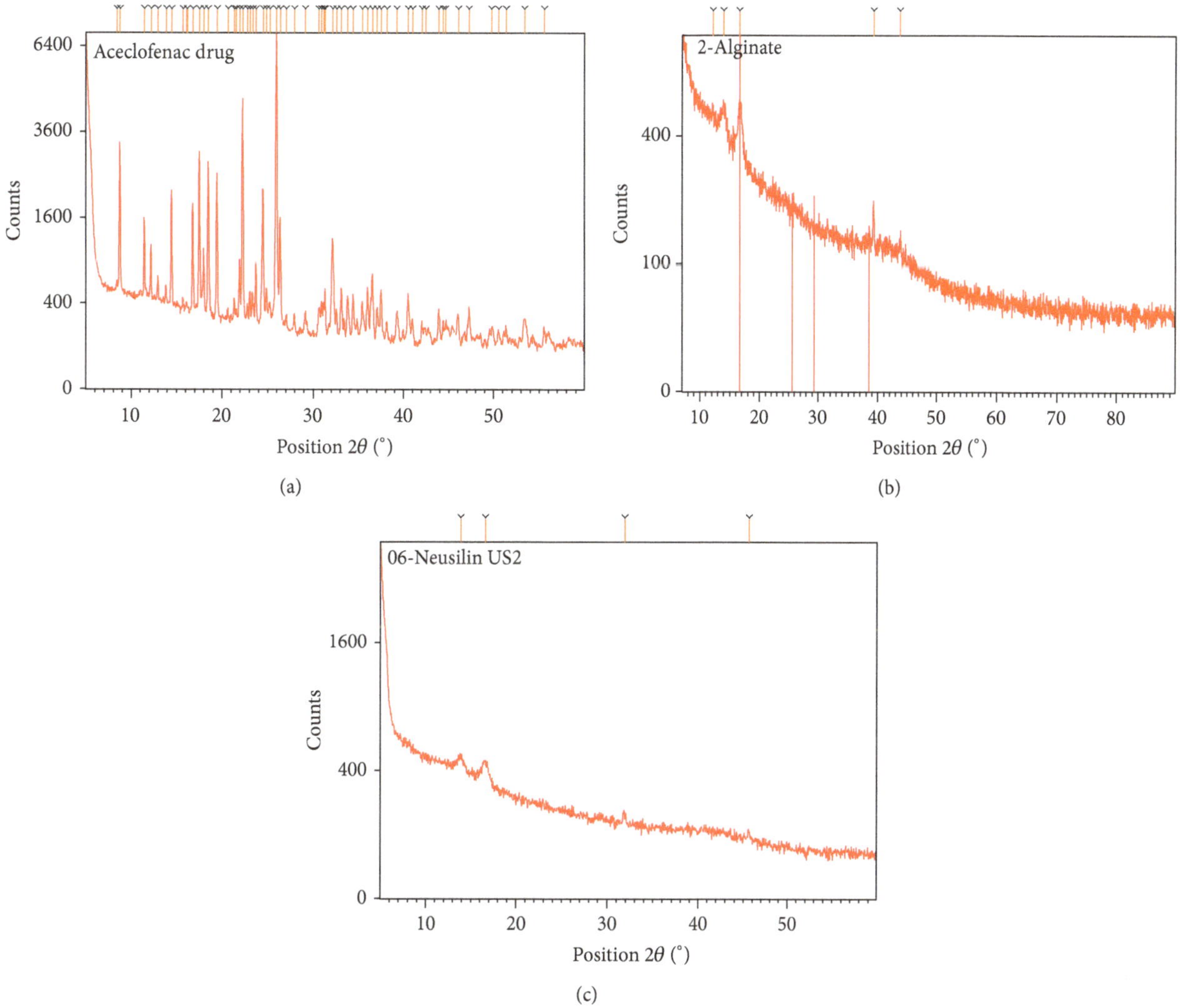

FIGURE 3: X-Ray diffraction patterns of (a) pure aceclofenac sodium, (b) CA drug loaded nanocomposite microbeads (AF-3), and (c) CA-Neusilin US2 drug loaded nanocomposite microbeads (AF-7).

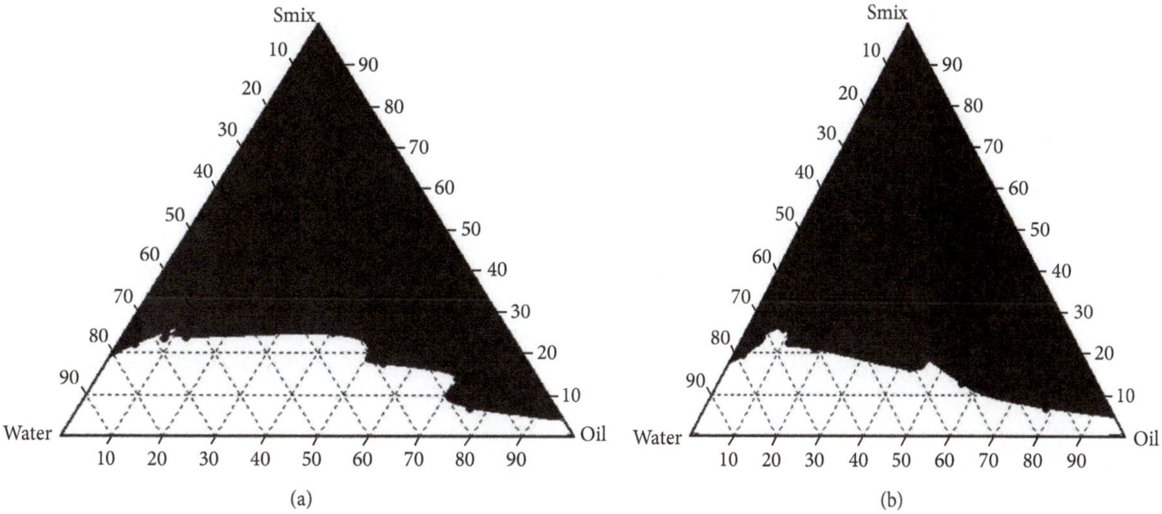

FIGURE 4: Pseudoternary phase diagram: (a) Km value 1 : 1 and (b) Km value 2 : 1.

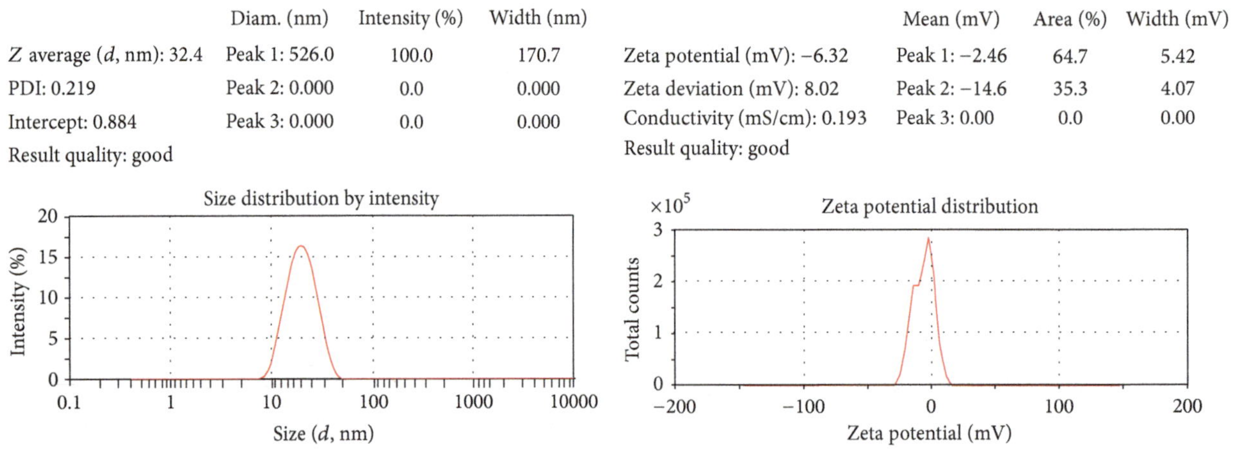

(a) (b)

FIGURE 5: (a) Globule size and PDI of aceclofenac sodium liquid microemulsion system. (b) Globule size and PDI of ACF-Na and SA polymeric dispersion.

TABLE 2: Micromeritic properties ACF-Na loaded nanocomposite microbeads.

Batch code	Mean particle size [μm]	Angle of repose [θ]	Bulk density [gm/mL]	Tapped density [gm/mL]	Carr's index [ci]	Hausner's ratio
AF-1	386 ± 1.22	31.21 ± 0.21	0.469 ± 0.95	0.585 ± 0.65	19.69	1.24
AF-2	552 ± 0.85	26.10 ± 0.37	0.556 ± 0.34	0.658 ± 0.64	15.50	1.18
AF-3	586 ± 1.02	20.80 ± 0.12	0.596 ± 0.38	0.688 ± 0.12	14.62	1.15
AF-4	667 ± 0.55	20.10 ± 0.32	0.602 ± 0.15	0.690 ± 0.33	14.45	1.14
AF-5	572 ± 0.80	23.30 ± 0.10	0.626 ± 0.64	0.756 ± 0.55	17.19	1.20
AF-6	568 ± 0.75	22.65 ± 0.20	0.597 ± 0.12	0.705 ± 0.85	15.32	1.18
AF-7	502 ± 0.45	19.65 ± 0.25	0.588 ± 0.62	0.685 ± 0.87	15.03	1.16
AF-8	496 ± 0.38	18.75 ± 0.62	0.562 ± 0.30	0.647 ± 0.54	13.29	1.15
AF-9	565 ± 0.22	25.45 ± 0.45	0.557 ± 0.42	0.678 ± 0.22	17.84	1.22
AF-10	536 ± 0.12	22.75 ± 0.82	0.545 ± 0.18	0.656 ± 0.12	16.92	1.20
AF-11	501 ± 0.15	20.15 ± 0.55	0.539 ± 0.23	0.638 ± 0.34	15.52	1.18
AF-12	488 ± 0.35	19.32 ± 0.22	0.529 ± 0.31	0.618 ± 0.58	14.45	1.16

Data are the mean ± S.D. $n = 3$.

It was observed that increasing the surfactant and cosurfactant ratio decreased the average diameter of oily droplets in the microemulsion. On the other hand, increasing the concentration of oil (Labrafac PG) of the average diameter of oily droplets slightly increased which influences the formation of large size microbeads. Moreover, it was observed that the spontaneous emulsion formation was not efficient with less than 2 : 1 concentration of surfactant : cosurfactant in L-MES. Hence, optimized formulation of preconcentrated L-ME contained Labrafac PG (10%), Labrasol: Span 80 (40%), and water (50%) which are used for the formulation of CA nanocomposite solid microbeads.

3.3. *Evaluation of CA-Neusilin US2 Nanocomposite Microbeads*

3.3.1. Micrometric Properties of Drug Loaded Microbeads. The rheological parameters like angle of repose, bulk density, and tapped density of all microbeads confirm better flow and good packaging properties. All the formulations showed excellent flowability represented in terms of angle of repose (<40°) 20 and compressibility index (<30) and Hausner ratio (<1.24). However, higher calcium chloride concentration in the curing medium influenced the formation of smaller beads because of shrinkage and formation of more compact matrix between SA/Neusilin US2 showed an increased angle of repose (Table 2). Bulk and tapped density of microbeads with Neusilin US2 showed good acceptable range indicating that they have good packability. Moreover, the density of the microbeads increases with increasing the concentration of SA/Neusilin US2 due to formation of more compact and less porosity microbeads than those prepared by SA alone (Table 2).

3.3.2. Scanning Electron Microscopy (SEM) Analysis. The SEM photomicrographs of the dried drug loaded CA nanocomposite microbeads are shown (Figure 6). Morphology of the drug loaded CA microbeads was discrete and

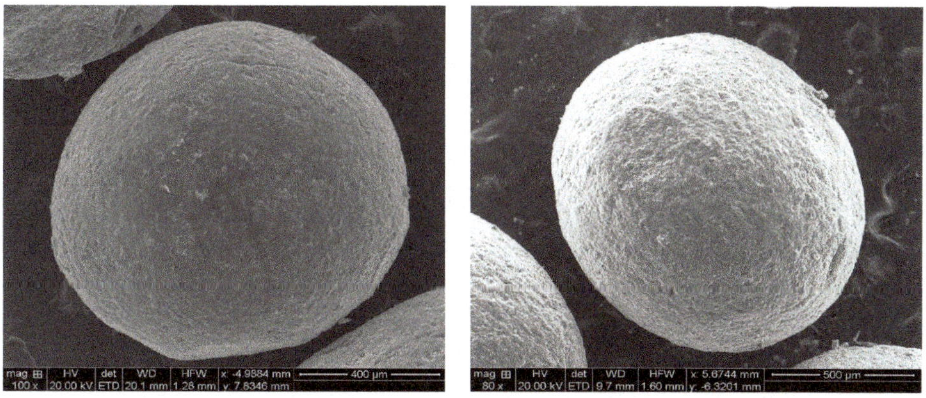

(a) (b)

FIGURE 6: SEM photographs magnifications 200x at 10 kv (a) CA drug loaded nanocomposite microbeads (AF-3) and (b) CA-Neusilin US2 drug loaded nanocomposite microbeads (AF-7).

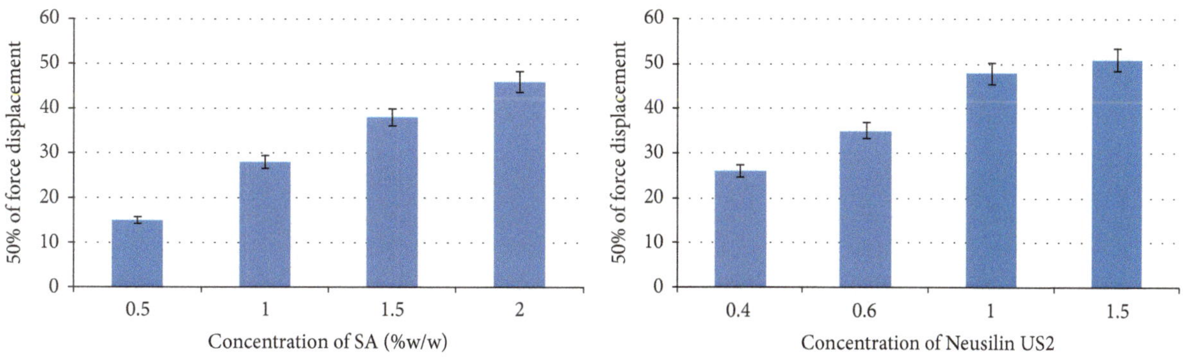

(a) (b)

FIGURE 7: (a) Effect of SA on mechanical strength of CA nanocomposite microbeads. (b) Effect of Neusilin on mechanical strength of CA nanocomposite microbeads.

spherical in shape with a rough outer surface and visible large wrinkles and pores having a sandy appearance due to less compactness (Figure 6(a)). In case of CA-Neusilin US2 nanocomposite microbeads are more spherical; absence of any pores, wrinkles, and also the drug is completely entrapped inside of the polymeric network due to interlocking of Neusilin US2 filler with SA gel (Figure 6(b)).

3.3.3. Mechanical Property of Microbeads. The maximum force for 50% displacement or breakdown was used to evaluate the strength of the microbeads. The mechanical strength of the CA nanocomposite microbeads was increased by increasing the concentration of SA in the formulation (Figure 7(a)). The maximum force for 50% displacement of the microbeads gradually increased with increasing concentration of Neusilin US2 content. The content of Neusilin US2 above 1.5% w/w did not show any greater changes in the strength of the beads due to complete saturation level of Neusilin US2 with SA. This result indicated that the Neusilin US2 interacts with SA adsorbing oil and water content in interior level of the beads during the cross-linking process and could create a dense matrix structure that reinforced the strength of the microbeads (Figure 7(b)).

3.3.4. Particle Size Analysis. The mean particle sizes of drug loaded microbeads were performed by optical microscopy, and mean particle sizes of the CA microbeads (AF1–AF12) were obtained in the range between 386 ± 1.22 and 667 ± 0.55 (Table 2). The results indicated that the proportional increase of SA in the formulations increases the mean particle size of microbeads. This could be attributed to an increase in relative viscosity at higher concentration of SA and formation of large droplets during addition of polymer solution to the curing medium. On the other hand, while increasing the concentration of Neusilin US2, the mean particle size significantly decreases. This may be due high water adsorption capacity of Neusilin US2 and formation of compact dense matrix with SA. Further, the concentration of calcium chloride increases in the curing medium would significantly decrease the mean particle size of nanocomposite microbeads (Table 2). It has been stated that when a drop of alginate solution comes in contact with calcium ions, gelation occurs instantaneously. As Ca^{+2} ions penetrate into interior part of droplets, water is squeezed out of the interior part of droplets resulting in contraction of microbeads [30]. The size of the spherical matrix could easily be controlled by varying the stirring

TABLE 3: Composition and physical characteristics of drug loaded nanocomposite microbeads.

Formulation code	S. A (%w/w)	Neusilin US2 (%w/w)	Calcium chloride (%w/v)	Actual drug content (mg/50 mg)	DEE (%w/w)
AF-1	0.5	—	4	29.56 ± 0.33	59.12 ± 0.35
AF-2	1.0	—	4	37.65 ± 0.15	75.30 ± 0.56
AF-3	1.5	—	4	44.85 ± 0.28	89.70 ± 0.36
AF-4	2.0	—	4	46.65 ± 0.62	93.30 ± 0.55
AF-5	1.5	0.4	4	45.95 ± 0.12	91.90 ± 0.25
AF-6	1.5	0.6	4	47.45 ± 0.55	94.90 ± 0.55
AF-7	1.5	1.0	4	49.25 ± 0.32	98.50 ± 0.09
AF-8	1.5	1.5	4	49.75 ± 0.25	99.50 ± 0.05
AF-9	1.5	1.0	0.5	47.30 ± 0.87	94.60 ± 0.69
AF-10	1.5	1.0	2	46.80 ± 0.74	93.60 ± 1.14
AF-11	1.5	1.0	4	45.40 ± 0.14	91.82 ± 1.04
AF-12	1.5	1.0	6	44.60 ± 0.42	89.20 ± 1.07

All the formulations contain 200 mg of aceclofenac sodium. Data are expressed ± S.D. $n = 3$.

speed and cross-linking time of the system (results are not reported).

3.3.5. Drug Entrapment Efficiency (DEE). As shown in Table 3, actual drug concentration in the microbeads was evaluated and was found to be in the range 29.56 ± 0.33 to 49.75 ± 0.25 mg/50 mg. The SA concentration increases; consequently, the actual drug loading is high due to increase in hydrophobicity leading to better adsorption of the microemulsion at the boundary phase of the droplets [AF-1 to AF-4]. When the concentration of Neusilin US2 increases the actual drug content predominately increases [AF-5 to AF-8] because of less leakage of drug from microbeads during the curing period with constant stirring speed (1500 rpm) due to the formation of dense matrix with SA and Neusilin US2. The effect of various process and formulation parameters on the drug entrapment efficiency of microbeads was investigated, by increasing the concentration of SA [AF-1 to AF-4]; the percentage of drug entrapment efficiencies was found to be in the range 59.12±0.35 to 93.30±0.55 w/w. It was observed that the drug entrapment efficiencies increased progressively with increasing the concentration of SA resulting in the formation of larger beads entrapping the greater amount of the drug. On other hand, the addition of Neusilin US2 drug entrapment efficiency of the CA nanocomposite microbeads is obtained in the range 91.90 ± 0.25 to 99.50 ± 0.05 [AF-5 to AF-8]. When the concentration of Neusilin US2 increases in the SA dispersions the percentage of drug entrapment efficiency progressively increases. The formation of hydrogen bonds between Neusilin US2 and SA to create numerous points of contact could produce a loose three-dimensional gel like structure throughout the composite dispersion. The higher the concentration of Neusilin US2, the greater the number of contact points in the dispersion. These interactions could result in an enhancement of the viscosity and thixotropic properties of the composite dispersions, more amount of drug adsorbed onto the Neusilin US2, increased the barrier to preventing the leaking of drug from the CA microbeads in the curing medium during the manufacturing process.

Increasing calcium chloride concentration, the percentage of drug entrapment efficiencies was found to be in the decreasing range 94.60 ± 0.69 to 89.20 ± 1.07 (Table 3). From the results, it is obvious that increasing calcium chloride concentration in the curing medium produced microbeads with higher levels of Ca^{2+} ions possibly due to shrinkage occurring during gelation period. This shrinkage could have led to a shorter path length for drug leakage and, therefore, higher drug loss [31]. On other hand, further increase in the concentration of calcium chloride above 6% w/w did not change the drug loading of microbeads (results are not reported). This could be due to possible saturation of calcium binding sites in the guluronic acid chain, preventing further Ca^{2+} ions entrapment and, hence, cross-linking was not altered with higher concentration of calcium chloride solution.

3.3.6. In Vitro Drug Release Studies. ACF-Na has been slightly soluble in water and showed very poor solubility in the acidic buffer media. However, the percentage of drug release from CA nanocomposite microbeads [AF-1 to AF-4] in SGF pH 1.2 within 2 h in the range of 32.54, 30.56, 28.35, and 26.55 w/w may be due to the stability of alginate at lower pHs and conversion of calcium alginate to the insoluble alginic acid to form tightening of the gel mesh work. On the other hand, the percentage of drug release in pH 6.8 PBS at 6 h is shown in the range of 52.33, 49.52, 44.25, and 37.65 w/w. Further, the percentage of drug release from microbeads in pH 7.4 SIF up to 12 h is 99.65, 97.12, 95.45, and 89.12 w/w (Figure 8(a)). As the concentration of SA increased, release rate of ACF-Na from the nanocomposite microbeads decreased, which shows biphasic pattern; that is, an initial rapid release (burst effect) phase was followed by a second slower drug release phase. The first phase might be disintegration of alginate in the presence surfactant and cosurfactant mainly based on drug diffusion through the small pores and cracks. The second phase exhibited slow release pattern, which was accompanied by diffusivity of polymer relaxation due to change in pH of the medium. The SA concentration in the formulation

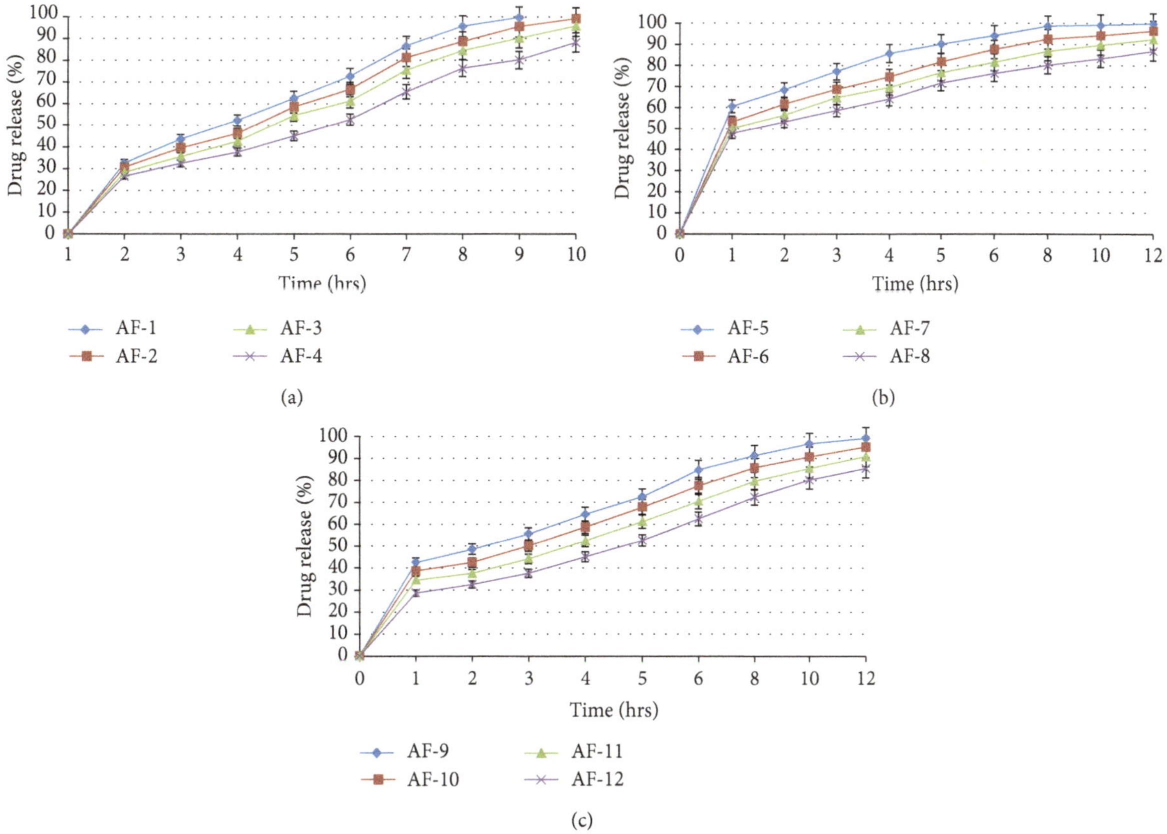

FIGURE 8: (a) Effect of SA on cummulative percentage of drug release from CA nanocomposite microbeads. (b) Effect of Neusilin US2 on cummulative percentage of drug release from CA nanocomposite microbeads. (c) Effect of calcium chloride on cummulative percentage of drug release from CA-Neusilin US2 nanocomposite microbeads.

greatly influenced the steady state release of drug from the nanocomposite microbeads.

The percentage of drug release from ACF-Na from CA-Neusilin US2 nanocomposite microbeads [AF-5 to AF-8] in SGF of pH 1.2 within 2 h was obtained in the range of 60.56 to 47.65 w/w. The results suggested that the presence of silanols on its surface makes it a potential proton donor as well as a proton acceptor, which increases the initial drug release by lower concentration of Neusilin US2 in acidic medium. The release rate during 6 h in pH 6.8 PBS and SIF of pH 7.4 after 6 h–12 h was decreased from 94.15 to 76.25 and from 98.96 to 86.75 w/w (Figure 8(b)). The observed results suggested that the hydrogen bonding between silanols and drug as well as interaction between the drug and metal ions on the surface of Neusilin US2 was stabilizing mechanism of ACF-Na in its amorphous state and increases the aqueous solubility at alkaline medium; due to this reason the maximum of drug releases in pH 6.8 PBS followed by sustaining SIF of pH 7.4 by electrostatic interaction between surface of the silicate layers of Neusilin US2 with negative charges of carboxylic groups of SA forms thick gel network which acts as a barrier to take prolonged time to diffuse the drug into bulk of the dissolution media.

The effect of cross-linking agent in the curing medium [AF-9 to AF-12] on percentage of drug release rate from CA-Neusilin composite microbeads in SGF of pH 1.2 was observed in range of 42.52 to 28.68 w/w. Further, observed the maximum amount of drug releases during at 6 h in pH 6.8 PBS is shown in the range 84.75, 77.55, 70.55, 62.54 and 99.12, 95.12, 90.75, 85.42 w/w at the end of 12 h in SIF of pH 7.4 (Figure 8(c)). The results indicate that rate and extent of drug release decreased with increase of concentration of calcium chloride, because sodium alginate as a linear copolymer consisting of β (1 $\rightarrow$ 4) mannuronic acid and α (1 $\rightarrow$ 4) L-guluronic acid residues; a tight junction is formed between the residues of alginate with calcium ions [32]. However, in case of higher calcium chloride concentration, the release of the drug from the beads decreased due to increased surface roughness and porosity and also poor entry of dissolution medium into the CA/Neusilin US2 nanocomposite microbeads.

3.3.7. Mechanism of Various Kinetic Models on Drug Release. The *in vitro* dissolution data were analyzed by different kinetic models in order to find out the n-value, which describes the drug release mechanism (Table 4). The values of correlation (r) were calculated and were found to be more linear for first-order release as compared to zero-order release. Cumulative % drug release was analyzed using PCP Disso-v2 08 software. The kinetic data was best fitted to Korsmeyer and Peppa's model and good regression coefficient was observed. The drug release from microbeads containing SA alone [AF-1

TABLE 4: Effect of various kinetic models on drug release.

Formulation code	Effect of various kinetic models on drug release					
	Zero-Order	First-Order	Higuchi matrix	Korsmeyer-Peppas	Korsmeyer-Peppas	
					n-values	k-values
F1	0.9117	0.9114	0.9124	0.9762	0.7248	2.7889
F2	0.9209	0.9174	0.9113	0.9801	0.7456	2.6783
F3	0.9392	0.9221	0.9108	0.9840	0.7515	2.4240
F4	0.9474	0.9329	0.9103	0.9950	0.7711	2.0693
F5	0.9521	0.9830	0.9097	0.9257	0.7764	1.9066
F6	0.9399	0.9803	0.9082	0.9291	0.6535	2.0130
F7	0.9372	0.9811	0.9088	0.9262	0.5449	2.1643
F8	0.9278	0.9801	0.9076	0.9217	0.5523	2.2625
F9	0.9129	0.9475	0.9702	0.9148	0.6482	2.4075
F10	0.9007	0.9568	0.9720	0.9115	0.7361	2.6019
F11	0.9826	0.9624	0.9842	0.9162	0.8704	2.8220
F12	0.9846	0.9700	0.9868	0.9153	0.8788	2.6173

All the results show S.D. $n = 3$; n: diffusion exponent (slope) related to mechanism of drug release, according to equation $Mt/M = K^{tn}$, and r: regression coefficient.

to AF-4] was followed by zero-order but in case of CA-Neusilin US2 nanocomposite microbeads [AF-5 to AF-8] continued to Korsmeyer and Peppa's model. The values of diffusion coefficient ranged between $n = 0.72480$ and 0.8788 indicating the drug release from the microbeads followed by case-II transport controlled by diffusion of CA-Neusilin US2 matrices [33].

4. Conclusion

From the investigation results, it can be concluded that the proper selection of optimized formulation conditions is very important to achieve high encapsulation efficiency and to control the release of ACF-Na from the CA-Neusilin US2 nanocomposite microbeads. As mentioned above, numerous studies have confirmed that microemulsion substantially improved solubility/dissolution, absorption, and bioavailability of poorly water soluble drugs. Hence, it was concluded that solid CA-Neusilin US2 nanocomposite microbeads can be efficiently formulated by microemulsification internal gelation technique. The SA and Neusilin US2 as solid fillers were used to convert L-ME preconcentrate into solid nanocomposite microbeads which could enhance drug entrapment efficiency, mechanical strength, and thermal stability, reduce initial burst release, and modulate drug release in both acidic and alkaline environments of gastrointestinal tract for water insoluble drug ACF-Na.

Conflict of Interests

The authors declare that they have no conflict of interests regarding this paper.

Acknowledgments

The authors thank Microlabs pharmaceuticals Ltd., Bangalore, for gift sample of aceclofenac sodium, Saint Priest Cedex, France, for providing the gift samples of Labrafac PG, Labrafil 2125 CS, and Labrasol, and Signet Chemical Corporation Pvt. Ltd., Mumbai, India, for providing a gift sample of sodium alginate. They are also thankful to the chairman and principal of TVM College of Pharmacy, Ballari, for giving the permission to conduct the research work with necessary facilities.

References

[1] K. Parfitt and W. Martindale, *Martindale. The Complete Drug Reference Part I: Anti-Inflammatory Drugs and Antipyretics*, Pharmaceutical Press, Philadelphia, Pa, USA, 32nd edition, 1996.

[2] D. Sharma, M. Soni, S. Kumar, and G. D. Gupta, "Solubility enhancement—eminent role in poorly soluble drugs," *Research Journal of Pharmacy and Technology*, vol. 2, no. 2, pp. 220–224, 2009.

[3] R. N. Gursoy and S. Benita, "Self-emulsifying drug delivery systems (SEDDS) for improved oral delivery of lipophilic drugs," *Biomedicine & Pharmacotherapy*, vol. 58, no. 3, pp. 173–182, 2004.

[4] A. A. Attama, I. T. Nzekwe, P. O. Nnamani, M. U. Adikwu, and C. O. Onugu, "The use of solid self-emulsifying systems in the delivery of diclofenac," *International Journal of Pharmaceutics*, vol. 262, no. 1-2, pp. 23–28, 2003.

[5] V. Agarwal, A. Siddiqui, H. Ali, and S. Nazzal, "Dissolution and powder flow characterization of solid self-emulsified drug delivery system (SEDDS)," *International Journal of Pharmaceutics*, vol. 366, no. 1-2, pp. 44–52, 2009.

[6] K. Kohli, S. Chopra, D. Dhar, S. Arora, and R. K. Khar, "Self-emulsifying drug delivery systems: an approach to enhance oral bioavailability," *Drug Discovery Today*, vol. 15, no. 21-22, pp. 958–965, 2010.

[7] C. M. Hentzschel, M. Alnaief, I. Smirnova, A. Sakmann, and C. S. Leopold, "Tableting properties of silica aerogel and other silicates," *Drug Development and Industrial Pharmacy*, vol. 38, no. 4, pp. 462–467, 2012.

[8] B. Tang, G. Cheng, J.-C. Gu, and C.-H. Xu, "Development of solid self-emulsifying drug delivery systems: preparation techniques and dosage forms," *Drug Discovery Today*, vol. 13, no. 13-14, pp. 606–612, 2008.

[9] T. Yi, J. Wan, H. Xu, and X. Yang, "A new solid self-micro emulsifying formulation prepared by spray-drying to improve the oral bioavailability of poorly water soluble drugs," *European Journal of Pharmaceutics and Biopharmaceutics*, vol. 70, no. 2, pp. 439–444, 2008.

[10] P. B. Deasy, "Microencapsulation and related drug process," in *Drugs and Pharmaceutical Science*, pp. 1–22, Marcel Dekker, New York, NY, USA, 2nd edition, 1984.

[11] H. H. Tønnesen and J. Karlsen, "Alginate in drug delivery systems," *Drug Development and Industrial Pharmacy*, vol. 28, no. 6, pp. 621–630, 2002.

[12] G. T. Grant, E. R. Morris, D. A. Rees, P. J. C. Smith, and D. Thom, "Biological interactions between polysaccharides and divalent cations: the egg-box model," *FEBS Letters*, vol. 32, no. 1, pp. 195–198, 1973.

[13] E. Josef, M. Zilberman, and H. Bianco-Peled, "Composite alginate hydrogels: an innovative approach for the controlled release of hydrophobic drugs," *Acta Biomaterialia*, vol. 6, no. 12, pp. 4642–4649, 2010.

[14] M. J. Fernández-Hervás, M. A. Holgado, A. Fini, and J. T. Fell, "In vitro evaluation of alginate beads of a diclofenac salt," *International Journal of Pharmaceutics*, vol. 163, no. 1-2, pp. 23–34, 1998.

[15] Fuji Chemical Industry, *Technical Newsletter*, Fuji Chemical Industry, 2007, http://www.neusilin.com/multicms/neusilin/pdf/news/29/2_neusilin_newsletter_nov07.pdf.

[16] S. G. Gumaste, S. A. Pawlak, D. M. Dalrymple, C. J. Nider, L. D. Trombetta, and A. T. M. Serajuddin, "Development of solid SEDDS, IV: effect of adsorbed lipid and surfactant on tableting properties and surface structures of different silicates," *Pharmaceutical Research*, vol. 30, no. 12, pp. 3170–3185, 2013.

[17] P. Balakrishnan, B.-J. Lee, D. H. Oh et al., "Enhanced oral bioavailability of dexibuprofen by a novel solid Self-emulsifying drug delivery system (SEDDS)," *European Journal of Pharmaceutics and Biopharmaceutics*, vol. 72, no. 3, pp. 539–545, 2009.

[18] M. K. Singh, V. Chandel, V. Gupta, and S. Ramteke, "Formulation development and characterization of microemulsion for topical delivery of Glipizide," *Der Pharmacia Lettre*, vol. 2, no. 3, pp. 33–42, 2010.

[19] B. K. Kang, J. S. Lee, S. K. Chon et al., "Development of self-microemulsifying drug delivery systems (SMEDDS) for oral bioavailability enhancement of simvastatin in beagle dogs," *International Journal of Pharmaceutics*, vol. 274, no. 1-2, pp. 65–73, 2004.

[20] V. Nekkanti, P. Karatgi, R. Prabhu, and R. Pillai, "Solid self-microemulsifying formulation for candesartan cilexetil," *AAPS PharmSciTech*, vol. 11, no. 1, pp. 9–17, 2010.

[21] M. J. Patel, N. M. Patel, R. B. Patel, and R. P. Patel, "Formulation and evaluation of self-microemulsifying drug delivery system of lovastatin," *Asian Journal of Pharmaceutical Sciences*, vol. 5, no. 6, pp. 266–275, 2010.

[22] M. Alfred, *Physical Pharmacy*, B.I. Waverly Private Limited, New Delhi, India, 4th edition, 1991.

[23] F. Edwards-Lévy and M.-C. Lévy, "Serum albumin-alginate coated beads: mechanical properties and stability," *Biomaterials*, vol. 20, no. 21, pp. 2069–2084, 1999.

[24] P. Trivedi, A. M. L. Verma, and N. Garud, "Preparation and characterization of aceclofenac microspheres," *Asian Journal of Pharmaceutics*, vol. 2, no. 2, pp. 110–115, 2008.

[25] P. T. Tayade and R. D. Kale, "Encapsulation of water-insoluble drug by a cross-linking technique: effect of process and formulation variables on encapsulation efficiency, particle size, and in vitro dissolution rate," *AAPS PharmSciTech*, vol. 6, no. 1, pp. 1–8, 2004.

[26] T. Østberg and C. Graffner, "Calcium alginate matrices for oral multiple unit administration. III. Influence of calcium concentration, amount of drug added and alginate characteristics on drug release," *International Journal of Pharmaceutics*, vol. 111, no. 3, pp. 271–282, 1994.

[27] P. Costa and J. M. Sousa Lobo, "Modeling and comparison of dissolution profiles," *European Journal of Pharmaceutical Sciences*, vol. 13, no. 2, pp. 123–133, 2001.

[28] C. Sartori, D. S. Finch, B. Ralph, and K. Gilding, "Determination of the cation content of alginate thin films by FTIR spectroscopy," *Polymer*, vol. 38, no. 1, pp. 43–51, 1997.

[29] Y. Murata, K. Tsumoto, K. Kofuji, and S. Kawashima, "Effects of natural polysaccharide addition on drug release from calcium-induced alginate gel beads," *Chemical and Pharmaceutical Bulletin*, vol. 51, no. 2, pp. 218–220, 2003.

[30] S. Puttipipatkhachorn, T. Pongjanyakul, and A. Priprem, "Molecular interaction in alginate beads reinforced with sodium starch glycolate or magnesium aluminum silicate, and their physical characteristics," *International Journal of Pharmaceutics*, vol. 293, no. 1-2, pp. 51–62, 2005.

[31] G. V. Joshi, B. D. Kevadiya, H. A. Patel, H. C. Bajaj, and R. V. Jasra, "Montmorillonite as a drug delivery system: intercalation and in vitro release of timolol maleate," *International Journal of Pharmaceutics*, vol. 374, no. 1-2, pp. 53–57, 2009.

[32] G. T. Kulkarni, K. Gowthamarajan, R. R. Dhobe et al., "Gums and mucilages," *Asian Journal of Pharmaceutical Sciences*, vol. 4, no. 5, pp. 309–323, 2009.

[33] R. S. Harland, C. Dubernet, J.-P. Benoit, and N. A. Peppas, "A model of dissolution-controlled, diffusional drug release from non-swellable polymeric microspheres," *Journal of Controlled Release*, vol. 7, no. 3, pp. 207–215, 1988.

17

Dry Powder Inhalers: A Focus on Advancements in Novel Drug Delivery Systems

Piyush Mehta

Dry Powder Inhaler Lab, Respiratory Formulations, Cipla R & D, LBS Road, Vikhroli (W), Mumbai, Maharashtra 400079, India

Correspondence should be addressed to Piyush Mehta; piyu053@gmail.com

Academic Editor: Ali Nokhodchi

Administration of drug molecules by inhalation route for treatment of respiratory diseases has the ability to deliver drugs, hormones, nucleic acids, steroids, proteins, and peptides, particularly to the site of action, improving the efficacy of the treatment and consequently lessening adverse effects of the treatment. Numerous inhalation delivery systems have been developed and studied to treat respiratory diseases such as asthma, COPD, and other pulmonary infections. The progress of disciplines such as biomaterials science, nanotechnology, particle engineering, molecular biology, and cell biology permits further improvement of the treatment capability. The present review analyzes modern therapeutic approaches of inhaled drugs with special emphasis on novel drug delivery system for treatment of various respiratory diseases.

1. Introduction

Development of inhalation technology for drug delivery has contributed immensely in treating various intrapulmonary and extrapulmonary diseases. This is supported by the lungs' unique geometry such as large surface area, thin alveolar epithelial lining, high vascularization, and avoidance of first-pass metabolism. Numerous inhalation delivery systems have been developed and studied to treat lung diseases such as asthma, COPD, and other pulmonary infections. Among them, three approaches, that is, nebulizers, pressurized metered-dose inhalers (pMDIs), and dry powder inhalers (DPI), are extensively scrutinized for the treatment of several lung diseases and pathological conditions. Each type of delivery has unique strengths and weaknesses in view of the class of drugs that can be applied, type of formulation that can be utilized, and the sum of respirable dose that can be delivered from devices. Utilization of nebulizers requires bulky compressors or a source of compressed air, while pMDIs have limitations such as sedimentation, crystal growth, and selection of appropriate propellant and they emit dosages at high velocity, which build deposition in the oropharynx most commonly where they are swallowed and enhance the risk of systemic absorption [1]. DPIs were introduced to defeat some of the weaknesses associated with nebulizers and pMDIs [2].

DPIs provide better physicochemical stability and deep lungs deposition using the patient's respiration. Additionally, they do not require cold chain storage or reconstitution of powders into solutions for nebulization [1, 2]. Lactose monohydrate is the most commonly used excipient (i.e., carrier) in DPI formulations. Mixtures of the lactose with drug are commonly described as ordered or interactive mixtures, which are simpler to handle during the manufacturing than micronized drug alone. The drug particles should loosely adhere to the lactose (carrier) particles and, during inhalation in the turbulent air stream which is produced, the drug particles detach from the lactose (carrier) particles and are made accessible for deposition into the lungs. The larger carrier particles normally impact the oropharyngeal region. The carrier also offers mass to the DPIs, which enhances the handling, dispensing, and actuation of the micronized drug, which is of actual significance for low dose DPIs such as steroids (typical dose per actuation: 50 μg to 500 μg) [3, 4]. In order to confirm effective delivery of drug, it is crucial that adhesive forces between the drug and carrier are not so strong that separation from the carrier is prohibited. The equilibrium between adhesive and cohesive forces should be in tune to confirm sufficient adhesion between drug and carrier so as to provide a stable formulation (homogeneous blend with good content uniformity) but with adequate detachment of drug from carrier on inhalation. It has been recognized that the efficiency of a DPI formulation is greatly dependent on the particle size distribution, fine-lactose content, lactose source, the inhalation flow rate, and dispersion capacity of the respective DPI device [3].

With the growth of disciplines such as biomaterials and materials science, nanotechnology, particle engineering, molecular biology, and cell biology have gotten rapid development in field of novel drug delivery systems (NDDS). These NDDS in the field of western medicine have been extensively studied and applied clinically. The development of NDDS based DPIs has the potential to overcome issues associated with carrier as a critical component of the formulation. Moreover, they are expected to accomplish various key requisites like aerosolization properties of the formulation, physicochemical characteristics of powder, stability, biocompatibility, and biodegradation without any adverse effect. Conservative delivery systems are unable to meet these demands. Developing various novel drug delivery systems, for instance, liposomes, solid lipid nanoparticles, polymeric nanoparticles, nanoaggregates, nanocomposites, polymeric microparticles, and microspheres, has offered a number of advantages for traditional dry powder inhaler, including physical and chemical stability, flow properties, dispersion, tissue distribution, and bioavailability. Several potential DPIs have been successfully delivered using NDDS approach. Therefore, in this article, an attempt has been made to touch upon different aspects related to the development of novel drug delivery systems including their impact on drug dispersion and disposition and other physicochemical properties are discussed in detail. This review offers a perspective on current reported studies to modify pulmonary deliveries for its better functioning.

2. Novel Drug Delivery System for DPI

2.1. Lipid Vesicles

2.1.1. Liposomes. Liposomes are typically self-enclosed small spherical arrangement composed of a single bilayer lipid membrane (unilamellar liposomes) or several bilayer lipid membranes (multilamellar liposomes) with a size range of 50 to 1000 nm. They have various functions ranging from drug delivery to food carrier [5]. They help improve the solubility, bioavailability, in vitro and in vivo stability, targeted delivery, and sustained release and, moreover, have ability to enhance the intracellular uptake of drug components and biodistribution pattern with protecting the encapsulated agent from the destructive action of the external environment [6]. Literature showed that numerous inhaled liposomal products are in various stages of clinical trials [7]. Site-specificity, biodegradability, biocompatibility, good safety profile, and potential to enclose both hydrophobic and hydrophilic particles are the prime reasons to choose liposomes in pharmaceutical industries [8].

Liposomes are widely scrutinized as vehicle for the dry powder inhalation delivery of various drugs for treatment of several diseases and pathological conditions. They can be easily aerosolized and provide prolonged retention of carriers and drugs in the respiratory track [22]. Liposomes seem mostly suitable for delivery of drugs to the lungs as they can be prepared from substances endogenous to the lung as elements of lung surfactant. Lung surfactant is a complex mixture, of which about 85% is phospholipid, generally dipalmitoyl phosphatidylcholine (DPPC), with phosphatidylglycerol as the next most widespread phospholipid. Surfactant is also composed of cholesterol and two groups of nonserum proteins which are believed to be important in the adsorption, spreading, and reutilization of surfactant. The mechanisms for the clearance and reutilization of lung surfactant are likely to be of major importance in determining the fate of liposomes deposited in the alveoli. The rate and extent of pulmonary uptake of liposomes are a function of their composition; significantly faster rates occur when liposomes contain phosphatidylglycerol [23]. In most cases, no considerable undesirable side effects were observed after the application of neutral or slightly negatively charged liposomes, though cationic liposomes were found to be toxic to human cells and potentially can introduce genetic aberrations [24]. Besides, adverse side effects of cationic liposomes considerably increased with an increase of positive charge of the particles. Still, because cationic liposomes normally are used for the formation of almost neutral complexes with negatively charged nucleic acids, such modification of cationic carriers usually prevents adverse effects on the cells [24]. Various investigations on liposomal formulations of inhaled drugs are listed in Table 1.

2.1.2. Proliposomes. Proliposomes are described as dry, free-flowing microparticles with a dispersed system which can easily form a liposomal vesicle when in contact with water or biological fluids. Simply, powdered drugs are prepared by the adsorption of phospholipids and drug moiety onto the microporous matrix of carrier particles [37]. Compared with conventional liposomes, proliposomes display more advantages in stability, drug release, and solubility [21]. Therefore, proliposomes would be a potential medium to enhance oral absorption of hydrophobic drugs. The primary mechanism allowing proliposomes to improve oral absorption might be partially explained by the presence of bile salts, which can interact with phospholipids in the gastrointestinal tract to construct mixed micelles for medium to augment the solubility of hydrophobic drugs [38]. Various investigations on proliposomal formulations of inhaled drugs are listed in Table 1.

2.1.3. Lipospheres. Lipospheres are also typically self-enclosed small spherical arrangement composed of water dispersible solid microparticles of particle size between 0.2 and 100 μm in diameter and a solid hydrophobic fat core stabilized by one monolayer of phospholipid molecules embedded in their surface. Due to their solid lipid matrix, controlled release from these carriers is achievable which is essential to provide the drug over a prolonged period of time with improved bioavailability and physicochemical stability [42].

Cyclosporine A (CsA) lipospheres based DPI was formulated using dipalmitoylphosphatidylcholine (DPPC) and dipalmitoylphosphatidylglycerol (DPPG) (75 : 25) phospholipids by spray drying method. Aerosol dispersion pattern

TABLE 1: Liposomes, nanoliposomes, and proliposomes inhaled formulation along with the key findings.

Drug	Method of preparation	Major ingredient	Assembly, device, capsules, and flow rate (L/min)	Percentage of FPF	Reference
		Liposomes			
Amikacin sulfate	RPE followed by LP	HSPC, CS, and stearylamine	TSI, Rotahaler®, #2, and 60	29.2 ± 2.10	[9]
Budesonide	TFH followed by LP and BM	Egg phosphatidylcholine, CS, and α-tocopherol	TSI, Rotahaler, #2, and 60	20.69 ± 1.50	[10]
Dapsone	TFE followed by SD	DPPC, CS, and hydrolyzed gelatin	ACI, #2 HPMC, and 28.3	75.6 ± 1.60	[11]
Gemcitabine hydrochloride	SE followed by LP	HSPC, DSPG, $mPEG_{2000}$-DSPE, and trehalose	ACI, #3 gelatin, and 60	56.12 ± 4.38	[12]
Ketotifen fumarate	TFH followed by FD	Saturated egg phosphatidylcholine, CS, and sucrose	TSI, #2, and 60 for 5 sec	21.59 ± 1.53	[13]
N-Acetylcysteine	RPE followed by SD	Phospholipid and CS	ACI, HandiHaler®, #3 gelatin, and 28.3 for 8.5 sec	35.34 ± 3.86	[14]
Recombinant secretory leukocyte protease inhibitor (rSLPI)	RE followed by LP and JM	1,2-Dioleoyl-sn-glycero-3-[phospho-L-serine] and CS	TSI, Spinhaler®, #2 gelatin, and 60	59.5 ± 5.40	[15]
Rifampicin	TFE, coated with chitosan and carrageenan, followed by SD	SPC, HSPC, and CS	NGI, Turbospin®, #2 gelatin, and 70	51.1 ± 2.30	[16]
Salbutamol sulfate	Vesicular phospholipid gel technique followed by LP and BM	SPC	TSI, Spinhaler, #2, and 60	41.51 ± 2.22	[17]
		Nanoliposomes			
Amiloride hydrochloride	TFH and then passed through HPH, followed by SD	HSPC, CS, and mannitol	ACI, Rotahaler, #2 gelatin, and 28.3	67.6 ± 0.60	[18]
Tacrolimus	TFE and then passed through HPH, followed by SD	HPC and CS	ACI, #2 HPMC, and 28.3	71.1 ± 2.5	[19]
		Proliposomes			
Isoniazid	SD	L-α-soybean phosphatidylcholine, CS, and 90% mannitol	ACI and 60	71 ± 2.0	[20]
Rifapentine	SD	HSPC and stearylamine	ACI, #2 gelatin, and 60 for 4 sec	92.5 ± 1.5	[21]

SD: spray drying; FD: freeze drying; LP: lyophilization; RE: rotary evaporation; TFH: thin film hydration; HPH: high pressure homogenizer; CS: cholesterol; SPC: soybean phosphatidylcholine; HPC: hydrogenated phosphatidylcholine; HSPC: hydrogenated soy phosphatidylcholine; DPPC: dipalmitoyl phosphatidylcholine.

was determined using a next generation impactor (NGI) with a HandiHaler device at 60 L/min using #3 HPMC capsules. The percentage of fine particle fraction (FPF), mass median aerodynamic diameter (MMAD), and geometric standard deviation (GSD) was found to be 52.99 ± 4.12%, 2.79 ± 0.47 μm, and 1.85 ± 0.05, respectively. In summary, compared to drug alone prepared co-SD CsA, DPPC/DPPG lipospheres displayed better physicochemical properties and aerosol dispersion with very low residual water content [63]. Singh et al. investigated the rifampicin loaded phospholipid lipospheres containing sulfphobutyl ether, β-cyclodextrin, and Vit. C formulated using spray drying technique. Prepared amorphous lipospheres showed spherical morphology with the size range of 1–5 μm. Aerosol dispersion pattern was concluded using Andersen cascade impactor (ACI) with device operating at 28.3 L/min using #3 HPMC capsules. The FPF and emitted dose (ED) were found to be 52.99 ± 4.12% and 85.40 ± 1.04%, respectively. Moreover, prepared lipospheres exhibited approximately ~2-fold improvement in antimycobacterial activity over MTB $H_{37}Rv$ strain compared to drug alone. Improvement in antimycobacterial activity may be attributed to the cyclodextrin-cholesterol matrix structure [64].

2.1.4. Lipid-Coated Particles. Liposomes, proliposomes, and lipospheres have been the platform of choice for pulmonary drug delivery applications over the past decade. However, extensive investigation has revealed their restrictions as drug delivery carriers. They have limitations. For instance, phospholipid may sometimes undergo oxidation and hydrolysis like reaction, short half-life, and poor mechanical stability due to leakage and fusion of the formulation [70]. To overcome these limitations, a hybrid class of lipid-coated particles has received good attention in recent years. Lipid coating offers better stability and higher encapsulation efficiency than liposomes. The existence of a low lipid coating level permits the preparation of powders with few excipients, thereby delivering more drug to the lungs. Additionally, the hydrophobic nature of neutral lipids (cholesterol) decreases the absorption of the ubiquitous vapor, leading to lessening the aggregation and the adhesion of particles [71].

Tobramycin lipid-coated particles were prepared using mixtures of cholesterol and phospholipids (75 : 25) by spray drying technique. Developed lipid-coated particles showed small, smooth surface properties and good flowability with a mean size of about 1-2 mm. Aerosol dispersion pattern was determined using a multistage liquid impinger (MSLI) with a Cyclohaler® device at 100 L/min for 2.4 s using #3 HPMC capsules containing 15 mg of tobramycin lipid-coated particles. The FPF of prepared lipid-coated particles was found to be 68% with approximately ~1.5-fold improvement in FPF compared to uncoated micronized tobramycin particles. Developed lipid-coated tobramycin DPI formulations required very low amount of excipient and produce better lung deposition. These formulations are mostly useful for drugs that are active at relatively high doses, for example, antibiotics, since they allow the delivery of a high concentration of antibiotic directly to the site of action while minimizing systemic exposure [71].

2.2. Nanoparticulate System. Nanoparticles are solid, colloidal particles comprising macromolecular materials that differ in size from 10 nm to 1000 nm in which the drug moiety is dissolved, encapsulated, and entrapped and/or to which the drug moiety is adsorbed, embedded, or attached, which can be administered in fluid form with a liquid carrier. A wide variety of delivery systems includes nanoparticles, polymeric nanoparticles, polymeric micelles, solid lipid nanoparticles (SLNs), nanostructured lipid carriers (NLCs), nanocapsules, nanospheres, nanoemulsion, and many more. They have the capacity to modulate both the pharmacokinetic and pharmacodynamic properties of drugs, thereby improving their therapeutic index. Nanoparticles help modify the biodistribution, in vivo stability, bioavailability, and penetration through biological barriers. Moreover, they also provide controlled and targeted drug release [81–83].

Inhalable nanoparticles are advantageous for the objective of improving the solubility, dissolution profiles, and pharmacokinetic profile and reducing premature mucociliary clearance of hydrophobic drugs [84]. The size, shape, and composition of nanoparticles are key features which determine their percentage retention and targeting properties [22]. Inhaled nanoparticles could be easily exhaled during administration due to their small diameter ($\ll$1 μm) and low inertia. Nanonization often conveys an enormous increase in Gibb's free energy due to the increase in surface area. Moreover, these particles have tendency to grow due to Ostwald ripening and can suffer from uninhibited agglomeration [85–88]. This issue has been resolved by transforming nanoparticles into inhalable microaggregates via numerous techniques like spray drying and spray freeze drying or with leucine, mannitol, and PVA as matrix components [89, 90]. Spray freeze dried microaggregates exhibited superior aerosolization performance compared to those produced by spray drying and this was credited to the porous structure and low density of the particles [91–93]. Various investigations on nanoparticulate formulations of inhaled drugs are listed in Table 2.

2.2.1. Solid Lipid Nanoparticles and Nanostructured Lipid Carriers. SLNs are the first generation of lipid nanoparticles. They are colloidal carriers made up of physiologically tolerated lipids components that remain solid at body and room temperature with mean diameter of 40 to 1000 nm [94]. Generally, SLNs are made up of 0.1–30% (w/w) lipid dispersed in an aqueous solution of 0.5–5% (w/w) surfactant as stabilizing agent. SLNs provide different advantage like physicochemical stability, protection of the incorporated drug from degradation, prolonged/sustained release profile with pseudo-zero-order kinetics, and low cytotoxicity, if well tolerated excipients are used [95, 96]. SLNs have disadvantages like low drug loading capacity and drug expulsion during storage. Drug expulsion takes place when the low ordered lipid modification of the particle matrix after manufacturing switches to the highly ordered β-modification during storage. The β-modification is characterized by a perfect crystal lattice with few imperfections and hence little room for drug accommodation. To defeat these SLNs related issues, the second generation of lipid nanoparticles, nanostructured lipid carriers, was developed [97]. NLCs are a delivery system

Table 2: Example of nanoparticulate inhaled formulation along with the key findings.

Drug	Method of preparation	Major ingredient	Assembly, device, capsules, and flow rate (L/min)	Percentage of FPF	Reference
			Nanoparticles		
Carvedilol	Antisolvent precipitation-ultrasonication followed by LP.	Pluronic F-127, sodium deoxycholate, and mannitol	ACI, Aerolizer®, #3, and 60 for 4 sec	81.90 ± 4.30	[25]
Calcium-disodium EDTA	Antisolvent precipitation followed by SD	Calcium-disodium EDTA and PVA	ACI, HPMC, and 60 for 5 Sec	67.35 ± 2.27	[26]
Salmon calcitonin	Ionic gelation method followed by SD	Sodium tripolyphosphate, chitosan, and Mannitol	ACI, glass inhaler device, and 60	63.50	[27]
			Nanoparticle agglomerates		
Budesonide	Antisolvent precipitation-ultrasonication followed by LP	Lecithin, cetyl alcohol, L-leucine, PVP, and Span 85	ACI and 60	95.9 ± 1.5	[28]
Levofloxacin	Emulsification solvent-evaporation method followed by SFD	Polycaprolactone, mannitol, and leucine	NGI, powder entrainment tube, and 85	30.00	[29]
Fluticasone propionate and albuterol sulfate (2 : 1 w/w)	Antisolvent precipitation followed by precipitation and homogenization	Lecithin, cetyl alcohol, L-leucine, PVP-K90, and Pluronic F-127	ACI, #3 gelatin, and 28.3 for 4 Sec	Fluticasone propionate, 84 ± 7, and albuterol sulfate, 70 ± 3	[30]
Theophylline (nanorods agglomerates)	Antisolvent precipitation-ultrasonication followed by LP	Stearic acid	ACI, Aerolizer, and 60	81.9 ± 4.30	[31]
			Microparticulate/nanoparticulate systems		
Azithromycin	co-SD	Methanol	NGI, HandiHaler, #3 HPMC, and 60 for 10 sec	53.45 ± 3.60	[32]
Paclitaxel	co-SD	DPPC and DPPG	NGI, HandiHaler, #3 HPMC, and 60 for 10 sec	86.7 ± 2.60	[33]
Paclitaxel	co-SD	DPPC and DPPE-PEG	NGI, HandiHaler, #3 HPMC, and 60 for 10 sec	77.9 ± 7.00	[34]
Tobramycin	co-SD	Methanol	NGI, HandiHaler, #3 HPMC, and 60 for 10 sec	28.48 ± 3.39	[32]
Tobramycin	Emulsion diffusion followed by co-SD	PLGA and PVA	MSLI, Turbospin, and gelatin	52 ± 1.00	[35]
Sodium cromoglicate	Liquid antisolvent precipitation followed by immediate SD	Deionized water	MSLI, monodose inhaler device, #3 HPMC, and 60	62.02 ± 2.12	[36]

SD: spray drying; co-SD: closed spray drying; FD: freeze drying; SFD: spray freeze drying; LP: lyophilization; PLGA: poly(lactic-co-glycolic acid); PVA: poly(vinyl alcohol); PVP: polyvinylpyrrolidone; DPPC: dipalmitoyl phosphatidylcholine; DPPG: dipalmitoylphosphatidylglycerol.

in which partial-crystallized lipid particles with mean particle size ≤100 nm are dispersed in an aqueous phase containing emulsifier(s). NLCs have a solid lipid matrix at room and body temperature which is composed of a mixture of a solid lipid and oil, preferable in a ratio of 70 : 30 up to a ratio of 99.9 : 0.1. Through mixing different kinds of lipids, a less ordered lipid matrix with high drug loading capacity for drugs is achieved [95].

Moreover, due to their controlled size, nanoparticles can be easily aerosolized into droplets with aerodynamically suitable properties, which permits adequate deep lung deposition of a drug. Furthermore, particle adhesion, accumulation, and retention in the pulmonary region as well as controlled release properties of SLNs and NLCs may lead to improved and sustained therapeutic outcomes, resulting in a longer dosing interval and better patient compliance [95, 98]. Considering these unique functionalities, researchers have developed several SLNs and NLCs based DPI formulations to enhance the therapeutic efficacy of inhaled drug molecules (Table 3).

2.3. Microparticulate System. The expression "microparticle" in drug delivery is usually designated to a particle with one or several micrometers in dimension. Based upon the method of preparation, the drug is entrapped, encapsulated, or simply dissolved to the microparticle template. Microparticle matrix contains many materials like polymers, ceramics, metals, and glass. This system is believed and accepted as a steady means to deliver the drugs to the target site with specificity [57]. Various delivery approaches involve microparticles, microspheres, solid lipid microparticles, polymeric microparticles [58, 99], surface coated microparticles [61], and so forth. In clinical practices, microparticles appreciably influence retention in the lungs and targeting properties of therapeutic agent, apart from the fact that active targeting microparticles also offer numerous advantages like masking, facilitation of handling, controlled dissolution profile, and protection [100]. Various investigations on microparticulate formulations of inhaled drugs are listed in Table 4.

2.3.1. Microsphere. Microspheres are microparticles of spherical shape without membrane or any distinct outer layer. They are small solid spherical particles made up of various natural and synthetic materials with mean diameter of 1 to 1000 μm. Microspheres may release drug at controlled rates for long periods of time. Microspheres are ideal vehicles for many controlled delivery applications due to their ability to encapsulate a variety of drugs, biocompatibility, high bioavailability, and prolonged/sustained drug release characteristics. Such techniques also offer various benefits over conventional methods of drug delivery, including protection of fragile drugs, tailoring of drug release rates, and increased patient comfort and compliance. Polymethyl methacrylate, acrolein, glycidyl methacrylate, lactides, poly(alkyl cyanoacrylate), polyanhydrides, poly(D, L-lactic-co-glycolic acid) and chitosan, poly(acryl) dextran, poly(acryl) starch, carrageenan, and gelatin are the commonly used polymeric agents for microspheres synthesis [101]. Microspheres based DPI formulations are listed in Table 5.

2.3.2. Mucoadhesive Microparticles. Mucoadhesion can be defined as the interaction of molecules with the mucous layer (biological tissue) in order to adhere to each other. Mucoadhesion techniques have received a good attention, in drug delivery system, due to their two prime requisites. First, they increase mean residence time of therapeutic agent. Second, they uphold a high concentration gradient of drug molecule across the epithelium. Mucoadhesion occurs via several mechanisms such as chain interlocking, diffusion, and chemical reaction (hydrogen bonding) [102]. These mucoadhesive agents are usually high molecular weight polymers which can interact with the mucin layer of the respiratory epithelium due to hydrogen bonding and electrostatic, hydrophobic, or van der Waals interactions. Chitosan, carbomer, poly(lactic acid), poly(D,L-lactic-co-glycolic acid), hydroxypropyl cellulose, and sodium carboxy methylcellulose are the commonly used mucoadhesive agents for inhalation drug delivery. The incorporation of therapeutic agents into these polymeric matrices regulates the drug pharmacokinetics by improving lung mean residence time. Even though the idea of mucoadhesion at the upper respiratory tract has been broadly studied, application to the lower respiratory tract has not been explored [103].

M. Mishra and B. Mishra formulated the doxycycline hyclate mucoadhesive microparticles using sodium carboxy methyl cellulose as mucoadhesive agents by spray drying technique. Developed microparticles showed moderately dimpled but spherical shape (1–5 μm) with 56.27% yield, 83.74 ± 2.31% encapsulation efficiency, and 4.16 ± 0.52% water content. Aerosol dispersion was examined using ACI with monodose inhaler device at flow rate of 60 L/min for 4 sec using #2 gelatin capsules. ACI analysis suggested good dispersion and deposition with the FPF, ED, and MMAD of 55.5 ± 4.2%, 80.2 ± 0.4, and 4.56 ± 0.10, respectively. Drug release from these mucoadhesive microparticles showed biphasic Fickian type of diffusion. Moreover, prepared microparticles exhibited good output in MTT assay on H1299 mammalian alveolar cells. Doxycycline hyclate containing sodium carboxy methyl cellulose mucoadhesive microparticles would be helpful dosage form for clinical treatment of respiratory infections with minimal adverse side effects [103]. Mucoadhesive beclomethasone dipropionate (BDP) microspheres for powder inhalation were formulated using hydroxypropyl cellulose (HPC) mucoadhesive polymer (1 : 4) by spray drying technique. This resulted in amorphous (aBDP/HPC) and crystalline (cBDP/HPC) microspheres with mean particle size of 2.5–2.9 μm. BDP's aqueous solubility was improved 25 times for aBDP/HPC, compared to cBDP/HPC. In antigen-induced asthmatic Guinea pigs, aBDP/HPC showed quick BDP absorption from the lungs (≥95% absorption for 180 min) with a greater metabolite (B17MP) formation, compared to cBDP/HPC, mainly due to the improved dissolution of aBDP/HPC. In contrast, 86.0% of BDP remained at 180 min following cBDP/HPC administration, indicating the prolonged retention of BDP in the lungs by virtue of poor dissolution (release) and delayed mucociliary clearance. cBDP (1.37 mg/kg) alone considerably inhibited eosinophil infiltration into the lungs of antigen sensitized and challenged Guinea pigs for only 1–6 h and at much lower drug dosage

Table 3: SLN and NLC based DPI formulations.

Drug	Method of preparation	Major ingredient	Assembly, device, capsules, and flow rate (L/min)	Percentage of FPF	Reference
Solid lipid nanoparticles					
Thymopentin	Double emulsion technique followed by co-SD	Glyceryl monostearate and SPC (1 : 1, w/w), poloxamer 188, mannitol, and leucine	TSI, #3 HPMC, and 60 for 10 sec	51.07 ± 1.21	[39]
Nanostructured lipid carriers					
Montelukast	Melt emulsification-homogenization followed by LP	Precirol ATO5, Capryol-90, and mannitol	ACI, Rotahaler, #3 gelatin, and 60 for 4 sec	90.22 ± 2.60	[40]
Rosuvastatin	Melt-emulsification and ultrasonication followed by LP	Lauric acid, Capryol-90, mannitol, and L-leucine	ACI, Rotahaler, #3 gelatin, and 60	91.25 ± 3.57	[41]

co-SD: closed spray drying; LP: lyophilization; SPC: soybean phosphatidylcholine.

TABLE 4: Example of microparticulate inhaled formulation along with the key findings.

Drug	Method of preparation	Major ingredient	Assembly, device and capsules, flow rate (L/min)	Percentage of FPF	Reference
		Microparticles			
Budesonide	SD	Lactohale 300 M : Pharmatose® 150 M (60 : 40)	ACI, Rotahaler, #3 HPMC, and 60 for 4 sec	34.50	[43]
Ciprofloxacin	co-SD	Mannitol	MSLI, Aerolizer, and 60 for 4 sec	43.5 ± 1.50	[44]
Ciclosporin	SFD	Tert-butyl alcohol and mannitol (5%)	ACI, Jethaler®, #2 HPMC, and 28.3 for 5 sec	36.4 ± 1.40	[45]
Dexamethasone	Vibrational SD	PCL and sodium deoxycholate	ACI, Aerolizer, #3 HPMC, and 28.3 for 8.5 sec	61.68 ± 1.28	[46]
Naringin	SD	Water-ethanol	TSI, Turbospin, #2 gelatin, and 60 for 5 sec	44.5 ± 1.54	[47]
Rifampicin	SD	Chitosan, ascorbic acid, and leucine	ACI, HPMC, and 60 for 10 sec	47.29	[48]
Rifampicin	SD	Dextran (Dex) and stearylamine grafted dextran	ACI and 60	77.51	[49]
Rifampicin	SD	Water : dichloromethane 80 : 20	ACI, Spinhaler, and 60 for 4 sec	58.00	[50]
Shuang-Huang-Lian corrugated particles	SD	D-Mannitol, lactose, and L-leucine	NGI, Cyclohaler®, #3 gelatin, and 60 for 4 sec	36.8 ± 1.90	[51]
Terbutaline sulfate	SD	L-leucine and low molecular wt. chitosan	MSLI, Spinhaler, #2 HPMC, and 60 for 2.5 sec	75.83 ± 2.59	[52]
Voriconazole	SD	Polylactide	ACI and RS01 dry powder inhaler	43.56 ± 0.13	[53]
		Solid lipid microparticles			
Salbutamol sulfate	SD	DPPC, CS, and L-leucine	TSI, Cyclohaler, gelatin, and 60 for 4 sec	42.70	[54]
Quercetin	O/W emulsification via a phase inversion technique followed by SD	Tristearin and phosphatidylcholine	NGI, Aerolizer, #3 gelatin, and 60 for 4 sec	20.5 ± 3.30	[55]
Budesonide	O/W emulsification via a phase inversion technique followed by SD	Pluronic F-68 and Compritol 888	MSLI, Aerolizer, #3 HPMC, and 60 for 4 sec	21.1 ± 0.60	[56]
		Biopolymer based microparticles			
Budesonide	Cation induced gelation method followed by LP	Sodium alginate, deacetylated chitosan, Pluronic F-68, and mannitol	ACI, Rotahaler, #3 HPMC, and 60 for 5 sec	60.09 ± 0.01	[57]
Budesonide	Cation induced gelation method followed by LP	Sodium alginate, deacetylated chitosan, Pluronic F-68, and mannitol	ACI, Rotahaler, #3 HPMC, and 60 for 5 sec	56.18 ± 0.01	[58]
		Miscellaneous microparticles			
Beclomethasone dipropionate ultrafine particles	Microfluidic antisolvent precipitation followed by homogenization and SD	NA	MSLI, Aerolizer, #3 HPMC, and 60 for 4 sec	68.39	[59]
Salbutamol sulphate sonocrystallized microparticles	Ultrasonication	Isopropyl alcohol	ACI, Rotahaler, gelatin, and 28.3 for 10 sec	44.21 ± 1.30	[60]
Salbutamol sulfate	Mechanofusion Process (dry coating processes)	MgSt	TSI, monodose inhaler device, #3 HPMC, and 60 for 4 sec	75.4 ± 1.00	[61]
B-Estradiol	SD	Lactose and leucine (6% w/w)	ACI, Spinhaler, #2 gelatin, and 60 TSI, Spinhaler, #2 gelatin, and 60	73.4 ± 1.00 85.0 ± 0.50	[62]

SD: spray drying; co-SD: closed spray drying; SFD: spray freeze drying; LP: lyophilization; PCL: poly(ε-caprolactone); CS: cholesterol; DPPC: dipalmitoyl phosphatidylcholine; MgSt: magnesium stearate.

TABLE 5: Microspheres inhaled formulation along with their key findings.

Drug	Method of preparation	Major ingredient	Assembly, device, capsules, and flow rate (L/min)	Percentage of FPF	Reference
		Microspheres			
Levofloxacin	SD	Chitosan and glutaric acid	NGI, HandiHaler, #3 gelatin, and 60 for 4 sec	32.3 ± 4.0	[65]
Montelukast sodium	SD	Xyloglucan	ACI, Rotahaler, HPMC, and 60 for 4 sec	43.8	[66]
Rifampicin	SE followed by FD	PLGA	NGI and 30 for 10 sec	52.00	[67]
Salbutamol sulfate	RE	Salbutamol sulfate coated by 2% MgSt, polycaprolactone, and PVA	TSI, Rotahaler, #3 gelatin, and 60	15.8 ± 1.5	[68]
Cisplatin	Emulsification and ionotropic gelation method	Chitosan	TSI, Rotahaler, #3 HPMC, and 60	34.4 ± 2.4	[69]

SD: spray drying; FD: freeze drying; RE: rotary evaporation; SE: solvent evaporation; PLGA: poly(lactic-co-glycolic acid); MgSt: magnesium stearate; PVA: poly(vinyl alcohol).

of cBDP/HPC (0.25 mg/kg) was capable of maintaining such inhibitory effects for 24 h following administration. The prolonged lung retention of BDP by the use of the cBDP/HPC microspheres was credited to prolonging its pharmacological duration without requiring increased drug dosage [104].

2.4. Solid Dispersions. Solid dispersions are one of the known approaches to improve drug solubility and release profile of poorly water-soluble drugs. It is a molecular mixture of drug in hydrophilic polymer wherein the drug physicochemical characteristics are regulated by the polymer properties [105]. Here, the drug dissolution profile may be enhanced by reducing the drug particle size to nearly a molecular level and by transforming the drug crystalline state to create a complete or partially amorphous state, both of which may improve drug solubility and bioavailability [106]. Commonly used polymers in formulation of solid dispersions are cyclodextrin, hydroxy propyl methylcellulose, hydroxy propyl cellulose, ethyl cellulose, silica, povidone, starch, and polyethylene glycols [107]. Solid dispersions act as a flexible platform for novel drug delivery systems.

Itraconazole (ITZ) SD based DPI was formulated using polymeric surfactant, that is, TPGS and hydrophilic agent, and mannitol by spray drying method. Prepared ITZ-SD-DPI compared with ITZ-SD-DPI without TPGS and bulk ITZ. ITZ-SD produced an improved dissolution rate and greater saturation solubility than bulk ITZ. The use of a polymeric surfactant (TPGS) was helpful in terms of solubility and dissolution profile but it also reduced FPF (47 ± 2% to 37.2 ± 0.4%). Additionally, device and capsule retention of ITZ-SD-DPI was significantly reduced when TPSG was used into the formulations. This may be due to lubricant effect of TPGS which improved device and capsule emptying by reducing the surface interaction and greater particle cohesion. Mannitol solid dispersions with optimized quantity polymeric surfactant may provide an effective platform for poorly soluble active ingredients DPI [108]. Cyclosporine A (CsA) amorphous solid dispersion was prepared by using wet-milling technique (WM/CsA) and jet milled with coarse lactose (Respitose SV003) to obtain desired aerodynamic particle size. WM/CsA-DPI exhibits the better dissolution profile as compared to pure CsA. Aerosol dispersion was examined using ACI with Jethaler device operating at a flow rate of 28.3 L/min. ACI analysis recommended good dispersion and deposition in the respiratory organs with the FPF and ED of 54 and 96%, respectively. Moreover, intratracheal administration of WM/CsA (100 μg CsA) in experimental animals led to 85 and 71% reduction of granulocyte recruitment in lung tissues and bronchoalveolar lavage fluids. In comparison to a commercially available CsA oral formulation, WM/CsA showed 10^2-fold reduction in AUC and Cmax values of plasma CsA at toxic concentration (10 mg/kg). WM/CsA-DPI would be effective dosage form for clinical treatment of airway inflammations with minimal systemic side effects [109]. Δ^9-Tetrahydrocannabinol solid dispersion was formulated using inulin in a mixture of tertiary butanol and water by spray freeze drying technique. Prepared formulation contains highly porous particles with specific surface area of 90 m^2/g. In vitro deposition of the powder formulations was determined with MSLI at flow rate of 60 L/min for 3 sec. FPF was found to be 50% for prepared formulation [110].

2.5. Thin Film Freezing. The particle engineering process, thin film freezing (TFF), has ability to produce low density pharmaceutical powders with a porous, matrix structure. In TFH, the particle morphology can be controlled by influencing the fluid dynamics and heat transfer characteristics upon spreading and freezing of liquid droplets on solid surfaces. When stabilizing excipients with high glass transition temperatures, for instance, PVP or HPMC, are incorporated in the formulation, the pharmaceutical powders can be turned into amorphous ones. These low density TFF developed powders have also been shown to be highly respirable when aerosolized with a marketed inhaler [111, 112].

Microstructured crystalline voriconazole (VRC) and nanostructured amorphous TFF-VRC particles [PVP K25 (1 : 3)] were formulated using thin film freezing technique. The prepared microstructured crystalline VRC and nanostructured amorphous VRC particles showed particle size of 0.45 μm and 0.05 μm, respectively. Powder dispersion was examined using NGI with single dose capsule based HandiHaler device operating at a flow rate of 60 L/min. NGI analysis showed better dispersion and deposition pattern for microstructured crystalline VRC (% FPF 37.80) compared to nanostructured amorphous VRC (% FPF: 32.40) particles. Microstructured crystalline VRC particles also showed approximately ~2-fold improvement in % FPF in comparison to micronized VRC with InhaLac® 70 (2% w/w). Moreover, in single dose 24 h pharmacokinetic studies (10 mg/kg) microstructured crystalline VRC particles showed 2.06-fold improvement in $AUC_{(0-24\,h)}$ of plasma compared to nanostructured amorphous VRC particles [111]. Similarly, an amorphous dry powder of tacrolimus (TAC) was prepared using thin film freezing technique. Aerosol dispersion of TFF-processed powder was performed using Miat® monodose inhaler device. TFF-processed TAC dry powder showed FPF and MMAD of 83.30% and 2.26 μm respectively. Although being of relatively large geometric size, the TFF-processed dry powder was capable of attaining deep lung due to its low density, highly porous, and brittle characteristics compared to a crystalline micronized TAC powder produced by milling technique. Additionally, in single dose 24 h pharmacokinetic study, TFF-processed powder showed better pulmonary bioavailability with prolonged retention time compared to a crystalline micronized TAC [112].

3. Protein, Peptides, and Vaccine Delivery

Numerous therapeutic proteins and peptides have been used for long time in routine clinical practice. These include insulin, human growth hormone (hGH), calcitonin, and parathyroid for treatment of diabetes, hormone deficiency, and osteoporosis, respectively. Due to recent advance in biochemical sciences and in the knowing of the physiopathology of many disorders, therapeutic biomolecules are likely to become of increasing significance. Pulmonary delivery of these proteins and peptides could compose an alternative to systemic delivery. In fact, direct administration to the lungs for local action allows high doses of protein and peptides to be distributed while preventing systemic adverse effects [113]. Another budding use of inhaled proteins and peptides is vaccination, as most antigens are macromolecules. Parenteral drug delivery is usually helpful in preventing systemic infections, but it fails to avoid the early interaction of pathogen and host and continual colonization at the mucosal surface. Mucosal immunization is the local and direct release of antigen to a mucosal surface to stimulate specific immunity versus an attacking pathogen. It has the ability to eradicate many of the difficulties linked with parenteral vaccinations [114]. For example, influenza vaccines have been shown in various animal models to induce appreciably superior mucosal antibody titres when served directly to the pulmonary region, equated with s.c. or i.m. injection [115, 116]. Additionally, pulmonary release can be utilized to offer systemic action of some proteins and peptides. Due to the high surface area of the lungs, the thin layer of the alveolar epithelium, and the high degree of lung vascularization, pulmonary delivery can present fast systemic absorption while ignoring the degradation mechanisms of the hepatic first-pass metabolism and gastrointestinal tract. Apart from this, pulmonary delivery offers advantages over injection in terms of both formulation and delivery technology, that is, patients' acceptance (needle-free delivery) and ease of administration [117].

However, delivery of proteins and peptides to the lungs presents some challenges. A prime issue with inhaled drugs is the necessity to provide the drug as microparticles (1–5 μm) to reach the lungs. Secondary question, which is specific to inhaled proteins and peptides, is that they can suffer physicochemical degradation. Physicochemical degradation can also happen during handing out of the proteins and peptides due to diverse stresses, such as exposure to extreme pH and temperatures. These physicochemical degradations can lead to loss of therapeutic activity. Another concern with these biomolecules is that they are prone to in vivo biological degradation due to the presence of enzymes (i.e., proteases) in the lungs and assorted clearance in the pulmonary area and the blood [95, 118]. To circumvent these issues, different strategies have been tried and tested for pulmonary applied proteins and peptides. An overview of these strategies along with their key achievements is denoted in Table 6.

4. Miscellaneous

Theophylline (THF) cocrystals DPI was prepared using various conformers like urea, saccharin, and nicotinamide by spray drying method. Aerosol dispersion was examined using NGI with Aerolizer inhaler device operating at a flow rate of 60 L/min for 6 sec. THF nicotinamide cocrystals show better aerosolization performance in comparison to other cocrystals. Micromeritic properties of THF cocrystals play important role in terms of the aerosol performance [119]. Voriconazole loaded large porous particles (VLPP) were prepared from polylactide polymer for treatment of invasive pulmonary aspergillosis. The optimized VLPP exhibited 4.85 ± 0.39% loading efficiency and 0.17 ± 0.02 porosity. Aerosol performance was examined using ACI. MMAD and FPF of optimized batch were found to be 2.85 ± 0.38 μm and 27.3 ± 2.7%, respectively. VLPP was shown to sustain the release of voriconazole for over 7 days with prolonging the residence time of VRZ at the site of action. Moreover, VLPP does not show any cytotoxic and inflammatory (IL-8) effect over A549 cells [120]. Methotrexate microspheres were fabricated using porous poly-L-lactide (MTX-PLLA-PMs) by emulsion combined precipitation of compressed CO_2 anti-solvent method. Prepared MTX-PLLA-PMs demonstrated a porous and uneven morphology with 81.6% of encapsulation efficiency. Additionally, obtained microspheres exhibited 79–85% porosity, 0.4 g cm^{-3} density, 10–25 μm geometric mean diameter, and FPF of 58–62%. Moreover, in in vitro antitumor assay MTX-PLLA-PMs possessed a sustained and better inhibitory activity compared with the neat MTX [121]. Inhalable dry powder composed of crystalline rifapentine and amorphous verapamil in presence of l-leucine was formed by spray drying method. When the dry powder was dispersed by an Osmohaler®, the total FPF of rifapentine and verapamil was 71.5 ± 2.0% and 77.4 ± 1.1%, respectively. Notably, the combination resulted in increased killing of *M. tuberculosis* H37Ra with acceptable IC_{50} values (62.5 μg/mL) on both lung alveolar basal epithelial (A549) and human monocytic (THP-1) cell lines. Furthermore, the dry powder was stable after three-month period in 0% RH at 20 ± 3°C [122].

5. Challenges and Future Perspectives

The successful delivery of any therapeutic agent to the pulmonary region via a DPI depends on four mutually dependent parameters: the formulation, the metering system, the inhaler device, and the patient's understanding/training. This review describes in detail the novel formulation aspects of DPI and merely touched other parameters. But there is an evenly appealing detailed story to be told regarding the inhaler devices, metering system, and patient's understanding/training. Various advantages and challenges in novel respiratory application are given in Figure 1.

Cochleates, a new type of lipid based drug delivery system, are applicable for administration through various routes and can be formulated in powder form. The interior of a cochleate structure remains considerably intact irrespective of outer enzymatic conditions. They have been reported to improve the systemic bioavailability and safety with good level of patient compliance compared to liposomes. There is a need to develop cochleates based dry powder inhaler formulations [70]. Ligand conjugated delivery system can also be explored to enhance the efficacy of the dry powder inhaler. This targeted multifunctional approach not only enhances bioavailability but also helps to deliver therapeutic agents exclusively to the diseased cells in the lungs collectively with suppressors of their resistance to the therapy. Research efforts in this segment led to developed ligand conjugated based dry powder inhaler with better targeting approach.

The growth in NDDS has already boosted the use of DPI for a variety of therapeutic aliments. A lot of novel drug delivery systems have been employed to increase the efficacy of DPI. Still, novel polymer synthesis, use of functionalized carriers, evolution in particle engineering,

TABLE 6: Summary of the pulmonary delivery of some therapeutic proteins and peptides.

Drug	Method of preparation	Major ingredient	Assembly, device and capsules, flow rate (L/min)	Percentage of FPF	Reference
Glucagon	JM	Pharmatose and erythritol	ACI, Jethaler, #2 HPMC, and 28.3 for 10 sec	33.9	[72]
Glucagon	JM	Citric acid and Respitose® SV003	ACI, Jethaler, #2 HPMC, and 28.3	25.0	[73]
Insulin	SD	Mannitol, bovine serum albumin, and aspartic acid	ACI, Turbospin, #2 HPMC, and 60	83.6 ± 4.7	[74]
Insulin	HPH followed by SD	Phospholipon® 90 H and hydrogenated soy lecithin	MSLI, Aerolizer, #3 HPMC, and 100 for 2.4 sec	63.0 ± 4.0	[75]
Influenza subunit vaccine	SD and SFD	Inulin	MSLI, Twincer®, and 53.7 for 3 sec	37.00 and 23.00	[76]
Pneumococcal surface protein	SD	*S. pneumoniae*	NGI, Cyclohaler, #3 HPMC, and 60 for 4 sec	74.31 ± 1.32	[77]
Unfractionated heparin	co-SD	L-Leucine (1% w/w)	TSI, Aerolizer, #3 gelatin, and 60 for 5 sec	13.23 ± 1.65	[78]
Recombinant human growth hormone	SD	Polysorbate 20, zinc chloride, and lactose	ACI, Spinhaler, #2 gelatin, and 60 for 4 sec	38.52	[79]
Recombinant antigen 85-B	SD	PLGA	ACI and 60 for 4 sec	68.9 ± 8.40	[80]

SD: spray drying; co-SD: closed spray drying; FD: freeze drying; SFD: spray freeze drying; LP: lyophilization; TFE: thin film evaporation; RE: rotary evaporation; SE: solvent evaporation; TFH: thin film hydration; HPH: high pressure homogenizer; CS: cholesterol; SPC: soybean phosphatidylcholine; HPC: hydrogenated phosphatidylcholine; HSPC: hydrogenated soy phosphatidylcholine; DPPC: dipalmitoyl phosphatidylcholine; DPPG: dipalmitoylphosphatidylglycerol.

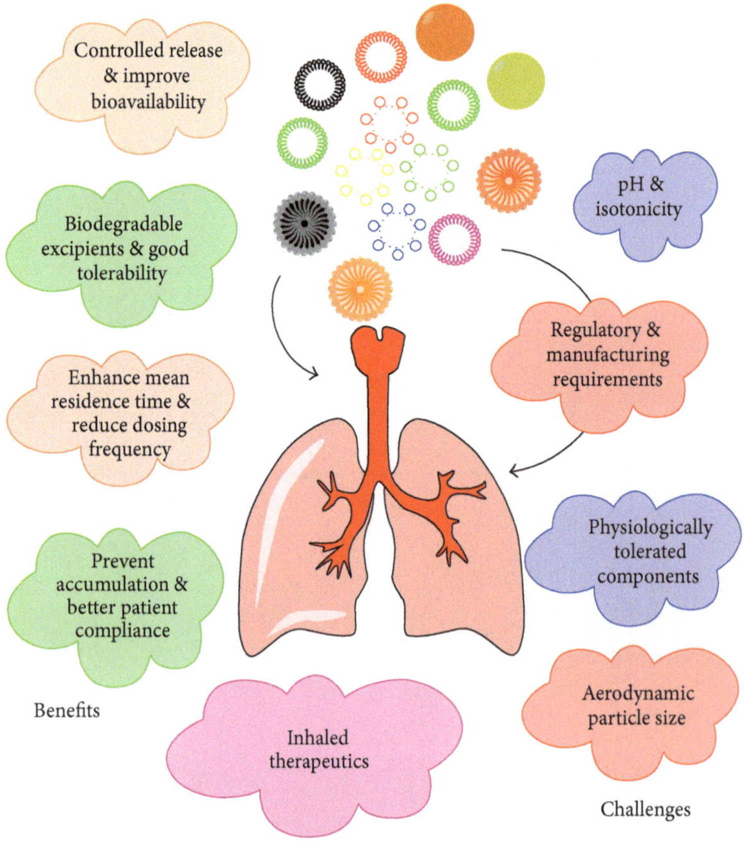

FIGURE 1: Advantages and challenges in novel respiratory drug deliveries.

and better knowledge of the structure function association have to be utilized to facilitate targeting of particles to predetermined lung cells. This may be tested by upholding of their structural integrity, biocompatibility, better stability in pulmonary fluids and enzymes, targeting ability, ease and safety of production, and regulatory requirements. For better localized targeting, ligand based drug delivery seems to have lot of prospect to reach the clinic in the near future. Ethosomes, cubosomes, and other vesicles as carrier systems are better alternative to extend the potential of DPI. Deposition efficiency, systemic toxicity, unfavorable PK/PD profile, and rapid lung clearance like critical issues can be defeated by improving the encapsulation efficiency and use of long circulating carriers. As detailed herein, there are a number of promising novel drug delivery options presently in the developmental pipeline, and if found to be safe, they will be valuable therapeutic alternative for clinicians to improve the end result and survival rates of patients with difficult-to-treat pulmonary infections.

Competing Interests

The author declares that there are no competing interests regarding the publication of this paper.

References

[1] J. Winkler, G. Hochhaus, and H. Derendorf, "How the lung handles drugs: pharmacokinetics and pharmacodynamics of inhaled corticosteroids," *Proceedings of the American Thoracic Society*, vol. 1, pp. 356–363, 2004.

[2] M. K. Al-Hallak, M. K. Sarfraz, S. Azarmi, W. H. Roa, W. H. Finlay, and R. Löbenberg, "Pulmonary delivery of inhalable nanoparticles: dry powder inhalers," *Therapeutic Delivery*, vol. 2, no. 10, pp. 1313–1324, 2011.

[3] A. M. Healy, M. I. Amaro, K. J. Paluch, and L. Tajber, "Dry powders for oral inhalation free of lactose carrier particles," *Advanced Drug Delivery Reviews*, vol. 75, pp. 32–52, 2014.

[4] M. Hoppentocht, P. Hagedoorn, H. W. Frijlink, and A. H. de Boer, "Technological and practical challenges of dry powder inhalers and formulations," *Advanced Drug Delivery Reviews*, vol. 75, pp. 18–31, 2014.

[5] X. Liu and G. Huang, "Formation strategies, mechanism of intracellular delivery and potential clinical applications of pH-sensitive liposomes," *Asian Journal of Pharmaceutical Sciences*, vol. 8, no. 6, pp. 319–328, 2013.

[6] A. Akbarzadeh, R. Rezaei-Sadabady, S. Davaran et al., "Liposome: classification, preparation, and applications," *Nanoscale Research Letters*, vol. 8, article 102, 2013.

[7] J. P. Clancy, L. Dupont, M. W. Konstan et al., "Phase II studies of nebulised arikace in CF patients with *Pseudomonas aeruginosa* infection," *Thorax*, vol. 68, no. 9, pp. 818–825, 2013.

[8] J. Sinha, S. Mukhopadhyay, N. Das, and M. Basu, "Targeting of liposomal andrographolide to L. donovani infected macrophages in vivo," *Drug Delivery*, vol. 7, no. 4, pp. 209–213, 2000.

[9] S. P. Shah and A. Misra, "Liposomal amikacin dry powder inhaler: effect of fines on in vitro performance," *AAPS PharmSciTech*, vol. 5, no. 4, pp. 1–7, 2004.

[10] M. R. Joshi and A. Misra, "Liposomal budesonide for dry powder inhaler: preparation and stabilization," *AAPS PharmSciTech*, vol. 2, no. 4, pp. 1–10, 2001.

[11] M. Chougule, B. Padhi, and A. Misra, "Development of spray dried liposomal dry powder inhaler of dapsone," *AAPS PharmSciTech*, vol. 9, no. 1, pp. 47–53, 2008.

[12] M. Gandhi, T. Pandya, R. Gandhi et al., "Inhalable liposomal dry powder of gemcitabine-HCl: formulation, in vitro characterization and in vivo studies," *International Journal of Pharmaceutics*, vol. 496, no. 2, pp. 886–895, 2015.

[13] M. Joshi and A. Misra, "Dry powder inhalation of liposomal Ketotifen fumarate: formulation and characterization," *International Journal of Pharmaceutics*, vol. 223, no. 1-2, pp. 15–27, 2001.

[14] A. F. Ourique, P. D. S. Chaves, G. D. Souto, A. R. Pohlmann, S. S. Guterres, and R. C. R. Beck, "Redispersible liposomal-N-acetylcysteine powder for pulmonary administration: development, in vitro characterization and antioxidant activity," *European Journal of Pharmaceutical Sciences*, vol. 65, pp. 174–182, 2014.

[15] A. Gibbons, N. G. McElvaney, and S.-A. Cryan, "A dry powder formulation of liposome-encapsulated recombinant secretory leukocyte protease inhibitor (rSLPI) for inhalation: preparation and characterisation," *AAPS PharmSciTech*, vol. 11, no. 3, pp. 1411–1421, 2010.

[16] M. L. Manca, D. Valenti, O. D. Sales, A. Nacher, A. M. Fadda, and M. Manconi, "Fabrication of polyelectrolyte multilayered vesicles as inhalable dry powder for lung administration of rifampicin," *International Journal of Pharmaceutics*, vol. 472, no. 1-2, pp. 102–109, 2014.

[17] W.-H. Huang, Z.-J. Yang, H. Wu, Y.-F. Wong, Z.-Z. Zhao, and L. Liu, "Development of liposomal salbutamol sulfate dry powder inhaler formulation," *Biological and Pharmaceutical Bulletin*, vol. 33, no. 3, pp. 512–517, 2010.

[18] M. B. Chougule, B. K. Padhi, and A. Misra, "Nano-liposomal dry powder inhaler of amiloride hydrochloride," *Journal of Nanoscience and Nanotechnology*, vol. 6, no. 9-10, pp. 3001–3009, 2006.

[19] M. Chougule, B. Padhi, and A. Misra, "Nano-liposomal dry powder inhaler of tacrolimus: preparation, characterization, and pulmonary pharmacokinetics," *International Journal of Nanomedicine*, vol. 2, no. 4, pp. 675–688, 2007.

[20] W. Rojanarat, N. Changsan, E. Tawithong, S. Pinsuwan, H.-K. Chan, and T. Srichana, "Isoniazid pro-liposome powders for inhalation-preparation, characterization and cell culture studies," *International Journal of Molecular Sciences*, vol. 12, no. 7, pp. 4414–4434, 2011.

[21] A. Patil-Gadhe and V. Pokharkar, "Single step spray drying method to develop proliposomes for inhalation: a systematic study based on quality by design approach," *Pulmonary Pharmacology & Therapeutics*, vol. 27, no. 2, pp. 197–207, 2014.

[22] O. B. Garbuzenko, G. Mainelis, O. Taratula, and T. Minko, "Inhalation treatment of lung cancer: the influence of composition, size and shape of nanocarriers on their lung accumulation and retention," *Cancer Biology and Medicine*, vol. 11, no. 1, pp. 44–55, 2014.

[23] K. M. G. Taylor and J. M. Newton, "Liposomes for controlled delivery of drugs to the lung," *Thorax*, vol. 47, no. 4, pp. 257–259, 1992.

[24] V. Shah, O. Taratula, O. B. Garbuzenko et al., "Genotoxicity of different nanocarriers: possible modifications for the delivery of nucleic acids," *Current Drug Discovery Technologies*, vol. 10, no. 1, pp. 8–15, 2013.

[25] A. A. Abdelbary, A. M. Al-Mahallawi, M. E. Abdelrahim, and A. M. A. Ali, "Preparation, optimization, and in vitro simulated inhalation delivery of carvedilol nanoparticles loaded on a coarse carrier intended for pulmonary administration," *International Journal of Nanomedicine*, vol. 10, pp. 6339–6353, 2015.

[26] N. Kumar, S. Soni, A. Jaimini, F. J. Ahmad, A. Bhatnagar, and G. Mittal, "Edetate calcium disodium nanoparticle dry powder inhalation: a novel approach against heavy metal decorporation," *International Journal of Pharmaceutics*, vol. 416, no. 1, pp. 376–383, 2011.

[27] C. Sinsuebpol, J. Chatchawalsaisin, and P. Kulvanich, "Preparation and in vivo absorption evaluation of spray dried powders containing salmon calcitonin loaded chitosan nanoparticles for pulmonary delivery," *Drug Design, Development and Therapy*, vol. 7, pp. 861–873, 2013.

[28] N. El-Gendy, E. M. Gorman, E. J. Munson, and C. Berkland, "Budesonide nanoparticle agglomerates as dry powder aerosols with rapid dissolution," *Journal of Pharmaceutical Sciences*, vol. 98, no. 8, pp. 2731–2746, 2009.

[29] K. Kho and K. Hadinoto, "Optimizing aerosolization efficiency of dry-powder aggregates of thermally-sensitive polymeric nanoparticles produced by spray-freeze-drying," *Powder Technology*, vol. 214, no. 1, pp. 169–176, 2011.

[30] N. El-Gendy, W. Pornputtapitak, and C. Berkland, "Nanoparticle agglomerates of fluticasone propionate in combination with albuterol sulfate as dry powder aerosols," *European Journal of Pharmaceutical Sciences*, vol. 44, no. 4, pp. 522–533, 2011.

[31] H. Salem, M. Abdelrahim, K. A. Eid, and M. Sharaf, "Nanosized rods agglomerates as a new approach for formulation of a dry powder inhaler," *International Journal of Nanomedicine*, vol. 6, pp. 311 320, 2011.

[32] X. Li, F. G. Vogt, D. Hayes Jr., and H. M. Mansour, "Physicochemical characterization and aerosol dispersion performance of organic solution advanced spray-dried microparticulate/nanoparticulate antibiotic dry powders of tobramycin and azithromycin for pulmonary inhalation aerosol delivery," *European Journal of Pharmaceutical Sciences*, vol. 52, no. 1, pp. 191–205, 2014.

[33] S. Meenach, K. Anderson, J. Hilt, R. McGarry, and H. Mansour, "High performing dry powder inhalers of paclitaxel DPPC/DPPG lung surfactant-mimic multifunctional particles in lung cancer: physicochemical characterization, in vitro aerosol dispersion, and cellular studies," *AAPS PharmSciTech*, vol. 15, no. 6, pp. 1574–1587, 2014.

[34] S. A. Meenach, K. W. Anderson, J. Zach Hilt, R. C. McGarry, and H. M. Mansour, "Characterization and aerosol dispersion performance of advanced spray-dried chemotherapeutic PEGylated phospholipid particles for dry powder inhalation delivery in lung cancer," *European Journal of Pharmaceutical Sciences*, vol. 49, no. 4, pp. 699–711, 2013.

[35] F. Ungaro, I. d'Angelo, C. Coletta et al., "Dry powders based on PLGA nanoparticles for pulmonary delivery of antibiotics: modulation of encapsulation efficiency, release rate and lung deposition pattern by hydrophilic polymers," *Journal of Controlled Release*, vol. 157, no. 1, pp. 149–159, 2012.

[36] J. Hu, Y. Dong, G. Pastorin, W. K. Ng, and R. B. H. Tan, "Spherical agglomerates of pure drug nanoparticles for improved pulmonary delivery in dry powder inhalers," *Journal of Nanoparticle Research*, vol. 15, no. 4, article 1560, 2013.

[37] V. Nekkanti, N. Venkatesan, and G. V. Betageri, "Proliposomes for oral delivery: progress and challenges," *Current Pharmaceutical Biotechnology*, vol. 16, no. 4, pp. 303–312, 2015.

[38] C. Chu, S.-S. Tong, Y. Xu et al., "Proliposomes for oral delivery of dehydrosilymarin: preparation and evaluation *in vitro* and *in vivo*," *Acta Pharmacologica Sinica*, vol. 32, no. 7, pp. 973–980, 2011.

[39] Y.-Z. Li, X. Sun, T. Gong, J. Liu, J. Zuo, and Z.-R. Zhang, "Inhalable microparticles as carriers for pulmonary delivery of thymopentin-loaded solid lipid nanoparticles," *Pharmaceutical Research*, vol. 27, no. 9, pp. 1977–1986, 2010.

[40] A. Patil-Gadhe, A. Kyadarkunte, M. Patole, and V. Pokharkar, "Montelukast-loaded nanostructured lipid carriers: part II pulmonary drug delivery and in vitro-in vivo aerosol performance," *European Journal of Pharmaceutics and Biopharmaceutics*, vol. 88, no. 1, pp. 169–177, 2014.

[41] A. Patil-Gadhe and V. Pokharkar, "Pulmonary targeting potential of rosuvastatin loaded nanostructured lipid carrier: optimization by factorial design," *International Journal of Pharmaceutics*, vol. 501, no. 1-2, pp. 199–210, 2016.

[42] T. Dudala, P. Yalavarthi, H. Vadlamudi, J. Thanniru, G. Yaga, and N. Mudumala, "A perspective overview on lipospheres as lipid carrier systems," *International Journal of Pharmaceutical Investigation*, vol. 4, no. 4, pp. 149–155, 2014.

[43] S. Naikwade and A. Bajaj, "Preparation and in vitro evaluation of budesonide spray dried microparticles for pulmonary delivery," *Scientia Pharmaceutica*, vol. 77, no. 2, pp. 419–441, 2009.

[44] H. Adi, P. M. Young, H.-K. Chan, H. Agus, and D. Traini, "Co-spray-dried mannitol-ciprofloxacin dry powder inhaler formulation for cystic fibrosis and chronic obstructive pulmonary disease," *European Journal of Pharmaceutical Sciences*, vol. 40, no. 3, pp. 239–247, 2010.

[45] T. Niwa, D. Mizutani, and K. Danjo, "Spray freeze-dried porous microparticles of a poorly water-soluble drug for respiratory delivery," *Chemical and Pharmaceutical Bulletin*, vol. 60, no. 7, pp. 870–876, 2012.

[46] M. C. Fontana, T. L. Durli, A. R. Pohlmann, S. S. Guterres, and R. C. R. Beck, "Polymeric controlled release inhalable powder produced by vibrational spray-drying: one-step preparation and in vitro lung deposition," *Powder Technology*, vol. 258, pp. 49–59, 2014.

[47] F. Sansone, R. P. Aquino, P. D. Gaudio, P. Colombo, and P. Russo, "Physical characteristics and aerosol performance of naringin dry powders for pulmonary delivery prepared by spray-drying," *European Journal of Pharmaceutics and Biopharmaceutics*, vol. 72, no. 1, pp. 206–213, 2009.

[48] A. Kundawala, V. Patel, H. Patel, and D. Choudhary, "Treating tuberculosis with chitosan microparticles loaded with rifampicin as respirable powder for pulmonary delivery," *Indian Journal of Novel Drug Delivery*, vol. 4, pp. 57–65, 2012.

[49] M. V. Vadakkan, S. S. Binil Raj, C. C. Kartha, and G. S. Vinod Kumar, "Cationic, amphiphilic dextran nanomicellar clusters as an excipient for dry powder inhaler formulation," *Acta Biomaterialia*, vol. 23, pp. 172–188, 2015.

[50] M. A. Darbandi, N. A. Rouholamini, K. Gilani, and H. Tajerzadeh, "The effect of vehicles on spray drying of rifampicin inhalable microparticles: in vitro and in vivo evaluation," *DARU Journal of Pharmaceutical Sciences*, vol. 16, no. 3, pp. 128–135, 2008.

[51] J.-J. Yang, C.-Y. Liu, L.-H. Quan, and Y.-H. Liao, "Preparation and in vitro aerosol performance of spray-dried Shuang-Huang-Lian corrugated particles in carrier-based dry powder inhalers," *AAPS PharmSciTech*, vol. 13, no. 3, pp. 816–825, 2012.

[52] T. P. Learoyd, J. L. Burrows, E. French, and P. C. Seville, "Sustained delivery by leucine-modified chitosan spray-dried respirable powders," *International Journal of Pharmaceutics*, vol. 372, no. 1-2, pp. 97–104, 2009.

[53] S. Arora, M. Haghi, C.-Y. Loo, D. Traini, P. M. Young, and S. Jain, "Development of an inhaled controlled release voriconazole dry powder formulation for the treatment of respiratory fungal infection," *Molecular Pharmaceutics*, vol. 12, no. 6, pp. 2001–2009, 2015.

[54] Z. Daman, K. Gilani, A. Rouholamini Najafabadi, H. R. Eftekhari, and M. A. Barghi, "Formulation of inhalable lipid-based salbutamol sulfate microparticles by spray drying technique," *DARU, Journal of Pharmaceutical Sciences*, vol. 22, no. 1, article 50, 2014.

[55] S. Scalia, M. Haghi, V. Losi, V. Trotta, P. M. Young, and D. Traini, "Quercetin solid lipid microparticles: a flavonoid for inhalation lung delivery," *European Journal of Pharmaceutical Sciences*, vol. 49, no. 2, pp. 278–285, 2013.

[56] M. Mezzena, S. Scalia, P. M. Young, and D. Traini, "Solid lipid budesonide microparticles for controlled release inhalation therapy," *The AAPS Journal*, vol. 11, no. 4, pp. 771–778, 2009.

[57] A. Kuzmov and T. Minko, "Nanotechnology approaches for inhalation treatment of lung diseases," *Journal of Controlled Release*, vol. 219, pp. 500–518, 2015.

[58] A. J. Mali, A. P. Pawar, and R. N. Purohit, "Development of budesonide loaded biopolymer based dry powder inhaler: optimization, in vitro deposition, and cytotoxicity study," *Journal of Pharmaceutics*, vol. 2014, Article ID 795371, 12 pages, 2014.

[59] L.-M. Xu, Q.-X. Zhang, Y. Zhou, H. Zhao, J.-X. Wang, and J.-F. Chen, "Engineering drug ultrafine particles of beclomethasone dipropionate for dry powder inhalation," *International Journal of Pharmaceutics*, vol. 436, no. 1-2, pp. 1–9, 2012.

[60] R. S. Dhumal, S. V. Biradar, A. R. Paradkar, and P. York, "Particle engineering using sonocrystallization: salbutamol sulphate for pulmonary delivery," *International Journal of Pharmaceutics*, vol. 368, no. 1-2, pp. 129–137, 2009.

[61] Q. Zhou, L. Qu, T. Gengenbach, I. Larson, P. J. Stewart, and D. A. V. Morton, "Effect of surface coating with magnesium stearate via mechanical dry powder coating approach on the aerosol performance of micronized drug powders from dry powder inhalers," *AAPS PharmSciTech*, vol. 14, no. 1, pp. 38–44, 2013.

[62] N. R. Rabbani and P. C. Seville, "The influence of formulation components on the aerosolisation properties of spray-dried powders," *Journal of Controlled Release*, vol. 110, no. 1, pp. 130–140, 2005.

[63] X. Wu, W. Zhang, D. Hayes Jr., and H. M. Mansour, "Physicochemical characterization and aerosol dispersion performance of organic solution advanced spray-dried cyclosporine A multifunctional particles for dry powder inhalation aerosol delivery," *International Journal of Nanomedicine*, vol. 8, pp. 1269–1283, 2013.

[64] C. Singh, L. V. S. K. Koduri, A. Singh, and S. Suresh, "Novel potential for optimization of antitubercular therapy: pulmonary delivery of rifampicin lipospheres," *Asian Journal of Pharmaceutical Sciences*, vol. 10, no. 6, pp. 549–562, 2015.

[65] M. C. Gaspar, J. J. S. Sousa, A. A. C. C. Pais et al., "Optimization of levofloxacin-loaded crosslinked chitosan microspheres for inhaled aerosol therapy," *European Journal of Pharmaceutics and Biopharmaceutics*, vol. 96, pp. 65–75, 2015.

[66] H. S. Mahajan and S. A. Gundare, "Preparation, characterization and pulmonary pharmacokinetics of xyloglucan microspheres as dry powder inhalation," *Carbohydrate Polymers*, vol. 102, no. 1, pp. 529–536, 2014.

[67] R. Diab, J. Brillault, A. Bardy, A. V. L. Gontijo, and J. C. Olivier, "Formulation and in vitro characterization of inhalable polyvinyl alcohol-free rifampicin-loaded PLGA microspheres prepared with sucrose palmitate as stabilizer: efficiency for ex vivo alveolar macrophage targeting," *International Journal of Pharmaceutics*, vol. 436, no. 1-2, pp. 833–839, 2012.

[68] R. A. Tuli, T. R. Dargaville, G. A. George, and N. Islam, "Polycaprolactone microspheres as carriers for dry powder inhalers: effect of surface coating on aerosolization of salbutamol sulfate," *Journal of Pharmaceutical Sciences*, vol. 101, no. 2, pp. 733–745, 2012.

[69] D. J. Singh, A. A. Lohade, J. J. Parmar et al., "Development of chitosan-based dry powder inhalation system of cisplatin for lung cancer," *Indian Journal of Pharmaceutical Sciences*, vol. 74, no. 6, pp. 521–526, 2012.

[70] A. Pawar, C. Bothiraja, K. Shaikh, and A. Mali, "An insight into cochleates, a potential drug delivery system," *RSC Advances*, vol. 5, no. 99, pp. 81188–81202, 2015.

[71] G. Pilcer, T. Sebti, and K. Amighi, "Formulation and characterization of lipid-coated tobramycin particles for dry powder inhalation," *Pharmaceutical Research*, vol. 23, no. 5, pp. 931–940, 2006.

[72] K. Endo, S. Amikawa, A. Matsumoto, N. Sahashi, and S. Onoue, "Erythritol-based dry powder of glucagon for pulmonary administration," *International Journal of Pharmaceutics*, vol. 290, no. 1-2, pp. 63–71, 2005.

[73] S. Onoue, K. Yamamoto, Y. Kawabata, M. Hirose, T. Mizumoto, and S. Yamada, "Novel dry powder inhaler formulation of glucagon with addition of citric acid for enhanced pulmonary delivery," *International Journal of Pharmaceutics*, vol. 382, no. 1-2, pp. 144–150, 2009.

[74] A. G. Balducci, S. Cagnani, F. Sonvico et al., "Pure insulin highly respirable powders for inhalation," *European Journal of Pharmaceutical Sciences*, vol. 51, no. 1, pp. 110–117, 2014.

[75] F. Depreter and K. Amighi, "Formulation and in vitro evaluation of highly dispersive insulin dry powder formulations for lung administration," *European Journal of Pharmaceutics and Biopharmaceutics*, vol. 76, no. 3, pp. 454–463, 2010.

[76] V. Saluja, J.-P. Amorij, J. C. Kapteyn, A. H. de Boer, H. W. Frijlink, and W. L. J. Hinrichs, "A comparison between spray drying and spray freeze drying to produce an influenza subunit vaccine powder for inhalation," *Journal of Controlled Release*, vol. 144, no. 2, pp. 127–133, 2010.

[77] N. K. Kunda, I. M. Alfagih, E. N. Miyaji et al., "Pulmonary dry powder vaccine of pneumococcal antigen loaded nanoparticles," *International Journal of Pharmaceutics*, vol. 495, no. 2, pp. 903–912, 2015.

[78] J. Shur, T. G. Nevell, R. J. Ewen et al., "Cospray-dried unfractionated heparin with l-leucine as a dry powder inhaler mucolytic for cystic fibrosis therapy," *Journal of Pharmaceutical Sciences*, vol. 97, no. 11, pp. 4857–4868, 2008.

[79] M. Jalalipour, K. Gilani, H. Tajerzadeh, A. R. Najafabadi, and M. Barghi, "Characterization and aerodynamic evaluation of spray dried recombinant human growth hormone using protein stabilizing agents," *International Journal of Pharmaceutics*, vol. 352, no. 1-2, pp. 209–216, 2008.

[80] D. Lu, L. Garcia-Contreras, P. Muttil et al., "Pulmonary immunization using antigen 85-b polymeric microparticles to boost tuberculosis immunity," *The AAPS Journal*, vol. 12, no. 3, pp. 338–347, 2010.

[81] A. Wicki, D. Witzigmann, V. Balasubramanian, and J. Huwyler, "Nanomedicine in cancer therapy: challenges, opportunities, and clinical applications," *Journal of Controlled Release*, vol. 200, pp. 138–157, 2015.

[82] F. Danhier, E. Ansorena, J. M. Silva, R. Coco, A. Le Breton, and V. Préat, "PLGA-based nanoparticles: an overview of biomedical applications," *Journal of Controlled Release*, vol. 161, no. 2, pp. 505–522, 2012.

[83] D.-C. Li, X.-K. Zhong, Z.-P. Zeng et al., "Application of targeted drug delivery system in Chinese medicine," *Journal of Controlled Release*, vol. 138, no. 2, pp. 103–112, 2009.

[84] J. Zhang, L. Wu, H.-K. Chan, and W. Watanabe, "Formation, characterization, and fate of inhaled drug nanoparticles," *Advanced Drug Delivery Reviews*, vol. 63, no. 6, pp. 441–455, 2011.

[85] N. Tsapis, D. Bennett, B. Jackson, D. A. Weitz, and D. A. Edwards, "Trojan particles: large porous carriers of nanoparticles for drug delivery," *Proceedings of the National Academy of Sciences of the United States of America*, vol. 99, no. 19, pp. 12001–12005, 2002.

[86] W. S. Cheow, M. L. L. Ng, K. Kho, and K. Hadinoto, "Spray-freeze-drying production of thermally sensitive polymeric nanoparticle aggregates for inhaled drug delivery: effect of freeze-drying adjuvants," *International Journal of Pharmaceutics*, vol. 404, no. 1-2, pp. 289–300, 2011.

[87] G. Kaptay, "The gibbs equation versus the kelvin and the gibbs-thomson equations to describe nucleation and equilibrium of nano-materials," *Journal of Nanoscience and Nanotechnology*, vol. 12, no. 3, pp. 2625–2633, 2012.

[88] B. E. Rabinow, "Nanosuspensions in drug delivery," *Nature Reviews Drug Discovery*, vol. 3, no. 9, pp. 785–796, 2004.

[89] W. Yang, J. I. Peters, and R. O. Williams III, "Inhaled nanoparticles-a current review," *International Journal of Pharmaceutics*, vol. 356, no. 1-2, pp. 239–247, 2008.

[90] J. C. Sung, D. J. Padilla, L. Garcia-Contreras et al., "Formulation and pharmacokinetics of self-assembled rifampicin nanoparticle systems for pulmonary delivery," *Pharmaceutical Research*, vol. 26, no. 8, pp. 1847–1855, 2009.

[91] Y. Wang, K. Kho, W. S. Cheow, and K. Hadinoto, "A comparison between spray drying and spray freeze drying for dry powder inhaler formulation of drug-loaded lipid-polymer hybrid nanoparticles," *International Journal of Pharmaceutics*, vol. 424, no. 1-2, pp. 98–106, 2012.

[92] S. M. D'Addio, J. G. Y. Chan, P. C. L. Kwok, B. R. Benson, R. K. Prud'Homme, and H.-K. Chan, "Aerosol delivery of nanoparticles in uniform mannitol carriers formulated by ultrasonic spray freeze drying," *Pharmaceutical Research*, vol. 30, no. 11, pp. 2891–2901, 2013.

[93] S. M. D'Addio, J. G. Y. Chan, P. C. L. Kwok, R. K. Prud'homme, and H.-K. Chan, "Constant size, variable density aerosol particles by ultrasonic spray freeze drying," *International Journal of Pharmaceutics*, vol. 427, no. 2, pp. 185–191, 2012.

[94] J. Pardeike, A. Hommoss, and R. H. Müller, "Lipid nanoparticles (SLN, NLC) in cosmetic and pharmaceutical dermal products," *International Journal of Pharmaceutics*, vol. 366, no. 1-2, pp. 170–184, 2009.

[95] S. Weber, A. Zimmer, and J. Pardeike, "Solid Lipid Nanoparticles (SLN) and Nanostructured Lipid Carriers (NLC) for pulmonary application: a review of the state of the art," *European Journal of Pharmaceutics and Biopharmaceutics*, vol. 86, no. 1, pp. 7–22, 2014.

[96] A. Pawar, S. Rajalakshmi, P. Mehta, K. Shaikh, and C. Bothiraja, "Strategies for formulation development of andrographolide," *RSC Advances*, vol. 6, no. 73, pp. 69282–69300, 2016.

[97] W. Mehnert and K. Mäder, "Solid lipid nanoparticles: production, characterization and applications," *Advanced Drug Delivery Reviews*, vol. 47, no. 2-3, pp. 165–196, 2001.

[98] R. R. Patlolla, M. Chougule, A. R. Patel, T. Jackson, P. N. V. Tata, and M. Singh, "Formulation, characterization and pulmonary deposition of nebulized celecoxib encapsulated nanostructured lipid carriers," *Journal of Controlled Release*, vol. 144, no. 2, pp. 233–241, 2010.

[99] A. J. Mali, A. P. Pawar, and C. Bothiraja, "Improved lung delivery of budesonide from biopolymer based dry powder inhaler through natural inhalation of rat," *Materials Technology*, vol. 29, no. 6, pp. 350–357, 2014.

[100] I. S. Chandiran, B. Pavan Kumar, and K. N. Jayaveera, "Design and development of microparticulate drug delivery system of Glimepiride for controlled release," *Drug Invention Today*, vol. 5, no. 3, pp. 235–240, 2013.

[101] N. K. Varde and D. W. Pack, "Microspheres for controlled release drug delivery," *Expert Opinion on Biological Therapy*, vol. 4, no. 1, pp. 35–51, 2004.

[102] M. F. Ali and S. Bakalis, "Mucoadhesive polymers for food formulations," *Procedia Food Science*, vol. 1, pp. 68–75, 2011.

[103] M. Mishra and B. Mishra, "Mucoadhesive microparticles as potential carriers in inhalation delivery of doxycycline hyclate: a comparative study," *Acta Pharmaceutica Sinica B*, vol. 2, no. 5, pp. 518–526, 2012.

[104] M. Sakagami, W. Kinoshita, K. Sakon, J. Sato, and Y. Makino, "Mucoadhesive beclomethasone microspheres for powder inhalation: Their pharmacokinetics and pharmacodynamics evaluation," *Journal of Controlled Release*, vol. 80, no. 1-3, pp. 207–218, 2002.

[105] R. Kamble, P. Palve, and P. Mehta, "Preparation and evaluation of amorphous olmesartan medoxomil with porous silica microparticles using spray-drying technique," *Journal of Advanced Pharmacy Education & Research*, vol. 4, pp. 65–71, 2014.

[106] C. Bothiraja, M. B. Shinde, S. Rajalakshmi, and A. P. Pawar, "Evaluation of molecular pharmaceutical and in-vivo properties of spray-dried isolated andrographolide-PVP," *Journal of Pharmacy and Pharmacology*, vol. 61, no. 11, pp. 1465–1472, 2009.

[107] V. Dhapte and P. Mehta, "Advances in hydrotropic solutions: an updated review," *St. Petersburg Polytechnical University Journal: Physics and Mathematics*, vol. 1, no. 4, pp. 424–435, 2015.

[108] C. Duret, N. Wauthoz, T. Sebti, F. Vanderbist, and K. Amighi, "Solid dispersions of itraconazole for inhalation with enhanced dissolution, solubility and dispersion properties," *International Journal of Pharmaceutics*, vol. 428, no. 1-2, pp. 103–113, 2012.

[109] S. Onoue, H. Sato, Y. Kawabata, T. Mizumoto, N. Hashimoto, and S. Yamada, "In vitro and in vivo characterization on amorphous solid dispersion of cyclosporine A for inhalation therapy," *Journal of Controlled Release*, vol. 138, no. 1, pp. 16–23, 2009.

[110] D.-J. Van Drooge, W. L. J. Hinrichs, B. H. J. Dickhoff et al., "Spray freeze drying to produce a stable Δ^9-tetrahydrocannabinol containing inulin-based solid dispersion powder suitable for inhalation," *European Journal of Pharmaceutical Sciences*, vol. 26, no. 2, pp. 231–240, 2005.

[111] N. A. Beinborn, J. Du, N. P. Wiederhold, H. D. C. Smyth, and R. O. Williams III, "Dry powder insufflation of crystalline and amorphous voriconazole formulations produced by thin film freezing to mice," *European Journal of Pharmaceutics and Biopharmaceutics*, vol. 81, no. 3, pp. 600–608, 2012.

[112] K. A. Overhoff, K. P. Johnston, J. Tam, J. Engstrom, and R. O. Williams III, "Use of thin film freezing to enable drug delivery: a review," *Journal of Drug Delivery Science and Technology*, vol. 19, no. 2, pp. 89–98, 2009.

[113] Y.-B. Wang, A. B. Watts, J. I. Peters, S. Liu, A. Batra, and R. O. Williams III, "In vitro and in vivo performance of dry powder inhalation formulations: comparison of particles prepared by thin film freezing and micronization," *AAPS PharmSciTech*, vol. 15, no. 4, pp. 981–993, 2014.

[114] F. Depreter, G. Pilcer, and K. Amighi, "Inhaled proteins: challenges and perspectives," *International Journal of Pharmaceutics*, vol. 447, no. 1-2, pp. 251–280, 2013.

[115] T. Sou, E. N. Meeusen, M. de Veer, D. A. V. Morton, L. M. Kaminskas, and M. P. McIntosh, "New developments in dry powder pulmonary vaccine delivery," *Trends in Biotechnology*, vol. 29, no. 4, pp. 191–198, 2011.

[116] J. Wee, J. Scheerlinck, K. Snibson et al., "Pulmonary delivery of iscomatrix influenza vaccine induces both systemic and mucosal immunity with antigen dose sparing," *Mucosal Immunology*, vol. 1, pp. 489–496, 2008.

[117] J. Huang, R. J. Garmise, T. M. Crowder et al., "A novel dry powder influenza vaccine and intranasal delivery technology: induction of systemic and mucosal immune responses in rats," *Vaccine*, vol. 23, no. 6, pp. 794–801, 2004.

[118] M. Witting, K. Obst, W. Friess, and S. Hedtrich, "Recent advances in topical delivery of proteins and peptides mediated by soft matter nanocarriers," *Biotechnology Advances*, vol. 33, no. 6, pp. 1355–1369, 2015.

[119] A. Alhalaweh, W. Kaialy, G. Buckton, H. Gill, A. Nokhodchi, and S. P. Velaga, "Theophylline cocrystals prepared by spray drying: physicochemical properties and aerosolization performance," *AAPS PharmSciTech*, vol. 14, no. 1, pp. 265–276, 2013.

[120] S. Arora, R. R. Mahajan, V. Kushwah, D. Baradia, A. Misra, and S. Jain, "Development of voriconazole loaded large porous particles for inhalation delivery: effect of surface forces on aerosolisation performance, assessment of in vitro safety potential and uptake by macrophages," *RSC Advances*, vol. 5, no. 48, pp. 38030–38043, 2015.

[121] A.-Z. Chen, C. Zhao, S.-B. Wang, Y.-G. Liu, and D.-L. Lin, "Generation of porous poly-L-lactide microspheres by emulsion-combined precipitation with a compressed CO_2 antisolvent process," *Journal of Materials Chemistry B*, vol. 1, no. 23, pp. 2967–2975, 2013.

[122] T. Parumasivam, J. G. Chan, A. Pang et al., "In vitro evaluation of inhalable verapamil-rifapentine particles for tuberculosis therapy," *Molecular Pharmaceutics*, vol. 13, no. 3, pp. 979–989, 2016.

18

Etodolac Containing Topical Niosomal Gel: Formulation Development and Evaluation

Gyati Shilakari Asthana, Abhay Asthana, Davinder Singh, and Parveen Kumar Sharma

Department of Pharmaceutics, M. M. College of Pharmacy, Maharishi Markandeshwar University, Mullana, Ambala, Haryana 133207, India

Correspondence should be addressed to Gyati Shilakari Asthana; gshilakari@gmail.com

Academic Editor: Philippe Maincent

The present study aimed to investigate the delivery potential of Etodolac (ETD) containing topical niosomal gel. Niosomal formulations were prepared by thin film hydration method at various ratios of cholesterol and Span 60 and were evaluated with respect to particle size, shape, entrapment efficiency, and *in vitro* characteristics. Dicetyl phosphate (DCP) was also added in the niosomal formulation. Mean particle size of niosomal formulation was found to be in the range of 2 μm to 4 μm. Niosomal formulation N_2 (1 : 1) ratio of cholesterol and surfactant displayed good entrapment efficiency (96.72%). TEM analyses showed that niosomal formulation was spherical in shape. Niosomal formulation (N_2) displayed high percentage of drug release after 24 h (94.91) at (1 : 1) ratio of cholesterol : surfactant. Further selected niosomal formulation was used to formulate topical gel and was characterized with respect to its various parameters such as pH, viscosity, spreadability, *ex vivo* study, and *in vivo* potential permeation. *Ex vivo* study showed that niosomal gel possessed better skin permeation study than the plain topical gel. Further *in vivo* study revealed good inhibition of inflammation in case of topical niosomal gel than plain gel and niosomal formulation. The present study suggested that topical niosomal gel formulations provide sustained and prolonged delivery of drug.

1. Introduction

Etodolac (ETD) is a nonsteroidal anti-inflammatory drug (NSAID) of selective COX-2 inhibitor class used for osteoarthritis and rheumatoid arthritis. Its therapeutic effects are due to its ability to inhibit prostaglandin synthesis ("as discussed by Inoue et al. [1]"). Prostaglandins are the chemicals which are responsible for pain and the fever and tenderness that occur with inflammation. It possesses poor solubility and also undergoes extensive first pass metabolism that could be the reason of its low bioavailability. Its terminal half life is 7 hrs and hence frequent dosing is required. Thus, to avoid aforementioned issues of ETD, it is desirable to encapsulate the drug in the vesicular system to prolong the existence of the drug in systemic circulation and perhaps increase the bioavailability. Continuous oral use of ETD causes serious gastrointestinal disturbance such as ulcer, stomach, or intestinal bleeding and chest pain which can be fatal. To avoid such problem there are other alternatives like coating of polymer that avoid release of drug molecule in gastrointestinal tract (GIT). Another approach to overcome such problem is changing the route of drug administration, namely, buccal route, topical route, nasal route, transdermal route, and so forth. Topical route is most preferable as easy to apply and provide high level of patient satisfaction. Transdermal route also avoid first pass metabolism associated with conventional route of drug administration. It also provides easy elimination of drug in case of toxicity and reduced fluctuation in plasma drug concentration level and thus decreased side effect. Various novel drug delivery technologies have been applied. Various novel delivery technologies including ethosomes ("as discussed by Chintala and Padmapreetha [2]"), microsphere ("as discussed by Kumar et al. [3]"), thermogels for rectal delivery ("as discussed by Barakat [4]"), and hydrophilic gel ("as discussed by Tas et al. [5]") have been reported for delivery of Etodolac.

Topical drug delivery means the application of drug to skin for localized effect. The skin is one of the most

TABLE 1: Composition of niosomal formulations at various ratios of cholesterol : Span 60.

Sr. number	Formulation codes	Drug : cholesterol : Span 60 (molar ratio)	Dicetyl phosphate (DCP) (mg)
1	N_1	1 : 0.5 : 1	5.0
2	N_2	1 : 1 : 1	5.0
3	N_3	1 : 1.5 : 1	5.0
4	N_4	1 : 1 : 0.5	5.0
5	N_5	1 : 1 : 1.5	5.0

widespread and freely available structures of the human body. Skin of an average adult body covers a surface approximately 2 m^2 and receives about one-third of the blood circulating through the body ("as discussed by Sharma et al. [6]"). It acts as a regulator in retaining the body heat, plays a part in regulation of blood pressure, and protects against the penetration of ultraviolet rays. Dermal drug delivery has number of advantages like longer duration of action, dosing flexibility, reduced side effects, uniform plasma levels, high patient compliance, and so forth but it has some disadvantages like possibility of local irritation effect, erythema, itching, and low permeability of drugs in the stratum corneum ("as discussed by Bhowmik et al. [7]"). Stratum corneum is outermost and top layer of epidermis which is impermeable to water and behaves like tough flexible membrane. It contains dead keratinized cells called corneocytes. For the permeation of drug to this barrier many technologies and systems have been investigated and one of the most promising techniques is the vesicular carrier for drug delivery through the skin.

Novel drug delivery carriers have great potential for dermal delivery. The lipidic and nonlipidic vesicular systems like liposome, transfersome, ethosome, and niosome are used to overcome the problem associated with topical conventional formulation. Drug delivery system using novel vesicular carrier, such as liposome or niosome, has distinct advantages over microspheres, nanoparticles, and other carriers in terms of better entrapment of drugs (payload characteristics), target site specificity, and handling premature drug release (burst effect). In 1985, niosomes were studied as an alternative to liposome because they offer some benefits over liposome such as being more stable, nontoxic, and economic due to low cost of nonionic surfactant as compared to phospholipids which are prone to oxidation. Incorporation of surfactants within niosomes may also enhance the efficacy of the drug, possibly by facilitating its uptake by the target cells. Niosomes are biodegradable, biocompatible, relatively nontoxic, and an alternative of liposome. They can be utilized in the delivery of wide variety of drugs as it has capability to entrap hydrophilic, lipophilic, and amphiphilic drugs. For transdermal route of administration NSAIDs, hormone, antibacterial, and antifungal drugs are most preferably used.

The objectives of the present study were to develop ETD loaded niosomal gel for transdermal delivery and to provide prolonged and sustained release of drug, so that required dose is decreased, and to avoid GI side effect and first pass hepatic metabolism.

2. Materials and Methods

2.1. Materials. Etodolac (ETD) was received as gift sample from IPCA Laboratories Ltd., Mumbai. Chloroform, acetone, potassium dihydrogen orthophosphate, sodium chloride, sodium hydroxide, methanol, Disodium hydrogen phosphate, and dialysis membrane were obtained from Himedia. Cholesterol, dicetyl phosphate (DCP), and Span 60 were taken from Sigma-Aldrich.

2.2. Preparation of Niosomal Formulation. In the present study, niosomal formulations were prepared by thin film hydration technique as reported earlier with slight modifications ("as discussed by Balakrishnan et al. [8]") by using various ratios of Span 60 and cholesterol as shown in Table 1. DCP (5 mg) was added in the formulation to keep the niosomal formulation stable for long period of time. Accurately weighted quantities of surfactants and cholesterol were taken to give the desired ratio and were dissolved in 10 mL chloroform in a round bottom flask and DCP was added to the above mixture. Then accurately weighed amount of drug was added into the solvent. The solvent was evaporated in a rotary flash evaporator under a vacuum of 20 inches of Hg at a temperature of 60°C at 120 rpm until a smooth, dry lipid film was obtained. Then film was hydrated with 10 mL of phosphate buffer saline (PBS) pH 7.4 for 3 hr at 60 ± 2°C with shaking on a water bath. The niosomal suspension was kept at 2–8°C for 24 hr. Developed niosomal formulation was evaluated with respect to particle size, shape, entrapment efficiency, and *in vitro* drug release profile.

3. Evaluation of Niosomal Formulation

Niosomes formulations were characterized with respect to shape, particle size distribution, entrapment efficiency, and *in vitro* release studies.

3.1. Particle Shape and Morphology. Shape and morphology of niosomal formulations were determined by optical microscopy and Transmission Electron Microscopy (TEM) and result were shown in Figures 1 and 2.

3.2. Particle Size. The particle size of the niosomal suspension was determined by optical microscopy. A drop of niosomal suspension was placed on a glass slide. A cover slip was placed over the niosomes suspension and evaluated the

FIGURE 1: Optical microscopy of niosomal formulation at 45x.

average vesicle size by an ordinary optical microscope using a precalibrated ocular eye piece micrometer ("as discussed by Firthouse et al. [9]").

3.3. Entrapment Efficiency. Entrapment efficiency of niosomal formulations was determined by centrifugation method. 10 mL niosomal suspension was poured into a stopper test tube and centrifuged by using cooling centrifuge at 10,000 rpm maintained at 4°C for 90 minutes and then filtered by using Whatman filter paper to obtain clear fraction. The clear fraction was used for the determination of free drug by using UV spectrophotometer at 278 nm ("as discussed by Sathali and Sangeetha [10]"). The encapsulation efficiency was calculated using the formula

$$\text{Entrapment Efficiency (\%)} = \left[\frac{(C_t - C_f)}{C_t} \times 100\right], \quad (1)$$

where C_t is concentration of total drug and C_f is concentration of unentrapped drug.

3.4. In Vitro Release Studies. In vitro release studies of niosomes suspension were carried out by dialysis bag method ("as discussed by Sathali and Rajalakshmi [11]"). A dialysis sac was washed and kept in distilled water for soaking. The vesicle suspension was pipetted into a bag made up of tubing and sealed followed by placing the dialysis bag into a beaker containing 500 mL of PBS pH 7.4. The beaker was placed over magnetic stirrer (50 rpm) and the temperature was maintained at 37°C ± 0.5°C. Samples were withdrawn at predetermined time intervals. Sink condition was maintained throughout the experiment by replacing the withdrawing sample with fresh medium. Samples were diluted and analysed for drug content by using UV/visible spectrophotometer at 278 nm ("as discussed by Sathali and Rajalakshmi [11]").

3.5. Formulation and Evaluation of Gels. Gel base was prepared by dispersing 1% w/w Carbopol 940 in distilled water and then was allowed to swell for 1 hour. After that glycerin was added to the dispersion with continuous homogenization. The pH was adjusted by triethanolamine ("as discussed by Solanki et al. [12]").

3.6. Preparation of Plain Topical Gel. Plain gel was prepared by adding drug (2% w/w) in 1% w/w Carbopol 940 base for the comparison with niosomal gel (N_2G).

3.7. Preparation of Niosomal Gel. The measured volume of N_2 niosomal formulation was centrifuged by using cooling centrifuge for 90 mins at 4°C and 12,000 rpm. The semisolid mass of niosomes was separated from supernatant and mixed in the 1% Carbopol gel base by using electric homogenizer ("as discussed by Solanki et al. [12]").

3.8. Evaluation of Topical Gel. The niosomal gel and plain topical ETD gel were characterized with respect to pH, viscosity, spreadability, and *ex vivo* permeation studies.

3.9. pH Measurements. The pH of the gel formulations was delivered by using digital pH meter. Before measurement pH meter was calibrated and readings were taken by dipping the glass rod into the gel formulations ("as discussed by Jain et al. [13]").

3.10. Viscosity Measurement. The viscosity of gel formulations was determined by Brookfield viscometer. 25.0 g gel was taken in beaker and spindle number 4 was rotated at 50 rpm and viscosity of the sample was determined ("as discussed by Jain et al. [13]").

3.11. Spreadability. The spreadability of gel formulations was determined by using spreadability apparatus. 1.0 g of gel sample was placed on the lower slide and upper slide was placed on the top of the sample ("as discussed by Jain et al. [13]"). The spreadability was determined by the formula

$$S = \frac{m \times l}{t}, \quad (2)$$

where S is spreadability, m is weight tied to upper slide, l is length travel by upper slide, and t is time.

3.12. Ex Vivo Permeation Studies. The *ex vivo* permeation studies of plain topical gel and niosomal gel were carried out with Franz diffusion (FD) cell using dehaired rat skin followed by hydration for 30 minutes in PBS pH 7.4 at room temperature to remove the extraneous debris and leachable enzymes. Then excised skin was placed between donor and receptor compartments of the FD cell. Gel was placed in donor compartment and PBS pH 7.4 was taken in receptor compartments as media. Temperature of cell was maintained at 37°C ± 0.5°C. The assembly was kept on magnetic stirrer and samples were withdrawn at time intervals of 1, 2, 3, 4, 6, 8, 12, and 24 h and replaced with equal volume of fresh media. Samples were analyzed by UV spectrophotometer at 278 nm and cumulative % of drug release was calculated ("as discussed by Srikanth et al. [14]").

3.13. Stability Studies. Niosomal formulation was selected on the basis of entrapment efficiency and *in vitro* release studies. Stability studies were assessed by keeping N_2 niosomal suspension and niosomal gel in sealed glass vials and storing

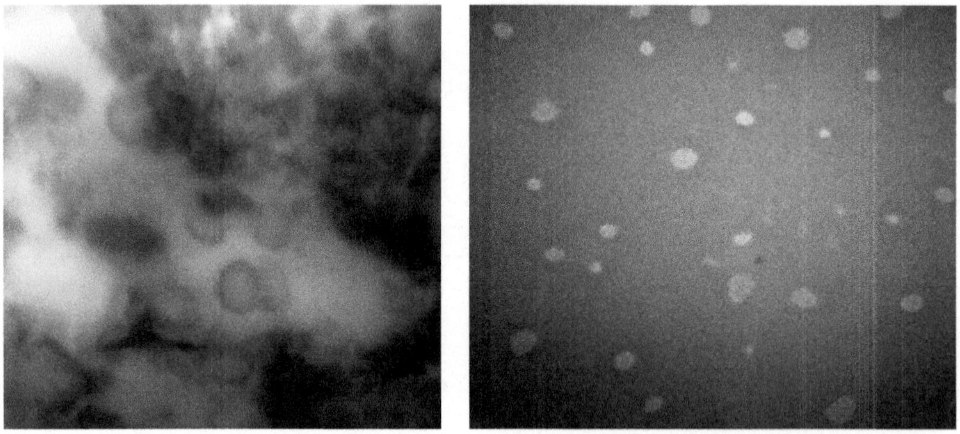

(a) (b)

FIGURE 2: TEM image of N_2 formulation at (a) 60,000x and (b) 18,000x.

them in two different storage conditions, that is, refrigeration temperature and room temperature for a period of 30 days. The samples were withdrawn at different time intervals over a period of one month and the residual content was determined spectrophotometrically ("as discussed by Arora et al. [15]").

3.14. *In Vivo Studies.* White Albino rats of either sex weighing between 180 and 200 g were selected for study. The approval of the Institutional Animal Ethical Committee CPCEA No. MMCP/IAEC/12/8 was obtained before starting the study. The animals were divided into four groups, each consisting of six rats. Groups II, III, and IV were subjected to topical gel of ETD drug, niosomal formulation, and topical niosomal gel formulation, respectively, whereas Group I was treated as control. Anti-inflammatory activities of the drug by developed formulations were determined by using paw edema method on the basis of the inhibition of the volume of the hind paw edema induced by phlogistic agent. For present study 1% w/v carrageenan solution in 0.9% w/v was used as phlogistic agent.

3.15. *Anti-Inflammatory Activity.* The animals were fasted overnight and all groups were treated by applying the formulations containing drug equivalent to 20 mg/kg body weight on the left paw of the rats, with respective gels. The area of application was covered with bandages and it was left in place for 3 hrs. The dressing was then removed and the gel remaining on the surface was wiped off with cotton. The animals were then injected with 0.1 mL of 1% w/v of carrageenan solution in plantar region of left hind paw and the paw volume was measured after 1 hr, 2 hr, 3 hr, 4 hr, 5 hr, and 6 hr and 8 hr, using modified or specially designed assembly which works on the Archimedes principle. The right paw served as a reference of noninflamed paw for comparison. The percentage difference between right and left paw volumes was taken as percent edema produced ("as discussed by Shinde and Kanojiya [16]"). The percent edema produced with test samples was subtracted from percent edema produced in control group to obtain percent edema inhibition by respective groups. Percent inhibition of edema is directly proportional to the anti-inflammatory activity.

4. Result and Discussion

4.1. *Evaluation of Niosomal Formulation.* Developed niosomal formulations were characterized with respect to particle size, shape, entrapment efficiency, and *in vitro* drug release profile.

4.1.1. *Shape and Morphology.* Shape and morphology of niosomal formulations were determined by optical microscopy. It was clearly observed from Figure 1 that niosomes are spherical in shape.

4.1.2. *Transmission Electron Microscopy (TEM).* Morphological characteristics of niosomal formulations were further confirmed by TEM analysis. TEM photomicrograph of (N_2) niosomal formulation at 60,000x and 18,000x magnification revealed the spherical shape of niosomes. Further it was observed from the TEM images that niosomes are hollow vesicular structure.

4.1.3. *Particle Size.* Particle size of niosomal formulation at different ratio of cholesterol and surfactant was shown in Figure 3. Mean particle size of the niosomal formulation was found to be in the range of 2 μm to 4 μm. It was clearly depicted from Figure 3 that particle size of niosomal formulations was increased on increasing the cholesterol content. Cholesterol content provides strength to the nonpolar tail of nonionic surfactant. At low cholesterol content, it is to be expected that the cholesterol and nonionic surfactant are in close packing with increasing curvature and reducing size. As the cholesterol content increases, it would reduce the content of surfactants and also increased the hydrophobicity of bilayer membrane thus increasing vesicles radius in a way to establish more thermodynamic stable form. Rigid structure of bilayer membrane due to cholesterol content

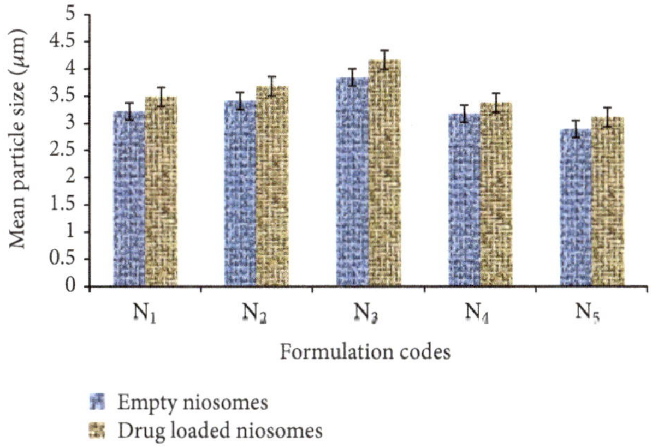

FIGURE 3: Particle size of niosomes containing Span 60.

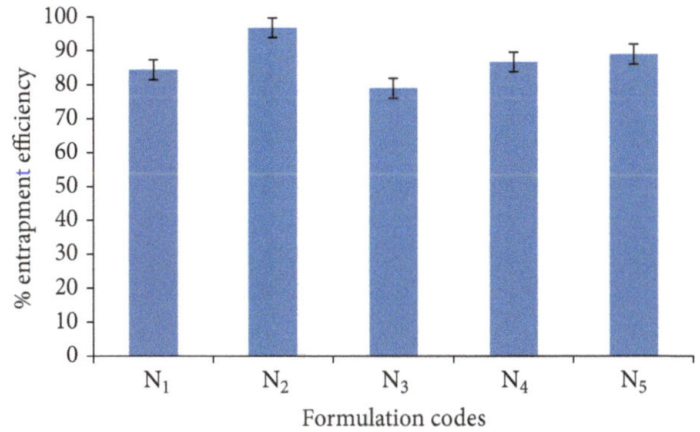

FIGURE 4: Entrapment efficiencies of various niosomal formulations containing Span 60.

also provides resistance to reduce size due to sonication and results in vesicles with bigger size.

4.1.4. Entrapment Efficiency. Entrapment efficiency of various niosomal formulations was determined at different ratio of cholesterol and surfactant by centrifugation method and result was shown in Figure 4. It was clearly depicted from the data shown in Figure 4 that entrapment efficiency of the niosomal formulation was increased on increasing the cholesterol ratio from 0.5 to 1 whereas on further increase in cholesterol ratio from 1 to 1.5 the entrapment efficiency was decreased. There could be two factors for such result: first, with increase of cholesterol ratio, hydrophobicity and stability of bilayers vesicles increase and permeability decreases which may lead to efficiently trapping the hydrophobic drug into bilayers as the vesicles formed. Secondly higher amount of cholesterol may compete with the drug for packing space within the bilayer, hence excluding the drug as the amphiphiles assembled into drugs ("as discussed by Balakrishnan et al. [8]").

Entrapment efficiency of niosomes was also influenced by varying the amount of surfactant. As the amount of surfactant in niosomal formulation increased, the decrease in leakage of drug results in enhancement of entrapment efficiency ("as discussed by Salih et al. [17]").

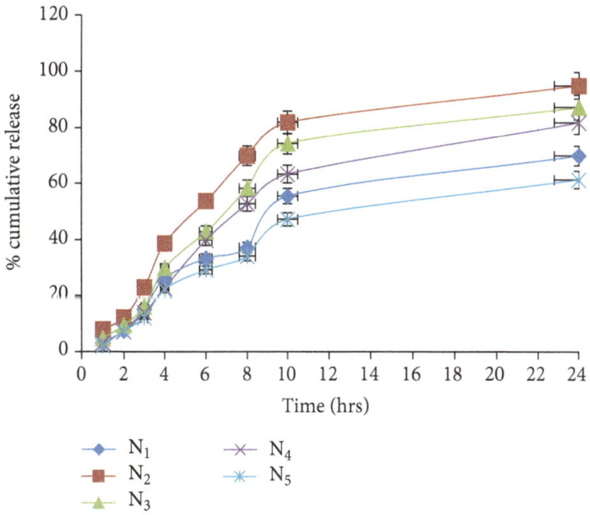

FIGURE 5: *In vitro* release profile of niosomal formulations.

4.1.5. In Vitro Studies. In vitro studies of niosomal formulations were carried out in PBS pH 7.4 by dialysis method on magnetic stirrer and results were shown in Figure 5 (see Table 1 of Supplementary Material available online at http://dx.doi.org/10.1155/2016/9324567). It was observed from the data that *in vitro* drug release of niosomal formulation was sharply increased up to 24 hr. It was found that N_2 formulation displayed maximum drug release that is 94.91% after 24 hr at 1:1 ratio of cholesterol to surfactant. Amount of surfactant varied in niosomal formulation affects the release profile of drug. As the ratio of surfactant increases from 1:1 to 1:1.5 (cholesterol:surfactant), the drug release from niosomal vesicles was decreased. This could be due to the fact that the increase in surfactant ratio acts as depot and reduces leakage of drug from niosomes to dissolution media ("as discussed by Salih et al. [17]").

On the basis of the above result it was found that N_2 possesses highest entrapment efficiency and *in vitro* release profile; thus it was selected for further study.

4.1.6. Characterization of Niosomal Gel Formulations

(1) Physical Examination. Gels were examined for physical appearance and results of the physical examination of the gel were shown in Table 2.

Plain gel and niosomal gel formulations were white in color, were homogenous, and had smooth texture.

(2) pH Measurement. pH of the niosomal gel and plain gel as shown in Table 2 lied in the normal pH range of skin to avoid any risk of irritation upon the application to the skin.

(3) Viscosity Measurements. The viscosities of the gel formulations are optimum as they provide good *in vitro* release of drug through the gel and results were shown in Table 2.

(4) Spreadability. Spreadability of the plain gel and niosomal gel formulation were found to be better as compared to plain

TABLE 2: Physical examination and other characteristics of plain and niosomal gel formulation.

Sr. number	Formulation codes	Color	Homogeneity	Texture	pH	Viscosity (cps)	Spreadability (gm·cm/sec)
1	N_2G	White	Homogenous	Smooth	6.70 ± 0.05	6831 ± 9.47	18.25 ± 1.24
2	Plain gel	White	Homogenous	Smooth	6.60 ± 0.08	6502 ± 8.51	13.71 ± 0.83

FIGURE 6: Spreadability studies.

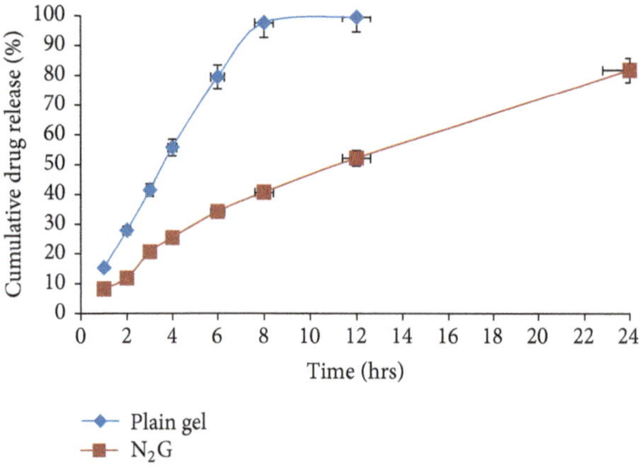

FIGURE 7: Comparative *ex vivo* permeation study of gel formulations.

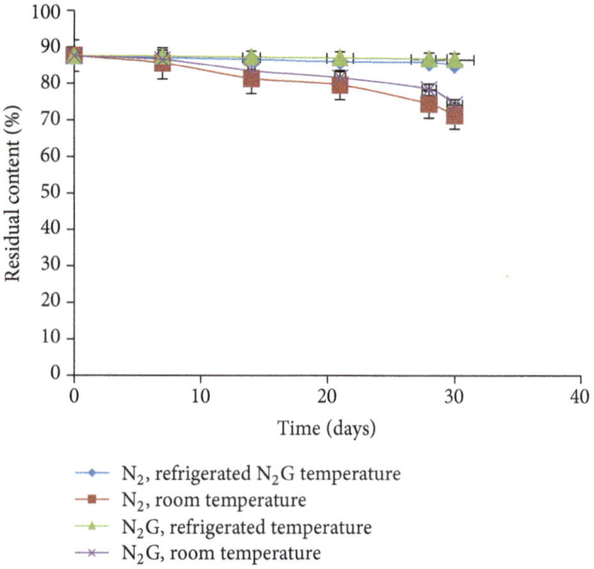

FIGURE 8: Stability studies of N_2 and N_2G formulation at different storage conditions.

gel as shown in Table 2 and Figure 6. This could be because of loose gel matrix of gel due to presence of vesicles.

(5) Ex Vivo Studies. The *ex vivo* skin permeation study of niosomal gel and plain gel was carried out with Franz diffusion cell using abdominal skin of male Albino rat by using PBS (pH 7.4) as quality media.

It was displayed from the data as shown in Figure 7 that from drug release 15.28% of drug release was reported from ETD topical gel after 1 hr and drug release was significantly increased from 15.28% to 97.57% up to 8 hrs; thereafter only 1.91% of drug was released in next 4 hrs, whereas in case of topical niosomal gel only 8.13% of drug release was observed after 1 hr and continuous and appreciable increase in cumulative drug releases was reported up to 24 hrs. After 24 hrs only 81.73% of drug release was recorded. These results show that the slow and sustained release of drug through the rat skin for prolonged period of time was obtained in case of niosomal gel formulation as compared to plain gel to ETD. Faster release of the ETD from the plain gel may be due to free drug being present in gel structure as compared to niosomal gel in which drug was entrapped into niosomal vesicular structure. In case of niosomal gel, drug permeated due to either the fusion of the niosomes with the intercellular lipid of the stratum corneum, direct transfer of drug from niosomes to the skin, or the penetration enhancement effect of the nonionic surfactant of niosomes ("as discussed by Shilpa and Vijay [18]").

(6) Stability Studies. Stability studies were carried out by keeping N_2 formulation and niosomal gel formulation (N_2G) for one month at different storage conditions. At different time points, sample was withdrawn and percent residual content was determined by UV spectrophotometer and results were shown in Figure 8.

It was observed from the results slight reduction in residual drug content at room temperature, whereas, in case of refrigerated temperature, no significant change was observed in residual content. Thus developed niosomal formulation was found to be stable at the end of the study on storage condition.

(7) In Vivo Studies. In vivo anti-inflammatory activity was determined by using carrageenan induced rat paw edema method. The percentage inhibition of edema was calculated from different formulations and results were shown in Figure 9 and Table 2 of Supplementary Material.

Maximum% edema inhibition was observed with niosomal gel formulation as compared to the niosome suspension and plain gel after 8 hrs. Although the difference observed is narrow at end point, however, improvement is consistent at all time points, which presents the significance of outcome. According to both *ex vivo* and *in vivo* studies N_2G gel showed the better permeation and effectiveness as compared to other

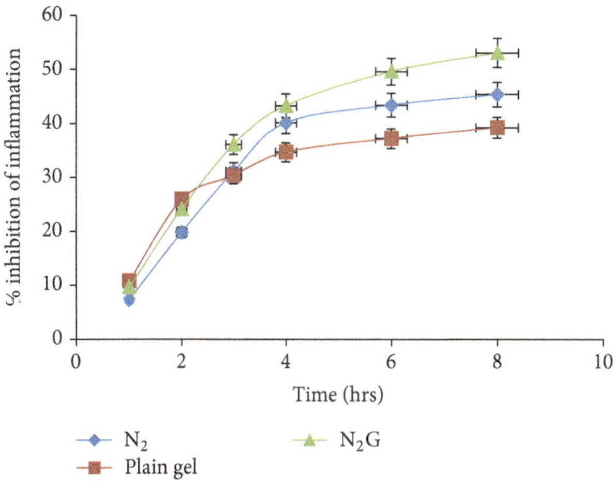

FIGURE 9: Comparative *in vivo* percentage edema inhibition.

formulations. This may be due to efficient hydration of thin film and more total amount of drug entrapped.

5. Conclusion

Niosomal formulation was successfully prepared by thin film hydration technique using different ratios of cholesterol and surfactant (Span 60) and dicetyl phosphate (DCP). It was found that niosomal formulation N_2 having cholesterol : surfactant ratio (1 : 1) showed better entrapment efficiency and *in vitro* release profile. Selected niosomal formulation was further incorporated in Carbopol gel base to prepare niosomal gel. Both niosomal formulation and niosomal gel were found to be stable at different storage conditions. Niosomal gel was prepared, exhibiting better skin permeation study when compared with plain gel. Further inhibitions in inflammation by developed niosomal gel were also found maximum when compared to plain gel and niosomal formulation. The result of present research work reveals that niosomal gel formulation could be the better choice for delivery of wide verities of drug for transdermal administration.

Abbreviations

ETD: Etodolac
DCP: Dicetyl phosphate
NSAID: Nonsteroidal anti-inflammatory drug
GIT: Gastrointestinal tract
TEM: Transmission Electron Microscopy
UV: Ultraviolet
RPM: Revolution per minute
FD: Franz diffusion.

Competing Interests

The authors declare that there is no conflict of interests regarding the publication of this paper.

Acknowledgments

The authors are highly thankful to IPCA Laboratory, Mumbai, for providing the gift sample of Etodolac and also thankful to Panjab University for providing TEM facility and MM University Mullana for giving the facility to carry out this research work.

References

[1] N. Inoue, M. Nogawa, S. Ito, K. Tajima, S. Kume, and T. Kyoi, "The enantiomers of etodolac, a racemic anti-inflammatory agent, play different roles in efficacy and gastrointestinal safety," *Biological and Pharmaceutical Bulletin*, vol. 34, no. 5, pp. 655–659, 2011.

[2] P. K. Chintala and J. Padmapreetha, "Formulation and *in-vitro* evaluation of gel containing ethosomes entrapped with etodolac," *International Journal of Pharmaceutical Science and Research*, vol. 5, no. 2, pp. 630–635, 2014.

[3] SS. Kumar, K. Masilamani, SS. Srinivas, and V. Ravichandiran, "Formulation and Physico-Chemical Evaluation of Ethylcellulose Microspheres Containing Etodolac," in *International Conference on Biotechnology and Pharmaceutical Sciences*, pp. 372–375, 2011.

[4] N. S. Barakat, "*In vitro* and *in vivo* characteristics of a thermogelling rectal delivery system of etodolac," *APPS Pharmaceutical Science and Technology*, vol. 10, no. 3, pp. 724–731, 2009.

[5] C. Tas, Y. Ozkan, A. Okyar, and A. Savaser, "*In vitro* and *ex vivo* permeation studies of etodolac from hydrophilic gels and effect of terpenes as enhancers," *Drug Delivery*, vol. 14, no. 7, pp. 453–459, 2007.

[6] N. Sharma, G. Agarwal, A. C. Rana, Z. A. Bhat, and D. Kumar, "A review: transdermal drug delivery system: a tool for novel drug delivery system," *International Journal of Drug Development and Research*, vol. 3, no. 3, pp. 70–84, 2011.

[7] D. Bhowmik, M. Chiranjib Chandira, B. Jayakar, and K. P. Sampath, "Recent advances in transdermal drug delivery system," *International Journal of Pharmaceutical Technology*, vol. 2, no. 1, pp. 68–77, 2010.

[8] P. Balakrishnan, S. Shanmugam, W. S. Lee et al., "Formulation and *in vitro* assessment of minoxidil niosomes for enhanced skin delivery," *International Journal of Pharmaceutics*, vol. 377, no. 1-2, pp. 1–8, 2009.

[9] P. U. M. Firthouse, S. M. Halith, S. U. Wahab, M. Sirajudeen, and S. K. Mohideen, "Formulation and evaluation of miconazole niosomes," *International Journal of PharmTech Research*, vol. 3, no. 2, pp. 1019–1022, 2011.

[10] A. A. H. Sathali and T. Sangeetha, "Formulation and evaluation of ocular niosomal in situ gel of levofloxacin hemihydrates," *Journal of Pharmacy Research*, vol. 4, pp. 4331–4337, 2011.

[11] A. A. H. Sathali and G. Rajalakshmi, "Evaluation of transdermal targeted niosomal drug delivery of terbinafine hydrochloride," *International Journal of PharmTech Research*, vol. 2, no. 3, pp. 2081–2089, 2010.

[12] A. B. Solanki, J. R. Parikh, R. H. Parikh, and M. R. Patel, "Evaluation of different compositions of niosomes to optimize aceclofenac transdermal delivery," *Asian Journal of Pharmaceutical Sciences*, vol. 5, no. 3, pp. 87–95, 2010.

[13] A. Jain, P. Deveda, and N. Vyas, "Development of antifungal emulsion based gel for topical fungal infections," *International Journal of Pharmaceutical Research and Development*, vol. 2, pp. 18–25, 2011.

[14] K. Srikanth, M. Nappinnai, V. R. M. Gupta, and J. Suribabu, "Niosomes: a prominent tool for transdermal drug delivery," *Research Journal of Pharmaceutical, Biological and Chemical Sciences*, vol. 1, no. 2, pp. 308–316, 2010.

[15] S. Arora, B. Prashar, H. Dhamija, A. Chandel, and V. Thakur, "Niosomes: the unique vesicular drug carriers," *Journal of Drug Delivery & Therapeutics*, vol. 2, no. 1, pp. 96–101, 2012.

[16] U. A. Shinde and S. S. Kanojiya, "Serratiopeptidase niosomal gel with potential in topical delivery," *Journal of Pharmaceutics*, vol. 2014, Article ID 382959, 9 pages, 2014.

[17] O. S. Salih, L. H. Samein, and W. K. Ali, "Formulation and in vitro evaluation of rosuvastatin calcium niosomes," *International Journal of Pharmacy and Pharmaceutical Sciences*, vol. 5, no. 4, pp. 525–535, 2013.

[18] D. J. Shilpa and K. P. Vijay, "Formulation, development and evaluation of niosomal drug delivery system for clindamycin phosphate," *Pharma Science Monitor*, vol. 5, no. 2, pp. 256–274, 2014.

19

Targeted Delivery of Glucan Particle Encapsulated Gallium Nanoparticles Inhibits HIV Growth in Human Macrophages

Ernesto R. Soto, Olivia O'Connell, Fusun Dikengil, Paul J. Peters, Paul R. Clapham, and Gary R. Ostroff

Program in Molecular Medicine, University of Massachusetts Medical School, 373 Plantation Street, Worcester, MA 01605, USA

Correspondence should be addressed to Gary R. Ostroff; gary.ostroff@umassmed.edu

Academic Editor: Jia You Fang

Glucan particles (GPs) are hollow, porous 3–5 μm microspheres derived from the cell walls of Baker's yeast (*Saccharomyces cerevisiae).* The 1,3-β-glucan outer shell provides for receptor-mediated uptake by phagocytic cells expressing β-glucan receptors. GPs have been used for macrophage-targeted delivery of a wide range of payloads (DNA, siRNA, protein, small molecules, and nanoparticles) encapsulated inside the hollow GPs or bound to the surface of chemically derivatized GPs. Gallium nanoparticles have been proposed as an inhibitory agent against HIV infection. Here, macrophage targeting of gallium using GPs provides for more efficient delivery of gallium and inhibition of HIV infection in macrophages compared to free gallium nanoparticles.

1. Introduction

Efficient targeted drug delivery systems are paramount for the development of novel and effective biopharmaceuticals and diagnostic agents. The advantages of targeted drug delivery and release include increased drug concentrations at the site of disease, limited side effects from off-target cell damage, and reduction in dose frequency and cost and length of treatment. A primary challenge for the development of drug delivery systems is the lack of optimal strategies to achieve selective and efficient cellular targeting.

Glucan particles (GPs) derived from Baker's yeast have been efficiently used for targeted payload delivery to macrophages and dendritic cells [1–11]. The hollow and porous nature of GPs (3–5 μm in diameter) allows for absorption and retention of payload molecules. The β-1,3-D glucan surface composition also serves as an effective means of recognition by cell surface receptors in macrophages (via dectin-1 (D1) and Complement Receptor 3 (CR3)) and other phagocytic innate immune cells, allowing for a receptor-mediated particle uptake mechanism [3, 12]. We have reported several methods for efficient encapsulation of a wide range of molecules inside GPs [1–11]. Water soluble macromolecules (e.g., DNA, siRNA, and proteins) can be efficiently encapsulated inside GPs by both polyplex and layer-by-layer (LbL) synthetic approaches [1, 2]. Neutral, small drug molecules have been encapsulated by embedding the payload in polymer hydrogels [7] and encapsulation within small nanoparticles prepared *in situ* inside GPs or loaded onto the surface of GPs in a piggyback approach [6]. These different drug loading strategies accomplish two important goals: (1) high encapsulation efficiency of the payload molecule using a synthetic approach that will provide protection of the payload inside GP during storage and in transit to macrophages and (2) efficient, sustained release at low pH (pH 5 or lower) to achieve payload escape from the GPs in the endosomal compartment following macrophage uptake. Here we describe a potential new application of GPs for macrophage-targeted delivery of gallium for enhanced inhibition of HIV infection in human macrophages compared to free gallium nanoparticles.

Gallium has been shown to be effective in the treatment of several disorders, including viral and bacterial infections [13]. Gallium salts are used in pharmaceutical applications for hypercalcemia, and there is also evidence of a gallium therapeutic effect against syphilis, trypanosomiasis, and tuberculosis [14]. Gallium's therapeutic activity stems from its similarity to iron (III), with the ability to substitute for iron (III) and interfere with critical enzymatic process in metabolism and the growth of proliferating cells due to the inability of gallium (III) to be reduced in redox-active enzymes [15]. This interference is responsible for gallium inhibition of proliferation of several pathogenic microorganisms, most notably species of *Mycobacterium.* Cell uptake of gallium-transferrin complexes by infected cells, particularly macrophages, diminishes iron (III) concentration essential to enzymes likely to be involved in various processes critical for viral and bacterial infection. Additionally, gallium's lack of redox activity reduces potential toxicity effects from gallium as it does not interfere with iron (II) bearing molecules, such as heme, or with oxygen transport. Gallium is also resistant to drug efflux pumps, allowing it to be less vulnerable to drug resistance mechanisms.

Recently, gallium nanoparticles have been proposed as an inhibitory agent against coinfection with human immunodeficiency virus (HIV) and *Mycobacterium tuberculosis* (TB) [16]. Nanoparticles of gallium (III) mesotetraphenylporphyrin chloride delivered to macrophages provided a long acting effect against HIV and HIV-TB coinfection. A limitation of this system was the inefficient targeting of the proposed particles to macrophages, thus requiring large concentrations of gallium for sustained effect on HIV inhibition.

In this publication we describe an effective approach for the encapsulation of gallium compounds in the form of large nanoparticle aggregates inside GPs. This approach provides for efficient cell targeting of gallium into macrophages by receptor-mediated uptake of GP. Macrophages are a major cellular target for HIV in tissues. For example, perivascular macrophages in brain tissue are heavily infected in subjects with HIV associated dementia [17]. The selected gallium compounds are insoluble at pH 7, but they react in the acidic endosomal compartment upon GP mediated cell uptake leading to release of water soluble gallium (III). This approach represents an effective strategy for the encapsulation and macrophage-targeted delivery of gallium that could be extended to other classes of inorganic nanoparticulate materials.

2. Materials and Methods

2.1. Materials. Glucan particles were prepared from Fleishmann's Baker's yeast (AB Mauri Food Inc., Chesterfield, MO) as previously described [1]. Gallium (III) chloride (99.999% purity) was purchased from Alfa Aesar. All reagents, solvents, and buffer solutions for the syntheses and characterization of gallium particles were purchased from Sigma-Aldrich and used without further purification. Tissue culture materials were purchased from Gibco.

2.2. Synthesis of Gallium Nanoparticles Inside Glucan Particles (GP-Ga Formulations). Gallium chloride was absorbed into GPs by swelling a dry GP pellet (5 mg) in a subhydrodynamic volume (5 μL/mg GP) of an aqueous gallium chloride solution. GP samples containing gallium chloride were incubated at room temperature for 1 hour to allow for diffusion into the GPs. The loaded GPs were then lyophilized and the loading and lyophilization steps repeated until target concentrations of gallium chloride within the GP samples were achieved. The dry GP-$GaCl_3$ pellets were then treated by wetting the pellets in a subhydrodynamic volume of trapping agent solution (sodium hydroxide, sodium bicarbonate, or sodium triphosphate) to produce insoluble gallium nanoparticles inside GPs. The GP-Ga particles were then washed with water to remove unreacted gallium chloride or small (<30 nm) gallium nanoparticles not trapped inside GPs. Samples were finally sterilized overnight in 70% ethanol and aseptically washed in 0.9% saline, and GP number was counted with a hemocytometer. Sample concentrations were then adjusted to 1×10^8 particles/mL in 0.9% saline and stored frozen.

2.3. Characterization of Glucan Particle Encapsulated Gallium Nanoparticles (GP-Ga)

2.3.1. Trapping Efficiency of Gallium in GP-Ga Formulations. Gallium was quantified using a spectrofluorometric assay [18]. Samples containing GP-Ga and empty GPs (negative controls) were suspended in 6 M HCl. Samples were centrifuged and the supernatants containing extracted gallium were mixed with rhodamine B solution in 6 M HCl (2 mg rhodamine B/mL) and incubated for 10 minutes at room temperature. The gallium-rhodamine B complexes were extracted with benzene. The fluorescence of the complexes in the organic phase was measured at an excitation wavelength of 553 nm and emission wavelength of 608 nm. GP-Ga samples incubated in aqueous rhodamine B solution were also prepared for fluorescence microscopy analysis to confirm formation of Ga-rhodamine complexes inside GPs.

2.3.2. Kinetics of Gallium Release from GP-Ga. Samples containing 1 mg of GP-Ga were incubated in 1 mL of phosphate buffer saline (PBS, pH 7) or in 0.1 M sodium acetate buffer (pH 5). The samples were incubated at 37°C for a total of 4 days. At specific times, 100 μL was aliquoted from samples and fresh buffer was added to maintain sink conditions. Gallium was quantified in these aliquots using the rhodamine B fluorescence assay as described above.

2.3.3. GP-Ga Cytotoxicity. To determine the effect of gallium on cell growth and viability, GP-Ga samples and empty GP controls were evaluated in a B6 immortalized murine derived bone marrow macrophage (iMac) cell line [19]. Particles were evaluated for particle cell uptake at a 10 : 1 GP : cell ratio to maximize phagocytic cell uptake. Free gallium nanoparticles were also evaluated in the same concentration range as GP-Ga formulations on a gallium weight basis. Samples were suspended in complete DMEM and added to 96-well plates containing 1×10^4 cells/well. The plates were incubated at 37°C under 5% CO_2 for 24 h. Alamar blue (10 μL) was added, incubated at 37°C for 30 min, and fluorescence was measured (excitation wavelength = 530 nm, emission wavelength = 590 nm). Fluorescence response is dependent on the reduction of the Alamar blue indicator by metabolically active cells and is a measure of cell number and viability. Growth arrest

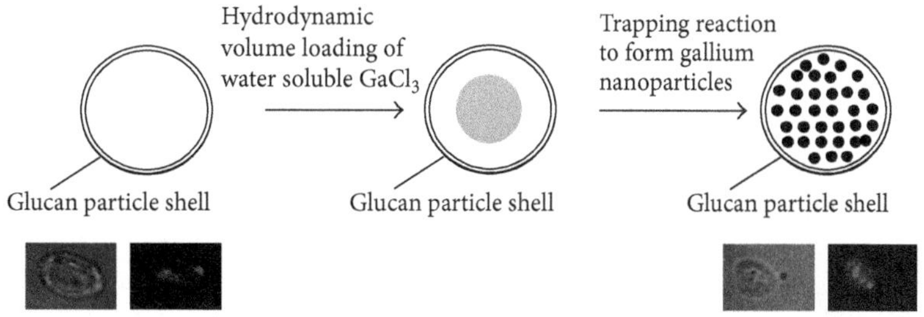

FIGURE 1: Schematic representation of gallium loading into GPs and trapping reaction to form gallium nanoparticles inside GPs. Microscopy images show complexes of rhodamine B with gallium trapped inside GPs (right image); minimum background fluorescence was observed from empty GPs (left).

was calculated from the fluorescence response of the sample relative to the response of control wells containing buffer (PBS) or empty GPs.

2.4. HIV Infected Human Macrophage Assay to Assess Inhibition of HIV Replication. Cotransfections of 293T/17 cells with env-minus NL4.3 backbone, pHIVec2/GFP reporter, and different envelope plasmids (Env17, B33, or B59) in pSVIIIenv were done with a $CaCl_2$ Promega Profection Kit (Promega Corporation, Madison, WI) [20]. Virus in supernatants was harvested 48 hours after transfection. Supernatants were collected and spun down at 1200 rpm for 5 minutes and 1 mL aliquots were made and frozen. Infectivity of each Env+ pseudovirus was estimated as GFP+ focus forming units via titration on HeLa TZM-BL cells [21].

Human monocyte derived macrophages were isolated and cultured using processed buffy coats from New York Biologics Inc. Briefly, 5×10^7 Ficoll-purified peripheral blood mononuclear cells (PBMC) from a buffy coat were plated into 15 cm bacterial culture dishes for 3 h before extensively washing away nonadherent cells, culturing overnight, and repeating the washes. The adherent monocytes were then cultured for 5–7 days in 10% AB+ human plasma in DMEM. The differentiated macrophages were treated with EDTA and transferred to 48-well tissue culture dishes the day prior to infection (day −1) at 1.25×10^5 cells/well. Cells were allowed to settle and adhere. After that, cells were treated with single (day −1) or multiple (days −1, 1, and 3) doses of different types of GP-$Ga_2(CO_3)_3$ formulations, empty GPs, or free $Ga_2(CO_3)_3$ nanoparticles. On day 0, all wells were infected with HIV Env+ pseudovirus carrying a GFP reporter gene following a laboratory standard protocol: 100 μL/well (20 μg/mL) DEAE dextran for 30 minutes at 37°C. HIV Env+ pseudoviruses were diluted 1 : 2 and added at 100 μL/well and then spinoculated at 1200 rpm for 45 minutes. On Day 7, cells were imaged and infected GFP-positive cells were counted using a fluorescent microscope at 20x magnification. Percent infection was calculated with B33 Env+ pseudovirus alone as the 100% infected value. The assay was repeated twice to confirm trends and values. Controls were done with HIV reverse transcriptase inhibitor Zidovudine (AZT) given in multiple doses similar to the gallium formulations (20, 10, and 5 μM).

3. Results

3.1. Synthesis of GP-Ga Formulations. A schematic representation of gallium loading and trapping inside GPs is shown in Figure 1. Dry GPs were swelled in a subhydrodynamic volume of a gallium chloride solution to load GPs by diffusion of the gallium solution into the particles through the porous structure of the glucan particle surface. The particles were then lyophilized and the loading cycle was repeated until achieving target gallium chloride concentrations inside GPs. Finally, the dry GP-$GaCl_3$ particles were swollen in a subhydrodynamic volume of a solution containing a suitable reagent for a rapid displacement reaction to produce insoluble gallium oxide (Ga_2O_3), gallium phosphate ($GaPO_4$), or gallium carbonate ($Ga_2(CO_3)_3$) nanoparticles inside GPs. Excess reagents and small (<30 nm) insoluble gallium salts were washed from the GP samples during purification and sterilization in 70% ethanol. It is likely that the water insoluble gallium materials trapped inside GPs correspond to mixtures of compounds. For example, the reaction of gallium chloride with sodium hydroxide produces gallium oxide (Ga_2O_3) and it has been reported to produce other gallium compounds such as amorphous $Ga(OH)_3$ and crystalline α-GaOOH [22]. Free gallium nanoparticles were also synthesized under the same stoichiometric conditions employed in the synthesis of gallium nanoparticles inside GPs. The objective of this work was to compare the effect of GP encapsulated gallium and free gallium nanoparticles on HIV infectivity inhibition in human macrophages. Future work will focus on complete characterization of the gallium materials in the most active GP-Ga formulation.

3.2. Characterization of GP-Ga Formulations

Gallium Encapsulation in GPs. The amount of gallium trapped inside GPs was quantified using a spectrofluorometric assay with rhodamine B. GP-Ga samples were digested in 6 M HCl to generate soluble gallium chloride. Gallium in acidic medium forms a stable complex with rhodamine B with higher solubility in organic solvents such as benzene. Fluorescence measurements of the gallium-rhodamine B complex extracted into benzene allowed for direct quantification of the concentrations of gallium trapped in GPs (Table 1). Figure 2 shows these quantitative results as percentage of gallium

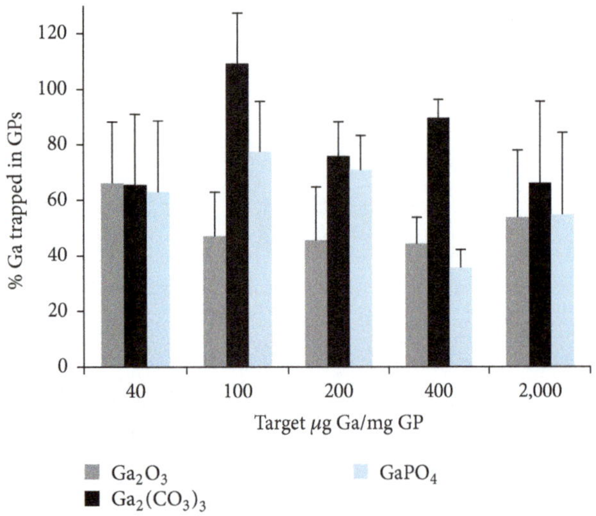

FIGURE 2: Efficiency of gallium trapping in glucan particles following reaction of gallium chloride inside GPs to yield the corresponding encapsulated water insoluble nanoparticulate gallium salt.

TABLE 1: Target and measured concentration of gallium trapped in glucan particles.

Target concentration μg Ga/mg GP	Measured concentration μg Ga/mg GP ± SD		
	Ga_2O_3	$Ga_2(CO_3)_3$	$GaPO_4$
40	26 ± 9	26 ± 12	25 ± 10
100	47 ± 16	108 ± 36	77 ± 18
200	90 ± 38	150 ± 28	140 ± 25
400	175 ± 38	355 ± 49	141 ± 26
2000	1063 ± 347	1308 ± 49	1085 ± 145

trapped in GPs relative to the target amount of gallium chloride loaded in GPs. Gallium carbonate was trapped more efficiently (>65% trapping at all target concentrations) than gallium oxide or phosphate. Additionally, Figure 1 shows fluorescent microscopy image of a GP-$Ga_2(CO_3)_3$ sample treated with rhodamine B confirming the trapping of the gallium salt as insoluble cores inside the hollow space of the glucan particles.

GP-Ga Cytotoxicity. We have previously shown that empty GPs and GPs encapsulating nanoparticles are nontoxic to cells at particle : cell ratios of up to 33 : 1 particle/cell [6]. We examined cytotoxicity of GP-Ga formulations by adding GP-Ga to the murine B6 macrophage cells at a ratio of 10 : 1 GP : cell and free Ga nanoparticles at an equivalent Ga concentration. The samples were incubated for 18–24 hours and cell viability was assessed using the Alamar blue viability assay. The results showed greater than 85% cell viability with all GP-Ga and free Ga nanoparticles formulations (not shown).

Kinetics of Ga Release from GP-Ga Formulations. The GP-Ga formulations were characterized for the effect of pH on kinetics of gallium release. The selection criteria for optimal GP-Ga formulations were stable formulations at pH 7 and sustained release at pH 5 (endosomal pH). Release kinetic results (Figure 3) show both GP-Ga_2O_3 and GP-$Ga_2(CO_3)_3$ are highly stable at pH 7 (<10% Ga released after four days of incubation at 37°C). The GP-$GaPO_4$ formulation showed a burst release of ~20% gallium and stability after the initial burst release. This burst release indicates that the gallium was not efficiently trapped as phosphate as gallium phosphate is water insoluble at pH 7. All formulations showed sustained gallium release at pH 5 with faster release for $GaPO_4$, followed by $Ga_2(CO_3)_3$, and slower release rate for Ga_2O_3. All samples released gallium efficiently at pH <3 (data not shown) due to a fast reaction under harsh acidic conditions to generate soluble gallium chloride.

GP-$Ga_2(CO_3)_3$ formulations were selected for HIV infection studies based on results showing higher efficiency of Ga trapping, stability at pH 7, and better sustained release at pH 5 than GP-Ga formulations of gallium oxide or phosphate.

3.3. Effect of GP-Ga Treatment on HIV Infection of Human Macrophages. We have previously demonstrated that GPs are effectively phagocytosed by macrophage cells via a receptor-mediated mechanism [3]. Experimental results with fluorescein labeled glucan particles using murine macrophages and dectin-1 knock-out murine macrophages demonstrated the role of the dectin-1 receptor for efficient particle uptake. The addition of a soluble beta-glucan receptor antagonist (laminarin) blocks uptake of GPs which also demonstrates that uptake occurs via a receptor-mediated mechanism. In this study, we used fluorescein labeled empty GPs (f-GP) to show that human macrophages are also capable of GP uptake. The fluorescent image in Figure 4 demonstrates efficient particle uptake by the primary human macrophages used in the HIV inhibition assays.

3.4. HIV Inhibition in Human Primary Macrophages with GP-Ga and Free Ga Nanoparticles. We next tested whether GP-Ga formulations could inhibit HIV infection of primary human macrophages. We selected GP-$Ga_2(CO_3)_3$ particles to investigate, since $Ga_2(CO_3)_3$ was trapped more efficiently compared to Ga_2O_3 or $GaPO_4$ (Figure 2). In addition, the profiles of gallium retention at pH 7 and release at pH 5 for GP-$Ga_2(CO_3)_3$ were superior to other formulations. Two different GP-$Ga_2(CO_3)_3$ dosing strategies were tested for their capacity to inhibit HIV-1 pseudovirions carrying R5 macrophage-tropic B33 envelope glycoproteins (Envs) [23, 24]. Macrophages were treated with GP-$Ga_2(CO_3)_3$ containing increasing amounts of Ga either in a single dose the day before infection (Day −1 dose) or 1 day before infection with additional doses 1 and 3 days after infection (Days −1, 1, and 3 dose). Increasing doses of GP-$Ga_2(CO_3)_3$ increased the efficiency of inhibition, with the three-dose strategy superior to a single dose (Table 2). Inhibition reached 93–95%, although complete blockade was not observed.

We next compared GP-$Ga_2(CO_3)_3$ to free $Ga_2(CO_3)_3$ as nanoparticles ($Ga_2(CO_3)_3$ NPs). It was previously reported that gallium in the form of gallium mesotetraporphyrin

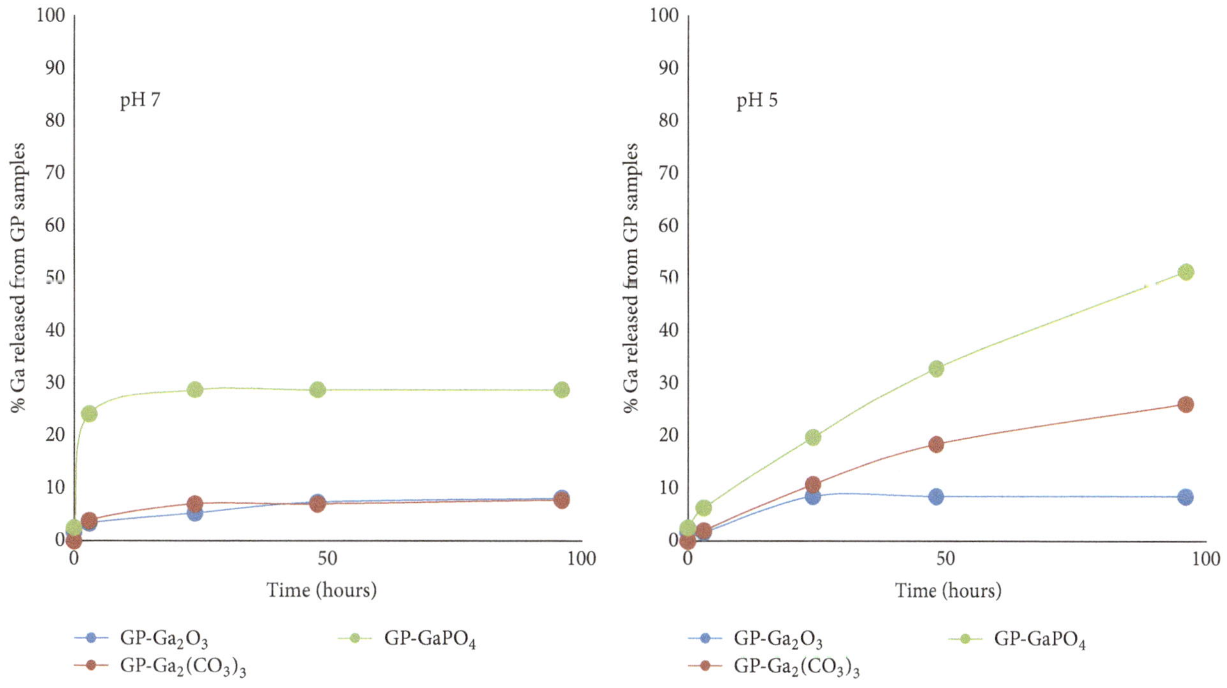

FIGURE 3: Release kinetics of gallium from GPs up to 96 hours at pH 7 (a) and pH 5 (b).

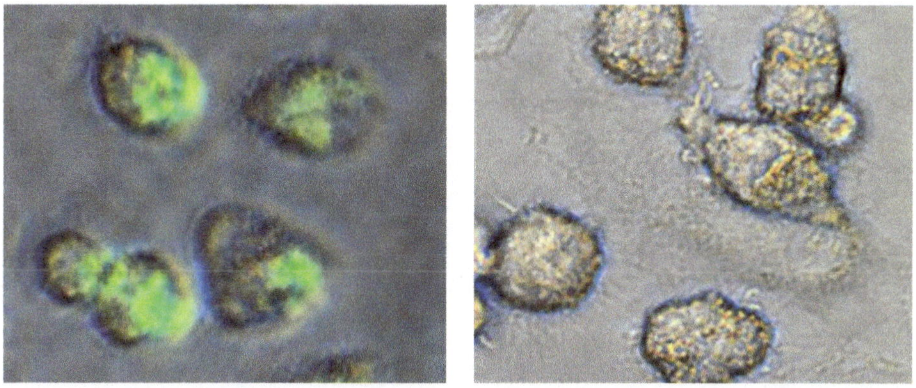

(a) (b)

FIGURE 4: Fluorescent photomicrographs showing efficient uptake of fluorescein labeled glucan particles by human macrophages (a). No significant autofluorescence was detected from control cells (b) when exposed to UV light for same exposure time as cells treated with f-GPs.

nanoparticles inhibited HIV infection of macrophages [16]. Figures 5 and 6 show that GP-$Ga_2(CO_3)_3$ inhibited HIV infection of macrophages significantly more efficiently compared to free $Ga_2(CO_3)_3$ NPs. Of note, Figure 6 indicates that empty glucan particles also inhibited infection, albeit only weakly compared to GP-$Ga_2(CO_3)_3$.

4. Discussion

We show here that glucan particles can deliver gallium carbonate into primary human macrophages, where it is released over time in the low pH of endosomes to inhibit HIV-1 infection.

Glucan particles have been utilized for macrophage-targeted delivery of a wide range of payloads such as DNA, RNA, proteins, and small drug molecules [1, 2, 4–6, 11]. Gallium in the form of gallium mesotetraphenylporphyrin nanoparticles has been recently proposed as an inhibition agent for both HIV and TB in macrophages [16]. However, these gallium nanoparticles lack specificity to target macrophage cells unlike glucan particles that are efficiently targeted to macrophages by a receptor-mediated uptake mechanism. The goals of using glucan particles as carrier of

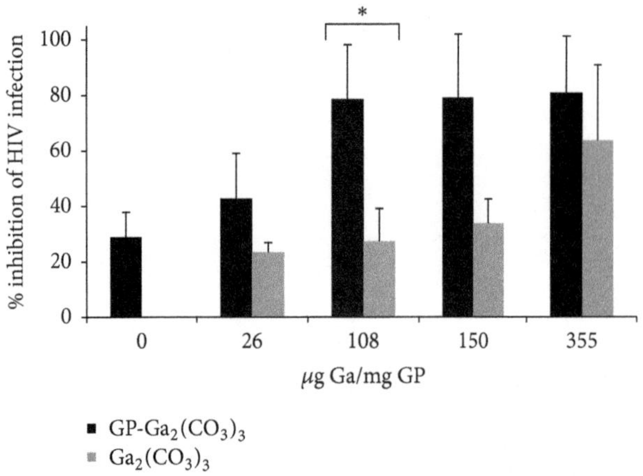

FIGURE 5: HIV infectivity inhibition in human macrophages following uptake of GP-$Ga_2(CO_3)_3$ or free $Ga_2(CO_3)_3$ formulations. Results are average of three experiments ± S.D. Statistical significance was determined by t-test; $^*P < 0.01$.

TABLE 2: Effect of dosage on HIV inhibition of macrophages using GPs containing gallium carbonate at different loading levels of gallium. Results are the average of three experiments. Statistical significance was determined by t-test, $^{a}P < 0.05$ statistical significance between GP-$Ga_2(CO_3)_3$ and GP control, and $^{b}P < 0.1$ statistical significance between dosing regimes.

Sample	μg Ga/mg GP	% HIV inhibition ± SD	
		Day −1 dose	Days −1, 1, 3 doses
GP	0	10 ± 9	19 ± 16
GP-$Ga_2(CO_3)_3$	108	45 ± 2[a]	74 ± 17[a]
GP-$Ga_2(CO_3)_3$	150	53 ± 19	92 ± 3[a]
GP-$Ga_2(CO_3)_3$	355	44 ± 19	91 ± 2[a,b]

gallium nanoparticles are to (1) provide receptor-mediated targeted delivery to macrophages and (2) reduce gallium dosage as uptake of a single GP provides for delivery of larger amounts of gallium than a free gallium nanoparticle.

We demonstrated efficient encapsulation of gallium in GPs by loading of water soluble gallium chloride into the particles followed by reaction with sodium salt or base to form insoluble gallium oxide, carbonate, or phosphate nanoparticles inside GPs (Figure 1). Efficient trapping of these materials requires the formation of gallium nanoparticles larger than 30 nm in diameter to prevent diffusion through the pores of the glucan particles. Gallium was encapsulated in GPs at concentrations as high as 1400 μg Ga/mg GP as shown in Figure 2.

We established that glucan particles loaded with $Ga_2(CO_3)_3$ had a superior combination of retention at pH 7 and release at pH 5 compared to other gallium salts. This experiment enabled us to devise a dosing schedule to enable $Ga_2(CO_3)_3$ release into endosomes before and after HIV infection. Using this approach, HIV inhibition of up to 95% was achieved.

Inhibition values higher than 80% were achieved with GP-$Ga_2(CO_3)_3$ formulations containing 108 to 355 μg Ga/mg GP (Figure 5). Macrophage cells in these experiments were treated at a ratio of 10 GPs/cell in each dose for a total of 3×10^7 glucan particles per 1×10^6 cells for the three-day dose treatment. The gallium concentration range added to the cells increases from 6.5 μg Ga/1 × 10^6 cells for the 108 μg Ga/mg GP-$Ga_2(CO_3)_3$ formulation to 21.3 μg Ga/1 × 10^6 cells for the 355 μg Ga/mg GP-$Ga_2(CO_3)_3$ formulation. A previous study with gallium nanoparticles showed HIV inhibition following maximum uptake of 25 μg Ga/1 × 10^6 cells. However, this gallium concentration in cells was achieved by loading larger doses of gallium nanoparticles to cells. Therefore, the use of GPs provides for more efficient delivery of therapeutic doses of gallium into macrophages.

It is unclear how gallium blocks HIV infection. As discussed above, gallium's similarity to iron may enable it to interfere with critical enzyme processes during HIV entry, nuclear localization, integration, and transcription. Here, we used an HIV-1 pseudovirus carrying a GFP reporter gene controlled by the LTR promoter and expressed from an early mRNA. The inhibitory effects of gallium here could therefore be imparted at any stage during viral entry through integration and up to the expression of spliced early mRNAs.

GP-$Ga_2(CO_3)_3$ particles therefore provide a potential delivery system to block infection of macrophages *in vivo*. Macrophages are a major target for HIV-1 infection in different tissues including the brain [17], lung [25, 26], and testes [27]. The role of macrophages during HIV transmission is less clear where CD4+ T-cells may form initial targets following sexual transmission [28]. Nevertheless, the potential of glucan particles for drug delivery at this stage in the form of microbicides would be attractive to protect against a range of sexually transmitted pathogens. Future work will address the characterization of the different phases of gallium trapped inside GPs in active formulations to correlate and optimize the effect of the gallium form with its biological activity.

5. Conclusions

We have developed a strategy for the encapsulation of gallium in glucan particles for targeted gallium delivery into phagocytic innate immune cells. Gallium was encapsulated in GPs in the form of gallium nanoparticles of gallium carbonate, oxide, or phosphate that are water insoluble at pH 7 providing stability and release gallium from the GPs at pH <5 (endosomal pH). GP-$Ga_2(CO_3)_3$ formulations showed better pH 7 stability and pH 5 release profiles, so we evaluated for their activity to inhibit HIV infection in human macrophages. The GP-$Ga_2(CO_3)_3$ formulations showed inhibition of HIV growth up to 95% and higher inhibition than free $Ga_2(CO_3)_3$ nanoparticles. The use of GPs as carrier of $Ga_2(CO_3)_3$ into macrophages therefore provides a potential delivery system to block HIV infection of macrophages.

Competing Interests

The authors declared no potential conflict of interests.

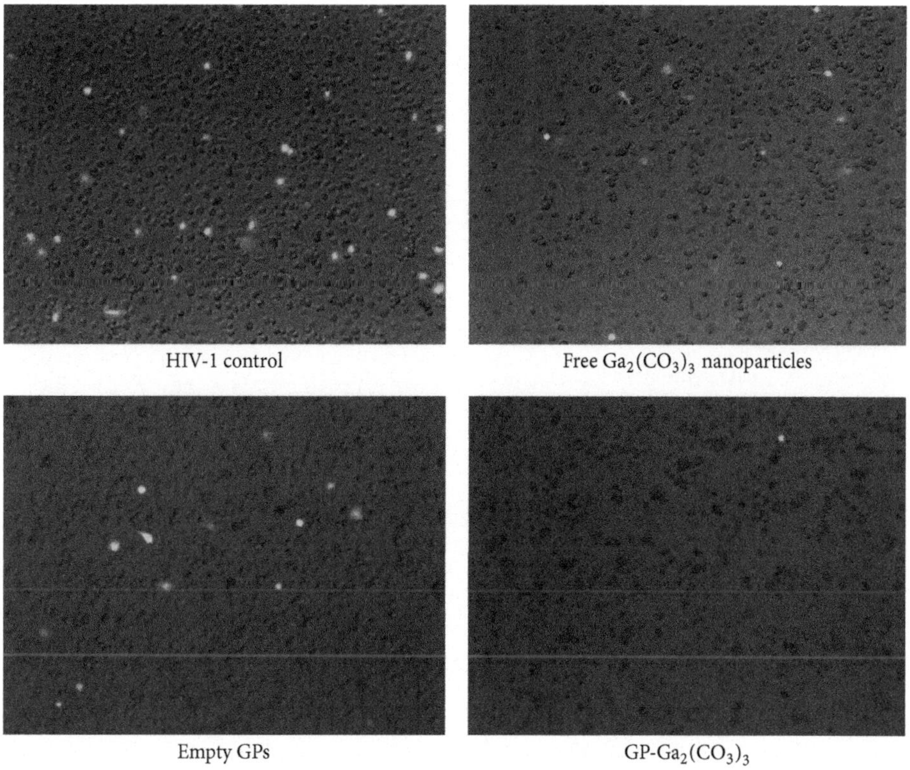

FIGURE 6: Fluorescence microscopy images showing effect of free $Ga_2(CO_3)_3$ nanoparticles, empty GPs, and GP-$Ga_2(CO_3)_3$ formulations on HIV growth inhibition compared to B33 HIV infected control.

Acknowledgments

The authors wish to thank Zeynep Mirza for technical assistance. This work was supported by the National Institute of Health (R01 Grant no. AI089334).

References

[1] E. Soto and G. Ostroff, "Characterization of multilayered nanoparticles inside yeast cell wall particles for DNA delivery," *Bioconjugate Chemistry*, vol. 19, no. 4, pp. 840–848, 2008.

[2] M. Aouadi, G. J. Tesz, S. M. Nicoloro et al., "Orally delivered siRNA targeting macrophage Map4k4 suppresses systemic inflammation," *Nature*, vol. 458, no. 7242, pp. 1180–1184, 2009.

[3] H. Huang, G. R. Ostroff, C. K. Lee, J. P. Wang, C. A. Specht, and S. M. Levitz, "Distinct patterns of dendritic cell cytokine release stimulated by fungal β-glucans and toll-like receptor agonists," *Infection and Immunity*, vol. 77, no. 5, pp. 1774–1781, 2009.

[4] G. J. Tesz, M. Aouadi, M. Prot et al., "Glucan particles for selective delivery of siRNA to phagocytic cells in mice," *Biochemical Journal*, vol. 436, no. 2, pp. 351–362, 2011.

[5] C. A. Specht, C. K. Lee, H. Huang et al., "Protection against experimental cryptococcosis following vaccination with glucan particles containing *Cryptococcus* alkaline extracts," *mBio*, vol. 6, no. 6, pp. 1–11, 2015.

[6] E. R. Soto, A. C. Caras, L. C. Kut, M. K. Castle, and G. R. Ostroff, "Glucan particles for macrophage targeted delivery of nanoparticles," *Journal of Drug Delivery*, vol. 2012, Article ID 143524, 13 pages, 2012.

[7] E. Soto, Y. S. Kim, J. Lee, H. Kornfeld, and G. Ostroff, "Glucan particle encapsulated rifampicin for targeted delivery to macrophages," *Polymers*, vol. 2, no. 4, pp. 681–689, 2010.

[8] H. Huang, G. R. Ostroff, C. K. Lee, C. A. Specht, and S. M. Levitz, "Robust stimulation of humoral and cellular immune responses following vaccination with antigen-loaded β-glucan particles," *mBio*, vol. 1, no. 3, Article ID e00164-10, 2010.

[9] H. Huang, G. R. Ostroff, C. K. Lee, C. A. Specht, and S. M. Levitz, "Characterization and optimization of the glucan particle-based vaccine platform," *Clinical and Vaccine Immunology*, vol. 20, no. 10, pp. 1585–1591, 2013.

[10] J. L. Cohen, Y. Shen, M. Aouadi et al., "Peptide-and amine-modified glucan particles for the delivery of therapeutic siRNA," *Molecular Pharmaceutics*, vol. 13, no. 3, pp. 964–978, 2016.

[11] R. De Smet, T. Demoor, S. Verschuere et al., "β-Glucan microparticles are good candidates for mucosal antigen delivery in oral vaccination," *Journal of Controlled Release*, vol. 172, no. 3, pp. 671–678, 2013.

[12] G. D. Brown and S. Gordon, "Immune recognition: a new receptor for β-glucans," *Nature*, vol. 413, no. 6851, pp. 36–37, 2001.

[13] L. R. Bernstein, " ^{31}Ga therapeutic gallium compounds," in *Metallotherapeutic Drugs and Metal-Based Diagnostic Agents: The Use of Metals in Medicine*, M. Gielen and E. R. Tiekink, Eds., chapter 14, John Wiley & Sons, New York, NY, USA, 2005.

[14] O. Olakanmi, B. E. Britigan, and L. S. Schlesinger, "Gallium disrupts iron metabolism of mycobacteria residing within human macrophages," *Infection and Immunity*, vol. 68, no. 10, pp. 5619–5627, 2000.

[15] L. R. Bernstein, "Mechanisms of therapeutic activity for gallium," *Pharmacological Reviews*, vol. 50, no. 4, pp. 665–682, 1998.

[16] P. Narayanasamy, B. L. Switzer, and B. E. Britigan, "Prolonged-acting, multi-targeting gallium nanoparticles potently inhibit growth of both HIV and mycobacteria in co-infected human macrophages," *Scientific Reports*, vol. 5, article 8824, pp. 1–7, 2015.

[17] J. E. Bell, "The neuropathology of adult HIV infection," *Revue Neurologique*, vol. 154, no. 12, pp. 816–829, 1998.

[18] H. Onishi, "Detection of gallium with rhodamine B," *Analytical Chemistry*, vol. 27, no. 5, p. 832, 1955.

[19] V. Hornung, A. Ablasser, M. Charrel-Dennis et al., "AIM2 recognizes cytosolic dsDNA and forms a caspase-1-activating inflammasome with ASC," *Nature*, vol. 458, no. 7237, pp. 514–518, 2009.

[20] T. Musich, O. O'Connell, M. P. Gonzalez-Perez, C. A. Derdeyn, P. J. Peters, and P. R. Clapham, "HIV-1 non-macrophage-tropic R5 envelope glycoproteins are not more tropic for entry into primary CD4+ T-cells than envelopes highly adapted for macrophages," *Retrovirology*, vol. 12, no. 1, article 25, 2015.

[21] X. Wei, J. M. Decker, H. Liu et al., "Emergence of resistant human immunodeficiency virus type 1 in patients receiving fusion inhibitor (T-20) monotherapy," *Antimicrobial Agents and Chemotherapy*, vol. 46, no. 6, pp. 1896–1905, 2002.

[22] T. Sato and T. Nakamura, "Thermal decomposition of gallium hydroxides," *Thermochimica Acta*, vol. 53, no. 3, pp. 281–288, 1982.

[23] P. J. Peters, J. Bhattacharya, S. Hibbitts et al., "Biological analysis of human immunodeficiency virus type 1 R5 envelopes amplified from brain and lymph node tissues of AIDS patients with neuropathology reveals two distinct tropism phenotypes and identifies envelopes in the brain that confer an enhanced tropism and fusigenicity for macrophages," *Journal of Virology*, vol. 78, no. 13, pp. 6915–6926, 2004.

[24] P. J. Peters, W. M. Sullivan, M. J. Duenas-Decamp et al., "Non-macrophage-tropic human immunodeficiency virus type 1 R5 envelopes predominate in blood, lymph nodes, and semen: implications for transmission and pathogenesis," *Journal of Virology*, vol. 80, no. 13, pp. 6324–6332, 2006.

[25] K. C. Jambo, D. H. Banda, A. M. Kankwatira et al., "Small alveolar macrophages are infected preferentially by HIV and exhibit impaired phagocytic function," *Mucosal Immunology*, vol. 7, no. 5, pp. 1116–1126, 2014.

[26] S. K. Cribbs, J. Lennox, A. M. Caliendo, L. A. Brown, and D. M. Guidot, "Healthy HIV-1-infected individuals on highly active antiretroviral therapy harbor HIV-1 in their alveolar macrophages," *AIDS Research and Human Retroviruses*, vol. 31, no. 1, pp. 64–70, 2015.

[27] V. Roulet, A.-P. Satie, A. Ruffault et al., "Susceptibility of human testis to human immunodeficiency virus-1 infection *in situ* and *in vitro*," *The American Journal of Pathology*, vol. 169, no. 6, pp. 2094–2103, 2006.

[28] S. B. Joseph, R. Swanstrom, A. D. M. Kashuba, and M. S. Cohen, "Bottlenecks in HIV-1 transmission: insights from the study of founder viruses," *Nature Reviews Microbiology*, vol. 13, no. 7, pp. 414–425, 2015.

20

Design, Characterization, and Optimization of Controlled Drug Delivery System Containing Antibiotic Drug/s

Apurv Patel, Hitesh Dodiya, Pragna Shelate, Divyesh Shastri, and Divyang Dave

Department of Pharmaceutics and Pharmaceutical Technology, K.B. Institute of Pharmaceutical Education and Research Center, Gandhinagar 382023, India

Correspondence should be addressed to Apurv Patel; patel.apurv.m@gmail.com

Academic Editor: Ali Nokhodchi

The objective of this work was design, characterization, and optimization of controlled drug delivery system containing antibiotic drug/s. Osmotic drug delivery system was chosen as controlled drug delivery system. The porous osmotic pump tablets were designed using Plackett-Burman and Box-Behnken factorial design to find out the best formulation. For screening of three categories of polymers, six independent variables were chosen for Plackett-Burman design. Osmotic agent sodium chloride and microcrystalline cellulose, pore forming agent sodium lauryl sulphate and sucrose, and coating agent ethyl cellulose and cellulose acetate were chosen as independent variables. Optimization of osmotic tablets was done by Box-Behnken design by selecting three independent variables. Osmotic agent sodium chloride, pore forming agent sodium lauryl sulphate, and coating agent cellulose acetate were chosen as independent variables. The result of Plackett-Burman and Box-Behnken design and ANOVA studies revealed that osmotic agent and pore former had significant effect on the drug release up to 12 hr. The observed independent variables were found to be very close to predicted values of most satisfactory formulation which demonstrates the feasibility of the optimization procedure in successful development of porous osmotic pump tablets containing antibiotic drug/s by using sodium chloride, sodium lauryl sulphate, and cellulose acetate as key excipients.

1. Introduction

Oral controlled drug delivery system can provide continuous delivery of drugs at controlled rate and predictable kinetics throughout the GI transit. Oral controlled drug delivery system targets drug delivery to a specific region for either local or systemic effect throughout the GI transit. This system also gives zero-order release profile [1].

Oral controlled release system can provide better effectiveness in treatment of chronic disease, reduce side effects, and improve patient compliance due to less frequent dosing interval.

Drug release from oral controlled release dosage forms are affected by pH of GI fluid, GI motility, and presence of food in GI tract. Drug release from osmotic drug delivery system is independent of pH and other physiochemical parameters and it is possible to modulate the release characteristic by optimizing the properties of drug and system [2, 3].

Osmotic pressure is used as driving force for osmotic drug delivery systems to release the drug in controlled manner. Osmotic pressure created due to imbibition of fluid from external environment into the dosage form regulates the delivery of drug from osmotic device. Osmotic drug delivery technique is the most interesting and widely acceptable among all other technologies used for the same purpose. Intensive research has been carried out on osmotic systems and several patents are also published. These systems can be used for both routes of administration, that is, oral and parenteral. Oral osmotic systems are known as gastrointestinal therapeutic systems (GITS). Parenteral osmotic drug delivery includes implantable pumps [3].

Dicloxacillin sodium and amoxicillin trihydrate are β-Lactam antibiotics. Dicloxacillin sodium and amoxicillin trihydrate have short half-life and high protein binding. The drug that shows linear pharmacokinetics is suitable for oral controlled release tablets and it would be advantageous to slow down its release in GI tract not only to prolong its therapeutic action but also to minimize side effects of drugs.

2. Material and Methods

2.1. Materials. Dicloxacillin sodium was obtained as gift sample from Suvik Hitek Pvt. Ltd. (Gandhinagar, India). Amoxicillin trihydrate was obtained as gift sample from Astral Life Care (Mumbai, India). Sodium chloride was purchased from Merck Pharmaceutical (Mumbai, India). Sodium lauryl sulphate was purchased from Bombay Tablet (Gandhinagar, India). Cellulose acetate and PVP K30 were purchased from Chemdyes Corporation (Gujarat). Magnesium stearate and talc were purchased from Suvik Hitek Pvt. Ltd. (Gandhinagar, India).

2.2. Differential Scanning Calorimetry (DSC). DSC studies were carried out for the pure drug, physical mixtures of drug and excipients, and placebo of the porous osmotic pump tablets to study the compatibility. The analysis was performed under nitrogen (nitrogen flow rate 50 mL/min) in order to eliminate oxidative and pyrolytic effects at a standard heating rate of 10°C/min over a temperature range of 50°C–400°C using Universal V4 5A TA instruments.

2.3. Preparation of Porous Osmotic Pump Tablet

2.3.1. Preparation of Core Tablets. Core tablets of dicloxacillin sodium were prepared by wet granulation method. All the ingredients were sieved through # 40 sieve. Individual ingredients, sufficient for a batch of 25 tablets, were weighed on a digital weighing balance as per Table 1. All the ingredients (except PVP K30, magnesium stearate, and talc) were mixed in mortar and pestle using geometric dilution method. The dry blend was granulated with sufficient quantity of PVP K30 which was dissolved in isopropyl alcohol. The powder mass was dried at 60°C in hot air oven for 6 h and passed through # 20 sieve. Then dried granules were mixed with magnesium stearate and talc for 3 min. Tablets were prepared by 9 mm concave die punch set using rotary tablet punching machine [4, 5].

2.3.2. Method of Preparation of Tablet Coat Solution. Cellulose acetate and PEG 400 were added to 3/4th of the total volume of acetone and stirred at 35 rpm using propeller stirrer for half an hour till the solution was clear. Magnesium stearate and coloring agent were triturated thoroughly in a mortar and added to the above solution and stirring continued further. Finally, the volume was made up with acetone [4, 5] (see Table 2).

2.4. Coating of the Core Tablets. Tablet coating was done using coating pan apparatus. Speed of coating pan was set at 30 rpm, and inlet air temperature and flow rate were 50°C and 3.2 kg/min, respectively. Spraying rate for coating solution was kept at 4-5 mL/min. Number of tablets per batch was fixed at 50 tablets. Ten tablets of test batch were mixed with 40 dummy tablets. Empty coating pan was run at above set parameters for 5 min. Tablets were loaded to the pan and allowed to gain equilibrium. Coating solution was sprayed at 5 mL/min rate for 2-3 seconds. Coating solution on the tablets was allowed to dry for 5 min and again sprayed. Approximately 100 mL coating solution was used for a batch of 50 tablets.

TABLE 1: Formulation of osmotic tablet.

Ingredient	Weight (mg)
Dicloxacillin sodium	244
Sodium chloride	100
MCC	60
Sodium lauryl sulfate	15
Sucrose	60
PVP K30	15
Magnesium stearate	3
Talc	3

Total weight of one tablet = 500 mg.
Number of tablets per batch = 20.

TABLE 2: Composition of coating solvent.

Ingredient	Composition
Cellulose acetate	2% w/v
PEG 400	2% v/v
TiO_2	0.2% w/v
Coloring agent	0.2% w/v
Acetone	Up to 100 mL

2.5. Characterization of Osmotic Tablet

2.5.1. Hardness. The fracture strength, which is defined as the force, was required to break a tablet by radial compression and was measured with a Monsanto tablet hardness tester in present study. The mean hardness is calculated and expressed as kg/cm^2.

2.5.2. Friability. The friability of the tablets was measured in a Roche friabilator. Tablets of a known weight (w_0) or a sample of 10 tablets are dedusted in a drum for a fixed time (100 revolutions) and weighed (w) again. Percentage friability was calculated from the loss in weight as given in equation as below. The weight loss should not be more than 1%. Consider

$$\% \text{ Friability} = \frac{w_0 - w}{w_0} \times 100. \quad (1)$$

2.5.3. Weight Variation Test. To study weight variation, 20 tablets of each formulation were weighed using an electronic balance individually, calculating the average weight, and comparing the individual tablet weights to the average. The tablets meet the IP test if no more than 2 tablets are outside the percentage limit and if no tablet differs by more than 2 times the percentage limit.

2.5.4. Thickness. The thickness of the tablets was determined using a Vernier caliper. 20 tablets were used and mean was calculated. Tablet thickness should not deviate by ±5%.

2.6. Determination of Drug Content. Ten tablets were accurately weighed and powdered. A quantity of the powder equivalent to 100 mg of dicloxacillin sodium was weighed accurately and extracted in 100 mL water by shaking for 20 min. After filtration through Whatman filter paper number 1 and sufficient dilution with water, samples were analyzed spectrophotometrically at 273 nm. Amount of drug present was determined from the calibration curve of dicloxacillin sodium [5].

2.7. In Vitro Drug Release Study. The release rate of dicloxacillin sodium from developed tablets was determined using USP dissolution testing apparatus I (Basket type). The dissolution test was performed using 900 mL 0.1 M HCl (pH 1.2) for 2 hr and then in pH 6.8 phosphate buffer for 10 hr, at 37 ± 0.5°C and 100 rpm. A sample (1 mL) of the solution was withdrawn from the dissolution apparatus hourly for 12 h, and the samples were replaced with fresh dissolution medium. The samples were passed through Whatman filter paper after dilution and the absorption of these solutions was measured at 273 nm. The cumulative percentage drug release was calculated.

2.8. Curve Fitting Analysis. For the determination of the drug release kinetics from the porous osmotic pump tablet, the in vitro release data were analyzed by zero-order, first-order, Higuchi, and Korsmeyer and Peppas equations [6].

2.9. Zero-Order Release Kinetics. To study the zero-order release kinetics the release data was fitted into the following equation:

$$\frac{dQ}{dt} = K_0, \quad (2)$$

where "Q" is the amount of drug release, "K_0" is the zero-order release rate constant, and "t" is the release time. The graph is plotted percentage cumulative drug release (% CDR) versus time.

2.10. First-Order Release Kinetics. To study the first-order release kinetics the release rate data are fitted into the following equation:

$$\frac{dQ}{dt} = K_1 Q, \quad (3)$$

where "Q" is the fraction of drug release, "K_1" is the first-order release rate constant, and "t" is the release time.

2.11. Higuchi Release Model. To study the Higuchi release model the release rate data are fitted into the following equation:

$$Q = K_H t^{1/2}, \quad (4)$$

where "Q" is the fraction of drug release, "K_H" is the release rate constant, and "t" is the release time. The graph is plotted as % CDR versus square root of time.

TABLE 3: Formulation of osmotic tablet (F1–F6).

Ingredient	Batch number					
	F1	F2	F3	F4	F5	F6
Dicloxacillin sodium (mg)	244	244	244	244	244	244
NaCl (mg)	150	150	150	150	150	50
MCC (mg)	30	30	90	30	90	30
SLS (mg)	20	10	10	20	10	10
Sucrose (mg)	90	30	30	90	90	30
PVP K30 (mg)	15	15	15	15	15	15
EC (%)	4	4	2	2	4	2
CA (%)	2	2	4	4	4	2
PEG 400 (%)	2	2	2	2	2	2
Magnesium stearate (mg)	3	3	3	3	3	3
Talc (mg)	3	3	3	3	3	3
Coloring agent	q.s	q.s	q.s	q.s	q.s	q.s

TABLE 4: Formulation of osmotic tablet (F7–F12).

Ingredient	Batch number					
	F7	F8	F9	F10	F11	F12
Dicloxacillin sodium (mg)	244	244	244	244	244	244
NaCl (mg)	50	50	50	150	50	50
MCC (mg)	30	90	90	90	30	90
SLS (mg)	20	20	10	20	10	20
Sucrose (mg)	50	90	90	30	90	30
PVP K30 (mg)	15	15	15	15	15	15
EC (%)	4	2	4	2	2	4
CA (%)	4	2	2	2	4	2
PEG 400 (%)	2	2	2	2	2	2
Magnesium stearate (mg)	3	3	3	3	3	3
Talc (mg)	3	3	3	3	3	3
Coloring agent	q.s	q.s	q.s	q.s	q.s	q.s

2.12. Korsmeyer and Peppas Kinetics. To study the Korsmeyer and Peppas release kinetics the release rate data are fitted into the following equation:

$$\frac{M_t}{M_\infty} = K_{KP} t^n, \quad (5)$$

where M_t/M_∞ is the fraction of drug release, "K_{KP}" is the release rate constant, "t" is the release time, and "n" is the diffusion exponent related to mechanism of drug release. The graph is plotted as log % CDR versus log time [6].

2.13. Selection of Polymers by Plackett-Burman Factorial Design. A Plackett-Burman design was adopted to selection of polymers of different category. In this design six factors were evaluated. Hence by applying Plackett-Burman factorial design, influence of six independent variables, osmotic agents (NaCl, MCC), pore forming agents (SLS, sucrose), and coating agents (cellulose acetate, ethyl cellulose), was studied over three dependent variables' drug release at 2 hr, 6 hr, and 12 hr and was checked [6, 7]. Formulation of osmotic tablets of factorial batches is shown in Tables 3 and 4.

TABLE 5: Formulation of osmotic tablet (F13–F20).

Ingredient	Batch number							
	F13	F14	F15	F16	F17	F18	F19	F20
Dicloxacillin sodium (mg)	244	244	244	244	244	244	244	244
NaCl (mg)	100	100	50	100	150	50	50	100
SLS (mg)	10	10	20	20	20	15	15	20
PVP K30 (mg)	15	15	15	15	15	15	15	15
CA (%)	4	2	3	4	3	4	2	2
PEG 400 (%)	2	2	2	2	2	2	2	2
Magnesium stearate (mg)	3	3	3	3	3	3	3	3
Talc (mg)	3	3	3	3	3	3	3	3
Coloring agent	q.s	q.s	q.s	q.s	q.s	q.s	q.s	q.s

TABLE 6: Formulation of osmotic tablet (F21–F27).

Ingredient	Batch number						
	F21	F22	F23	F24	F25	F26	F27
Dicloxacillin sodium (mg)	244	244	244	244	244	244	244
NaCl (mg)	100	150	150	50	150	100	100
SLS (mg)	20	15	10	10	15	15	15
PVP K30 (mg)	15	15	15	15	15	15	15
CA (%)	2	2	3	3	4	3	3
PEG 400 (%)	2	2	2	2	2	2	2
Magnesium stearate (mg)	3	3	3	3	3	3	3
Talc (mg)	3	3	3	3	3	3	3
Coloring agent	q.s	q.s	q.s	q.s	q.s	q.s	q.s

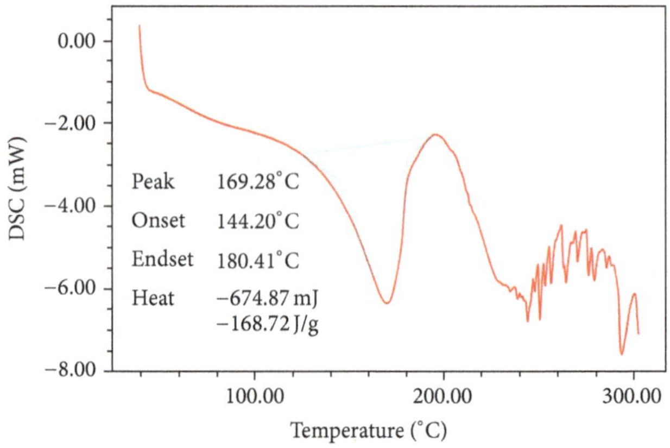

FIGURE 1: DSC spectra of pure drug (dicloxacillin sodium).

2.14. Optimization of Osmotic Tablet by Box-Behnken Factorial Design. In this optimization technique, the desirability approach was used to generate the optimum settings for the formulation. From the trial batches, three independent variables were found to affect drug release significantly. Concentration of coating agent (NaCl) and pore forming agent (SLS) and concentration of coating agent (cellulose acetate) were taken as independent variables [8, 9]. For the optimized formulation, the drug release at 2 hr, 6 hr, and 12 hr and release exponent (n) were kept in target. Formulation of osmotic tablets of factorial batches is shown in Tables 5 and 6.

2.15. Effect of pH on Drug Release. The optimized formulation of porous osmotic pump tablets was tested for the effect of pH on drug release. The best formulations were undergone in dissolution studies in 0.1 N HCl, 6.8 pH phosphate buffer, 7.5 pH phosphate buffer, and distilled water in rotation speed of 100 rpm and 37 ± 0.5°C using USP dissolution test apparatus type 1.

2.16. Effect of Agitation Intensity Drug Release. The optimized formulation of matrix and porous osmotic pump tablets are tested for the effect of agitation intensity on drug release. The best formulations are undergone in dissolution studies by maintaining different rotation speed of 50, 100, and 150 rpm and at 37 ± 0.5°C in 7.5 pH phosphate buffer for 8 h using USP dissolution test apparatus type 1.

2.17. Stability Studies. The stability studies were carried out as per the ICH and WHO guidelines of stability testing. Optimized formulations were kept inside the stability chamber maintained at 45°C and 75% RH for the period of 30 days. At the end of the stability study period, samples were analyzed for parameters like physical characteristics, drug content, and in vitro drug release.

3. Result and Discussion

3.1. Drug Polymer Compatibility Studies Using DSC. DSC thermograms of pure drug (dicloxacillin sodium) and physical mixtures of drug and excipients (NaCl, SLS, and CA) were studied for their interactions. It was observed that there was no significant drug polymer interaction observed among drug, NaCl, SLS, and CA even at higher temperature. From DSC study, we can see that there is no change in drug's melting peak (169.28°C–172.77°C) after the preparation of mixture. There is the no interaction between drug and excipient shown in this study. So, we can conclude that drug is compatible with all polymers. DSC thermograms were shown in Figures 1 and 2.

TABLE 7: Physiochemical parameters of factorial batches.

Batch code	Diameter (mm)	Thickness (mm)	Hardness (kg/cm^2)	% friability	Uniformity of weight (mg)	% drug content (% w/w)
F1	10.0 ± 0.05	5.2 ± 0.5	6.3 ± 0.2	0.54	540 ± 2.7	103.2 ± 2.1
F2	10.1 ± 0.05	4.9 ± 0.5	6.8 ± 0.4	0.39	470 ± 4.8	99.3 ± 3.6
F3	10.1 ± 0.05	5.1 ± 0.2	6.5 ± 0.5	0.72	530 ± 2.9	98.2 ± 4.3
F4	10.1 ± 0.05	5.2 ± 0.5	6.3 ± 0.7	0.43	540 ± 3.1	97.3 ± 4.7
F5	10.0 ± 0.05	4.6 ± 0.4	6.8 ± 0.3	0.11	385 ± 3.4	100.3 ± 2.2
F6	10.0 ± 0.05	5.4 ± 0.3	6.9 ± 0.2	0.47	590 ± 1.8	99.5 ± 1.4
F7	10.1 ± 0.05	4.7 ± 0.5	6.8 ± 0.2	0.52	380 ± 4.4	101.4 ± 1.2
F8	10.0 ± 0.05	4.9 ± 0.5	6.8 ± 0.5	0.65	500 ± 2.5	96.3 ± 3.3
F9	10.0 ± 0.05	4.8 ± 0.4	6.5 ± 0.2	0.83	430 ± 3.7	98.4 ± 1.4
F10	10.0 ± 0.05	5.2 ± 0.2	6.8 ± 0.4	0.49	540 ± 1.2	99.2 ± 3.8
F11	10.1 ± 0.05	4.8 ± 0.5	6.8 ± 0.5	0.57	430 ± 5.1	97.7 ± 2.6
F12	10.0 ± 0.05	4.8 ± 0.5	6.5 ± 0.3	0.34	440 ± 2.9	97.2 ± 1.3

All values are mean of three readings.

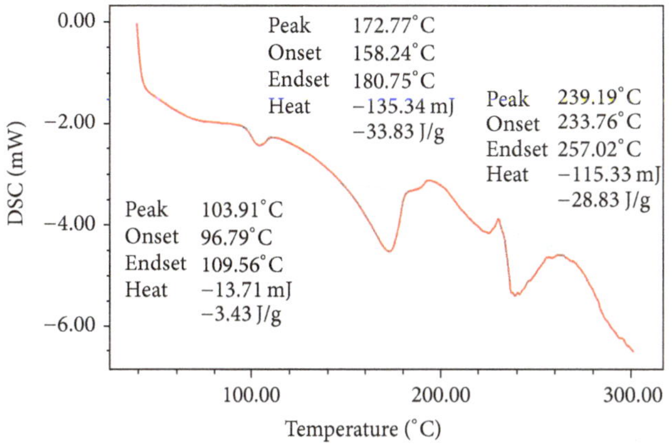

FIGURE 2: DSC spectra of drug and polymers.

3.2. Screening of Polymers by Plackett-Burman Factorial Design

3.2.1. Physicochemical Properties. Twelve batches were prepared for screening of polymers. The mean values of hardness, friability, thickness, weight, and drug content of prepared porous osmotic pump tablets are shown in Table 7.

3.2.2. In Vitro Dissolution Study. To study all the possible combinations of all factors at all levels, a six-factor, two-level Plackett-Burman factorial design was constructed and conducted in a fully randomized order. Six factors, NaCl($X1$), MCC($X2$), SLS($X3$), sucrose($X4$), EC($X5$), and CA($X6$), were selected as independent variables. Twelve batches were prepared to study Plackett-Burman factorial design for osmotic tablets. Two checkpoint batches were also evaluated to validate the design. The dependent variables (responses) studied were % drug release after 1 hr, 6 hr, and 12 hr of dissolution. Results of the drug release profile obtained for osmotic tablets are shown in Figures 3(a), 3(b), 3(c), and 3(d).

Effect of formulation variable on drug release at 1 hr, 6 hr, and 12 hr was carried out using Design-Expert Software (Version 7.1.6, Stat-Ease Inc., Minneapolis, MN).

Effect of Formulation Variable on Drug Release at 1 hr (Y1). From the equation, factor value of $X1$ was +2.08 and $X2$ was −1.41 indicating that $X1$ had more effect on drug release than $X2$. Factor value of $X3$ was +5.75 and $X4$ was +0.41 indicating that $X3$ had more effect on drug release than $X4$. Factor value of $X5$ was +0.08 and $X6$ was +0.53 indicating that $X6$ had more effect on drug release than $X5$. Positive sign of $X1$, $X3$, and $X6$ indicates positive effect on drug release. Figures 4(a)–4(d) show contour plot and 3D surface plot for $Y1$ suggesting effect of variables as described above. Consider

$$Y1 = 2.08X1 - 1.41X2 + 5.75X3 + 0.41X4 + 0.08X5 + 0.53X6. \quad (6)$$

The relationship between formulation variables ($X1$ and $X2$) and $Y1$ was further elucidated using 3D surface plot. From Figure 4(b) it can be concluded that factor NaCl($X1$) had more osmotic effect on drug release while MCC($X2$) had no significant effect on drug release.

The relationship between formulation variables ($X3$ and $X4$) and $Y1$ was further elucidated using 3D surface plot. From Figure 4(d) it can be concluded that factor SLS($X3$) had more pore forming effect on drug release while sucrose($X4$) had no significant effect on drug release.

Effect of Formulation Variable on Drug Release at 6 hr (Y2). From the equation, factor value of $X1$ was +6.66 and $X2$ was −3.66 indicating that $X1$ had more effect on drug release than $X2$. Factor value of $X3$ was +12.66 and $X4$ was +0.66 indicating that $X3$ had more effect on drug release than $X4$. Factor value of $X5$ was −0.16 and $X6$ was +3.83 indicating that $X6$ had more effect on drug release than $X5$. Positive sign of $X1$, $X3$, and $X6$ indicates positive effect on drug release. Figures 5(a)–5(d) show contour plot and 3D surface plot for $Y2$ suggesting effect of variables as described above. Consider

$$Y2 = 6.66X1 - 3.66X2 + 12.66X3 + 0.66X4 - 0.16X5 + 3.83X6. \quad (7)$$

The relationship between formulation variables ($X1$ and $X2$) and $Y2$ was further elucidated using 3D surface plot. From

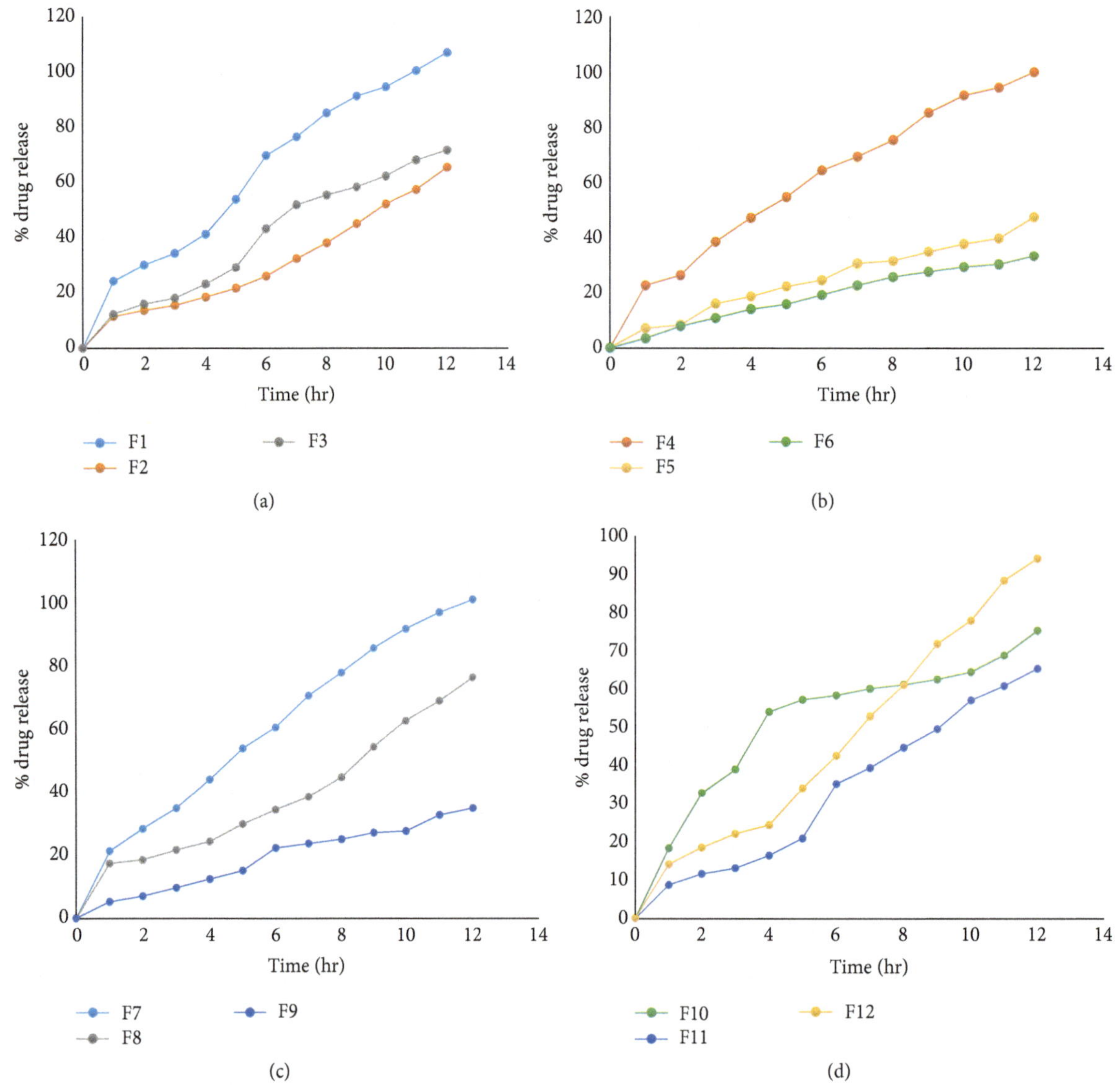

FIGURE 3: (a) Drug release profile for batches F1 to F3. (b) Drug release profile for batches F4 to F6. (c) Drug release profile for batches F7 to F9. (d) Drug release profile for batches F10 to F12.

Figure 5(b) it can be concluded that factor NaCl($X1$) had more osmotic effect on drug release while MCC($X2$) had no significant effect on drug release.

The relationship between formulation variables ($X3$ and $X4$) and $Y2$ was further elucidated using 3D surface plot. From Figure 5(d) it can be concluded that factor SLS($X3$) had more pore forming effect on drug release while sucrose($X4$) had no significant effect on drug release.

Effect of Formulation Variable on Drug Release at 12 hr ($Y3$). From the equation, factor value of $X1$ was +5.08 and $X2$ was −5.19 indicating that $X1$ had more effect on drug release than $X2$. Factor value of $X3$ was +19.75 and $X4$ was −1.08 indicating that $X3$ had more effect on drug release than $X4$. Factor value of $X5$ was +2.41 and $X6$ was +7.25 indicating that $X6$ had more effect on drug release than $X5$. Positive sign of $X1$, $X3$, and $X6$ indicates positive effect on drug release. Figures 6(a)–6(d) show contour plot and 3D surface plot for $Y3$ suggesting effect of variables as described above. Consider

$$Y3 = 5.08X1 - 5.19X2 + 19.75X3 - 1.083X4 + 2.41X5 + 7.25X6. \quad (8)$$

The relationship between formulation variables ($X1$ and $X2$) and $Y3$ was further elucidated using 3D surface plot. From Figure 6(b) it can be concluded that factor NaCl($X1$) had more osmotic effect on drug release while MCC($X2$) had no significant effect on drug release.

The relationship between formulation variables ($X3$ and $X4$) and $Y3$ was further elucidated using 3D surface plot. From Figure 6(d) it can be concluded that factor SLS($X3$) had more pore forming effect on drug release while sucrose($X4$) had no significant effect on drug release.

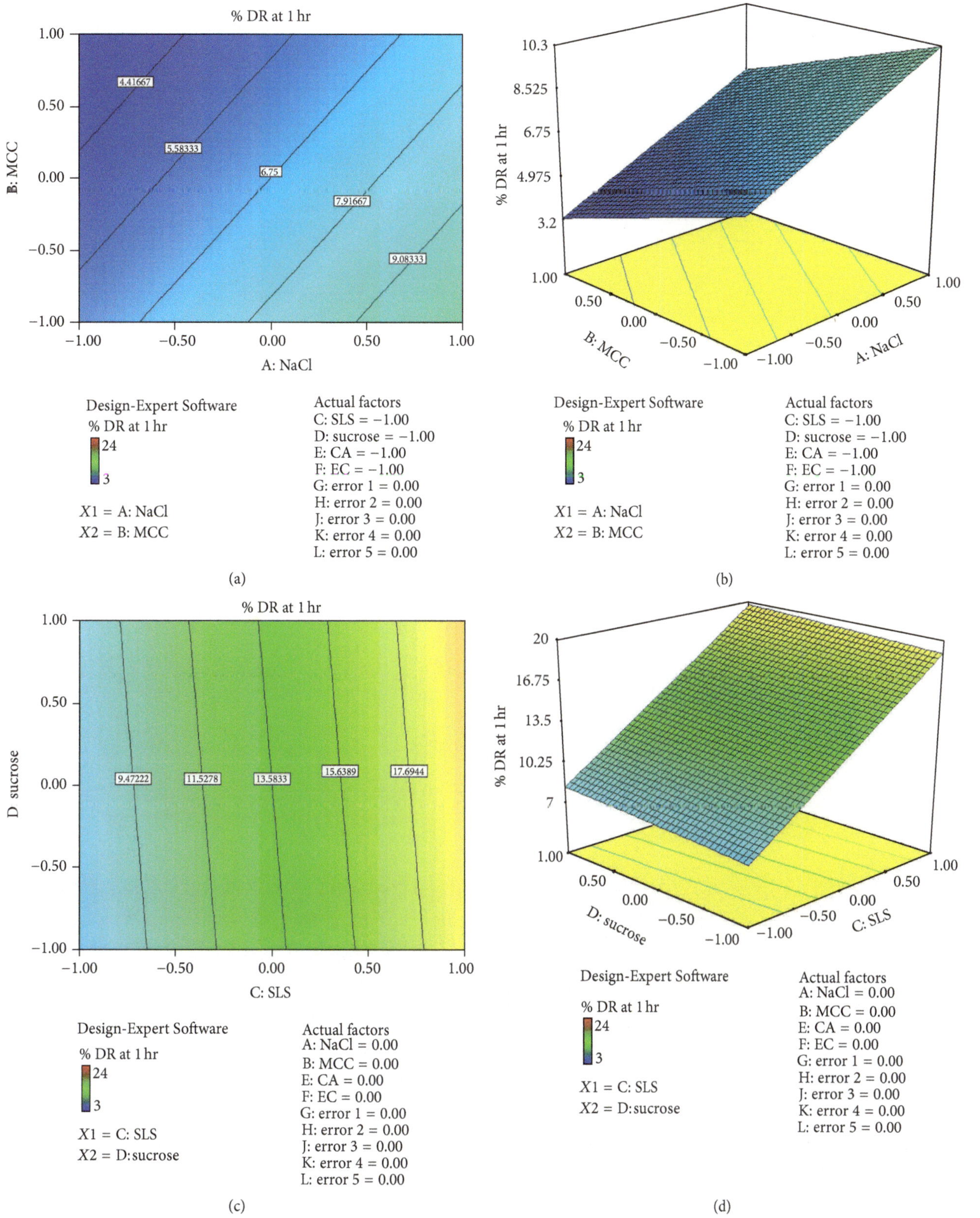

FIGURE 4: (a) Contour plot for response $Y1$ (drug release at 1 hr) (for $X1$ and $X2$). (b) 3D surface plot of response $Y1$ (drug release at 1 hr) (for $X1$ and $X2$). (c) Contour plot for response $Y1$ (drug release at 1 hr) (for $X3$ and $X4$). (d) 3D surface plot of response $Y1$ (drug release at 1 hr) (for $X3$ and $X4$).

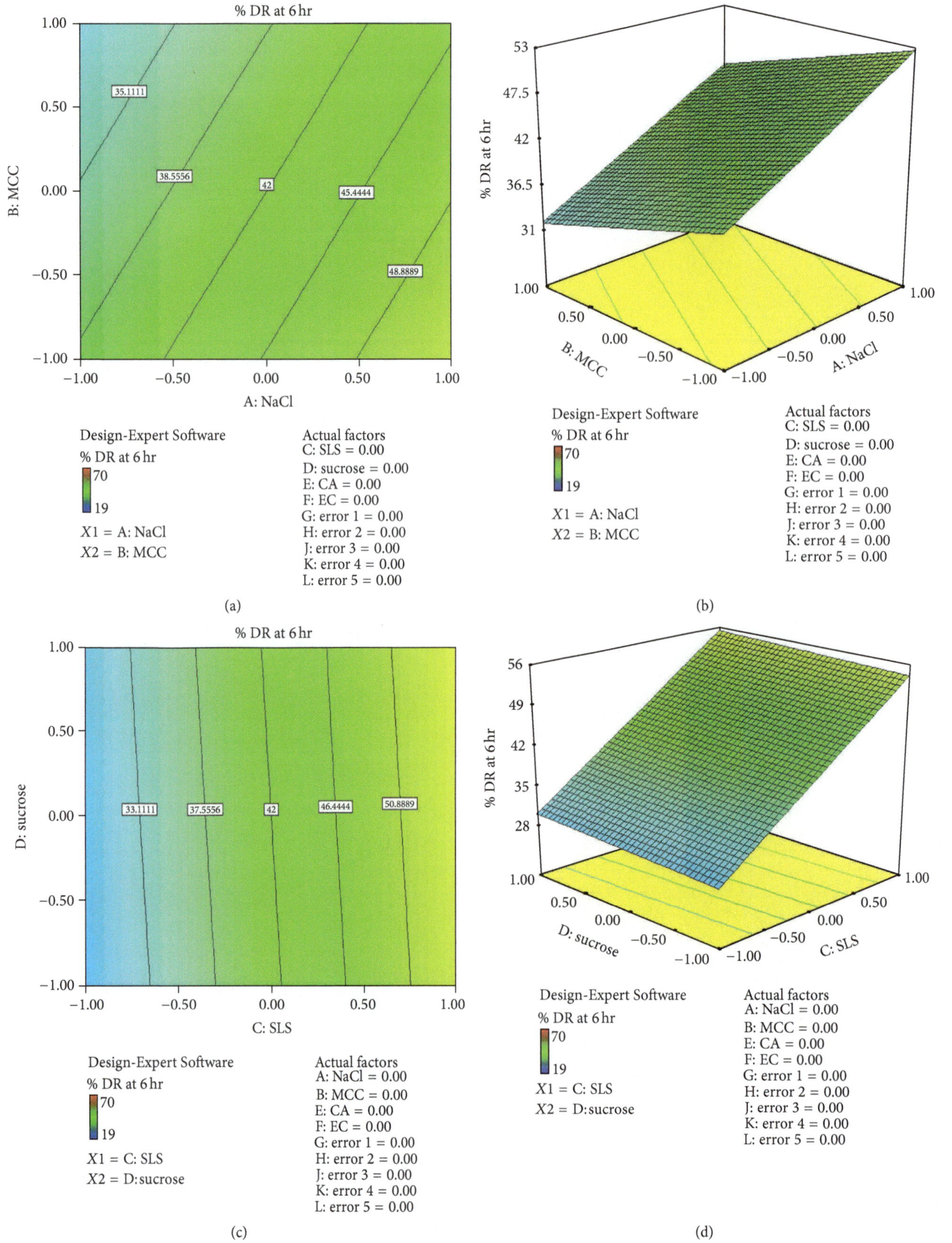

Figure 5: (a) Contour plot for response $Y2$ (drug release at 6 hr) (for $X1$ and $X2$). (b) 3D surface plot of response $Y2$ (drug release at 6 hr) (for $X1$ and $X2$). (c) Contour plot for response $Y2$ (drug release at 6 hr) (for $X3$ and $X4$). (d) 3D surface plot of response $Y2$ (drug release at 6 hr) (for $X3$ and $X4$).

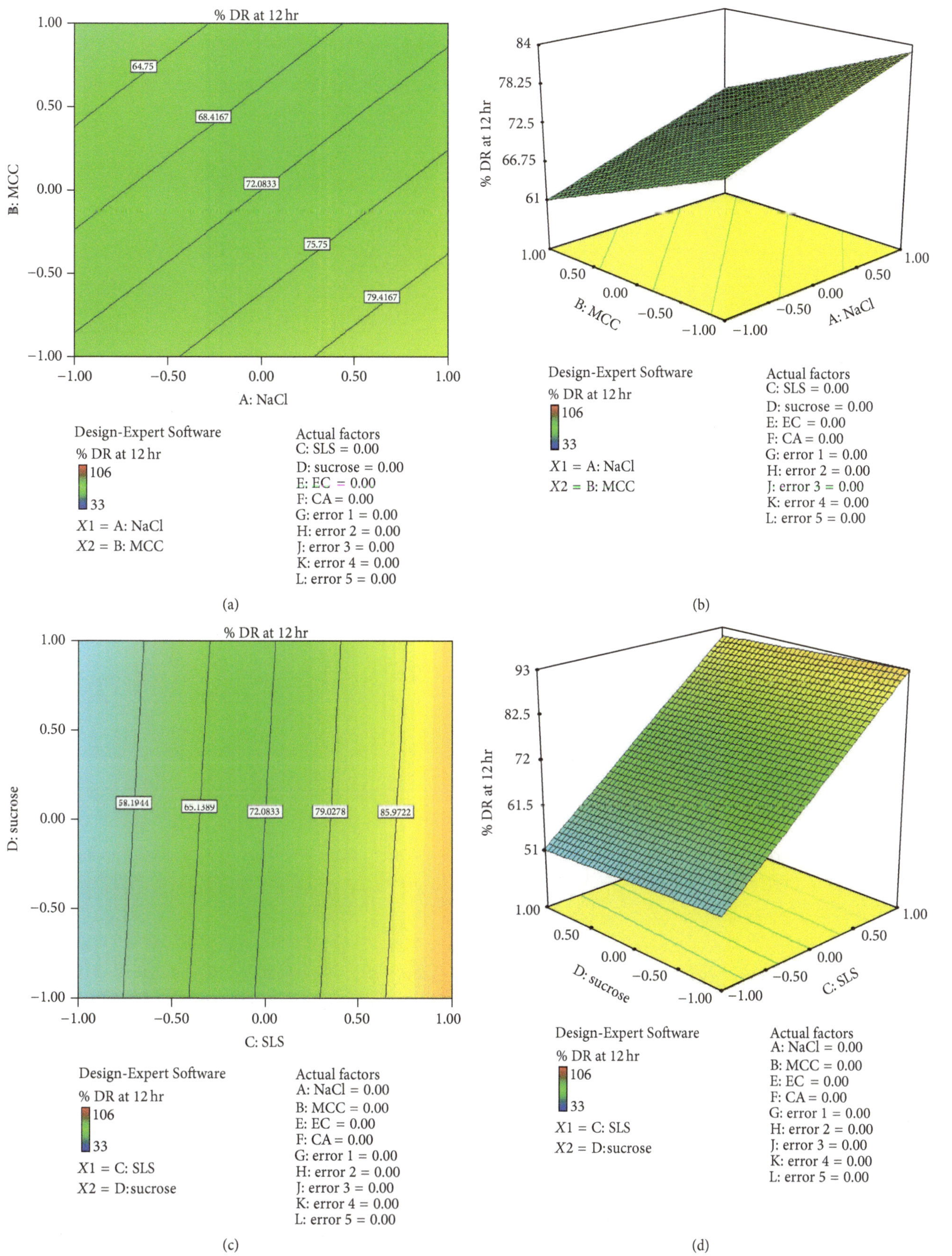

FIGURE 6: (a) Contour plot for response $Y3$ (drug release at 12 hr) (for $X1$ and $X2$). (b) 3D surface plot of response $Y3$ (drug release at 12 hr) (for $X1$ and $X2$). (c) Contour plot for response $Y3$ (drug release at 12 hr) (for $X3$ and $X4$). (d) 3D surface plot of response $Y3$ (drug release at 12 hr) (for $X3$ and $X4$).

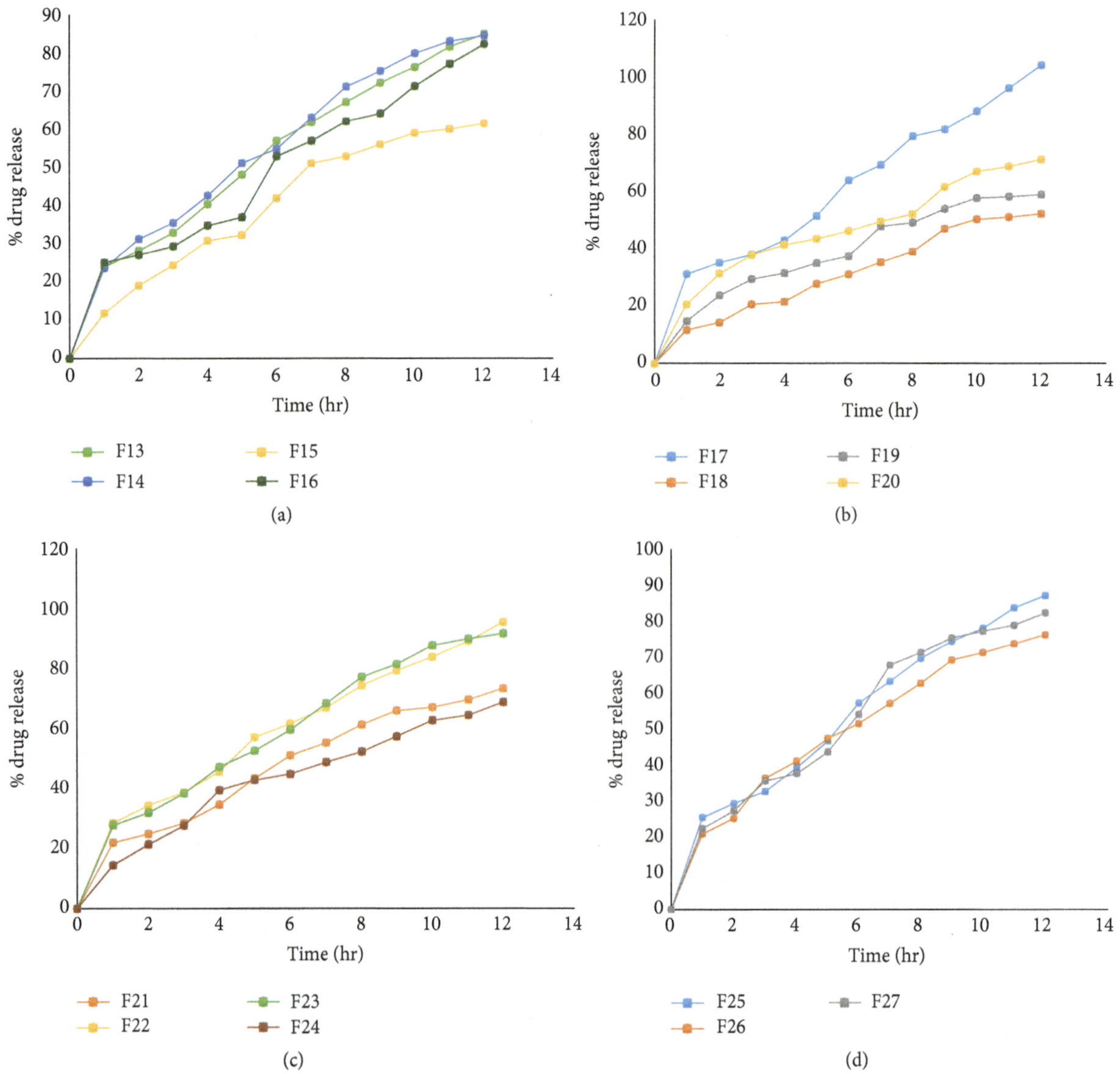

FIGURE 7: (a) Drug release profile for batches (F13–F16). (b) Drug release profile for batches (F17–F20). (c) Drug release profile for batches (F21–F24). (d) Drug release profile for batches (F25–F27).

3.3. Optimization of Osmotic Tablet by Box-Behnken Factorial Design

3.3.1. Physiochemical Parameter. 15 batches were prepared for optimization of osmotic tablets. Tablets were evaluated for uniformity of weight, uniformity of contents, tablet thickness and diameter, and hardness and friability. Results of the physiochemical tests obtained are shown in Table 8.

3.3.2. In Vitro Dissolution Study. To study all the possible combinations of all factors at all levels, a three-factor, three-level Box-Behnken factorial design was constructed and conducted in a fully randomized order. Three factors, NaCl($X1$), SLS($X2$), and CA($X3$), were selected as independent variables. 15 batches were prepared to study Box-Behnken factorial design for osmotic tablets. Two checkpoint batches were also evaluated to validate the design. The dependent variables (responses) studied were % drug release after 1 hr, 6 hr, and 12 hr of dissolution. Results of the drug release profile obtained for osmotic tablets are shown in Figures 7(a), 7(b), 7(c), and 7(d).

Figure 7(a) contains dissolution profile for batches F13–F16. Figure 7(b) contains dissolution profile for batches F17–F20. Figure 7(c) contains dissolution profile for batches F21–F124. Figure 7(d) contains dissolution profile for batches F25–F127.

Effect of Formulation Variable on Drug Release at 1 hr (Y1). Equation shows that coefficients b_1 and b_2 bear a positive sign and b_3 bears a negative sign and coefficient value for $X1$ is 7.50, $X2$ is 0.25, and $X3$ is −0.50. So it indicates that $X1$ has more effect on drug release than $X2$ and $X3$. Figures 8(a) and

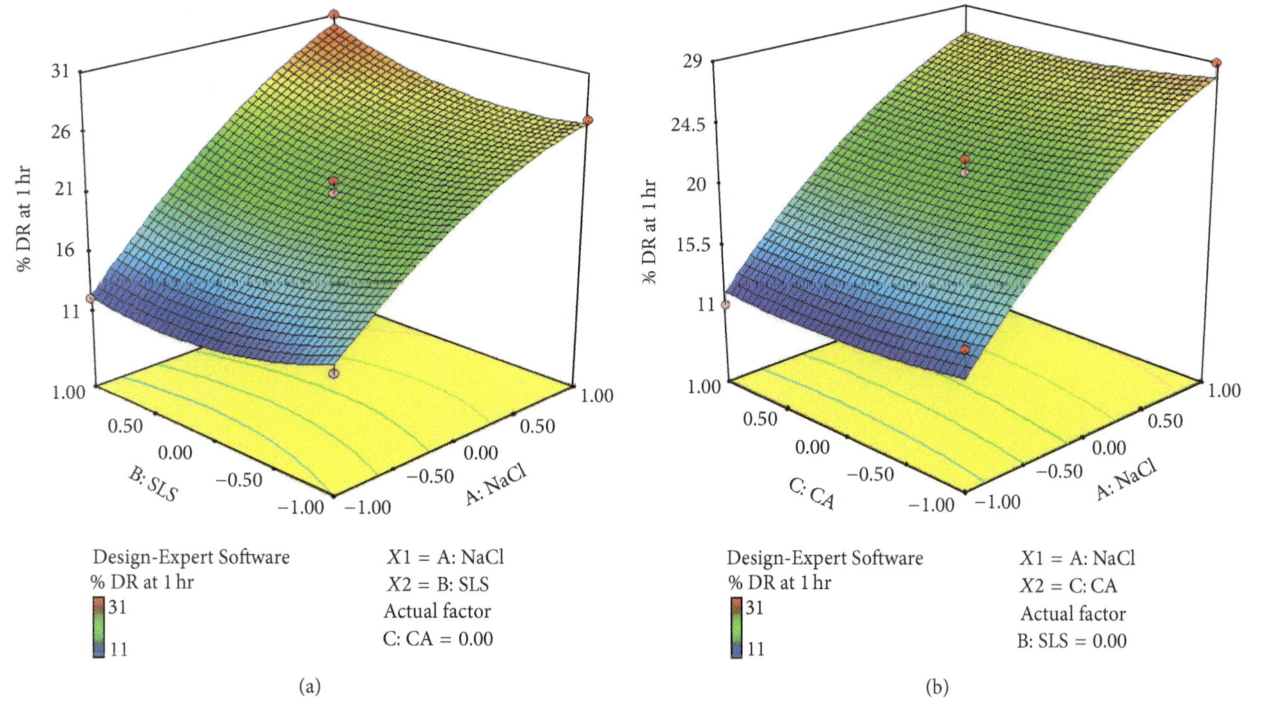

FIGURE 8: (a) 3D surface plot of response $Y1$ (drug release at 1 hr) (for $X1$ and $X2$). (b) 3D surface plot of response $Y1$ (drug release at 1 hr) (for $X1$ and $X3$).

TABLE 8: Physiochemical parameters of factorial batches.

Batch code	Diameter	Thickness	Hardness	% friability	Weight variation	% drug content
F13	10.1 ± 0.05	4.6 ± 0.5	6.8 ± 0.3	0.54	375 ± 2.6	101.2 ± 2.3
F14	10.1 ± 0.05	4.6 ± 0.3	6.4 ± 0.3	0.39	375 ± 4.8	98.3 ± 3.6
F15	10.0 ± 0.05	4.2 ± 0.2	6.5 ± 0.3	0.72	335 ± 2.9	99.2 ± 4.1
F16	10.0 ± 0.05	4.7 ± 0.5	6.3 ± 0.5	0.43	384 ± 3.1	95.3 ± 4.4
F17	10.1 ± 0.05	5.1 ± 0.4	6.8 ± 0.2	0.11	435 ± 3.4	103.3 ± 2.5
F18	10.0 ± 0.05	4.2 ± 0.3	6.9 ± 0.3	0.47	330 ± 1.8	97.5 ± 1.7
F19	10.0 ± 0.05	4.3 ± 0.5	6.8 ± 0.5	0.52	330 ± 4.4	101.4 ± 1.2
F20	10.1 ± 0.05	4.7 ± 0.5	6.8 ± 0.4	0.65	380 ± 2.5	98.3 ± 3.5
F21	10.1 ± 0.05	4.8 ± 0.4	6.5 ± 0.2	0.83	385 ± 3.7	99.4 ± 1.4
F22	10.0 ± 0.05	5.0 ± 0.2	6.8 ± 0.2	0.49	430 ± 1.2	97.2 ± 3.8
F23	10.1 ± 0.05	4.9 ± 0.5	6.9 ± 0.3	0.57	426 ± 5.1	98.7 ± 2.6
F24	10.0 ± 0.05	5.2 ± 0.5	6.5 ± 0.2	0.34	440 ± 2.9	98.2 ± 1.3
F25	10.1 ± 0.05	4.2 ± 0.4	6.6 ± 0.5	0.43	325 ± 1.3	99.4 ± 5.4
F26	10.1 ± 0.05	4.7 ± 0.1	6.9 ± 0.2	0.61	380 ± 3.4	98.5 ± 1.7
F27	10.0 ± 0.05	4.7 ± 0.5	6.8 ± 0.1	0.53	380 ± 2.7	99.9 ± 2.3

All values are mean of three readings.

8(b) show cube and 3D surface plot for $Y1$ suggesting effect of variables as described above. Consider

$$Y1 = 7.50X1 + 0.25X2 - 0.50X3 + 1.50X1X2 + 0.00X1X3 + 0.50X2X3 - 1.92X1^2 + 1.58X2^2 + 0.58X3^2. \quad (9)$$

The relationship between formulation variables ($X1$, $X2$, and $X3$) and $Y1$ was further elucidated using cube and 3D surface plot. From Figure 8(a) it can be concluded that factor Nacl($X1$) has more effect on drug release than SLS($X2$). From Figure 8(b) it can be concluded that factor $X3$ (Coating agent) has negative effect on drug release. As we increase the level of $X3$, it decreases drug release.

Effect of Formulation Variable on Drug Release at 6 hr (Y2). Equation shows that coefficients b_1 and b_2 bear a positive sign and b_3 bears a negative sign and coefficient value for $X1$ is 11.62, $X2$ is 0.38, and $X3$ is −0.75. So it indicates that $X1$ has

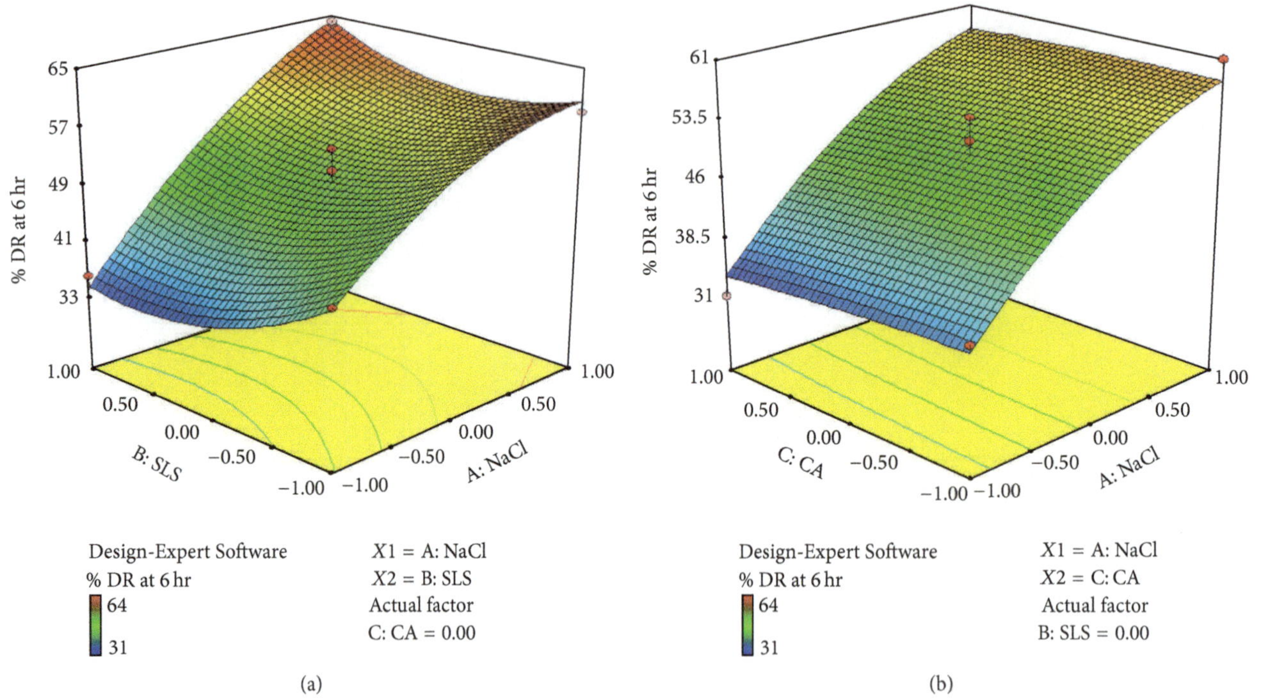

FIGURE 9: (a) 3D surface plot of response $Y2$ (drug release at 6 hr) (for $X1$ and $X2$). (b) 3D surface plot of response $Y2$ (drug release at 6 hr) (for $X1$ and $X3$).

more effect on drug release than $X2$ and $X3$. Figures 9(a) and 9(b) show cube and 3D surface plot for $Y2$ suggesting effect of variables as described above. Consider

$$Y1 = 11.62X1 + 0.38X2 - 0.75X3 + 3.25X1X2 + 0.50X1X3 + 0.00X2X3 - 3.54X1^2 + 3.96X2^2 - 0.96X3^2. \quad (10)$$

The relationship between formulation variables ($X1$, $X2$, and $X3$) and $Y2$ was further elucidated using cube and 3D surface plot. From Figure 9(a) it can be concluded that factor NaCl($X1$) has more effect on drug release than SLS($X2$). From Figure 9(b) it can be concluded that factor $X3$ (Coating agent) has negative effect on drug release. As we increase the level of $X3$, it decreases drug release.

Effect of Formulation Variable on Drug Release at 12 hr (Y3). Equation shows that coefficients b_1 and b_2 bear a positive sign and b_3 bears a negative sign and coefficient value for $X1$ is 17.50, $X2$ is 0.88, and $X3$ is −0.80. So it indicates that $X1$ has more effect on drug release than $X2$ and $X3$. Figures 10(a) and 10(b) show cube and 3D surface plot for $Y2$ suggesting effect of variables as described above. Consider

$$Y3 = 17.50X1 + 0.88X2 - 0.80X3 + 5.00X1X2 - 1.00X1X3 + 2.25X2X3 - 1.29X1^2 + 5.96X2^2 - 1.04X3^2. \quad (11)$$

The relationship between formulation variables ($X1$, $X2$, and $X3$) and $Y3$ was further elucidated using cube and 3D surface plot. From Figure 10(a) it can be concluded that factor NaCl($X1$) has more effect on drug release than SLS($X2$). From Figure 10(b) it can be concluded that factor $X3$ (coating agent) has negative effect on drug release. As we increase the level of $X3$, it decreases drug release.

TABLE 9: Desirable values selected for dependent variables.

Dependent variables	Desirable values	
	Lower limit	Upper limit
$Y1$ (% drug release at 1 hr)	20	30
$Y2$ (% drug release at 6 hr)	50	60
$Y3$ (% drug release at 12 hr)	90	100

3.4. Selection of Optimized Batch. Selection of best batch was carried out using *Design-Expert Software (Version 7.1.6, Stat-Ease Inc., Minneapolis, MN)*. After statistical analysis the desirability function was applied to select the best batch. The desirable values selected for dependent variables $Y1$, $Y2$, and $Y3$ are given in Table 9.

Desirable value range selected that was 5% varies from optimum value.

Batch F22 came closest to satisfying all the selection criteria. The results were further reinstated using the overlay plot in Figure 11. The yellow region of the plot indicates the area where all the selection criteria are satisfied. *Batch F22* falls in this yellow area, indicating the formulation having amount of osmotic agent (150 mg), pore forming agent (15 mg), and coating agent (2%) that possessed the desirable characteristics.

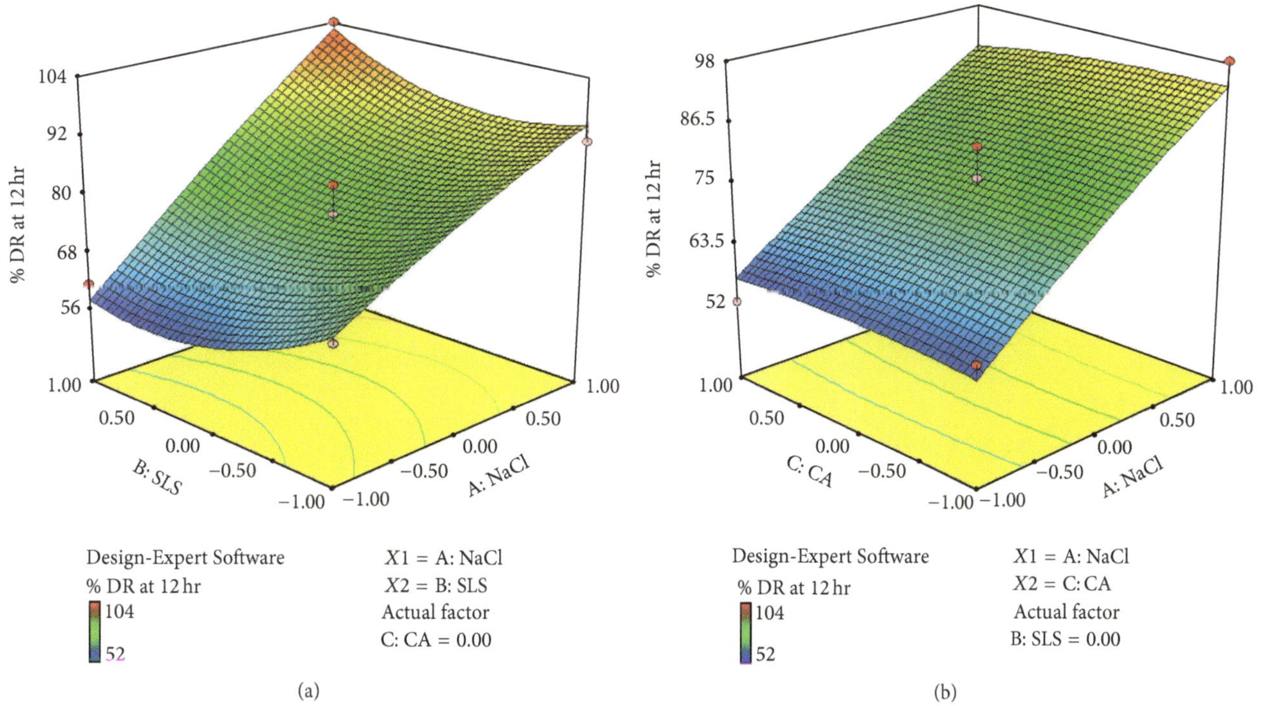

FIGURE 10: (a) 3D surface plot of response $Y3$ (drug release at 12 hr) (for $X1$ and $X2$). (b) 3D surface plot of response $Y3$ (drug release at 12 hr) (for $X1$ and $X3$).

3.5. So F22 Batch Was Selected as Optimized Batch

3.5.1. Effect of pH on Drug Release. When formulation F22 was subjected to in vitro release studies in buffers with different pH and distilled water, no significant differences in the release profiles were seen compared to that in phosphate buffer pH 6.8. Thus the fluid in different parts of the GI tract will scarcely affect drug release from the osmotic system.

3.5.2. Effect of Agitation Intensity on Drug Release. The release profile of dicloxacillin sodium from the optimized formulation F22 was independent of the agitational intensity of the release media.

4. Osmotic Tablet of Amoxicillin Trihydrate

Optimized batch of amoxicillin trihydrate was prepared using F22 batch composition of Box-Behnken design batches. From the drug release data and also release pattern shown in Figure 12 it can be concluded that there is no significant difference between two drug release profiles.

5. Release Kinetics and Release Mechanism

Six kinetic models were used for controlled release curve fitting to select the most appropriate model. The dissolution data for optimized batch was fitted to the zero-order, first-order, Higuchi, Hixson-Crowell, Korsmeyer-Peppas, and Weibull models. Best fitting model was selected on the basis of highest correlation coefficient and lowest F value.

TABLE 10: Comparison of drug release profiles of dicloxacillin sodium and amoxicillin trihydrate.

Time (hr)	Dicloxacillin sodium	Amoxicillin trihydrate
0	0	0
1	28.56	30.07
2	34.38	35.98
3	38.72	38.72
4	45.72	43.72
5	57.23	57.23
6	61.81	60.37
7	67.04	69.84
8	74.53	72.53
9	79.45	77.75
10	84.02	82.09
11	89.39	90.39
12	95.72	93.88

Comparative statistical parameters for all the models were obtained as shown in Table 11. Drug release mechanism was explored on the basis of release exponent (n) value.

Model fitting results revealed that the Korsmeyer-Peppas model was best fitted to the release kinetics (r^2 = 0.9960, highest; F = 6.8629, lowest). Higuchi model was also close to the Korsmeyer-Peppas model. Hence F test was performed for both models. It revealed significant difference between the two models. Hence Korsmeyer-Peppas model was finally selected as best fitted model. Release exponent n was found

TABLE 11: Kinetic modeling of drug release.

Parameter	Kinetic model					
	Zero-order	First-order	Higuchi	Hixson-Crowell	Korsmeyer-Peppas	Weibull
Sum of residuals	1314.416	346.8983	205.599	336.2533	**75.4920**	258.9369
Correlation coefficient (r)	0.9781	0.9821	0.9905	0.9877	**0.9960**	0.9860
R square (r^2)	0.8595	0.9629	0.9780	0.9635	**0.9918**	0.9719
F	109.534	28.9081	17.1332	28.0211	**6.8629**	25.8936

Model fitting results revealed that the Korsmeyer-Peppas model was best fitted to the release kinetics (r^2 = 0.9960, highest, F = 6.8629, lowest). Higuchi model was also close to the Korsmeyer-Peppas model. Hence F test was performed for both models. It revealed significant difference between two models. Hence Korsmeyer-Peppas model was finally selected as best fitted model. Release exponent n was found to be 0.580, indicating that the drug was released from the formulation by *anomalous (non-Fickian) mechanism*.

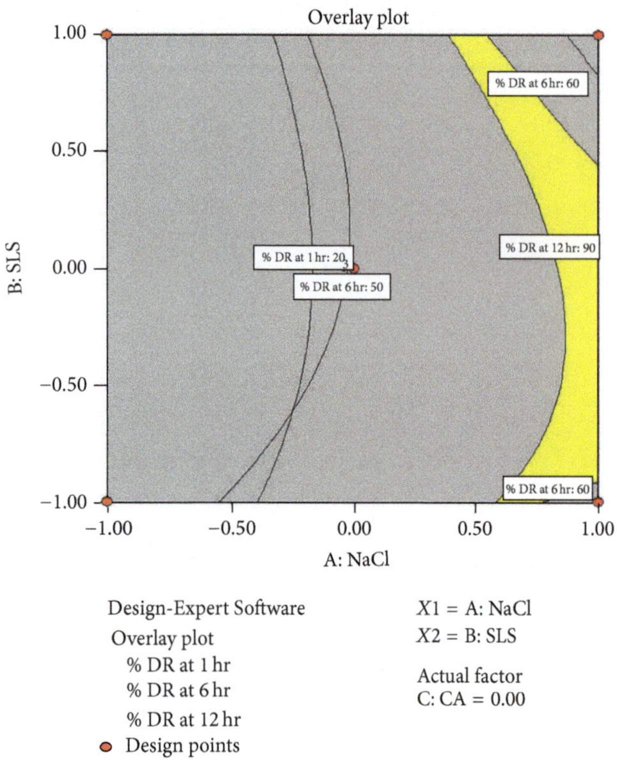

FIGURE 11: Overlay plot of $Y1$, $Y2$, and $Y3$.

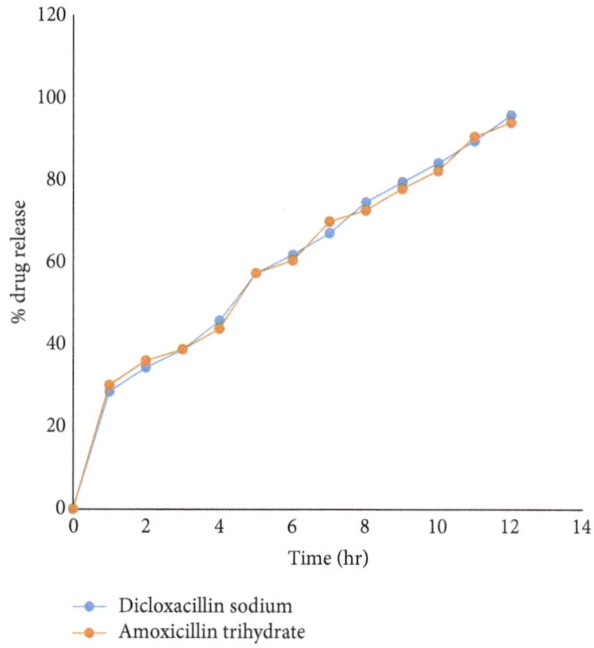

FIGURE 12: Drug release data of dicloxacillin sodium and amoxicillin trihydrate.

TABLE 12: Results of stability study of optimized batch (F22).

Evaluation parameters	Initially	After 30 days
Weight variation (n = 10)	430 ± 1.2	429 ± 3.3
Diameter (mm)	10.0 ± 0.05	10.0 ± 0.05
Thickness (mm)	5.0 ± 0.2	5.0 ± 0.1
Hardness (kg/cm^2)	6.8 ± 0.2	6.7 ± 0.5
Friability (%)	0.49	0.52
% drug content	97.2 ± 3.8	97.0 ± 1.3
$Y1$ (% drug release at 1 hr)	28.56%	30.07%
$Y2$ (% drug release at 6 hr)	61.81%	60.37%
$Y3$ (% drug release at 12 hr)	95.72%	93.88%

to be 0.580, indicating that the drug was released from the formulation by *anomalous (non-Fickian) mechanism*.

6. Stability Study

After the 1-month storage of formulation F22, values of all parameters like hardness, diameter, thickness, % drug content, and friability were checked periodically and found to be almost similar to the initial values. The drug profile was similar to the initial profile shown in Figure 13. There was not any significant change in any value and also no changes in the physical appearance. So it can be said that formulation is stable (see Table 12).

7. Conclusion

The observed independent variables were found to be very close to predicted values of optimized formulation which demonstrates the feasibility of the optimization procedure in successful development of porous osmotic pump tablets containing dicloxacillin sodium and amoxicillin trihydrate as model drug by using sodium chloride (150 mg) as osmotic

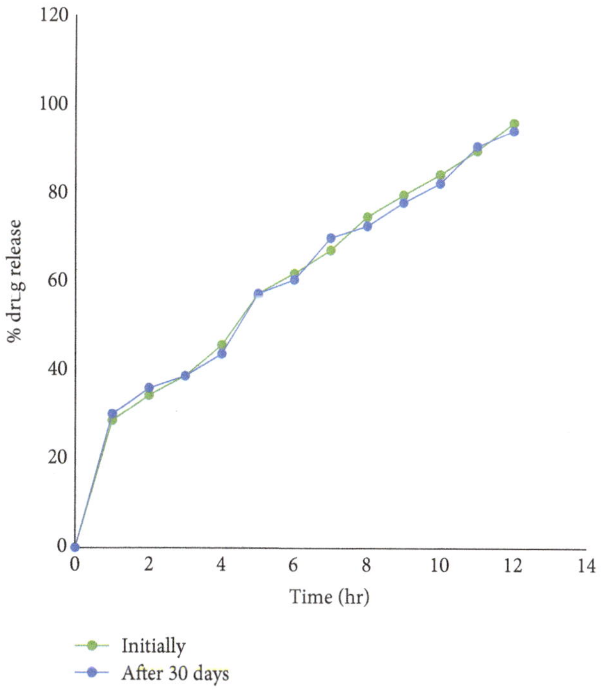

FIGURE 13: Drug release data for stability study of osmotic tablet (F22).

agent, sodium lauryl sulphate (15 mg) as pore former, cellulose acetate (2%) as coating agent, and control membrane permeability. Batch F22 was selected as optimized batch. Stability studies also revealed that optimized formulation is stable.

From the comparison of dissolution profile of optimized batch for both drugs (dicloxacillin sodium and amoxicillin trihydrate) it can be concluded that there was no significance difference in drug release observed, so it concludes that porous osmotic pump tablets of antibiotic drugs were successfully developed (see Table 10).

Competing Interests

The authors declare that they have no competing interests.

References

[1] P. Srikanth, N. Raju, S. Wasim Raja, and S. Brito Raj, "A review on oral controlled drug delivery," *International Journal of Advance Pharmaceuticals*, vol. 3, no. 1, pp. 51–58, 2013.

[2] C. L. Stevenson, F. Theeuwes, and J. C. Wright, *Handbook of Pharmaceutical Controlled Release Technology*, Edited by D. L. Wise, Marcel Dekker, New York, NY, USA, 2007.

[3] S. Gupta, R. P. Singh, R. Sharma, R. Kalyanwat, and P. Lokwani, "Osmotic pumps: a review," *International Journal of Comprehensive Pharmacy*, vol. 2, no. 6, pp. 2–8, 2011.

[4] B. P. Gupta, N. Thakur, N. P. Jain, J. Banweer, and S. Jain, "Osmotically controlled drug delivery system with associated drugs," *Journal of Pharmacy & Pharmaceutical Sciences*, vol. 13, no. 4, pp. 571–588, 2010.

[5] S. Edavalath, K. Shivanand, K. Prakasam, B. P. Rao, and G. Divakar, "Formulation development and optimization of controlled porosity osmotic pump tablets of diclofenac sodium," *International Journal of Pharmacy and Pharmaceutical Sciences*, vol. 3, no. 1, pp. 80–87, 2011.

[6] C. B. Sanford Bolton, *Pharmaceutical Statistics Pratical and Clinical Application*, vol. 135, 4th edition, 2004.

[7] S. P. Jain, P. P. Singh, S. Javeer, and P. D. Amin, "Use of Placket-Burman statistical design to study effect of formulation variables on the release of drug from hot melt sustained release extrudates," *AAPS PharmSciTech*, vol. 11, no. 2, pp. 936–944, 2010.

[8] S. L. C. Ferreira, R. E. Bruns, H. S. Ferreira et al., "Box-Behnken design: an alternative for the optimization of analytical methods," *Analytica Chimica Acta*, vol. 597, no. 2, pp. 179–186, 2007.

[9] N. Aslan and Y. Cebeci, "Application of Box-Behnken design and response surface methodology for modeling of some Turkish coals," *Fuel*, vol. 86, no. 1-2, pp. 90–97, 2007.

Permissions

All chapters in this book were first published in JDD, by Hindawi Publishing Corporation; hereby published with permission under the Creative Commons Attribution License or equivalent. Every chapter published in this book has been scrutinized by our experts. Their significance has been extensively debated. The topics covered herein carry significant findings which will fuel the growth of the discipline. They may even be implemented as practical applications or may be referred to as a beginning point for another development.

The contributors of this book come from diverse backgrounds, making this book a truly international effort. This book will bring forth new frontiers with its revolutionizing research information and detailed analysis of the nascent developments around the world.

We would like to thank all the contributing authors for lending their expertise to make the book truly unique. They have played a crucial role in the development of this book. Without their invaluable contributions this book wouldn't have been possible. They have made vital efforts to compile up to date information on the varied aspects of this subject to make this book a valuable addition to the collection of many professionals and students.

This book was conceptualized with the vision of imparting up-to-date information and advanced data in this field. To ensure the same, a matchless editorial board was set up. Every individual on the board went through rigorous rounds of assessment to prove their worth. After which they invested a large part of their time researching and compiling the most relevant data for our readers.

The editorial board has been involved in producing this book since its inception. They have spent rigorous hours researching and exploring the diverse topics which have resulted in the successful publishing of this book. They have passed on their knowledge of decades through this book. To expedite this challenging task, the publisher supported the team at every step. A small team of assistant editors was also appointed to further simplify the editing procedure and attain best results for the readers.

Apart from the editorial board, the designing team has also invested a significant amount of their time in understanding the subject and creating the most relevant covers. They scrutinized every image to scout for the most suitable representation of the subject and create an appropriate cover for the book.

The publishing team has been an ardent support to the editorial, designing and production team. Their endless efforts to recruit the best for this project, has resulted in the accomplishment of this book. They are a veteran in the field of academics and their pool of knowledge is as vast as their experience in printing. Their expertise and guidance has proved useful at every step. Their uncompromising quality standards have made this book an exceptional effort. Their encouragement from time to time has been an inspiration for everyone.

The publisher and the editorial board hope that this book will prove to be a valuable piece of knowledge for researchers, students, practitioners and scholars across the globe.

List of Contributors

Jason A. Ellis, Matei Banu, Sean D. Lavine and Jeffrey N. Bruce
Department of Neurological Surgery, Columbia University Medical Center, New York, NY 10032, USA

Shaolie S. Hossain
Department of Molecular Cardiology, Texas Heart Institute, Houston, TX 77030, USA

Rajinder Singh-Moon
School of Engineering and Applied Science, Columbia University, New York, NY 10032, USA

Shailendra Joshi
Department of Anesthesiology, Columbia University Medical Center, New York, NY 10032, USA

Piyush Sanghai, Tanaji Nandgude and Sushilkumar Poddar
Department of Pharmaceutics, Dr. D. Y. Patil Institute of Pharmaceutical Science and Research, Pimpri, Pune, Maharashtra 411018, India

Harika Ryakala, S. Dineshmohan and Alluri Rameshand
Vishnu Institute of Pharmaceutical Education and Research, Vishnupur, Narsapur, Medak, Telangana 502313, India

V. R. M. Gupta
Department of Pharmaceutics, Pulla Reddy Institute of Pharmacy, Annaram, Hyderabad 502313, India

Faithful Makita-Chingombe
School of Pharmacy, University of Zimbabwe, P.O. Box MP167, Mount Pleasant, Harare, Zimbabwe

Sara L. DiTursi
School of Pharmacy and Pharmaceutical Sciences, University at Buffalo, Buffalo, NY 14214, USA

Hilliard L. Kutscher
The Institute of Lasers, Photonics and Biophotonics, University at Buffalo, Buffalo, NY 14260, USA
Center for Integrated Global Health Sciences, Translational Pharmacology Research Core, New York State Center of Excellence in Bioinformatics and Life Sciences, University at Buffalo, Buffalo, NY 14203, USA

Gene D. Morse
Center for Integrated Global Health Sciences, Translational Pharmacology Research Core, New York State Center of Excellence in Bioinformatics and Life Sciences, University at Buffalo, Buffalo, NY 14203, USA
School of Pharmacy and Pharmaceutical Sciences, University at Buffalo, Buffalo, NY 14214, USA

Charles C. Maponga
School of Pharmacy, University of Zimbabwe, P.O. Box MP167, Mount Pleasant, Harare, Zimbabwe
Center for Integrated Global Health Sciences, Translational Pharmacology Research Core, New York State Center of Excellence in Bioinformatics and Life Sciences, University at Buffalo, Buffalo, NY 14203, USA
School of Pharmacy and Pharmaceutical Sciences, University at Buffalo, Buffalo, NY 14214, USA

Martina Aduenimaa Bonsu, Kwabena Ofori-Kwakye, Samuel Lugrie Kipo,
Mariam El Boakye-Gyasi and Mary-Ann Fosu
Department of Pharmaceutics, Faculty of Pharmacy and Pharmaceutical Sciences College of Health Sciences, Kwame Nkrumah University of Science and Technology (KNUST), Kumasi, Ghana

Shawn Riechers, Nai-Ning Yin, Arpad Karsai and Gang-yu Liu
Department of Chemistry, University of California, Davis, CA 95616, USA

Qian Zhong and Sandro R. P. da Rocha
Department of Chemical Engineering & Materials Science,Wayne State University, Detroit, MI 48202, USA

Roche C. de Guzman and Sina Y. Rabbany
Bioengineering Program, Department of Engineering, Hofstra University, Hempstead, NY 11549, USA

Babajide A. Tytler
Department of Pharmaceutics and Pharmaceutical Microbiology, Ahmadu Bello University, Zaria, Nigeria

Partap G. Bhatia
Department of Pharmaceutics and Pharmaceutical Microbiology, Usmanu Danfodiyo University, Sokoto, Nigeria

Michael U. Adikwu
University of Abuja, Abuja, Nigeria

Emmanuel O. Olorunsola
Department of Pharmaceutics and Pharmaceutical Technology, University of Uyo, Uyo, Nigeria
Department of Pharmaceutics and Pharmaceutical Microbiology, Ahmadu Bello University, Zaria, Nigeria

Marcus J. Goudie, Alyssa P. Ghuman, Stephanie B. Collins, Ramana M. Pidaparti and Hitesh Handa
College of Engineering, University of Georgia, Athens, GA 30602, USA

Majid Abrishami
Retina Research Center, School of Medicine, Mashhad University of Medical Sciences, Mashhad, Iran

Asma Mahmoudi, Navid Mosallaei and Mohammad Vakili Ahrari Roodi
School of Pharmacy, Mashhad University of Medical Sciences, Mashhad, Iran

Bizhan Malaekeh-Nikouei
Nanotechnology Research Center, School of Pharmacy, Mashhad University of Medical Sciences, Mashhad, Iran

Mojtaba Abrishami
Retina Research Center, School of Medicine, Mashhad University of Medical Sciences, Mashhad, Iran
Eye Research Center, Farabi Eye Hospital, Tehran University of Medical Sciences, Tehran, Iran

Md. Sohel Rana
Department of Pharmacy, Jahangirnagar University, Savar 1342, Dhaka, Bangladesh

Swarnali Islam
Department of Pharmacy, University of Asia Pacific, Dhanmondi, Dhaka 1209, Bangladesh

Irin Dewan
Department of Pharmacy, Jahangirnagar University, Savar 1342, Dhaka, Bangladesh
Department of Pharmacy, University of Asia Pacific, Dhanmondi, Dhaka 1209, Bangladesh

Adam Carie, Bradford Sullivan, Tyler Ellis, J. Edward Semple and Taylor Buley
Tara Lee Costich, Richard Crouse, Suzanne Bakewell, and Kevin Sill Intezyne Technologies, 3720 Spectrum Blvd. Ste. 104, Tampa, FL, USA

Elizabeth Schaefer, Mary Walsh, Donna Newman, Jacklyn Salmon and Brian Gilger
North Carolina State University, Raleigh, NC, USA

Santhi Abbaraju and Rasidul Amin
Symmetry Biosciences, Research Triangle Park, NC, USA

Sidney Weiss, Ulrich Grau and Poonam Velagaleti
i-novion, Inc., Randolph, NJ, USA

Deepak Sharma
Department of Pharmaceutics, Rayat Bahra Institute of Pharmacy, Hoshiarpur, Punjab 146001, India

Gurmeet Singh
2ISF College of Pharmacy, Ghal Kalan, Moga, Punjab 142001, India

Dinesh Kumar
Institute of Microbial Technology, Sector 39-A, Chandigarh 160036, India

Mankaran Singh
Quantum Solutions, Chandigarh 160101, India

Anubha Khare, Inderbir Singh and Kanchan Grover
Chitkara College of Pharmacy, Chitkara University, Chandigarh-Patiala National Highway, Rajpura, Patiala, Punjab 140401, India

Pravin Pawar
Gourishankar Institute of Pharmaceutical Education & Research, Limb, Satara, SurveyNo. 990, Near NH-4, Satara 415020, India

Manjanna Kolammanahalli Mallappa
Department of Pharmaceutics, TVM College of Pharmacy, Bellary, Karnataka, India

Rajesh Kesarla
Department of Pharmaceutics, Parul Institute of Pharmacy, Limda, Gujarat, India

Shivakumar Banakar
Department of Pharmaceutical Chemistry, B.L.D.E College of Pharmacy, Bijapur, Karnataka, India

Piyush Mehta
Dry Powder Inhaler Lab, Respiratory Formulations, Cipla R & D, LBS Road, Vikhroli (W), Mumbai, Maharashtra 400079, India

Gyati Shilakari Asthana, Abhay Asthana, Davinder Singh and Parveen Kumar Sharma
Department of Pharmaceutics, M. M. College of Pharmacy, Maharishi Markandeshwar University, Mullana, Ambala, Haryana 133207, India

Ernesto R. Soto, Olivia O'Connell, Fusun Dikengil, Paul J. Peters, Paul R. Clapham and Gary R. Ostroff
Program in Molecular Medicine, University of Massachusetts Medical School, 373 Plantation Street, Worcester, MA 01605, USA

Apurv Patel, Hitesh Dodiya, Pragna Shelate, Divyesh Shastri and Divyang Dave
Department of Pharmaceutics and Pharmaceutical Technology, K.B. Institute of Pharmaceutical Education and Research Center, Gandhinagar 382023, India

Index